Pretending to be
Somebody Else

An Actor's Journey

by

Terry Wale

First published in Great Britain in 2020
by SNB Publishing Ltd
57, Orrell Lane,
Liverpool L9 8BX

Copyright 2020 Terry Wale

Acknowledgements

There are many people without whose help and encouragement this book would not have been possible. First and foremost, I am indebted to my wife, Lesley Mackie, not only for letting me access her diary as an aide-memoire, but for all the days, weeks and months she spent tirelessly proof-reading and editing my story. Thank you darling.

Many of those who helped me throughout my career are mentioned in the pages, most notably my mother and father who supported me throughout all those early years.

I also thank my old friend, Alan Murgatroyd, for introducing me to my publisher, Nick Broadhead, whose input, both technically and editorially, knew no bounds.

I would also like to acknowledge the positive contributions made by Fiona Bruce, Marjorie Clark and Marion Webster after reading the proof copy.

So many of the photographers whose photos grace these pages are no longer with us, nor have I any way of recalling their names, except for Louis Flood Senior and Louis Flood Junior, both from Perth, who took most of the photos at Perth Theatre and the Pitlochry Festival Theatre from the 1970s onwards. I cannot bring this to a close, however, without mentioning the late Ronald Searle who provided me with his delightful cartoon of my earliest days as an actor, and which is now here for all to see.

I have tried to seek permission to reproduce photographs for which I do not own the copyright and will happily rectify any omissions at the earliest opportunity.

Terry Wale
October 2020

With love & thanks
for your friendship,
Lesley + Jimmy —
not to mention
Edmund!
X

To my dear wife and soulmate, Lesley,
And our beloved children, Katy and Oliver
I dedicate this book,

Together with the following sonnet by
William Shakespeare

When to the sessions of sweet silent thought
I summon up remembrance of things past,
I sigh the lack of many a thing I sought,
And with old woes new wail my dear time's waste:
Then can I drown an eye, unus'd to flow,
For precious friends hid in death's dateless night,
And weep afresh love's long since cancell'd woe,
And moan th'expense of many a vanish'd sight;
Then can I grieve at grievances foregone,
And heavily from woe to woe tell o'er
The sad account of fore-bemoaned moan,
Which I new pay as if not paid before.
But if the while I think on thee, dear friend,
All losses are restor'd, and sorrows end.

One

The number 187 bus from Alperton to Hampstead Heath via Kensal Rise, and very often with my father at the wheel, used to pass the top of Acacia Road in St. John's Wood. That was back in 1951, and for all I know it still does, although Dad gave up driving buses in the early '60s when he was appointed a full-time officer of the Transport & General Workers' Union, by which time I had in any case moved away and have never had occasion to board a number 187 again.

Strolling down leafy Acacia Road from St. John's Wood underground station you will eventually come upon a house on the left-hand side of the road that was once the home of the actor, Bernard Miles and his wife, Josephine Wilson. That was also back in 1951, the year of the Festival of Britain when an estimated eight million people visited the funfair in Battersea Park, or made their way to the South Bank to gawp at the Dome of Discovery and the Skylon, highlights of a huge and flamboyant exposition designed to lift the spirits of the British people out of the gloom of post-war austerity. Only a very select handful, however, were aware of the tiny but infinitely more exquisite gem that was being fashioned at the same time in Acacia Road. Behind Duff House, as it was called, stood a large and empty hall which, more than 50 years earlier, had formed part of a girls school. Sometime during the summer of 1950 Miles took his house guest, the celebrated Wagnerian soprano, Kirsten Flagstad, to look at the hall from which, following an enthusiastic exchange of ideas, they both emerged with a dream. By September 1951, the substance of their dream was realised when the Mermaid Theatre opened its doors for the first time.

I was a 13 year-old schoolboy at the time, and one for whom the die had already been cast. Kilburn Grammar School had a fine reputation, not only academically and for its sporting achievements but also for its annual Shakespearean production staged, with a careless disregard of theatrical tradition, at Christmas. As a first-year pupil, I had been completely enthralled by a production of *Macbeth,* from which I emerged with the strains of Mussorgsky's *Night on a Bare Mountain* ringing in my ears, and a dream of my own. I also, by-the-by, emerged with a huge crush on the Lady Macbeth which, disconcertingly, was not entirely laid to rest when I saw him the following day in school uniform. We were fortunate, however, in having for our close neighbours, the Brondesbury and Kilburn High School for Girls, so I never seriously doubted on which side my bread was buttered!

After the initial impact of my first brush with Shakespeare came the shock waves. The words I had heard spoken on the stage that night, in a language I barely understood, stayed with me, an intriguing and frustrating hotchpotch of half-lines and misquotes. I persuaded my parents to give me a 'Complete Works' for Christmas and by Easter I knew every line of *Macbeth* together with a handful of soliloquies from *Hamlet*. I clearly remember leaning up against a wall in the playground with my 'Complete Works', all other boyish activities spurned in favour of learning, 'O, what a rogue and peasant slave am I…' Laurence Olivier's film had only recently been released, and while the story didn't have quite the same dramatic effect on me as *Macbeth*, Olivier's performance did and from that day on, and for some considerable time afterwards, I could never quite accept that William Shakespeare and Laurence Olivier were different people. At any rate, they both share the credit for inculcating in me a passion for our language which has never cooled even in a world that appears to place less and less value on the spoken word.

At that time, my previous experience as a performer had been limited to the occasional concert staged in the garden of my Auntie Elsie's prefab in Harlesden, and the somewhat thankless part of the Lord Chamberlain in *Four-and-Twenty Blackbirds* at Kensal Rise Junior School. Notwithstanding this I was determined to play a role, however minor, in the next Shakespearean production at Kilburn Grammar School. Even when *The Tempest* was chosen I lost none of my enthusiasm, despite the fact that I scarcely understood a word of it and didn't think too much of the story either. I must have got the gist, however, for I knew instinctively that Prospero and Caliban were the 'heavies' and, consequently, well outside my range. The actual process that led me to audition for the part of Ariel is lost in the mists of time, although I probably owe the idea – as I owe so much else – to the keen interest of Peter Wright, an inspirational teacher of English, and an equally inspired interpreter of Shakespeare's plays. By the time school broke up for the summer holidays in the July of 1950, I knew that I had been cast as Ariel and that I had six weeks to contemplate the challenge and to make some kind of sense of it before rehearsals began at the start of the Autumn term.

Meanwhile, back in St. John's Wood, only a couple of miles due west, plans for the construction of the Mermaid Theatre were beginning to take shape. Bernard Miles' agent, Derek Glynne, had enlisted the support of the impresario, Peter Daubeny, who in his turn had persuaded Ivor Novello to lend his name and his reputation to the enterprise. With such an illustrious figurehead, who sadly did not live long enough to witness the fruits of his patronage, it was not long before subscriptions started to pour in. The sums raised would have been laughable by today's inflated standards, but given that there were, in those far-off days, a number of gifted people prepared to donate their services freely to a project they believed in, there was enough in the kitty by the end of 1950 to begin the conversion of the disused hall behind Duff House into a small Elizabethan playhouse. Research and design for the theatre were the responsibility of C. Walter Hodges and Michael Stringer and, under their supervision, the portable stage was built in a film studio during the winter months. The Mermaid never claimed to be a faithful evocation of any particular Elizabethan theatre but all the elements were there, including a central tiring house and a gallery so that an Elizabethan actor, transported through time on to its stage, would have felt almost at home there except, that is, for the addition of a roof. True, the ceiling was painted, in the best of theatrical traditions, with clouds and cherubs set in a blue firmament and adorned with the signs of the Zodiac, but I doubt if that would have fooled even a moderately gullible or short-sighted Elizabethan actor! Artistic decisions were, in part, dictated by Kirsten Flagstad's enthusiastic involvement, and so it was decided that the first of the two opening productions would be Purcell's opera, *Dido and Æneas*, with Flagstad singing the role of Dido, and for which her fee would be two pints of oatmeal stout a day. This largesse obviously filtered down to the other performers for there was no one, as far as I know, who was offered, or demanded, more than the most basic of expenses.

It was agreed fairly early on that Bernard Miles would produce the opera and that Julius Gellner would be brought in to direct the second of the two productions which was to be *The Tempest*. Casting began in the spring of 1951, a mammoth task when you consider that reputable singers and actors were being asked to commit some months ahead to a short season in a theatre which still didn't exist, and by a management that was offering them precisely nothing in the way of financial remuneration. Somehow or other they succeeded, and the quality of the companies that were assembled for both productions remains to this day a tribute, not only to the persuasiveness of Bernard Miles and his fellow pioneers, but also to an age in which money was not the only and exclusive inducement to work.

One of Julius Gellner's earliest decisions, supported by Bernard Miles, was that the part of Ariel in *The Tempest* should be played by a boy, so a campaign was launched and a search began, initially limited to those bastions of fledgling talent, the Arts Educational School, Italia Conti and the now defunct Corona School. When none of these establishments yielded up the Ariel that Miles and Gellner were looking for, they were obliged to cast their net wider. At the same time, they were beginning to entertain serious doubts about the wisdom of entrusting a major and complex role like Ariel to an inexperienced child.

1951 The Tempest - The Mermaid Theatre. Cartoonist Ronald Searle.

It was Sports Day at Kilburn Grammar School, and I was sitting on the sidelines lost in my own thoughts and occasionally rousing myself to cheer on my more athletic classmates. Not that I was completely useless in that area. I was, in fact, quite capable of leaving a number of my peers behind in the 100 yards sprint, but I was never equipped to compete with the best and consequently the event held little interest for me. To be perfectly honest, apart from a mild and occasional flirtation with cricket, and latterly football, sport has played no significant part in my life. Besides, I now had other fish to fry.

4

Playing Ariel in the school production of *The Tempest* had left me strangely elated and, at the same time, curiously unfulfilled. I knew I wanted to be an actor but I had no idea what that meant. My working-class background offered no clues as, apart from my Uncle Harry, a keen amateur, no one I knew had ever 'trod the boards'. At the age of 18 my mother was something of a beauty and even later, when she was in her thirties and I was but a lad, I was aware of how attractive and stylish she was. At the right time, and in the right place, she might easily have been considered for a stage or film career. But from the age of 14, she was obliged to contribute to her family's expenses by working in a laundry, hardly a window of opportunity in 1925 although, due to the vagaries of time and the advent of television, being an untrained laundress would probably be enough to ensure her stardom these days! All I knew was that I wanted to act to the exclusion of anything else and that, with such a fire raging inside me, I was finding it difficult and painful to weather the year-long gap between school plays. The next one hadn't been chosen yet so I couldn't even find solace in reading it and deciding what part I would audition for. I had enjoyed *The Tempest* even beyond my expectations and, as Ariel, I had come out of it, if not exactly covered in glory, certainly with more than my fair share of praise. I had also developed a healthy respect for the power and beauty of Shakespeare's poetry, although I still had serious reservations about the plot. I believe to this day that *The Tempest* is pretty well unstageable, although I was not troubled by such empirical judgements at the time; it just wasn't my cup of tea, that's all. Had Shakespeare tackled the story earlier in his career, it would probably have ended in a bloodbath and I suppose, as a normally ghoulish 13 year-old, I would have found that more to my taste!

Sitting on the terraces at Willesden sports ground, a mere spectator, I suddenly knew that at least I was about to learn the title of the next school play. Why else would Peter Wright be walking towards me with a smile on his face?

"Not running today, Wale?" he asked, quite unnecessarily.

"No, sir", was my equally redundant reply.

"I suppose you're just waiting for the next school play, are you?"

"Yes, sir".

The exchange was threatening to run out of steam, and I was thinking 'why doesn't he just tell me what the play is and put me out of my misery?', when his dialogue took an entirely different turn. "There's a chance," he said, "just a chance, that you might not have to wait that long. I read in a newspaper that Bernard Miles is looking for a boy to play Ariel at the Mermaid Theatre, so I telephoned and arranged an audition for you. I've spoken to your parents and they're perfectly happy about it, so it's up to you. Well, would you like to audition?" I have wondered on occasion since that day what might have happened to me had I said, "If it's all the same to you, sir, I think I'd rather concentrate on my education, and make those kind of decisions when I'm a little older." Of course, it never entered my mind at the time!

Had I not lived through the Blitz, and spent my formative years negotiating dangerous bomb sites, I would have found it all but impossible to imagine the obstacle course where I auditioned was to become the Mermaid Theatre. I clambered over sawn-off lengths of timber, and stumbled over pots of glue to the accompaniment of electric drills, saws and hammers. Silence was obviously enforced while I did my audition, but as I have no recollection whatsoever of the event, I shall leave it to Peter Daubeny in his book, *Stage by Stage,* to summarise the occasion:

'At the very first sight of Terry Wale, Bernard Miles felt that here was the Ariel of whom he had dreamed. Julius Gellner (the director), too, had no sooner seen him than he felt sure the search had ended. So Terry Wale became our Ariel ... his first major part in what I feel confident will prove to be a successful professional career ...'

Memories of my five weeks at the Mermaid Theatre in the late summer of 1951 are, of course, fragmentary; I know I was delivered every morning to Duff House by my father, although how he managed this while he was on shift work is still a mystery to me.

I remember the thrill of my first journey by car, of being driven at the outrageous speed of 60 miles an hour up the A1 to Letchworth in Hertfordshire where I was fitted for a harness at the parachute factory. As Ariel, in the guise of a harpy, I was to be flown down from a platform constructed in the roof of the theatre, and suspended high above the stage, from where I would deliver the speech that begins, 'You are three men of sin ...' I also remember being photographed on numerous occasions and for various newspapers standing beside this rather large and generously proportioned woman called Kirsten Flagstad, of whom, of course, I had never heard, although I understood she was to be singing the leading role in the opera, *Dido and Æneas*. I knew nothing about opera either. In fact, I was profoundly ignorant about most things which, I suppose, was hardly a capital offence at the age of 13, although I do recall suffering agonies of embarrassment about it. On one particular occasion when I was invited, as guest-of-honour, to dine at a famous public school, I was paralysed with fear by the sight of four sets of cutlery. Julius Gellner's daughter, Joan, was my escort for the evening, and somehow or other she managed to rescue me. From across the table, and with absolute discretion, she directed my every move. Like father, like daughter! I have no idea what persuaded Joan Gellner to take me under her wing, but I accepted her interest in me without question at the time and only much later, too late as it happened, did it occur to me that I had never thanked her for opening so many doors to me. Joan was a strikingly good-looking young woman in her mid-twenties with just a hint of the middle-European accent bequeathed her when she was but a child. It was in 1933, the year of Hitler's rise to power, that Julius Gellner had given up his post as artistic director of Munich's Kammerspiele and, with his then eight year-old daughter in tow, came to England.

Amongst many other things, Joan introduced me to the 'cinema' which, I discovered, was not quite the same thing as going to the 'pictures.' For a start, cinema involved making a choice, and possibly even booking a seat. It also meant seeing a film from the beginning. I had been going to the pictures regularly, and totally indiscriminately, since I was six or seven. Most of the time I had no idea what I was going to see or when the programme started; I'd simply wander in somewhere in the middle of a film and stay there until I experienced a sense of *déjà vu*. I often accompanied my mother to the pictures, a habit that had begun when we were both evacuated to Cheshire during the war. The up-side of this arrangement was that I got to see a lot of 'A' Certificate pictures without having to stand outside the cinema and beg some total stranger to take me in. The down-side was that I never got to see the film through twice because my mother, with her unerring ear for dialogue, would always lean across and say, "This is where we came in." But 'cinema' was a much more serious business, none the less pleasurable for that, and all the more so in Joan's stimulating company. I confess that I have, to this day, always had a sneaking preference for 'going to the pictures' although, over the years, these two not unrelated experiences have probably merged. That's education for you!

Joan also took me to see several plays. As a family we seldom went to the theatre. I have vague memories of seeing a show called *Soldiers in Skirts* at the Shepherd's Bush Empire and a production of *Aladdin*, starring Arthur Askey, at the Golders Green Hippodrome. Intended as a Christmas treat, the experience induced in me a chronic case of Pantophobia from which I have never fully recovered. Not that Joan's tastes were exclusively highbrow. She took me to see *The Mousetrap*, I remember, during the first week of its interminable run. Even at the age of 13, and even with Mr. and Mrs. Richard Attenborough heading the cast, I found it pretty unremarkable and, had I been asked, would have consigned it to theatrical history within a matter of weeks. This uncanny knack of mine for predicting theatrical success has, I am proud to say, never deserted me! We also went to see a production of *Much Ado About Nothing* with John Gielgud and Diana Wynyard which was superior in every respect, and which consequently ran for only six weeks!

Sadly, Joan died of cancer in her early forties, and I saw little of her in the intervening years. I remember her, though, with affection and with gratitude, for her kindness and her patience and for introducing me to a world of experiences that helped to pave my way towards manhood better equipped to deal with it than I might otherwise have been.

The most far-reaching and, arguably, the most important influence Joan exerted over me was her determination to rid me of all the horrible north London vowel sounds that were obviously coming out of my mouth, and of which I was quite unconscious, of course. I had actually been born in the City of London Hospital in the Borough of Finsbury, and well within the sound of Bow Bells, which meant that, by birth at any rate, I was a cockney. But I grew up in the Willesden area of north-west London where the accent is less precise and the vowel sounds are drawn out in something approaching a whine. For anyone fortunate enough to play Eliza Doolittle in *Pygmalion* or indeed, in *My Fair Lady*, it's worth remembering that, far from being a cockney, she was born in Lisson Grove, NW1, and while I cannot claim to have suffered from those kind of extremes, Henry Higgins would almost certainly have detected the similarities. For all that Joan Gellner was essentially foreign, she was aware of them too. It was, however, no part of Joan's plan to pass me off as a duchess. She simply wanted to help me do justice to Shakespeare's verse, and she invested a considerable amount of time and effort to that end. Had I known that, within a matter of five or six years, authentic regional accents of all shades would become the actor's *passe-partout,* and that hideous vowel sounds would eventually replace Standard English, I might have held my ground. But few, if any, were aware of even the distant rumblings in that late summer of 1951 when Osborne, Behan, Pinter, Wesker *et al* had not, as yet, raised their heads above the barricades, the ground still held by the likes of Coward, Rattigan, Fry and Anouilh. At that time a 'workshop' was where the scenery was built, and certainly no place for actors, who still turned up at rehearsals wearing suits and ties or, at their most casual, blazers with cravats. Actresses dressed to kill, and were always alluringly perfumed, even after six hours in the rehearsal room. Those siren-like creatures could have lured me onto the rocks any time they had a mind to, even at that early age. Some things never change, although I have often thought how much easier it must be for a young actor to concentrate on his work now that both sexes, when dressed at any rate, are all but indistinguishable.

Rehearsals for *The Tempest* took place on the stage whenever possible, but we had to share the space with the *Dido and Æneas* company. Construction work was also still going on, and so we found ourselves, more often than not, in a room above a local pub. My experience of the inside of public houses was, at that time, limited to a rather large function room adjoining *The Swan* in Sudbury, Middlesex, to which the members of Kensal Cricket Club and their families would adjourn following a home match on the nearby Vale Farm sports ground. My father was a keen cricketer in those far-off days when the women were only too happy to make the sandwiches, or pretended to be. My mother certainly enjoyed the evening sessions at *The Swan* where, with a gin and orange rocking precariously on top of the piano, she would accompany anyone who had a mind to sing something. Fortunately, for mum's repertoire was not vast, it usually turned out to be the same people singing exactly the same songs as they did the last time. My Uncle Chris was no cricketer, but he had a very pleasing light baritone voice and his rendition of *The Story of a Starry Night* was both melodious and romantic. He was, as I remember, quite a good-looking bloke with a full head of wavy hair which, some few years later, he left behind on the pillow when he got up one morning. Some hair turns white overnight, but Uncle Chris's just fell out, every last strand of it. I don't know if he ever sang 'Starry Night' in public again, but somehow I doubt it. He was quite a vain man and the permanent beret was not an image he would have wanted to promote. Somewhat later in the evening, one of my aunties, normally quite restrained, would regale the company with a ditty, the title of which I'm not sure I ever knew, but which opened with the following couplet:

'Show me your winkle tonight,
Out in the pale moonlight.'

We kids, of course, had usually been despatched to play hide-and-seek in the pub garden by this time. Out of sight and out of mind, they were free to chortle and snigger at their rude songs while we were equally at liberty to exercise our own preference for a game called 'Sardines'!

The atmosphere in the room above the pub in St. John's Wood was not nearly so earthy and daily reverberated to the sounds of Purcell and Johnson's version of *Where the bee sucks, there suck I*. Strangely, I have little or no recollection of the rehearsal process. But I do recall that the grown-up actors were, in general, very kind and helpful, and that I was in awe of every single one of them. I am bound to remember Clifford Evans, who played Prospero, as our on-stage relationship was very close. His easy authority and his mellifluous Welsh voice made a great impression on me, but I have no idea how successful his performance was, or anybody else's for that matter, as I had nothing to measure them against at that time.

Memory is a funny thing. I remember, for instance, with remarkable clarity, standing outside a butcher's shop in the Harrow Road while my mother was inside, negotiating our weekly meat ration. It was a warm summer's day and I was looking up into a blue, cloudless sky where two fighter aircraft were engaged in a dog-fight. As far as I was concerned, their life and death struggle on that beautiful sunny morning was no more than a pleasant diversion, and it did not occur to me until many years later that what I had actually witnessed was an incident in the Battle of Britain, which took place in the August and September of 1940, when I was about two and a half years old. Nowadays, I usually have to go through the alphabet letter by letter, in order to remind myself of the name of an actor with whom I shared a dressing-room most recently, and I cannot for the life of me remember two lines of the part I was playing at the time. And yet, perversely, I need neither diary nor programme to summon up an all-but-complete cast-list from those early days in the theatre. To prove the point, I remember that Miranda and Ferdinand in *The Tempest* were played by Josephine Griffin and Kenneth Fortescue, Stephano and Trinculo by Wensley Pithey and Toke Townley, Sebastian and Antonio by Bryan Coleman and that doyen of middle-eastern villainy in a score or so of British films, Ferdy Maine. Bernard Miles himself played Caliban and, both as himself and as Caliban, he managed to scare the pants off me. It wasn't that he was unpleasant or cruel in any way but, from one moment to the next, he was totally unpredictable. Not that I was altogether unfamiliar with that curious phenomenon known as the 'English eccentric' as Kilburn Grammar School boasted its fair share of them. 'Bunny' Rhodes, our Geography master, for instance, was a man of uncertain temper, whose habit of hurling hard-backed blackboard dusters at wayward pupils was legendary, although his aim was mercifully inaccurate; Mr. Merlyn-Smith, our fiery music teacher, refused to curb his smoking habit even for the duration of his class, with the result that the top of the piano was furrowed with deep cigarette burns; and while we minnows hugged the walls for safety, Mr. Gould, the senior Classics master, tall and gaunt, would sweep along the school corridor, his white hair standing on end and his black gown billowing out behind him, vampire-like, for all the world like a character out of *Tom Brown's Schooldays*. Even the relatively normal Peter Wright had acquired the sobriquet of 'Lefty', due to his habit of carrying a copy of *The Daily Worker* in his jacket pocket. It was, in fact, such a permanent and conspicuous feature, one could have been forgiven for thinking it part of the jacket's original design. But none of this, colourful though it certainly was, had prepared me for the eccentricities of Bernard Miles. His well-known rural persona, on both film and radio, was a very effective mask, and while he could be as genial as Joe Gargery one moment, he could change in an instant into the very reincarnation of W.C.Fields. I never knew where I was with him and, rather than risk a confrontation with 'Uncle' Bernard's alter ego, I found ways and means of keeping out of his way.

Several years later, when I was trying to re-enter the acting profession as a young adult following an enforced absence of two years, I sought Bernard's assistance, and instantly regretted it. I went to meet him in what passed for his office in the much larger and altogether less lovely manifestation of the Mermaid Theatre situated on the Thames at Puddle Dock. The charming and eternally attractive Mrs. Miles was also there, so that Bernard had an audience of two for his monologue, which went almost as follows, "Well, look who's here, Josephine. My word, hasn't he grown? Well, that's what National Service does for you. RAF, wasn't it? Imagine that, eh, Josephine – our Ariel in the RAF. My goodness, you were very good, wasn't he, Josephine? His Ariel, *you* remember. Very good, it was. My word, yes. So ... looking for a job, are you? Well, we'll have to see what we can do, eh Josephine? Yes. *(Pause)* Mind if I give you a bit of advice, young Terry? You see, times have changed a bit since you went away. You don't want to wear a suit and tie, you know. When you go for an interview or an audition these days, you don't want to go wearing a suit and tie. Oh, no. What you want to wear is a pair of jeans and a sweater. That's what they're wearing these days. More relaxed, you see. I should do that, if I were you. Stroll in, all casual-like, in your jeans and sweater, plonk yourself down without waiting to be asked. Put your feet up on the table. Nothing rude, mind!" Bernard was obviously determined to be part of the recently unleashed theatrical revolution, although he couldn't bring himself to feel entirely comfortable about it. It almost goes without saying that I never worked with Bernard again, although I came pretty close to it on one occasion. Nor did he give me any really useful help or advice. I still wear a suit and tie when I consider it appropriate, and I have never put my feet up on my own table, let alone anyone else's. Call me a rebel, if you like!

But back to 1951: *Dido and Æneas* opened on September 9th in front of an audience almost entirely made up of critics, and even they had to be hand-picked due to the limited number of seats available. The seating, as I remember, had caused enormous problems. Plush velvet armchairs were out, not only because of the expense, but because they would have looked absurd in the context of an Elizabethan playhouse, and made an already restricted space even smaller. There was a suspicion, however, that hard wooden benches might give offence to the bottoms of the glitterati who would be making up a sizeable proportion of the audience, many of whom were also subscribers. In the end, there was no real alternative but benches, which allowed for a capacity audience of around 180, and which were painted a smart red, although I am sure this didn't make them any softer!

I had already been introduced to the music of Purcell, courtesy of Mr. Merlyn-Smith whose repertoire included that lovely song, *Fairest Isle*, which we sang, or so it seemed, in the course of every music lesson we ever had. But I was in no way prepared for the operatic experience of *Dido and Æneas*. Needless to say, I had never witnessed an opera before; nor had I consciously ever heard singing of the kind that filled the Mermaid Theatre that night. We were a 'Light Programme' family and, apart from the doleful and dreaded Sunday night excursion into light classical music with Tom Sanders and his Palm Court Orchestra, my musical knowledge at the time was pretty well restricted to the recordings of Frankie Laine and Guy Mitchell. There were, apparently, a number of people who feared that Kirsten Flagstad's powerful Wagnerian voice would blow Purcell's delicate music to pieces. I knew nothing of that; only that Flagstad singing was an earth-shattering experience, and especially when she eventually arrived at the exquisite *When I Am Laid in Earth*, and that Maggie Teyte as Belinda was as delightful on-stage as she was off. I was also somewhat relieved to see the flying equipment being tested by Murray

Dickie as the Attendant Spirit, particularly as he was obviously a good deal heavier than me! What really hooked me, though, was the performance of Edith Coates as the Sorceress. With everyone else singing so beautifully, the abrasive quality of her voice, and her all-round malevolence chilled me to the marrow, and was the one single reason for the fact that, although I never saw it from the auditorium again, I never missed a single performance of *Dido*. I suppose that I must have worn my enthusiasm on my sleeve, although I have no particular memory of it, but I was asked if I would like to operate the thunder-sheet which introduced and punctuated the Sorceress's scenes, and it was with great relish and, I imagine, with some little training, that I undertook the task for the rest of its run, delighted that I was now able to contribute to the atmosphere of those spine-tingling scenes. Several years later, I saw Edith Coates again, equally compelling as the Old Lady who, amongst other things, loses one of her buttocks in Leonard Bernstein's musical, *Candide*, and it was nice to know that my earlier approbation had not been so very wide of the mark.

Memories of my own first-night are hazy by comparison, and the only incident I can recall with anything like clarity is being flown down from the roof to take my curtain-call. The entire company, with the exception of Prospero and Caliban, was on-stage and gesturing towards me as I made my descent. My feet had no sooner touched the ground than a rose, thrown from the audience, landed in front of me. In my innocence, I hadn't the faintest idea how it had got there, or why, so I simply took my bow, turned away and left it where it had fallen. Fortunately, one of the ladies in the company rescued it and gave it to me afterwards, telling me that it had been thrown by Madam Flagstad. What an idiot I felt! Joan Gellner had certainly not prepared me for that eventuality.

The remaining two weeks flew by in something of a blur, and I can only rely on the recollections of Peter Daubeny to fill in what is essentially a blank in my own memory:

'The weather was kind. Throughout the season we had only two wet days. We were thankful. The hall was water-tight enough, but a wet season would have meant much discomfort for at least half the cast who, for lack of proper dressing-rooms, were obliged to dress in Bernard Miles' house and walk over in their costumes... On rainy nights innumerable umbrellas were used, not only for the artists who hurried between house and theatre, but also to keep dry those who had to climb the ladder onto the garage roof in order to reach the flying platform. An Ariel sheltered beneath an umbrella is a pretty fancy which will long remain in my memory.'

There is no doubt that it had been a thrilling début, and a unique opportunity. I don't suppose for one minute that I entertained any thoughts as to where it all might lead at the time. Those kind of considerations would come a little later. For the moment, I was happy that I had been asked to do it, and sorry that it was all over. Still, I had my memories, plus a Boy Scout sheath-knife presented to me by Bernard Miles, a wilting rose thrown by Kirsten Flagstad, and my first professional review by Elizabeth Frank of the late, and still lamented, *News Chronicle*:

'Never was there such a sprite as this Ariel – 13 year-old Kilburn Grammar School boy Terry Wale, son of a London bus driver. His performance was magical and enchanting. I think we have not heard the last of Master Wale.'

oOoOo

Two

I was not yet 14 and I had already reached a crossroads in my life. During my season at the Mermaid Theatre, I had attracted the interest of a London agent, a lady called Rita Cave, who saw my immediate future in terms of film studios rather than theatres. To this end she accompanied me to a meeting at the Savoy Hotel where I was introduced to Irving Allen, the producer of a forthcoming picture about an American convict on the run who meets up with a young London boy and, as a result of their relationship, undergoes a personality change. The star of the picture, John Garfield, was also there and I recall reading several scenes with him. Now, had it been James Cagney or Humphrey Bogart, I would probably have been rendered speechless, but John Garfield, albeit a major star, was all but unknown to me, and I don't think I was unduly rattled in his presence. In any event, I was offered the part a few days later and so, subject to approval by the powers-that-be, I was all set to make my motion picture début!

At the same time, I was invited to audition for the part of Puck in *A Midsummer Night's Dream* at the Old Vic Theatre. Someone must have thought this was a good idea, but it certainly wasn't Rita Cave, who was trying to push me in the general direction of Ealing and Shepperton rather than the Waterloo Road. I can only assume that, once again, my old English teacher, Peter Wright, had had a hand in making the decision that led to me being ushered onto the stage of the Old Vic Theatre one morning early in October, 1951. Even now, all but seventy years later, I still look on the Old Vic as a kind of Mecca, the one single theatre that can be guaranteed to set the Leichner running through my veins again! The effect on me at the time was totally awe-inspiring, especially as I found myself auditioning in the middle of the set for Donald Wolfit's *Tamburlaine the Great,* which consisted of several vast tents, their tops reaching up so high that they disappeared out of sight, even from where I was standing on the stage. If my first impression was of a world of Swiftian dimensions, it was given further substance when, after my audition, I was joined on the stage by the director, a giant of a man called Tyrone Guthrie. He must have been six feet four or five, but with a disproportionately small head which made him appear, in false perspective, even taller. His voice, however, was not the voice of a big man, and there was something of the leprechaun in his manner. I liked him immediately although, of course, I had no idea who he was, nor of his place in the theatrical establishment of the day. I would have been much more impressed, in any case, had I known that he was the cousin of Tyrone Power, the swashbuckling Hollywood film star whose *Zorro* had left its mark on me some years earlier.

Although I didn't know it at the time, I was obviously living a charmed life for, only a couple of days later, I was offered the part of Puck in *A Midsummer Night's Dream*. The only problem was that the dates clashed entirely with the dates of the film and that, consequently, I would have to give one of them up. The decision was not really mine to make, although the prospect of joining my idols up there on the 'Silver Screen' was obviously the more alluring of the two. I had, after all, just finished playing one Shakespearean fairy. In this, I was at one with my agent who pulled out all the stops to persuade those powers-that-be to let me do the picture. They were, in this case, members of the London County Council (LCC) Education Authority, whose job it was to grant or withhold performing licences to children of school age. Clearly none of them had ever queued up outside the Odeon, the Palace or the Gaumont on the outside chance of getting in, or traded in their jam-jars for the price of a ticket, for while they appeared happy enough to grant me a licence to appear in Shakespeare at the Old Vic, they refused to countenance any absence from school for the purpose of making a motion picture. I was, of course, deeply disappointed, as was Rita Cave who promptly lost all interest in my future. As it turned out, however, I would have suffered something more than disappointment had the decision gone the other way. Several weeks later, John Garfield suffered a heart attack, and while I am almost a hundred per cent certain that it had nothing to do with the fact that I was no longer going to play opposite him, it did mean that the picture had to be indefinitely postponed and that, for all the wrong reasons, the LCC Education Authority had made the right decision.

The part of Puck was to be, in the long term, one of the most significant in my career as an actor, although it would be another ten years before I was able to grasp the many and varied opportunities afforded by that extraordinary creature, William Shakespeare. The last Old Vic production of *A Midsummer Night's Dream*, also directed by Tyrone Guthrie, had been before the war in 1937, when John Mills, already in his late twenties, had played Puck. There is no doubt that, at 13 going on 14, I was too young for the role, and that those qualities in me that had meshed so well with the character of Ariel, left a whole swathe of Puck's multifaceted features unexplored and undiscovered. Ariel is an airy spirit; Puck, on the other hand, is decidedly earthbound.

When he announces that he is about to 'put a girdle round about the earth in forty minutes', you are left in no doubt that he means to achieve this by running very fast on his feet. Ariel appears and disappears 'with a thought', and only exists on this plane because Prospero has captured him through the power of his magic. He performs his master's bidding unquestioningly and to the letter because, in return, he has been promised his liberty. But he is quite disinterested and has no understanding of the human emotions involved, only curiosity, and no identifiable experience of anything except the pain of confinement and the joy of freedom – recognisable enough concepts for any average schoolboy! Puck does as he is told too, but manages to serve his own interests at the same time by putting his own twist on things. He is well acquainted with human frailty and exploits it for his own pleasure. Ariel serves Prospero because he has no choice; Puck serves Oberon because it gives him status and because he knows what's best for him. He is sophisticated, independent and experienced in the ways of the world. Later on, I would come to grips with some, if not all, of these characteristics, but at the time I simply played what I saw, and what I saw, wearing the blinkers of extreme youth, was just the tip of the iceberg. One newspaper review said: 'It was a brave and intelligent notion to cast a 14 year-old boy as Puck, and Terry Wale bravely and intelligently rewards the notion.' So, on account of my tender years, I managed to get away with it. I certainly enjoyed playing the part. It was more fun than Ariel and, of course, I was happily ignorant of my shortcomings. In those halcyon days, acting simply meant getting up and doing it. In any case, I was far too busy accumulating the experiences that would, in time, serve me well in an altogether more disingenuous interpretation of Robin Goodfellow.

I was chaperoned across London by a very attractive young woman whose services I was obliged to share with 15 boys from a school in Highgate who had been cast to play the other fairies in 'The Dream' and with whom I consequently shared a dressing-room. This led to occasional mayhem, such as the day when several of them decided to swing from the sprinkler system, setting off the alarm and flooding not only our own dressing-room, but also Douglas Campbell's on the floor below. Douglas was not particularly well disposed towards any of us after that episode although, to be perfectly honest, I don't recall him going out of his way to seek our company prior to the flood. There were also several confrontations between me and some of the other boys, exacerbated, no doubt, by our cramped conditions, but triggered by the preferential treatment meted out to me by our chaperone, and my tendency to side with her in any dispute. I was not, I hasten to add, and I never have been, a goody-goody or a teacher's pet. At the time, her motives seemed perfectly clear to me. I was playing a large and demanding role, and she saw it as part of her duty to protect my interests. My own motives were somewhat more ambiguous and disturbing. During the rehearsal period, I had developed strong feelings towards her, both emotional and physical.

1951 Midsummer Night's Dream - The Old Vic Theatre playing Puck.

I wanted to spend time with her, and would seek her out in breaks from rehearsal; felt thwarted if she was engaged in conversation with other grown-ups and even suspected she was doing it on purpose. In fact, I was thoroughly confused about the whole thing. Although I had never heard of the word, I was clearly infatuated, and hadn't the remotest idea how to handle my burgeoning sexuality. I'd experienced a bit of kissing before, of course, but with girls of my own age who'd laugh and run away at the first hint of heavy breathing. This was quite different, and the most tantalising thing about it was that she knew, and far from being shocked or censorious, she was gently amused and, heaven help me, mildly flirtatious.

A Midsummer Night's Dream opened on December 26th, 1951. The technical dress rehearsal took place several days before, and went on into the early hours of the morning. Union rules have since imposed limits on working hours, even in the theatre, but at that time directors like the indefatigable Tyrone Guthrie were free to work actors and crew until they dropped, which is precisely what he did. I remember Guthrie leaping up onto the stage sometime after 2am in order to sort out yet another technical problem, and turning his impish gaze onto the actors who were lying around in various stages of mental and physical collapse. "Oh," he said, gleefully clapping his hands together, "isn't it fun putting on a play!" And curiously, it was.

Guthrie's production of *A Midsummer Night's Dream* was not, as I recall, particularly well received by the critics. It was too austere. The 'wood near Athens' resembled a landscape in the immediate aftermath of an atomic explosion; the trees were leafless and twisted, affording no shade or comfort, let alone mystery or, indeed, any sense of being inhabited by a bunch of wrangling fairies. It could be argued, I suppose, that it was ahead of its time, but coming as it did in a period of post-war austerity, it didn't accord too well with peoples' expectations. Sets and costumes were designed by the superb Tanya Moiseiwitsch, with whom I would be lucky enough to work again. 'The Dream', however, was not one of her more notable triumphs.

Neither was it one of Kenneth Griffith's, whose intense and highly-strung Oberon was ill-matched with Jill Balcon's serene and rather lovely Titania; the wonder of it being not so much how they managed to effect a reconciliation at the end of the play as how they ever got together in the first place! In the right part, Ken was pretty well peerless, but Oberon was not the right part, and being on stage with him which was where, as Puck, I very often found myself, was not the most comfortable place on earth to be, especially for someone as inexperienced as I was. His delivery of the lines was somewhat erratic, and his behaviour was unpredictable to say the least. At one performance I went on stage, expecting to be greeted at Titania's bower with the lines, "Welcome, good Robin. See'st thou this sweet sight?", and found myself completely alone. Once I had decided there was nothing I could do to further the plot without someone else to talk to, I left the stage and went to Ken's dressing-room where I tentatively knocked on the door and suggested, ever so politely, that maybe he ought to join me on stage. My abiding memory of that moment is of the sheer panic that suddenly overtook him, and remained with him for the rest of his performance, which was even damper and more tremulous than usual. It was a reaction quite alien to me at the time. But that's the insouciance of youth for you! Nevertheless I had, and still have, a great regard for him. His numerous appearances in British films of the period were memorable, and none more so than his hen-pecked, cowering, yet bitterly resentful librarian in *Only Two Can Play*, which was an absolute gem of a performance. I also much admired his later television documentaries, on subjects as diverse and controversial as the Boer War and the IRA, notable for their complete lack of objectivity, and presented with that same Welsh passion and nervous intensity that made his Oberon so difficult to relate to.

My memories of the production itself are necessarily hazy, and are largely confined to personalities, incidents and, of course, to the quality of the acting. Watching Irene Worth (Helena) and Paul Rogers (Bottom), both in rehearsal and in performance, was worth three years at any drama school, and it was a great privilege to work, if only once, alongside that splendid and strangely underrated actor, Alan Badel. Ah, if only our modern television audiences and critics had seen him play D'Arcy in the first TV adaptation of *Pride and Prejudice* back in the '60s, they wouldn't be so ready to heap praise on his successors. By all accounts, Badel was not a particularly loveable man, and was given to occasional bouts of violence. I was told that, during the run of 'The Dream', he beat up a troublesome drunk outside Waterloo station. But I saw nothing of that side of the man. I only recall a gentle, bewildered Peter Quince and, later, a dashing and stylish Romeo to Claire Bloom's Juliet, with Peter Finch as a swashbuckling Mercutio. I remember too his passionate portrayal of a French poet opposite Irene Worth, in a now forgotten play called *The Other Heart* by James Forsyth. Around about the same time he also starred in a short and quirky picture called *The Stranger Left No Card*, directed by Wendy Toye. It was about the arrival in a small town of a weirdly dressed eccentric who, by playing the fool, wins acceptance by the townspeople. But he is really there to commit murder. It's many years since I last saw it, but it made a lasting impression on me, as did Badel's mesmerising performance.

The only fly in my own particular pot of ointment was Robert Shaw, who played Lysander, and became the bane of my life during those few weeks when, night after night, whilst lying 'asleep' on the stage, he would grab hold of my ankle as I applied the love-potion to his eyes, and refuse to let go. Leaving aside the obvious consideration that as I wasn't experienced enough to deal with it and that he ought to have picked on someone his own size, it was the sheer mind-numbing repetition that finally got to me, so that I ended up dreading that particular scene. It has to be said, I suppose, that Mr. Shaw himself was quite young at the time, and had I not come across him some years later, a well-established star by then, and discovered that he was just as boorish as I remembered him, and with an ego that, in my opinion, more than matched his talent, I would have put it all down to coltishness, and probably have forgotten it by now. Funny the things that stick in your mind! I remember, for instance, that Mr. Shaw enjoyed something of a reputation with the ladies, and that his amorous adventures included sexual congress with one of Hippolyta's handmaidens in the Old Vic scene dock, deserted at the time except for George Murcell's parrot. It was all gossip, of course, and in any case, if the scene dock had indeed been deserted, how come everyone seemed to know about it? Unless, of course, George Murcell's parrot was only pretending to be monosyllabic!

I grew up very quickly at the Old Vic. Well, it was an adult world, and very few of my fellow actors had the time or the inclination to make concessions to my extreme youth. There were exceptions, of course, and particularly amongst the ladies. Jill Balcon, for instance, the daughter of film producer, Michael Balcon, and wife to the then Poet Laureate, Cecil Day-Lewis, thence becoming the mother of Daniel Day-Lewis, was always prepared to talk and offer advice. Even now, I can hardly believe that I had the nerve to go knocking on her dressing-room door as often as I did, but she never discouraged me and was always charming, attentive and, to my mind, extremely wise. Wisdom by the bucketful also came in the shape of the Old Vic's stage-door keeper, Ernie Davis. Ernie was the archetypal stage-door keeper against whom all other stage-door keepers have since been measured and, to a greater or lesser degree, found wanting. Pickwickian in appearance, with silver hair and rosy cheeks, Ernie was always ready to lend an ear or even half-a-crown until pay-day. He was part of the brickwork, and even some 30 years later, on a return visit to the Old Vic, I was irrationally disappointed not to find him there. It was, after all, his welcome that introduced you to the unique atmosphere of that loveliest of theatres. Still vivid in my memory after all these years are the warmth of his smile, as you left the chill drabness of the Waterloo

Road behind, and his cheery greeting, which always made you feel that he was genuinely pleased to see you. It was more like a homecoming than a trip to the workplace. Ernie was never the kind of stage-door keeper from whom you just picked up your key and tipped at the end of the week simply for being there. His little cubbyhole was a constant hive of activity, and no gratuity, however large, could have recompensed him for the services he provided. Part doctor, part philosopher, part storyteller, Ernie was one of the most truly generous people I have ever come across. He also taught me one of my earliest professional lessons, although I was unaware of his part in it at the time. In general terms, I'm sure my behaviour was far from irreproachable, but Ernie was never censorious. His way of dealing with any kind of misdemeanour was altogether more oblique. I was about to leave the theatre after the performance one evening, when I heard the gabble of voices from outside on the pavement. "Oh, no," I complained. "Not autograph hunters *again!*" A lesser mortal would have torn me off a strip, and sent me out there to do my duty with a sizeable flea in my ear. But that wasn't Ernie's way. He smiled sympathetically and said, with earnest solicitude, "Don't you worry about it. Just you wait here." He then left his cubbyhole and went outside, where I heard him raising his voice above the general hubbub. "Anyone here want Puck's autograph?" he inquired. There was silence, and the slightest of pauses, before a concerted and unanimous "No!" rang in my ears. Ernie came back in, still pretending he was on my side. He winked at me. "Off you go then," he said, "they won't give you any bother." I was completely devastated, of course, and knew, for the first time in a life replete with blows to the ego, what it was like to have the wind well and truly taken out of your sails. I also learned that it was a rare honour to be asked for your autograph, warmly welcomed on many a cold and rainy night in Nuneaton, Sunderland, Peterhead or wherever, when the sight of even one bedraggled person outside the stage door asking for my signature on their soggy programme, would have sent me back to my dingy digs with more of a spring in my step. The other thing I learned, but not until much later, was that Ernie had silently instructed them in that resounding chorus of disapproval, for which hard lesson I thank him from the bottom of my heart. I wept when the run of *A Midsummer Night's Dream* came to an end. I almost always did in those far-off days when being in a theatre was pure joy, and acting little more than a glorious game. But the Old Vic was special, and remains so, and I had no idea as I said goodbye to Ernie for the last time in February 1952, carrying my make-up box and a heavy heart to Waterloo Station and thence by way of the Bakerloo line to my home in Kensal Rise, that I would be coming back before too long. Meanwhile, however, there were more hard lessons to be learned.

The Innocents, by William Archibald, adapted from the Henry James novel, *The Turn of the Screw,* began its life at the Q Theatre, adjacent to London's Kew Bridge. The 'Q' presented many new plays in its 30 year history, a forerunner, if you like, of 'fringe theatre.' Sadly, unable to meet local authority requirements, it closed in 1956. Stephen Mitchell of London Theatrical Productions was already financially involved, and subsequently decided to mount a full-scale production of *The Innocents* for the West End. This meant, amongst other things, a change of cast, and fast upon the heels of my engagement at the Old Vic, I auditioned for the part of Miles in March 1952. I didn't know it at the time – or at least I think I didn't – that the part of Miles was already cast, and what I was, in fact, auditioning for was the job of understudy. It's very easy, with the benefit of hindsight, to say that I should have walked away from that particular opportunity, as I was to do in similar circumstances just over a year later. There's no doubt that my education was suffering, and although it was undeniably fun to be able to put my hand up in the middle of a maths class and say, "Excuse me, sir, but I've got a matinée", I really ought to have taken my schooling more seriously. Later, much later, I would realise that I had a lot of catching up to do, but meanwhile I only wanted to act. The irony behind my decision to accept the understudy job was that, for the next nine months, I did virtually no acting whatsoever.

Somewhere around this time, I made my television début. During the early fifties, television was not a particularly rich area of employment for actors; the boom in television drama was yet to come, although Children's TV did offer a few opportunities, and I recall one job in particular, a children's serial called *Peter in the Air* for Associated-Rediffusion, in which Ronnie Barker and I played two Mexican peasants who kept wandering in and out of the action leading a donkey. I have no recollection of our part in the story. In fact, I have no idea what it was all about anyway; I even wonder if I did at the time! My actual début was with the BBC, in a charming little play called *Young Chippie,* directed by Joy Harington. It was the story of a country boy from a poor family who manages to save up 27/6d (£1.37½) in order to buy a bicycle. Ignoring the kindly advice of his parents, played by that veteran of dozens of British war movies, Sam Kydd, and the lovely Maureen Pryor, he goes to the local auction rooms and finds, as they had feared, that all the bicycles fetch considerably more than 27/6d. At the end of the afternoon, however, with everyone at the auction by now aware of his plight, even the most obdurate and hard-hearted collector cannot bring himself to bid against the boy who ends up cycling away on the newest and brightest bike of them all! I only mention this because it is almost inconceivable that such a delightfully sentimental, naïve and warm-hearted tale could find its way on to our television screens today, and not even in a children's programme!

Which brings me back, rather neatly I think, to *The Innocents*. Set in the late 19th century, it is the tale of two children, possessed, or so it would appear, by the ghosts of their former governess, and their absentee guardian's late valet, Peter Quint who, when they were alive, got up to all manner of unspeakable, and unspoken things, with which the children, Miles and his younger sister, Flora, were apparently acquainted and, consequently, tainted. Or so it seems. The arrival of a new governess, Miss Giddens, coincides with the expulsion of Miles from school for unmentioned, and unmentionable, misdemeanours. *The Turn of the Screw* hinges on whether the children are genuinely haunted or whether Miss Giddens, a repressed and unworldly Victorian spinster, drives them in that direction with her suspicions and neurotic fantasies. *The Innocents,* as adapted by William Archibald, wisely goes for the former, more theatrical, option. Well, with both ghosts plainly on view, it's difficult to imagine – even if Miss Giddens is guilty of mishandling the situation – how it can be treated otherwise; or at least it was, until I saw a production (in which my own daughter played Flora) of the same adaptation, in which the director desperately and misguidedly tried to return the play to its literary origins and which, of course, fell uncomfortably between two stools. There was no room for ambiguity in the original London production, directed by Peter Glenville, in which the ghosts were all too real, their malevolent influence over the children undeniable and, in Miles' case, unstoppable this side of the grave. Miles, and to a slightly lesser extent, Flora, were inhabited by evil, and it was altogether understandable, and probably inevitable, that the young actors who played them – not to mention their understudies – were going to be adversely affected by this over a period of nine months.

Peter Glenville and Stephen Mitchell had assembled a small, though distinguished, cast for the West End production, led by Flora Robson as Miss Giddens, and supported by the redoubtable Barbara Everest as the housekeeper, Mrs. Grose. The children were to be played by Jeremy Spenser and a pretty little thing called Carol

Wolveridge. These, plus the two ghosts, played by Sheila Wynn and Leslie Wright, myself and Carol's understudy, Gillian Gale, made up the entire company. As I have already suggested, I was quite sure that Jeremy had been cast to play Miles long before the auditions took place, and that they were, from the start, only looking for someone to understudy him. It made perfect sense, of course, for besides already being something of a film-star, Jeremy's looks, voice and stage presence were pretty well unrivalled amongst his peers. I can still remember with great clarity his first entrance, standing in front of the French windows, looking like a Midwich Cuckoo with his dyed blond hair, wearing an immaculate Victorian suit, and greeting the new governess with polite but icy condescension, as he slowly removed first one glove, and then the other. It was an utterly compelling, and truly chilling moment, giving more than a hint of what was to come, and a glimpse to Miss Giddens of the devil she might be up against. God knows, I saw the show often enough in my professional capacity, and I never tired of that moment, nor of wondering how Jeremy managed to achieve that effect. With all the confidence that goes hand in hand with inexperience, I knew perfectly well that I could play the part, and that I would be good in it but, with something approaching perception, I realised that I would find it difficult, if not impossible, to act being mesmeric. Later, of course, I came to learn about that indefinable something that you either possess or you don't, star quality if you like, and Jeremy Spenser, as a child performer, had it in spades. Memorable, too, was the deceptively conventional setting by Oliver Smith, with its winding staircase, its top landing innocent enough by day, but something like hell's threshold after dark. That staircase haunted my dreams at the time, replacing the nightmare-inducing severed hand that played the piano in *The Beast With Five Fingers*. But that may well have been because I had finally got around to closing the lid of my mother's piano in my bedroom at night!

Before opening at Her Majesty's Theatre, Haymarket, in July, 1952, *The Innocents* went on the road, on what was described as 'a short pre-London tour'. For all sorts of reasons, I found it interminable, although by far the biggest reason was Jeremy's mother, Caryl Spenser. Chaperones had, of course, to be provided for the children, and since nothing on earth could have prised Mrs. Spenser from Jeremy's side, it was agreed that she would be my chaperone too. With Caryl Spenser I was introduced to that theatrical peculiarity – the 'Stage Mother', and it was a baptism of fire. She was, in almost every respect, a monster, who made Rose in the musical *Gypsy* almost winsome by comparison!

Sharing her, in any case, was a bad idea to begin with since, as Jeremy's mother, she was bound to take his side in all things, and favour him in every way to my disadvantage. This I could almost cope with, although I knew that my own mother, in similar circumstances, would have been even-handed to a fault. But I was not equipped to deal with the constant accusations that I was trying to engineer Jeremy's infirmity so that I could play the part. She would frequently hem me in with her huge bulk, point an accusing finger in my face, and tell me in venomous tones that she *knew* I'd tried to trip him up, push him down the stairs, and take the only towel (*my* towel) away from the beach in Blackpool so that he would catch pneumonia! Some time later, during the London run, I arrived at the theatre to be told that Jeremy was very ill, that the doctor was with him in his dressing-room, and that he probably wouldn't be able to go on for that performance. I don't know if I rejoiced at the prospect, but even if I did, my celebrations were short-lived, for on my way upstairs I met Mrs. Spenser coming down. Out came the finger, "Think you're going on, do you? Over my dead body!" she hissed. Needless to say, I didn't get on at that performance, nor indeed at any other, although it was very nearly over her son's dead body that she achieved this Pyrrhic victory. It was in Leeds, I think, that she invited Miss Jessel's ghost, the hapless Sheila Wynn, to afternoon tea in their hotel room. Sheila sat on the bed and had no sooner eaten her cream cake and downed her second cup of tea when she was leapt upon by a high-spirited Jeremy who, to peals of laughter and the occasional fond admonishment from his mother, simulated the sex act while lying on top of her. Sheila was far too polite to knee the little bugger in the crutch, which was what he deserved, but she was plainly mortified by the experience, and even I was appalled, not so much by Jeremy's antics, as by the fact that his mother appeared to condone them.

For those who have spent a fair amount of their professional lives 'on the road', memories of Sunday train calls tend to merge, but on tour with *The Innocents* they were distinguished by the regular and frequent disappearances of Jeremy and Carol Wolveridge. A full-scale search of the train would be mounted, and they were invariably found, sooner or later, locked together in one of the toilets. I never doubted that it was anything other than a game, devised by Jeremy to pass the time and create mayhem amongst the adults, but while Carol's chaperone and auntie, Margaret Blue, was guaranteed to have the vapours, Mrs. Spenser always found it hugely entertaining, and probably wouldn't have been unduly perturbed even if everyone else's worst fears had been confirmed. Jeremy's elder brother, David Spenser, had somehow managed to extricate himself from his mother's embrace somewhat earlier, and went on to become a well-respected radio producer, and an extremely nice man. I believe Jeremy won his freedom too eventually, although it must have cost him dear. My happily brief relationship with Caryl Spenser reduced me to frequent tears, drove me to tobacco, and introduced me to the unhappy realisation that life in the theatre was not always going to live up to my wide-eyed expectations.

There was no way, of course, that four children, all of school age, were going to be allowed completely off the leash as far as schooling was concerned. The Education Authority had seen to it that, in common with Miles and Flora, we had our very own governess, an unfortunate woman who went by the singular name of Bertha Cwybel, and who must have rued the day that she ever applied for the post. It was Bertha's job, for four hours every day, to keep us abreast of the school curriculum, and since Jeremy and I were both 14, while the girls were a year or two younger, it was no easy task, a task which all four of us took great delight in making even more onerous. If Miss Giddens suffered untold misery in her fictional dealings with the manipulative Miles and Flora, poor Miss Cwybel must have gone through similar real-life agonies at the hands of her four insufferable charges. A room was usually set aside as a schoolroom in whatever theatre we were playing, and there, for four hours every day, we would throw ourselves whole-heartedly, and mercilessly, into the task of making Bertha's life a misery. We would taunt her, ignore her, argue with her over every little thing, and in one climactic burst of appalling barbarity, we even tied her to a chair and performed a kind of war dance around her. We enjoyed nothing more than the visits she planned to various museums and galleries, because it gave us the opportunity, just as soon as her back was turned, to give her the slip and keep her just out of reach for next hour or two as she sought us, with mounting anxiety, from room to room. I can only imagine what kind of anguish she must have suffered at our hands, and hope I simply wasn't capable of imagining it at the time.

For some unfathomable reason, Bertha thought that I was redeemable. My work was certainly of a higher standard, all three of them being products of various stage schools, but my general behaviour was just as bad, and I resented any attempt she made to drive that particular wedge between us. Three floors up in Manchester's Opera House, she sent me to an adjoining room where I would be free from Jeremy's influence, and better able to get on with my work. I was furious, and immediately climbed out of the window, edged my way precariously along the narrow ledge high above busy Quay Street until I arrived outside the window of the schoolroom, and tapped on the glass, grinning evilly. Bertha reeled backwards with shock, and I was subsequently and severely reprimanded by the management. Nothing, however, could take away the pleasure I felt at my suddenly enhanced reputation amongst the other children, and particularly with Jeremy who, for the first time, saw me as a potential rival. He was, after all, the instigator of all things, good or bad, and where he led, we would inevitably follow. But after that incident I was considered an equal, which was just as well, otherwise I might have spent the rest of my life blaming Jeremy for everything. It was easy, too, to make a scapegoat of the play, and to some extent our daily contact with the nature of evil in *The Innocents* must have had some effect on us, although I cannot confidently assert that our conduct would have been any more acceptable had we been appearing in *The Sound of Music*. I have often thought, since then, how profusely I would apologise to Bertha Cwybel were our paths to cross again. But they never did, and I can only hope she didn't bear the scars of that encounter for too long afterwards.

The Innocents opened to favourable reviews in London, although I don't recall reading any of them, and I certainly wouldn't have kept them even if I had, as my name wouldn't have been mentioned. Those were the days when I actually underlined any references to myself, obviously because I thought no one would be remotely interested in reading anybody else's reviews!

During the run of the play at Her Majesty's Theatre, life returned to something approaching normality. I was back at school, mixing with ordinary boys, and living at home with my blessedly normal parents. Every evening, I would take the Number 6 bus from Kensal Rise to Lower Regent Street, and spend the next two and a half hours in my dressing-room. As soon as Jeremy went on stage for his final scene, I was free to take the Number 6 back to Kensal Rise, from where I would depart for school again the following morning. There was something reassuring about this relatively dull routine although, as the weeks turned into months, it became more and more irksome, especially when rehearsals began for the school play, and I couldn't be in it! Memories of the tour began to fade, although they left a sour taste for a long time afterwards, but Mrs. Spenser's shadow no longer fell across me or, at least, on the odd occasion that it did, I was no longer threatened by it. My world had suddenly expanded beyond the narrow confines of that stifling relationship, while Jeremy was still hemmed in by it. Now that I had other points of reference, his influence over me also evaporated. But it was somehow shocking, and distinctly unsettling, to ponder on how easily led, and ultimately, how corruptible I had been when removed from the familiarity of my everyday world.

The routine was broken up once a week by a day off from school to attend understudy rehearsals prior to the mid-week matinée, a welcome chance to act, even if there wasn't an audience to act for. They were made even more rewarding when, on the odd occasion, Flora Robson came in, quite voluntarily, to work with us. She may have been a bit too mature to play Miss Giddens, although that thought never crossed my mind at the time, but she was a marvellously powerful actress, and it was thrilling to play Miles opposite her, especially that last, terrifying scene when, left alone together in the big house, she takes on herself the role of exorcist and finally, but fatally, forces Miles to confront the ghost of Peter Quint. With a soul-rending cry of, "Leave me, leave me, ah, leave me!" he dies in her arms. Oh, what I wouldn't have given to have played that scene in front of a huge Saturday night audience!

It was immediately after that final confrontation, as the curtain fell on one particular matinée performance, that an uncharacteristically perturbed Miss Robson, later to become Dame Flora, approached the stage manager to complain, hesitantly, that Jeremy had spent the best part of the scene staring at her bosom. The stage manager politely suggested that, as it was such a personal matter, it would be better broached on a personal level, and that since Jeremy was still on stage, there was probably no time like the present. Flora Robson was a gentle, and rather strait-laced lady, hence her agitation as she approached Jeremy with caution. "I don't want to make a fuss, Jeremy," she began diffidently "but I find it very difficult to play that last scene when you keep staring at my ... well, I don't even know if you're aware of it yourself, but all through the scene, you were staring at my ... oh, dear ... at my ..." she gathered all her strength and finally took the plunge, "at my bosom!", she declared, almost against her will. "It's very off-putting, and I would be most grateful," she added, more assertively, "if you didn't do it again." Jeremy blushed, a deep scarlet, and turned away from her. Without a word, he slowly climbed that ominous staircase and, having reached the landing, turned. His face was now, by contrast, deathly white, as he looked down at Miss Robson, who was still waiting for an apology or, at the very least, some kind of acknowledgement. "Huh!" he uttered darkly instead, "Wishful thinking!" With that, he turned and disappeared into that dark chasm beyond the staircase, no doubt to be congratulated on his performance by Peter Quint! By that stage of the proceedings, some six months into the run, Jeremy and the character of Miles had become virtually inseparable; in fact, I'm not altogether sure they were total strangers to begin with.

What it was that made me write a play is now long forgotten. Maybe it was simply to while away the long hours spent in the dressing-room, waiting in vain to be told that Jeremy had developed some highly contagious disease that necessitated, despite his mother's protests, his immediate removal from the theatre. Or maybe it was belated revenge on Mrs. Spenser, best eaten cold, that drove me to put pen to paper. But then again, the creative urge might well have been inspired by Flora Robson. It was certainly she who promised she would try to persuade the management to allow me to stage a performance of the play if ever I should finish it. In any event, my evenings at the theatre took on a new purpose, and the days sped by as I laboured with love, and with a new kind of energy, to write my first play.

At Furleigh House, which probably lasted no longer than 35 to 40 minutes, was a story of avarice and retribution. Flora Robson had suggested that I try to write parts for as many people as possible, only excluding the actual cast of *The Innocents* and, with this in mind, the plot took shape. The members of a large family meet and wrangle over the will of the head of the household, who is missing, presumed dead. All their characters, good or bad, are laid bare, and just when it seems that evil, in the shape of the matriarch and her two greedy offspring, is about to win the day, the missing man returns, alive and well, rewards those who have been loyal to him, and punishes his wife and his errant children with forgiveness. Simple fare, owing more to all the plays I had either seen, read, or been in, than to any artistic vision of my own. But it was a workmanlike effort, at the very least in its preparation. I had written it all by hand in an exercise book and, in the absence of a typewriter and the basic skills that go with it, I had even painstakingly penned, in my neatest handwriting, all eight copies!

True to her word, Flora Robson had persuaded Stephen Mitchell of London Theatrical Productions to let me produce the play, for one performance only, on the stage of Her Majesty's Theatre between a matinée and an evening performance of *The Innocents*. I no longer recall the rehearsals that led up to it, nor the event itself with any great clarity which, considering the fact that I was not only the author, but also the director, the stage-manager, the prompter and the one who raised and lowered the curtain, is not altogether surprising. But I do remember some of the performances. Caryl Spenser, in particular, was so good as the avaricious and malevolent mother that the part might have been written with her in mind. The fact that everyone knew that it was, except for Mrs. Spenser herself, gave me some satisfaction and a feeling that, one way or another, I had paid her back for some of the wrongs she had inflicted on me. There is no doubt that it was the best part in the play – written, as it was, from the heart! The rest of the cast, which included Fredric Bayco, the theatre organist (an absolute *must* for any reputable theatre in those days!), and the two spotlight operators, Kip Carpenter and Ronald McMaster, played with zest and enthusiasm. History does not record how well the play was received by its small, though distinguished, audience, and I no longer possess a copy of the script to be embarrassed by, but everyone was very kind about it and, as a memento, I received a book by Henry James, containing both *The Turn of the Screw* and *The Aspern Papers*, with an inscription by Flora Robson, which read: 'To Terry Wale, to commemorate the production of his first play *At Furleigh House* on August 23rd, 1952 at Her Majesty's Theatre. With love from all the Company of *The Innocents*, including ghosts, seen and unseen.' There followed the signatures of practically everyone involved, either backstage or front of house, which explains how, being no diarist, I can still remember their names! As a relatively polite child, even after six months on *The Innocents*, I am sure I must have been suitably appreciative. Had I known that it would be almost 35 years before my second stage play would be seen in the West End, I would have been lost in wonder at my good fortune!

Prior to the death of King George VI in February 1952, the theatre had been known as *His* Majesty's. Almost a year later, together with the other understudy, Gillian Gale, I was standing in the foyer of *Her* Majesty's Theatre, collecting for the King George VI Memorial Fund, when I saw Irene Worth come in off the street, accompanied by Robert Quentin, the Old Vic's Production Manager. They both saw me too, and stopped in their tracks. After exchanging a look, they came over and greeted me. When Robert Quentin subsequently asked me when I would be free, I told him that the play was due to close in two weeks. They exchanged another look, followed by a mutual nod. "How would you like to come back to the Old Vic?" Robert asked. "Very much," I replied, rather too moderately in view of the sudden leap of excitement I must have felt. They both smiled happily. I had obviously solved a problem. "I don't know why we didn't think of you before", said Irene.

Had I not been collecting for the King George VI Memorial Fund in the theatre foyer at that particular moment, but had instead been cooped up in my dressing-room on the third floor of Her Majesty's Theatre, would they, I wonder, have thought of me at all? I don't know, but somehow I doubt it. Which just serves to demonstrate that the first and most important attribute for an actor – talent and training notwithstanding – is always to be in the right place at the right time!

oOoOo

Three

Returning to the Old Vic was pure, undiluted joy and, following nine months in what had felt like a strange and alien country, more like a homecoming than ever. Never had Ernie's smile of welcome at the stage-door meant more to me that it did on that first day. I was also looking forward to acting in front of an audience again, and in a part that represented something of a professional landmark – my first Shakespearean mortal! I had been invited back to play Lucius, servant to Brutus, in Hugh Hunt's production of *Julius Caesar*, and at a salary of £10 a week, 30 shillings (£1.50) more than I had been paid to play Puck. At a time when the national average wage was barely £7 a week, this was a pretty fair offer, and particularly when you consider that Lucius, nice part though it was, did not come into the same 'leading role' category as Puck. Not that money was of any great consequence to me at the time. Apart from my train fares on the Underground, and a bit of pocket money, my parents wisely saved the rest in a Post Office savings account, which they subsequently handed over to me, not so wisely, on my 17th birthday!

There were lots of familiar faces around; actors who had stayed on with the company since *A Midsummer Night's Dream*, together with a handful of new ones – well, new to me at any rate. Robin Bailey, a good actor by anybody's reckoning, was strangely miscast as Mark Antony. I seem to remember that he was not very persuasive, either as an orator or as a soldier. He certainly didn't impress me nearly as much as did William Devlin as Brutus. His performance was both strong and authoritative and, more to the point since most of my scenes were with him, he was an extremely nice man. But it was once again Paul Rogers, Bottom in 'The Dream', and now a wonderfully 'lean and hungry' Cassius, who stole the honours as far as I was concerned. I worked with Paul on only three occasions but, as a frequent member of the audience at the Old Vic during the early to mid-fifties, I saw him give a number of performances, all of which I found thrilling and inspiring. I particularly remember his convincingly 'honest' Iago, opposite Douglas Campbell's Othello; also his hilarious performance at the centre of Labishe's comedy, *The Italian Straw Hat*, and especially his urbane and elegant Pandarus in Guthrie's famous Edwardian production of *Troilus and Cressida*, observing the battle for Troy through binoculars and looking, for all the world, like a spectator at Royal Ascot. Paul had a richly mellifluous voice that seemed to wrap itself around the words, and a physical presence that was both striking and yet subtly malleable.

Ramrod-straight and poker-faced or well-upholstered and droll, Paul Rogers was my kind of actor, and still is, except that in a world where versatility is no longer as highly prized as it once was, there aren't too many of his kind around any more.

If the two parts of *Henry IV* are known as 'The smoking-room of Shakespearean drama', then *Julius Caesar* must surely be the billiard hall. Aside from the relatively minor intrusions of Portia and Calpurnia, it is an exclusively masculine play and, with 33 named characters, it imposes something of a strain on dressing-room resources. During rehearsals I had celebrated my 15th birthday, which meant that I still had a year to wait until I was allowed to share a dressing-room with the adult members of the company. This regulation, doubtless framed by people who had my best interests at heart, was a mystery to me at the time. I couldn't fathom what it was that men said or did in the privacy of their dressing-rooms that could possibly be worse than the goings-on behind the bicycle sheds in any ordinary boys' school! In any event, it caused something of a dilemma on this particular occasion, due entirely to the absence of a spare dressing-room. The problem was eventually solved when I found myself quartered in a partitioned-off area of the wardrobe department, three floors above stage level. What the wardrobe mistress, Antoinette Mara, thought of this, or whether she was even consulted about it, I never knew but, since I was intruding into her private domain, I can't imagine that she gladly welcomed my presence. Nevertheless, Mrs. Mara and I, separated by a hessian curtain, kept ourselves to ourselves, and the arrangement seemed to work quite well. Well, for most of the time it did.

There was no such thing as a Tannoy system in 1953, certainly not at the Old Vic, so that actors were unable to hear a relay of the show in their dressing-rooms or receive their calls directly through that system from the prompt corner. The responsibility for making sure that actors arrived on stage in time for their entrances lay with the call-boy who would have to trudge from dressing-room to dressing-room announcing each call in person. This still happens in certain venues that aren't equipped with a Tannoy system, of course, or on the odd occasion that it breaks down, but in 1953 it was the *status quo*, and the call-boy's job was held to be an extremely responsible one. First and foremost, however, it was – and is – down to the actor alone to be on stage at the right time, in the right costume and speaking the right words, an obligation that cannot be delegated no matter what system is in operation. At the age of 15, I was blithely unaware of this unwritten law, and utterly dependent on the good offices and proven efficiency of the Old Vic's call-boy – or, to put it in its more accurate context – the Old Vic's call-*girl!*

Ann Spiers was in her early twenties at the time, a petite brunette whose delicate fragrance lingered in the backstage corridors long after her black dirndl skirt, her crisp white blouse and her pony tail had vanished around a corner, up the stairs to the next floor or, indeed, to wherever her duties as call-girl took her. She was, in her designated task, swift and super-efficient and, apart from the seductive whisper of skirt and petticoat, utterly silent in her ballet-pumps as she pursued it. Off-duty or in rare moments of stillness, Annie had eyes that were full of laughter, a smoky saloon-bar voice, full soft lips that were made for kissing, and a mole on her chin that I preferred to call a beauty-spot. She also had a fondness for Guinness which, together with her other attributes, made her a great favourite amongst the men. She was certainly a great favourite of mine, and in my testosterone-led way, I was already half in love with her. She was aware of this, of course, and while she did nothing to encourage me (apart from simply being herself), she didn't discourage me either. She was far too warm and generous to do that. I also like to think that, in her own way, she was really quite fond of me, and consequently prepared to tolerate my attentions, possibly even found them quite appealing for, while I secretly lusted after her, I was never importunate. Instinctively, I suppose, I must have known that it would have been a waste of time, and in any case I was far too much in awe of my feelings for her to do anything that might rock the boat.

What I never took into account was that my dressing-room on the third floor added an extra dimension to Annie's job, i.e. one more flight of stairs than she was accustomed to climb. Nor did it occur to me that there was just a chance she might, if only once, forget to make that unfamiliar journey. Consequently, I was sitting with my feet up on the dressing-table in my corner of Mrs. Mara's eyrie one evening, reading *William and A.R.P.* by Richmal Crompton, confidently awaiting my call for Act II Scene IV of *Julius Caesar.* I even remember looking at my watch on the dressing-table and wondering, without being even remotely troubled by it, why it was taking so long for her to get there at this particular performance. Suddenly, and from three floors below, I heard Annie's voice, distant but nonetheless stentorian in its urgency – "Terry – you're off!" It took a moment to register but then, having nearly fallen backwards off my chair, I threw the book aside and raced out of the room towards the staircase, desperate to close the distance between me and the stage as quickly as I possibly could without breaking a leg or twisting an ankle, I eventually reached stage level in what must have been record time. But where I landed was stage-right and I knew that all my entrances were from stage left so that I still had some distance to cover, along the back corridor and through various pass-doors, most of which had to be pulled open rather than pushed, slowing me down and adding to the panic that had already seized me and which now prevented me, having at last reached the stage-left wing, from stopping and trying to regain a little composure. I simply flew onto the stage, motivated by nothing except blind faith; but the stage was empty. The panic had driven everything except the need to get there out of my head, so I hadn't the remotest idea what scene I was supposed to be playing. In fact, the only thing I knew for certain was that I was never on stage by myself; so where were the other actors? Their presence would, at least, have given me a clue. I looked around again but there was no doubt about it, I was entirely alone. I felt certain that, if only I could calm down and start thinking rationally, the answer would come to me in a blinding flash, so I began walking slowly around the stage, oblivious to all else but the overriding desire to get on with the play. Dimly, as if through a closed door, I thought I heard murmurs from the audience, but I wasn't going to let myself be distracted. I needed to concentrate all of my mind on the job in hand. Not that I was having much luck. In fact, having described a complete circuit of the Old Vic stage, I had to face the truth, and the truth was that I was completely and utterly at sea. I walked off-stage and into the prompt corner, leaving the audience to speculate on the meaning of the apparently meaningless scene they had just witnessed, as I bared my soul to the assistant-stage-manager on the book. "I'm sorry," I confessed, abjectly, "I just don't know where we are." "Act II Scene IV," she hissed. "The scene with Portia. You need your lute." My lute! Of course! Suddenly everything fell into place. It was the lute that had done it. Funny how a simple thing like a prop can hold the key, and I didn't even have to play the damn thing in Act II Scene IV, I just had to hold it! If someone had been on hand to thrust it at me when I first arrived, there wouldn't have been a problem, but luteless I was lost. I rushed across to the props table, and grabbed hold of the instrument. Helen Cherry, as Portia, could have rescued me sooner. The scene was, after all, a two-hander and, even although I had used the wrong entrance, we could have played it virtually anywhere. She also had the first line, 'I prithee, boy, run to the senate house ...' If only I'd heard those words, I later ruminated, everything would have been fine. But for reasons best known to Miss Cherry, she chose to prevaricate. Maybe she panicked too, but by the time she decided to make the best of a bad job by making her entrance, she was just in time to see me disappear into the prompt corner. Now it was her turn to hold the stage alone which, I have to say, she did with a good deal more assurance than I had done. She simply stood her ground, calling out, "Lucius! Lucius!" over and over again, knowing that sooner or later I was bound to return. What she didn't know was that, as soon as I had grabbed my lute, I made for the nearest entrance, ending up right behind her. "Madam!" I yelled, and Helen spun round, stifling a scream. "I prithee, boy, run to the senate house," she said, now on familiar ground, although it had never sounded quite as high-pitched as that before. I had no idea how long the nightmare had lasted. These kind of things usually seem much longer than they really are when you are the perpetrator or the victim. But I was later told that the anachronistic clock which linked the previous scene with ours, and which was meant to strike nine on the morning of the Ides of March, had struck 22 before the scene finally got under way!

I did not have long to enjoy the relief that flooded over me as I came off at the end of the scene. An avenging angel, in the shape of Tom Brown, the company's Stage Director, loomed up out of the darkness, obviously bent on devouring me whole! At which point, Annie Spiers leapt forward, putting herself between Tom and me. Voices were necessarily hushed, as we were still in the wings, only a matter of feet away from the stage where Douglas Campbell, as Caesar, was about to be felled. "It wasn't Terry's fault, Tom," she pleaded, "I forgot to call him." I think that was the moment when I fell *completely* in love with her! But Tom was not to be cheated of his prey, even if she had succeeded in removing something of his sting. He moved her aside and, putting his face very close to mine, he hissed, "Calls are a privilege. It's an actor's responsibility to be on time, and he'd better learn that right now if he wants to make a career in this business!" At that particular moment I would sooner have been a Trappist Monk, and I suggest that, had I been obliged to live through that experience a few years later, the trauma would probably have persuaded me to give up any notion of a future in the theatre. But 15 year-olds are amazingly resilient, and once I had apologised to Helen Cherry, as per instructions from Tom Brown, and had been forgiven by that very charming lady, I was able to put the episode behind me. The long-term effect of the incident, if there was one, was to develop over the years something approaching a fetish for punctuality. Oh, I've had my fair share of thrills and spills since then, but I have never missed an entrance, the very thought of which still brings me out in a cold sweat.

Missing entrances (being 'off') and forgetting your lines ('drying') in Shakespeare, presents you and your colleagues with the unenviable and, some would say, insuperable task of ad-libbing, more often than not, in iambic pentameter. That late-lamented actor Dennis Quilley had a line up his sleeve, or so I heard, that can be used in moments of extreme crisis, and when *sauve qui peut* is the only way out. You should address your fellow actors thus: "Forswear no longer, make we hence amain!" After which you should quickly depart, leaving them to sort out the mess which you probably created in the first place. Not many, however, could aspire to the dizzy heights achieved by Nicholas Selby as the Prince in *Romeo and Juliet,* upon whom it falls to bring the play to an end with the following, deceptively simple, couplet:

'For never was a story of more woe
Than this of Juliet and her Romeo.'

The trouble with this is that the play is known as *Romeo and Juliet* and not the other way around, making it appallingly easy to get wrong. This is the stuff of actors' nightmares; but not for Nicholas Selby who, falling headlong into the trap, declaimed

"For never was a story of more woe
Than this of Romeo and his Juliet ..."

And then, after the briefest of pauses, concluded triumphantly:

"A tragic tale which we shall ne'er forget."

In a scene from a famous production of *King Lear,* the eminent actor of the eponymous role failed to make his scheduled appearance, leaving only various non-speaking Lords and soldiers on stage to forward the plot. After a lengthy silence, one of the Lords took it upon himself to fill the vacuum and, no doubt, earn himself a bit of kudos in the process. He walked up to one of the soldiers and, playing it fairly safely, said, "Where is the king?" The hapless soldier who had, until that moment, been hanging onto his spear and minding his own business, certain that the problem had nothing whatsoever to do with him, was naturally appalled. He stared blankly and silently back at the Lord, until it began to dawn on him that the entire audience was waiting on his reply. After what must have seemed like an eternity, he finally came up with, "I don't know, but I expect he'll be back in a minute!" He was obviously guilty of being unprepared, for which he probably paid a heavy price, at least in the Green Room afterwards, but I sincerely hope that the actor playing that non-specific Lord was brought to justice for his unspeakable cruelty and that, at the very least, he never worked again!

Another personal mishap that occurred during the run of *Julius Caesar* was that my voice broke, and consequently the song that I was requested to sing to Brutus in his tent before the appearance of Caesar's ghost, accompanied by that aforementioned lute, had to be lowered by a semitone at each performance, until it was finally cut altogether, leaving Brutus with no alternative but to settle for a lute solo. The production, as I remember, was well received, although I have no recollection of any reviews, except for a tiny unattributable extract: 'Even the boy, Lucius, played by Terry Wale, makes an unforced mark on the memory.' And the only reason I can remember that little snippet is that I probably underlined it at the time!

It is a well-known truism that the most exciting aspect of acting as a career is being offered a job. It's certainly true that, following that sublime moment when your services are requested, things are apt to go wrong; in fact, the pitfalls are legion, and the only wonder is that actors, terminal optimists all, go on believing that the next job will be the one that proves the rule. Being a child actor, however, is somewhat different. Certainly you share with your elders that same glow of satisfaction, that boost to the ego and that sense of excitement and keen anticipation on being offered employment. But, almost always, your hopes and your expectations are fulfilled. You have a great time during rehearsals, you can't wait to go on stage every night, and you are left feeling utterly bereft when it all comes to an end. Then, joy unconfined, you are offered another job that turns out to be even more fun than the last one. Well, that's certainly how it was for me when I was invited to stay on at the Old Vic for Tyrone Guthrie's production of *Henry VIII*.

I think the LCC Education Authority had probably given up on my academic development by this time, as they raised no objections to an extension of my contract, even although I was not being offered a major part in *Henry VIII*. In fact, I had been offered several parts, the most prominent being Cardinal Wolsey's Page. Wolsey was to be played by that notable Canadian actor, Alexander Knox, and it says a great deal for the unquestioning acquiescence of youth that, even to this day, I am convinced that Cardinal Wolsey spoke with a soft transatlantic accent.

'Tony' Guthrie was at his flamboyant best on *Henry VIII*, moving the play along at a relentlessly cracking pace and handling the crowd scenes with his fabled prowess. He was also at his most wickedly mischievous. He shamed all the men and embarrassed all the ladies one day by leaping up onto the stage during rehearsals and demonstrating the difference between the rather genteel tea-party they were offering him and the 16th century orgy that he wanted it to be. Notable amongst the ladies of the company at that time were Phyllida Law and Barbara Grimes who, along with another Old Vic favourite, Andrée Melly, were known collectively, and affectionately (I think!), as 'Filthy, Grimy and Smelly!' But it was another of the ladies, Sonia Graham, who was Guthrie's hand-picked and red-faced partner in this particular demonstration. He was quite outrageous, but never was he offensive. His natural ebullience had an almost childlike and gleeful innocence about it, motivated by a sense of fun, which was utterly contagious. Looking back now, over a long and chequered career, I can honestly say that the sheer, unadulterated joy of putting a show together goes, more often than not, hand in hand with the success of the show. It was certainly true of Guthrie's production of *Henry VIII*, which was a delight from beginning to end, and a huge hit into the bargain. Tanya Moiseiwitsch was also in her element, designing the glorious costumes, gold and white predominating, echoed in the flags, the banners and the hangings, coincidentally reflecting the traditional Old Vic posters of the time which adorned the outside walls of the theatre.

A few years ago I was presented with one of those posters, a gift from a friend who had come across it in a shop specialising in theatrical memorabilia. It adorns the wall of my study, and I am looking at it even now, more than 60 years later, mulling over the names, some of which would become, over the next few years, even more familiar to me, others that would go on to achieve fame of one sort or another, many no longer with us, most of them remembered with a clarity which seems almost to deny the years between. Eric Thompson, for instance, who later married Phyllida Law, sired Emma Thompson, became a director of some distinction and died far too soon, but will be best remembered for his voice(s) in the TV series, *The Magic Roundabout* ... the pretty and amply-bosomed Jeanette Sterke, who played Anne Bullen (Boleyn) and, quite startlingly, went on to become the wife of another King Henry VIII in the guise of actor, Keith Michell, which was courting disaster if you like ... Patrick Wymark, who also died too young, but not before achieving considerable success in the classical theatre and a bit of celebrity too in the TV series, *The Power Game* ... James Ottaway and John Warner, whose paths I was destined to cross and re-cross in time to come. I recall one particular moment during a dress rehearsal of *Henry VIII* when, having reached the divorce scene, John Warner as the Papal Emissary, Cardinal

Campeius, was holding forth when Gwen Ffrangcon-Davies, dignified and imperious as Queen Katharine, called out to the director: "Tony, what should I be doing during this pause while Campeius is speaking?" Then there was an up-and-coming young actor called Alan Dobie who almost, but for some reason, never quite fulfilled his early promise, although he did make a considerable impression in the television adaptation of Tolstoy's *War and Peace*. I remember Alan and I being summoned to a recording studio somewhere in London's West End by a distinguished American gentleman who, acting on behalf of a theatrical company in Washington DC, had been instructed to obtain a recording of our voices as Hubert and Arthur from *King John*, a production of which was scheduled for later in the year, always provided that Alan and I, on whom its financial backing depended, were both available and prepared to accept the offer that would follow upon receipt of the tape. After several weeks of complete and utter silence, we learned that the man had no connections with a theatrical company in Washington DC, did not come from the USA at all, and that he had departed, destination unknown, without paying for the use of the recording studio, its engineers or equipment. Furthermore, we discovered that the gentleman in question had built up a considerable reputation for the employment of similar scams. While acknowledging that people take their pleasures in all sorts of strange and often puzzling ways, I have never quite been able to fathom that one!

Rehearsals for *Henry VIII* went swimmingly, but the most exciting aspect of the production – and those careful guardians of my educational future doubtless took this into account when granting me a license to perform in it – was that it would open on Wednesday 6th May, 1953 in the presence of Her Majesty Queen Elizabeth II, and in honour of her coronation. It was, all things considered, a very special night, topped off by the official presentation on stage, when the Queen said to Paul Rogers, effortlessly donning the gargantuan mantle of Henry VIII after shedding the lean outline of Caius Cassius, "I'm not sure that King Henry had such red hair as yours." Being a royal observation, this fairly banal remark was quoted in practically every newspaper the following morning, as though it were an epigram worthy of Oscar Wilde. Not that I myself was aware of the distinction at the time, and would have been more than happy to touch the royal glove, a privilege restricted to the leading members of the company.

Following the London season, *Henry VIII* was taken out on a provincial tour, a prospect that filled me with joyful anticipation, and for several reasons. In the first place, since the tour was coincidental with the school holidays, I was allowed off the leash for the first time in my life without chaperone or governess; I could book my own accommodation and spend my free time any way I chose to. But, uppermost in my mind was the prospect of being out on the road with Annie Spiers, with whom I might even get to share those digs. Indeed I did, and it was in Leeds, I think. Anyway, wherever it was, my fantasies remained disappointingly unrealised.

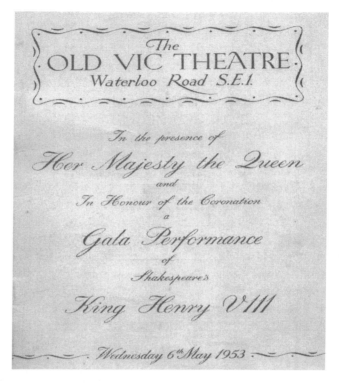

The
OLD VIC THEATRE
Waterloo Road S.E.1.

In the presence of
Her Majesty the Queen
and
In Honour of the Coronation
a
Gala Performance
of
Shakespeare's

King Henry VIII

Wednesday 6th May 1953

I also paid a return visit to that most singular of theatrical landladies, Mrs. McKay, of Daisy Avenue in Manchester. I had stayed there during the tour of *The Innocents*, along with Flora Robson, who used to send me out every morning to the local corner-shop for her daily supply of Kensitas cigarettes. Now I was sharing with Margaret Courtenay and several other members of the company, and I only wished that one of them would dispatch me on a similar errand – preferably to the Antipodes so that I could get away from Mrs. McKay who, warm and generous though she was, and imbued with genuine North Country hospitality, was given to describing, in minute, gorge-rising detail, the events leading up to her mother's latest hospitalisation, not omitting the colour and texture of her bile, the frequency and consistency of her motions, followed by a blow-by-blow account of the subsequent operation in all its gory particulars; every one of these disclosures timed perfectly to coincide with breakfast. Maybe it was her way of limiting the consumption of eggs and fried bread, actors being notorious gannets, or it could be that she was spurred on by the somewhat earthy and Rabelaisian personality of Maggie Courtenay. She certainly hadn't been nearly as forthcoming in Dame Flora's presence!

At the then New Theatre in Oxford, I made a dangerous discovery – the presence of a bar close to the stage from which it was quite possible to buy alcoholic drinks during the performance.

It seemed like a good idea at the time and so, in keeping my new-found independence, I treated myself to a glass of cider in the middle of a matinée, blithely unaware that the actors in the company steered well clear of the place, and that it was only the hard-drinking members of the choir who indulged during the show. The news spread like wildfire, and when I made my next entrance, carrying Cardinal Wolsey's train into the divorce scene, I heard Patrick Wymark, as the Earl of Surrey, mutter, "Here comes Wale, pissed again!" I looked up, caught his eye and grinned at him, whereupon I missed my footing on the steps, tripped and fell headlong onto the train, bringing Alexander Knox's progress to an abrupt halt. I know for an absolute fact, and I knew it even then, that the accident was brought about by a momentary lapse of concentration and had nothing whatsoever to do with the half-pint of cider I had consumed shortly before the scene, but received opinion would not have it so. My presumed over-indulgence went into the show report, and I was severely reprimanded. Worse, much worse than this, Ann Spiers refused to speak to me for 24 hours! A couple of days later, however, soft-hearted woman that she was, she relented and took me on a 'dutch' treat to see *Hans Christian Anderson* at the local cinema. Not only that, but she allowed me to hold her hand throughout the picture, giving me quite the wrong idea about the wages of sin!

Annie and I remained friends for a while, even after my time with the Old Vic Company came to an end, and until our paths finally and inevitably diverged. I remember cycling down to visit her in Croynge, as she called the suburban no-man's-land between Croydon and Penge that was her home. I assume that she was pleased to see me, but even had I arrived uninvited – not entirely beyond the realms of possibility – she would have made me feel welcome, because that's the way she was. Annie and I were to meet again, ever so briefly, some years later, and not in the happiest of circumstances. As far as I know she never married, although she was surely besieged with suitors, and I can only assume that that was the way she wanted it to be.

The Old Vic was about to enter a new phase under the direction of Michael Benthall, while Guthrie himself was off to fresh fields and pastures new in Canada where he was to co-found, with Tanya Moiseiwitsch, the Shakespeare Festival Theatre in Stratford, Ontario. Benthall's first season in the Waterloo Road was to include a production of *King John*. My appetite having already been whetted by the bogus American's recording session, I was naturally keen to play Arthur. I also had every reason to believe that I would be offered the part. Was I not, after all, the Old Vic's obvious choice when it came to casting boys' parts? And what was good enough for Guthrie would surely be good enough for Michael Benthall. What I had overlooked or, more strictly, never knew at the time, was that most directors, and certainly directors of a certain persuasion, came with their own child actors in tow. The casting of Arthur was already a *fait accompli* long before I even knew it was on the cards, and I didn't even get to audition for it. Instead, I was invited to understudy Nicholas Edmett in the role, and to play various bits and pieces during the rest of the season. The question then became, could I afford to be absent from school for yet another protracted period during the run-up to my G.C.E. 'O' Level Examinations? At least, that's the way I put it to the Old Vic Management. Nearer to the truth was that I had no desire to understudy anybody after my dismal experience of the job in *The Innocents*, and least of all was I prepared to understudy somebody I'd never even heard of in *my* theatre, and in a part that could have been written for me! Robert Quentin, the Production Manager, guessed, I think, that my decision had more to do with wounded pride than a sudden rush of academic fervour, and he tried to persuade me to reconsider my decision in the light of my long-term career as an actor. Having learned a little about the nature of the business I had chosen to be part of, I suspected that his concerns had more to do with his own short-term casting problems than they had to do with my future, and so it was without regret, and with many happy and fond memories, that I exchanged the lights, the make-up and the glamour for the altogether shadier olive groves of Academe. And all that really meant was that I went back to Kilburn Grammar School at the end of the summer holidays, and almost immediately auditioned for the school play!

oOoOo

Four

'A little learning is a dang'rous thing' wrote Alexander Pope, and I always thought that it meant dang'rous only to those on the receiving end; victims of the semi-skilled brain surgeon or the semi-literate critic, for instance. It took me years to realise that it is just as deleterious to the subject himself, he of little learning, painfully insecure, aware of his shortcomings, caught between the justifiable assurance of the highly educated on the one hand, and the entirely unwarranted confidence of the totally ignorant on the other. Nowadays, of course, with ignorance having gained the upper hand, this agonising dilemma is all but extinct. Opinions grow on trees, and young people who can't even spell 'erudition' let alone lay claim to any, feel themselves free to express them – and in mixed company too! I must have been at least 25 before I was bold enough to air my views on any serious topic, and then only amongst friends, and even then, more often than not, I wished I hadn't. To this very day, although experience has to some extent filled in the big black hole that was my formal education, I still feel disadvantaged in conversation with university graduates, particularly of the Oxbridge variety, and not so much by the intellectual content of their argument which, as a rule, I can more or less rise to, but by their eloquence, their style and their unassailable self-confidence. I have seldom fallen victim to envy or regret, but oh, how I once envied them, and how I still regret missing out on the possibility of a university education.

As I entered my fifth and, as it turned out, my final year at Kilburn Grammar School, not one single person offered me this advice, not even my enlightened and usually well-informed English teacher, Peter Wright. To be fair, he and the rest of the teaching staff had probably given up on me by that time, and not without good reason; I was completely blinkered to anything that might divert me from the business of acting. I suppose they could have told me that a university education would have better equipped me to deal with life in whatever my chosen profession, but I doubt if I would have taken any notice. Had they been aware of it, they could also have told me that a university education, and particularly at Oxford or Cambridge, would have provided me with an incomparably prestigious shop-window for my talents, and moreover furnished me with a host of influential contacts from amongst my fellow undergraduates who, within a few short years, would be running the theatres I would want to work in.

But this was all unknown to them and to me at the time and, in any case, having fallen so far behind in so many subjects, it would have taken a Herculean effort on my part to pass the entrance exam into a university of any kind. Besides, my mind was made up. I was determined to go to drama school which was, after all, the traditional training ground for the vast majority of actors, and a much more attractive prospect, to my mind, than any number of dreaming spires or punting trips up the river to Granchester. Meanwhile, I applied myself to the irksome chore of doing just about enough to ensure that I would stumble over the hurdles of the 'O' Level course, while applying all my energy and enthusiasm to the infinitely more gratifying task of playing Katharina in *The Taming of the Shrew.*

1953 - The Taming of the Shrew - Kilburn Grammar School.

Taking on a female role at the age of 15 might have been a more daunting proposition if I hadn't known that Laurence Olivier had also played Katharina at exactly the same age, and in a school production too, which had subsequently been performed at a special matinée to celebrate Shakespeare's birthday on the stage of the old Shakespeare Memorial Theatre in Stratford-upon-Avon. That was back in 1922. There's a marvellous picture of him in his autobiography, *Confessions of an Actor,* wearing a quite outrageous head-dress, scowling darkly into the camera and looking like some ill-tempered gypsy. I would probably have gone for that look too, had I seen the photograph at that time but, with Hollywood as my only reference point, I ended up in a red wig and consequently bore more than a passing resemblance to Rhonda Fleming! One more reassurance, along the lines of 'a trouble shared,' was that my best school-friend, Duncan Drown, was assigned to play the part of the Widow, while yet another boy, whose name I have now forgotten, was saddled with Bianca. I was grateful for these small mercies although, truth to tell, I revelled in the experience and threw myself headlong into the part of Katharina which, in common with all of Shakespeare's women, had been written for a boy to play in any case.

There were other diversions in that late summer of 1953, apart that is from England winning the Ashes from Australia for the first time since the Bodyline Series of 1932/3, and the coming to power of Nikita Kruschev in the USSR. At the Brondesbury and Kilburn High School for Girls, a certain fifth year pupil was beginning to cast her spell over several of her male counterparts across the road, myself included. Her name was Barbara Sonia Warby, a name that will forever be engraved on my mind, possibly for no other reason than the time it took me to engrave it on my desk! Being a fifth-former at that time was rather like emerging from an educational cocoon into a world that wasn't quite as rigidly disciplined as you had been led to believe it was. True, we still had to wear our school uniforms, caps and blazers sporting the school badge – Bishop's mitre atop a shield containing crossed swords, all enclosed in a laurel wreath, and bearing the exhortation *Pasce Agnos Meos* (Feed my lambs) – but in the fifth year you suddenly discovered, quite mysteriously, that you could get away with wearing them in your own special way, and that the girls, equally mysteriously, were doing something very similar. We boys would comb our hair into the fashionable '50s quiff, held firm in anything up to gale force winds by a massive amount of Brylcreem, and wear our caps perched behind the quiff on the back of our heads. This, together with a sadly neglected blazer, on which both badge and motto were so worn and faded as to be all but indecipherable, was held to be extremely attractive to the opposite sex. The opposite sex, meanwhile, had discovered that they could do all sorts of wild and wonderful things with the brims of their hats so as to enhance the shape of their faces and to better show off their hair, suddenly transformed by regular washing from greasy rats' tails into a glorious adornment. They had also somehow learned that their legs, previously only useful when playing hockey, were capable of driving boys into something approaching a frenzy. Now, while Barbara Sonia Warby was by no means the comeliest or, indeed, the most personable fifth-form pupil at the Brondesbury and Kilburn High School for Girls, beyond question she wore her hat and flaunted her legs with a difference. On top of which, it was rumoured that she was more liberal with her favours than any of her classmates and, without quite having the nerve to put it to the test, I was not alone in hoping to become another notch on her gun-barrel. But, unhappily, it was no secret that Barbara Sonia Warby was currently immune to the concerted drooling of 5A because of her predilection for Mick Page, the class athlete, a blond-haired, blue-eyed, demi-god, covered in mud and glory from his recent exploits on the rugby field. It was ever thus, I realised, and I was relatively stoical about it, confident that she would, sooner or later, see beyond the mud to the essential philistine within. Besides, rehearsals for *The Taming of the Shrew*, once again under the inspired direction of Peter Wright, were more than enough to keep carnality at bay for the time being.

After school hours, two or three times a week, fortified by a mug of tea and a slice or two of bread and jam in the dining-hall, we would adjourn to the Creighton Hall, and give ourselves over to the totally absorbing task of putting Shakespeare's comedy on the stage. They were halcyon days, made all the more euphoric by the uncommonly high standards of both the production and the acting. For some reason, not entirely clear to me then or now, Kilburn Grammar School had already fostered several careers in the performing arts. That well-known broadcaster, Richard Baker, he of Sunday evening's *Melodies For You*, was an Old Creightonian too, while Leon Eagles, whose younger brother, Brian, was at that very moment rehearsing alongside me as Lucentio in 'The Shrew', had gone on to drama school only a year or two earlier. Playing opposite me as Petruchio, another close friend, Paul Kriwaczek, was even then in fairly constant demand by the BBC World Service, broadcasting plays to Germany, a fact which lent to our relationship a very healthy competitiveness, an obvious bonus in the war of words between Katharina and Petruchio.

Paul was one of a number of Jewish boys amongst my classroom acquaintances, although his background was more impecunious than most. Having lived through the war, albeit as an infant, I knew just a little about the Jews, had a vague idea about the Holocaust and had seen documentary footage of the liberation of prisoners from the Concentration Camp at Bergen-Belsen. But I never actually came across a Jew, not consciously at any rate, until I went to Kilburn Grammar School which, due to its location on the fringes of kosher Brondesbury, attracted a fairly substantial number of them. They came, surprisingly to me at the time, in all shapes and sizes, and from a rich diversity of backgrounds and degrees of orthodoxy. The one thing they shared was a determination to make the most of their education and an awareness of its importance to them in their future careers. I was on friendly terms with quite a few Jewish boys, even visited their homes which, to my amazement, and regardless of their social standing, were all, to a greater or lesser extent, decorated with books. and even in some cases, with paintings. Our walls at home were decorated with wallpaper, and the only books (apart from my recently acquired *Complete Works of William Shakespeare)* that I can remember seeing very occasionally, for they were always hidden away in a cupboard, were a copy of the Bible, and a huge, unwieldy tome called *Everything Within,* which offered detailed instructions on everything from the treatment of head lice to the laying of linoleum, potted biographies of important historical figures like Albert Einstein, and translations of legal phrases such as *sub judice* and *habeas corpus.* Although no *Encyclopædia Britannica,* it was obviously a very useful book to have around and was frequently taken from its cupboard when something needed either flattening or propping up. My mother, a not infrequent reader of romantic fiction, held firmly to the belief that, in general, books were for returning to the library when you had finished with them, and definitely *not* for cluttering up the home. Being a pupil at Kilburn Grammar School, albeit an academic also-ran, had a decidedly civilising effect on me, and if I emerged at the age of 16 a little less barbaric than I had been at the age of 11, and with, at least, a cultural aspiration or two, then I owe it to the friendships I made there as much as to the quality of the teaching. But then again, any institution can only be as good as the sum of its parts, and by any standards, Kilburn Grammar School was a fine institution.

The Taming of the Shrew was well received and, for my performance as Katharina I was rewarded with two prizes. At the end of term, the headmaster presented me with the Hicks-Bolton

Shakespeare Prize, a copy of the *Concise Oxford Dictionary*, not quite as heavy as *Everything Within*, but a useful addition to our home library, and which, to this day, still sits in my bookcase, its spine damaged, and the school insignia faded beyond anything I managed to achieve with the badge on my blazer, but still in regular use. Returning to school after the Christmas holidays, I was awarded my second prize – the undivided attention of Barbara Sonia Warby! Remembering my own juvenile crush on the boy who had played Lady Macbeth, I had no trouble with the fact that Barbara Sonia Warby's sudden interest in me had been engendered by my performance in a female role. It would have happened, I told myself, had I been playing any leading part, the key word being 'leading', and the consequent celebrity that came with it. She was very into 'stars' was Barbara Sonia Warby and, with mine in the ascendant, at least for the time being, the athletic prowess of Mick Page seemed to have lost some its allure. Not that our relationship developed to any great extent over the following weeks which were largely taken up with school work. In fact, it was limited to an exchange of messages and to stilted conversations across the 'moat', which separated the windows of her classroom from the pavement of Chevening Road which ran alongside the girls' school. Twice a day, weather permitting, in the mornings and at lunchtime, I would park my flashy turquoise-blue Philips *Kingfisher* bike against the fence and, with my cap perched precariously on the back of my head, wait for her friends to summon her to the window. Unfortunately, most of them opted to stay there, and their incessant giggling imposed even greater restrictions on our dialogue. For an over-sexed youth, on the verge of his 16th birthday, the cumulative effect of these long-distance meetings was agonisingly frustrating, and probably unsustainable, except for the tantalising promise held out, like a carrot, in front of us both. A school trip to the French Alps had been arranged for the Easter holidays, and the fifth form boys of Kilburn Grammar School were to be joined by their female counterparts from the Brondesbury and Kilburn High School for Girls. Barbara Sonia Warby and I had already booked our places and, if she felt even remotely the way I was feeling, then we were both looking forward to it with keen anticipation!

Meanwhile, the results of my GCE 'O' Level exams were as catastrophic as I feared they would be, with only two passes, in English and in French. Even then I knew that I owed my success in French to the oral part of the examination which gave me an actor's opportunity to show off my accent. Had the result depended entirely on my knowledge of French grammar, then I'm sure that subject would have gone down the drain along with all the others. Maths was always going to be a lost cause, my initial aptitude for basic arithmetic eventually having been squeezed out by my total block-headedness when it came to algebra, geometry and trigonometry. I should have passed in History, which has always been one of my strongest subjects and, in certain areas, has since become a passion. I'm pretty sure I would have passed too if they had chosen any subject other than 'The Corn Laws', which I found excruciatingly dull and, since I had not the slightest intention of becoming a baker, completely irrelevant! Kings and Queens, battles and conquests ... that was my kind of history and, to some extent, it still is, although my interest in the social ramifications did blossom eventually. That's the trouble with education; for some of us, it comes too early. I would have been an exemplary student in my early thirties, and better still in my late forties. Anyway, it's all spilt milk now, and I'm really grateful for the amount and the quality of the education that was on offer to me at Kilburn Grammar School, even if I chose to side-step most of it. I believe that doors were opened for me at that time which remained open until I was ready to go through them, years later. Even my scant knowledge of Latin and Greek, in both of which subjects I failed dismally, has been surprisingly useful to me, socially as well as professionally. With the exams behind me, however, and with Spring on the horizon, my superficial wounds were soon licked better, and my fancy lightly returned to thoughts of love.

Having briefly and enticingly glimpsed Paris for the very first time whilst en route by foot from the Gard du Nord to the Gard de l'Est, our party arrived in the early hours of the following morning at St. Gervais les Bains, a tiny mountain resort near Chamonix at the foot of Mont Blanc in a region of France known as the Haute Savoie. I had never been abroad before, and I was overwhelmed by it all. Looking out of the hotel window at the snow-capped peaks that dominated the view in every direction was a truly awesome sight, and yet here we were, nestled in a valley between the slopes, seemingly cut off from the rest of the world, like the inhabitants of Shangri-La or Brigadoon. The tiny streets were crammed with even tinier shops, adorned with colourful awnings and displaying signs with exotic-sounding words on them, like 'Boulangerie' and 'Patisserie,' their windows crammed to overflowing with all manner of delicious and mouth-watering confections. Even the shop that called itself 'Tabac,' was altogether more seductive and glamorous than its English equivalent. It was an Alpine wonderland, little short of paradise to a bunch of goggle-eyed schoolchildren from a country still bearing the visible scars of a recent war, and still suffering the privations of food rationing. We were collectively enchanted by it, and I was lucky enough to be able to share the experience with my best friend, Duncan Drown, in whose pleasant company I was just about able to live with the fact that Mick Page, fresh from some muddy triumph, and unluckily with us on the trip, had recaptured Barbara Sonia Warby's affections. 'Frailty, thy name is woman!' There was, of course, a lesson for life to be learnt from this, although I was far too busy being resentful at the time, and not at all in the mood for any kind of analysis. Had I been in a more rational frame of mind, I would have weighed my somewhat distant and ever-receding moment of fame as Katharina with Mick Page's more recent and on-going glory on the rugby field, and come to the conclusion that you simply have to seize the moment, because – and more especially in the narrow confines of the professional world I was about to enter – people have notoriously short memories.

At the party which marked our final night in St. Gervais les Bains, I am pretty sure that I was persuaded to perform a party-piece. I cannot swear to it, of course, but I would hate to think that I had dreamed it up myself. The general idea was that I should make my appearance in 'drag', and attempt to hoodwink the rest of our party as to my true identity. Bearing in mind my recent theatrical success in the field of female impersonation, this wasn't nearly as outré as it might seem, and I was obviously buoyed-up by the fact that at least *somebody* remembered it. Truth to tell, I would have done virtually anything in my power to re-claim the spotlight which had turned its beam elsewhere, and I was determined to prove that I could do it successfully too. Where the clothes and make-up came from, I have no idea, but I have a pretty good idea that the hotel staff must have become involved in the conspiracy, since there is no conceivable way that any of the girls from the Brondesbury and Kilburn High School would have had hidden away in their suitcases the glamorous and sophisticated *haute couture* in which I finally made my entrance. Having parked myself on a barstool, I ordered a *crème de menthe,* lit a cigarette at the end of an outrageously long holder, crossed my knees as decorously as I knew how, and awaited the arrival of the rest of our party. Eventually, they drifted down in their familiar groups, casting glances in my direction, some more obviously lascivious than others, but all with varying degrees of curiosity, and none – *not a single one* – with recognition. I pushed my luck to its limits that evening, and it held out for longer than I had dared hope until, finally, I unmasked to scenes of wild acclaim. Oh, the sweet smell of success! But there was more yet to come, and as the others drifted away to pursue their own activities, their approbation still ringing in my ears, I was left face to face with my most fervent admirer who suggested – nay, insisted – that she accompany me to my room to help me remove my make-up and to assist me in the even more delicate task of changing my clothes. I was obviously far too intent on 'seizing the moment' there and then to take any conscious note of this particular eccentricity of hers, but down the years I have, from time to time, wondered what life held in store for Barbara Sonia Warby. However, bearing in mind my own penchant for cross-dressing, and my apparent willingness to do it at the drop of a hat, so to speak, she may well have had her doubts about *my* future too!

The summer term at Kilburn Grammar School was unremarkable, although rife with the usual rumours about the school play, all of them finally laid to rest when, following a read-through, Peter Wright announced that it was to be *Hamlet,* and that, despite an embarrassing slip of the tongue when I had mispronounced the word 'misled' as 'mizl'd', I was to play the title role. Needless to say, I was thrilled but, at the age of 16, not even remotely awed by the enormity of such a challenge. It could not have been more than a few weeks later, however, that I learned I had been awarded a scholarship to the Webber-Douglas Academy of Dramatic Art, and so Hamlet – together with my elevation into the sixth form – was abandoned in favour of the opportunity to study, full-time, the art of acting. Had I known, perhaps, that not only would I never be asked to play Hamlet again, but that the art of acting did not feature strongly in the syllabus at the Webber-Douglas Academy of Music and Dramatic Art, *circa* 1954, then I might have had second thoughts, although I doubt it. I was starry-eyed about the prospect of spending whole days doing nothing except what I had chosen to do, and sharing my time with people who, like me, thought, talked and dreamed of nothing but acting. The decision had been made long before the opportunity arose, and so it was with no real thought at all, let alone a second one, that I forsook my satchel and my school uniform and, after one final burst of the school song – 'Kilburn Grammarians, muster your forces, shoulder to shoulder, happy and strong!' – headed off for fresh fields, where it is commonly held that the grass is supposed to be greener.

Roughly halfway between Gloucester Road and South Kensington underground stations, if you cut the corner at Old Brompton Road by walking along Clareville Street and Clareville Grove, you would have passed the Webber-Douglas Academy of Dramatic Art, possibly without even noticing it, except that on a fine day you would have been hard pushed to ignore the crowd of students, sitting on the steps leading up to the front door, spilling out on to the pavement, and thronging the basement area. The Webber-Douglas was a bijou establishment, uncomfortably, and somewhat incongruously squeezed into what is essentially a residential area of Regency terrace houses. Nowadays, of course, these houses are occupied by the seriously rich for whom the proximity of a drama school, full of unruly extroverts, was at the very least an inconvenience. The walls of the tiny Chanticleer Theatre had to be thickened in more recent years, lest the sounds of Chekhov, or the gunshot that invariably marks the passing of one of Ibsen's heroines, should disturb the neighbours and distract them from their God-given right to think of ways to make even more money. But back in 1954, these problems were yet to surface. Unimaginable though it is today, all college activities, classes, rehearsals, performances, took place at that time within the four walls of that minute building which, incredibly, even found room for a student common room with a bar that served occasional refreshments. The neighbours were *real* people in those days too, people who not only took kindly to a bit of theatrical exuberance in their street, but who also offered accommodation to students on very reasonable terms; happy days indeed, unthinkable even 30 years later when most students had to trek into college from digs only just affordable in distant and remote places such as Streatham or Queen's Park.

My arrival on the first day of term at the Webber-Douglas Academy of Music and Dramatic Art in September 1954 augured well. I was accosted on the steps leading up to the main door by a lanky young man with sandy-coloured hair and a strange accent, which could have derived, to my untutored ear, from anywhere west of Ballyferriter, but which turned out to be Canadian, with distinctly English aspirations. "Are you Terry Wale?" he asked, as I drew level with him on the top step. It was almost as though he had been waiting for me. "Yes, I am," I replied, wondering if, where and when I'd met him before. "*The* Terry Wale?" he persisted, apparently awed by the possibility. Well, I'd seen enough Hollywood movies to know that our North American cousins were capable of charming the birds out of the trees if they chose to, and that English girls had been particularly susceptible to this kind of expertise during the war years, but this was my first personal experience of it, and I was appropriately flattered. It transpired, with elaboration, that not only did the Canadian government equip its young student ambassadors with the gift of making lifelong friends, but also with an enviably generous financial grant, which not only enabled them to live out their student days in relative comfort, but also to pursue their studies in the field, so to speak, and which, in Sandy Black's case, meant going to see as many shows in the theatre as there were days in the week. Arriving in the U.K. a few weeks before he was due to present himself at the Webber-Douglas, Sandy had visited the Edinburgh Festival and, whilst there, had seen a production of Marlowe's *Edward II*, by the Oxford University Players, and in which I played the part of Prince Edward, later King Edward III.

James Maxwell, an actor I first worked with in *Julius Cæsar* at the Old Vic, had recommended me to Casper Wrede, the director, and so I was invited, during the summer holidays, to join the other professionals, James Maxwell himself and Patricia Kneale, in what was otherwise essentially an amateur production of Marlowe's play, although it has to be said that the standards of both production and acting in *Edward II* were far from being amateur in any deprecatory sense of the word – hardly surprising when you consider that the OUP was an off-shoot of the long established, and highly esteemed Oxford University Dramatic Society (OUDS). In fact, my association with them during that summer of 1954 gave me my first inkling of what I might have missed out on by putting all my eggs, so early in my life, into one basket. Looking at the cast-list now, it's surprising that not one single member of that company, to my knowledge, took up acting as a career. However, it did boast a couple of estimable future directors in Michael Elliott and Ronald Eyre, not to mention Jack Good, at that time President of OUDS, who went on to produce two of the earliest pop music shows on TV, *Six-Five Special* and *Oh Boy!* and whose greatest claim to fame was to persuade Cliff Richard to shave off his sideburns, and to abandon his guitar, leaving his hands free to plead for sympathy, thereby converting the former rock 'n' roller into a tame family entertainer. Jack played the assassin, Lightborn, in *Edward II*, clothed in pink and minus his eyebrows. It was an incredibly effective performance, and chillingly sinister, echoing his victim's homosexual proclivities, initially in fellowship, but finally as a taunt.

As part of the official Edinburgh Festival Fringe, although more selective and smaller in number than today's largely indiscriminate scrum, we were accommodated in the distinctly non deluxe surroundings of the City Lighting & Cleansing Department in Advocate's Close, just off the Royal Mile. A huge room had been converted into a dormitory, furnished with bunk-beds, and it was to this room that we all returned after the show, and in the privacy of which I was introduced to the polemics of Oxford University undergraduates, even imagined myself one of them, a fantasy which was difficult to sustain in the face of my appalling ignorance on most subjects.

Anyone who has been in Edinburgh during the Festival knows how exciting it can be, a coming together of time and place that seems to have been ordained rather than cultivated, like *Mardi Gras* in New Orleans, if somewhat more eclectic. It is even more exciting when it's your first time there, and even more so when you are involved in a successful production. 'Tremendous, Tremendous, Tremendous!' began one of the reviews. 'The opening performance of Christopher Marlowe's *Edward II* in the hall of George Heriot's School last night ... had a splendour about it no other 'fringe' event this year has achieved.' Some of that splendour was certainly attributable to Malcolm Pride's sumptuous costumes, but a large slice of the credit must go to Casper Wrede who, as director, took his disparate company along with him in a determined attempt to scale the heights of Marlowe's most human of tragedies. James Maxwell's Edward was, quite simply, magnificent in every respect; his vulnerability, his anguish and his final degradation achingly poignant, winning us to his side despite a purblind arrogance and haughtiness in the early stages of the play that demanded retribution.

James Maxwell, or Max, for so I came to know him, was a graduate of the Old Vic School under Michel St. Denis, as was Casper Wrede, who had been, or so I was told, a Baron in his native Finland. In spite of his limited and heavily accented English, Casper was mysteriously articulate, and even now I find it difficult to avoid being fanciful when I describe his method of communicating with actors as anything other than telepathic. He would say, "Terry, at this moment ... I would like you to be ... more ... *(after a wave of the hands)* ... you know?" And the extraordinary thing was that, somehow or other, you did know. It was, I see now, a rare gift that many an indigenous director, with a suitcase full of adverbs, adjectives and literary references, plus the ability to string them all together, simply does not possess. How else do you explain his ability to achieve from a company largely untrained, and in a language foreign to him, 'The magnificence of their diction...?' The same review went on to say, ' ... the blank verse rolled off their tongues in a rich torrent of poetry.' Casper was also responsible for one magnificent *coup de théâtre*, forced upon him by the fact that the audience in the hall of George Heriot's School were seated on three sides of the acting area, making it virtually impossible to kill Edward in the historically accurate way, easily achievable in a proscenium-arch theatre, by sticking a red-hot poker up his bum without actually doing it. So Casper reverted to the original stage directions and produced a very different, but almost equally appalling death for the pathetic creature who had been king, which had the audience on all three sides gasping in horror and wide-eyed with incredulity. Two 'heavies' who accompanied the assassin, Lightborn, to Edward's cell, turned a heavy wooden table upside-down and placed it across the prostrate Edward's chest. They then climbed up onto it and, without in any way faking it, they jumped relentlessly up and down until the life was crushed out of him. James Maxwell only survived this deadly assault on his person courtesy of two steel bands around his chest, and I remember only too clearly how, night after night, we all prayed that the metal wouldn't finally give way under the pressure or, perhaps even more feasibly, that this wasn't the night that Max had forgotten to put the steel rings on!

For a child actor with heroic ambitions, there can be no better part in all Elizabethan drama than Prince Edward in Marlowe's *Edward II*. Set up as a bit of a booby, easy meat for his mother and her lover, Mortimer (once his father has been removed), the young King Edward III grasps his sceptre more firmly than anyone could have imagined, sends Mortimer off to his execution and his mother to the Tower to await trial for complicity in his father's murder. Not only that, but he has the last lines in the play:

'Sweet father, here unto thy murdered ghost
I offer up this wicked traitor's head;
And let these tears, distilling from mine eyes,
Be witness of my grief and innocency.'

And as if this wasn't enough to be going on with, being at the centre of the gloriously costumed coronation scene was an incredibly intoxicating experience. Then there was that review ... 'The splendid entry of 16 year old Terry Wale as the new king into the tail of the action is, where one had anticipated disappointment, the crown-piece of this terrible drama.' All this might well have turned my head. In fact, it probably did to a certain extent, except that even then I suspected Christopher Marlowe might have had more to do with it than me. In any event, it was an idyllic way to spend the summer holidays, and all the more gratifying to be reminded of it as I stood on the steps outside the Webber-Douglas Academy of Dramatic Art on the first day of my first term as a drama student.

During her time as a pupil at the Blessed Sacrament Convent in

New York, the celebrated critic, writer and wit, Dorothy Parker, learned that if you spit on a pencil eraser, it will erase ink. That, she claimed, was the sum total of her education there. I learned a lot more than that at the Webber-Douglas, but not a great deal about acting. I suppose we must have had voice classes and movement classes, although I have no recollection of any. What I do remember, all too clearly, is a class called 'Gesture' which seemed to take up a disproportionate amount of time, and which was dedicated exclusively to teaching us what to do with our hands while reciting the opening Chorus speech from *Henry V*. So dogmatic was our tutor, whose name happily escapes me, that I was left firmly believing, along with all the other students, I suppose, that there was no personal choice to be made, that the gestures as laid down in her class were irreplaceable and vital to the proper illustration of the text. Even now, some sixty-odd years later, engraved as they were on my young mind, I know that if I were ever asked to play the part of Chorus in *Henry V*, I would have to spend the first week of rehearsals with my arms strapped to my sides. I remember, too, a fencing master called Frank something-or-other, whose understandable, if slightly misguided, preoccupation with the opposite sex led to entire lessons being spent in teaching the girls how to hold their foils correctly by wrapping his arms around them from behind. For different reasons this practice led to a great deal of resentment from both sexes.

But the fundamental problem with the Webber-Douglas at that time, led by its co-founder, W. Johnstone-Douglas, was simply that it had become old fashioned. In its pre-war heyday, it had nurtured the talents of such future stars as Stewart Granger who, for obvious reasons, had to change his name from James Stewart, and had also provided the theatrical world with one of its most famous married couples, Michael Denison and Dulcie Gray. But times were changing, and the none-too-distant tom-toms were all but unheard within the precincts of the Webber-Douglas where too many members of the staff had little or no contact with the outside world. Not that they lacked distinction. Ellen O'Malley had been one of George Bernard Shaw's favourite actresses, and was his original Candida, a role in which Sybil Thorndike had actually understudied her. It was a great honour to be directed by her even if, in her eighties by then, she didn't have a great deal to say, and fell asleep quite frequently. Doris Johnston was also something of a relic, although being on the receiving end of her wrath, delivered in her gin-sodden, chain-smoker's growl, was an education in itself. Only Helen Lowry, retaining her evening job as

Stage Director for HM Tennent, brought a breath of contemporary theatre into the building with her. For Helen, I played the eponymous role in a Spanish play by the Quintero brothers called *A Hundred Years Old*, a performance which, given at the age of 16, must have asked of the audience a paranormal suspension of disbelief, despite masses of 'lake' shadowing and a liberal application of Johnson's Baby Powder on my hair. But Helen Lowry aside, I was already, by the end of the first term, beginning to entertain doubts about staying the full course. I may have been one of the youngest students, if not *the* youngest, ever to be given a place at the Webber-Douglas, but I had already accumulated quite a bit of experience out there in the real world, and had more than a sneaking suspicion that, in the absence of some really useful training in voice and movement, I would learn more working alongside other, even more experienced, professionals. Not only that, but I would be getting paid for it.

What I did learn, however, and took great pleasure in learning, was how to be a student and it was, if nothing else, a welcome interlude. The Webber-Douglas was part retirement home, part finishing school and part – by far the largest part – a glorious social club. For starters I learned to drink wine, albeit of the cheap and cheerful variety, at an endless stream of parties, thrown by other students in their digs, scattered across south-west London, and even once or twice, by me at my home in Kensal Rise on the odd occasion my parents and my brother weren't there. These were, generally speaking, bottle parties, and we would arrive at about 8 o'clock in the evening, clutching our bottles of *Entre Deux Mers*, and either end up on the floor or stagger home at about three in the morning. There was, however, one exception to this general rule. Todd Thomson was not only a rather mature student, but also the son of an enormously rich Australian sheep farmer, and when Todd decided it was his turn to throw a party in his rather swell Earl's Court apartment, bringing bottles of *Entre Deux Mers*, or anything else for that matter, was definitely *de trop*. His bath was always filled with ice, and literally bristled with countless bottles of champagne. Needless to say, we all looked forward very much to Todd's parties, and were somewhat in awe of his sophistication and his wealth, not to mention his boundless generosity, which was just as well as he couldn't act for toffee! To my great surprise, there were quite a few students in my year, mainly female, who failed to demonstrate any marked ability in the acting stakes. Largely middle to upper-middle class girls they were, whose parents had bowed to their wishes and sent them to drama school instead of to Cheltenham Ladies College. I often wonder what became of Olivia Carruthers, a charming girl whose natural poise always somehow got lost on her way to the stage. I can't ever recall seeing her name in a theatre programme, and imagine that she probably married a career diplomat, and ended up being called upon to recite 'O, for a muse of fire…', with appropriate gestures, at various embassy soirées!

In the intervals between student parties, I went to the theatre. In fact, I went to the theatre more often than I went to parties, and this was entirely due to my friend Sandy's comparatively lavish Canadian government grant, and his own reluctance to go by himself. My own personal grant was a 'fees only' award which was pretty measly back in the 1950s. The fact that I was still living at home was, of course, a major financial bonus, but without Sandy's generosity I certainly wouldn't have seen Orson Welles' *Moby Dick,* Terence Rattigan's *Separate Tables, An Evening with Beatrice Lillie,* Giraudoux's *Tiger at the Gates* and Robert Dhéry's brilliant revue, *La Plume de ma Tante,* in close succession. This illustrates how indebted I am to Sandy Black and, of course, to the Canadian government, for much of my theatrical education. At some point, Sandy and I also went to see Peter Brook's production of *Titus Andronicus,* transferred to the West End from Stratford-upon-Avon, and containing a performance which was seminal in my development as a worshipper of idols, a weakness to which I succumbed with religious fervour, and which might well have led, in later life, to a crippling inferiority complex, but for the fact that there are no longer any idols left for me to worship.

It was the first time I had seen Laurence Olivier in the flesh, and the effect of his performance on me was little short of cataclysmic. I remember particularly a moment when, his grief boiling over, Olivier rolled his eyes skyward until only the whites were visible, as he cried, "I am the sea", and what he did with that word 'sea' was nothing short of Olympian, certainly way beyond any conception of human pain that I, in my short life, could even have begun to comprehend. I do know that it actually knocked the breath out of my body, and that his performance left me, at the end of the evening, feeling totally wrung-out and yet, at the same time, exhilarated. Kenneth Tynan's words can better describe the experience than any number of my fumbling adjectives: 'Sir Laurence Olivier's Titus … is an unforgettable concerto of grief. This is a performance that ushers us into the presence of one who is, pound for pound, the greatest actor alive. As usual, he raises one's hair with the risks he takes … a hundred campaigns have tanned his heart to leather, and from the cracking of that heart there issues a terrible music, not untinged by madness. One hears great cries, which, like all of this actor's best effects, seem to have been dredged up from an ocean-bed of fatigue. One recognised, though one had never heard it before, the noise made in its last extremity by the cornered human soul.'

A couple of years later, the theatrical barricades having fallen, and the *ancien régime* having been consigned to periodic, and largely provincial, revivals, Olivier bravely crossed the bridge from the 'old and tried' to the 'new and untested' when he appeared at the Royal Court Theatre as Archie Rice, the 'dead behind the eyes' comedian, in John Osborne's *The Entertainer*. I saw the play on its transfer to the Palace Theatre in Shaftesbury Avenue, and once again I was mesmerised and rendered breathless by the power of Olivier's acting. There was a moment when, leaning against the proscenium arch, he learns of his son's death as a National Serviceman in Egypt. In the scene leading up to it, he had been telling his daughter of a Negress he once heard singing in a night-club, rising above the wretchedness of her existence by 'making the most beautiful fuss in the world.' Now, without making any significant or, for that matter, any remotely predictable movement, he slid slowly, almost imperceptibly slowly, down the proscenium arch, until – Tynan again – 'he crumples, and out of his gaping mouth come disorganised moans that slowly reveal themselves as melody. Archie the untouchable is singing the blues.' It was a moment of pure theatrical genius, a marriage of truth and technique that made public Archie's private grief so that, for a moment, we were able to share his loss, and suffer it with him. Several years later, I actually got to meet the great man, whose general appearance reminded me of nothing so much as a middle-aged bank manager, a revelation that, far from denting my admiration, only served to confirm the miraculous nature of his talent, and to further deify him in my eyes.

I think I can truthfully say that the only really useful skill I learned during my time at the Webber-Douglas was eating spaghetti which, although not part of the curriculum, has served me better, and played a far greater part in my life, than anything else I managed to glean while I was there. I took my first, faltering steps with spoon and fork in Sandy's handsome flat in Belsize Park Gardens, NW3, where the carpet must have paid a heavy price for my inexperience. It was not long, however, before I was ready to go public which, in the case of students from the Webber-Douglas Academy, meant the occasional visit to Dino's *Ristorante Italiano*, situated on the corner of Gloucester

Road and Stanhope Gardens. Dino's was one of the first generally accessible Italian restaurants to be established in London and where, in 1954, you could buy a *spaghetti bolognese,* together with French bread and butter and a cup of the then unfamiliar and exotic cappuccino coffee for two shillings and ninepence (14p or thereabouts!). The Gloucester Road Dino's has gone, although I believe its sister restaurant in South Kensington still exists. But for years afterwards, until its closure, I took great pleasure in returning whenever I was in the area, and ordering exactly the same meal plus the odd glass of red wine – even if the price had risen over the intervening 45 years, by something like 3,400%!

I was invited, once again through the medium of James Maxwell, to play the part of Jim Hawkins in *Treasure Island* for director, Frank Dunlop, with the Piccolo Theatre Company in Chorlton-cum-Hardy, a suburb of Manchester. Rehearsals and performances fell conveniently within the Christmas holiday period and so, with the blessing of Mr. Johnstone-Douglas, I headed off at the end of term for what turned out to be an enjoyable return to the professional stage. I shared digs in a large Victorian house with Max and his wife, Avril Elgar, and managed, during my short stay, to see them both in productions of *Twelfth Night* and *Dial M for Murder,* by virtue of the fact that the Piccolo Theatre Company was weekly repertory, a much maligned system which was already on the wane by then, although it has to be said that it encouraged a far greater degree of audience loyalty in provincial theatre than anything we've come up with since. Give or take the odd variation, it involved opening a production on Monday evening, and then meeting the following morning for a read-through of the next play which the director would aim to have blocked by the end of rehearsals that day with the indispensable aid of a French's acting edition of the script which gave you all the moves. On Wednesday you would work through and run the first act, and on Thursday repeat the process with Act Two, leaving Friday for Act Three or, if you were fortunate enough to be rehearsing one of those newfangled two-act plays, for a complete run-through, followed by a welcome Saturday morning off. Otherwise a run-through was scheduled for Saturday morning, prior to playing a matinée of the current production, followed by a technical rehearsal on Sunday, and then one or two dress-rehearsals on Monday, followed by an opening night. In between times, of course, there were lines to be learned, food to be eaten and sleep to be taken. But, amazingly, actors in weekly rep somehow also managed to enjoy a social life of sorts, even if it was confined to a quick visit to the local pub after the show before staggering back to their digs and eventually falling asleep over their scripts. If I was affected at all by this cloistered existence, having been engaged for only one production, it was manifested in the budding relationship I enjoyed with the attractive actress playing my mother in *Treasure Island,* which began and ended in the cupboard of the Admiral Benbow Inn, where we both hid from the pirate, Black Dog (or was it Blind Pew?), for all of ten minutes, during which time we indulged in the kind of cuddles that were neither filial on my part nor, by her ready acquiescence, even remotely maternal on hers! There was, however, no time to pursue this relationship beyond its budding, which was probably just as well as my penchant for older women was in danger of getting out of hand. Somehow or other, we did manage to get to see a matinée performance of the musical, *Wonderful Town,* at Manchester's Opera House together, and held hands throughout the performance as I recall, but it was a fleeting romance, and one I might very well have forgotten all about, had it not lent a whole new meaning to the phrase 'cupboard-love'!

Wonderful Town was an early Leonard Bernstein musical and, significantly, my very first acquaintance with musical theatre, a genre that came to mean more and more to me over the next few years. A musical adaptation of the play *My Sister Eileen,* it teamed Bernstein with Betty Comden and Adolph Green who had together been responsible for the score of that wonderful 1949 screen musical, *On the Town.*

Treasure Island was great fun and full of derring-do, as Jim Hawkins manoeuvred his way in and out of dangerous situations, hiding in apple-barrels (alone!), and climbing up the ship's rigging, shooting and being shot at by various pirates, and finally ending up on the winning side, taking his last farewell of that perennially appealing and charismatic rogue, Long John Silver, played in that particular production with great charm and insidious treachery by another former colleague from the Old Vic days, Eric Thompson who, I learned, was also a graduate of the Old Vic School. In fact, it seemed that practically everyone I worked with at that time had studied under Michel St. Denis, and so influenced was I by them all that, had the school still been up-and-running, I would have applied for an immediate transfer. As it happened, internecine squabbles amongst the powers that be at the Old Vic had led to its closure, and so Michel had picked up his marbles and left Britain to run the *Centre Dramatique de l'Est* in Strasbourg. There was no alternative for yours truly then but to return, as I did, to the Webber-Douglas Academy, once the good ship

Hispaniola had made its last voyage back to Bristol, and Jim Hawkins into the waiting arms of his mother!

It was during my time at the Webber-Douglas that I first came across, or at any rate consciously encountered, homosexuality, which was at that time illegal. Two young men in my year, obviously seeing what they were looking for in each other on the first day of term, had set up home together in Onslow Gardens very shortly afterwards, and I became a frequent visitor to their flat. John Harry and Peter Mackriel were both delightful and civilised people, and the fact that they were a homosexual pairing did not in any way affect my relationship with them. This was contrary to all my previous education on the subject, which was something along the lines that all homosexuals are, by their very nature, predatory. God knows, I have happened upon a fair number of importunate homosexuals in my time, but in all probability they number no more and no fewer than their heterosexual counterparts.

It was through the medium of these two young men that I began to develop a taste for popular music of a certain kind, a taste which essentially remains mine to this day: the music of Coward, Gershwin, Cole Porter, Rodgers and Hart and Jerome Kern, to name but a few of that gifted generation of songwriters who emanated from what I still refer to as 'The Golden Age of Popular Music.' Until I was introduced to them by way of a mammoth (or so it seemed to me) collection of long-playing records of which I possessed none at the time, my musical education had been haphazard to say the least. From a childhood dominated by the songs of Vera Lynn, and my particular wartime favourite, *Run, Rabbit, Run,* I had graduated, courtesy of my music teacher, Mr. Merlyn-Smith, to a mild appreciation of classical music, songs by Bach and Purcell, as well as from his native Wales – *David of the White Rock,* for instance, which I loved, and even got to sing in Welsh, at a school concert. My brush with Purcell's *Dido and Æneas* at the Mermaid Theatre had further fed my interest in classical music. But my affections really and truly lay with popular music. I have fond memories of a family holiday, taken to coincide with a T&GWU conference in Whitley Bay, when, leaving my parents and my baby brother basking in the sun, I furtively sneaked away from the beach every couple of hours or so, clutching another sixpence in my hand, ostensibly for an ice-cream, and sought out the nearest juke-box to satisfy my junkie-like craving for Frankie Laine's latest hit record, *Jezebel!*

John and Peter weaned me away from this kind of thing, and

introduced me to more refined melodies and infinitely more sophisticated lyrics. It was also in John and Peter's company that I visited a cinema in Bromley that was showing *A Star is Born*. I had, of course, been acquainted with the films of Judy Garland for some years, and was practically weaned on *The Wizard of Oz*, but this in no way prepared me for her performance as Esther Blodgett/Vicki Lester in *A Star is Born,* or for the unfathomable and long-lasting effect it would have on me, culminating many years later, and long after her death, in a relationship with Judy Garland, intimate yet obviously distant, which I could not, even in my wildest imagination, have dreamed of at the time. Suffice to say that my crush on Doris Day, engendered by her delicious performance in *Calamity Jane* which I'd seen more than a year earlier, came to an abrupt end that evening in Bromley when Judy Garland took her place in my affections, a very special place from which, to this day, she has never been ousted.

My disaffection with what was on offer at the Webber-Douglas had been made all the sharper as a result of my brief sojourn with the Piccolo Theatre Company and, despite the friendships I had made, and the social life which I continued to enjoy, I found I was asking myself more and more often what I was doing there. I had arrived at my 17th birthday, only too well aware that my days as a child actor were running out. True, I still looked quite young for my years, but ahead of me, only a couple of years away at the most, lay the prospect of National Service, two years out of my life, after which I knew, even then, that things would never be the same again. I was afraid of missing out on the few opportunities that were left, a concern that only niggled away at me because I felt I was wasting my time at the Webber-Douglas Academy.

In the Easter holidays, Sandy and I went off on a hitch-hiking tour, a trip we'd been planning throughout the previous term, equipping ourselves with walking shoes and haversacks, and studying the route we were to take. The weather was unseasonably warm for most of the time – or perhaps early spring was always like that in those days. We made our way down through Somerset and Devon, as far as the Minack Theatre carved out of the cliffs in Porthcurno, on the very furthest tip of Cornwall. We stayed in youth hostels for the most part, treating ourselves once or twice, after an especially foot-weary day, to the comforts of a proper hotel. Our return route took us through North Devon to Bristol and Bath and northwards as far as Oxford, where we paid a visit to the New Theatre and caught the pre-London tour of *Kismet,* which is the reason I embarked upon this diversionary tale in the first place.

If *Wonderful Town* had been my introduction to musical theatre, *Kismet* was the show that put the seal on my lifelong devotion to that particular form. I have seen many wonderful musicals since then, but none that excited me more than *Kismet* did at that particularly impressionable time in my life. The overture, borrowed from Borodin, as was the rest of the musical score, sent the adrenaline racing through my body, as it still does today when I hear it, possibly more in fond remembrance than for any other reason. I found myself transported by it, longing to be part of it, trapped in a well-worn cliché that was nonetheless only too real to me at the time. The lights dimmed, and on came the beggar-poet, Hajj, played by Alfred Drake. Of course, I didn't have a clue who Alfred Drake was, or that he had originated the part of Curly in *Oklahoma* and played the Petruchio character in the first ever production of *Kiss Me Kate*. But from that very first moment I was aware that I was watching a star of the first magnitude; a relatively small man, as it turned out, who bestrode his narrow world like a colossus. He stood centre stage and began to sing the prologue, a haunting melody called *The Sands of Time*, during which he lifted his arms and, with the most elegant of gestures, magically opened the gates to the city of Baghdad, where the story is set. I have never seen a performer occupy a stage so completely and with such easy assurance. I was hypnotised by him in the first five minutes, and by the end of the show, I was a devoted fan. His performance, stylish and witty, passionate and philosophical by turns, was described at the time as 'bravura', which was accurate enough, I suppose, but fell far short of expressing the effect it had on me. His acting was so remarkably good, in fact, that there was a danger of taking for granted that wonderfully rich baritone voice which lay at the centre of his performance. I made a point of being present at the Stoll Theatre several weeks later for the West End opening of *Kismet,* and went on to see the show a further six times, the last following Alfred Drake's return to the USA, and with the role of Hajj now in the hands of a perfectly capable British replacement, I was made painfully aware of how lacklustre it all seemed without him.

Events during the summer term at the Webber-Douglas were eclipsed very early on by an offer from Frank Dunlop, who had recently taken over from Frank Hauser the artistic directorship of the Midland Theatre Company in Coventry. I had no doubts, no second thoughts, no hesitation in accepting the offer. The only problem was that I would have to confront the principal, Johnstone-Douglas, an unapproachable man at the best of times. The interview was just as bad as I had imagined it would be. J-D was appalled, astounded and reproachful by turns. He could scarcely countenance the fact that one of his students, and the youngest one at that, was prepared to throw in the towel only halfway through the course. I was as diplomatic as I knew how to be, but my mind was made up, and there was nothing he could say to change it, although he tried his damnedest to browbeat me into submission. I knew what I wanted to do, and although he, of course, had been unaware of it, I had been dreaming of a rescue mission such as this for months and months. I finally emerged from his office, battered but resolute.

Sandy Black and I remained in close contact, although he eventually returned to his native Canada and ended up running the technical department at Ryerson College in Toronto, one of Canada's leading drama schools. He was never much of an actor, an opinion I knew he shared, but his talents led him in another, not unrelated, direction, where he achieved a great deal of success and distinction, which I always knew he would. I was sorry, of course, to have to say goodbye to many of the friends I had made while at the Webber-Douglas. Some of our paths would cross in the future, others I would never see again, although I cannot honestly say that any of these melancholy thoughts troubled me as I boarded the Coventry-bound train at Euston in August 1955, and headed off for what was to be, amongst many other things, a date with destiny.

oOoOo

Five

Over the years, Coventry has played a fairly significant part in my life and, although I never really liked the place, time has taken the rough edges off my memories, and left me with a quite irrational affection for it. Back in that summer of 1955 it was little more than a shell of a city, having barely recovered from one of the most devastating air-raids of the war. On the night of the 14th November 1940, German bombs had virtually reduced the place to rubble, and while the process of reconstruction was well under way, its former standing as a major commercial and industrial centre in the heart of the Midlands had been blitzed out of existence, never to return.

At the same time, many of its native inhabitants had, one way or another, disappeared, to be replaced by migrant workers, very few of whom had any intention of putting down roots in the city. At the centre of the terrible destruction wrought upon it on that fateful night lay the ruins of its beautiful medieval cathedral, the 15th century walls and North Tower of which remain standing to this day, the only really tangible evidence, apart from the statue of Lady Godiva, that Coventry had a history at all. The new cathedral, designed by Sir Basil Spence, which now stands alongside the ruins of the old, wasn't finally consecrated until 1962 and, as I arrived for what was to be the first of many return visits, even the Belgrade Theatre was three years away from celebrating its inauguration as the first of Britain's new civic theatres. Devoid of hindsight or a crystal ball, my first impression was simply that Coventry was a bit bleak and decidedly unlovely.

The Midland Theatre Company was a triangular operation, the apex being Jedburgh House, which accommodated the administrative offices and, way up at the top, the costume department.

Opposite Jedburgh House, on one corner of the adjacent road, was the Technical College which housed the stage and the auditorium, more suited perhaps to prize-giving ceremonies than to theatrical presentations, while on the other were the workshops and a church hall used for rehearsals. It was here that we gathered that first day, a company of around 15, presided over by Frank Dunlop, fresh from his success at Chorlton-cum-Hardy. He had taken over the job of artistic director from Frank Hauser, now removed to the Oxford Playhouse, where he formed the Meadow Players, one of the most successful regional companies of the post-war period.

Sitting round in a circle at the beginning of a season with people you had never met before but with whom you were about to share a most peculiar intimacy, was all part and parcel of a working actor's life in those far-off days. I don't suppose it happens much any more, outside the purlieus of the Royal Shakespeare Company, and even if it did, the circle would, of financial necessity, be somewhat smaller. But Frank Dunlop's projected season was, if not ground-breaking, certainly drawn large, and included productions of Thornton Wilder's *The Matchmaker,* Anouilh's *The Lark, The Comedy of Errors* and, for the Christmas season, *Treasure Island,* in which I was to be enlisted again as cabin-boy on board the *Hispaniola.* Strangely, I cannot for the life of me remember who played my mother on this occasion, nor do I have any recollection of the famous cupboard, although by the time Christmas came around, my fancies lay beyond the walls of the *Admiral Benbow Inn,* and I had no need of such a trysting-place. It was reassuring to see at least a couple of familiar faces on that August morning. Eric Thompson was there, no doubt to play Long John Silver again amongst other things, and Bernard Kilby, who had been a member of the Old Vic Company in 1953. Otherwise, they were all unknown to me, although not for long, as I had already learned that close relationships, if only of a temporary nature, are forged faster in the theatre than in any other walk of life, except maybe in the armed forces or in prison. I was to share digs, nay a bedroom, with Ronald Fraser, one of the leading members of the company, and nothing brings two people closer together than that! But by the same token, it has to be said, lasting friendships are not so easy to make or sustain; rather I believe as a consequence of the nomadic lifestyle of an actor than the superficiality with which we are often tarred. In those far-off days, with television in its infancy, most actors plied their trades in regional repertory companies, living in lodgings far from home, and working together for 12 hours a day, very often for months on end. So it's hardly surprising that they became fairly adept at making quick and easy friendships. You'd think that with the vast majority of actors now living in London or the Home Counties, and depending largely on television work to meet their mortgage repayments, such friendships would be easier to hang on to, but they're not, as anyone who has ever tried to get from Muswell Hill to Wimbledon Common and back in time for bed will tell you.

Another peculiarity belonging to that era was the existence of the Acting Assistant Stage Manager. Nowadays if you are a member of the stage management team, then that is what you do, and trying to persuade an A.S.M. to go on stage during a performance except to shift a piece of furniture is as difficult as trying to persuade an actor to shift a piece of furniture. The lines have long been drawn, and to our mutual benefit it has to be said, but it's a pity that young actors, outside of certain drama schools, don't get the opportunity to try their hands at stage management, if only to widen their experience and teach them to value its proper practitioners. It was not any kind of altruism, however, but sound economics that were responsible for the existence of the Acting Assistant Stage Manager back in the 1950s, for who in their right minds would pay two salaries if they could get away with paying one? In theory, of course, the young actors assigned to these duties would not, as actors, be burdened with major roles, but that wasn't the way it worked out – at least, not in the Midland Theatre Company under Frank Dunlop – and to the detriment, more often than not, of the stage management side of things. In retrospect, the array of acting talent employed for the season in that dual capacity (not counting myself, of course!) was pretty formidable, but in the way of cleating flats together, connecting lights, making props and giving cues, much was left to be desired. To be fair, the fact that we were a three-weekly touring company didn't make the job any easier, and by the time we had two productions under our belts, group fatigue was already beginning to set in. This was the routine: we would set up at the Technical College on Sunday and play there for a week, while beginning rehearsals for the next production, then strike the set after the final performance on Saturday night and, early Monday morning, drive in the stage management pantechnicon to Nuneaton, some ten miles away, where we would put the set up in the Co-op Hall and, with the arrival of the rest of the company in the afternoon, run the play technically prior to opening on Monday evening. We would then return to Coventry and continue to rehearse the following day, commuting to Nuneaton for an evening performance until Wednesday night when we would strike the set, return to Coventry and, early on Thursday morning, drive to Netherton, a dismal journey through Birmingham pre Spaghetti-Junction, and via Dudley Zoo, where we would again set up, this time in the Public Library, performing in that cheerless venue until Saturday night before striking the set and returning to base for yet another early start on Monday, the prelude to a comparatively luxurious week at a delightful little theatre in Loughborough, marred only by the fact that the get-in was through an access about 15 feet up the side wall of the building. Another downside to this particular week was that, because of the length of the journey, rehearsal time was cut even shorter and also that we seldom arrived back in Coventry before midnight. Needless to say, we had to strike the set on Saturday night, making it even later, although no concession was made to this, and we were called early on Sunday to begin the process all over again with the next production. But we were all young and comparatively resilient, and for the most part managed to keep going throughout the season, suffering little more than varying degrees of exhaustion. I have fond and vivid memories of a very young Alan Bates, who had been seconded to 'Electrics', wandering, apparently aimlessly, backwards and forwards across the stage on set-up days with coils of cable slung over his shoulder. To the casual observer, his progress may well have looked purposeful, but it didn't fool me, as I was giving precisely the same semi-comatose performance while pretending to carry out my own duties only a few feet away from him. It's worth pointing out that, as well as attending to his stage management duties, Alan was required to play, amongst other things, the juvenile lead in Denis Cannan's comedy, *You and Your Wife,* the opening play of the season, as well as one of the Antipholuses in *The Comedy of Errors,* and Squire Trelawney in *Treasure Island.* Also on the stage management team were James Culliford and Alfred Lynch, a couple of lads from the East End of London who became, and remained for the rest of their lives, close friends, besides being two of the nicest people I have ever met. Jimmy was ex-navy while Alfie had served his time in the Royal Artillery, so neither was afraid of hard work and they were probably the most effective members of the team. There is little doubt, however, that without Bernard Kilby, our lunatic stage manager, the scenery would seldom have been up in time for the performance or, in the unlikely event that it had been, that it would have fallen down before the end. Bernard was a natural company man, good-natured, humorous and companionable. He was also a very good actor, particularly outstanding that season as the Dauphin in *The Lark.* But with his stage manager's hat on, he became Mr. Hyde. He ranted, raved, and sweated profusely, driving himself and the rest of us, but especially himself, to ever more strenuous endeavours, as if he was trying to overcome a terrible and secret handicap or break some kind of record only he knew about. I was never quite sure whether he was engaged in a battle with his own inadequacies or with ours, but working under him was an alarming and a demoralising experience; never more so than when he would roughly push you aside in order to carry a 12 foot 'flat' up four flights of stairs alone and unaided, as he almost always did during the 'get-in' at the Co-op Hall in Nuneaton. Bernard was married to actress, Gillian Rain who, after his untimely death a few years later, went on to become Leonard Rossiter's wife, and it's a funny thing, but there was always something about Len's acting – brilliant though it was – that recalled Bernard Kilby's high-voltage performance as stage manager.

There was only one female Acting A.S.M. on the team, a young lady called Patricia Healey, an attractive if somewhat brittle, 19 year-old. Naturally enough, I sought her out, even took her to the pictures on one occasion (I think), but she wasn't even remotely interested, and for some reason I wasn't particularly bothered either, although we remained on friendly terms for the rest of the season. Years later, I heard that she was involved in a relationship with the writer, Shelagh Delaney, and although that could have presented me with a face-saving explanation for her lack of interest, I'm not entirely sure that Patsy had already orientated herself back in 1955. Truth to tell, our mutual lack of real enthusiasm and a marked absence of any chemistry between us augured badly from the start, for outside the ranks of the acting company Patsy had been the only possible option, ascertained on the very first day as we all sat round in that circle which long-established theatrical tradition had ordained for introductions, read-throughs, and for sorting out your sex-life! For very obvious reasons, Charmian Eyre and Rosalind Knight – the future Mrs. Michael Elliott – were never in contention, and while I thought that Sheila Ballantine was attractive in a fluffy kind of way, there was something rather prim and proper about her that did not invite the kind of approach I might have had in mind. I subsequently worked with Sheila on several occasions over the years, and became very fond of her. I also noticed that a sea-change had taken place since our first season together. It had come to pass, apparently, that following the end of a long and rather staid relationship, Sheila had taken off on her own for the Costa Brava, or somewhere very like it, where she was accosted on the beach one day by a lusty young Spaniard who asked her three questions, to wit: "You like hot sun?" "You like hot sand?" and "You like hot boys?" Whether she intended to reply in the affirmative to all three questions, or was simply mesmerised by his accent, Sheila came back home a changed woman, or so legend has it, and I'm only sorry that I didn't meet her for the first time *after* her Spanish holiday!

Across the road in Jedburgh House, and four narrow flights up, under the eves and completely isolated from the rest of us, was the kind of eyrie traditionally set aside for people who make costumes in the theatre, on the not unreasonable grounds, I imagine, that they will seldom have the opportunity to come down. This little kingdom in the clouds was ruled over by a formidable lady called Riette Sturge-Moore.

Her lieutenant, and chief cutter of costumes, was an extremely attractive young woman called Dawn Pavitt who was, like nearly everybody else I worked with in those days, a graduate of the Old Vic School. Before I get carried away, and for future reference, it is worth pointing out that Dawn was very good at her job, and extremely conscientious in all matters relating to it. That aside, and more to the point, she was such stuff as dreams are made on; well, *my* dreams at any rate. But dreams they were likely to remain, and I was under no illusions about it, for although Dawn was only 21 at the time, she was possessed of a poise and sophistication that placed her more than a few rungs up the ladder of unattainability, at least as far as I was concerned. She was also, if not exactly aloof, somewhat detached from the extrovert camaraderie of the acting company, and not only because she was physically removed from it, but because she didn't seem to need it and never sought it out. At the same time she was always perfectly friendly, while costume fittings which, of necessity, demand an unusual degree of physical proximity became, instead of the usual irksome experience, a consummation devoutly to be wished. A smile bestowed by Dawn during one of these sessions would fire my imagination for the rest of the day, fuelled by the memory of her perfume, a subtle and lingering fragrance called *Indiscret*. Whether Fate played a hand in it or not, there was only one free seat on the coach back from Loughborough when I boarded it following the opening there of one of our early productions, and I found myself sitting next to Dawn for the hour-long journey back to Coventry. Neither Fate nor alcohol can be held responsible for the irresistible impulse that made me reach out and take her hand, and I suppose that it must have been by her own free will that she chose not to take it back. In any case, there it remained for the entire journey, and the rest, as they say, is history. I have been dying to include a little verse, originally written and performed by the great Max Miller, and which, in my opinion, ought to have found its way into *Palgrave's Golden Treasury* by now. It exemplifies, and a good deal more succinctly than anything penned by Donne, Herrick or Marvell, the kind of woman to whom I have always been fatally attracted ...

'I like the girls who do;
I like the girls who don't;
I hate a girl who says she will, and then she says she won't.
But the girl I like the best of all, and I think you'll say I'm right,
Is the girl who says she never does,
But she looks as though she might!'

These days, or so it seems, they either do or they don't, and they'll let you know one way or the other without any help from you, thank you very much. Mystery and allure, those essentially feminine masks, have been tossed aside, and the art of flirtation is all but extinct. The very notion of the hunter and the hunted is anathema to most modern women, who see it as a distasteful relic of the pre-feminist age when women only did what they did, dressed how they dressed and appeared to enjoy it, because that is what men demanded of them. Well, I'm sure there's a grain of political truth in there somewhere, but what it perversely overlooks and throws out with the bathwater is the fact that a large number of men played by the same rules, and also appeared to enjoy it. They spent a similar amount of time grooming themselves in order to attract the opposite sex, they held doors open for them, pulled chairs out from under tables in restaurants for them, gave up their seats on public transport for them and, in order to protect them from being splashed or otherwise inconvenienced by the traffic, they walked on the outside of the pavement. The objective was still the same, of course, but I believe that before lassies evolved into ladettes, they were treated with a good deal more respect in pursuit of it. Back in the '50s, when a young man was expected to exercise a degree of patience, the course of a relationship and the speed at which it was allowed to develop was largely dictated by the woman, upon whom it fell to either sanction or prohibit. It was agonisingly frustrating for us blokes, of course, but it was the way of the world, and in weighing up the pros and cons of being in love for the very first time at the age of 17 back in 1955, with all its agonies, as against any amount of today's easy and casual coupling, be it on the island of Ibiza, the Greek resort of Kavos, or anywhere else for that matter, eternal youth is not a gift I would thank anyone for!

I certainly had to exercise a great deal of patience, and not only in deference to female prerogative, but also because our working hours were long and, more often than not, at variance. We did have the occasional Sunday though, which almost always began with lunch at The Friars, probably the only affordable restaurant in Coventry at the time, and where the menu offered up roast posk [sic] and apple sauce at 2/6d (12½p) which became a firm favourite. On our combined salaries of £9 a week or thereabouts, eating out on a regular basis was something of an indulgence, even at those prices, but with the help of my newly acquired Post Office savings book, and to the utter bewilderment of the rest of the company, we certainly indulged ourselves. We went to the pictures quite often too, a fine and relatively private place where we held hands and embraced our way through a number of forgotten films, and were content simply to hold hands through a few memorable ones: *Carmen Jones,* for instance, *New Faces* with Eartha Kitt and *Seven Brides for Seven Brothers.* We also spent a lot of time talking to each other in a way that was quite new to me, almost as if we had been saving it all up for each other like long-separated lovers, and out it all came, thoughts and ideas previously unexpressed, opinions never before sought, stories untold. Moreover, and of even greater significance, we made each other laugh.

Dawn had come to Coventry via Stratford-upon-Avon, where she had worked on the costumes for Olivier's *Macbeth.* During the technical dress-rehearsal, at which she had been present, the familiar problem of Banquo's ghost had reared its head. It's relatively easy to make the ghost appear and take people by surprise because they're not looking for it, but once you have achieved this – and in that particular production they employed a pair of rubber doors between which the actor was able to squeeze through no apparent aperture – how the hell do you get him off again with all eyes glued on the door? This dilemma clearly had to be resolved before the rehearsal continued, and so everything ground to a halt while the director, Glen Byam Shaw, bent his mind to it. Out of the protracted silence that followed, and the absence of anything like an idea to fill it, Olivier's voice was raised, "Glenny baby," he said, "how would it be if I were to leap up onto the table for 'Hence, horrible shadow, unreal mockery, hence!' and then describe a complete circle with my cloak? The audience's eyes will be taken by that, and Banquo can go back the way he came." This extravagant offer would probably have been greeted with derision had it come from a lesser mortal, but it had been made by Laurence Olivier, and therefore commanded a certain amount of attention. "Sounds good, Larry," said the director, "but can you do it?" Whereupon Olivier leapt onto the table, spoke the lines, described a complete circle with his cloak, and Banquo vanished. The effect, according to Dawn, was quite astonishing, and all the more so in that he was able to repeat it at every performance thereafter. I have never tired of retelling that story as an example of supreme technical skill, and had I not already deified him, his place at the top of Olympus would have been assured from the moment I first heard it. I was, of course, sick to my stomach that I had not seen the performance myself, and so turn again to Kenneth Tynan to articulate what I sadly missed, 'Last Tuesday, Sir Laurence shook hands with greatness and within a week or so the performance will have ripened into a masterpiece … On the battlements his throttled fury switches into top gear, and we see a lion, baffled, but still colossal. 'I 'gin to be a-weary of the sun' held the very ecstasy of despair, the actor swaying with grief, his voice rising like hair on the crest of a trapped animal. 'Exeunt, fighting' was a poor end for such a giant warrior. We wanted to see how he would die; and it was not he but Shakespeare who let us down.'

No matter where Dawn and I had been, or what we had done or seen during those palmy Sundays, we always ended up sitting on the wall outside the house she was staying in, and where we said our protracted 'goodnights.' She couldn't invite me in, she said, because she didn't yet have a table. It says a lot about the manners of the time, not to mention my own scant knowledge of the female psyche, that I never questioned the need for one. I simply accepted it as an insurmountable problem and, having extracted the last ounce of pleasure afforded by the cold hard wall, made my euphoric way back from Prince of Wales Drive to my own digs in Spencer Road, a considerable distance measured by the fact that I could just about sing the entire vocal score from *Carmen Jones* before I got there, steeling myself to face the inevitable inquisition from Ronnie Fraser. It was on one of those idyllic Sundays, several weeks later, that I received a visit from Sandy Black, my old friend from the Webber-Douglas. He'd stopped off on his sight-seeing way to Kenilworth or Warwick, or some such place, and I was anxious for him to meet Dawn, so he joined us for lunch at The Friars where we no doubt enthusiastically recommended the roast posk! It was a very pleasant occasion, as I recall, enhanced by the fact that I was probably basking in the certain knowledge that Sandy would find my female companion as mature, intelligent and devastatingly attractive as I did, and was probably wondering how the hell I had 'gotten so lucky!' In any event, Sandy eventually left to visit one of those medieval piles so envied by our cousins from the New World, and having made no plans until the evening, Dawn and I strolled back to Prince of Wales Drive where, without the slightest hesitation, she opened the door and invited me in. It must have been at least an hour or so later that I was first able to take stock of my surroundings, and I was somewhat puzzled to notice, although of course I didn't mention it, that she still didn't have a table!

Dawn celebrated her 22nd birthday on October 16th, and around about the same time we became engaged. It was a declaration, however, made without any real intent, for Dawn had no immediate desire to be married, and I was too young. Besides, the prospect of

National Service was already casting its shadow over my future, and long-term plans of any kind had to be put on hold. So we simply exchanged rings, further eroding my savings, and vowed eternal love. Of course, I would have married her there and then, and with no thought for the consequences. I was so completely besotted that, even after only a few short weeks, I found it well nigh impossible to imagine a future without her. Dawn, on the other hand, older, wiser and a good deal more circumspect than I, was simply marking our relationship down as more important than any that had gone before. I didn't know that at the time, of course, and in any case, several feet off the ground as I was, I certainly wouldn't have appreciated the distinction.

Meanwhile the season ground on as the days became murkier, the nights darker, and my duties as an Assistant Stage Manager even more irksome. Everyone on the team – apart from Bernard Kilby, of course – was running out of steam, and even with extreme youth on my side, I was probably suffering more than anyone, on account of my extra-curricular activities. These were the talk of the company needless to say, a topic that I was hardly in a position to refute when I habitually arrived for fit-up on Monday morning wearing my best Sunday clothes. It was at about this time, too, that a notice was posted in the rehearsal room banning members of the acting company from visiting the wardrobe department except on official business. There was nothing ambiguous about it, as there clearly was about the director's motives for putting it there, and in any case, a private word in my ear would have served the same purpose, but Frank Dunlop never brought the subject up. He chose, instead, to take out his 'whatever-it-was' on Dawn who, as I have already said, was never less than super-efficient and conscientious when it came to her work. But he began to subject her to a studied campaign of non-communication, addressing all his remarks to her through Riette Sturge-Moore who had the unenviable task of repeating them to Dawn who was perfectly capable, it has to be said, of playing him at his own game, and she did.

Nevertheless, and whatever his real motives, it felt like a pretty unpleasant and malicious way to conduct a working relationship, and fully justified the sobriquet of 'Spider,' which became attached to him at about that time – and not only by Dawn and me. One of my abiding memories of that season in Coventry is the sight of Riette, tall and dignified, walking up the Butts towards the centre of town, with 'Spider' Dunlop lumbering along at her side, like an attendant goblin. He did some good work, however, and one of the highlights of the season was his production of *The Comedy of Errors,* freely adapted and with songs by George Hall, not only a member of the acting company but also a gifted musician, who went on to become the Principal of the Central School of Speech & Drama. I have particularly fond memories of Jimmy Culliford at the opening of the show steering his gondola across the back of the stage and singing in his lovely baritone voice a haunting little song called *Early Morning on the River.* To play my twin Dromio, Frank had imported a young actor called Brian Smith, who had preceded me as resident boy-actor at the Old Vic in the late 1940s, had made several films, and was regarded as something of a celebrity by the rest of us. The fact that both Alfred Lynch and Alan Bates went on to achieve celebrity of their own shortly afterwards, and that Brian's star faded with the onset of adulthood, is just one of the vagaries of a business that is crammed with them. I also suspected, even then, that Brian was somewhat older than he appeared to be. He had certainly been around a good few years longer than I had and all the accumulated experience of those years he brought to bear upon the part of the Syracusian Dromio, so that working alongside him, as well as being fun, was something of an education. Together we closed the show by singing a duet, words and music by George Hall, which I make no apologies for including here, if only because I don't think there's a single living soul who will remember it at all, let alone with such astonishing clarity; except perhaps for Brian Smith!

'I'm Dromio of Ephesus,
And I'm the boy from Syracuse.
The fact that he's my double
Is sure to lead to trouble;
We'll plot and plan, do all we can
To muddle and confuse;
We'll play terrible tricks,
You can't believe how we'll mix you,
We'll be known throughout the town as regular terrors;
For without a doubt, we're sure to bring about
Many a similar Comedy of Errors!'

In *The Matchmaker* there is a scene between Horace Vandergelder and his two apprentices, Cornelius Hackl and Barnaby Tucker in which, having decided to marry Dolly Levi, Vandergelder tells them that they are to have a mistress. Barnaby, appalled, replies, "But I'm too young, Mr. Vandergelder!" It got one of the biggest laughs in the show although, as I was playing Barnaby, it also managed to raise more than a few eyebrows backstage. And in truth, I was finding it increasingly difficult to get the balance right between business and pleasure, and was guilty of burning my candle, not only at both ends, but in the middle too! On one occasion, as Barnaby, I fell asleep while hiding under the restaurant table, missed an important cue, and was brought to my senses by a sharp kick in the ribs, delivered by Charmian Eyre who, as Dolly, obviously felt that she couldn't get on with the scene without hearing me sneeze, or whatever it was I was supposed to do at that moment. As an English soldier in Anouilh's *The Lark*, required to stand still and say nothing for what seemed like an eternity, there were occasions when I caught myself swaying perilously, and I learned – if nothing else – how to maintain my equilibrium while taking a nap on my feet at the same time. I remember an autumnal journey to Netherton in the company coach which was forced to crawl along through a particularly nasty combination of rain and fog. The members of the company, almost without exception, were slumped in their seats in various attitudes of fatigue, demonstrating a decided reluctance to get up on stage and perform. As the coach nosed its way cautiously through the murk into the centre of the town, Rosalind Knight rose from her seat, wound the window down, and shouted, "People of Netherton! Come to the Library Theatre, and let us bring a little drabness into your colourful lives!" It goes without saying that we had Ros to thank for helping us get through that particular performance.

Increasingly I valued those Sunday oases, and not only for the more obvious reasons, but also for the serene interludes they provided in the otherwise gruelling régime of a three-weekly touring repertory company. In the warmth and comfort of Dawn's room, still lacking a table, although equipped with a compact record-player, I was introduced to the songs of Charles Trenet, and in particular to *Que Reste-T'il de Nos Amours?* and *Douce France*. The other record in her small collection of 78s that made a great impression on me was Frank Sinatra's early recording of *Ma'mselle*. I had obviously heard Sinatra sing before, but this was a completely new experience, and the birth of yet one more god in my personal pantheon. Over the years I have come to appreciate his singular talent more and more, but there was something special about that first occasion, and only later did it come to me that you never *really* hear Frank Sinatra until you're in love.

But Dawn's job was becoming daily more difficult to face, made so by Frank Dunlop's persistent and intolerable persecution. Obviously he wanted her to go, and go she did. At one of those gatherings, peculiar to regional theatres at the time, where the audience get to mingle with the actors, Dawn confronted him, and told him precisely what he could do with his job. She handled it quite beautifully, I thought, and had it not been for the tell-tale sight of her hands nervously playing with her shawl behind her back, which only I could see, she carried it off with a calm dignity that only enhanced her standing in my eyes. Frank's imperturbable expression barely masked his glee. His ploy had paid off, and Dawn had become ensnared in his web. What he didn't expect, and what was clearly beyond his calculations and his understanding, was that I would follow up Dawn's resignation with my own. Actors, and more particularly, young actors, didn't do that kind of thing. But, aside from the matter of personal loyalty, I wanted to put a spoke in his wheel by thwarting what I felt were his intentions. Maybe it wasn't the wisest move I could have made, but wisdom played no part in a decision that was taken with all the careless impetuosity of youth. Truth to tell, by the time the final curtain fell on *Treasure Island* in mid-January 1956, I had had enough of Coventry, enough of being an Assistant Stage Manager, enough of three-weekly touring, and more than enough of working with a man I had come to despise.

Greater love hath no man than this, that he should lay down his job for his fiancée! But I didn't regret it, even though I had no other work lined up. Nor did Dawn for that matter. She returned to her parental home in Southend-on-Sea, and I went back to Kensal Rise. But having exhausted my savings, and feeling bound to contribute something towards household expenses, the need to find work took on a whole new meaning. Luckily, I was rescued from immediate penury by a couple of television offers, courtesy of Muriel Cole, casting director for Associated-Rediffusion, who had long taken a keen interest in my fledgling career. I was also invited down to Guildford for one play, and stayed for five. I even briefly returned to the Midland Theatre Company – not, I hasten to add, at the behest of Frank Dunlop, who had since departed – to play the young King in Terence Rattigan's *The Sleeping Prince,* which had also been the last of my five roles at that lovely old theatre, long ago gutted by fire, in Guildford's North Street. Oddly, I remember nothing at all about my return visit to Coventry, except for the play itself which was a joy to perform, as are most plays by Rattigan, that most actor-friendly of playwrights.

What I do remember is that 1956 was not a year that was primarily about acting, or advancing my career, so much as nurturing my relationship with Dawn which had, all of a sudden, become the single most important thing in my life. Fenchurch Street Station, hardly the most romantic place on earth, became our very own Grand

Central, the scene of many passionate reunions and lovelorn farewells. All the stops on the Southend line, places unknown to me except by names I would never be able to forget – Billericay, Rayleigh, Pitsea, Benfleet, – were each encountered on a rising scale of expectation, although on the return trip they were more like the stations of the cross. Not that my visits to Southend-on-Sea were all milk and honey. Sunday lunches with my parents in Purves Road were always genuinely warm and relaxed occasions. At 242 Central Avenue, the home of Rose and Jack Pavitt, the atmosphere was usually prickly, to say the least. Their front-door mat proclaimed a welcome which, for Dawn's sake, they observed to the letter. But it was a thin veneer that barely masked the disapproval which, particularly from her father, hung over the proceedings like a sullen sky. I have no idea whether they liked me or not and, in any case, it was largely irrelevant. I was simply the last person on earth they wanted for their beloved daughter and only child, and who could blame them? Well, I did, of course, but looking back, I can see they had a point. Dawn was an extremely eligible young woman, not only the winner of a local beauty competition, but intelligent and gifted to boot. I was an impecunious actor, four and a half years her junior, whose only immediate prospect was a two year run in H.M. Armed Forces. Not only that but, although our backgrounds were similar, the Pavitts had moved a rung or two up the social ladder and, in common with many others who had emigrated to that recently discovered territory called 'The Lower Middle Class,' they had become a bit sniffy about anyone whose working-class origins were still showing.

Rose and Jack were, it has to be said, a strangely ill-matched couple who didn't appear to have a great deal in common. He was the foreman at a local family-run timber merchant's business whose aspirations to management were likely to be frustrated, if for no other reason, because he wasn't a member of the family. He was also, and possibly with those ambitions in mind, a Freemason and, horror of horrors, although fairly predictably, a Tory! I found him dull and uncommunicative, only really animated on those occasions when his disapproval of me rose to the surface. Dawn's mother was a different kettle of fish altogether, and some of her nicer characteristics were reflected in her daughter who was happily free of the less appealing ones. Rose was much easier to handle than Jack and, at the same time, much easier to offend. She was a tightly wound-up conglomeration of unfocussed energy, unrealised ambitions and bitter disappointment. Her life, or as much of it as I came to know, was full of complaint. She also possessed the most ultra-sensitive antennae I have ever come across, so that even the slightest transgression, a word out of place, a gesture made or omitted, became the reason for prolonged periods of tight-lipped and glacial silences which no amount of reparation would bring to an end, until she herself was good and ready to forgive, if not forget. Over the years I have come into contact with a good many such self-centred people who make the rules you are expected to play by and, while none of them are friends, just occasionally they become important to you and, although deeply resenting it, you learn to play the game their way when it really matters. It certainly mattered in the case of Dawn's mother to whom she was bound, if not uncritically, with very strong ties. A generation later, Rose Pavitt would probably have had a career of her own. She undoubtedly had the intelligence, the drive and the organisational ability to have held down a fairly high-powered job, which no doubt would have given her a sense of achievement and cancelled out most of the reasons for her overbearing dissatisfaction with life. Jack may have been partly to blame for this, but it was Rose who made the rules, not Jack, and according to her rules, married women shouldn't have to go out and work. She saw it as demeaning, not only in itself, but also in its implicit acknowledgement that her husband was unable to provide for her. Thus, all of her not inconsiderable energies were bent on the home, a small bungalow that was so crammed with highly polished furniture that a journey across the living-room to the kitchen was as fraught with danger as any SAS obstacle course! One of the most puzzling things about Rose and Jack Pavitt, emotionally disabled as they were, was that somewhere back in the past they had mutually experienced at least one moment of glorious abandon when they had bestowed upon their daughter the middle name of Desirée!

My call-up papers came through towards the end of the year and, subject to a medical examination, I would begin my National Service with the Royal Air Force in February, 1957. The RAF was my preferred choice for two very good reasons. Memories of the Battle of Britain, and of dashing young men taking to the skies in Spitfires and Hurricanes to defend our island against the invader, were infinitely more romantic and glamorous than anything the army had to offer. The fact that the army was doing all of its fighting equally gallantly on foreign soil, and therefore out of sight and earshot, didn't really occur to me. The second, and the more determining reason for choosing the RAF, was the colour of the uniform which, since it matched the colour of my eyes, would obviously suit me a whole lot better than khaki.

In the run-up to my medical, I was regaled by many stories about the lengths people would go to in order to avoid military service. One of these involved a friend of a friend who, although thoroughly heterosexual, had stopped off on his way to be examined and found a public convenience where he applied a complete make-up. Together with a liberal application of perfume, he appeared in front of the medical officer with his coat draped around his shoulders and a ready lisp to complete the picture. Needless to say, he was told that his services were surplus to requirements. Had the doctor been made aware of the extreme measures he had taken, I believe that he would not only have been snapped up and immediately promoted out of the ranks, but awarded a medal for bravery – not so much for seeing the interview through to the end, but for the time he spent in the waiting-room beforehand, surrounded by dozens of other less imaginative young men. I also heard that some people deliberately perforated their own ear-drums, learned how to flatten their feet, simulated insanity and, in extreme cases, even contrived to lose one of their toes or fingers. But I had no desire to be found unfit for military service. To tell the truth, I was actually looking forward to it. It was, after all, a new experience, a rite of passage, and I would have felt curiously thwarted had I been rejected for one reason or another. Over and above everything else, it was a new part to play and a different costume to wear, and had it been for two months instead of two years, I might well have enjoyed it. Offers of work had, in any case, dried up as the year neared its end, partly because I was all but unavailable, partly because I had given up looking, but mainly, I think, because I had entered that no-man's land between being a child actor and a member of the grown-up variety, where parts are notoriously difficult to come by, and across which an alarming number of erstwhile child actors fail to make the journey.

oOoOo

Six

By the time I returned to civilian life, about a week or so before my 21st birthday, the theatrical landscape had changed almost beyond recognition. True, *The Mousetrap* was still running, and it was entirely possible to visit a West End theatre once a month and see nothing other than drawing-room comedies, murder melodramas and barrack-room farces. But thanks largely to the English Stage Company at the Royal Court, and to Joan Littlewood's ensemble at Stratford East, contemporary realism was advancing on all fronts in a determined attack upon the bourgeois tastes of the past. The fact that, almost seventy years later, it is still pretty much the same audience, if a little less spruce, and more inclined to treat the auditorium as their own private domain, says more about the nature of theatre than it does about its content.

But by far the most important change that took place during those two years was that I grew up. When I re-entered the profession in February 1959, it was no longer as a member of that small and privileged group of child actors, but one of a multitude of grown up ones, in a business where supply has always grossly exceeded demand. Had I known what was in store for me in my chosen profession, I might well have embraced the womb-like comfort and security of service life and its petty irritations. I might well have grown to enjoy it. I certainly would have exploited the opportunities it presented for further education and travel. As it was, I resented it. From the moment that I looked on in horror as I was all but scalped by the RAF barber, and exchanged my civilian clothes for a uniform which may well have been blue, but was made of a material that bore no resemblance to those worn by Battle of Britain pilots, I resented it. As time went by, I resented it more and more for having robbed me of two years of my life, for keeping me away from Dawn, for turning me from Terry Wale, actor, into 5040978 Aircraftman Second-Class Wale. This negative attitude was doubtless responsible for making the days drag, but there was nothing I could do about it. It was simply the way I felt. The fact that, in due course, the RAF went out of its way to accommodate me and my talents did little to appease me, or to stop me from scoring off the days of my incarceration on a calendar. During those two years, I learned to duck and dive, a useful enough skill, but apart from that, and the ability to make up a bed with hospital corners, an accomplishment that became all but redundant with the advent of the duvet, I took nothing of any value from the experience. That was entirely my fault.

I was posted to Bridgnorth in Shropshire for basic training, but it might just as well have been the Outer Hebrides or the wastes of Siberia. For eight weeks I saw nothing beyond the perimeter fence. It was an unremittingly miserable time although I withstood it better than most. True, I didn't take all that kindly to the lack of privacy that goes hand-in-hand with barrack-room life, but at least it wasn't the first time I'd been away from home. I was surprised by the number of young men, most of them bigger and uglier than I was, who sobbed themselves to sleep at night, presumably because they were missing their mums. I suppose I have Jeremy Spenser's mother to thank for making me pretty well immune to those kind of sentiments. Having toured the country under that lady's shadow, and been all too often on the receiving end of her venomous tongue, I also found it hard to be intimidated by the various NCOs whose job it was to bellow, shout and generally scare the shit out of us. I did as I was told for the most part because life was easier that way. Keeping a low profile is the first lesson in the art of ducking and diving. Mind you, it doesn't always go according to plan.

Corporal Pottinger was our flight NCO, the man responsible for making sure that we and our billet were ready for inspection first thing in the morning, and that we arrived, duly inspected, on the parade ground immediately after breakfast, there to be inspected again before being marched backwards and forwards and round in circles, taught to salute, to present arms, to slope arms, to come to attention, to stand at ease, to fix bayonets, unfix bayonets, and a whole host of other skills which may have been appropriate in the army, but none of which included showing us an aeroplane, let alone teaching us how to fly one. I may be wrong, but I don't recall ever seeing RAF personnel marching into battle, or combat troops advancing across no-man's land with bayonets fixed wearing air force blue. All this aside, I didn't much like Corporal Pottinger, although just occasionally I caught a glimpse of something that resembled a human being under the surface. For the most part, however, he managed to look and behave like an SS Obersturmbannführer and, while acknowledging that he had a job to do, I couldn't help feeling that he enjoyed it a bit too much. It was virtually impossible for anyone to escape unobserved from Corporal Pottinger's gimlet eye, and on one occasion I was summoned to his quarters, a private room at the end of our billet, to account for some major infraction of the rules, like failing to properly square off my bed-pack or something like that. He was lounging on his bed when I went in, looking relaxed and in the mood for a nice informal chat. He seemed keen for me to tell him about my career as an actor, asked a lot of reasonably intelligent questions, and demonstrated what seemed to be a genuine interest in the theatre. An hour later, without having once asked me to stand at ease, he abruptly dismissed me, no doubt congratulating himself on his Machiavellian ploy to keep me standing to attention for a whole hour. What he had overlooked, however, with his limited understanding of show business, was that there is nothing an actor likes better than talking about himself, even if he has to do it hanging upside-down from a meat-hook!

Our drill sergeant was altogether less subtle, but at least you knew where you stood with him. He was not a particularly large man, unusual in a drill sergeant, and probably because of this he had clearly worked hard and over a good many years at being a bully, an art he had all but perfected by the time he rose to the rank of sergeant in the RAF. He was, of course, and of necessity, a complete and utter bastard. But he was also a wonderful choreographer, although I don't think he would have thanked me for pointing that out. There's many an actor, though, would have given his right eyebrow for a pair of lungs like his, which surely must have been transplanted from an altogether bigger man's chest. With one unambiguous command, 100 disparate, shambling, and largely uncoordinated, individuals, responded as one. At the slightest hint of any individuality, however – an arm swinging in the wrong direction or a foot out of step – he would approach the culprit, and at the same time become very quiet and confidential. This was even more unnerving because you knew that when the pay-off came – and pay-off there was sure to be – it would not only be delivered with such force as to send birds shrieking from the trees for miles around, but would begin its journey only two inches from your face. He approached me one day on the parade ground, looked me up and down, and said, far too gently for my liking, "Can eagles fly upside-down, airman?" I think I said something like, "Not as far as I know, sergeant." Whereupon he ripped a button from my tunic, shoved it into my top pocket, and roared, "Then sew your fucking button on the right way up then!" The fact that I knew for certain I had never sewn a button on the tunic and that if, indeed, the eagle embossed upon it had been flying upside-down, then that's the way it had been when issued to me, was largely irrelevant, for not only had the evidence already been destroyed, but it would have been unwise, in any case, to dispute the matter with our drill-sergeant. Back in those far-off days, and in such an enclosed society, authority may have been subverted in a number of devious ways, but it was seldom openly challenged. On the odd occasion that it was, usually by some complete numbskull, retribution was swift and draconian. I sometimes wonder how easy it would be to tame today's anarchic rabble, especially with the threat of a penal colony hanging over any parent or teacher who so much as frowns at them. With that creeping conservatism that seems to afflict many ageing lefties, I suspect that the re-introduction of National Service could well be the only thing that might instil some much-needed discipline into them. But then again, maybe I'm still a 'lefty' at heart, and I simply want to get my own back on all those little Hitlers who tormented me during those eight interminable weeks.

They came to an end at last, as did the winter of 1957, both at about the same time. I'm not saying I would have actually enjoyed basic training had it taken place in balmier weather, but getting up at 6am in February and March, washing and shaving in cold water, slipping or slushing your way to the cook-house every morning, only to be fed by people who'd been up even earlier and who were, if anything, more miserable than you were, queuing in sub-zero temperatures to be issued with rifles you didn't want, and ending up on a parade ground across which the icy wind cut like a knife, only to be told to report to the duty officer because your buttons and your badges weren't brassed enough, your webbing not blancoed enough, your boots not polished enough, or your hair not short enough, was as close to hell on earth as I ever wish to be. On the subject of boots, it's worth noting that all recruits were issued with boots, the toe-caps of which were covered with little pimples. In order to produce the mirror-like surface demanded by those in authority, it was essential to get rid of the little pimples first because only then, with liberal application of spit and polish, could you achieve the required sheen. This time-consuming and utterly mindless process was undertaken with the aid of a dessert spoon which had to be heated on the stove and then applied to each individual pimple (and there were dozens of them on each toe-cap), which by virtue of combined heat and pressure would be melted flat. Why RAF boots were issued with pimples which were surplus to requirements in the first place was, and remains, one of the unsolved mysteries of service life.

Afternoons were an improvement, if only because they afforded more variety. A great favourite, as I recall, was bayonet practice. Skewering an 'enemy' dummy which, in my mind's eye, bore a remarkable resemblance to Corporal Pottinger or to our drill sergeant, was entirely therapeutic. I also enjoyed my time on the shooting range, and would have scored a notable success with the Bren gun had I not fired all my rounds into someone else's target. And at least we occasionally got to sit down in the afternoons, when we pretended to listen to the numerous talks we were given on a host of subjects, most of which concerned the various career options that were open to us during our two year sojourn in the RAF. Not surprisingly, better prospects were on offer if we chose to extend our stay, but very few were tempted, and needless to say I was not amongst them. Having quite early on ascertained that pilot training was not on the cards, even had I chosen to stay on for a further seven years, in keeping with my low profile policy I decided to opt for a clerical job, and was duly posted to Hereford where I would undergo training as a Clerk (Personnel).

1957 RAF Training Centre in Hereford (far right, back row).

Turning my back forever on Bridgnorth is probably the happiest memory I have of service life. The fact that it took place on a fine Spring day, and that it was prologue to a week's leave, only served to enhance the experience. I had no inkling at that moment, of course, that in very different circumstances I would grow quite fond of the county of Shropshire. It would have been unthinkable at the time in any case, and I couldn't wait to put it and its dismal associations behind me.

RAF Hereford, officially designated No. 2 School of Admin Trades was, in a manner of speaking, only just down the road from Bridgnorth, but it might well have been on a different planet. For a start, most of the officers and NCOs in charge of running the place were either short-termers looking forward to the day when they could swap their 'paper-clips, clerical staff for the use of' for ordinary civilian paper-clips, or professionals taking early retirement or time out from the more rigorous demands associated with flying aeroplanes. Discipline was fairly relaxed and since most of my colleagues were, like me, dedicated to making the least of their opportunities, it was an altogether more congenial experience than I expected it to be. During my six weeks at Hereford, I learned how to type and even passed the necessary qualifications test. Unlike riding a bicycle, however, I quickly forgot how to do it when it transpired that my newly acquired skill was surplus to requirements. In fact, for the remainder of my two years National Service, I was never asked to handle anything more complex than a rubber-stamp. Apart from that, I can't honestly say that I learned anything else during that time, and although reason tells me that we must have been instructed in other aspects of office administration, I have no recollection of any of them. All I do remember about that particular slice of service life is that every weekend we were given a 36 hour pass, and at 12 noon every Saturday, following the regulation parade, a weekly ritual which not only served to remind us and our superiors that we were in the armed forces, but also effectively prevented us from enjoying a forty-eight hour pass, I hitch-hiked my way to Stratford-upon-Avon where Dawn was once more ensconced in the wardrobe department of the Shakespeare Memorial Theatre, although she was now promoted to senior cutter of costumes.

Hitch-hiking became, of financial necessity, the accepted mode of travel for National Servicemen, who would only be issued with travel warrants for postings and official leaves. I became quite adept at it and, in fact, mostly enjoyed the challenge it presented, not to mention the variety it offered. In a single journey you could easily exchange the cab of a noisy lorry for the sleek and silent luxury of a Mercedes-Benz saloon, and the majority of drivers who stopped to pick you up did so out of a genuine desire to help you on your way and probably because they welcomed a bit of company for at least part of their journey. The only drawback, as I soon learned from bitter experience, was that the comparatively short distance between Hereford and Stratford took twice as long to achieve if I tried to accomplish it in civilian clothes. This, of course, meant that I would arrive in the theatrical Mecca of Stratford-upon-Avon looking like the proverbial duck out of water in my RAF uniform and carrying a change of clothes in a hold-all. I later took to leaving them in Dawn's flat where a quick-change into tight black jeans and sweater was effected, a bit of eye-pencil applied to the place where my sideburns had once flourished, together with a dab or two of cologne behind the ears, before I was allowed to emerge, swan-like, and camp as a row of tents, into theatrical society!

One of the things I had already learned about Dawn and which I now found was common to all wardrobe ladies at that time and who shared a similar art school background, was that they liked to design their men-folk and, being Colette addicts to a woman, were determined to make them all look like *Chéri*, or as near as damn it given the raw material to hand. Being neither too short nor too tall, very youthful, and fairly good-looking – even if my hair didn't quite suggest the blue sheen of a blackbird's plumage – I had all the essential qualifications and, having achieved the required transformation, Dawn enjoyed the unequivocal approval of her colleagues. For my part, having no real identity outside the enclosed world of the Royal Air Force, I was putty in her hands and more than happy to play along with this rather effeminate image just so long as I was allowed to prove myself a real man when it mattered most! But by far the most important thing I learned on my frequent visits to the wardrobe department, where Cyril Kegan-Smith kept his harem of cutters and seamstresses hard at it day and night, was the degree of esteem in which different actors were held simply by the way they conducted themselves at costume fittings. For those who just stood there, allowing themselves to be manipulated, grudging the time it took, and complaining at the very first fitting that the basic shape didn't even remotely resemble the original design, the utmost contempt was reserved. For those happy few who were able to transform that basic shape into the finished article simply by the style with which they wore it, and who made it known that they understood the care that had been lavished on each and every costume by those traditionally underpaid and undervalued professionals, no praise was high enough. Prince among these actors at that time was Michael Meacham, every wardrobe lady's dream, supervision of whose costume fittings was variously envied and ruthlessly fought over. Whilst I could never aspire to such soaring accolades, I would like to think that my long and intimate association with at least one costume maker, had endowed me with a trace of the Meacham magic, and that wardrobe ladies down the years have at least not groaned when they saw that my name was next on the list for a fitting.

But for all Dawn's fairy dust there was no disguising the fact that I was a fish out of water. I mixed with the actors on various social occasions, went to their parties, drank with them in that famous theatre hostelry, *The Dirty Duck*, and sat around with them late into the night listening to imported recordings of the latest Broadway musicals, but I could neither share their preoccupations, nor take part in their conversations. Their lives were entirely taken up with the rehearsal process and with performing, and while I desperately wanted to be part of it and deeply resented the circumstances that excluded me from it, there was no getting away from the fact that I was an outsider. The gulf between their world and mine was unbridgeable, made all the more painful for me because it was their world I knew I really belonged to and desperately wanted to re-inhabit. I think it was being tongue-tied in their company that depressed me most, but their conversation flowed so easily, prompted by familiarity and by shared experience, that the very idea of silencing it and having all eyes turned on me in various expressions of startled expectation, froze the blood in my veins. Besides, I knew I had nothing to say and no opinions to offer even had they been sought which, as far as I can remember, they never were.

Although things would never again be quite as bad as that, for reasons that will soon become clear, I suffered a lot at the time, and went on suffering to a somewhat lesser extent from the same malaise for the next 18 months. If I'd had any sense, I would have applied to be posted three thousand miles away, or at any rate far beyond any possibility of hitch-hiking to Stratford-upon-Avon.

It would have saved me a good deal of heartache. But being in love and having good sense do not usually come as a package, and so I continued to hitch-hike to Stratford-upon-Avon and indeed to wherever Dawn was whenever I could. My return journey to Hereford, usually undertaken in the dead of night, instead of being filled with the adrenalin rush of anticipation, was a doleful progress, and not only because it was more difficult to get lifts from people in the dark whether you were wearing a uniform or not, but also because I was feeling pretty miserable anyway. I somehow knew, although I refused to face it, that my relationship with Dawn was changing, and not for the better. Circumstances dictated that I was no longer at the centre of her life, and for how long can you sustain a relationship that is made up almost entirely of brief encounters? Encounters, moreover, in which I was able to play no significant part. I am nothing, however, if not dogged, and my refusal to accept the apparently inevitable is buried deep in my character. I believe that's what made me put up with the almost constant heartache of separation, just as much as my romantic belief in the all-conquering power of love. And so, instead of using those dread hours on the road to try and come to terms with reality, I found solace in the words of some of my favourite poet-lyricists, piercing the night's dull ear with my own Sinatra-based versions of *In the Wee Small Hours of the Morning* and *I've Got it Bad And That Ain't Good!*

Only once during those six weeks do I recall my 36 hour pass being threatened. As a result of some minor infraction of the rules long since forgotten, but probably something to do with the Saturday morning parade, our flight commander decided to curtail my freedom by ordering me to turn over the earth surrounding our hut, a task that he must have known would take me the rest of the day. I was distraught, of course, and not least because I had been invited to a party in Stratford that evening. So it was with heavy heart that I began to dig, wondering if there was even the remotest possibility of getting it finished before sunset. Then I noticed that, due to the long dry summer we were enjoying, there was no perceptible difference in the colour of the earth that I was turning over, and it gradually dawned on me that to reveal any dampness at all, I would probably have to dig down a couple of feet at least. Not being any kind of a gardener I couldn't swear to it, but I was pretty certain that nobody dug that deep unless they were planting an extremely determined root vegetable, or else burying somebody. So I left it, hid the fork and, in the almost certain knowledge that Flight Lieutenant Woodall would not be interrupting *his* 36 hour pass to inspect my progress, I hit the road for one more weekend of self-flagellation in Warwickshire.

Towards the end of my time at Hereford, having passed the qualification exam, I was promoted to AC1 (Aircraftman First Class) and designated a Clerk (Personnel). At about the same time, and don't ask me why, we were all issued with forms on which we were required to state our three posting preferences. In a fanciful mood, born no doubt out of a reasonable scepticism rather than any real desire to go there, I put (not necessarily in order of preference):

1. Supreme Headquarters Allied Powers in Europe, Fontainbleau.
2. Air Ministry Detachment, Washington DC.
3. Air Ministry, London.

Needless to say, I wasn't posted to any of these exotic locations, but instead to the RAF Reception Centre at Cardington in Bedfordshire, the place where I had begun my National Service career nearly six months earlier, only fifty-odd miles from London, and well within easy hitch-hiking distance of Stratford-upon-Avon.

RAF Cardington is situated on the A800, three or four miles south of Bedford, and was noteworthy, not only on account of the superannuated Spitfire parked on the lawn outside Station Headquarters, but for the two enormous hangers that dominated the camp, originally built to house the giant airships, the R100 and the R101. In October 1930 the R101 crashed into a hill near Beauvais during a violent rain storm, and the R100 was subsequently scrapped. All that remains as testament to the brief era of the British airship are those two vast hangers, used mainly (or so they were in 1957) for motor transport maintenance and volley-ball. They certainly lent a bit of character to the otherwise characteristically drab landscape that was to be my home for the next 18 months.

One of the first things I did once I'd settled in was to audition for the part of the young blackmailer in RAF Cardington Dramatic Society's forthcoming production of *The Shop At Sly Corner*. I was to learn that they took their drama very seriously at Cardington, and that they had acquired something of a reputation for quality, at least within the confines of Technical Training Command. I was also to learn that membership of the Society consisted largely of officers, their wives and senior NCOs. While this made rehearsal room camaraderie and dressing-room badinage a bit tricky – I mean, "Are you really going to say it like that?" loses something of its edge when you have to add "Sir" – there were also decided advantages. For instance, rehearsals were given top priority and, much to the chagrin of my immediate superiors, I usually found I was otherwise engaged when it came to some of the less tasty aspects of service life. I even began to grow my hair again, secure in the knowledge that, as a member of the Dramatic Society, I could always claim that I'd been given permission to grow it for my next part. The fact that Cardington, reception centre for all raw recruits, had been the scene of my induction into the RAF, and that the very same barber who had so brutally separated me from my hair a few short months before and was still practising his black art on other poor souls while mine grew virtually unchecked under his very nose, was not without a certain fairy-tale irony. Not that discipline was entirely absent. There were even occasions when, short of being cast as Jesus, I would have found it difficult to justify the total disappearance of my collar under my hair, and was obliged under threat of something long forgotten, but doubtless unspeakable, to get it at least trimmed. But even then, I would somehow prevaricate until the weekend and get it done by a civilian hairdresser in Stratford or in London. I cannot for the life of me remember what a haircut cost in those days, but it must have made a considerable hole in the 27/6d (£1.37½) which was my weekly pay as an AC1. But such was the price of vanity!

There was also the day I went AWOL (absent without leave) to attend the opening night of Judy Garland's season at the Dominion Theatre, Tottenham Court Road. It was October 16th 1957, and before I lay claim to total recall, I should confess that I have a 45 rpm record here beside me that commemorates the occasion. It was a free handout and consists of only one rather corny song, *It's Lovely to be Back in London,* written for her by her lifelong friend and musical mentor, Roger Edens, which contains the following lines:
'When the tourists crowd the gates outside the Palace,
You may rest assured that I will lead the pack;
And should the Queen ride by me,
I'd holler out "Cor Blimey",
I'm so glad I'm back.'
And builds to a climax with:
'Just to feel the feel of London,
I always come all undone.
But so glad, so glad I'm back.'
But the rest of the concert was memorable for altogether more joyful reasons, and being made up almost entirely of hard-core Judy Garland fans, the audience was happy to allow her (and Roger Edens) this one little lapse. Truth to tell, most of them seemed to love it. This spirit of forgiveness, however, did not extend to the RAF. I was sentenced to seven days CB (confined to barracks) which required me to do a lot of menial, tiresome and repetitive jobs during my spare time and which not even a rehearsal call could countermand. But the thrill of seeing Judy Garland live on stage for the first time was worth every mind-numbing minute of it.

Life at Cardington wasn't going to be too bad after all. In fact, it was destined to get better. For the time being I found myself working in quite a comfortable office with reasonably civilised people and presided over by a little Maltese Flight-Sergeant, whose knowledge of our way of life was entirely confined to Queen's Regulations. His world was simple, blue, and unquestioningly hierarchical. When the edges became blurred, he became puzzled. I don't think I ever saw him angry, but quite often bewildered, and in particular by my increasingly unorthodox relationship with commissioned officers and their ladies. On one particular morning, he announced that my posting had come through. Still living in that fantasy land common to most actors, I immediately thought – Fontainebleau? Washington? London? "Where to, Flight?" I asked. "Cyprus", he said. My heart sank, but not because I have anything against Cyprus as such, but Cyprus in 1957 was not the sun-drenched and carefree holiday destination it is today. It wasn't the Cyprus of Paphos or Agia Napa or the golden sands of Coral Bay. It was the Cyprus of Archbishop Makarios and the struggle for union with Greece and independence from Britain. It was the Cyprus of heavily guarded RAF stations in places like Nicosia, Limmasol, Akrotiri and Famagusta, excursions out of which in anything less substantial than a tank left you at the mercy of EOKA terrorists, for whom any British serviceman, no matter how reluctant, was a legitimate target. No, Cyprus was the last place on earth, with the possible exception of Bridgnorth, that I wanted to visit in 1957.

Limping along behind these cowardly considerations was the fact that I was also in the middle of rehearsals for a play. It was my very first directorial assignment, and I was naturally anxious to make a success of it, so the timing of this little bombshell couldn't have been worse. I was gloomily pondering the inevitable end of my career with the RAF Cardington Dramatic Society, not to mention my life, when the telephone rang. Our flight-sergeant answered it, and was immediately struck dumb. Had it been possible for someone with so swarthy a complexion to go pale, then that's what he did. Finally, he managed to stammer out a few incoherent words, cupped his hand over the receiver and, clearly way out of his depth, said in tones of awed disbelief, "It's the C.O. He wants to speak to you, Wale." The Commanding Officer was Group Captain C. R. Lousada, an imperious and exalted figure in whose presence it would have been more appropriate to genuflect than to pass the time of day. The only way of communicating with your commanding officer, in the unlikely event that you ever needed to, was through the Station Adjutant, and it was inconceivable that he himself would ever deign to exchange words with a non-commissioned officer, let alone a mere airman. Not since the siege of Malta had our poor Flight Sergeant's world felt so insecure.

Group Captain Lousada was, in fact, quite a genial man, his status conferred upon him by his rank alone, and certainly not by any demonstration of superiority. In my limited experience of service life the same thing went for most high-ranking officers, and for those who wore wings on their tunics. Generally speaking, it was only the junior officers, usually on short-term commissions, who took advantage of their little brief authority. In the hush that had descended, I took the phone from our Flight-Sergeant, and had the following conversation with Group Captain Lousada:

"I had no idea you'd put in for a posting, Wale."

"I didn't, sir."

"I've got it here in front of me. Cyprus."

"I didn't ask for it, sir."

"Pity it's come when you're in the middle of rehearsals."

"Yes, sir."

"Any objection if I got it postponed for a few weeks?"

"No, none at all, sir. I'd appreciate that."

"Good. Get the play on first. I'll see what I can do."

"Thank you, sir."

"Listen, why do you want to go at all?"

"I don't, sir."

"Right then. Leave it with me. I'll have a word with the A.O.C."

"Thank you, sir."

And that was the last I heard of Cyprus. No doubt Group Captain Lousada and the A.O.C., who must have been at least an Air Commodore, maybe even an Air Vice Marshal, had held a high-level meeting to discuss my case, and came to the conclusion that my particular talents were of more value to the RAF Cardington Dramatic Society than they were to stemming the tide of resurgent nationalism in the Southern Mediterranean. The fact that the Group Captain's wife, Elizabeth Lousada, was playing one of the leading roles in the play I was directing might have had something to do with it too!

For my début as a director I had chosen a play called *You And Your Wife,* a light comedy by Dennis Cannan, well suited to the somewhat restrained talents of the cast. Fortunately, membership of the society was not restricted, and so there were always at least a couple of NCOs around to play whatever low-life was required. One of these was the Station Warrant Officer, a hawk-nosed individual called Reg Glover. Not that I ever called him Reg, and woe betide me if I'd ever tried to. As it was, I paid in kind for every note (an instruction from the director) I ever gave him. He knew how to bear a grudge, did Reg.

He accepted his notes with ill grace and was constantly baiting me in an attempt to lure me into insubordination, always finishing off with a barely concealed sneer that said 'I'll get you for that, laddie.' And one way or another, he almost always did. I thought he'd decided to bury the hatchet on one occasion; I was serving behind one of the bars at the Officers' Mess Ball, and Reg bought me a drink and gave me a big smile. "I think you've earned this", he said. Needless to say, of course, it was a Mickey Finn, and 20 minutes later, having drunk the bastard's health, I collapsed behind the bar and was carried ignominiously to the guard room where I awoke the following morning, not only with the mother of all hangovers, but on a charge for being drunk on duty. Luckily, Reg wasn't at all a bad actor so I was able to be reasonably economical with the notes I gave him thereafter.

As a director who was out-ranked by every member of his cast, some method had to be devised whereby I could wield a little authority without being clapped in irons every time I raised my voice. Clearly it wouldn't work if I had to keep on addressing everybody as 'Sir' or 'Ma'am' or 'Corporal,' so it was decided that as long as I referred to everyone by the name of the character they were playing, I could say pretty well what I liked, and no one would take it personally. As far as I can remember, the system worked quite well, except that Reg was playing a character called Reg, so I ended up not speaking to him at all, which he didn't like either.

The thing that set our Dramatic Society apart from other theatrical ventures in the RAF was that at Cardington, being the Reception Centre for all new recruits, we played to a constantly changing audience, not only confined to the camp for a week before being sent off for basic training, but deprived of any other entertainment since we used the stage of the Astra cinema for our productions. The only other option open to them was to while away the long evenings drinking in the NAAFI (Navy, Army and Air Force Institutes – the recreational establishments for British armed forces), but few could afford to do that while the price of admission to the Astra was made and kept deliberately affordable. Hence we always played to packed houses, largely made up of young men, most of whom had probably never been to the theatre in their lives before. Whether this experience had any lasting effect on them is open to question, and I doubt very much that *You and Your Wife,* a rather bland, light-hearted English take on *The Desperate Hours,* changed many lives. Nevertheless it was, by all the accepted standards, a success, and shortly afterwards, following the overseas posting of the officer in charge, I was invited to take over the day-to-day running of the RAF Cardington Dramatic Society, as well as being responsible for all its future productions. This was the first time in its history that it had been run by a lowly airman, and for a few heady moments I thought I might be offered a commission to go with it. But I doubt whether, for all his undoubted influence, even Group Captain Lousada was capable of swinging that one. It was suggested at the time that I might like to consider extending my stay with the RAF for a year or three – the inference being that if I did, a spell at OCTU could be arranged from which I might well emerge as a Pilot Officer. But for all its allure – not least being able to wear a proper RAF uniform – I was definitely not in the market for remaining one day longer than was strictly necessary. As it was, my promotion to LAC (Leading Aircraftman) followed on the heels of my appointment and although it didn't do much to alter my status, it allowed me to wear twin propeller blades on each sleeve, conferring upon me about as much authority as a Lance-Corporal in the army, and even that's stretching it a bit. In view of the administrative work involved, not to mention the perusal of scripts and the essentially solitary task of planning a production schedule, I did however request removal to a private room. I was sick of barrack-room life in any case, and while I didn't hold out too many hopes, it seemed to me entirely justifiable that my new responsibilities ought to merit, if not elevation from the ranks, at least a little privacy. I was nonetheless taken aback when my request was granted without demur, and I was allowed to move my goods and chattels into a room at the end of one of the huts reserved for new intakes. This simple move enhanced the quality of my life considerably, if only because I was able to lock my own door whenever I felt like it. It also had a knock-on effect I hadn't anticipated. Every week a bunch of new recruits moved into the hut over which I appeared to preside. They didn't have a clue who I was, but I obviously had to be someone special to enjoy such a privilege, so they regarded me warily, and treated me with respect. Not that I took advantage of their deference; I knew only too well what lay in store for the poor buggers after they left Cardington, and if anything I went out of my way to help make their stay there a pleasant memory.

My first assignment in charge of the dramatic society was to choose a one-act play for entry into the Technical Training Command Drama Festival. I immediately pounced on a Tennessee Williams one-acter called *This Property is Condemned,* a play I'd worked on at the Webber-Douglas Academy with my old friend, Sandy Black. My reasons for choosing it were pretty obvious. I could bet with a fair degree of certainty that, whatever our rivals might choose to do, it was unlikely they would go for something quite so eccentric and, moreover, that didn't require a box-set. In my enthusiasm, I had quite overlooked the problem of finding a girl within the confines of RAF Cardington capable of carrying the play virtually on her own and in a Mississippi accent, while convincing us that she is 13 years old pretending to be 23, 'laughing frequently and wildly and with a sort of precocious, tragic abandon'! In the end, I settled for Elizabeth Aitken, the pretty but rather too demure young wife of Flight Lieutenant Aitken, the first real pilot I had come across, and the absolute personification of 'Johnny, head in air.' We often rehearsed at their home in the officers' married quarters, and it struck me that, besides being charming and hospitable, there was something disconcertingly fey about him, and I half expected to hear Nicholas Brodsky's music from *The Way to the Stars* every time he came into the room. It was as though half of him – the vital half – was still up there in the clouds, while the other more shadowy half had been projected down in order to perform certain mundane functions. Some years later, I heard that he had been killed when his aircraft had crashed, and somehow there seemed to be something sadly inevitable about it. It certainly explained, if only partly, that aura of 'other-worldliness' that appeared to surround him.

Elizabeth was a sweet lady who, early on in the process, realised that I had bitten off more than she could chew. She tried to withdraw, but I persuaded her to stick at it, and little by little we managed to bring the unattainable marginally closer. It was never going to work entirely; Elizabeth had neither the skill, the training nor the imagination to take the kind of risks that were inherent in the part, and I knew then that I had been crazy to choose such a difficult play. The only other part was Tom, little more than a feed whose main purpose it is to encourage the girl to talk. I decided to play the part myself, if only because he spends almost the entire play with his back to the audience in listening mode, hardly a tempting proposition for anyone else, although it placed me on stage and in the director's chair at the same time, which couldn't have been more ideal. Much to my astonishment, we won second prize, although I imagine that it was our audacity, rather than any significant achievement, that was being rewarded. I was even more astounded when I was voted best actor of the Festival. I can only assume, although I undoubtedly wallowed in it at the time, that it was intended as a comment on the generally low standards, rather than a wholehearted accolade for my back acting!

Another little bonus was about to come my way as I embarked upon the second year of my National Service. There was apparently some regulation that obliged the RAF to either provide, or make allowance for training courses which were meant to re-introduce us to our chosen civilian occupations. They aimed to fulfil this requirement, as far as was possible, on site, but of course there were quite a number of jobs that fell outside their expertise, so a good few were packed off to college in Bedford for one evening every week. Sadly, neither Bedford nor RAF Cardington could boast a voice teacher while those in London were far too expensive. Since the RAF was obliged to foot the bill, I suggested that it would make more sense economically if I were to have lessons with Denne Gilkes, voice coach at the Shakespeare Memorial Theatre, Stratford-upon-Avon. They would have to pay my fare to Stratford, of course, but it would still work out cheaper than going to London for classes, and in both cases, because of the distance, it would have to take place on a Saturday morning. They happily accepted this as a generous compromise on my part and gave it their blessing. The fact that I was now guaranteed a forty-eight hour pass every weekend, missing out on the statutory monthly parade, went unnoticed and unremarked.

The quality of my weekends in Stratford improved considerably as a result of this, and not only because my weekly voice class with Denne Gilkes provided a new sense of purpose and helped me to feel less of an outsider, but also because Dawn had moved from shared digs into a self-contained flat in St. Gregory's Road which, to all intents and purposes, became my second home. Not that the lonesome road back to Cardington in the early hours of a Monday morning was any the less wearisome, but at least I was going back to a room of my own, and to the prospect of rehearsals for something or other. In fact, it probably sounds as though I must have had a pretty cushy time in the RAF, more privileged than put upon, and to a certain extent that was true. But I was still part of a world that, no matter how congenial, I had no desire to inhabit, and as 1958 wore on I grew more and more impatient to be free of it, crossing off the days on the calendar, which only seemed to make them go slower. The familiar phrase 'Get some in,' (a boast about the comparative length of time served) had now been replaced by 'Get some out,' referring to the length of time left to serve, and as with the calendar, it did nothing to hasten the end. In the early days, I had felt alienated from my own world by a degree of imposed separation that was now beginning to reverse itself so that I found I was becoming more and more alienated from service life, although by far the biggest slice of my life was still being spent in uniform and behind a perimeter fence. The result of all this essentially negative thinking had a negative effect of course, so that one interminable day trudged heavily in the wake of another, while the weekends appeared to fly by on wings, adding fuel to my growing resentment, despite the fact that Providence did bestow the occasional blessing. After a week's leave, most of which I spent at home with my family in London, I returned to Cardington, feeling decidedly under the weather. I reported sick as little red spots started to appear all over my face, and was diagnosed as having contracted chicken-pox and immediately quarantined. I had my little brother, Peter, to thank for this. After ten days isolation in sick quarters, which I spent reading and sleeping, I was given a fortnight's sick leave, which meant that by the time I eventually returned to my duties I was able to score a whole month off my calendar. So I really did have every reason to be genuinely grateful to my little brother!

On another trip to London at about that time, I visited the Old Vic Theatre to see a production of *Twelfth Night*. Dawn had already booked tickets for the opening night of the same play at Stratford some few weeks later, and I was keen to see how the two different companies would handle it. I remember being impressed by the Old Vic production, and especially by Barbara Jefford's authoritative performance as Viola and John Neville's astonishing transformation from matinée idol into Sir Andrew Aguecheek. I told Dawn that the Stratford production would have to go some to equal the Old Vic Company's achievement, and even as I accompanied her to the opening night in my newly-acquired Italian suit (courtesy of Hector Powe of Regent Street!), I was more than ready to carp.

Some 50 years later Peter Hall's production of *Twelfth Night* at Stratford still ranks as one of the finest productions of a Shakespeare play that I have ever seen, and certainly the best production of *Twelfth Night* that I am ever likely to see. The lights came up on what could have been a Van Dyke painting of Orsino's court, the Duke himself and his attendant lords languidly poised, as if for the painter's benefit, and in the process of drinking hot chocolate from the most delicate of porcelain cups, while their spirits wallowed in the melancholy mood set by the music. A mixture of self-indulgence, ennui, and neglect pervaded the scene, reinforced by the dust hanging in the strained sunlight as it filtered through the windows on the painted backcloth. It was quite the most breathtaking and illustrative stage picture I had ever seen, and from that moment on and until the final curtain when, to the

accompaniment of Feste's closing song, the characters seemed to evaporate before our eyes, I was completely entranced. The contribution made by Lila de Nobili, not only as set designer, but also responsible for the ravishing Caroline costumes in muted greens, browns and golds, was immeasurable. So were the performances. Michael Meacham as an understandably narcissistic Orsino, Geraldine McEwan as a delightfully bewildered Olivia, Patrick Wymark, giving the performance of his all too short life as Sir Toby Belch, Richard Johnson as Sir Andrew, demonstrating, like John Neville, a gift for character and comedy that was somehow lacking when in more familiar heroic mould, and, oh … Dorothy Tutin's Viola! I have no idea what the rest of the audience, or indeed Orsino, must have thought, because she was quite obviously playing it entirely for my benefit. She certainly had eyes for no one else, nor I for anyone else but her while she was on stage. I had to resist the urge to call out and let her know that her brother was alive and well because I had read the rest of the play. She was vulnerable yet plucky, gauche and graceful, plus a host of other delightful contradictions, not to mention the heart-stopping moment when she, gender disguised, oh so nearly steps over the edge with:
'Holla your name to the reverberate hills,
And make the babbling gossip of the air
Cry out 'Or…livia.'
All these qualities combined to bring the main romantic thread of the play back into focus with a vitality and a freshness that belied its age and familiarity, and made Olivia's infatuation – little more than a dramatic device, or so I thought – not only believable, but inevitable. Boy or girl, this Viola/Cesario was born to be loved and cherished. Enough to say, before my prose gets even purpler, that Dorothy Tutin placed a flag on the part of Viola that night which will never – *could* never – be replaced.

I was in for another revelation too. One Saturday evening, in the weeks leading up to that memorable night, Dawn and I were invited to dinner by Lynne Holm, employed in the wardrobe department for the season by virtue of the fact that her husband, Ian, was a member of the acting company. We arrived at their flat, clutching a bottle of wine, and appropriately hungry, only to be offered baked beans on toast, albeit garnished with a sprig of parsley, and nothing else. No pudding – nothing! Aside from the fact that this would have been a fairly unusual way to entertain guests, even during the years of immediate post-war austerity, it is worth noting that Ian Holm was not present. I assumed he was playing at the theatre that evening, and in all probability, he was. Two other possible reasons, however, suggested themselves in the aftermath of that Lenten repast, the first being that he had sneaked off for a decent meal with his friends from the theatre; the second being that, almost entirely without social skills, he had no intention of spending his evening off chatting inconsequentially to a colleague of his wife's from the wardrobe department, and to a 20 year-old National Serviceman. I already had some evidence of his sullen behaviour from our occasional meetings in the street, when he would either walk three feet behind the rest of us, or three feet in front, but preferably in the middle of the road, to avoid engaging in any kind of conversation. Naturally, I took it personally, and I confess I found it difficult to warm to him, but in retrospect I should, perhaps, allow that anyone exposed over a long period to his wife's culinary shortcomings, was entitled to be a bit grumpy! I mention this episode, not only because, for all its triviality, it has inexplicably lodged itself in my memory all this time, but mainly because the very last thing I would have expected from that surly little fellow was a performance that not only challenged some of my preconceptions about acting, but provided me with the inspiration I needed as I contemplated my longed-for return to the profession.

The part of Sebastian in *Twelfth Night* is, or was, commonly held to be 'thankless.' I venture to suggest that there are a great number of actors who still hold that view, and in my opinion mainly because, for one reason or another, they didn't get to see Ian Holm play it. Well, in Ian Holm's hands, this *Twelfth Night* was just as much about Sebastian's survival and subsequent adventures as it was about his sister's. From the very first moment we set eyes on him, it was perfectly clear that Viola had modelled her Cesario on him, her most obvious point of masculine reference. Throughout the play they complemented each other beautifully, her attempts at male assertiveness suddenly revealed with Sebastian's arrival on the scene as a pale shadow of his all-too-real masculinity; his initial bewilderment and finally fatalistic acceptance of Olivia's romantic claim on him, perfectly echoing Viola's own puzzlement. Never before – or since – have I seen the reunion of Viola and Sebastian at the end of the play as anything much more than a cause for general celebration, usually stretching the audience's credulity to the limits. But on this occasion, Geraldine McEwan's 'Most wonderful!', crammed to bursting with innuendo, spoke for us all. For there they stood, brother and sister, 'one face, one voice, one habit, and two persons.' So far was it from being the customary theatrical device that I suspected trick photography, except that there wasn't a camera to be seen. No, it was the acting. So perfect were they both that, again for the first time, I understood why, after being first struck dumb with amazement, they were so genuinely overjoyed to see each other again. It was more than affection. They were two sides of the same coin, and consequently incomplete without each other. Like some kind of miracle, the true climax of the play was revealed to me. The wonder of it is that Dorothy Tutin and Ian Holm pulled it off, not only by being so perfectly matched, but by making it seem that we had never seen or read the play before. During the course of 1958, I saw a considerable number of shows in London, and for the life of me I can't think how I managed to cram them all in, given that, apart from official leaves, I only had Saturdays and Sundays. But it was Stratford that had me under its spell and, culminating with the impact of that *Twelfth Night*, the one and only place I was determined to work – preferably as part of a company that included Dorothy Tutin!

Back at Cardington, I was soon casting my next production, Terence Rattigan's *The Deep Blue Sea*. Fortunately, I had no trouble casting the part of Hester Collyer, as it seemed to me that, after being somewhat overstretched in the Tennessee Williams piece, Elizabeth Aitken had earned the right to play something which, in a few years time, she would be absolutely right for; and in any case there was no one else within striking distance of the part. The casting of Freddie, the ex-Spitfire pilot, was a different matter altogether. Restricted as it was to RAF personnel, I was faced with a veritable *embarras de richesses*. In the end, however, I settled for a short-term education officer who had been no nearer to sitting in a cockpit than I had. Neither was he in many respects ideally cast as Freddie, although he was certainly the best actor around, and on that quaintly old-fashioned premise, I asked him to play it. I like to think that I recognised it at the time, although with memories of a friendship that lasted for more than 30 years, it might perhaps be more truthful to say it was pure chance that Flying Officer Chris Fulford and Freddie Page shared at least one vital characteristic in that they were both fundamentally irresponsible. On the face of it, Chris was a happily married, if mildly hen-pecked, man whose French-born wife, Margot, was at that time expecting their first child. She was altogether more mature and seemed less fun than Chris, although she was perfectly hospitable and her cooking was superb. During the rehearsal period and, indeed, right through to the end of my days with the RAF, I enjoyed many hospitable evenings in the comparative comfort of their married quarters when, following the culinary delights on offer, Chris and I would sit up into the early hours, listening to a recording of Olivier's *Richard III*, knocking back the wine, and discoursing enthusiastically on a variety of topics until, inevitably, his eye-lids drooped, and he gave up the struggle to stay awake. He was an extremely sociable man, for whom the difference in our ranks soon became irrelevant in the face of a rapport which I don't think either of us had managed to establish with anyone else in uniform. Having no real responsibilities myself at the time, I had no reason to see him in any critical light, but as the years went by, and with the RAF behind us both, I began to view things more from Margot's point of view and, having cast her as a bit of a party-pooper, I was forced to reconsider this in the light of his inability to grow up, and finally recognised her as a kindred spirit, albeit somewhat tougher, of Hester Collyer.

Chris was by no means a womaniser, any more than Freddy is in *The Deep Blue Sea,* but he was nevertheless addicted to self-indulgence which, in his case, took the form of insatiable acquisitiveness. He had a perfectly good, and relatively new camera, for instance, but as soon as a newer and slightly more sophisticated version appeared on the market, Chris simply had to have it. The same thing went for television sets, hi-fi equipment, motor cars and, as his means increased in line with his promotion to head teacher at a large comprehensive school in Croydon, so did his appetite for spending money on the very latest of practically anything. Margot's increasing complaints, which I began to see as perfectly reasonable, were invariably met by sulky resentment, and finally, three children plus a whole lot of consumer goods later, he left her. Our friendship was very much intact when all this happened and he was often on the phone, seeking to justify his actions and feeling the need, for some reason, to solicit my approval. Margot called quite often too, mainly I think because she saw me as one of Chris's closest friends, and thought that I might possibly be able to act as go-between or, at least, throw some light on his extraordinary behaviour. I suppose I did what little I could for both of them. I was sad when they split up although, to be honest, I was only really surprised in the end by who left who. When Chris set up home with another lady shortly afterwards, it seemed for a while that he might have settled down at last but, all too soon, he upped and left her as well, this time for a younger woman, and I confess that I then lost patience with him. I wasn't being judgemental – or, at least, I don't think I was – I simply couldn't bear the thought of having him on the phone again, trying to make me see it from his point of view when, in fact, I no longer really cared. Chris and I didn't fall out; we simply drifted away from each other. When he died, some years ago now, I reproached myself for having allowed the gulf between us to widen. We had, after all, enjoyed each other's company over many years, and that Peter Pan-ish quality of his, while it was at the root of many of his problems, was also very appealing and, whether I recognised it at the time or not, cast him in precisely the same mould as Freddie Page, a part he played as to the manner born in a performance that hit exactly the right note and which had more than a little to do with the success of the production.

Service life had by this time clearly taken something of a back seat in favour of my other activities, which now also included a radio show, providing me with the opportunity to infuriate the other inmates by interrupting the otherwise incessant barrage of inane pop and noisy rock 'n roll for one hour every week with my own choice of songs from the shows, alongside record tracks by personal favourites like Frank Sinatra, Ella Fitzgerald, Peggy Lee, Lena Horne and, of course, Judy Garland. And it wasn't merely as a DJ that I functioned. I took time out to talk about the songs, and to compare the interpretation of, say, *My Funny Valentine* by Sinatra on the one hand, and Ella Fitzgerald on the other, which meant, of course, that I had to play both tracks. I must have been extremely unpopular, and no doubt radios were turned off in disgust all over the camp. But I enjoyed the experience hugely and, as far as I can remember, I never received a single death threat!

For the last six months of my National Service I was elevated to the rank of SAC (Senior Aircraftman), which was about as high as you could hope to get in two years without resorting to blackmail or prostitution. But, apart from adding a couple of shillings to my weekly pay packet, and allowing me to add one more propeller blade to the two I already sported, it didn't make any significant difference to my life, nor to the way I was treated by those who out-ranked me, and by whom I was still massively outnumbered. Nor did it relieve me of regular duties outside office hours which operated on a roster system, although once you'd been round the block a few times, you were bound to get acquainted with ways and means of exchanging your duty or even – if you were either flush or desperate – buying someone else's services as a stand-in. I had noticed, for instance, at the end of the previous year, that most of my fellow airmen were dismayed when they saw their names on the Christmas duty list and were only too happy to part with a fiver if you offered to take their place. Now there were duties and duties, of course, and some of them came more expensive than others. Guard-room duty, for instance, was pretty well non-negotiable as it meant spending your time under the highly critical and retributive gaze of the SPs. Fire picket was another no-go area, not only because it meant patrolling the perimeter fence throughout the night in the middle of winter, but also waking the cook-house staff in time for their breakfast, and at least a couple hours before yours. Duty-clerk, however, based as it was in the comparative comfort of Station Headquarters, was an altogether more congenial proposition and, always provided there weren't too many phone calls, you could pretty well gamble on a good night's sleep. But far and away the cushiest of them all was guard-room duty. Two of you were designated for this duty which involved being locked in the station armoury all night, well provided with tea, coffee and food-stuffs while preventing members of the IRA from breaking in and stealing all the guns. Periodically, the duty officer and his little patrol would pass by to ensure that you were still alive by knocking three times and whispering a coded message through the locked door to which, if you were not dead, or a member of the IRA, you would give the correct reply. Apart from these occasional interruptions, you were left to your own devices, which included playing cards, brewing up, reading and sleeping. The only disadvantage was the absence of alcohol which for obvious reasons was strictly forbidden. In company with a particularly cunning fellow one evening, however, we managed to unscrew the hinges on the back door which was never inspected in any case, and took it in turns to go down to the NAAFI for a well-earned pint. Only on one occasion, I recall, were we put to the test by an over zealous duty officer, who threatened us with unspeakable torture and summary execution if we refused to open the doors. But his Irish accent was so appalling we didn't even bother to reply. Given the relative pros and cons of the various duties, I was more than happy to take the money and stand in for someone over Christmas because it meant that I would be given leave in lieu over the New Year, an altogether livelier time to be out and about. Another plus was that Christmas dinner in the cookhouse was the best meal of the year, certainly comparable with anything you'd get at home. Not only that, but it was served to you at your table by officers who, short of washing your feet, were there to answer all your needs in the true spirit of Christmas.

But, having honed to perfection my skills in ducking and diving, I cannot in all honesty say that militarism in any way, shape or form intruded too heavily into my life during those last few months. My weekly visits to Stratford for voice classes with the gloriously eccentric, pipe-smoking Denne Gilkes, continued unabated, and gave at least a sense of purpose as well as the stamp of approval to my otherwise illicit weekends, although it has to be said that the illicit side of things was distinctly lacking in ardour of late, and not nearly as passionate as Denne's exhortations to breathe and to articulate properly. I, of course, part ostrich and part believer in the eternal nature of love, refused to see this as anything other than a temporary problem, and one that would be quickly resolved once I'd managed to get rid of that accursed uniform, and was back in the swing of things again. I simply refused to accept that our relationship, if not exactly over, had changed in a fundamental way, in spite of the fact that there was plenty of evidence to support this, the most compelling being on our visit to the Edinburgh Festival in the late summer of 1958.

It was my last period of leave before demobilisation, and I was anxious to spend some time with Dawn away from her work and from the tightly-knit community of the Shakespeare Memorial Theatre, as enclosed in its way as any RAF camp. It augured well that she was only too happy to come along. We booked separate rooms in a boarding house, more out of deference to the social customs of the time than to any overt or, at any rate, mutual decision to stay apart. That we remained separate for the entire week, and that any suggestion from me that we might break the rules now and again was neatly side-stepped, became distressing, to say the least. The fact that it was never discussed, that she never made an excuse, not even citing the proverbial headache, but remained affectionate and companionable throughout, should have made it dazzlingly clear that her feelings for me had undergone a sea change. But still I refused to accept it, choosing instead to suffer the frustration, fearful of losing her altogether on the one hand, and stubbornly confident on the other that I would not be the only loser were I to walk away. Half lap-dog, half Doberman, that's me and always has been, although it is only now, with the Doberman side of me only occasionally capable of showing its teeth, that I can afford to be a bit more objective about it.

Such excruciatingly painful inner turmoil did not make it easy to enjoy what was on offer at the Edinburgh Festival although, for what became obvious reasons, I recall a fringe production by the Oxford University Dramatic Society of a new play by Willis Hall entitled *The Disciplines of War*. This later went on to reap West End success, having lost its original stark title in favour of the cheerier *The Long and the Short and the Tall*. It also exchanged its wonderfully raw cast of unknowns in favour of a starry line-up giving predictably starry performances, not to mention its inspired but untried director in favour of a fashionably safe pair of hands. The difference between the two productions can best be described by saying that it was like seeing two different but distantly related plays, the first a harsh, no-punches-pulled account of an anonymous bunch of squaddies, trapped in the middle of the Malayan jungle, surrounded by the advancing Japanese, and living out what little is left of their lives with the kind of intensity that only the condemned can know, while the second was a more polished affair, perfectly entertaining, and played with great panache by the likes of Peter O'Toole, oddly cast as the cockney, Bamforth, while cockney Alfred Lynch played Taffy, the Welshman, and Robert Shaw who, of course, played himself. But the sting had been removed with its transition to the West End, the gritty realism of the original replaced by anodyne commercial packaging, and as I walked down St. Martin's Lane, only minutes after the final curtain had fallen, my mind was already on other things, like why the hell they hadn't invited the original director, Peter Dews, to bring it to London, if not with the same cast who were, after all, still at university, then at least with a handful of professional actors better suited to serving the interests of the play.

We met the aforementioned director after the show in Edinburgh and, having been fairly bowled over by the production, I was all set to be overawed by his presence. I was somewhat taken aback, therefore, when he pre-empted my adulation by not only knowing who we were, but by seeming to be genuinely surprised and delighted that we had taken the trouble to come and see the play. Not only that, but he steadfastly refused to address me by my name, rank and number, opting instead to treat me as a working actor with whose curriculum vitæ he was so thoroughly acquainted that he might well have written it himself. He also knew where Dawn was working, where she'd trained and how we'd met. It was a most extraordinary meeting and providential too, for although I didn't know it at the time, I was to be treated to many more such displays. Peter Dews was a moon-faced Yorkshireman, overflowing with humour and with a zest for all things theatrical that was totally infectious. His phenomenal memory was but one of his many gifts, and for those of us who were privileged enough to work with him during the height of his powers, he proved to be truly inspirational. He certainly inspired me. Even from that first meeting, intended as homage from a mere National Serviceman, I was the one who emerged feeling somehow more estimable. As far as Peter Dews was concerned, his was the privilege, and when he said that he hoped we would work together once I had rejoined the human race, I knew without a shadow of a doubt that he meant it.

Inspired by this boost to my ego, as well as by the play I had just seen, I was able to take something positive away from what was otherwise, and for various reasons, a pretty depressing week in Edinburgh. On my return to Cardington I threw myself into preparations for my final production with the Dramatic Society, Christopher Fry's *A Sleep of Prisoners*, a choice inspired more by *The Disciplines of War* than by any lurking affection for the military life or the uniforms that go with it. In a flurry of self-indulgence, born out of a state of growing euphoria as my own days in uniform dwindled, I decided not only to direct that play but also to play a major role in it, the part of Private David King. The rest of the small cast was entirely male and made up of young men from the ranks, amongst whom was a young airman called Julian Fox, the only other professional actor I came across during my time in the RAF. The nature of the play, of course, as well as its history, dictated that it should be performed for maximum effect in a church, so the Astra cinema was free to stick to its programme of films. Somehow or other, a small tour was organised, and we were bussed around to various churches, most of them relatively nearby, but culminating (don't ask me how!) in a special performance of the play in St. George's Chapel, Windsor Castle. This was quite a coup, as I recall, and much talked about, even if no members of the Royal Family were there, and not one single corgi was sent to represent them.

Following an extremely pleasant Christmas in the armoury and at table, waited upon by a host of seasonally festive officers, I was able to count off my last few weeks in an atmosphere of genial comradeship, which almost made the lure of service life not only comprehensible, but also quite appealing. Well, almost! I no longer felt the need to cross the days off on my calendar as they were no longer to be wished away, but revelled in. Final dinners with my officer friends in married quarters, a little farewell party thrown in my honour by the Dramatic Society, all those protracted 'goodbyes' and the more or less permanent smile on my face; all these things were to be relished. I even sought permission to take my leave of the Commanding Officer, although I kept this outrageous breach of Queen's Regulations away from our Flight Sergeant who would undoubtedly have fainted away. But Group Captain Lousada was a most charming man, and as he had been instrumental in making my life at Cardington not merely tolerable, but occasionally enjoyable, it would have been churlish to leave without acknowledging this. He shook my hand warmly and sincerely wished me all the best.

My final memory of National Service was more typical, I'm glad to say, otherwise I might well have been left with residual regrets and mild nostalgia. I was standing with my colleagues at the NAAFI wagon on the morning prior to the day of my departure, ordering my final bacon bap, and watching the tea flow from the urn into my permanently tannin-dyed mug for the very last time, when I was tapped on the shoulder. I turned round and found myself face-to-chest with an enormous RAF Regimental sergeant. "Fuck me," he said, "I thought you was a fuckin' WAAF!" I smiled up at him. "Sorry to disappoint you, sarge," I said. The little flicker of humour in his eyes guttered and died. "Get your fuckin' hair cut, airman, and report to me first thing tomorrow mornin' with it done." I went on smiling as he gave me one last malevolent glare and stomped away. "Yes, sarge," I said to his retreating back, secretly and blissfully aware that the only thing he was likely to see of me tomorrow morning was the dust raised by my heels.

oOoOo

Seven

Returning to Coventry wasn't part of my game plan. After two years away, and on the threshold of a new beginning, my ambition burned a little brighter than that. I had written numerous letters, of course, in the months leading up to my demobilisation, but nothing had come of any of them and, contrary to expectation, no London agents were vying with each other to represent me. Augury and omens aside, it should have been pretty clear to me that while a week may be a long time in politics, two years in show business is an eternity. Not only that, but a theatrical revolution had overtaken me, in which French windows had been ousted in favour of kitchen sinks, and there was little point in protesting my working-class cockney origins when I'd gone to so much trouble covering them up.

At the height of my powers i/c drama at RAF Cardington, I had no reason to set a limit on my dreams. I'd even written a letter to Laurence Olivier Productions, staking my claim to the part of the young King in the *The Sleeping Prince,* which I'd heard was to be made into a film. I was quite unreasonably affronted when, without even auditioning me, the part was given to Jeremy Spenser. It didn't occur to me at the time that, as Jeremy had played the part alongside Olivier and Vivien Leigh in the West End, and had obviously been very good in it, there would be absolutely no reason, short of his sudden demise, to recast it. My seething resentment probably had something to do with a sense of rivalry between us that had begun during *The Innocents,* but was very definitely connected to the fact that his career had not been interrupted by National Service. I'm not suggesting that his mother, who had forced him onto the stage with a temperature of 104°, had personally punctured his eardrum or flattened his feet with a hammer, to keep him out of the forces, but in any event, I wrote a somewhat petulant letter of complaint and, to my complete astonishment, received a reply on personal notepaper from Sir Laurence himself. Typed very badly and with several mistakes which, in those days, had to be covered over with a row of 'x's, he made the very points that I have already mentioned. If he had been at all put out by the tone of my letter, he didn't show it, but very kindly went out of his way, not only to justify his decision, but to smooth my ruffled feathers. Having himself served in the Fleet Air Arm during the war, he too might have been just a bit suspicious about Jeremy's exemption from military service. The letter concluded with all good wishes for my future, and was signed 'L. Olivier.' Unfortunately, along with Kirsten Flagstad's rose, the letter has long since disappeared and was either lost or, with too much handling, simply disintegrated, so you'll just have to take my word for it. I eventually persuaded myself to go and see *The Prince and the Showgirl* as it was retitled, and as a postscript to the story I would like to record the fact that Jeremy Spenser's performance was just as good as I feared it would be and that no one, not even me, could have played it better!

This pill, sweetened though it was with kindly words from Olympus, was but a foretaste of the many I would have to swallow now that I had joined the swelling ranks of a profession that could only boast a 20% employment rate at any given time. My membership of that small band of privileged child actors had well and truly expired and, as if to prove the point, it was some little time later, during a lengthy period of unemployment, that I telephoned my old friend, Muriel Cole, the casting director at Associated-Rediffusion who had been the source of most of my television work before I joined the RAF. I called her a couple of times in as many months, and on the second occasion, she said, "If you're out of work, Terry, you shouldn't be wasting your pennies calling me." Funny, isn't it, how a tiny moment like that assumes a significance that, many slings and arrows later, still epitomises that sharp sting of rejection.

So I had every reason to consider myself extremely lucky (although I didn't appreciate it at the time) that scarcely having shed my uniform, I walked straight into a job – even if it was in Coventry. And this was no Midland Theatre Company engagement either, which had in any case long since disbanded. Nor were performances to take place in the dreary Technical College, but on the spanking-new stage of the Belgrade Theatre on Corporation Street which had only opened its doors a year earlier, and was the first of Britain's civic theatres, so named in recognition of a gift of timber from the capital of what was then Yugoslavia. It was an attractive and commodious building with a 900 seat auditorium, and even included accommodation for the resident company although, typically, most of the best flats had gone to members of the management team, while many of the others were set aside for visiting notables. Company members, by and large, still had to hunt for digs in the remoter suburbs, or on the recently completed by-pass, which is where I found myself in early March 1959, having just had time to celebrate my 21st birthday at home with my family. The offer of a season had come from the artistic director, Bryan Bailey, for whom I had worked on several productions at the old Guildford Repertory Theatre back in 1956, my last period of prolonged employment before I was called up. Since, of all the letters I had written, the one to him was alone in bearing fruit, my reservations about returning to Coventry were set aside. I was simply, and enthusiastically, looking forward to joining a theatre company again, instead of being on the outside looking in.

I was on a 'play-as-cast' contract, not unusual in those days of long seasons and permanent companies, and certainly appropriate in my case, as Bryan probably didn't have a clue how he would use me over a period of several months and in seven or eight plays. Initially, he played safe by casting me as Antony's servant and Young Cato in *Julius Caesar* which he was to direct himself. I would rather have played Lucius again, of course, but obviously the years had taken their toll, and I was supplanted by a 17 year-old. His youthfulness notwithstanding, I didn't think he was as good as I had been, and he couldn't sing for toffee. His name was Michael Crawford! Otherwise, my memories of the production are all but extinct. The backbone of the acting company was provided by a nucleus of relatively young hopefuls, amongst whom Charles Kay stood out as the strongest and the most versatile. But they were an extremely sociable and fun-loving bunch, and friendships, albeit for the most part superficial, were cemented fairly quickly.

The season began to go wrong for me fairly early on, although I didn't see it as a trend at the time, and indeed it wouldn't have amounted to one had not a certain visiting director stayed on for two extra productions. James Roose-Evans came to see *Julius Caesar* and the following day cast me as the Fourth Knight and the Fourth Tempter in T. S. Eliot's *Murder in the Cathedral,* a re-working of his recent amateur production of the play at the Maddermarket Theatre in Norwich. My obvious delight was curtailed when I realised shortly after rehearsals began that it hadn't been my brief appearance in *JC* that had caught his eye, but the even briefer chiton I wore as Antony's servant. I think I began to suspect ulterior motives when he kept calling me for extra rehearsals in the evenings, and while I was perfectly happy to admit that I may have needed them, I wasn't convinced that his approach was entirely relevant. It took three or four of these extra-curricular meetings before I was able to persuade him that he and I didn't bat on the same team, and when he finally realised I wasn't just playing hard to get, his interest in me and, indeed, in my performance came to an abrupt end. No longer in need of extra rehearsals, I was left to consider the heady proposition that I must have achieved perfection as the 4th Tempter.

Our relationship, if you can call it that, remained glibly polite, and while he was never less than silkily charming, he made it all too clear that rejection was something 'up with which he would not put'. He was a pretty condescending creature in any case, but from that point on an extra layer of superciliousness was added for my benefit. As far as I was concerned, this would have been neither here nor there, had he not stayed on to direct the next play, a fairly silly piece called *Bridge of Sighs* by a man called Thomas Muschamp (pronounced 'Meecham'). It purported to address the plight of refugees but did no such thing. Two young people, a married couple with a young baby, are trapped in the middle of a bridge guarded on one side by an Eastern European soldier, played by Charles Kay, and on the other by Richard Martin as his opposite number from the West. The young couple, lacking the proper papers or the wherewithal to offer a bribe, are told they can neither cross the bridge nor return from whence they came. The substance of the play is a long-winded discussion between the guards who, in the semi-literate way of soldiers, and in thick middle-European accents, try to defend their conflicting ideologies, interrupted from time to time by the simple humanitarian pleas of the couple. It was naïve and it was unbelievably fatuous, but worst of all, it was mind-numbingly dull. Stuck centre stage for the duration, and with nothing much to say, Jacqueline Wilson and I undoubtedly had the worst of it, although I have no reason to doubt that the four of us made the best of a bad job.

After the first dress-rehearsal, we sat in the auditorium while the director gave us our notes. I was conspicuously ignored throughout the session and, not until he was on the point of winding up, did he even condescend to glance in my direction. With what I can only describe as a smirk, he said, "Far too camp, Terry." And that was it. The breath was literally knocked out of my body, and by the time I had regained anything resembling composure, James Roose-Evans had departed, leaving me to be comforted by my fellow actors. All to no avail, of course. They were nice people, and were perfectly happy to call our director all the shits under the sun, just so long as he wasn't there to hear it, but I had no way of knowing for certain that, deep down, they hadn't agreed with him, even if they took issue with his way of communicating it. I was, at best, thoroughly confused, and by the time the curtain rose on our second dress rehearsal, I had pored over the text, looking for potentially ambiguous moments, thoroughly examined my performance for vocal inflections and physical mannerisms that might be sending the wrong message, entertained doubts about my previously undoubted masculinity, even questioned my ability to act at all. None the wiser, but completely demoralised, I wound up giving much the same performance, although lacking the same degree of confidence, as I had at the first dress rehearsal. Afterwards, completely ignoring me as before, the director gave his notes to the rest of the company before he finally turned his gaze upon me, his smirk having given way to a smile of such appalling condescension that, for a bewildering moment, I thought he might be about to pat me on the head. Instead, he said, "Oh, Terry, the opposite of camp isn't butch, you know."

I suffered the first night with the kind of stoicism that has served me well in times of stress throughout my life, and if James Roose-Evans had thought to unhinge me, he was obviously unaware of my 'fuck it then' approach to all things outside my obvious control. I knew, in any case, that *Bridge of Sighs* was not about to set Coventry alight, and that my performance, camp, butch or simply inadequate, would hardly cause a ripple on the water. I also knew, with equal certainty, that his treatment of me had been motivated by nothing more nor less than spite. And if I had any remaining doubts on that score, they were laid to rest the following morning when I arrived at the theatre to find an envelope addressed to me in the letter rack. Inside were three typed foolscap pages of notes from the director on how I should have played the part, none of which he had given me during the rehearsal period or had even been broached as a subject for discussion. Incensed as I obviously was by this outrageous assault on my tolerance, never mind my intelligence, I went into the stage management office and typed a similar number of pages which, bordering on the abusive, dwelt lustily on his inadequacies, not only as a director, but also as a human being. With grim satisfaction, I thrust the note into the letter rack, and effectively sealed my fate at the Belgrade Theatre. Not that I paid the penalty immediately, but having turned my back on the unwritten 'know thy place' clause in any actor's contract, I should have known that my days were numbered.

As a postscript to this particularly unsettling episode, I was invited, only a couple of years later, to play the Messenger in *Hippolytus* by Euripides at the Hampstead Theatre Club, to be directed by none other than James Roose-Evans. For obvious reasons I said I was not available, although I actually saw the production on its first night as Dawn had been responsible for designing both set and costumes, and I rather enjoyed it. Afterwards, civility being required of the designer's guest, I congratulated the director, and told him that I thought Michael

Deacon, who played the Messenger, was very good. James smiled warmly at me, and without a hint of condescension, said, "Not nearly as good as you would have been." Well, like they say up north, "There's nowt so queer as folk"!

As if Ossa wasn't bad enough, Pelion arrived in the shape of the thoroughly obnoxious John Dexter, who was in Coventry to direct the world premiere of Arnold Wesker's play, *Roots*. He'd been up the year before to direct *Chicken Soup with Barley*, and would return in 1960 to complete the trilogy with a production of *I'm Talking About Jerusalem*. I knew little about the man, except that he was one of the 'new' boys, nurtured in the bosom of the English Stage Company at the Royal Court Theatre, and that he had served a brief term in prison for unlawful sexual congress with a 15 year-old boy. Legend has it that on his release he was picked up by film director, Tony Richardson, in an ostentatiously large and luxurious limousine from which, as it was about to pull away, he shouted to a prison guard who was on the point of mounting his bicycle outside the prison gates, "You see, crime *does* pay!" I suppose it was quite funny, in a ghoulish kind of way, and the humour effectively disguised, albeit thinly, the true nature of the man. When I was first introduced to him outside the stage-door of the Belgrade Theatre, he pre-empted any courtesies by saying; "Aren't you Terry Wale, the East End slut?" Well, clearly he was a very rude man, and despite his alleged sally outside the gates of Wandsworth, the Scrubs, or wherever it was, he could also be pretty witless too. Our relationship, such as it was, never really moved on from there, and if he ever bothered to address me at all, it invariably took the form of foul-mouthed insults or equally gross sexual advances. Since I had never, to my knowledge, offended him in any way, I could only suppose it was all part of some primitive mating ritual.

One of the many wonderful things about growing older is that you eventually cease being a prey to predatory poofs, an alliterative temptation I couldn't resist, but which shouldn't be interpreted as a sign that I was turning, or have since turned, into a homophobe; far from it, in fact. I mean, some of my best friends etc. It's just that I've always believed in the mutuality of sexual relationships, and the very idea of foisting yourself on a reluctant or unwilling partner is, to me, not only abhorrent but the ultimate turn-off. Oh, I'm sure I've been as importunate in my time as any testosterone-led male, but I like to think I always knew when to back off, and without bearing any grudges either. If John Dexter had bothered to make a few preliminary enquiries about my personal preferences, who knows but he might have said, "How do you do?" when we met and wished me the occasional "Good day", although somehow I doubt it.

Fortunately – and I was in dire need of a bit of good luck by then – there wasn't a part for me in *Roots*, and so I never had to suffer the notoriously repressive atmosphere of a John Dexter rehearsal, in which actors were frequently berated for their lack of imagination on the one hand, and roundly castigated for not doing as they were told on the other. In spite of, or maybe because of this, *Roots* was a great success at the Belgrade, but even more so when it transferred to the Royal Court. I loved the play, and especially the character of Beatie Bryant, as played by Joan Plowright. The fact that Miss Plowright had obviously spent her formative years considerably further north than Beatie's Norfolk origins mattered not a jot. The final moments of the play when, instead of resorting to the words of her pseudo-intellectual left-wing lover as she had throughout, she triumphantly discovers her own passionate and articulate voice which, while falling on deaf ears up there on the stage, certainly found at least one all too receptive pair out there in the auditorium. Wesker's plays may have been quick to date, at least in terms of form and structure, but the prophetic nature of his message, powerful enough at the time, has well and truly come to pass. In Beatie's words: 'Anything's good enough for the workers,'cos they don't ask for no more! The whole stinkin' commercial world insults us and we don't care a damn! ... it's our own bloody fault. We want the third rate – we got it! We got it! We got it!' And Arnold Wesker hadn't even heard of TV's *Big Brother* when he wrote those words!

Meanwhile, I had been enjoying a relatively angst-free time on Wycherley's *The Country Wife*, in which, according to words purported to have been uttered by John Dexter (and he certainly wouldn't have told me himself), I was the only member of the cast to have accurately captured the real spirit of the period. As I was horribly miscast as the Quack, I can only assume that my squalid appearance, augmented by a liberal application of blood and gore, together with a wig that looked like a nesting place for vermin, all giving rise to an impression of pungent malodorousness, must have struck him as more authentic than the Restoration finery and perfumed elegance of the other actors. It certainly could have had nothing to do with my performance. *The Country Wife* was my introduction to Restoration Comedy and, although Edward Burnham's production may not have been grubby enough to win approval from the *nouvelle vague* practitioners of Sloane Square, it was a revelation to me, not only for its style, but also for its substance and attention to detail, and it's largely due to him that it remains to this day my favourite example of the genre. I remember being particularly impressed by Patricia Routledge, imported into the company for the sole purpose of playing Lady Fidget, and by Charles Kay's deliciously paranoid Pinchwife, Patsy Byrne's delightful Margery, the quintessential country bumpkin, although – and with all due respect – I found it hard to believe that Alan Howard's rapacious, though discriminating, Horner would have gone to such lengths to bed so dumpy and unattractive a girl, unless it was simply to torment her husband.

In a season of relative hits and near-misses, Alan was at his most convincing as Horner; hardly surprising when you consider that, give or take 300 years, the part could have been written for him. Alan's reputation as something of a Lothario had gone before him and, as with others of his ilk, I have always puzzled over what it was exactly that made him so irresistible to women. Yes, all right, he was good-looking in a kind of way, I suppose. He was tallish. He was chronically short-sighted which, I have since discovered, allows you to be a bit off-hand with people without actually appearing rude which, in its turn, endows you with the kind of mystique that women find fascinating in a man who, more often than not, will turn out to be an uncaring and unprincipled shit. Not that I'm suggesting that Alan Howard was unprincipled, or that I put my friendship with him under a microscope at the time. I simply liked him and enjoyed his company, along with others – Patrick O'Connell and Kenton Moore come to mind – whose uncompromising maleness provided a safe haven for me. For obvious reasons, I was only too happy to be associated with a clique whose pretty well exclusive preoccupation was with the opposite sex.

Following its run at the Belgrade Theatre, and at the height of that glorious summer of 1959, we took *The Country Wife* to the Arts Theatre, Cambridge for a week, where we took full advantage of those long, idyllic days with indulgent pub lunches, either slept off in the sun or worked off with punting expeditions up the River Cam, following in the wake of Rupert Brooke all the way to Grantchester on one occasion, and queuing for what seemed like forever at the refreshment stand, only to be told, "Sorry, dear, honey's off!"

I lost most of my mates over the next couple of weeks when *Roots* transferred to the Royal Court, taking with it not only Alan, but also Charlie Kay and Paddie O'Connell, leaving only Kenton Moore, Clinton Greyn and myself to hold the fort against the massive, star-studded, invasion from London that heralded the main event of the season. In conjunction with Laurence Olivier Productions, the Belgrade Theatre was to present the world premiere of A.L.Pattisson's play, *Dispersal*, clearly intended as a try-out prior to a guaranteed West End transfer. Well, that's what we assumed when the distinguished director, Lindsay Anderson, arrived with his set designer, Sean Kenny, both fresh from their critically acclaimed production of Brendan Behan's *The Hostage* in London, and trailing in their wake a positive galaxy of star names, including Daniel Massey, Jill Bennett, Victor Maddern, Stratford Johns, Peter Bowles, Sylvia Kay and John Lee (by kind permission of Associated British Picture Corporation Ltd). I mean, surely none of them would have chosen to spend five weeks in Coventry unless they knew they were en route for Shaftesbury Avenue, would they?

My first doubt arose when I opened the script and ran my eye down the *dramatis personæ*, noting characters with names like 'Wing Commander Johnny Johnson', 'Johnny Jackson, a pilot,' 'Jackie James, a pilot,' and yet another pilot, the part to which I had been assigned, called – and surely it had to be a misprint – 'Jammie Gimson.' But no, it wasn't, and even now I recall fighting a half-hearted battle during rehearsals to have my surname pronounced with a hard 'G' , all to no avail, of course, as our director maintained that the author, an ex-WAAF officer, lately deceased, had clearly intended bulk alliteration; though whether Lindsay Anderson had ascertained this prior to the lady's demise or after, he wasn't prepared to say. My second doubt, which amounted to heresy, bearing in mind that I was surrounded by theatrical heavyweights, all of whom had thrown their considerable and collective weight behind this project, crept up on me as I read the script. Set on an RAF Bomber Command station during World War II, and written, incredibly, in blank verse, it was, page for page, one of the worst plays I had ever read. But could this possibly be true, or had I taken leave of my senses? I read it again. The author had obviously been influenced by Terence Rattigan on the one hand and by Christopher Fry on the other; either that, or she hadn't heard of either of them. The story, such as it was, and I remember very little of it now, vaguely resembled Rattigan's in *Flare Path* and *The Way to the Stars*, but without even a hint of his humanity, his humour or, indeed, his talent. The dialogue, unwisely and pretentiously manipulated into a verse form with which the author was ill at ease, read and sounded even more banal than it would have done had she chosen to write it in ordinary conversational prose. I checked out my findings with my friend, Clinton Greyn, who was widely in agreement with me, although he was a bit more circumspect about it. Having been seduced by the model rather than the actor in him, I suspected, the prospect of appearing on stage in the glamorous guise of an RAF bomber pilot, circa 1942, seemed to outweigh all other considerations. And in all fairness, I have to admit that he did look very fetching in his flying jacket.

There remained the mystery of how so many estimable and well-established people had been deluded into accepting an engagement which was so obviously doomed from the outset. Well, of course, it all came down to the Olivier connection; there could have been no other explanation. Actors, by and large, have never been famous for knowing a good (or bad) script when they see one, so it goes without saying that, if the biggest and the best of them thought it was worth putting money into, then it simply had to be worth doing. Which brings me to the most perplexing mystery of all; what the hell was it that Laurence Olivier saw in the play that I didn't? Quite clearly, he was right and I was wrong, or else he was just as fallible as the rest of us, which was unthinkable, of course. Something magical was obviously going to happen during rehearsals that would transform this lump of lead into coin of purest gold. After all, that's what theatre is all about – the sleight of hand, the conjuring trick, the transformation – and that's why such a distinguished bunch of magicians had been assembled. They were, all of them, of course, well aware of the task that lay ahead, had taken it on with their eyes wide open, and were about to perform miracles. I, on the other hand, a minnow by comparison, and a very small cog in the wheel, had no significant part to play in this metamorphosis, and was therefore free to watch and learn. That's what I told myself, anyway.

I was mercifully divorced from the main thread of the story, my part being confined to several clandestine meetings with Jenny, a young WAAF, under the tail piece of a Lancaster bomber which protruded onto the stage and was Sean Kenny's uncharacteristically simple and effective setting for the airfield's dispersal area, from which the play derived its title. I was teamed once again with Jacqueline Wilson, my erstwhile wife from *Bridge of Sighs,* in a romantic relationship that was destined to end tragically, and predictably, in a bombing raid over Frankfurt or Dortmund or somewhere. In truth, the relationship ended tragically and predictably under the tail piece of that bomber, grounded by the awful dialogue, and further hindered, not only by a complete absence of directorial help, but by bouts of giggling from Lindsay Anderson and his asinine assistant, Anthony Page. Whether they were reduced to helpless laughter by the script or by our performances was a subtle distinction they didn't bother to share with us, but given that we were the ones who had to get up and do it every night in front of an audience, it was irrelevant in any case. Their crass behaviour effectively undermined what little confidence we had in ourselves and in our scenes together, and I have no doubt that I, at least, was less than convincing in them. It's hardly surprising, in the circumstances, that I began to wonder if, during my two year absence, the job description for directors had changed, and that making actors' lives as difficult and as miserable as possible, had now become a condition of employment.

There were compensations, of course, as there always are in the theatre. The vintage summer of 1959 continued with unabated sunshine, and we took full advantage of it during breaks from rehearsal by utilising the roof terrace of the theatre as a gathering place. The wonderful camaraderie that exists between actors, even when they scarcely know each other, is a well-worn cliché, but is nonetheless true for all that, and it certainly applied to the majority of that more or less distinguished crew who, although disappointingly possessed with no supernatural powers as far as the play was concerned, turned out to be extremely convivial company. More often than not, Jill Bennett, the only one amongst them who exhibited snooty tendencies, would hold court unbidden until called away, leaving behind a muted sigh of relief, as well as the overpowering smell of her none-too-subtle perfume. More delicate by far, and far more seductive, was the fragrance that emanated from Sylvia Kay, a delightful young woman in the visiting company whose long brown legs were, along with the sun, one of the main attractions of the roof terrace, for me at any rate.

I should, perhaps, explain at this point that, while Dawn and I were still enjoying a relationship of sorts, the barrier she had erected between us during our visit to Edinburgh the previous year, give or take the occasional breach, was still in place. With the benefit of hindsight, I don't think that, had I chosen to cut loose at that time, she would have raised any passionate objection, or made any serious effort to keep us together. Whether she would have regretted that or not I have no way of knowing. In any case, and certainly as far as I was concerned, choice didn't come into it. I had made a commitment, and short of being given my marching orders, there was no question I was going to walk away from something I instinctively knew was important to both of us. Nevertheless, Dawn had made it pretty clear, in both word and deed, that our relationship, although valued, was no longer exclusive and, painful as that obviously was, I certainly no longer felt constrained by any notions of physical fidelity myself. Besides, she had moved down to London and was no longer working in Stratford which, being a mere 19 miles from Coventry would have been an easy and irresistible weekend trysting place. London was further away and much more expensive to reach. Consequently, our times together were fewer, and shorter, and inevitably we were less answerable to each other for the times in between.

Another unlooked-for diversion came in the genial shape of Peter Dews, who had uncannily divined, not only my whereabouts, but also my sagging spirits, and arrived on several Sunday mornings to transport me in his car to Birmingham where, in his Edgbaston flat, he plied me with food and drink, music and conversation. His kindness and his tacit understanding were all the more surprising in that they were unconditional, while his enthusiasm for all things musical and theatrical was boundless and entirely contagious. Although Peter was still a radio producer with the BBC in Birmingham, he talked passionately, and in great detail, about his plans to produce a television series, the first of its kind, culled from Shakespeare's history plays, and entitled, *An Age of Kings,* and while these plans were still in the formative stage, and there was as yet no commitment from the BBC, his vision was so exciting and so completely compelling that I had no doubt that it would finally come to pass. I did not even dare to dream, however, that I might become involved in it.

Meanwhile, the much heralded opening night of *Dispersal* arrived, accompanied by the stirring sound of an RAF band, assembled for the occasion to play outside the theatre where a Spitfire had also been parked for the duration, presumably to prepare the audience, in case they didn't already know, that they were coming to see a play about the Battle of Britain. In the end, of course, it might just as well have been the Battle of Lockjaw Creek for all that audiences and critics alike thought of it. As is the way, however, we had to go on performing it night after night in the almost certain knowledge that it was heading nowhere except into well deserved, and long overdue, oblivion. As is also the way, Lindsay Anderson and his acolyte vanished the following day, never to be seen again.

In the crowded backstage bar one night, following a performance, Sylvia Kay and I exchanged one of those looks that can be interpreted as either significant or meaningless, depending to a great extent on how confident you are feeling about yourself at the time. Having just struggled through another dismal reminder of my shortcomings as an actor, I chose the latter interpretation. And even when, a short time later, after rummaging through her handbag, she complained that she had lost her keys, and asked me if I would be kind enough to climb through the window into her flat, I thought that it was entirely due to the fact that nobody else would be small enough to squeeze through it. Sylvia and, indeed, most members of the visiting company, had been allocated theatre flats whose kitchen windows were, to say the least, economically proportioned. I, of course, agreed to help, and followed her up the stairs to her flat where I managed, without difficulty, to climb through the window and let her in. It was several hours later, however, before I managed to find the front door again and let myself out. My memories of that particular encounter are somewhat hazy and, in any case, recalling them in this context would be unbecoming. I do remember, however – and what man whose ego was in dire need of a boost wouldn't? – that she said I looked like 'a beautiful young medieval knight'!

1959 Dispersal - Outside the Belgrade Theatre, with Clinton Greyn.

On our last Saturday morning in Coventry, Sylvia and I headed off by bus for nearby Kenilworth, which boasted a large open-air swimming pool. We had a matinée performance at 5pm, and reasoned that by catching the 3 o'clock bus back to Coventry, we would arrive in plenty of time for the half-hour call. It was another glorious day, and we had a lovely time, sunbathing, swimming, enjoying each other's company, and contemplating (or at least, I was) what might lay in store following the evening's performance. I was not alone in being committed to someone else, so we both knew that whatever happened between us belonged to those few weeks alone, and could not be allowed to spill over into the future. I know, of course, that many such intentions have paved the way to Hades, but I think we both believed we could cope with it, and happily settle for a brief and carefree interlude. In any case, our resolve was destined not to be put to the test. We were back at the stop well before the 3 o'clock bus to Coventry was due, and we passed the time in light-hearted conversation. We both knew that, while *Dispersal* was to end its run at the Belgrade that evening, an extra week at the Cambridge Arts Theatre lay before us and, although by no means eager to prolong the agony as far as the play was concerned, memories of Cambridge still loomed large, and the prospect of saying a protracted goodbye against such a romantic backdrop held out the promise of an enticing week. It was 3.30 before we realised that the bus still hadn't arrived, and that no one else was waiting at the stop. We didn't panic, but were concerned enough to question a passer-by, who told us that we were wasting our time as all the buses had been diverted round the town due to the carnival. He then gave us directions to the railway station before going on his way, with a cheery, "You'll be lucky if you get there, though!" Concern gave way to worry at that point, and we headed off in the general direction of the railway station, breaking into a run as it gradually dawned on us that the trains probably didn't run as frequently as the buses, and that Coventry station was, in any case, a good ten minute's walk from the theatre. It was only then that we suddenly understood what our friendly passer-by had meant with his parting shot, as we ran headlong into the carnival. Huge clowns on stilts, jugglers and brass bands, floats full of carnival queens, all loomed before us, travelling in the opposite direction, of course, and bringing our progress to a virtual halt. Several times I lost sight of Sylvia in the crowd, and when I did see her, tears were streaming down her face. Panic had really set in by now.

Recognising, finally, that the railway station was, indeed, beyond our reach, and seeing a telephone kiosk tantalisingly close by, I grabbed Sylvia by the hand and managed to extricate us from the throng. The very least we could do was to make contact with the theatre and advise them of our dilemma. It being a Saturday, however, the administration offices would be closed, of course, and neither of us knew the number of the stage door phone, so I dialled the box-office number. It was engaged. By this time, I was more concerned about Sylvia's state of mind than anything else. The fact that she was in the opening scene of the play, and that I didn't make my first entrance until the beginning of the second act in no way mitigated my anxiety. I felt an overwhelming sense of responsibility for her, and besides, the half-hour call was not only mandatory, but deeply entrenched. So, as standing still was not an option, I said, more in hope than in expectation, "Let's see if we can find a taxi," before taking hold of her hand again and whisking her off, away from the crowds, and up a side street where the odds against finding any kind of conveyance, let alone a waiting taxi cab, must have been astronomical. Twice more I stopped at a telephone kiosk and on both occasions the box office number was still busy. We'd played to half empty houses ever since the blasted play opened, I thought with mounting frustration, and suddenly there's an overwhelming demand for tickets. For a fleeting moment, I thought I saw the top of a policeman's helmet in the crush and, hoping against hope that it was a real policeman and not some carnival representation of PC Plod, we flew back into the crowd and forged a path towards him. At last, there he stood, the very image of composed and kindly authority, directing traffic at a busy crossroads. As succinctly as I could, I related our story, trying to impress upon him our desperate need to get back to Coventry as quickly as possible. Whether he rated an appointment at the theatre as a matter of life or death, or was more influenced by Sylvia's noisy and very obvious distress, was of no consequence. He stopped the very next car, and asked the driver if he was heading for Coventry, and if so, would he be kind enough to give a couple of his friends a lift. Before the driver had time to reply, the nice policeman had opened the door and ushered us into the back of the car, waving us on our way with an amiable smile.

The couple in front were quite elderly, obviously in no hurry, and anxious to engage us in conversation as we trundled along the Kenilworth-Coventry road, getting stuck behind lorries and being overtaken by practically everything else on wheels. As a token of my gratitude for the lift and, I suppose, as a result of some deeply ingrained social conscience, I tried to participate in the chit-chat without burdening them with our problems, a difficult enough task in the circumstances, made all the more taxing by Sylvia's now voluble and incessant weeping which, for very English reasons, I suppose, the couple never mentioned. By the time we were dropped off just opposite the theatre, I had managed to achieve a more or less stoical acceptance of the situation. We had, after all, not only missed the half-hour call, but the quarter of an hour call, the five minute call, beginners and curtain up, and there was nothing we could do, or any more we could have done, about it. Nevertheless, having offered perfunctory thanks to our tardy rescuers, we tore across Corporation Street and down the side of the theatre to where a group of people were waiting outside the stage door. "Quick!", one of them shouted, "we've held the curtain!" Whereupon Sylvia was whisked away to be speedily transformed into a WAAF called Zoë, and I collapsed onto the ground where superficial stoicism quickly gave way to hysteria. Anyone with a jot of imagination, and a modicum of sympathy and understanding, would have recognised my laughter, tinged as it was by madness, as a symptom of relief following a bout of extreme anxiety. Bryan Bailey, however, who was suddenly towering over me, chose to see it as further evidence of my lack of respect for the theatre, first engendered, or so I suspected, by a certain letter I had written to a certain director several months before. As far as he was concerned, I'd probably been laughing all the way from Kenilworth, and as he poured forth a stream of invective, refusing to listen to either my apologies or my proffered explanation, accusing me of "Disgraceful Behaviour," "Unprofessional Conduct," and threatening to report me to Equity, I found myself wishing I had been laughing.

My only real regret, in looking back, was that this unfortunate episode cast a shadow over my relationship with Sylvia Kay, and effectively brought it to an end. We were affectionate enough with each other during that last week in Cambridge and, as the nightmare receded, even managed to raise a few genuine smiles as we recounted the story to other members of the company, but neither of us felt inclined to rekindle the fire, and when we finally said goodbye, it was as if nothing of any consequence had ever taken place between us. In fact, my only substantial memory of that final week was when, on the penultimate night, Laurence Olivier himself arrived to formally announce that *Dispersal* would not be transferring to the West End. I remember that he spent a long time in Daniel Massey's dressing-room while the rest of the company assembled in the green room, to await the pronouncement that had, in any case, been inevitable since the author had first put pen to paper. When he finally emerged, and despite my recent and disappointing discovery that he was only a human being after all, I found myself overawed by his presence. Without a word, he cast a rueful smile around the room, a smile that spoke volumes and rendered words superfluous, and which only subtly changed when it alighted on me. I can only imagine that my idolatry must have been writ large in my face, for he smiled a different kind of smile, full of amusement, but not without warmth, and he said – to me and me alone – "Hello" – after which, he departed.

I enjoyed a brief trip to London before returning to Coventry the following Monday to begin rehearsals for the next play. I arrived at the stage-door to check the cast list on the notice board, as was customary at the beginning of each new production, and discovered that my name was not on it. I went straight to the production office, where I learned that I was not in the next play, nor were there any plans to cast me in anything else for the rest of the season. I was naturally shocked, and also more than a little angry that I had been allowed to go to London and return to Coventry without being told that my services were no longer required. Not having an agent, and possessing little or no knowledge of the theatre's obligations under a 'play as cast' contract, I was unsure of my rights, although I knew without a doubt that Bryan Bailey's decision to do it that way was both deliberate, and thoroughly nasty. However, being possessed of that uncrushable, and totally unjustified resilience I had obviously been born with, I turned round, left the theatre, went to pick up my belongings from the digs, and headed straight back to London, where nothing awaited me but the dole queue, although believing, and with true Panglossian certainty, that my abrupt and unceremonious departure from the Belgrade was 'all for the best in this best of all possible worlds', and praying fervently that never again would I have to return to that benighted city.

oOoOo

Eight

During the long autumn months that brought 1959 to a close, I found myself hopelessly out of work which was cause enough, if not to regret, at least to question my impetuosity. Looking back over a long career, however, I cannot in all honesty accuse myself in general terms of being too forthright for my own good. I am acquainted with several actors, and good ones too, who have paid the price for speaking their minds and, whilst I admire their courage and their self-confidence, I do not count myself amongst them. Even at the age of 21 I had bitten my tongue more often than I'd allowed it to run free, as I was already well aware that the 'grovel factor' plays a significant part in an actor's career, often determining its progress – or lack of it. So short of biting my tongue off altogether, I learned very early on to keep my own counsel about most things. I was well aware that, by speaking out when I did, I had probably ruined my chances of ever working with Bryan Bailey or James Roose-Evans again but, despite the bleakness of my immediate prospects, I had no regrets about that. As far as Bryan Bailey was concerned, my theory was never put to the test, as he was killed in a car crash on the newly-opened M1 shortly afterwards while returning to Coventry from a visit to the Theatre Royal, Stratford East.

Not that I was unemployed for long, even if the job I took wasn't exactly what I had in mind. But I was living at home with my parents again, and although never pressed on the subject by either of them, I felt conscience-bound to pay something towards my keep. So I became a clerk in the stores of an engineering factory on the North Circular Road, dealing mainly with orders for machine tools and various other mysterious items whose functions were, and remained, unknown to me. But the job was undemanding enough, and my immediate superiors, fascinated by having an actor on the pay-roll, were both courteous and strangely deferential. Thus it was that during the few months I spent in their company I managed to work my way through the entire works of Euripides, Sophocles and Aeschylus. I suppose it seemed as good a way as any of passing the time. Nor did I impose too much on my parents' hospitality, as most of my evenings and weekends were spent with Dawn, who had recently moved from her up-market accommodation in South Kensington to the top-floor flat of a terraced house in Luna Street, situated at the 'wrong' end of the King's Road, in an area known as 'World's End.' There would be little point in looking for it now though, as Luna Street has long since disappeared, its houses demolished, and the entire area from Blantyre

Street down to the river at Cheyne Walk completely re-modelled, so that you would be hard pushed to imagine it was ever there. Dawn shared the flat with Penny McVitie, a colleague from the wardrobe department at Stratford. They had a room each with shared bathroom and a common oven which was situated on the landing between their rooms. I loved the flat, if only because it was there that our relationship blossomed again. It was the first time we had lived in the same town since our early days together in Coventry and, to borrow a phrase, 'nothing propinks like propinquity'.

No promises were exchanged, however, and no commitments made. We just enjoyed each other's company and rediscovered shared interests. The fact that our tastes in most things were pretty much the same was hardly surprising, given that I'd had very few of my own before we met. In truth, I could only lay personal claim to my sense of humour, and that we continued to laugh at the same things made life in each other's company preferable to any alternative. On top of which, and without – as far as I can recall – any reference to it, the platonic restrictions she had imposed on our relationship were removed, and life together assumed an altogether rosier hue.

An additional interest came in the shape of her neighbours, a young couple with a small child and a somewhat larger Alsatian dog who lived on the ground floor. Ken and Leila were real Londoners, and consequently very open and friendly besides being irrepressibly cheerful. Leila was a good-looking woman, extremely tough and capable. Archetypically, she ruled the roost while cosseting her little girl outrageously and bestowing on her man unconditional support, both socially and in all his professional endeavours. Ken was also good-looking in a boyish kind of way, with fair hair, blue eyes and an extremely engaging smile. He was also – for a while anyway – a good provider. That is, until the law finally caught up with him, for Ken was a professional thief. This came to light when Dawn managed to lock herself out of her flat one day and, on seeking advice from Leila, was dissuaded from engaging the services of a locksmith, given a cup of tea, and told that Ken would deal with it as soon as he got home, which he did, gaining access to Dawn's flat with astonishing ease and with the aid of nothing more than a bit of plastic. Sensing, alongside her gratitude, a degree of alarm, he sought to reassure her with disarming sincerity that he would never dream of breaking into a private home in pursuit of his trade. In fact, he was dead against it with a passion bordering on the evangelical. In our many subsequent meetings with him over innumerable cups of tea, sometimes up in

Dawn's flat, and occasionally downstairs where, under Leila's proprietorial eye, he would show us the tools of his trade, which mainly consisted of a drawer full of keys of all shapes and sizes and another crammed with pairs of white cotton gloves. Ken enthusiastically expounded on the nature of his calling while ingenuously defending its morality. He had nothing but contempt for burglars who gave professional thieves a bad name, while bank robbers who invariably threatened violence also put themselves beyond the pale. Hanging was too good for those kind of villains, Ken maintained, and you got the impression that he would have been only too happy to spring the trap himself. I think Ken saw himself more in the mould of a latter day Robin Hood, except that the poor amongst whom he distributed his righteously appropriated booty usually began and ended with his own friends and family. I recall over the next few months being offered a number of diverse items at knock down prices, so I obviously qualified as a friend by this time. But both he and Leila, with true Puritan zeal, drew the line at turning their daughter, however innocently, into a receiver of stolen goods. I have seldom seen a child so pampered with the latest fashions and the most expensive toys, none of which, they both vehemently insisted, had fallen off the back of a lorry, but had been bought at the full retail price, and almost always from Harrods! Ken's pick 'n' mix principles, however, did not embrace commercial enterprises whose bosses failed to insure their property and their products adequately, for insurance companies were his prime targets. There was nothing Ken enjoyed more, apart from thieving, than arguing his case, which he did with absolute conviction and with an *Alice in Wonderland* approach to ethics that defied even the most elementary logic. Put simply, it was his contention that since businesses paid hefty premiums to insurance companies in exchange for a guarantee against loss, they were entitled to be reimbursed for these losses, while the insurance companies only existed because they'd been paid these hefty premiums in the first place, so in effect the businesses were only getting their own money back, and the only ones to suffer were the insurance companies, racketeers of the worst kind, according to Ken, although he reserved his most withering scorn for those businesses that refused to pay 'protection money' to the insurance companies. "Well, that's *their* problem, ennit?" was his rejoinder when questioned about their status on his hit list. "I mean, they should've got themselves insured, shouldn't they?" There was, of course, no answer to that one, and Ken smiled happily in the knowledge that he had successfully made his point.

Ken's associates, all of them with names that sounded like characters out of a Damon Runyon story, came from either Chelsea, which was his own patch, or across the border in Fulham. Such borders were always jealously guarded and the police, according to Ken, were well paid to keep intruders out. Indeed, he claimed a very special relationship with the Chelsea police, whose patronage extended as far as giving him the occasional lift to a job, waiting for him round the corner, and then helping him to escape, although with the police providing the getaway car, it was never quite clear to me who he was supposed to be escaping from. That he enjoyed such immunity while restricting his activities to the Chelsea area was a matter of fact as far as Ken was concerned, and he would only shake his head sadly at our lack of worldliness when we expressed any doubts about it. In truth, if there was no substance to his claims, then Ken's downfall was brought about by nothing more nor less than the long arm of coincidence. On the face of it, joining forces with the boys from Fulham seemed like a good idea. After all, their leader, Spanish Jim, laid claim to a similar relationship with the Fulham police, which meant that both groups could extend their activities, increase their revenue, and enjoy cross-border immunity courtesy of their mates from the neighbouring borough. What this arrangement didn't take into account was the huge propensity amongst thieves for falling out with each other when things go wrong. Unfortunately for Ken, things went badly wrong on a job in Fulham – something to do with putting a brick through the window of a television show-room just as a bobby was approaching on his beat, then dropping the looted television set onto the pavement where it exploded, before leaping into a passing taxi, leaving the bobby, in all innocence, to requisition the getaway car that the thieves had obviously forgotten they had, telling the driver to, "Follow that cab!" and only realising his mistake when they ended up in a cul-de-sac with the taxi nowhere to be seen. And if this reads like a sequence from an Ealing comedy, all I can say is that's the way Ken told it. Needless to say, however, the incident required some kind of response from the Fulham police, and Spanish Jim fingered Ken for the job, presumably on the grounds that it had been Ken who'd panicked and dropped the television set, although he may well have had other reasons for wanting him out of the way. All this we heard from Ken himself after he'd been charged and was out on bail prior to his trial at the Old Bailey. Not that he was unduly worried about the outcome. Apart from some pretty robust invective against the treachery of Spanish Jim, and a bit of self-flagellation for allowing himself to stray beyond the boundaries of

Chelsea, he took it all in his stride, made the necessary arrangements with his solicitor, and promptly forgot all about it. In fact, he didn't remember he was due to appear in court until half an hour before his appointed time, whereupon he grabbed his dog and ran from the house, yelling out as he went, "See you later!" After another hour or so had passed, there was a knock at the front door, and Leila went to answer it. She came upstairs immediately afterwards, and told Dawn that it had been a copper from Chelsea nick, an old friend by all accounts, who'd said, "Is Ken at home, Leila? 'Cos he was due at the Bailey half an hour ago, and he ain't turned up." Leila appeared to find it all quite amusing. "Oh, ain't he terrible", she said, clearly meaning the opposite. Nothing more was heard until late in the afternoon when another policeman turned up with Ken's dog. "Sorry, Leila", he said, "Ken's got 18 months". Apparently, he'd arrived at the Old Bailey, already late for the hearing, handed the dog's lead to a policeman on duty outside, saying he'd pick him up again in a few minutes, and disappeared inside, never to re-emerge. How long the PC had been standing there holding onto the dog before he began to suspect that Ken's optimism might have been misplaced is not on record. What was fairly obvious, though, was that Ken's connections – even if they weren't influential enough to get him off – certainly ensured his dog's safe return to Luna Street! We never saw Ken again. By the time he was released, we had all moved on. In the meantime, we got a running commentary on his welfare from Leila whose frequent visits to Wandsworth prison were reported with a mixture of pride and affection, only slightly marred by a hint of resentment, and then only on behalf of their little girl who had, by all means, to be protected from the truth, who never accompanied her mother to Wandsworth, and was simply told, "Daddy is away on business." The reason I have such vivid memories of this episode is that Dawn and I decided to write a television play about it. I have no idea if we ever finished it, but nothing came of it in any event. What we learned from the experience, however, was that we had a natural affinity when it came to collaborating as writers, a revelation that was entirely limited, at that time, to the pleasure of discovering that it was one more thing we had in common.

Although it is generally held by the educated that decades are measured in periods of ten years, it would be a mistake to think that the '50s came to an end in 1959 or that what we look back on as the '60s began the following year. It would certainly be more convenient if they had, but life has a way of rough-hewing our ends, shape them how we may, and I'm sure that most commentators would agree that the 'fab' sixties didn't really kick in until 1963 when *The Beatles* burst onto the scene, and suddenly everybody started doing the 'Twist'. It was even later when the mini-skirt, that emblematic symbol of female emancipation in the '60s, made its first brief appearance. Of course, it had nothing whatsoever to do with emancipation. Quite the reverse, in fact. It was simply an instinctive and deeply primitive response to 'The Peacock Revolution,' as it was described by Cecil Beaton, when male flamboyance reached its apogee in the late '60s with a degree of ostentation that hadn't been seen since the days of Charles II. In the late 17th century, women had responded by revealing more of their bosoms, but with tits not being much of a feature in the '60s, there was only one thing left to flaunt in order to guarantee that men would go on looking at them rather than at each other. I never much cared for the mini-skirt. For a start, it discriminated cruelly – not only against girls whose legs weren't exactly their best feature, but also against girls whose legs were perfectly shaped for anything *except* a mini-skirt. On top of this, it took away from the opposite sex much of their mystery and allure and, worse still, made the wearing of tights *de rigueur* for at least two-thirds of the year, which rendered obsolete that delightful, if only occasional, prospect of glimpsing stocking-tops. All of which is undeniable, irrefutable and, of course, totally subjective!

The reason I embarked upon this particular topic – apart from the obvious one – is that the mini-skirt, and all that it was claimed to represent, perfectly illustrates a decade that wasn't all that it was cracked up to be. The much-maligned years between 1950 and 1959, however, for all that they have been painted historically in shades of grey, represented as perpetually foggy, and described as bleakly austere, contained more genuine innovation, more real energy, and considerably more revolutionary zeal than they are given credit for. Contrary to popular belief, there was also a lot more fun to be had in those days too, and if Philip Larkin really meant it when he declared that 'sexual intercourse began in nineteen sixty-three', then I'd dearly like to know what the hell it was I was doing in 1955! But then, of course, all this is pretty subjective too. After all, I did most of my growing up in the 1950s, formed most of my opinions, developed most of my tastes which, with minor adjustments, are much the same today as they were then. Laurence Olivier remains the greatest actor I have seen on stage, and my favourite movie, all in all, is still *On the Waterfront,* released in 1954. The advent of Rock 'n Roll, together with its exponents, including Elvis Presley, may have fallen on my deaf ears, but I am still bewitched by the voices of Ella Fitzgerald, Peggy Lee, Lena Horne, Judy Garland and, above all, by the incomparable Frank Sinatra, who cast a lifetime spell on me with those flawless recordings he made for Capitol Records back in the mid-fifties. By the same token, the songs he and the others sang were written by my favourite song-writers and, albeit most of them were the products of even earlier decades, it was during the '50s that I was introduced to them. An abiding passion for the American musical was engendered during the same period, which encompassed a string of evergreens, including the near-perfect *Guys and Dolls,* and which reached a thrilling climax when, in 1958, Dawn and I were present at a preview performance of Leonard Bernstein's *West Side Story* at Her Majesty's Theatre. Nothing – not even my familiarity with the music had prepared me for the tremendous impact it made, not only on me and thousands of others like me, but on the future of musical theatre.

I had, earlier that same year, seen the superlative *My Fair Lady* at Drury Lane, a delightful show in every respect, and especially for Rex Harrison's definitive performance as Professor Higgins, but it was essentially a distinguished contribution to a well-established tradition, whereas *West Side Story* broke new ground. Not only was the music redolent of those mean streets the characters inhabited, but the production, and especially the choreography by Jerome Robbins, fairly vibrated with raw energy. Of course, I was already acquainted with this relatively new approach to dance, having first come across it in Michael Kidd's acrobatic routines for the film, *Seven Brides for Seven Brothers* but, not being an *aficionado*, and never having even heard of Martha Graham, I'd not seen anything remotely like it on stage before. The effect was mesmerising, all the more so because it wasn't diluted by close-ups of a lot of nice-looking boys from ballet school as it was in the movie version which came out a couple of years later. I mean, the idea of Russ Tamblyn knowing what a flick-knife was, let alone using one, was a difficult concept to come to terms with. At a distance, the boys on stage were both dangerous and deadly, their latent violence masking their technical virtuosity, so that you ended up completely believing that street kids in New York really did move like that, with all the grace and sure-footedness of prowling alley-cats. It's difficult, so many years later, to recapture, let alone share, the elation I felt as I left the theatre that night, all the more so because *West Side Story* is old news now, its well-deserved place in the pantheon taken for granted. The fact that never before had dance been used in such a fully integrated way, and that as a result of this, musical theatre would never be quite the same again, is a matter of historical record. What it doesn't convey is the sheer exhilaration of seeing it for the first time. That its immediate impact was anything but academic, is best illustrated by the fact that, at that particular performance, two of the three interval bells were redundant, as the entire audience had already returned to their seats, breathless with anticipation.

Then there was the legitimate theatre, undeniably languishing during the first half of the decade, although Terence Rattigan gave us two of his finest plays, *The Deep Blue Sea* and *Separate Tables*, during this period. But there wasn't much else happening on the domestic front until, in 1956, John Osborne's *Look Back in Anger* burst onto the scene and, quite suddenly, we were catapulted into an altogether different kind of theatre, its vitality undoubtedly inspired by a resurgent Broadway, dominated throughout the '50s by Tennessee Williams and Arthur Miller, several of whose plays had been enlivening the West End from the late 1940s onwards. But both Osborne and then Arnold Wesker, while by no means punching the same weight, found their own distinctive voices and their own decidedly home-grown preoccupations. Osborne's Jimmy Porter and Wesker's Beatie Bryant, chalk and cheese in all other respects, shared a passionate refusal to accept the status quo; Jimmy in a determined attack on middle-class values, Beatie in an impassioned assault upon the ignorance and apathy of her own class. In short, neither of them was prepared to accept the role in which society had cast them; no longer were they going to play supporting characters in someone else's drama. So it was goodbye to French windows, drawing-rooms, and dressing for dinner. Even more radically, it was goodbye to dressing for the theatre. Potential patrons from across the social spectrum were encouraged to lay aside their preconceptions and their glad rags and to come as they were. This was to be the dawning of a new age of inclusiveness and accessibility, and it was exciting while it lasted. As was Joan Littlewood's bold, even revolutionary, attempt to establish a peoples' theatre in Stratford East which, for a while, did manage to attract a substantial working-class audience, with its rumbustious fare, including plays by Brendan Behan, *The Quare Fellow* and *The Hostage,* as well as *A Taste of Honey* by Shelagh Delaney, all of which were so successful that they transferred to the West End, along with several other Theatre Workshop productions. This development was, of course, anathema to Miss Littlewood, not at all what she had in mind when she founded the company, but 'fings bein' what they always was', I suppose she needed the money.

In the long term, of course, mainstream theatre remained the province of largely middle-class audiences who carried on dressing up for the occasion, while Beatie's kin stayed away, as ignorant and apathetic as ever they were. Nevertheless, it was in the 1950s that these ideas flourished, and that everything seemed possible. Even Samuel Becket's bewilderingly elusive, yet strangely compelling *Waiting For Godot* was possible, probably unthinkable until then, and certainly not at a theatre in the middle of Piccadilly Circus. Unthinkable too, from a personal point of view, that I should see three Chekhov masterpieces in their original language and understand what the characters were talking about. Not only that, but finding them funny. Chekhov? Funny? And in Russian? I confess that I had to be dragged along to the Sadlers Wells Theatre to see *Uncle Vanya,* as performed by the Moscow Art Theatre. But I returned of my own free will to see *Three Sisters* and *The Cherry Orchard.* One of the most remarkable things in a truly remarkable season, and especially from a young English actor's perspective, was that the man who played the title role in *Uncle Vanya* went on to lend his considerable weight and talent to relatively minor roles in the other two plays, and the same rules seemed to apply to the rest of the company. The result was that the acting achieved a quality in depth that only pure fluke could have replicated in our own rigidly hierarchical system. Some years later, an attempt was made to establish an ensemble such as this in London, and for a while it shone out like a beacon. It was formed in 1972 by a small group of distinguished actors whose task it was to choose the plays and cast the directors, thus turning our cherished system on its head, and firmly placing the director back where he belonged in the not-too-distant past. As Simon Callow avers in his book *Being an Actor* 'instead of being the *fons et origo* of the entire enterprise he would have been chosen – employed, to be blunt – by the actors specifically for his knowledge of the world of the play and its performing traditions.' But how, oh how, were such first-rate directors going to be persuaded to surrender the jealously guarded power they had gathered unto themselves, when that was one of the main reasons most of them had become directors in the first place? It would have been easier to persuade Caligula to abdicate. And then again, having had the stuffing knocked out of them, and their initiative surgically removed by a lot of self-appointed martinets, how on earth could a new generation of actors be expected to shoulder this new burden of responsibility? No, it was pretty well doomed from the outset. On top of which, it has to be said, the Actors' Company harboured its own built-in booby-traps, primed by a tradition that owes more to the star system than it does to genuine ensemble playing. In an otherwise well-presented and well-cast production of Feydeau's *A Flea in her Ear*, the relatively small part of the hotel bell-boy was played by Ian McKellen, a founder of the company and, even then, one of the finest young actors of his generation. Nothing wrong with that, except that, in a stunningly detailed display of vocal and physical mannerisms, he managed to steal every scene he was in, dazzled the audience with his comedic skills, and consequently succeeded in upsetting the balance of the play. This wasn't deliberate, you understand; he simply couldn't resist the challenge of making something out of very little. Olivier would have done the same, Irving too, probably, and certainly Anthony Sher. It's the way we've been brought up, and there's not much we can do about it. All the more surprising then, that in a company of superlatively talented Russian actors, there were no show-offs, no overt demonstrations of technical virtuosity, and no star performances. The only star, in fact, was Chekhov, acknowledged by the actors as such in that every word, gesture and nuance of their performances was selflessly dedicated to serving his intentions. Again I turn to Kenneth Tynan for these last, and infinitely more telling, words on the subject: 'They (the actors) have become, with long rehearsal, the people they are playing; they do not need, as our actors do, to depend on the lines alone for their characterisation. We act with our voices, they with their lives. Where we leave off, they begin .... This is not verbal acting, like ours, but total acting ... Read the play before going, and you will be safe. Safe, and enriched.'

No, the '50s were not, by any stretch of the imagination, a decade in the doldrums. And even if none of these things had happened, on a very personal level they were the years in which I did most of my growing-up, and in which I conceived my twin passions for the theatre and for the opposite sex, although not necessarily in that order! Not that the '60s were entirely without incident, devoid of pleasure or, indeed, lacking in opportunity or achievement. In fact they got off to a pretty auspicious start when, early in the New Year, I heard from Peter Dews that he had been given the green light by the BBC for his television Shakespeare series, and that he would like me to become a member of the permanent company. I was euphoric, of course, and always allowing for the occasional ordinary day, euphoria was to be my constant companion for the next seven or eight months. *An Age of Kings* was a mammoth undertaking, the scale of which is best described by Peter Dews himself, its intrepid producer: 'In screening eight of Shakespeare's histories in serial form, the British Broadcasting Corporation not only presented history, they made it. Never within living memory in the British Isles had it been economically possible to mount the whole of the great double tetralogy in sequence, either in the theatre or on the screen. When I began to make my plans the obstacles seemed endless: the best place to present Shakespeare will always be the theatre; Britain has yet no colour TV; I had 600 parts to cast; I did not know if everyone's stamina would endure 30 weeks continuous rehearsal and performance; worst of all, no one had ever done what we were about to do.'

I was one of 20 young or youngish actors who had been invited to form the nucleus of a company whose task it was to undertake a bewildering variety of roles throughout the series, which was made up of eight historically consecutive plays, covering the reigns of seven kings over a period of 86 years from 1399 to 1485. The company was to be augmented by guest artistes who would play, not only the eponymous monarchs, but other strongly featured characters who would then depart, having been deposed, murdered, or otherwise disposed of. The series – or serial, for it was Peter's intention to present it in that form – would consist of 15, 50-minute episodes, each episode rehearsed over a period of two weeks before recording it for transmission only a matter of days later. The reason for this unseemly haste was that, having committed to a time-scale, the BBC realised that the studio allotted to the series at the Television Centre in Wood Lane, which was under construction at the time, would not be available to us immediately, and that consequently the first three episodes would have to be transmitted 'live' from the Riverside Studios which, at that time, had no VTR (video-tape recording) facilities. Not that there was anything unusual about 'live' television back then. In fact, there were elements at the BBC that held stubbornly to the belief that it was somehow superior, like steam engines and wooden ships, and went on making a virtue of it long after the necessity had disappeared. *An Age of Kings,* however, presented unusual problems, not only with the movement of a large number of actors from one area to another, very often with only seconds to spare, but also with television cameras that were not nearly as mobile or manoeuvrable as they are today. By the time we moved up the road to the Television Centre, therefore, the first three episodes had already been shown, and the 'Beeb' was obliged to go on transmitting them at fortnightly intervals. On the plus side, however, the transition to VTR did afford us the comparative luxury of strolling across the studio for the next scene during a tape break, instead of rushing hell for leather down a corridor and inevitably running into a camera being pushed along at breakneck speed in the opposite direction. Pre-recording also provided the opportunity for a limited number of retakes at the end of each session, so stress levels all round were considerably reduced which was a blessing from everybody's point of view, especially as we had discovered from very early on that undue stress was likely to have a volcanic effect, sometimes of Vesuvian proportions, on our otherwise jocular and genial producer!

It was April, 1960 when we took up residence in the Territorial Army Drill Hall in Bulwer Street, Shepherd's Bush, and for the next 30 weeks this was to be our headquarters, our rehearsal room and, indeed, our second home. In those days, the streets around Shepherd's Bush were relatively free of traffic, Bulwer Street being no exception until, that is, on the days before we moved into the studio when the 'extras' were called to be put into various scenes, and suddenly there wasn't a parking space to be had. I had always assumed that extras, supernumeraries, walk-ons, or whatever you care to call them were just biding their time, itching to become proper actors. How I managed to square this assumption with the almost certain knowledge that few, if any of them, would be able to afford to run a car if they were to achieve their ambitions, is just one of those self-delusive peculiarities that lead people to become actors in the first place. Not that we were badly paid on *An Age of Kings;* I received about £45 per episode, more than double what I'd been earning at the Belgrade Theatre the previous year, and that's not taking into account the occasional overtime payments, repeat fees and residual payments from overseas sales, so that I ended up more than quadrupling my original fee. The fact that I was still without an agent also meant that I didn't have to part with a penny of it. On top of this, and arguably even more attractive, was the sheer joy of working in London for seven months on an exclusive diet of Shakespeare, and with an inspired director whose passion for the plays was matched, not only by his minutely detailed knowledge of them, but by a genuine desire to share all this with his actors.

I already had good reason to respect Peter's retentive memory from the time we first met in Edinburgh two years earlier, and as we gathered that April morning in the Drill Hall for the first read-through of Episode One, I was about to witness an even more impressive exhibition of it. There must have been about 30 of us, and maybe more, gathered round on that first day, including members of the permanent company, guest artistes, designers and studio management. Peter rose to his feet, and instead of asking us to introduce ourselves, a common and acceptable enough practice with large companies, he proceeded in a clockwise direction to name each and every one of us, dwelling briefly on our functions, without even the slightest hesitation, and without making a single mistake. It was an awesome achievement, and it fully deserved the ovation he received when he finally came full circle. But it wasn't just a party trick. If you happened to forget your lines during rehearsals, irrespective of the play, and no matter what part you were playing in it, even down to the 2nd Messenger in Act 4, Scene 3 of *Henry VI, part 2,* Peter would be able to prompt you, and without referring to the script. His memory was phenomenal and, in time, it became the stuff of legend. He was also a marvellous raconteur, and I wonder even now that someone has not produced a collection of the stories, off-the-cuff remarks and jokes with which he captivated all, or very nearly all, who worked with him. On the down side, he was famous for his rages as well, which, infrequent though they might have been, were heart-stopping even when they were directed at someone else. I recall two particular examples, probably engraved on my memory because their visual impact at the time was so extreme. The first involved an unfortunate young man whose job it was to operate the tape-recorder, playing incidental music and working from a cue sheet by his side. It was a first run-through in the rehearsal room, and a certain amount of tension was already in the air when the lad made his first mistake, bringing in the music far too early, eliciting from Peter nothing more than a look, although for those of us whose antennae were pretty well extended by then, those basilisk eyes, together with an onrush of blood into the face that surrounded them, were dangerously portentous. Seemingly impervious to the warning signs, the young man or, come to think of it, it may even have been a young woman, for Peter did not discriminate, fell into the same trap, not once but twice more, whereupon our esteemed director fell upon the machine, and hurled it down the stairs. He then turned his fury on the perpetrator of the crime, now transfixed with terror, and snarled, "You do that just once more, and you'll bloody well follow it!" Fortunately, it was an empty threat as the tape-recorder was damaged beyond repair, and I have no recollection how long it took to replace it, by which time, in any case, we had a new and super-efficient operator. Fast-forward to the end of the series, to the very last episode, in fact, for the other occasion that was seared into my memory. Tensions were again running high in the lead-up to the Battle of Bosworth at the end of *Richard III.* The battlefield was represented in the studio by a huge tank of mud through which we had to fight our way to victory or to defeat, depending whose side we were on, and in which Paul

Daneman's Richard had to die, lying face down, for what seemed like forever, although it probably seemed much longer than that to Paul who was the one who had to do it. The scene was fraught with problems, not the least being that the costumes would be ruined by the mud, and that consequently, recording it had to be accomplished in one take. Our allotted studio time was fast running out, and Peter implored us all from the control room above to be patient and quiet while cameras were lined up and sound levels checked. For those of us who had lived through 86 years of English history by then, survived 7 monarchs, and emerged unscathed from numerous 15th century battles, this was the ultimate test, and we wisely obeyed his instructions to the letter. Two extras, however, mistaking an edict for a request, decided to carry on with their conversation, probably about the relative fuel consumption of their cars. Suddenly, a door slammed, footsteps were heard running down the gantry stairs, and Peter appeared, red-faced with fury. He rushed straight up to the two malefactors, both of them sturdy lads and a good few inches taller than he was, and banged their heads together, before turning and running back up the stairs to the control room. A deathly hush fell over the studio floor, eyes were averted in a cowardly refusal to become involved, and The Battle of Bosworth was fought without further incident, Lancastrian forces winning the day as intended, despite the unscheduled intervention of one particularly aggressive Yorkshireman. The mud of Bosworth Field, I should perhaps point out, owed nothing to historical record, but rather to Peter's decision to tackle the problem of studio-bound battles by setting each of them against a different backdrop, his entirely justifiable argument being that there are only a limited number of ways you can shoot a medieval army at war in a television studio. From the Battle of Shrewsbury at the end of *Henry IV, Part I* to Bosworth which brought the series to a close, *An Age of Kings* incorporated about a dozen battles whose common denominator was swordplay, which can get a bit repetitive no matter how many angles you shoot it from. So, apart from the climactic mud bath, we fought the Battle of Wakefield in deep snow, the second Battle of St. Alban's against a city in flames and the Battle of Barnet in dense fog, although it may well have had viewers adjusting their sets, under the impression they'd lost the picture altogether!

The real success of *An Age of Kings* depended, to a large extent, on creating a unity of style and purpose from eight separate plays, historically sequential, but written at very different periods in Shakespeare's working life, and certainly not in sequence. The three parts of *Henry VI,* for instance, were amongst his earliest works, followed by *Richard III,* and then *Richard II.* The two parts of *Henry IV* and *Henry V* were written later, his early dependence on rhyme having given way to a more confident and altogether freer employment of both verse and prose.

1960 Henry VI - An Age of Kings, as Edmund Mortimer.

Having a permanent company of actors, of course, helped to create a wholeness out of these fairly disparate parts, as did the narrative, swept along by sometimes ruthless editing of the text, particularly in the three parts of *Henry VI,* which was both scholarly and, at the same time, instinctively theatrical. Peter's decision to present the 15 episodes in serial form, seeking a suspenseful ending for each episode, may have owed much to Francis Durbridge and his ilk, but the plays lent themselves readily to this kind of treatment, and its success was measured by viewing figures you wouldn't normally associate with televised Shakespeare. Some of the endings were fairly low-key domestic affairs, deceptively trivial, some presaged huge events, some were darkly ominous, others were outrageously melodramatic. My favourite of them all came at the end of Episode 14, as Richard, Duke of Gloucester, having resolved to usurp the crown, is seen limping down a corridor and coming to a halt outside a chamber door from which the sound of children's voices can be heard singing *Oranges and Lemons*. After the final line of the song, 'Here comes a chopper to chop off your head – chop, chop chop …' all goes quiet, and a nurse emerges, carrying a double candelabra, which Richard takes from her. After watching her depart, he then goes into the chamber and stands by the bed, looking down at the peacefully sleeping figures of the two young Princes. For a moment or two he regards them with apparently avuncular affection; then he blows out both candles, and the closing titles roll. Great stuff!

Many years ago I received a letter from a lady called Jan Dines. She had first seen *An Age of Kings* when she about 14 years old, and it had clearly made a huge impression on her. Since then, she had followed the fortunes of the actors involved in it whom she insisted on addressing by the names of the main characters they had played. She addressed me as 'Dear Edmund,' for instance, and has done ever since, in deference to my performance as Edmund, Earl of March in *Henry VI,* one of the few named parts I played in the series. Having also played Wart in *Henry IV, Part 2* and the Second Murderer in *Richard III,* I was obviously quite content to be called Edmund. Anyway, Jan Dines had heard that the National Film Theatre was to present a special showing of *An Age of Kings,* and she was keen to promote a reunion of as many of the cast as possible to coincide with this event. I was amazed, in the first place, to learn that the series still existed on tape. After all, more or less forty years had gone by since it was first shown, and in black and white, so I was quite convinced that the BBC would long since have wiped it. I was disappointed too, that circumstances prevented me from being there. I was living in Scotland by then and, in any case, I was too busy at that particular time to make the trip. Sadly, there were others whose absence was due to a more permanent engagement. But it was, by all accounts, a happy occasion, and Jan followed it up by asking the BBC if they would be prepared to copy the series onto video tape and make it available to any members of the company who might wish to own it. The BBC obliged and, for a token fee, supplied those of us who expressed an interest, with all 15 episodes, now a possession treasured by at least one member of the permanent company for whom *An Age of Kings* remains to this day more than just a fond memory.

It's hardly surprising that the series, in technical terms, now looks as though it was actually recorded while the Wars of the Roses were being fought, and not entirely because of the absence of colour. God knows, there are any number of black and white movies that can still hold their own in the cinema. No, it's rather a lack of camera mobility that dates it, so that you get a lot of set pieces from which the camera has to stand back, or a variety of closer shots, and not a lot in between, certainly no sense that the camera is part of the action, but more like a spectator at a promenade performance. To a certain extent, this feeling of inertia is off-set by an ingenious composite set, designed by Stanley Morris, comprising corridors, ante-chambers, throne rooms, gardens, council chambers, or any combination of these, around which, and through which, the action is allowed to flow pretty well seamlessly. Much of the acting, however, does stand the test of time, with exemplary performances throughout the series from members of the company and guests alike. It's quite startling to watch, all these years later, actors who were so obviously responsible for setting standards which I now acknowledge as my own, particularly as I was unaware of their influence on me at the time. Edgar Wreford's dying words as John of Gaunt still sound as if they had never been spoken before or, indeed, since, and certainly never better. Geoffrey Bayldon, outstanding as the vacillating Duke of York in *Richard II* and as the incorruptible Lord Chief Justice in *Henry IV pt 2*, William Squire's hot-blooded Owen Glendower, as fiery now as ever it was, and his Justice Shallow as seedy and obsequious as I remembered it. In fact, the Gloucestershire scenes from *Henry IV, pt 2* are amongst the least affected by the passing of time, possibly because they are so gloriously timeless themselves. Frank Pettingell's Falstaff, too endearing by half perhaps, nevertheless truly inhabits these scenes, and those in the Boar's Head tavern, as comfortably as he inhabited the rehearsal room, where he always changed into his carpet slippers before going to work. Both on-screen and off, he was full of warmth and humour. The Baddeley sisters, Angela as Mistress Quickly, and Hermione as a deliciously over-the-hill (and over-the-top) Doll Tearsheet, are still great value, as are Gordon Gostelow as a perpetually inebriated Bardolph and George A. Cooper as a totally off-the-wall Pistol.

Cannily cast in his first Shakespearean role, and quite naturally 'thick of speech', a pre-Bondian Sean Connery remains as effective a Hotspur as I thought he was at the time, while the first of our two dames-to-be, Eileen Atkins, still chills with her portrayal of the possessed Joan La Pucelle whose demons appear, not existentially, but reflected in her eyes as the camera moves into a big fat close-up – a remarkable effect in those fairly low-tech days. Then, of course, there are the eponymous monarchs: Paul Daneman as Richard III, managing to emerge from Olivier's shadow (cast over anyone attempting the role at that time), creates an image that is more hedgehog than bottled spider, although none the less effective for that, and it remains a pretty impressive performance forty years on, as does Tom Fleming's Henry IV, whose fairly stolid and unimaginative Bolingbroke grows in complexity as the character gradually disintegrates, weighed down by guilt, by his son's apparent fecklessness, and by the threat of constant rebellion. Henry VI's artlessness is beautifully captured for the small screen by Terry Scully, and Robert Hardy's Henry V, more irritatingly mannered than I found it at the time, is still supreme in the wooing scene, aided and abetted as it is by another future Dame, Judi Dench who, even if hindsight plays some small part, gives a performance that marked her out for certain stardom even then. But it is David William's Richard II that weathers the ravages of time most successfully, and remains to this day a near perfect account of that sorry creature whose tragedy is that his downfall is not tragic, but merely pitiable. 'O! that I were as great as is my grief' is the nearest this Richard comes to any real self-knowledge; the rest is petulance and posturing, and an obdurate refusal to accept that the Divine Right, of which he makes so much, comes with responsibilities attached to it. It is a beautifully judged performance that even succeeds in investing Richard, especially in the later scenes, with a majesty and a dignity that overrides the fatal flaws in his character, engages our sympathy, and makes those who have engineered his well deserved overthrow appear brutish and self-seeking. If it had been Peter Dews' intention, and I'm sure it was, that Richard's cruel fate should cast a long shadow over the rest of the series, as it did in reality over the events of the 15th century, then David's performance well and truly rewarded that intention. There were other sterling performances, of course, too numerous to mention, that make *An Age of Kings* worth another visit, not only to bear witness to the recent sad decline in the quality of spoken Shakespeare, but for many infinitely rewarding moments; for the unflagging and contagious energy and enthusiasm of a director in his element, and for a bunch of actors who, pound for pound, were equal to anything Stratford or the Old Vic could have thrown together, and certainly amongst the best I've ever worked alongside. Peter Dews again: 'The results, in the United States and in the Commonwealth as in Britain, exceeded our wildest hopes. We found a new audience for Shakespeare. And on a more personal level, we all found a great new friendship. For a very happy year we were a very hard-working ensemble. Now we are a band of brothers.'

There was even an *Age of Kings* tie which we all wore with pride, save for one disaffected member of the company who, having been unceremoniously dumped following one run-in too many with our beloved director, offered up his for sale in the personal column of *The Daily Telegraph*!

And it wasn't all hard work, either. Friendships were forged, some of them lasting, and I have many happy memories of sitting in the sun outside the rehearsal room during that summer of 1960, enjoying occasional lunches at Bertorelli's on Shepherd's Bush Green, and exchanging gossip and confidences over coffee in the 'green-room' which adjoined the rehearsal room. Sex, of course, was a regular item on the agenda, during one such session, Anthony Valentine let it be known that he had once been seduced in a BBC dressing-room by an older lady, an actress well-known to us all for her prodigious experience in that particular arena, who had afterwards told him that, in two years, he would undoubtedly be the most sought-after lover in London. On being asked when this had happened, Tony replied that it must have been about two years ago. He went on to defend himself against a charge of undue *amour propre* by protesting that they were the lady's words, and certainly not his. There was no way of proving or disproving this, of course, although what it did prove was that Anthony Valentine would never need to employ the services of a publicity agent! Patrick Garland was another notable contributor at these forums. I had first come across Patrick, still an undergraduate at Oxford, when he played Private Bamforth in Peter's production of *The Disciplines of War* at the Edinburgh Festival two years earlier, a performance I'd greatly admired at the time. Patrick enjoyed telling stories, some of them about his life, and most of them at odds with his somewhat laid-back and deceptively camp way of telling them. There were several, for instance, that related to his brief spell as a cockle and whelk salesman on Southend sea-front, and even now the very idea of Patrick selling cockles and whelks anywhere, let alone in Southend-on-Sea, is so bizarre, I suspect he might well have invented it. On one occasion, about halfway through the series, he arrived for rehearsals one morning, fairly bursting with news. He had been to the cinema the previous evening, he told his breath-bated audience, taking with him a young lady of manifold charms whom he scarcely knew, but upon whom he had medium to long-term designs. His short-term ambitions were more modest, stretching as far as a goodnight kiss, maybe, and a future assignation, certainly no more than that. The fact that all his plans, short, medium and long-term, were realised immediately after the closing titles was not only a cause for rejoicing, but for sharing with his colleagues the secret of his success which, he believed without a shadow of a doubt, was the movie itself, Louis Malle's *Les Amants*. Well, we all knew that *Les Amants* had caused quite a stir and had encountered censorship problems at the time, and I for one found it easy to imagine that any film of an erotic nature starring Jeanne Moreau was bound to be worth seeing. What I hadn't considered was that it might possess magical, even miraculous, aphrodisiac properties that swept away all inhibitions, turned relative strangers into crazed fornicators, and rendered the age-old custom of wooing, redundant, and all in 88 minutes, which Patrick assured us was the case. He urged us, we being naturally sceptical, to try it out for ourselves if we didn't believe him. He even identified key moments in the film which, with the benefit of experience, he told us we would be well advised to take advantage of, for the purposes of breaking down what little resistance she might still be clinging on to; i.e. we should take her hand on such-and-such a line, put an arm around her shoulders during such-and-such a scene, etc. He could not, he insisted, be held responsible if we got the timing wrong. I have no idea how many of us took up the challenge. I'm not even a hundred per cent certain that I did myself, but never having been one to look a gift horse in the mouth, I more than likely did. I certainly went to see the film at about that time, although it could well have been with my mother for all I can remember of the occasion. What I do recall is that the the project was a dismal failure, and that Patrick's success was not replicated in one single case. The ladies concerned were, without exception, entirely unresponsive to the formula, some of them even anticipating those 'special' moments by moving further away. It was, in fact, a sad, sorry and thoroughly demoralised bunch of would-be Don Juans who met in a series of de-briefing sessions over the next week or so, and finally dismissing as unlikely the possibility that all of these ladies had known each other, had been advised of our intentions, and had voted unanimously to thwart our evil designs, we could only come to one conclusion: Patrick's companion had obviously been up for it anyway and needed no encouragement from Louis Malle nor anyone else for that matter, and would probably have leapt on him even if they'd been to see *The Nun's Story*. But Patrick would have none of it. We had failed where he had succeeded, and his smiling condescension over the following weeks was hard to bear. As George, Duke of Clarence, however, his sins finally caught up with him and, although I had to wait until Episode 14, I took considerable personal pleasure in helping to drown him in a butt of Malmsey!

Memories of those palmy days tumble over each other to get out, mostly in fragments, and far too many to record. Our accident-prone stuntman, Derek Ware, many of whose body parts were, at one time or another, bandaged or plastered as the result of bad falls or mistimed parries, rhapsodised frequently about the stunts performed by various film stars. Alan Ladd was his particular hero, and he was wont to go on at great length about the incredible feats performed by his idol in *Shane*, describing in even greater detail every punch and every tumble, as though he were recounting the labours of Hercules. Then he'd say, "Of course, it wasn't Alan Ladd who did them, it was a stuntman", his admiration for the star's athletic feats in no way diminished by this strange paradox.

Then, of course, there were the parties. With *An Age of Kings* being more or less simultaneously transmitted, we enjoyed a bit of celebrity for a while, and were honoured guests at all sorts of social events where we could count on being plied with drink, and surrounded by fans and admirers of the series. At one such gathering, although I have no idea now where or whose it was, I was button-holed by a rather intense young man, who was obviously a student of some kind. He was tall and gangling and severely acned. He would also have been extremely boring if he hadn't wanted to talk about me and my career for the entire evening. As it was, I was quite happy to bask in his undivided attention, modestly demurring when his flattery was in danger of getting out of hand, telling second-hand anecdotes as if they were my own, and generally patronising the poor bugger who was obviously suffering from an acute case of hero-worship. I suppose it must have been the prick of conscience that finally prompted me to ask what he was studying and where. When he told me he was a student at RADA, I was initially struck dumb, and then overwhelmed with compassion. How on earth did this unfortunate creature think he could become an actor? What parts could he possibly play? Who had practised such a cruel deception on him? Pity gave way to embarrassment in the end, but I think I made good my escape without making it too obvious, shaking his hand warmly and wishing him luck before grabbing my coat and leaving the party altogether, just in case we should happen to bump into each other again. Only five years later, he was widely acclaimed as the Hamlet of his generation at Stratford-upon-Avon. His name was David Warner. Clearly, my uncanny knack for picking a winner hadn't deserted me!

At some point, and it must have been relatively early on, late spring or early summer anyway, I left the parental home. I'd been thinking about it for quite a while, but I had neither the financial resources nor a good enough reason. Now I had both. The house in Kensal Rise had, for some time, been a convenient and congenial bolt-hole, somewhere to come home to on leave from the RAF and between jobs in the provinces. But I was now spending more time in Luna Street than I was in Purves Road, and with a longish spell of London-based work ahead of me, I decided the time had come to make the break complete. I don't think my parents put too many obstacles in my way, and with my newly teenage brother Peter in residence, they may well have been pleased to see the back of me. In any case, I had no intention of moving too far away; close enough in Notting Hill Gate to visit regularly and, very often with Dawn, to enjoy mum's wonderful Sunday roasts!

It was Michael Graham Cox, a fellow member of the permanent company, who suggested that I take a bed-sitting room in the house where he was living, a substantial early Victorian property in Palace Gardens Terrace. Strictly speaking, it was only a stone's throw from the Bayswater Road, but as it joined Church Street only a little further down, we were not above telling people we lived in Kensington. What made 39 Palace Gardens Terrace such a remarkable house was not entirely due to its tenants who, apart from the steady ebb and flow of actors, included the mysterious figure of young Prince Omer, who inhabited an eyrie on the top floor, and was reputedly the sole surviving member of the Ottoman dynasty. He kept himself to himself, adding to the mystery, but when we eventually met him he turned out to be disappointingly Anglicised and distinctly un-mysterious. It was, in fact, our landlady Evelyn Chetwynd, or rather, *Lady* Evelyn Chetwynd, who regularly offered us a glass of sherry in her first-floor apartment and kept us in thrall with tales of her exotic past. Approaching 70, Eve was clearly a bit of a fantasist, although there were obviously elements of truth in her stories, and we had great fun in the aftermath of one of her sessions, trying to sort the wheat from the chaff. That she was the widow of a British diplomat, Sir Stephen Chetwynd, stood up to close scrutiny, but that they had met in Cairo where she was appearing as a high-kicking Bluebell Girl tested the imagination, while her claim to have been known as 'The wickedest woman in Cairo' was, without doubt, a flight of fancy too far. She was nevertheless a delightful landlady, slightly dotty perhaps, but with an air of grandeur about her that lent credence to her having moved in diplomatic circles, and when she was in full flow, animated and flirtatious, you could well believe that 30 or 40 years earlier she had been a very lively and attractive young woman. When she died, not long after we had all moved on, Michael Graham Cox and I, together with another ex-tenant, Elric Hooper, met in the saloon bar of what had been our 'local' at the Notting Hill Gate end of Palace Gardens Terrace. Naturally, our conversation was all about Eve, and actors being actors we probably shared it with the rest of the customers. An elderly lady, appropriately attired and extremely dignified, came up to our table, apologised for the intrusion, and having ascertained that we were talking about Evelyn Chetwynd, said: "Oh, I've known Eve for many years. We were in Egypt together. She was the wickedest woman in Cairo, you know." As she departed, the epitome of genteel respectability, we were left to contemplate the very real possibility that perhaps she too had once been a Bluebell Girl!

Vivid though my memories are of that particular time, I didn't stay long in Palace Gardens Terrace. On my daily walk up to Notting Hill Gate tube station, I had become fascinated by the development of a new tower-block, situated almost on the corner of Pembridge Road. It was little more than a building site when I first took note of it, but day by day it took shape and grew until it became, by late summer, a very intriguing, if somewhat skeletal structure. Little balconies had begun to appear which, although on the east side of the building may have offered nothing more enticing than a view of Shepherd's Bush, on the west side probably afforded the most wonderful views of Kensington Gardens, Hyde Park and, from the very top of the building on a clear day, maybe even as far as Marble Arch. My interest, it has to be said, was motivated by little more than curiosity. After all, Notting Hill wasn't exactly famous for its sky-scrapers, and I wondered what kind of people would live in a place like that. It was a fairly safe bet that I would never be one of them. Then the phone rang. It was my old mate from the Belgrade Theatre, Clinton Greyn who, undeterred by any such considerations, asked me if I would like to go with him to view one of the few remaining flats in what was already known as Campden Hill Towers. It seemed like a pretty good way of satisfying my curiosity, so I went, and two months later Clinton and I moved into No. 43, situated on the fifth floor or, more accurately, the fifth and sixth floors as they were not so much flats as maisonettes. I have no idea how it happened, and I imagine that impetuosity must have played a significant part in it, particularly as the rent was a staggering £123.15 a quarter which, even when split down the middle, was a sweat-inducing commitment for two impecunious actors back in 1960. But obviously there were overriding factors. The upper floor, for instance, with two decent-sized bedrooms and a fairly spacious bathroom, made it seem like a house, and I'd never lived in a house before. Then there was the living-room downstairs, with a small screened-off dining area and a door leading out onto the west-facing balcony from which the view was just as extensive as I had imagined it. Being more practised in the culinary arts than I, the kitchen was very much Clinton's domain, and he appeared to be well satisfied with the facilities. I was simply overwhelmed, and especially by the existence of a Tweeny Food Waste Disposal unit, which was certainly the clincher as far as I was concerned, while the very act of leaving or returning home through the vast waste of deeply carpeted lobby, presided over by a uniformed concierge, was simply the icing on the cake!

As luck would have it, however, my tenancy had to be suspended, and with the paint scarce dry on the bedroom walls, I was forced to sub-let my half of the flat, to Clinton's very obvious displeasure, when I auditioned for, and was offered, a season with the Royal Shakespeare Company in Stratford-upon-Avon. I was, of course, reluctant to leave my new home, however temporarily, but the choice was not really mine to make. Having all too frequently been on the outside looking in, and having dreamed more often about being a member of that particular company than any other in the whole wide world, it would have taken more than four walls and a roof, however 'des' the 'res', to stand in the way of a dream come true.

oOoOo

Nine

It's tempting to say that the dream became a nightmare from day one, which obviously wasn't true. But looking back across all the chequered years: the highs, the lows, the agonies, the ecstasies, and everything in between, that's probably the way I would sum up my season with the Royal Shakespeare Company were I pressed on the subject. There must have been pleasurable moments, of course, and rewarding moments too, even if I am at a loss to bring just one of them instantly to mind. Never having kept a diary, I cannot turn the pages and read entries such as 'What a laugh we had in rehearsals today!' or 'Peter Hall was inspirational this morning!' But even if I had such an *aide memoire* and were to read therein two such entries, it would only serve to cast doubt on my sanity, either then or now. No, it is only by digging deep into the hidden recesses of my mind that I might be able to uncover the odd nugget or two and, give or take the occasional flourish provided by hindsight, that is what writing a memoir is all about, isn't it?

Having conceded then, that day one, a cold February day in 1961, was probably warmed by happy expectations and by that familiar tingle of excitement that I always felt on arriving in Stratford-upon-Avon, when did things begin to go wrong? Was it when Michael Langham, directing *Much Ado About Nothing*, the first play of the season, fell backwards off his chair in rehearsals having suffered a heart-attack, leaving Peter Hall to take over the production? Or was it when Peter Wood, with everything to live for, took on the mantle of suicide bomber and destroyed his own production of *Hamlet* together with everyone in it? Or could it have been the arrival of William Gaskill who, fresh from contemporary theatre's Mecca in Sloane Square and barely on nodding terms with the works of Shakespeare, decided to give the text of *Richard III* a very wide berth for as long as possible, or was it Peter Hall himself for ... ? But I don't want to give away too much of the plot. Besides, the die must have been well and truly cast long before Mr. Hall got his hands on *Romeo and Juliet*.

Before opening all these cans of worms, however, I had better set the scene from a personal perspective. In the autumn of 1960, the closing titles having rolled for the last time on *An Age of Kings,* I paid a brief visit to the Marlowe Theatre, Canterbury, to play a couple of nice character parts in Molière's *Le Malade Imaginaire.* For some extraordinary reason, a fellow actor from the series, Leon Shepperdson, and I decided to do a joint audition – the tent scene from *Julius Caesar,* as I recall. Whether we had given any thought to the distinct possibility that only one of us might be offered a job, or considered how the other one would deal with that, is not on record. Fortunately, we were both employed, and it was lovely to get back on stage again after so many months in front of a camera. It was also very nice to get back in front of a camera again, and in something that wasn't Shakespeare, when I was asked to appear in an episode of *Probation Officer,* a very successful television crime series back in those days, starring an actor called John Paul. I was to play the part of Johnny Cazzo, described as 'The most vicious bloke in the Harrow Road.' This was something of a challenge, particularly as I had spent much of my young life trailing up and down the Harrow Road, with and without my mother, and had never come across anything more vicious than the waitresses in Lyons' Tea Rooms, nor even lurking in the murky purlieus of the Ha'penny Bridge!

I also enjoyed the company of Brian Murray, who was playing a fellow-delinquent. Brian, it turned out, had also been offered a season with the Royal Shakespeare Company, and so we decided, as incurably optimistic actors will, even on first acquaintance, to look for accommodation together in Stratford. This turned out to be in the High Street, a top-floor flat in the 15th century home of Denne Gilkes, fondly remembered alibi for my illicit trips to Stratford when I was in the RAF. Denne was, by this time, on the verge of retirement and had been somewhat sidelined as voice teacher for the company in favour of Iris Warren, commemorated in my mental scrap-book as the woman who added a new and deeper register to Geraldine McEwan's voice which made her sound, on occasion, and sometimes inappropriately, like Joan Greenwood. Beatrice's injunction to 'Kill Claudio' from *Much Ado About Nothing* is a difficult enough line at the best of times, and the odd thing is that I don't think Geraldine ever quite understood why it was getting even more laughs than usual. I continued to take my lessons from Denne, and not only out of loyalty or because she lived downstairs, but because Iris Warren's diary was kept pretty full, her clientèle coming largely from the upper echelons of the company. Not that I had anything against the billing system that operated in Stratford at the time. It is, after all, part of our theatrical tradition and, were I a star, I would be the first to insist on my name being higher up and bigger than anyone else's on the poster. It is only with the manifestation of such a system within a company that I take issue, and particularly when Top Billing, Middle Billing and Bottom Billing become barely disguised euphemisms for First Class, Economy and Steerage. I was firmly rooted in Economy, my line of parts being neither substantial enough nor of such inconsequence as to qualify for either of the two extremes. However, my relationship with flat-mate Brian Murray who, with Horatio, Richmond and Benvolio in his contract, was obviously a First-Class ticket holder, did afford me an occasional entrée into the *beau monde*. I particularly remember one party, probably because it was the only one I was ever invited to, at which Christopher Plummer, newly arrived from Canada and feeling, no doubt, a little insecure, and justifiably bewildered, not to say somewhat pissed at the time, began hurling bread rolls around the room, all the while shouting, "I come all the way *(hurl)* from Stratford-On-fucking-tario *(hurl)* to Stratford-on-fucking-Avon *(hurl)* to work with a bunch of *(hurl)* fucking amateurs!" But that didn't happen on day one either.

In fact, day one was full of promise. *Much Ado About Nothing* was in the more than capable hands of Michael Langham, a protégé of Guthrie's and his successor as artistic director at Stratford Ontario. Even at the read-through, Christopher Plummer's Benedick promised to be witty, urbane and decidedly charismatic, exuding confidence, and clearly happy to be working with a familiar director from back home. Moreover, he was surrounded by a pretty strong company, with Geraldine McEwan as Beatrice, Ian Richardson as Don John and Noël Willman as Don Pedro, the baser comedy being entrusted to the hugely experienced Newton Blick as Dogberry and to Clifford Rose as Verges. I was entrusted with 2nd Watch, not a part on which the success or failure of the production was going to hinge exactly, but alongside Bill Wallis as 1st Watch, it was fun to do, and with fun being at something of a premium that season, I found myself, as the weeks turned into months, treasuring the two performances a week of *Much Ado About Nothing*. I also understudied Barry Warren, sadly remembered less for the quality of his performance as Claudio than for the night when, on witnessing what he thought was Hero *in flagrante delicto* on the balcony, he expelled his dentures onto the stage.

Within a week, and in tandem with *Much Ado,* we started rehearsals for the second production of the season, *Hamlet,* directed by Peter Wood. Immediately prior to the read-through, he talked about the play and his own vision of it at great length and with such enthusiasm and intellectual clarity that I was thoroughly convinced – and I was not alone in being convinced – that we were to be a part, however small, of something quite momentous, and even of possibly lasting significance. The vital ingredient was, of course, as it always has been, the casting of the title role, and during the early days of rehearsal, Ian Bannen promised to be every bit as electrifying as Peter Wood, in his opening talk, had clearly foreseen. Here was a man, close to madness from the start, whose dilemma was rather to grasp and hold on to what was left of his sanity than to camouflage himself with an 'antic disposition'. Being in this Hamlet's company was decidedly unsafe and, although we were later to discover that being on stage with Ian Bannen was unsafe no matter what he was playing, it was as thrilling as a roller-coaster ride at the time and, as far as I was concerned, made Hamlet's prevarication more psychologically understandable than in any other performance I'd seen before or, indeed, have ever seen since.

Idle pursuits were also high on the agenda in those early days, and along with what promised to be an extremely sociable bunch of people, I was well and truly involved in the chase. *The Dirty Duck* was, of course, as it has been for countless seasons, a favourite meeting place in the evenings, and from where a small and select group would often retire to somebody's lodgings, usually mine, where we would while away the rest of the evening casting aspersions on anyone who wasn't there, playing word games, drinking coffee and making contact with 'those on the other side,' a very fashionable indulgence at the time. Not surprisingly, and despite being a dedicated sceptic, I soon imposed a ban on seances since, having bid them all goodnight, I was the one who was left alone in the wee small hours of the morning in the attic of a 15th century house in the middle of Broomstick County!

Very much at the centre of our little group and, indeed, at the centre of many little groups that sprung up in the course of that season, was a young woman called Georgina Ward, daughter of Viscount Ward of somewhere or other and consequently the *Honourable* Georgina Ward, an extremely attractive, gutsy, raven-haired and fun-loving girl, who had most of the young men in the company, myself included, at her feet from day one. I myself fell victim to her charms when, only ten days or so into the season, she threw a surprise party to celebrate my 23rd birthday at the storybook cottage she rented some distance away in Long Compton, and at which she presented me with an expensive Ronson cigarette lighter. Her generosity, of which this was but one example, sprang, I believe, not only from a genuine warmth, but also from an upper-class compulsion to demonstrate largesse. A dozen years later, our paths having diverged rather dramatically during the Stratford season, we met again in a working situation at the Hampstead Theatre Club and immediately became the best of friends again. It was as though not only the intervening years, but the circumstances surrounding our eventual estrangement at Stratford had never happened. We chose each other's company pretty well exclusively, both inside the Hampstead Theatre Club and out of it, enjoying an intimacy that was well-nigh unique in my experience as it had nothing whatsoever to do with sex. Well, maybe that's not entirely true, but whatever part it may have played remained well and truly locked inside my head, as I had no intention of putting our rediscovered friendship at risk by attempting to change the boundaries. When our season at Hampstead came to an end, Georgina flew off somewhere for several weeks, leaving her very chic bright red Alpha-Romeo sports car for me to drive around in during her absence, a typical Georgina flourish. We lost touch with each other eventually, and the last I heard, many years ago now, was that she had given up acting (at which, it has to be said, she was no great shakes) and had gone to Spain to become a matador which, strangely enough, didn't at all surprise me.

Back in Stratford, I'd had to share Georgina's attention with several other young men, equally in thrall to her undeniable magnetism. But that wasn't the reason, or the main reason, for my self-imposed exile from her presence. In the wake of some pretty bad reviews early on in the season, and in the absence of a unifying figurehead, morale took a nose-dive, and the company was already beginning to fragment. But the crunch, as far as my relationship with Georgina was concerned, undoubtedly came when, having run over and killed a man who was painting lines down the middle of the road, she suddenly became the focus of so much sympathy, understanding and support from her little band of courtiers that she might well have been mistaken by an outsider for the victim rather than the perpetrator of that terrible accident. I am not, of course, suggesting that she herself did not suffer remorse and a dozen other traumatic after-effects including, not unnaturally, fear of the legal consequences from which, it has to be said, she emerged unaccountably unscathed. But I withdrew at that point, somehow repelled, although not by her so much as by the kind of slavish loyalty she inspired in others. It was a great pity, and all the more so as the rift was bound to widen during that interminable season. The Royal Shakespeare Company of 1961 was not known, nor will it be remembered by those who took part in it, as a place of reconciliation.

The first hammer-blow fell during the latter stages of rehearsals for *Hamlet*. The company had somehow managed to survive Michael Langham's sudden indisposition, and *Much Ado* appeared to be back on track again, in spite of Peter Hall's determination to redirect it in his own autocratic way with a little over a week to go before opening. Nevertheless, it was obviously going to be all right and, given that *Hamlet* was clearly ear-marked for distinction, the mood of the company was fairly buoyant. On a personal level, I was thoroughly enjoying my principal role as the Player Queen, opposite Tony Church, and with Russell Hunter as Gonzago. It was not my first, nor would it be my last, venture into the questionable world of cross-dressing, although in this particular case the character was at least called upon to appear as a boy first. We were, in fact, rehearsing the scene following the first exit of the Players, leaving Hamlet alone to deliver his 'Oh, what a rogue and peasant slave am I' speech, and we were, as usual, mesmerised by Ian Bannen's intensity, and again transfixed as he delved into the costume skip left behind by the Players in a desperate attempt to assimilate the passion artificially summoned up by the Player King in his account of Priam's death as witnessed by his wife, the 'mobled queen'. 'What's Hecuba to him or he to Hecuba that he would weep for her? What would he do had he the motive and the cue for passion that I have?' At this point, Hamlet's torment was interrupted by Peter Wood, who then proceeded to take Ian apart and, in front of the entire company, described his performance as having, "the consistency of a bowl of cold porridge". That this was patently untrue was evident. That he should choose to humiliate his leading actor in such a public way was outrageous. Peter Wood was many things. He was undoubtedly brilliant, both intellectually and theatrically. He could also be charming, witty and entertaining. That he was capable of being arrogant, acid-tongued and casually spiteful was par for the course with many overweening theatre directors, but that he may have been stupid didn't even warrant serious consideration. Why, then, did he deliberately set out to undermine the fragile confidence of an actor upon whose shoulders rested the success or failure of the entire production? An actor, moreover, with whom he had previously worked, notably in his highly praised production of Eugene O'Neil's *The Iceman Cometh* only a couple of years earlier? Surely he must have known, as we all did on a much briefer acquaintance, that Ian's stability was akin to that of a tightrope walker, precarious in the extreme, and thrillingly so, but deeply personal, and in need of very careful handling. Nor was the safety net of technique available to him in the event that he should fall, the ever-present danger of this being one of the things that had made him so breathtakingly watchable during rehearsals. That he didn't fall in the end but was pushed, and pushed deliberately by a man who must have known better than any of us what he was risking, was one of the two reasons that, at that very moment, an entire company was struck dumb. The other reason being the indisputable fact that he was wrong. But, actors being actors, and directors being employers, we uttered not a word of protest, nor did we rush to Ian's support with assurances that the man in whom he had placed his absolute trust was talking a load of shit. No, we just sat there and watched him fall apart in front of our very eyes.

Hamlet opened to poor reviews, the casting of Ian Bannen in the central role being held largely to blame for the production's failure to rise to the occasion. Ian failed to turn up for the next performance and was not seen anywhere near the theatre for the following four or five weeks; he simply vanished, leaving his understudy, a woefully o'er parted and under-rehearsed Barry Warren, to face the music. This disappearing act did not exactly endear him to the company, already shell-shocked in the wake of such a pounding by the press. But 'soldiering on' was not something Ian Bannen was equipped to do, not psychologically, and certainly not technically. For the record, he did eventually return from his retreat, which rumour held to have been in a monastery, and took up the reins again as Hamlet, displaying occasional flashes of the old brilliance but, for the most part, giving a performance that had all the consistency of – well, cold porridge, really! The fact that Ian could not tell the difference between these two extremes, and that he was fundamentally incapable of recognising and reproducing something of value, was a handicap to say the least, and one that I became more and more aware of as the season went on. Watching from the wings during a performance of *Romeo and Juliet* several months later, I was treated to a moment of stunning brilliance as Ian, a perfectly good Mercutio in any event, took hold of the Queen Mab speech and made it his own for the very first time. It suddenly became a very personal vision imbued with the same sense of danger and knife-edge insanity that we had glimpsed in those earlier *Hamlet* rehearsals. When he came off the stage, I told him I thought it had been wonderful, and he said, "Was it, heart? Why, what did I do?" And he was being serious too, which was a great pity, because it meant that, except by accident, chances were we'd probably never see anything like it again.

It's a challenging dichotomy in a profession that can be, and very often is, extremely cruel, necessitating a thicker than average skin as well as an impenetrable self-belief, that a deep-seated vulnerability is also, and quintessentially, part of an actor's make-up. The problem is getting the balance right, and not only, or even principally, to achieve success, but to ensure survival. Ian Bannen's failure to get it right, while far from being unique, was monumental. In one of the few private moments that we shared during the season he talked about his dread of having to return to 'The sweetie factory' where he had obviously once been obliged to work. And it wasn't an exercise in Scottish whimsy, or a patronising reminder from on high of his humble origins, but a very genuine fear, and an imminent one at that. Of course, it's hardly surprising that a degree of uncertainty plays its part with any young actor worth his salt when contemplating a season of major roles with the Royal Shakespeare Company, but what was incomprehensible to me at the time was that Ian appeared to be as tormented by success as most actors are by the absence of it.

My own personal memories of *Hamlet* in performance, having eventually come to terms with its failure to live up to expectations, were by no means unhappy. The Players inhabit their own world in any case, and apart from their patron's tendency to keep sticking his oar in, Elsinore is just another gig as far as they are concerned, so as one of them you're bound to feel a bit semi-detached from all the heavy stuff going on around you. Besides, I enjoyed swanning around in drag if only because it enabled me to stand out from the crowd for a few hours every week. In between times I was twinned with Paul Bailey as a household servant. Dressed identically in Elizabethan lovat, we shifted furniture, ushered people into their seats on formal occasions and generally tidied up the mess left by Claudius and his step-son. In an inspired moment, Paul christened us 'Elsie and Doris Nore'. Sharing a dressing-room with Paul, along with Sebastian Breaks and Ronald Scott-Dodd, was a joy, notably on account of the laughter that filled it much of the time, a rare commodity elsewhere in the theatre during that season. The tone, having been set by Paul, was unremittingly camp, and occasionally quite cruel, only redeemed by Paul's essential humanity. Narissa Knights was a sweetly pretty girl in the company, fatally flawed in Paul's book by an intense approach to acting that was earnest in the extreme and for which crime she became known as Dame Freda Best. So apt was this sobriquet that it stuck and, to give Narissa her due, not only did she accept it without complaint, but in time she actually answered to it! The boys in the dressing-room next door to us were not nearly so forgiving. Being uniformly 'butch' and somewhat dour, they were incensed by the shrieks of laughter that came through the wall, probably assuming (and with some justification) that they were the object of such mirth. It was widely known and accepted, thanks to Paul's networking skills, that whereas their dressing-room was characterised by the smell of sweaty jockstraps, ours was permeated by nothing more offensive than the seductive and vaguely exotic aroma of Mitsukiku, Paul's chosen fragrance at that time, which became so popular with the rest of us that it was soon wafting its way along the corridors of Elsinore, another example, along with an addiction to Rhenish wine, of Denmark's growing decadence!

All this was pretty silly, of course, and at this distance even sillier, but at the time it provided a needful antidote to the doom-laden atmosphere of that relentlessly oppressive season. Without Paul's companionship, which blossomed into a long-lasting friendship, my memories of that year would be almost undeviatingly grey. Certainly, little relief was to be found at home where domestic bliss had long since given way to an irksome and persistent battle of the wills between Brian Murray who, surprisingly, turned out to have homosexual leanings, and myself who – possibly just as surprisingly – had none. This wouldn't have bothered me had he not chosen to lean in my direction, and it wouldn't have continued to bother me had he been able to take no for an answer. But the almost nightly confrontations began to take their toll on our friendship and, while he remained as nice as ever he was, his overtures never less than courteous, I found myself dreading the inevitable encounter and contriving to stay out as late as possible every night in the hope that he would have retired to his bed by the time I got home. It was not, in short, a situation that could go on for ever. Meanwhile, and with no little degree of apprehension, we embarked on rehearsals for *Richard III*, at this stage minus a Duke of Buckingham, due to Ian Bannen's protracted absence which, in the end, and for reasons about to unfold, turned out to be to be entirely fortuitous.

In 1961, no director was more qualified and better equipped to stage *Richard III* at Stratford-upon-Avon than was Peter Dews, and following his landmark production of *An Age of Kings* on BBC Television the previous year, he was undoubtedly the obvious choice, which is probably why they offered it to William Gaskill, a protégé of George Devine's English Stage Company at the Royal Court Theatre, and a stranger to Shakespeare. There was no general rush to judgement, however, and even after his stumbling introductory talk, the company remained firmly on his side. We were, after all, in dire need of a success, and most of us had had our fill of smooth-talking intellectuals and their empty promises. In any case, there was something vaguely appealing about a director who was obviously and visibly nervous. It made him appear almost human. For a start, he was clearly over-awed by the presence of Dame Edith Evans, insanely cast as Queen Margaret ("I simply cannot go on stage and hate solidly for 15 minutes!"), and he couldn't refrain from deferring to her at every opportunity. "I'm sorry, Dame Edith, did you say something?" "No, dear boy, I was just talking to my handbag." And he won us over completely with his closing remark: "Finally I'd like to say, Dame Edith, how delighted I am to have this opportunity of working with you at least once before you – before I die." Such was the quality of Bill Gaskill's production of *Richard III* that nothing about it was as memorable as that glorious *faux pas*.

What I do remember, and with crystalline clarity, was his determination to avoid any contact with the text for as long as possible. Following the read-through, which was probably forced upon him in any case, he threw himself (and us) with missionary zeal into two solid weeks of improvisation. He was, after all, in the vanguard of the post-modernist movement, or the Theatre of Portentous Pauses, in which a monosyllabic reply to an equally monosyllabic question masks layers of unspoken meaning and innuendo, only uncovered, and not necessarily even then, by an investigation into the mind and the motivation of the character who says 'Right' when, in other circumstances, or having enjoyed a happier childhood, he might well have said 'Left'. This is fertile ground for improvisation, as are pregnant pauses, but Shakespeare does not lend himself easily to this kind of approach. I mean, when a character says 'I am determined to prove a villain/And hate the idle pleasures of these days,' then that is precisely what he means, and the reasons behind it are perfectly clear because he has spent the previous 29 lines explaining them. There are ambiguities, of course, and a very great deal that is open to interpretation, which is why Shakespeare continues to intrigue and challenge us more than 400 years down the line, but they can only be illuminated by an investigation of the text, and while improvisation is without doubt a useful tool in many dramatic contexts, I believe that it is as futile to impose it on plays in which the author's meaning is perfectly clear, as it is in plays where it remains enigmatic because that's what the author intends it to be. It can be a dangerous exercise too, as many an actor has found to his cost when trying to come to post-Freudian terms with the poisonous character of Iago in *Othello*, whose last lines are:

'Demand me nothing: what you know, you know:
From this time forth I never will speak word.'

In other words, leave well alone. As an actor, you may well be able to justify Iago's machinations for yourself by referring them to the psychiatrist's couch, or attributing them to a homosexual obsession, but as sure as eggs are eggs, by bringing these discoveries to bear on your performance, you'll only succeed in diluting the impact of the character and diminishing his effect on the play. If Shakespeare had intended him to be driven by unrequited love or some psychotic disorder, he would have told us so.

Sadly, Mr. Gaskill didn't ask me for my thoughts on this subject. In any case, I don't think I held any strong opinions on it at the time. Besides, we were enjoying ourselves. At least, we were for the first few days. At the beginning of the second week, however, when it became clear that our director had nothing planned for us but more of the same, doubts began to spring up, privately at first, followed by whispered conversations in the Green Room. Our main concern was for Christopher Plummer, saddled as he was with the title role, and who, as the days went by, appeared to be showing symptoms of a relapse into his earlier condition. The relative success of *Much Ado,* due in no small measure to his delightfully witty and urbane performance as Benedick, had done much to acclimatise him, and it was with an easy assurance that he approached the part of Richard, even allowing for the empty space at his side that should have been filled by the Duke of Buckingham. But, already well into the second week of rehearsals, the cracks were beginning to reappear, the old uncertainties rising to the surface again, his temper becoming more brittle with each passing day and the entirely justifiable choice of open rebellion thwarted by his own self-doubt. At the start of week three, and with no indication from the director that we should maybe bring our scripts to rehearsal next time, a sense of desperation, tinged with hysteria, began to filter through the rank and file as a now almost robotic leading man continued to jump through the director's hoop, demonstrating his achievement to date, best illustrated by a brief extract from the wooing scene, taken from the Sloane Square Folio version of the play:

Richard: Lady Anne, you're a very attractive woman.

Anne: I'm not listening to you.

Richard: I want to fuck you, Lady Anne.

Anne: Oh, you terrible man!

What we sorely needed there and then, if ever this production was going to open, was a miracle or, better still, a new director or, even better than that, an actor of considerable stature, well respected, quietly authoritative, astute enough to recognise the problem, and brave enough to take control of the situation. Moreover we needed him to walk through the door at that precise moment which, most improbably, is exactly what happened when Eric Porter made his entrance, having been seconded from the RSC's London base at the Aldwych Theatre to take over the part of Buckingham. "Enough of all this," he said, or words to that effect, "let's start working from the text." And so it came to pass that two weeks later *Richard III* opened, a pretty drab production to be sure, but respectable enough, and respectfully received.

I have wondered from time to time whether Christopher Plummer ever fully appreciated the debt he owed to Eric Porter, whose timely intervention not only saved the day as far as the production was concerned, but enabled him to assume his rightful place at the centre of it, a story that uncannily reflected their on-stage relationship. Never before, surely, has a Richard owed more to his cousin of Buckingham than this one did. The fact that Eric didn't lose his head at Salisbury, but went on to play opposite Chris in Anhouilh's *Becket* at the Aldwych later in the year, suggests a degree of trust and a mutual regard at the very least.

Looking back on *Richard III* in performance, my memories are almost exclusively light-hearted, an understandable reaction to the gloom that descended on us whenever we were required to perform it. On stage, I had nothing more demanding to focus my attention on than the Scrivener, a part that is excised more often than not, who tells us what we already know, and only exists to give Richard a breather. Otherwise, along with my fellow-travellers in Economy Class, I was either cloaked and hooded, dressed raggedly, or armed with pike. The secret, of course, with roles such as these, is to achieve absolute anonymity, easy enough when shrouded in monks' habit while accompanying the coffin of Henry VI, and providing an ideal opportunity to enjoy the odd private joke, count the house, and observe Chris Plummer making considerably more progress with the delicious Jill Dixon by using Shakespeare's words rather than his own. As citizens of London, forming the crowd that is asked to give its approval to Richard's claim to the throne, we were anonymous in any case, having been mystifyingly placed out of sight under the stage, probably because we didn't amount to much of a crowd anyway. Our only representative at stage level was the Mayor who, along with the Duke of Buckingham, had to shout down to us through this big hole in the ground, giving the impression that all Londoners were subterranean creatures, heard but never seen. It was an irksome task, interrupting much more important activities, such as a second cup of coffee or another hand of bridge in the Green Room. Having had our earnest entreaties to be replaced by a tape recording turned down, we decided to take matters into our own hands, devising a roster which allowed for each of us in turn to take a night off. For a while, this system worked very well, the rest of us being charged to make up in volume what we lacked in physical presence. And oh, what a treat it was when your turn for a night off came around! Unfortunately, stage management eventually got wind of it, and sent one of their number up to the Dress Circle where, by standing just inside the door, a head count could be made of the citizens down the hole. To be spied upon in this way gave rise to a feeling of outrage amongst us, and we set about devising ways to circumvent their underhand behaviour including, at one point, making a dummy which, Colditz-like, would be hidden somewhere under the stage, and retrieved as we passed on our way to the hole. Matters came to a head, however, when Ronnie Scott-Dodd, seized by a fit of righteous indignation, having spotted the tell-tale shape of an assistant stage manager, stomped through the pass-door, fully costumed, into the front-of-house area, climbed the stairs to the Dress Circle, opened the door and whispered into the ASM's ear: "You're wasting your time, you know. We're all there!"

Eric Porter was, of course, everybody's darling, not only for breathing life into a dying show, but for his general demeanour during its run. Not having been engaged for the entire season like most of the rest of us, however, he only popped up from London once or twice a week and was blessedly ignorant of the in-fighting, the factionalism, and the low morale of the company. It was, in fact, only when Eric was around that it felt like a company at all. He was consistently cheerful, friendly and sociable, superbly authoritative on stage and completely free from pretension off it. His attitude towards acting appeared to be so relaxed that, performance after performance, he would sit on in the Green Room in order to complete a hand of bridge long after his call had been announced over the tannoy. I recall many times sitting at another table, open-mouthed, as he made no attempt to move from his seat, and wondering just how long he would leave it this time, toying with the idea of giving him a nudge, just in case he hadn't heard it. But he always made it in the nick of time, and I still cherish the memory of him running into the wings, the skirts of his medieval gown held high, and lisping, "Excuse me, girls!" to anyone standing in his way, before dropping his skirts, crossing an invisible line onto the stage, and saying, in a suddenly rich and deeply resonant voice, "Will not King Richard let me speak with him?" I also fondly remember the occasional lift he gave me to London in his car following a Saturday evening performance, not only because it gave me the chance to visit my barely lived-in flat and to see Dawn for a few brief hours, but because the journey itself was always entertaining and informative. Strangely, I can recall nothing of what was said on those occasions, except that he told me once I would never really make it as an actor until I had acquired two deeply furrowed lines running down my face on either side of my nose. It goes without saying, of course, that Eric boasted the definitive pair himself and, even if he wasn't being entirely serious, it was a theory that certainly held true in his case.

The arrival of Vanessa Redgrave in Stratford carried with it a personal significance that I couldn't possibly have dreamed of at the time, let alone predicted. What I knew for a fact was that it heralded the start of rehearsals for *As You Like It,* the fourth play of the season, which also happened to be my play out, promising days of leisure and nothing to do with them, except to organise a cricket team which I then led to six consecutive defeats during that summer, one of my more notable achievements with the RSC! For those unfamiliar with Stratford-upon-Avon, I should point out that in those days, and probably even now, it was a very difficult place to get to and, without transport of your own, virtually impossible to get out of, and particularly late at night. So, apart from cadging the odd lift to London from Eric Porter and, just occasionally, from Peter McEnery in his flashy, open-topped Sunbeam Alpine, I was pretty-well stuck there. Gone were the days of my visits to the Shakespeare Memorial Theatre under Glen Byam-Shaw when I saw it as a haven, cut off from the world, yes, but populated almost entirely by kindred spirits. Great heavens, that was why I'd auditioned for the company in the first place! Under new management, however, it had become oppressively claustrophobic, Prospero's island bequeathed to a smiling Caliban, and getting away from it had become a major imperative. That's why I purchased a second-hand Lambretta from goodness knows where, but it must have been a bargain because I was only being paid £17.10s a week. Ronnie Scott-Dodd, who had a superficial acquaintance with these machines, gave me a few preliminary lessons, but a journey on my own beyond the Clopton Bridge remained out of my reach for quite some time.

Meanwhile, at one of those parties thrown up at Avoncliff, the home of Peter Hall and his wife, Leslie Caron, a well-known film star of French origins, who cared even less about the lower echelons of the company than her husband did, making sure that her guests were restricted to those who enjoyed top-billing. Anyway word got out, as rumours will, that they'd played party games such as 'postman's knock' and 'hide and seek,' and that Brian Murray had come across Vanessa Redgrave in a cupboard or somewhere and, being the only man in the company tall enough to reach up to her mouth, he'd kissed her and they'd ended up getting engaged.

I could probably have come nearer to the truth had I asked Brian himself but, in all honesty, I didn't really want to know, and I certainly didn't want to risk any emotional outpourings, intimate revelations or, worse still, vehement denials. In any case, the evidence spoke for itself, as Brian and Vanessa were scarcely out of each others company from that moment on, both at rehearsals and into the wee small hours. I don't imagine for a moment that my peace of mind contributed in any way to their euphoria, but they had made a young man very happy all the same. I could go home at night in the certain knowledge that, even if Brian returned from an assignation before I had gone to bed, his mood would be buoyant, and his company entirely congenial. So naturally I wished them joy, and a long life together – always provided that he was still alive at the end of the season, which was by no means guaranteed. For some little time, in performances of *Richard III,* he had been on the receiving end of increasingly vicious attacks from Chris Plummer at the Battle of Bosworth where Brian, not by any stretch of the imagination type-cast in the heroic mould as Richmond, cowered against the proscenium arch while Chris, still a man of uncertain temper, rained blows upon him with his broadsword, threatening not only decapitation, but the course of English history!

But back to the climax of the story which came about some weeks later, well after *As You Like It* had opened. No longer required for rehearsals, Vanessa started commuting from London, phoning nightly when she wasn't in Stratford. Its clarion call would send Brian scampering down the stairs, from where he would bound up again half an hour or so later, wreathed in smiles, a perfect advertisement for some life-enhancing elixir, ebullient to the point of ecstasy. The trouble with Brian was that he had to demonstrate all his moods, and I was never quite sure whether I was expected to join in, give sympathetic ear to his story, or ignore him. One way and another, I had discovered that living under the same roof as Brian Murray was a wearing and wearying experience. The last straw landed on my back one night a couple of weeks later when I heard, to my utter dismay, the sound of Brian's heavy footfall on the stairs as he returned from the telephone. In fact, such was the heaviness of his footfall that, rather than being a personal expression of his sorrow, it was clearly meant to convey it to an audience, and since I was the only audience in the vicinity, I realised that some kind of response would be expected. I imagined him framed in the doorway, looking woebegone, and saying, "It's all over. I don't want to talk about it. If you don't mind, Terry, I think I'll just go to bed." Wishful thinking on my part, of course. But even in my wildest imaginings, I could not have foreseen the drama that actually unfolded before my eyes, desperately averted as I tried, not entirely successfully, to carry on reading my book. Not a word did he say as he came into the room. He simply walked over to my record-player, selected one of my LPs, *Love is a Now and Then Thing,* its cover depicting a lovelorn Anthony Newley standing by an upturned dustbin, and placed the needle onto a track entitled *I Get Along Without You Very Well.* He then proceeded, without any reference to me, nor even acknowledging my presence, to go into a dance routine, reflecting the bitter-sweet mood of the song, using the 15th century beams to swing himself from one end of the room to the other, clumsily pirouetting as he changed direction in a grotesque parody of Gene Kelly in something or other. Then, as the lyrics wound down to their inevitably doleful conclusion ...

'I get along without you very well, of course I do,
Except perhaps in Spring;
But I should never think of Spring,
For that would surely break my heart in two.'

... he slowly crumpled onto the floor, where he lay for some considerable time, wracked with sobs, as I closed my book, went into my bedroom, packed my suitcase and, early the following morning, took advantage of a long-standing offer from Ronnie Scott-Dodd to share his tiny cottage on the Banbury Road. It transpired that, whilst in London, Vanessa had met the celebrated director, Tony Richardson, who was a good deal taller than Brian Murray.

As You Like It was a huge success. In fact, it threatened to become the highlight of the season, which I sincerely hoped had nothing to do with the fact that I wasn't in it. But it was a delightful production, directed by Michael Elliott, alongside whom I had appeared in *Edward II* at the Edinburgh Festival seven years earlier when he was but an Oxford undergraduate. Max Adrian, who had just joined the company, was a deliciously lugubrious Jacques, and even Ian Bannen appeared to be at ease as a charming, if slightly wayward, Orlando. But it was Vanessa Redgrave's performance that shone out most brightly, her Rosalind the sum and substance of all those qualities in women that make men like me go weak at the knees. She was courageous, resolute, playful, wise, vulnerable and oh, so romantic. When, following Orlando's exit in Act IV, scene I, Rosalind says to Celia, 'O coz, coz, coz, my pretty little coz, that thou didst know how many fathom deep I am in love,' Vanessa invested it with such a depth of feeling and such a compendium of mixed emotions that it remains to this day one of the most sublime moments I have ever witnessed on stage.

A short time later, during a break from rehearsals of *Romeo and Juliet*, I found myself sitting at a table in the Green Room with a few other people, including Dame Edith Evans, while a matinée performance of *As You Like It* was taking place to which we were half listening over the tannoy system. At one point, possibly even the moment described above, Dame Edith, herself a notable Rosalind back in the 1920s, said, "Romance isn't what it used to be, you know." She then went on to tell us about the time she had accompanied an old friend to the railway station to see the friend's young daughter off on her first trip abroad. After fond farewells had been exchanged, and the train was about to pull away, the friend called out to her daughter from the platform, "I hope you haven't forgotten to take some contraceptives with you". "You see," said Dame Edith, "romance isn't what it used to be." Clearly, Dame Edith was not as taken with Vanessa's Rosalind as I had been.

One of the best things about moving to the Banbury Road was that I had a proper place to park my Lambretta, and a long, straight road to practise on. One of the worst things was that, before you could say knife, I realised that I had jumped out of the proverbial frying-pan. For how much longer, I asked myself, would I have to go on making the same mistake? The answer to that was pretty well for ever. In my defence, I had been given no reason to believe that Ronnie was anything other than a voracious heterosexual. Even at the cottage, he was just as likely to arrive home with a couple of girls he'd abducted from the stage door as he was to come back empty-handed and jump on me. My problem was, and always has been, recognising and acknowledging bisexuality. I know that it has a long pedigree, going back at least as far as ancient Greece and across different cultures even now, but I have no patience with it. I think it's self-indulgent, confusing and often emotionally damaging to others. I'm not saying, as many of my persuasion might, that I would choose complete abstinence on a desert island populated exclusively by members of my own sex, but Stratford-upon-Avon did not exactly suffer from a dearth of women, so my back wasn't against the wall, so to speak – except that it was, of course, and that's where it was staying! I just think people should make up their minds on which side their bread is buttered, that's all. Anyway, Ronnie's assaults on me were physical, rather than psychological, and being small, he was easily thwarted, so I wasn't unduly bothered, and he soon tired of it. This process was helped along, no doubt, by Dawn's occasional visits, transported from London on the pillion seat of my Lambretta. Oh, what a joy it was, and what a sense of freedom I experienced as I climbed onto its seat, kick-started the engine, and left Stratford behind me for the very first time under my own steam, with nothing but the moon and the stars above me and the cool breeze of a summer's night for company. On one of my last trial runs along the Banbury Road, I had forgotten to change to a lower gear as I approached Sun Rising, a steep hill, flanked by the site of the Battle of Edgehill, fought in 1642 between Royalist and Parliamentarian armies. Inevitably, the engine stalled when I was about halfway up, and I decided to call it a day. I manipulated the gear-change into neutral, wheeled the scooter to the other side of the road, put it up onto its stand, and tried to kick-start it. But it wouldn't respond to my repeated efforts. As I stood there, contemplating my next move, I became aware of my surroundings. The night was incredibly still, but quiet and peaceful it certainly wasn't. The atmosphere was, in fact, heavily laden with what I can only describe as an ominous silence. I knew my history, of course, and chastised myself for an over-active imagination. It was then that I heard the heavy tread of feet slowly approaching the hedge in the adjoining field. It had to be an animal of some sort, I told myself, not even daring to contemplate the alternative. I listened hard and with bated breath as the sound drew closer to the hedge and, consequently, closer to me. I tried hard to visualise the animal that was making it, but couldn't for the life of me think of an indigenous animal that walked on two feet, and the sound of two feet was what I was undoubtedly hearing. As it ineluctably closed the distance between us, I heard, for the first time, the sound of its heavy breathing. Only a matter of a couple of yards away from me now, and with only a hedge between us, I panicked, jumped onto the Lambretta and, as it rolled away, forced it into second gear. I was shaking like a leaf all the way back to the cottage, and arrived there in a cold sweat, not to mention a blue funk. My scepticism had been seriously challenged. The hairs on the back of my neck, however, did not stand on end until I was told shortly after, having recounted the story, that only relatively recently a ritual murder had taken place in that very spot. The body of a man – a farmer, I think – had been discovered with a pitchfork through his heart, his dog found hanging from a nearby tree. Somehow or other, I managed to rationalise this experience over a period of time, and I have never seriously believed it was anything more than a flight of fancy, given wings by the well-known reputation of Warwickshire as a centre of witchcraft and dark deeds. A month or two later, while driving in the early hours of the morning through neighbouring Shropshire, I misjudged a bend in the road, drove through a hedge, and ended up on my back, the wheels of my upturned Lambretta spinning in the night air. I had no sooner recovered my composure, having inspected both myself and my transport for serious damage, than I became aware of an entirely different atmosphere. Despite my predicament, the discomfort of a few bruises, a damaged lamp, and the time it would take me to put things right, I was reassured and comforted by the friendliness of the environment. There was nothing oppressive about it, no sense of foreboding, no heavy footsteps. It was haunted by nothing, in fact, but by a feeling of tranquillity, undisturbed and entirely benevolent. I have given some thought to this over the years, and while I still stubbornly refuse to entertain superstition of any kind, I would not ever again willingly saunter through the Warwickshire countryside alone and at night, although I remind myself that I did so on many occasions, and without incident, before my encounter with who knows what on a hill called Sun Rising in the summer of 1961.

Thus the story goes: a young Indian actor by the name of Zia Mohyeddin, who had already won acclaim for his performance in a stage adaptation of E. M. Forster's *A Passage to India,* which I was fortunate enough to have seen at the Comedy Theatre only a year or so earlier, received a wonderful review from Kenneth Tynan for his performance in a new play entitled *The Guide* at the Oxford Playhouse, in the course of which Tynan suggested, somewhat disingenuously, that perhaps Mr. Mohyeddin should be considered for one of Shakespeare's Mediterranean roles. He knew, of course, that Peter Hall was about to direct *Romeo and Juliet* at Stratford, and that he had not, as yet, found his leading man. It is reported, possibly with a touch of bias, that Mr Hall laid his copy of The Observer aside, jumped into his E-Type Jaguar, drove down to Oxford and offered the part of Romeo to Zia Mohyeddin. I was given to understand, by way of the horse's mouth, that Zia, although flattered, demurred on account of the fact that Romeo is not a foreigner and, while he would be delighted to play the part in an entirely Indian production, he thought it would be a bad idea to mix cultures, not to mention messages. This was an altogether relevant point, made all the more irrefutable in that Dorothy Tutin, the archetypal English Rose, was already cast as Juliet. It was then, or so I was told, that Peter Hall uttered the two words which ought rightly to result in the immediate suspension from duty of any director caught saying them. "Trust me," he said, and instead of saying, "No, thanks," Zia said, "All right." A little over three weeks later, Peter Hall stopped a rehearsal of the balcony scene to compliment Zia on his reading of the text, its clarity and precision, but said he was finding it hard to believe that his Romeo was actually in love with Juliet. As Zia's understudy, I had a ringside seat at all of his rehearsals, and could not but agree with our director. This Romeo was polite, well-mannered and beautifully spoken, but next to Dorothy Tutin's highly-charged Juliet, he was a bit of a cold fish, and you wondered what kind of spark had lit the flame between them in the first place. Peter Hall then suggested that Zia should put aside his single-minded concern for the text and allow some passion to inform his performance. Zia nodded and cast a rueful glance in my direction, having shared a few confidences with me on this very subject, it being the main reason he'd had reservations about playing the part in the first place. What happened next was so extraordinary that it defies description. Zia's way of expressing passion was, as he knew it would be, so completely out of tune with any European concept, that Shakespeare had to move over and make room for Paul Scott, the story of Romeo and Juliet being suddenly transported to the Raj, which would have been perfectly acceptable had Peter Hall chosen to set his production in Simla or Rawalpindi instead of being firmly rooted in 15th century Verona. It was a bizarre experience, and I left rehearsals that afternoon more than a little puzzled. How on earth was this dilemma going to be resolved? I arrived at the theatre the following morning, and saw through the door into the conference room, where we held our rehearsals, Dame Edith, Juliet's nurse, sitting in a high-backed chair cradling Dorothy Tutin's head in her lap. I thought they were rehearsing, so I tip-toed into the room, only to discover that Tutin's tears were no fiction, no dream of passion, but entirely real. Zia Mohyeddin had been sacked, his contract terminated overnight. The reason for his hasty departure from the cast, and from Stratford-upon-Avon, was given out to the press as a viral infection. The real reason was that he had been right and Peter Hall had been wrong, but no one was going to admit to that, least of all Peter Hall.

My first thoughts were, naturally enough, for Zia. I had liked him, and he was a good actor, his career prospects now severely damaged, and whatever compensation he had been offered, if indeed he had been offered any, could hardly make amends for such a loss of prestige. My second thoughts which, with a sudden shock, followed hard upon the first, were for myself. I was, after all, his understudy. Surely they wouldn't ask me to take over? Certainly, I knew the lines and I knew the moves, but I hadn't rehearsed them. But nor had anyone else, and neither did anyone else know the lines. But then again, I wasn't top billing. They were hardly going to ask a middle-ranking actor to take over a leading role, except for the odd matinée perhaps, but not for the rest of the season – and definitely not for the opening night. Nevertheless, I knew that I must have been considered, and that Peter Hall would undoubtedly take me aside and tell me what decision he had made, one way or the other, before announcing it to the company. He didn't, of course. He didn't even acknowledge my presence, let alone my vested interest. He told the company that Brian Murray would be taking over the part of Romeo, and asked us all to give him our support in this difficult undertaking. Even then, I anticipated something a bit more personal, a sympathetic gesture, or some kind of explanation. To tell the truth, I experienced a surge of relief when the announcement was made. I didn't want to play Romeo very much, and I certainly didn't want to play it opposite Dorothy Tutin who was more an object of worship in my eyes than an object of passion. I wasn't old enough, experienced enough or confident enough to share the stage with such a luminary, and I would almost certainly have been inadequate, probably more so than Brian Murray who at least, as a member of the upper echelon, had a kind of *droit de seigneur* on his side. Peter Hall could have told me all this, nay more, and I would have thanked him. The fact that he totally ignored me and didn't even favour me with one of his token smiles, made me angry. I think I realised at that moment that I had never been in contention for the part, nor consciously by-passed, because Peter Hall was not even aware of my existence. I was prompted by this to approach him, if only to see if his memory could be jogged. As near as I can recall, this is what I said, "You're obviously going to be very busy getting Brian up to speed, so I'd be more than happy to work on other scenes which might, in the process, get a bit neglected, because – as I'm sure you know – I'm understudying Romeo." He looked at me blankly for a moment or two, confirming my suspicions, and then said, his voice reflecting the blankness of his expression, "Yes. Thank you." Needless to say, he neither called me by my name, nor did he avail himself of my services.

Romeo and Juliet, the fifth and penultimate production of the season, fared better than might have been expected, largely due to a few fine performances, and one that was touched by greatness. Looking back, I would have to admit that my season at Stratford, nightmarish in so many respects, was worthwhile in at least two. It opened a door that led more or less directly to one of the most exciting and fulfilling periods of my career as an actor, and it allowed me the opportunity to see and hear at close hand, and as often as I wished, Dame Edith Evans' performance as the Nurse. In the end, it didn't really matter how many times I saw it, because I was never able to analyse it, and was consequently unable to learn anything from it. The nearest I can come to any kind of definition, for what it's worth, is that it was like watching a miracle take place, as opposed to a brilliant conjuring trick. I simply had no idea where the character came from. It certainly bore no resemblance whatsoever to the *grande dame* we had become so accustomed to backstage. This nurse was a peasant, with a peasant's wisdom, largely informed by a peasant's ignorance, indomitable and stupid, infuriatingly blinkered, yet possessed with occasional insights and a deeply felt, unconditional love for her charge, sentimentally indulgent on the one hand, and austerely reproving on the other. From what well of experience she drew this character, so complex in its simplicity, I have no way of knowing and, I suspect, neither did she. The world-renowned Spanish guitarist, Andres Segovia, once said of British guitarist, John Williams, that his forehead had been touched by the finger of God. I think I know what he meant, even if I can't relate to the imagery. But that is precisely the way I felt as I watched Dame Edith, night after night, from the wings, awestruck by what I can only, and more prosaically, call her genius. No one is more of a sucker for the pyrotechnical personality performance than I am, but the kind of acting that achieves, by some mysterious process, a metamorphosis is just as breath-taking in its own way, and considerably rarer. I have come across it once or twice at close quarters, fleetingly in a rehearsal room and never to be seen again, or just occasionally during a long run. I had to wait a quarter of a century, in fact, before I witnessed at close quarters and over a sustained period of time, such an uncanny transmutation again. It was to be an experience made all the more memorable in that it was far, far closer to home.

Not that we entirely lost sight of the *grande dame,* who made her reappearance occasionally, and most notably during the technical dress rehearsal when she missed her entrance twice by failing to mount the revolving stage in time. She then refused point blank to get onto it at all while it was moving and, being Dame Edith Evans, the bloody thing made a request stop just for her. The rest of us had to cope with it as best we could, the window of opportunity being open for only a couple of seconds as a narrow gantry on the revolve met up with a static one that ran off-stage, and upon which we waited in single file, our hearts in our mouths, like so many parachute jumpers. It was a ludicrous and entirely inappropriate set, designed by the almost obligatory Sean Kenny, during a period when the set designer and the director vied with each other for supremacy in the battle for influence, fought over the bodies of entirely expendable actors. I remember the hapless Barry Warren, as Paris, being almost crushed to death when the heavy and cumbersome backing for the churchyard scene came adrift from its guy ropes and fell on him during a performance. More significantly, however, and certainly more importantly in the scheme of things, the incident probably provided an inspirational moment for Sean Kenny who went on to design the sets for Lionel Bart's musical, *Blitz*, the following year.

1961 - Royal Shakespeare Company - entire cast and crew.

In the end, Peter Hall's accident prone production of *Romeo and Juliet* turned out to be respectable enough, enhanced as it was by a few outstanding performances, but I found it hard to equate this rather uninspiring man with the director who had introduced Samuel Becket so successfully to the West End of London, and who had been responsible for the most perfect production of *Twelfth Night* that I had seen or, indeed, have ever seen since. More than anything, however, his production of *Romeo and Juliet* suffered by comparison. Only a year earlier, the Italian director, Franco Zeffirelli, had changed our view of the play forever at the Old Vic. Heavily pruned, rather too ruthlessly on occasions, his production had fairly galloped apace, events overtaking people slowed down by the influence of a fierce Mediterranean sun, yet quick to take offence. Seeing it from the auditorium, breathless and sweating in sympathy, you became aware that this story could not have unfolded in quite the same way in an English climate. It was the very hot-bloodedness and volatility of the Italian temperament that created the inevitability of tragedy. How then did Shakespeare know so well what so many of his interpreters had failed to grasp? In the end, it took a real Italian to understand the very nature of the play. There was no time for circumspection in this production, nor any inclination amongst its characters towards reconciliation. If there had been, the story simply wouldn't have turned out the way it did. It was a quite brilliant piece of theatre and we, of the Royal Shakespeare Company, were keenly looking forward to the arrival of Franco Zeffirelli in our midst – for he was to direct the final production of the season.

oOoOo

Ten

In 1634, John Milton's masque, *Comus*, was first performed at Ludlow Castle. Such was its commercial success that it was next performed in the ruins of that same castle 324 years later in 1958, not exactly in response to public demand, but rather to celebrate the 350th anniversary of the poet's birth. It was directed by David William and the costumes were designed by Dawn Pavitt. The setting, of course, was already in place, and what a wonderful setting it was, conceived, designed and built by the Normans in the 11th century, with subsequent alterations made by the Lancastrian army when they sacked the town in 1459, and by that most effective of all design partnerships, Time and Neglect. In 1722, Daniel Defoe described it as 'The very perfection of decay.' I saw that production of *Comus* – the revival, I hasten to add, not the original – when I was on leave from the RAF, and three years later I returned to see *Macbeth,* the main attraction of what had by then become known as the Ludlow Festival. I fell in love with Ludlow and its castle at first sight, and mounted my more-often-than-not trusty Lambretta to hie me there from ill-starred Stratford at every opportunity, and not exclusively because that's where I would find Dawn, plying her needle, and putting the finishing touches to her magnificent creations, but also because it was, and remains, one of the most beautiful and beguiling of English market towns, wearing its history on its sleeve for all who have an interest in such things to revel in. It was on one such occasion, sitting on the grass of the castle's outer bailey during her lunch break, that Dawn asked me if I still wanted to marry her. For all that we both still wore the rings we had exchanged in Coventry six years earlier, marriage had never really been on the agenda. For one thing, it had never seemed to be the right time and, in any case, I knew she'd probably say, "Maybe we will, one of these days," for the simple reason that she'd said something like that before when the subject had come up in a purely academic way. Why that particular day turned out to be the day in particular, I never did discover, and I never asked. In fact, I didn't much care. I'd fallen in love with Dawn when I was 17 years old and, at 23, I still felt the same way, only much more than that by then. I can't remember exactly what I said, but it was probably something as unremarkable as, "Yes."

We decided to get married in London, and as soon as possible after the end of my Stratford season, allowing time for all the arrangements to be made, and for her parents to get used to the idea. Having done their level best to discourage our relationship from its earliest days, they were not going to be exactly overjoyed. In fact, the first thing her father said to me some little while later, was, "I must say, Terry, the thought of having you for a son-in-law unnerves me." Nothing, however, not even the thought of having to return to Stratford, took the shine off my euphoria, and in Ludlow at least we were surrounded by friends and well-wishers. Foremost among them was my dear friend from Webber-Douglas days, Sandy Black who, having returned from a course at the Centre Dramatique de l'Est in Strasbourg, then under the aegis of Michel St. Denis, was working as David William's assistant on *Macbeth*. There was also Dawn's new landlady, Zoë Zajdler, an elderly lady with a past and whose present was almost entirely focused on a host of young men, university graduates by and large, and all with theatrical connections. In the vanguard of this cohort was David William, and it was pretty well accepted by all who knew them, that where David went, Zoë was bound to follow, hence her presence in Ludlow. It was David, I believe, who effected the introduction between Dawn and Zoë, and when Dawn and Penny McVitie decided to give up their flat in Luna Street, Zoë offered Dawn accommodation in her spacious Westminster flat, where I had been an occasional visitor on my flying visits to London from Stratford. Zoë was a Polish countess, Irish by birth, who had fled Poland with her husband, a high-ranking officer in the Polish army, shortly after it had capitulated to the Nazis in 1939. En route to England, their ship had been intercepted by a German E-boat. Being in possession of an Irish passport, Zoë was allowed to continue her journey, but her husband was taken away, and she never saw him again. She wrote a book anonymously, published under the title, *My Name Is Million,* an account of that journey, and the plight of the Polish people at that time. I never did read it, nor did Zoë ever encourage me to, although she did insist that I read to her from the works of William Shakespeare for which task I needed no encouragement whatsoever. I was, to all intents and purposes, only an honorary member of Zoë's coterie, having neither the educational qualifications, the willowy appearance, nor the sexual orientation that seemed to be a prerequisite for full membership. And I certainly wasn't looking for a mother figure on whom to confer unconditional deference, something that Zoë's very existence demanded. But she was extremely fond of Dawn whose credentials were, after all, impeccable, and as I was part of Dawn's baggage, she had little option but to take me to her bosom. I like to think that I repaid this singular honour to some extent with my readings of several of Shakespeare's plays in their entirety, although I couldn't help feeling a little bit miffed when, having prepared to read *Julius Caesar* at her insistence, she suddenly decided she didn't want to hear it because it was all about ambition, politics and blood-letting, subjects which held a particular and unwelcome resonance for her. Fair enough, but what did she think it was about when she asked me to read it? In truth, my callow reaction to her *volte face* was prompted by disappointment. I'd been looking forward to getting my teeth into Brutus, Cassius and Mark Antony, any one of which I would have given my right arm to play, let alone all three together! But Zoë was very generous in many respects and, although she could be insufferably imperious at times, she was also extremely loyal. Besides, she thought Dawn and I were meant for each other, and was genuinely delighted by the prospect of our marriage, which meant that she was okay as far as I was concerned.

Looking back, it seems to me that the world was full of women like Zoë Zajdler at that time, elderly ladies of some quality who, finding themselves bereft of contemporaries, sought out the company of a younger generation, usually of the opposite sex. The reasons behind this were doubtless many and complex, ranging from the Queen Bee syndrome, to the delusory fantasies of women like Ninon de Lenclos, as commemorated in verse by Dorothy Parker:

'So bring my scarlet slippers, then,
And fetch my powder-puff to me.
The dear young men, the poor young men –
They think I'm only seventy!'

There was obviously something of the Queen Bee about Zoë but, unlike my erstwhile landlady, Evelyn Chetwynd, nothing of the Ninon de Lenclos. But then Eve had been a Bluebell Girl and her enduring femininity was her strongest card. With the benefit of hindsight, however, I can see now that in none of these relationships was it just a case of age battening onto youth in a vain attempt to turn back the clock, but of a mutual desire on the part of a younger generation to maintain some link with the past, to reverence it in some cases, and certainly to be enriched by the experience and occasional wisdom associated with those who had inhabited it. The bridges that existed between generations then are sadly, or so it seems to me, all but derelict, rendered so by a more recent generation for whom history doesn't extend beyond last week.

These musings aside, it's worth recording that somehow or other I also managed to get to Ludlow for the opening night of *Macbeth*, probably because it coincided with an *As You Like It* performance at

Stratford. It was a memorable occasion, made so largely by the spine-tingling marriage between play and setting, the guttering torchlight visible through the gaping windows of the Great Hall, reflecting the banquet within, the coronation robes of Macbeth and his lady, startlingly blood-red against the grey medieval stone and, in the fading light, the flock of wild geese that, unrehearsed and for one night only, swooped low over the stage during Macbeth's words,

'Light thickens, and the crow
Makes wing to the rooky wood;
Good things begin to droop and drowse,
Whiles night's black agents to their preys do rouse.'

All of these images were printed indelibly on my mind, as was the spectacular death of Young Siward, his lifeless body falling from the battlements onto the stage below, happily represented by a lifelike dummy, actors being less expendable in Ludlow than might have been the case in an RSC production! At the centre of all this was a fine performance by Alan Dobie, especially in the first half of the play, it being notoriously difficult for any actor to embrace both halves before achieving middle-age, by which time he's too old to play it at all.

A colleague of mine from my days as a child actor at the Old Vic, Alan Dobie, was also one of a rather distinguished list of actors considered by Franco Zeffirelli for the part of Iago in his Stratford production of *Othello*. None of them, however, turned out to be quite what Franco had in mind. "You see, Peter, what I'm-a-looking for ...," he said to Peter Hall in his outrageously over-the-top Italian accent, "what I'm-a-looking for is a man, you look in his eyes an' you trust him. Every thing you got, your wife, your house, your money, you trust with this man because, you see, Peter, in his eyes he is honest. But, underneath, Peter – *underneath* – the dagger. *(long pause)* Tell me, Peter, do you act?" Apocryphal? Possibly. But it contained what many of us saw as the essence of Peter Hall, and that's why the story took root. Many years later, I found myself sharing a table in the BBC canteen with Jonathan Miller, celebrated not only for his emergence onto the scene as one of a quartet of seriously talented comic actors in the Cambridge Footlights revue, *Beyond the Fringe,* but for his growing reputation as an actor-friendly director, of both drama and opera. On top of which, he was also a qualified Doctor of Medicine, something of a raconteur, and witty with it. Needless to say, I was overawed by his entirely unexpected presence at the table and, although reconciled to being nothing more than an appreciative audience, I tried to justify my own presence in such exalted company by desperately trying to think of something amusing to say. Eventually, on hearing Peter Hall's name come into the conversation, I seized my chance and, heart in mouth, re-told the story, conjuring up from somewhere a reasonably authentic Italian accent, and hanging onto the pause for as long as I dared. It was a big hit and, much to my delight, no one laughed louder or for longer than Jonathan Miller. Obviously, the story held some personal significance for him too.

I was not alone in wondering at the time why John Gielgud wanted to play Othello. Apart from the essential nobility of the character and the monumental language Shakespeare had put into his mouth, I could not, and still cannot, imagine what had attracted him to a part that, neither physically nor vocally, was he ever intended to play. He had, I believe, flirted with the idea a few years earlier, but his chosen director, Peter Brook, had had other fish to fry, which was a pity because Franco Zeffirelli was definitely not the captain to whom he should have looked for safe passage on such a hazardous voyage. For a start, Franco's knowledge of the English language was, at best, sketchy, and he quite failed to recognise how significantly different it was from the language of *Romeo and Juliet,* thus determining to approach *Othello* in much the same way. Nor could Sir John have chosen, had the choice been his, a less compatible travelling companion than Ian Bannen who, in the absence of a suitable alternative, had finally been cast as Iago. But enough of these second-hand, and now distantly remote reminiscences. This is Gielgud himself, taken from his published letters: 'Zeffirelli is extraordinary – maddeningly undisciplined and more unpunctual than Peter Brook and Binkie (Hugh Beaumont) put together ... his work is quite brilliant, but he dallies and dickers, and everything's behindhand, scenery, dresses, as well as the play itself ... Ian Bannen, the Iago ... is overtired, neurotic, a converted Catholic, tricky, a bad study, interfering, inefficient and impertinent, and makes rehearsals a misery when they could be really very stimulating, I've had one or two real rows with him already, and fear there may be more in the offing. If the production fails it will be largely his fault. The rest of the cast is weak but willing ...'

And two days later, 'Don't talk to me about Iago – he is a neurotic, tiresome boy ... shouts or mumbles and capers about in jackanapes fashion, impossible to help, and well-nigh impossible to act with – no sense of timing or rhythm and madly in love with tricks and business ... the director clever and fascinating, though alas no good on the SPEECH. I fear it will be uneven and unbalanced, though less ignoble, I *hope*, than the four current productions, which are a disgrace. (Peter) Hall is young and has none of the discipline and control of Tony Q(uayle) and Glen (Byam Shaw). It's a great hazard for me. *As You Like It* is the best thing here. The Redgrave girl is very charming and talented, though dreadfully tall. She will have the same difficulties as Phyllis Neilson-Terry had – no leading man capable of topping her. No Shakespearean joke intended!'

Leaving aside his apparent lack of judgement in allowing himself to be faced with such a dilemma, we all felt a keen sympathy for Sir John – or at least, I did. He was a delightful man and a true gentleman. Ian Bannen's behaviour was indeed not only disrespectful, but outrageously and gratuitously rude. I'm tempted to say that he'd been perfectly sane at the beginning of the season but, on reflection, he had always been teetering on the edge of madness, although it was probably the dreadful experience of living through the season that tipped him over. Having absconded from *Hamlet,* reneged on *Richard III,* and somehow or other got his act together, or at least spasmodically, for *Romeo and Juliet* and *As You Like It,* what but a demon could have possessed him to undertake, at the tail end of an exhausting season, the largest part that Shakespeare ever penned? Ian Bannen's mind, without question unbalanced, was as nothing, however, compared to the sheer lunacy of those who asked him to play it. Surely this could not have been the Iago of Franco's dreams? At times, however, it seemed that he and Ian were involved in a conspiracy to torment the life out of poor JG, vying with each other in their complete disregard for punctuality, and their mutual determination to invade his space. Ian's Iago was forever clapping Othello on the back and hugging him to Gielgud's total discomfiture and to Franco's obvious delight, while his constant paraphrasing of the text went unchecked. On one occasion, having arrived at rehearsals ahead of Ian, although still late himself, Franco borrowed all of our wrist-watches and lined them up along the edge of the stage, a humorous reprimand entirely lost on Ian, who didn't even offer an apology to Sir John, never mind the rest of the company, when he eventually arrived. Had Gielgud not been the thorough professional that he unquestionably was, and had he not enjoyed the support and the solace of two dear friends, Peggy Ashcroft and Dorothy Tutin, who were curiously marginalised in this ramshackle production as Emilia and Desdemona, he might well have walked away. He certainly had good enough reason.

I might as well confess here and now that I was entirely captivated by Franco Zeffirelli, which might have had something to do with the fact that I was not in any way personally affected by his cavalier approach to the play, having been assigned the role of a Cypriot sailor whose duties terminated at the end of Act Two. Nor was I required to understudy anyone, so I was a more or less a disinterested observer, and counted myself extremely fortunate in view of the potential disaster that loomed larger with every passing day. But Franco's enthusiasm was infectious, his charm was effortlessly bestowed on all and sundry, and all and sundry were thus pretty much under his spell. Several years later, shortly after the release of his movie version of *Romeo and Juliet,* I was asked, along with a dozen or so other RSC veterans, to attend a post-production dubbing session at Elstree Studios. It transpired that Franco, unhappy with the Italian interjections in all the crowd scenes, shot in the most wonderfully authentic settings, wanted to replace them with Shakespearean English. Paramount Pictures, needless to say, as the film's distributors, were none too happy, baulking at the extra expense, especially as the picture was already up and running in the West End. But Franco was adamant, and said that if Paramount wouldn't pay for it he'd pick up the tab himself, a characteristically flamboyant gesture which may or may not have persuaded Paramount to back down. In any event, I was booked for the session and arrived to find Paul Hardwick handing out foolscap sheets upon which was typed a fairly comprehensive list of the Shakespearean phrases, exhortations and aphorisms that were to be dubbed onto the soundtrack at various appropriate moments. Paul had joined the company at Stratford late in 1961, principally to take over Claudius in *Hamlet* from Noël Willman. He had stayed on for *Othello,* and I believe it was he who put my name forward for inclusion in what turned out to be a hugely enjoyable day. Zeffirelli was in great form, typically playful, treating it as a social occasion, and seeming to enjoy our company as much as the job in hand. We partook of a very nice lunch, courtesy of Franco, or possibly Paramount, and we enjoyed a good many laughs along the way. The fact that I remember such a brief interlude with such undiluted pleasure speaks volumes, I think, as does the smile that returns to my face whenever I see a re-run of the movie and hear my disembodied voice calling out for Romeo in the streets of medieval Verona after the Capulets' party, or urging Tybalt to keep his rapier up and 'go to't' in the fight scene, my words coming out of an Italian mouth that was clearly saying something quite different!

Had I been in Sir John's shoes, I would certainly have been more circumspect in my admiration of Zeffirelli, and never more so than when I saw the set for the first time, designed by *l'huomo* himself, and more appropriate, perhaps, to the Verdi than to the Shakespearean version of the play, all heavy drapes and huge pillars, behind one of which Gielgud was obliged to wait for what must have seemed like an eternity before making his first entrance. At the technical rehearsal, as I stood chatting to the girl on the book in the prompt corner, I saw Sir John float onto the stage in costume for the first time, and fully 'blacked-up' for the role. He was wearing a full-length gown, happily concealing his famously weak knees, and I thought he looked magnificent. I also thought I'd tell him so, conjecturing that, having been put through the mill one way or another during the rehearsal process, he would be happy to hear it, even from the likes of me. So I walked onto the stage, and offered my compliment, whereupon he grasped me by the arm, squeezed it tightly, and looked into my eyes for a very long time, the expression on his face fixed in what I can only describe as a pained smile. Then, following a beautifully timed and entirely enigmatic pause during which I became completely unnerved, he said with great warmth and with the wicked humour for which he was also famous, "We aim to please." I never felt quite as sorry for him after that, recognising his strength and the resilience of a born survivor. He knew better than anyone that he was about to fail in a part he should probably never have played, and in a production that should never have left the drawing-board, but he also knew that it was all in a day's work, that failure should be treated with the same degree of scepticism as success and that, in fact, there was something to be learned from both. Of course, I'm making all of this up, based on the studied flippancy of his response to my somewhat presumptuous compliment. It was, after all, hardly a moment of shared intimacy, although that's what it felt like at the time. And so, in deference to that illusion, I shall stand aside and allow my intimate friend, Sir John Gielgud, to tell you about the opening of *Othello*:

'We had a terrible time with *Othello* thanks to a ghastly number of mishaps on the first night, which lasted four hours. The impossibility of working with Ian Bannen, and Franco's irresponsible and irrepressible charm, mixed with his dreadful lack of discipline and punctuality, wasted important time in every department ... Except for (Harold) Hobson and (Victor) Cookman, who gave me very good notices indeed, the entire press was disastrous, Zeffirelli attacked violently, and Dorothy and Peggy almost ignored. The settings are beautiful but cumbrous, the dresses ditto, and the pace is snail-like. Far too many blackouts, realistic business and pauses as if playing Chekhov, and no earthly good in Shakespeare ...'

None of this meant a great deal to me, of course, being

somewhat semi-detached from the production. In fact, it was only significant as far as I was concerned in that it was the last play of the season, the light at the end of the tunnel. I do recall, however, many an evening when, having disembarked Othello's luggage in Cyprus, I would retire to the saloon bar of *The Dirty Duck* until closing time, occasionally enjoy a leisurely Indian meal in Sheep Street, or even from time to time take in a double-feature at the local cinema, from where I would return to the theatre only to discover, more often than not, that Desdemona was still in the land of the living. Mostly, I would keep well out of the way, however, just in case the company manager should change his mind and 'suggest' that I ought to hang around for the curtain-call!

From quite early on in the season, those of us who had not been exactly overburdened with responsibility on stage, were given classes in Shakespearean verse-speaking by John Barton, Peter Hall's resident teacher, dramaturg or whatever, with whom he had shared a similar background at Cambridge University. Over the next few years, he went on to acquire a considerable reputation as a director himself, first coming to prominence with *The Wars of the Roses,* the RSC's answer to *An Age of Kings,* and for the enormously successful royal anthology, *The Hollow Crown,* which he also devised. Clearly, the classes were introduced, not merely to keep us off the streets, but to establish a unity of approach to verse-speaking in RSC style, if you like, although my recollections do not really bear this out. I had chosen as my test piece Richard II's speech, from Act 3 Scene 2, the one that begins, 'No matter where, of comfort no man speak ..' and I think I can truthfully say that, give or take the odd change of inflection, the addition of a bit more variety in tone and pace, all of which I would probably have discovered for myself in time, my delivery of the speech remained pretty much the same as it had been at the beginning of the season. All in all, and putting his subsequent track-record to one side, John Barton's classes were dull and uninspiring, or they would have been had it not been for the entertainment value derived from his utterly amazing lack of physical and spacial awareness. When lecturing us, or giving us notes from his chair on the stage of the Conference Room, you could be absolutely certain that, as soon as he decided to get up, he would trip over the book he had laid on the floor five minutes ago. Similarly, having missed his footing whilst climbing up onto the stage to give someone a bit of close attention, it was inevitable that, in backing away, he would fall off the edge of the stage and into the front row of chairs which, for obvious reasons, we chose never to use. The extraordinary thing was that he never mentioned it, nor did he appear to suffer any embarrassment. He simply picked himself up, fell over something else that was in his way, and went on talking. I don't know of any condition, drunkenness aside, that could have produced such a degree of physical ineptitude. John Barton was perfectly capable of standing still; it was only when he started to move that disaster struck, and we would sit there, holding our collective breaths, as every step took him closer to the fire bucket, or whatever. On one occasion, having placed his mug of coffee on the floor beside him, a sudden burst of intensity propelled him from his chair to the edge of the stage where, to everyone's relief, he managed to stop. Having got whatever it was off his chest, he then returned to his chair which, for some unknown, but obviously compelling reason, he decided to move. Even as he lifted it, we knew with a certainty born of familiarity, that the unbelievable was about to happen, which it did. In replacing the chair, he somehow contrived to put one of its front legs into his mug of coffee. The fact that he executed this without knocking the mug over, spilling a single drop of coffee or, indeed, knowing what he had done, was the icing on the cake as far as we were concerned, and the only reason it was not greeted by a round of applause was that John Barton was not exactly noted for his sense of humour. All the more ironic then, that it was for the farcical element, rather than the instructive, that his classes were unmissable.

As the season began to wind down, we were informed that Peter Hall had expressed a desire to acquaint himself with what we had been doing with John Barton for the last six months, and had suggested that perhaps we would like to recite our speeches in front of him. On the face of it, a not unreasonable request, and had it been made by anyone other than Peter Hall, looked on without suspicion as a genuine, if somewhat belated interest in the company he had assembled. However, the fact that he had timed his little bombshell to explode amongst us just when rumours about casting for the following season were rife, did nothing for his reputation, either as kindly uncle or as a Machiavell. There were distinct rumblings below deck; not exactly mutinous – you'd be hard-pushed to find a Fletcher Christian in any acting company where the chances are that most of the crew would end up siding with the captain – but ominous enough to cause alarm bells to ring on the bridge, and for Chief Petty Officer Maurice Daniels to call a meeting at which he assured us that we were not being covertly invited to audition for next season but simply to demonstrate what progress we had made under John Barton's tutelage. The fact that Peter

Hall was in no position to gauge any progress or lack of it for the simple reason that he had never shown an active interest in the classes and certainly, unless he had been concealed behind a curtain, had never witnessed any, was passed over without comment. CPO Daniels went on to guarantee that, under no circumstances, would our speeches be taken into account when offers were made for the following season. To further sweeten the pill, he insisted that Peter Hall had issued an invitation, not a command, and that anyone who did not wish to participate was free to decline without prejudice. This was followed by tots of rum all round and a sullen murmuring which, nonetheless, signified grudging assent, as we all returned to swabbing the decks.

It is anthropologically worth noting, I think, that not one single actor took issue with Maurice Daniels' obviously flawed statement, that not one single actor decided to test it by refusing the invitation, and that not one single actor raised his voice in protest when, only two days after we had delivered our speeches in the presence of Mr Hall, offers were made for the following season. Was this pure coincidence, or had we been more subtly manipulated than we imagined? Was it possible that the artistic director of a theatre dedicated to the works of a man who was an actor as well as a playwright, could hold actors in such contempt? Well, yes, it clearly was. But what of the actors themselves? This is probably not the time, nor possibly the place, to embark upon a detailed analysis of the actor's psyche. To begin with, a certain amount of objectivity would be required, and it is only as I write this, at a distance of almost sixty years, that I can even begin to articulate my own state of mind at the time, let alone speak for a couple of dozen others or, indeed, presume to be speaking on behalf of my entire profession. Suffice it to say that the very last thing I wanted to do, as chill November winds spoke of imminent freedom, was to return to Stratford-upon-Avon where I had endured nine months of almost unrelenting misery, at least as far as my employment was concerned. True, I had been allowed the opportunity to work alongside a few of the 'greats'; Gielgud, Ashcroft, Edith Evans and the divine Dorothy Tutin, experiences I would treasure for the rest of my life, but in the absence of any humane leadership, I had been made to feel anonymous, my work unacknowledged, my very identity in doubt. Earlier in the season, someone had remarked that, as Peter Hall had never taken the trouble to learn our names, we might just as well have worn numbers on our backs. In such a situation, and over such a considerable period of time, the thin veneer of self-confidence, essential for an actor's survival, had been completely eroded, leaving me with nothing to fall back upon except the power to say, "No", and this I had determined to do in the unlikely event of being asked to return the following season. I would most certainly have spurned any suggestion that I audition for that singular privilege, but having been deceived into doing just that, and having subsequently been told that my services would not be required, I had been robbed of even that tiny prerogative. By way of compensation, I imagine, I had been invited to 'play as cast' in Chekhov's *The Cherry Orchard* at the Aldwych Theatre, the RSC's London venue, and so completely undermined was my ego by this time, that I found myself actually considering it. After all, I reasoned, I'd be in London and on salary for a while, which was surely better than embarking on a marriage unemployed, even if I did end up playing a cherry-picker's assistant with no lines.

I was sitting alone at a table in the Green Room one morning, nursing a third cup of coffee, and pondering my situation while trying to pin-point the line that separates total humiliation from utter degradation in order to determine whether or not I had crossed it, when Sir John Gielgud came in and, after casting his eyes around the other tables, approached me.

"I believe you have played Puck," he said.

"Yes, Sir John, a long time ago", I replied. "In Tyrone Guthrie's production at the Old Vic".

"Do you remember any of it?" he asked.

Silly question, I remembered it all, and even now, all these years later, I'm still pretty-well word-perfect on all of the major speeches.

"Yes, I think so – some of it, anyway" I answered diffidently.

"Come and do a bit of it for me," he said, and promptly turned away, leaving me to follow him out of the Green Room and into the wings, where he gestured me onto the stage before disappearing through the pass-door and into the auditorium. Fragments of various speeches flashed through my mind as I stood there on the empty stage and, by the time he had settled himself, I had made my decision.

"Whenever you're ready," he encouraged, and I began, having instinctively decided to go for a performance rather than a recitation. The speech I had lighted upon was the one that begins, 'My fairy lord, this must be done with haste,/For night's swift dragons cut the clouds full fast,/And yonder shines Aurora's harbinger ...' I came to the end of it, reasonably satisfied that, in the circumstances, I had done it justice, my sense of being a real actor again revived in an instant, even if I hadn't the remotest idea why he had asked me to do it. Moments later, he came onto the stage. "That was very good," he said. "Would you like to play it at Covent Garden?"

Somewhat bewildered, I desperately tried to decide which, of all the theatres in and around Covent Garden, he could possibly mean by simply referring to it as Covent Garden.

"Covent Garden?" I asked, finally obliged to admit my ignorance.

"The Royal Opera House," he said, without a trace of condescension, "In my production of Benjamin Britten's opera." He must have sensed my utter disbelief, probably from the look of utter disbelief on my face. He smiled. "Puck is a non-singing role," he said reassuringly. I could think of nothing appropriate to say that my stunned silence hadn't already made obvious – except, "When does it start?" Sir John's smile, warm and genuine, was manna in the wilderness. "We begin rehearsals next week" he said, taking it for granted, as I had given him every reason to, that I had accepted his offer.

The glorious uncertainty that goes hand in hand with being an actor is, rather like the game of cricket, one of its most alluring aspects and, combined with incurable optimism, the actor's *sine qua non,* one of the reasons that make it so difficult to quit. Had I been given irrefutable evidence that all I had to look forward to were carbon-copies of the season I had just suffered, I might well have considered doing just that. But as it was, and quite out of the blue, I had been presented with a new and exciting challenge which, along with the 'happy ever after' expectations of marriage to Dawn, made the prospects for December 1961 and thereafter look suddenly and decidedly rosy. I also had the deliciously petty pleasure of turning down the RSC's measly offer, thereby restoring my sole prerogative as an actor, as well as allowing me the last word on the subject.

It could be argued, I suppose, that my expectations had been unrealistic, based as they were on an outsider's impressions, a bit like Mole looking in through other people's windows on Christmas Day and assuming, from what he saw, that everyone was having a lovely time except him. But perhaps they weren't. Perhaps the lights on the Christmas tree, the warmth of the fire in the hearth and the smiles on the faces of all those families as they gathered round the table to enjoy their Christmas dinner, was nothing but a sham, an idyllic picture painted for the benefit of outsiders, masking all sorts of misery and unpleasantness. Who knows, but maybe the seemingly palmy days of the Shakespeare Memorial Theatre under Glen Byam Shaw, which I had glimpsed, as it were, through the window, had been just such a sham: the camaraderie, the absence of rancour, the enthusiasm and the joy of rehearsing and performing in all those wonderful plays, just a façade, put on for my benefit, and instantly cast aside the moment I left, hitch-hiking my way back to RAF Cardington, my head filled with false dreams. But somehow I don't think that was the case. The fact that the 1961 season at Stratford had been, with the exception of *As You Like It,* an unmitigated disaster in artistic terms was unfortunate, of course, and had I been associated with one of the many successful seasons that followed, I might have felt very differently about my time with the RSC. My state of mind at the end of its inaugural season, however, had less to do with a 'slew of bad reviews,' than it did with a growing, yet still hazy, awareness that the theatre was undergoing a sea-change; certainly *had* changed since I first came into contact with it ten years earlier. I know now, of course, that what I had witnessed at first hand, and indeed been prey to, was not just a question of personal antipathy, but one more stage in the gestation period of what is now accepted as the status quo. Simon Callow was to call it the 'hi-jacking of the theatre by the director'. Another reputable actor, whose identity I will not reveal just in case he wants to work again, calls it 'a usurpation, a colonisation, the rape of one culture by another'. I knew nothing of this at the time, of course, save for a feeling of acute disappointment and a vague presentiment, born of the fact that I had already had a whiff of the smoke without which there is no fire during my season at the Belgrade Theatre in Coventry. So it was with a lightness of spirit I had not felt since putting National Service behind me almost three years earlier, that I turned my back on Stratford-upon-Avon, its hold on my imagination broken, left with no desire ever to work there again which, but for a very brief visit in the not-too-distant future, I never did.

oOoOo

Eleven

I think I can say, without fear of contradiction, that I am one of a very few actors to have performed at the Royal Opera House, Covent Garden, and of even fewer to have appeared there in a principal role. Not that Benjamin Britten's Puck is William Shakespeare's by any stretch of the imagination. Most of the magic has gone, along with most of the language, and what's left is a prankster with a penchant for gymnastics. It soon became clear that one of the reasons Sir John had asked me to do it was his love for the words, or what was left of them, and his desire to hear them spoken well. By the same token, I believe that Britten was less impressed by my performance, having been deprived of the boy acrobat he had set his sights on. When I later heard the recording of the original Covent Garden production from the year before, I can only say I was glad, for professional as well as personal reasons, that Sir John had got his own way the second time around. Not that my Puck was without agility. I was pretty fleet of foot in those days and, while triple somersaults in mid-air were never a speciality of mine, I reckon I could still have put a girdle round about the earth in 40 minutes or thereabouts, given a marginal suspension of disbelief, and without ever leaving the ground!

One of my earliest recollections on arriving at the Opera House was seeing that the posters advertising the production, and featuring my name, were already being displayed. I stopped to look, and there it was – WALE – no first name, just WALE. The last time I'd been addressed by my surname had been in the RAF, and I'd never been too happy about it. On that basis, I ought to have been deeply affronted, but I wasn't; quite the reverse in fact, and I can only imagine I must have thought that what was good enough for CALLAS, GOBBI, SUTHERLAND and BJÖRLING was good enough for me. Not that any of these illustrious names featured on the poster I was looking at, although it was a pretty impressive cast list nevertheless: Geraint Evans was returning to the role of Bottom, Jenifer Eddy and, later, Joan Carlyle were to sing Tytania (Britten's spelling and, for obvious reasons, sung as a 'y' rather then an 'i'!), John Dobson and Peter Glossop as Lysander and Demetrius, and Jeanette Sinclair, replaced at some performances by Heather Harper, as Helena. Another newcomer to the Royal Opera House, besides myself, was a young man called Grayston Burgess. Having conceived and written the part of Oberon for a counter-tenor, Benjamin Britten had clearly not reckoned with the dearth of such an endangered species in the 20th century, and so with neither Alfred Deller nor Russell Oberlin being available, both of whom had sung the part before, he was obliged to call on the services of a non-operatic singer. Grayston was, in fact, a member of the famous St. Paul's Choir, whose delightfully mellifluous voice had, no doubt, enhanced many a recital of madrigals and *cantiones sacrae* in hallowed halls or from the choir stalls of various churches, but it was too small an instrument for Covent Garden, where the first imperative is to be heard above a 100 piece orchestra. The second imperative is, without question, being able to match up, at least in terms of volume, to some pretty big female voices, voices trained for, and naturally developed in the world's greatest operatic arenas. Poor Grayston was at a decided disadvantage here with both his Tytanias, but especially singing opposite Joan Carlyle who produced such a magnificent sound that it simply overwhelmed his delicate alto tones. Never mind the altered seasons, forget about the Indian boy, this ill-matched couple left you in no doubt as to who wore the trousers in that particular bower, and you didn't have to look much further than that to account for the Fairy Kingdom's current malaise! For my part, I loved Grayston's voice, but as I spent a large part of the evening either standing or kneeling next to him, I was obviously in a better place than anyone else to hear it.

The Royal Opera House was like no other theatre I had worked in, largely because opera singers bear little or no resemblance to actors. My memories of the rehearsal period are about as detailed as snapshots really, which is not surprising as it only lasted for just over a week. Most of the singers turned up knowing exactly where they were supposed to enter and exit, and where they were supposed to stand once they had come on. They also knew their parts, although this had to be taken on trust to some extent as none of them bothered to sing the notes until the final rehearsal, content to mouth their way through solo arias, duets, quartets and whatever else the musical score demanded. I found this rather odd and more than a little frustrating as I was obliged, being new to the game, to give my all on a daily basis whilst learning the moves and dealing with gentle but constant reminders of my shortcomings from the Assistant Director, such as, "This is where Leonid executed three cartwheels followed by a handspring; do you think you could manage that?" In the end, they had to settle for the occasional somersault, and I wasn't exactly over the moon about having to do that, and not because I couldn't, but because I'd always thought of Puck as a very practical creature, not given to self-indulgent, meaningless, and time-wasting displays of that kind.

192

But the oddest thing about opera singers was that, while understandably reluctant to indulge in equally meaningless and needlessly strenuous displays of their vocal dexterity during rehearsals, they talked incessantly during breaks and, almost exclusively, about their voices. The women tended always to sit together, not a bit like actresses who would mix freely and, more often than not, seek out members of the opposite sex to socialise with, but deliberately segregated themselves, more like a meeting of the W.I. than a theatrical gathering. This impression was strengthened by those amongst them who, having meandered and mimed their way through a scene, would then retire to a chair and pick up their knitting! The men, meanwhile, would stand around in groups, hands buried deep in their pockets in the absence of a pint glass to hold, and would remain equally segregated from their female colleagues. In fact, the only thing these two groups appeared to have in common was this singular preoccupation with their voices; they talked of little else. A few months later, we took the production to the Coventry Theatre for just one performance, and after it was over, I was offered a lift back to London by André Turp, who had by then replaced John Dobson as Lysander. I sat in the back of the car and, for the entire length of the journey which must have taken two-and-a-half to three hours in those days, my presence was entirely ignored as André Turp and his other passenger, Joan Carlyle, talked incessantly and passionately about throat lozenges. They discussed the pros and the cons of various brands; they compared, they recommended, they disparaged, talked about their beneficial effects, side effects, placebo effects and after effects, and never once did either of them show any inclination to change the subject. Certainly, actors are known to be more cavalier about their vocal equipment, not to mention their physical well-being, than either singers or dancers, which is reprehensible no doubt, but at least you can have a decent conversation on a variety of subjects with most of them. Astonished, and grudgingly overawed as I was by this fanatical dedication to their art, my growing respect for opera singers in general was somewhat dented when, having been given a dressing-room recently vacated by the celebrated German baritone, Dietrich Fischer-Dieskau, I was greeted on arrival by the unmistakable aroma of stale cigarette smoke, although I suppose it might well have been left there by the cleaner.

The opening night on December 16th 1961 was, for me, an awesome experience. The sheer size of the orchestra in front of me, for a start, and the audience beyond, 2,000 of them, tier upon tier, would have been enough to stop me in my tracks had I given it any thought at the time. But all I was aware of, apart from the overwhelming sounds coming from the orchestra pit and from the mouths of singers, all but mute until now, was that my Mum and Dad were out there. They had never seen an opera before, and probably never would again, and I wondered what they would be making of it, Benjamin Britten being perhaps not quite as accessible to the uninitiated as Puccini, for instance. I found Britten's music pretty difficult myself although inevitably, as time went by, I grew to like it more and more. My appreciation of serious music hadn't extended much beyond my introduction, courtesy of Peter Dews, to Carl Orff's *Carmina Burana,* but while I never became a complete fan of Britten's work, I certainly began to understand it during my time at the Royal Opera House, and derived a great deal of pleasure from some of it. I particularly remember Bottom's awakening, sung and acted with great skill and perfect comedy timing by Geraint Evans, and for many years afterwards I was able to give – and did at the drop of a hat – a fair rendition of Oberon's aria, 'I know a bank whereon the wild thyme blows ...' until at last, having lost much of my upper register, I was forced to abandon it as a party piece. But playing the composer's version of Puck was, on the whole, an unsatisfactory experience, the character having lost at least one and a half of his three dimensions and most of his complexity in translation. Virtually all of his lines have to be delivered *allegro vivace,* in tempo, often accompanied by a snare drum or some such, which doesn't allow any space for interpretation or changes of mood, and undoubtedly accounts for the fact that most of his lines, i.e. those that don't lend themselves to such a restrictive approach, are missing. On the plus side, I soon discovered that Puck was not entirely a speaking part, as Sir John had assured me it was. When leading Lysander and Demetrius away from each other in the woods I was required, as in the play, to imitate their voices, so I can claim, with some justification, to have sung both tenor and baritone parts at the Royal Opera House, Covent Garden!

Dawn and I were married on December 9th, a week before the opening of *A Midsummer Night's Dream,* so not only did I have my parents in the audience on that occasion, it was also graced by the presence of my wife – another first for me! The wedding took place at the Friends Meeting House in St. Martin's Lane, a Quaker wedding which, for those unfamiliar with the rites of that particular sect or, more to the point, the absence of them, is performed without the benefit of clergy, the two parties being considered perfectly capable of making that public commitment in the presence of their 'Friends' and, as in all their religious dealings, in direct communion with their God. For legal reasons, of course, there has to be a registrar present and, as with any contract, witnesses to the act, but otherwise it is a refreshingly simple and grown-up way of going about it. The wedding itself takes place within the context of an ordinary Meeting for Worship, and consequently you are bound to find yourselves in unfamiliar company or indeed, as with us, in the company of complete strangers, being neither Quakers ourselves, nor of that 'parish.' We had our families there, of course, together with a few friends of our own, including Peter Dews, who had kindly agreed to be my Best Man, but otherwise the supporting cast was made up of members of the local Quaker community, any of whom is free to stand up and speak during the meeting as 'The spirit moves them'. In fact, several did, and it was remarkable, as much is remarkable about that most persuasive of all Christian sects, how in tune the speakers appeared to be, and not just with the occasion, but with us, strangers to them. Why a Quaker wedding? Well, it was Dawn's idea, really. Having become attached to a family of Quakers whilst working in Ludlow – a hotbed of Quakerism, if you can imagine such a thing – she had come to admire their way of life, their inner strength and their no-frills approach to religion. I suppose I should come clean at this point, and confess that I have never adhered to any faith beyond a childhood acceptance of Christianity as being somehow compulsory. I was baptised a Roman Catholic, for the simple reason that it was my mother's inherited faith although, to my almost certain knowledge, she never practised it and, consequently, neither did I. I took part in all the ordinary C of E church services whilst at school, sang regularly in St. Laurence's Church choir, adorned in cassock and surplice, and may well have done that even if I hadn't been paid fourpence a time for my services. During the years that followed, and particularly when I enlisted in the RAF, I remember struggling with my conscience when it came to filling in forms that required you to declare your religious denomination. For reasons that now bewilder me, 'don't know,' 'agnostic' or 'atheist' were unacceptable in those days, and may well still be if you're thinking of joining the armed forces. In fact, even as I write this, a friend tells me that he felt constrained to remove the word 'atheist' from his Facebook page because of the amount of hate-mail he received. But, in any case, I had no strong opinions at the time, and certainly not strong enough to call myself, with any degree of conviction, an atheist. So in the end I always opted for C of E, mainly because it was the easy way out;

nobody questioned it and, apart from a modicum of lip-service, no one expected anything from you. I suppose that's the unavoidable risk taken by Established Churches all over the world. They represent conformity and provide a safe haven for the uncommitted. That's one of the reasons, probably the main reason, I was attracted to the Quakers or, to give them their proper title, the Religious Society of Friends. No safe haven and no soft options are to be found amongst them; unless, of course, you are able to contemplate a lifetime of self-deception. They have done away with symbols of any kind, right down to the exchanging of rings at a wedding ceremony although, having eschewed didacticism as well, they allow you the choice. They are strongly opposed to gambling and famously, of course, known for their adherence to pacifism. But, here again, they allow for conscience, making each individual responsible for his or her own decisions, answerable only to that 'Inner Light' which lies at the centre of their beliefs. Fellowship, without doubt, plays a large part in their religious lives, but beyond that there are no points of reference outside the Scriptures, no refuge to be found in ritual and no absolution to be had from the confessional. For someone like me, who even then was fascinated and yet, at the same time, repelled by the kind of mumbo-jumbo associated with a lot of other faiths, Quakerism represented Christianity in its purest form. Not that I had any illusions about becoming a member. For a start, I was well aware that the apparently laissez-faire principles on which the Society's rules were founded, placed a huge burden on the individual, at the very least in ascetic terms, and I knew I simply wasn't up to it. No doubt they wouldn't have raised any objections to my shortcomings, and would still have welcomed me with open arms. On one point, however, they were obdurate. They insisted on a belief in the existence of a loving and compassionate God, and even at the age of 23, I entertained far too many doubts on that score to qualify for membership.

Dawn and I began our married lives at 43 Campden Hill Towers, along with a delightful Siamese kitten called 'Bosie', purchased from Harrods as a wedding present, and so named, I can only surmise, on account of our recently having seen *The Trials of Oscar Wilde*, starring an impossibly glamorous Peter Finch.

Our marriage couldn't have got off to a better start, both of us being gainfully employed and, as far as I was concerned, in particularly dilettante fashion as the immediate future held nothing more demanding for me than the occasional appearance in *A Midsummer Night's Dream* at Covent Garden, giving only one performance a week more often than not, and for which I was paid the princely sum of £50 a time. Nevertheless, the rent still had to be found, and with Clinton Greyn's departure to a flat in Bayswater with his girl-friend, the search for a lodger became something of a priority. We were lucky; Dawn's connections with the BBC Television design department led to a visit from a charming young man called Darrol Blake who, being equally charmed by the accommodation, decided to move in. Over the months we got to know and like Darrol, who remains a friend to this day, and it transpired quite early on that he and a colleague, also from the design department, and desirous of a career change, had decided to apply for the television director's course. In the fullness of time, having all but completed the course, they were given a minimal budget and required to cast and direct a short piece of their own choosing by way of demonstrating their newly acquired skills. The rules for this exercise were very specific. No film was to be employed, no outside locations used. It had to be a studio production with a specially designated crew. Unfortunately, there was nothing Darrol could offer me in his test piece, although he felt sure that his colleague, who had opted to direct an excerpt from that powerful First World War drama, *Paths of Glory*, would be bound to find something for me, which he did. I ended up playing one of the witnesses in the court-martial scene, dominated by that fine television actor, Keith Barron, as the defending officer, originally played by Kirk Douglas in the 1957 Stanley Kubrick film. Now, whereas Darrol stuck to the rules, and ended up directing perfectly respectable but essentially routine television drama for the rest of his days at the BBC, his colleague threw caution to the winds and flouted the regulations by hiring his own crew and filming battle scenes on Clapham Common. It was thrilling stuff, but he should, of course, have been disqualified for cheating; instead of which he eventually became Sir Ridley Scott! I don't think Æsop covered that particular scenario, or did he? Anyway, needless to say, having contributed in a small way to Ridley's meteoric rise, he never asked me to work for him again, and I'm not sure he ever asked Keith Barron either. Darrol, on the other hand, made me several offers over the years, for which I was duly grateful.

In the early months of 1962, after having spent the best part of the previous year in Warwickshire, the last thing I wanted to do was to leave home and hearth again so soon. But an offer came up that, for some reason, I found irresistible. It came by way of my new agent, whose name I can no longer remember, but whose services on my behalf did not, in any case, survive the fiasco I was about to embark upon. For some strange reason, not uncommon with events seen through the wrong end of a telescope, I look back on it now with a kind of indulgent affection, although I'm sure I didn't feel that way at the time.

Terence Fitzgerald, whose particular claim to fame was that he managed to combine, under one umbrella, a Theatrical Production Company and a Domestic Cleaning Service, had decided to tour a play called *Cry For Love,* by someone called Robert Owen, a play that owed more than a little to the better known, and infinitely better written Emlyn Williams play, *Night Must Fall,* the rights to which must surely have been unavailable at the time. It was to be a five week tour, opening at the Sunderland Empire, co-starring Susan Shaw (erstwhile daughter of Jack Warner and Kathleen Harrison in the popular post-war *Huggett* pictures), and me. Come to think of it, that's why I accepted the offer, of course, and so puffed up was I by the prospect of co-starring, it didn't even enter my head to ask 'why me?' My memories of that particular engagement are few, but nonetheless vivid, and most of them centre upon Miss Shaw herself, still a very attractive woman, although the bloom of her celebrated youth had by then left her, hastened in its departure by an over-fondness for whisky. As Huw Prosser, a young Welsh psychopath – yes, it strayed that close to the original – I spent a good deal of the play in her seductive embrace until, that is, I decided to do away with her on the sofa. The trouble was that, while she was quite alluring from a distance, the miasma created by what I can only describe as a walking distillery, was difficult to handle in a clinch, testing my acting skills to the limit. I was also kept on my toes trying to guess by which door, if any, she was going to enter, and for that reason alone, I have to say, I became increasingly thankful for the waft of Johnny Walker that announced her arrival on stage.

It was rumoured amongst the company although, as far as I know, no evidence was ever offered to support the claim, that *Cry For Love* was, in fact, written by a young John Osborne, and that Robert Owen was merely a *nom de plume.* It was a nice idea, but while I could sympathise with Mr. Owen's desire to become a figment, I found it hard to believe that John Osborne could have had any sane reason for hauling it out of his bottom drawer and selling it to Terence Fitzgerald. In any case I was persuaded at the time that 'inside knowledge' had confirmed it as the truth and so, with my fellow actors, I was perfectly happy to go along with it, taking some satisfaction from the idea that, instead of trying to breathe life into a piece of third-rate plagiarism, we were engaged in the altogether more prestigious exercise of staging 'an early Osborne'!

Opening the tour at the Sunderland Empire was not a very bright idea, it being one of the largest, if not *the* largest, theatre on the Moss Empire circuit, and although my assertion that we played to £40 worth of ticket sales during the week might be slightly exaggerated for the sake of making a point, I can't have been that wide of the mark. Not that we had any reason to be surprised. Susan Shaw's celebrity, such as it was, was already verging on the antique, whilst my name would have meant nothing to anyone in the north-east or, come to that, at any other point of the compass, and with John Osborne being determinedly coy about his authorship, our fate was pretty well sealed. Even the handful of bums that found their way onto the seats of the Empire were not exactly choice. I had occasion, during one performance, to stop the play in order to admonish four young men in the front stalls for creating a disturbance. I had only recently been told of a similar incident during a performance of *Billy Liar* in the West End when Albert Finney, playing the title role, had told certain members of the audience that if they wished to continue their conversation, they were free to do so by removing themselves from the auditorium. Provoked as I undoubtedly was, I decided to emulate Mr. Finney's dignified protest. But while the disruptive element at the Comedy Theatre was suitably chastened, allowing the play to resume, and the rest of the audience to enjoy it in peace and quiet, the four young men in the front stalls at the Sunderland Empire were only too happy to accept my invitation. They got up and left, depriving us of approximately 25% of our audience! At another performance, as the play (and mercifully the week) drew to a close, Huw Prosser was in the process of being cornered by the local Methodist Minister, determined to force a confession from the boy. I backed up the staircase, as was my wont, with that splendid and genuinely Welsh actor, Artro Morris, in close pursuit, and grabbing hold of a banister rail, found myself in sudden possession of the entire rail, it having come adrift from the staircase. Obviously, the actors weren't the only things that came cheap in that production. However, I was at least spared the humiliation of it being greeted by derisory laughter, as there were never enough of them out there to create such a sound. It was, nevertheless, a fitting end to our week in Sunderland and, as it turned out, to the entire tour; the citizens of Bradford, our next port-of-call, having succumbed to an outbreak of smallpox. I cannot recall any tears being shed by the members of the cast or, indeed, any questions being asked about why we shouldn't pick up the remainder of the tour a week later. Perhaps we all felt we'd sufficiently plumbed the depths of *Cry for Love,* or that the durability of the set, following the banister incident, could not be guaranteed in transit. Personally, I prefer to attribute our acquiescence to a premonition that smallpox, or some other notifiable disease requiring quarantine, would suddenly, and without warning, break out in the rest of the towns we were due to visit, their populations being miraculously spared only if we decided not to go there. Another reason for not lamenting the cancellation of the tour was that, having been seduced by the aforementioned Welsh actor into visiting most of the betting-shops in Sunderland, I was in grave danger of becoming an addict and, having already spent a week at the Roker Park Hotel, accommodation befitting my 'star' status but way beyond my meagre salary, I would have returned to London substantially out of pocket, giving my father-in-law further cause to question the sanity of his daughter. As it was, I found myself obliged to accept an offer of employment in that other branch of Terence Fitzgerald's entrepreneurial empire, cleaning the flats of perfectly able-bodied ladies of leisure in Swiss Cottage and St. John's Wood. This came to an end, somewhat peremptorily, a couple of weeks later when I suggested to a particularly officious customer, after she had followed me from room to room, criticising my efforts, peering into corners I had recently hoovered, running her fingers across surfaces I had just cleaned, and even finding fault with the way I held the vacuum-cleaner, that if she had so much time on her hands, and was clearly such an expert, maybe she should seriously consider cleaning her own flat; or words to that effect.

I was rescued from the Chadwick Street Labour Exchange shortly after this by my old colleague from *An Age of Kings,* Patrick Garland, recently turned director, who asked me if I would like to play Puck in a concert version of Mendelssohn's *A Midsummer Night's Dream,* a one-off performance with the Birmingham Symphony Orchestra at the Royal Shakespeare Theatre, Stratford-upon-Avon, of all places. Well, as it turned out, and contrary to expectations, it was good to go back, independent of the régime, and as one of a select group of actors, four or five of us at the most, including Tony Church and Elizabeth Sellars, prominent members of the company during my season there. I can recall little of the event itself, except that it allowed me to work, albeit briefly, alongside the legendary Robert Atkins, whose Bottom had been exposed on numerous occasions and almost every summer in Regent's Park. In fact, Robert Atkins had run the

Open Air Theatre there for almost 30 years, and had only just handed over the reins to David Conville, under whose aegis, in 1962, the New Shakespeare Company was born.

I knew nothing of David Conville at that time, save that he had had the wit and the wisdom to engage David William as his artistic director for that first season and who had, in his turn, been wise enough to invite Dawn to design the costumes for the opening production which was to be, surprise-surprise, *A Midsummer Night's Dream*. It says a great deal about the character of the Open Air Theatre, Regent's Park, that throughout its history, going back to its beginnings in 1900 under the direction of Ben Greet, right on through the decades and up to the present day, *A Midsummer Night's Dream* has been by far the most oft repeated play in its repertoire. True, 'The Dream' has a more popular appeal than many other of Shakespeare's plays, but the main reason is surely that it sits more comfortably in that arena, open to the sky, and with its greensward stage surrounded by natural foliage, than any other I can think of. And what other play, especially in its closing moments, is served so perfectly by nature's stage management, daylight giving way, almost imperceptibly, to candle-lit night and the approach of fairy-time. Throughout its long history, and despite its more recent modernisations and reconstructions, the conversion of the adjacent tent, previously used as an alternative auditorium in the event of rain, had become a rather smart restaurant presided over by the eccentric and fashionable restaurateur, Clement Freud. Mulled wine now became the perfect antidote to chilly summer evenings. Together with the subsequent raking of its 1,100 seat auditorium and the introduction of more complex settings, plus a more sophisticated, state-of-the-art lighting rig, the magic of that entirely natural effect has never been improved upon, and remains to this day reason enough by itself to make the trip.

Dawn had already worked on a previous production of the 'The Dream' with David William only a couple of years earlier at Ludlow Castle, although those ancient stones provide a more fitting backdrop for Shakespeare's history plays than for his Sylvan comedies. Legend has it that David, having cast a host of Shropshire lads and lassies as the fairies, addressed them prior to rehearsals as they sat cross-legged and eager-eyed on the grass outside the castle walls. This is what I was told he said, "You may well imagine that there is something effeminate about playing fairies. You would be quite wrong. What I am looking for from you all is a kind of courtly humour". You can see them all, can't you, turning to each other, heaving a sigh of relief, and saying, "Phew!

Thank goodness for that!" I saw the production, but can remember little of it, except that Terry Scully, fresh from his success as Henry VI in *An Age of Kings,* had played Puck. On this occasion, however, having seen my performance at Covent Garden, David offered the part to me, and I jumped at the chance. It would, after all, be an opportunity to play it in its entirety, and without orchestral backing. Besides, having missed out on the Ludlow experience, and only witnessing it from Dawn's perspective, I desperately wanted to work with David. I had admired much of his work at Ludlow, knew him as an actor, and was aware, again courtesy of Dawn, that he was held in high esteem as a director by other actors, even by those who had crossed swords with him. Stories of his almost daily clashes with Alan Dobie during *Macbeth,* had filtered through to me, strongly featuring an uphill struggle to convince his leading man that a belief in the supernatural, if only for the duration, was a decided asset when tackling that particular role, an argument refuted by Alan who was not, perhaps, the brightest button in the box, but obdurate as any brick wall, as I myself was to discover a decade or so later. I too, had clashed with David on one memorable occasion. Having left Stratford, with Dawn riding pillion, following a Saturday matinée, and in good time to reach Ludlow for the final performance of *Macbeth,* my Lambretta suffered a breakdown, as did Dawn who was better acquainted with David than I was, and knew for a fact that 'mechanical failure' would have no place in his lexicon, and that using it as an excuse for missing the last performance of their production, would be to invite nothing but contempt. We did, in fact, miss the show, although we arrived in time for the last night party, and Dawn was, of course, quite right. Accepting my responsibility as keeper of the machine, I offered my apologies for failing to deliver his costume designer at the appointed time, whereupon David brushed aside my excuses and proceeded to launch into a full-scale verbal assault on Dawn for what he chose to call her disloyalty. We were sitting down by this time, on either side of a table, and I was astonished by David's apparent sincerity, and the vehemence with which he relentlessly pressed home his attack. I was also troubled by Dawn's obvious distress. I knew that she held David in high esteem, both as a friend and as a working colleague, and that nothing he said, of whatever nature, would be easily laughed off. But his charges against her were so outrageous, and so clearly bordering on the Kafkaesque, I began to suspect that, instead of making a genuine case, he was simply indulging in a favourite game at her expense. In my newly acquired role of fiancé, I decided to intervene, even knowing as

I did, with looming certainty, that I was about to put my featherweight intellect into the ring against an acknowledged heavyweight. But I am nothing if not chivalrous, even on occasions to the point of recklessness, and so in I jumped, accusing David of concocting a trumped-up case simply to satisfy his own desire to dominate and wound, while his deliberate choice and subsequent misuse of the word 'loyalty' was nothing short of despicable. I should admit right here and now that I probably said nothing of the sort, and that I have purposely put a gloss on it, in order to highlight the dénouement. Whatever it was that I did say I remember being quite happy about, as well as being somewhat proud too that I had managed – or so I thought – to control myself throughout the diatribe; David had, at least, been silenced. He regarded me throughout with just the hint of a smile on his face, although I suppose it could have been the trace of a smirk. When I had finished, he looked down at my hands which were resting – or so I thought – on the table, and there was certainly a smirk on his face as he said, "Why do you keep fidgeting with your cigarette packet, Terry?" Well, that was it, I'm afraid. All poise, all dignity, and whatever vestige of self-control was left to me departed as I stood, leaned across the table, and yelled, "Listen, do you want to come outside?" The warmth of the smile that replaced the smirk was quite genuine, and proclaimed his victory. Although, come to think of it, the subject of Dawn's loyalty did not arise again. It was almost impossible to score points off David, whose armoury, as well as a pretty unassailable intellect, consisted of a cornucopian vocabulary, so that if you were momentarily stuck for a word, even if it were to use against him, he would instantly supply it. He had also acquired, no doubt from his public-school days, a well-rehearsed superciliousness that was brought into play whenever he sensed you were out of your depth or, indeed, on those all-too-rare occasions when, perhaps, you were getting too close to the truth. Above all, however, and by way of remission, he was possessed of great warmth and a keen sense of humour, never too far below the surface, and verging at times on the kind of silliness that is the almost exclusive preserve of the extremely clever, public-school educated university graduate.

He had meanwhile, at the Open Air Theatre, assembled a pretty impressive cast for *A Midsummer Night's Dream,* led by Patrick Wymark as Bottom and Heather Chasen as Helena, both of whom I knew well. In fact, I had only recently worked alongside Patrick in a BBC Television adaptation, directed by Peter Dews, of Robert Graves' book, *They Hanged My Saintly Billy,* in which he had played the notorious

Staffordshire murderer, William Palmer. Another colleague from way back was James Ottaway as Peter Quince. Relatively new faces belonged to Edward Petherbridge and Bernard Lloyd, as Demetrius and Lysander, while David himself, as well as directing the production, was to play Oberon. If I had entertained even the slightest notion that I was about to embark upon a familiar and well-charted journey, I was quickly disabused. The rehearsal process proved to be arduous and challenging, both physically and mentally. The fact that I had played the part, or versions of it, on several previous occasions and very recently too, was not acknowledged, and any attempt on my part to take short cuts was dealt with swiftly and decisively. As far as David was concerned, I had never before even approached the level of commitment he was demanding, and never before had I examined the text in anything like the detail he insisted upon. Far from being an advantage, my previous experience of playing Puck was turning out to be something of a handicap and, as David ruthlessly set about kicking the props I had been depending upon from under me, I began to feel very vulnerable indeed. I have good cause to remember what happened next, for the simple reason that it has never happened to me since. I have witnessed, on several occasions over the years, an actor being stripped bare of preconceptions, mannerisms, and all those myriad habitual quirks that constitute a safety-net, and almost as often I have seen the trust engendered by such a painful, yet willing surrender betrayed by a director who was either incapable of building on the ruins he had created or, for other more subterranean reasons, disinclined to do so. Not so with David William, for whom the task began there, not by imposing a performance on me, far from it, but by forcing me to dig deeper and discover in myself resources I didn't know I possessed. There were times, I have to say, when I desperately wanted to say "enough is enough", but every time I tried to close the door, David would kick it open again. He never allowed me to settle for anything and, even in performance, whilst playing Oberon, his directorial eye – and just occasionally his voice – urged me on. The end result was that I gave a performance, the like of which I had never given before and, while my approach to acting certainly underwent a sea-change from that point on, I am not entirely sure I have ever given since.

Playing Puck in the Open Air Theatre, Regent's Park, was an exhilarating experience. In a delightful production, enhanced by the pretty pastel shades of her Watteau-inspired costumes, Dawn had created for me a second skin in the form of a body-stocking, attached to the lower half of which was animal fur, and from the waist up, leaves and foliage of one sort or another had been appliquéd so that, in the words of one critic, '… it would be no surprise to discover that he actually lived in, or under, Regent's Park'. Half-masked and with a wig that was distinctly fox-like, both in colour and in shape, I was 'akin to Debussy's faun', according to another review, or if you chose to read *The Financial Times*, '…looking like some sharp, adolescent Papageno, spanning the earth, we really do believe' (or at least R.B. Marriott did), 'impish, droll, a sprite to touch the heart' or, to complete this brief anthology, '… truly a merry – and sinister – wanderer of the night.'

Costume designer Dawn Pavitt with her designs for 'The Dream'.

There was an element of the unexpected in the almost universal praise heaped upon the production by critics and public alike. The Open Air Theatre had become a bit of a joke in recent years. Uninspired and poorly dressed productions watched by relatively sparse audiences in assorted deckchairs were the order of the day, and even with the coming of the New Shakespeare Company, expectations could not have prepared them for what they were about to see. The following extract from a review in the *News Chronicle*, one of many in similar vein, captures the surprise with which David's production was greeted: 'Magic returned last night to Regent's Park. After years of Shakespeare in an atmosphere of cocoa and stale cake, he is now served with strawberries and champagne.

1962 'The Dream' - Regent's Park Open Air Theatre with Barbara Latham as the First Fairy.

As we saw with the summer's first production ... everything is improved. The wide stage with its melancholy little hedge has gone. The eye is now concentrated on a small crescent lawn dominated by an elegant and baroque staircase. All suspicion of an impoverished church pageant in which actors seem to have rummaged through a very old costume skip is completely banished. There are gleaming new clothes, specially designed. And, far more important, the acting and the production by David William are really worthy of the author and the setting. The poetry sang – yes, this is really Regent's Park I'm talking about! – and the comedy was uproarious ... The play danced along to an ecstatic climax when the fairies seemed to be flitting through the branches of the star-spangled trees. Take overcoats, blankets, hot water bottles, and snow-shoes, if you have to, but see this *Dream.'*

Perhaps not surprisingly, the production was revived the following year with a few cast changes, but essentially it was the same, although if anything, it had matured. Certainly most of the critics seemed to think so, and while a favourable review in *The Stage*, our long-established trade paper, is unlikely to be read by many who have not come near to treading the boards themselves, I cannot resist quoting from it on this occasion '...Terry Wale is surely one of the finest Pucks of all time; certainly, I would say, the finest of our time.'

There were two other shows during that first season. Denis Carey's production of *Twelfth Night,* having played at the Ludlow Festival, came into the Park with an entirely different company, some of whom remained to join those of us who were invited to stay on for David William's final production of *Love's Labour's Lost.* I was offered the part of Costard, the Clown, which turned out to be something of a rest-cure after the rigours of playing Puck. My relationship with David during rehearsals for 'The Dream' had been so intense and demanding that I'd scarcely had time to take in all those other aspects of the production that were going on around me. Now it seemed that, from time to time, I had the leisure to sit back and watch him in his element, coaxing and cajoling performances out of other actors with sympathy and understanding, often playful yet always disciplined. David's unsurprising empathy with actors, being one himself, was entirely matched, on this occasion, by his affinity with the deliciously indulgent, and rarely performed play. *Love's Labour's Lost* takes place in the hothouse world of academia, where the four young men at the centre of the play take an oath to forsake worldly pleasures and to embrace nothing but cloistered study for three years, in spite of the fact that they are expecting a visit from the Princess of France and her three equally desirable ladies-in-waiting. Needless to say, their high-minded ambitions falter in the face of rising testosterone levels, and the ladies, equally in thrall but far less airy-fairy than their male counterparts, send each of them packing for 'a twelve month and a day' as a forfeit for breaking an oath they should never have been silly enough to take in the first place. It's a delightful piece of what must have been, with all its verbal conceits, elitist entertainment even in the late 16th century, although it says a great deal for the aspirations, or at least the catholic tastes, of the groundlings at that time that it eventually found its way out of the rarefied confines of the court and into the playhouse. No one, I suggest, was better equipped to bring it to life in the 20th century than was David who, after all, had at least one foot in that esoteric world himself. Sharing the experience was a complete joy, watching performances grow under his careful tutelage, seeing them eventually take flight on wings of their own, making complete sense of a play which, only a short time before, had probably mystified most of them as much as it bewildered me. I remember particularly Bernard Lloyd's Berowne, edged with cynicism, but falling harder and more irreversibly in love than any of his colleagues, and Edward Petherbridge as Dumaine, whose effete and scholarly pretensions give way, in the face of new-found love, to the writing of passionate sonnets. Then there was Peter Whitbread's gloriously fantastical and thickly accented Spaniard, Don Adriano de Armado, and Michael Blakemore's wonderfully pedantic schoolmaster, Holofernes, ill-equipped in that hot-house world to join in the cut and thrust of erudite word-play with the best of them, and settling, instead, for the unquestioning approbation of the Curate, Sir Nathaniel, a beautifully obsequious performance from James Ottaway. Michael Blakemore, of course, went on to become a distinguished director, and subsequently published his own Memoir, *Arguments with England,* in which he, too, looks back on that episode in his life, drawing a picture of David in rehearsal with such insight and perspicuity that I cannot resist quoting from it:

'Guiding us we had a director who might have been born to do this play, whose own love of language, playfulness and sense of honour had a shining mirror in the text. We were all quick to recognise that, in a certain way, he owned it, and we were happy to put ourselves in his hands. David William was an actor-director with, on first acquaintance, a haughty, rather prancing manner like an over-bred horse, which left you unprepared for the humour and firm benevolence with which he ran a rehearsal room. It was a pleasure to come to work because you knew you were going to get justice. His authority had the transparency which comes, not from egotism, but from a passionate concern for the greater good. He never hesitated to intervene when he felt that mistakes were being made, or when a scene could be improved, but he also had the modesty when rehearsals were going well, to simply watch and become, in Guthrie's phrase, an ideal audience of one.'

It was while I, too, was watching these and other delightful performances, too numerous to mention, take shape and grow before my eyes, that I realised David hadn't said a word to me about my own burgeoning performance as Costard. Having been under the lash pretty well without remission during rehearsals for 'The Dream', I began to experience a feeling of insecurity, fast followed by a gnawing sense of my own inadequacy. Why was David not giving me any notes? Obviously because he thought my performance was beyond salvation. It took me a while to pluck up the courage to confront him, and when I did, all he said was that he thought I was very good, but that he didn't have much to contribute, Costard being 'low comedy.' It was rather like the lord of the manor offering reassurance to a lowly servant, while at the same time generously acknowledging my superior knowledge of life 'below stairs'. Having been put firmly in my place, I doffed my cap, and got on with the job, remembering as I did so, that he hadn't had much to say to the rude mechanicals in *A Midsummer Night's Dream* either.

The critical reception for *Love's Labour's Lost* was, if anything, more rapturous than that we had received for 'The Dream', for the simple reason that David had astonishingly made this seemingly remote and largely archaic verbal confection entirely accessible to a modern audience. The redoubtable Bernard Levin, in a review which was headlined, 'A Labour of Love and Joy Beyond All Praise,' went on to say, 'I cannot recall more than half a dozen occasions at the theatre in my life which were productive of so much unalloyed delight.'

It had been a triumphant first season for the New Shakespeare Company. On a very personal level, it had restored my faith in the relationship between actor and director to the extent that it became a benchmark for the rest of my professional life. We were, it has to be said, a very good company of actors, young and untried for the most part, but full of enthusiasm, and with an ability to speak Shakespeare's verse that, even then, was compared favourably to what was on offer at the Old Vic and at Stratford-upon-Avon. But above all else, and quite deservedly, it had been a triumph for David William who had inspired us, brought out the best in us, and left us all, I'm sure, feeling privileged to have been part of it.

Many years later, at a party in Regent's Park hosted by David Conville to celebrate the 40th anniversary of that first season, and while those of us who were still around ate and drank in the rather chic restaurant that had by then replaced the tent, fondly reminiscing and lamenting those who were no longer with us, I found myself sitting next to David William, who had returned from his home in Canada for the occasion. He was older of course, and somewhat less imperious than I had remembered him, but none the less iconic for all that. We talked of many things, but mainly of the past, and I reminded him of his address to the fairies in Ludlow, memories of which, obviously long dormant, made him cringe with embarrassment. I then asked him if he remembered a meeting between us, a couple of years after our sojourn in Regent's Park and which took place, for some reason long since forgotten, in a coffee bar close to Aldgate underground station. He had invited me to take part in a season at the Mermaid Theatre, still under the aegis of Bernard Miles who was to direct *Macbeth,* while David himself was going to direct a production of Dekker's *The Shoemaker's Holiday.* Having been prepared for this meeting, I had read the play and, when David asked me what I would like to play in it, I had no hesitation in declaring my interest in the part of Firk, very sharp, very London and, consequently, or so I thought, very much up my street. "I'm afraid that part has already been cast", he said. "How would you like to play Rafe?" Well, it was a good enough part, to be sure, but not one that had leapt off the page as particularly right for me. Still, if David thought I could do it ... "And what would you like to play in *Macbeth?*" he asked. "Malcolm", I said, but with a lack of conviction that was immediately justified when he said, "That's already been cast too". The very same actor, as it happened, and who David went on to name, had been invited to play both parts. The fact that I had no great respect for the actor in question seemed somehow irrelevant in the circumstances, so I'd said, probably with a hint of irritation in my voice, "You keep asking me what I want to play. Why don't you just tell me what I'm being offered?" "Fleance," he replied, without a moment's hesitation. "Fleance?" I said, clearly astonished. "But, David, Fleance has only got two lines!" At which point, David had risen to his full height without getting up, and with all the indignation of a schoolmaster outraged by his pupil's ignorance, he'd looked down his nose at me, and said in icy reproof, "But Terry, Fleance is the hope of Scotland!" I don't know what reaction I expected upon recounting that story forty years on in Regent's Park, but David didn't disappoint me. After considering it for a few moments, a familiar smile, or was it a smirk, returned to his face, and he said, with just a hint of the old hauteur, "I think I can live with that!"

While we were enjoying this reunion, a matinée performance

was going on in the adjacent theatre, still under the banner of the New Shakespeare Company, still flourishing all those years later. It was surely something worth celebrating, and I know I wasn't alone in thinking that. Looking back on my time at the Open Air Theatre, with all that has happened to me since, I count myself singularly blessed to have been part of a venture so ambitious, so true to the spirit of the plays, and so personally enriching. In bringing this particular episode in my life to a close, I am bound to turn again to Michael Blakemore, who entirely reflects my own thoughts and feelings, but in words more precise and infinitely more expressive than I could possibly summon up:

'The rain that fell on us was the same English rain that had once fallen on performances at the Globe, and attested to what is always true about theatrical enterprise – its riskiness and the quixotic gallantry that is sometimes needed to sustain it. In the open air all performances begin badly. Broad daylight is not kind to actors and their pretences, and the dramatic propositions they bring on with them can seem ludicrously simplistic in a setting of indubitably real trees and open sky. You wonder if disbelief will ever be suspended. Then, slowly, the darkness falls, and the surrounding world begins to close down to that small patch of illuminated grass. The see-saw of credibility begins at last to tilt in favour of the players, as they extract a single strand of drama from that which surrounds them, and is now receding into the shadows – the world's chaos … The last hour of a good production in the open air can have a power all its own as, against the odds, the idea of theatre slyly raises its banner.'

oOoOo

Twelve

In the early months of 1963, Darrol Blake left 43 Campden Hill Towers, having married and opted for a transpontine life in Barnes. Dawn and I were consequently faced with the prospect of looking for another lodger who would inevitably up and go, leaving us to go through the same ritual time and time again; and besides, Darrol had become a friend. There was no guarantee we would go on being that lucky, and the idea of sharing our home with a series of random transients did not appeal to either of us. In any case we were newly-weds and didn't really want to share our home with anybody – except for the cat, of course. Bosie had made it perfectly clear that running up and down the corridor outside the flat, although acceptable for a kitten, was no longer a viable alternative to exploring the world, only tantalisingly glimpsed from the windowsill until now. And so it was, to some extent, with his needs in mind, that we went to look at a self-contained ground-floor flat in rural Buckinghamshire, which Dawn had seen advertised in one of the 'posh' Sundays. We took the train from Marylebone Station to Great Missenden, from where a fairly infrequent bus service took us to the tiny hamlet of Ballinger, en route to Chesham.

Ballinger Grange was a substantial country house, divided into four flats, with extensive and well-kept communal gardens to the front, featuring a pretty, trellised archway interwoven with flowers, and equally extensive grounds to the rear, although these were overgrown and completely neglected. There was no doubt that Flat 4, situated as it was on the ground floor, was the most desirable, being possessed of a sitting-room that not only looked out onto the front gardens, but gave immediate access to them by way of a door, giving the impression that the occupants of that particular flat enjoyed, if not ownership of the gardens, at least proprietorial rights. It was an impression, I should say, that our neighbours did nothing to contradict while we lived there. Strangely, and unusually, I have no recollection of our neighbours at Ballinger Grange. We hardly ever saw them and, to my almost certain knowledge, never in those lovely gardens. The flat itself, being a conversion, was oddly shaped but spacious, and consisted of two bedrooms, one of which was immediately requisitioned by Dawn as a workroom, her skills as a cutter of theatrical costumes designed by others as well as by herself, providing our only more or less regular income. The flat also had a good-sized kitchen/dining-room, and all of this came for £4 – or it might have been guineas – per week!

Bosie was the first to make himself at home. After one or two tentative forays beyond the front door, and then, having thoroughly explored the immediate area, he would disappear, much to our consternation, for hours at a time. But he always returned, exhausted but unscathed, at the end of the day. Our only real concern was that he wasn't eating. We tried everything, switching brands of cat food, even offering him morsels from our own plates, but he just sniffed at them and walked away. We even considered the possibility that he was hunting his own food, but given that he'd lived such a cloistered and somewhat pampered existence until then, we dismissed that idea as ludicrous. The oddest thing of all was that he looked perfectly fit and well nourished. The mystery was finally solved when I ran into the judge's wife from the even more imposing house next door. "Is that your Siamese cat who comes visiting?" "Yes, probably", I said. "I hope he's not making a nuisance of himself." "No, not at all. We've discovered he loves pheasant, so we leave some out for him every day. You should try it," she suggested, a touch patronisingly, and I couldn't quite make up my mind whether she meant try it on the cat, or try it ourselves. Anyway, I got the distinct impression that not only did she think pheasant was probably too good for us, but that a cat of such refined tastes was too good for us as well. Clearly, he had 'Harrods' stamped all over him!

While Bosie took to country life with a vengeance, and with more than a hint of rent-a-cat in his shameless search for *haute cuisine*, Dawn and I were finding it more difficult. In fact, I'm not entirely sure that we ever felt we belonged there. Not that we didn't like the flat or the surrounding countryside; nor were we particularly bothered by the lack of friends or even the potential for making any in the neighbourhood. But the absence of shops in Ballinger, together with the infrequent bus service between Great Missenden and Chesham, proved to be wearisome, and having said goodbye to my Lambretta some time back, it soon became clear that I was going to have to take driving lessons before long and get myself a car. I don't know if we ever discussed the necessity of commuting to London, but it must have occurred to us that rural Buckinghamshire was not exactly the pulsating centre of anything very much, and certainly not of the entertainment industry. The problem was not quite so urgent as far as Dawn was concerned, although her less frequent trips were more burdensome, involving as they often did the transportation of finished costumes to London, and a return trip with a case full of fabric, invariably purchased from Borovic's in Berwick Street market, for the making of more. Her day jobs, including a spell as lecturer and occasional designer at the London Academy of Music & Dramatic Art, which she thoroughly enjoyed, and a brief period in the BBC Television costume department which, in spite of a decent salary, holiday pay and a superannuation scheme, she did not enjoy at all, had come to an end, and she had reverted to her former status, happily and determinedly freelance. As far as I was concerned, however, it was not long before I found myself commuting by train to London on a daily basis, occasionally sharing the platform with Clement Attlee, former Labour Prime Minister, but by then Earl Attlee of Walthamstow, although we never shared a compartment and I cannot even claim that he ever acknowledged my presence. In any case, we parted company at Marylebone, whence he undoubtedly made his way to the House of Lords, whilst I headed in the opposite direction towards Shepherd's Bush and an engagement at the BBC Television Centre.

Following the success of *An Age of Kings,* the BBC had commissioned Peter Dews to produce another Shakespearian television series, this time with a Roman theme. Three plays, *Coriolanus, Julius Caesar* and *Antony and Cleopatra* were to be split up into nine separate episodes under the generic title, *The Spread of the Eagle.* The format was to be much the same, with a nucleus of actors playing a variety of parts throughout the series, together with a handful of star names in the major roles. On this occasion, however, the names were a good deal starrier than they had been in 'Kings'. Robert Hardy's services had been retained from the earlier series to play the politically incorrect Caius Martius Coriolanus, while that doyen of British horror films, Peter Cushing, was enlisted to play Cassius in *Julius Caesar,* alongside Paul Eddington as Brutus and Keith Michell as Marc Antony. Other substantial personages, no doubt attracted to the enterprise by the sweet smell of success enjoyed by *An Age of Kings,* were Roland Culver, Beatrix Lehmann, Barrie Jones, Brian Oulton and Mary Morris, a powerfully masculine Margaret of Anjou in the previous series, and now perhaps more questionably cast as the powerfully feminine Cleopatra. There were old friends and new in the company; Bernard Lloyd from Regent's Park, and Paul Bailey from the RSC had both been enlisted, while David William was summoned back from an untimely death at Pomfret castle to play Octavius Caesar. Jerome Willis, Frank Pettingell, George Selway and Noël Johnson, whose performance as the legendary *Dick Barton – Special Agent* had kept my ear glued to the radio throughout several of my formative years, together with a few other members of the Peter Dews Repertory

Company had also returned, including myself in a variety of roles, but notably as Antony's messenger in *Julius Caesar* who then becomes, for the sake of continuity, Eros in *Antony and Cleopatra*. For those amongst us who had thought that we were about to embark upon a familiar journey, *The Spread of the Eagle* was bound to disappoint. There were many reasons for this and, to be fair, working on the series was, for those of us who had been involved in *An Age of Kings*, not only a salutary lesson in the chemistry of success, but also a rewarding experience on its own account. That we returned to the Territorial Army Drill Hall in Bulwer Street for rehearsals was perhaps, with hindsight, not a very good idea. There were too many ghosts, and far too many reminders of halcyon days, so that comparisons were inevitable and, while *The Spread of the Eagle* was by no stretch of the imagination a failure or, indeed, an unhappy experience, it certainly suffered by comparison. For a start, the three plays are not historically sequential. In fact, more than 400 years separate the events in *Coriolanus* from the other two plays and, although Peter Dews stressed from the very beginning that the concept of Rome as an ideal would be at the centre of the series, in much the same way that the English crown had been emblematic throughout *An Age of Kings*, it was not nearly as cohesive, depriving Peter, for the most part, of opportunities to serialise the episodes, as he had done so successfully with the history plays. I do recall, however, at the end of one particular episode, following the assassination of Julius Caesar, Barry Jones' lifeless body sliding to the ground, his fingers leaving a trail of blood on a plinth engraved with the letters *SPQR* over which the titles rolled. It was a nice touch, although the fact that I remember it so well is largely because, with the plays not lending themselves quite so readily to that kind of punctuation, it was a rare one. The lack of cohesion in the concept was also reflected in the structure of the company. In *An Age of Kings*, Peter had assembled a group of actors, many of whom were strangers to each other at the outset, but who were known to Peter, both professionally and personally. We were, if you like, his chosen comrades on that journey, sharing with him its hazards as well as its rewards, and the empathy that existed between us from day one as a result of that common link was matched by a mutual respect and, in most cases, a personal allegiance to Peter himself. It was not until my season with the Royal Shakespeare Company a year later that I came to understand, by the complete absence of it, how much a company of actors depends on the quality of its leadership, and especially over a long period of time. But the injection of star names into *The Spread of the Eagle* introduced a hierarchical element which, although insignificant when set alongside the Stratford system, did create a division within the company. Not that any of our celebrities were anything other than perfectly amiable, although in a slightly distanced kind of way. At an end-of-season party, Paul Bailey and I were largely responsible for putting together a cabaret for which we rewrote the lyrics to several well-known popular songs, including *Thanks for the Memory* which, if I remember correctly, went something like this:

> 'Thanks for Paul Eddington,
> And every other star who glittered from afar,
> One even smiled at me one night in the BBC Club bar.
> Oh, thank you so much.'

A more ominous arrival on the scene was Peter's newly acquired wife. Not that anyone seriously begrudged Peter the solace of marriage although, to be honest, there were those amongst us who had worked with him frequently, counting ourselves as his more or less intimate friends, who had our doubts on that score and, disregarding his own personal feelings, had been somewhat relieved when rumours of various romantic attachments had come to nothing. To us he had become a kind of totem, exemplifying all those qualities we were far too wrapped up in our own private lives to emulate. His passion, his energy, his single-minded commitment to whatever was his current project gathered us all to his banner, and we feared that nest-building would somehow blunt his edge and distract him from his real purpose which was, of course, to motivate us. Such considerations, selfish and alarmist though they might have been, did not really prepare us, however, for the shock to come, for Peter had chosen as his bride a Bradford hairdresser. Not, I hasten to add, that I have anything against hairdressers, not even from Bradford, but I would like to think that, had I married the owner of any business with which I was unfamiliar, I might have taken the trouble to learn something about that business before I considered myself qualified to offer opinions, make judgements, or indeed – however playfully – to threaten some poor employee who had maybe spoken out of turn, with an uncertain future in my wife's employ. But not for Ann Dews (née Rhodes) the rigours of a learning curve, however shallow. On numerous occasions during rehearsals, she would arrive, tweedily twin-setted, and hold court, as if her marriage to Peter had conferred upon her some kind of divine right to command our attention. She wore the mantle of director's wife as though it were a chain of office and, with that curious mixture of courtesy and self-preservation peculiar to actors, we indulged her. I am reminded that, some years later, having been invited to attend a Gala evening at the Open Air Theatre, Regent's Park, I was expected, along with a whole bunch of other actors, to attend upon the guest of honour, HRH Prince Edward who, during the interval, had the temerity to regale us with some of the most excruciatingly boring stories I had ever heard, all based upon his own thespian activities at university. We dutifully smiled, one or two of us even managing to summon up the odd chuckle. Besides, it was only a brief encounter, whereas Ann Dews was obviously going to be around for some considerable time, probably seeing herself as the guardian of Peter's best interests, but effectively distancing him from us.

1963 The Spread of the Eagle with Keith Michell and David King.

Meanwhile, *The Spread of the Eagle* had reached its climax with *Antony and Cleopatra* in which I had my featured part as Eros. During rehearsals, Keith Michell and I enjoyed a fairly light-hearted relationship, full of banter, during which, for reasons best known to himself, I took on the role of Thumper, presumably to his Bambi, a double act that culminated in a party trick in front of the entire company. Keith stood at one end of the rehearsal room, clapped his hands and shouted, "Come on, Thumper!" Whereupon, I ran towards him from the other end, the pay-off being that, instead of catching me in his outstretched arms, all six feet two of him leapt into mine, a feat that could not have been achieved with such apparent ease had he not been as light as a feather due to his macrobiotic diet. It was all pretty harmless and good-natured fun, although it was another, altogether less playful, Keith Michell who emerged as soon as we went into the studio when suddenly the only relationship that seemed to matter to him was with several strategically placed monitor screens. Viewing himself from every conceivable angle, adjusting the tilt of his head, keeping a watchful eye on his profile, he made sure that when he was obliged to share the screen with another actor, it was always to his advantage. In a scene with Mary Morris sitting at his feet, a mixture of single and two-shots, Keith became so familiar with the camera plot that he chose to stroke her face just as it cut away to a solo shot of her, now dominated by his hand. Following Antony's defeat at the Battle of Actium, as he lay sprawled in despair on a man-made hillock, and I was offering comfort whilst precariously perched on its slope, I felt his foot against mine. His attention was on a nearby monitor, and I suddenly became aware of his foot exerting pressure on mine, so that, with no purchase for either feet or hands, I slid slowly and inexorably down the hill and out of shot, no doubt to his complete satisfaction. Luckily, it was only a camera rehearsal, and by the time we came to record it, I had adjusted my position so that a repeat performance would have been all but impossible for anyone other than a professional contortionist. Outside of Hollywood legend, I had never come across such outrageous behaviour, and certainly not at the BBC Television Centre in Wood Lane. Retribution was at hand, however, when Keith's narcissism was celebrated in our end-of-season cabaret. A member of the company was persuaded to mime, while gazing into a mirror, Keith's recording of *Our Language of Love,* his hit song from the musical, *Irma La Douce.* History does not record Keith's reaction to this, although I don't recall him being around at the end of the party, and it was to be many years before our paths crossed again.

For some weeks prior to the end of the series, we had known that Peter had been invited to take 'his company' to *Chicago* the following summer to present a season of Shakespeare's plays, comprising *Hamlet, Henry V* and *Twelfth Night,* at the Ravinia Festival. Since it was obvious that the invitation had come about as a direct result of the success of *An Age of Kings* on American television, those of us who had been involved in the series, and who consequently saw ourselves as being partly responsible for the impact it had made, nurtured hopes of being included in that company, hopes that were voiced in our very own version of the song, *Chicago,* which brought the cabaret to a close. Memories of that particular lyric are pretty sketchy, although dimly remembered lines surface, such as: 'Bet your bottom dollar you'll work for Dews in Chicago, Chicago' and 'You'll have the time, the time of your life, with Hamlet the Dane and Henry the Fife' – lines which may, or may not, be worth recording for posterity.

But a lot of water, and a good deal of blood, was to flow under the bridge before that particular carrot was dangled before me. A revival of *A Midsummer Night's Dream* in Regent's Park had long been on the cards, and was received with, if anything, more critical acclaim than it had been the previous year. But prior to that I was offered the part of Conrade in David William's production of *Much Ado About Nothing,* which was to open the season. I would probably have done it too, despite the fact that Conrade is not exactly a part to send the blood coursing through the veins. As it happened, however, I was given a choice, and the alternative turned out to be, for a variety of reasons, a good deal more alluring. Peter Dews was to direct *Richard II* at Ludlow Castle, with David William, hot-foot from Regent's Park, assuming once again the part which, possibly more than any other, he was born to play. Moreover, Dawn had been engaged to design the costumes, and the prospect of actually working together in that loveliest and most authentic of settings, the very place where our future together had been sealed, proved to be irresistible. I was to play Green, one of the Caterpillars of the Commonwealth, along with Bushy and Bagot, after whose demise I was to end the play as Richard's groom, a nice little cameo and none too strenuous, affording David and I, once the play had opened, ample opportunity to brush up on the fairy scenes from 'The Dream', prior to returning to Regent's Park for the second half of the season there.

Dawn and I stayed at the Ludlow Arms Hotel, which specialised in delicious home-made curries, and was situated just on the far side of the River Teme, within earshot of the weir, whose unceasing music lulled us to blissful sleep every night more infallibly than a hatful of sleeping pills. It was a delightful place, and only a stone's throw from the castle where Richard's story was played out in the remains of an edifice that had been standing in that very same place for nearly 300 years before Richard himself, the son of *Cœur de Lion,* had been born. It was, as I had imagined it would be, an uncanny experience, the ghosts of 1,000 years of English history having, in a sense, more substance there than we poor shadows could hope to achieve in recreating them. There were, notwithstanding, moments of extraordinary power, and none more so than the sight of Richard, standing atop the crenellated walls of the Round Chapel, while Bolingbroke's followers gathered below, gazing up in awed silence at the spectacle of pure majesty outlined against the sky, the very embodiment of that divine right to rule which is at the centre of the play. It was, indeed, a moment to cherish.

But 1963 was to leave its mark for more than personal reasons. It was the year, as I have already mentioned, in which that celebrated decade, the Decade of Change, came to fruition, an assertion that was certainly borne out by scandals that rocked the Tory government to its foundations, led to the resignation of the war minister, John Profumo, made real life porn-stars out of Christine Keeler and Mandy Rice-Davies, and culminated in the suicide of Stephen Ward, convicted at the Old Bailey for being a pimp on such flimsy evidence that it was impossible to believe he was anything other than a scapegoat for the whole sorry mess. It was also the year in which the Beatles released their first single, *Please Please Me*, and in which their second, *From Me To You*, reached the number one spot where it stayed for six weeks, and to which I tirelessly 'twisted' the night away in Ludlow, the *Twist* being the only dance I have ever been able to master with any degree of proficiency. 1963 was also, and most memorably, the year in which the U.S. President, John Fitzgerald Kennedy, was assassinated.

It was some time during the late summer or early autumn, following my return to the Open Air Theatre, that I was offered a very nice part in Jack Rosenthal's play, *Green Rub*, for Granada Television. I don't think you'll find it in any list of the author's more notable achievements, but it was a very funny and well-written little play. A young sailor, home on leave after a long absence, finds that his family do not exactly live up to his dreams of homecoming, and returns to his ship, somewhat demoralised, but ultimately happy about his choice of career. John Ronane, obligatory casting for practically any leading role on TV during the '60s until Michael Caine came along, played the disenchanted sailor, with Jack Smethurst as his suddenly estranged best friend from way back, while I had a lovely time playing his younger sister's fairly objectionable boyfriend. It was certainly the best part I'd had in a modern television play up until then and consequently I was eagerly awaiting its transmission, following which I had reasonable expectations of being spoiled for choice in the work market. Dawn and

I had invited two newly-acquired friends from a nearby village to come and watch it with us, and so it was that in the early evening of November 22nd I sauntered along to our local pub and, from its off-license, purchased a bottle of wine. "Terrible news, isn't it?" said the landlady. "What is?" I asked. "Haven't you heard?", she said. "President Kennedy's been shot." I rushed back home and switched on the television just in time to catch the sombre announcement from outside the Cedars of Lebanon Hospital in Dallas, Texas, that he had died. I naturally assumed that, in the wake of such an appalling tragedy, solemn music and news updates would be the order of the day on all radio stations and television channels, and that an inappropriate trifle such as *Green Rub* would, with a bit of luck, be shelved for a happier occasion. But it was not to be. In their wisdom, the powers-that-be decided to show it, and I can only imagine that the vast majority of unsuspecting viewers were as astounded as we were, and either switched to another channel, or sat watching it in numbed disbelief as we did, immobilised by shock, and certainly in no mood for laughter.

The fact that Kennedy turned out to be not nearly as Arthurian as we had been led to believe he was – even to the extent of the White House, during his administration, being referred to as 'Camelot' – had little or nothing to do with the overwhelming sense of loss, even of grief, that was felt at the time, and not only by me and those I knew, but right across the world. Certainly, revelations about his private life which emerged during the months and years following his death chipped away at that iconic image. But if 1963 saw the birth of sexual intercourse, it also witnessed the death throes of a kind of political innocence. An unprecedented freedom of the press saw to it that, during the latter half of the century, no one who was not entirely blameless would escape scrutiny and exposure, down to the most intimate details of their private lives. Never before had the power of the Press been so unbridled, not only to make or break, but to create graven images of its own. Burgeoning television coverage of every incident under the sun also had its part to play, not so much in a consciously manipulative way at that time but because of its growing ubiquity and immediacy, certainly in a way that has increasingly desensitised our response to cataclysmic events.

Television certainly came of age in the early sixties, and in more ways than one. Political satire, for instance, was born again in late 1962 with BBC Television's ground-breaking *That Was The Week That Was*, featuring a host of talented people and David Frost who, in the words of the veteran journalist and broadcaster, Malcolm Muggeridge, 'rose without trace' and who was never very good at anything, for which distinction he eventually received a knighthood. The show, which was considered controversial enough to be removed from our screens in the run-up to the General Election in 1964 was, in truth, a reasonably mild-mannered affair compared with the vicious blood-letting we are accustomed to witnessing these days. It nevertheless laid aside its less than deadly weapons, and reached its apogee, in my opinion, with an extremely emotional and hastily put-together tribute to Kennedy on the very day after his death, reflecting an almost universal mood of desolation and reducing me to tears with Millicent Martin's rendition of *The Battle Hymn of the Republic.*

But before these observations become a treatise, I had best move on, leaving the subject with a fairly inconsequential and entirely personal postscript which, for some reason, remains in my memory, ineradicably linked to the events of those few days. It was on the morning of November 23rd that Dawn and I, feeling we had to do something to lift the overwhelming torpor that had settled on us, made a trip to nearby Chesham where we purchased *With the Beatles,* their first album, which turned out to be the sure-fire antidote to misery that we had hoped it would be.

Another effective distraction came in the shape of an invitation to play Ratty in the West End production of *Toad of Toad Hall,* a matinées only Christmas season at the Comedy Theatre, directed by David Conville, who had obviously decided to combine the responsibilities of producer and director, and under whose baton I was destined to go on playing Ratty for a good few years at a variety of London theatres, and apparently breaking the Ratty record.

Toad of Toad Hall is, of course, A. A. Milne's take on Kenneth Grahame's *The Wind in the Willows* which, for perfectly valid theatrical reasons, sidelines the rural idyll which is at the centre of the novel in favour of Toad's adventures and misadventures. By 1963, this adaptation, first performed in 1929, was already showing signs of age although, it has to be said, much of its charm and a good deal of its humour is essentially archaic in any case. The time was fast approaching when, with copyright restrictions having been removed, a plethora of new adaptations would see the light of day, some more successful than others, but none, I would suggest, destined to experience the longevity enjoyed by *Toad of Toad Hall.* A strong link with the past, providing us with a tangible sense of continuity, was the presence of Richard Goolden, who had first played the part of Mole in that original production, and who had grown, or perhaps shrunk would be more accurate, to resemble that tiny burrowing creature more closely with every passing year. He did, in fact, confide to me on one occasion that he had at first been offered the part of Badger, but I was never sure if he meant me to take him seriously. He had obviously always been a small man, a characteristic now exaggerated by the atrophy that goes with old age. But he remained pretty nifty on his feet, and maintained an almost permanent twinkle in his eye except when he fell asleep during the trial scene, which he did at almost every performance, relying on Ratty to nudge him awake in time to say his lines. Over the years, Dickie had assumed a proprietorial watch over the play which seemed to include in its searchlight beam anyone and everything to do with the production except for himself, who had been gifted by the author, or so it seemed, with *carte blanche* to do and say exactly what he wanted to at any given time, and to cultivate a relationship with the audience that left his fellow actors stranded until such time as he decided to return to the script. In one particular scene, Toad having returned in a state of shock following his car crash, and having collapsed into a chair, I was instructed to remove his hat, to which a pair of driving goggles were attached, and place it, ever so accidentally, onto a cottage loaf sitting on a nearby table. This had been Dickie's idea during rehearsals, an idea that had been well and truly tried and tested in past productions, according to him. Mistaking the hatted and goggled loaf of bread for a disembodied head, he would stagger back in fright, and thereby bring the house down. That was the premise, but needless to say, it didn't work. Rather than give it up as a lost cause, however, he decided to embellish it at the next performance by adding a double-take on the loaf, but still to no avail. The scene, which had its own momentum, had already stalled by the time Dickie had added a further take coupled with a gasp of shock and horror, and when that failed to provoke any kind of response, he trotted down to the footlights during the next show and addressed the audience thus: "What's that?" he said, pointing upstage to what was obviously a loaf of bread with a hat on. Well, clearly we had all had enough of it by then, and none of us more so than poor old Martin Friend as Toad. It was, after all, supposed to be Toad's scene, containing a lot of genuinely funny jokes, not to mention a storyline that was now in danger of grinding to a halt. Quite out of character, being an equable sort of person, but obviously at the end of his tether, Martin rasped in reply, "Its Mrs Bun, the Baker's wife, she's always loafing around!" The largely juvenile audience erupted with laughter and Dickie, somehow sensing that he had merely provided the feed line for someone else's laugh, never attempted it again, and neither did he ever mention it. But there was more to Richard Goolden than in the portrait I have just painted of him. Yes, he was a selfish old actor, and working alongside him, as the tirelessly good-natured and tolerant Ratty has to do for most of the play, was in the main an exhausting and thankless task. But he was extremely generous in other respects. It was, mercifully, a limited season, although with two shows a day, virtually back to back, it sometimes felt like an interminable Dantean punishment. Consequently, there was nothing we looked forward to more than shutting our doors and closing our eyes between shows in an effort to regenerate enough energy to get us through the second one. But not Dickie. No sooner had the curtain fallen than hordes of children would appear at the stage door and, thwarted in their attempts to meet Badger, Toad and Ratty who had all gone into hibernation, were ushered into Moley's dressing-room where they were royally entertained with little stories about life on the river bank, and then plied with sweets, a prolonged invasion of his privacy that, for some eccentric reason, Dickie appeared to welcome. That he managed to catch up with his sleep at various moments during the play didn't alter the fact that he was more than twice as old as any of us and apparently twice as resilient. But we were already well aware of his amazing powers of recovery. Our opening performance took place at the obscenely early hour of 10am before an audience made up almost entirely of members of the I-Spy Club. It had gone quite smoothly, and as we approached the home strait, the penultimate scene in which our four heroes engage in a battle to repossess Toad Hall from the Wild Wooders, we were looking forward to a well-deserved lunch when Dickie, all fired up with enthusiasm and blood-lust, let go with his foot and kicked a ferret, otherwise engaged in a life and death struggle with Toad, up the backside. Whether Dickie had improvised this moment or not, the ferret was caught unawares and, failing to respond, stood his ground, whereupon Dickie bounced off him, teetered away backwards, and fell into the orchestra pit. Led by the members of the band who simply stopped playing, the whole company fell silent. I happened to be on the fore-stage at the time, and could see down into the pit where poor old Moley was lying flat on his back with a pool of blood blossoming around his head. Anthony Bowles, our Musical Director, a rather pale young man at the best of times, had turned ashen. Laying his baton aside, he removed his jacket and placed it over Dickie's head. This gesture was greeted, not surprisingly, with an almost choral intake of breath from on stage. Then David Conville leapt up from the auditorium and took control of the situation, explaining to the audience that Mr. Mole had had an accident, and that we wouldn't be be able to finish the show, and asking them to leave the theatre as quickly and calmly as possible so that poor old Moley's wounds could be attended to. This was accomplished with the minimum of fuss, the members of the I-Spy Club having been reassured by our director that it was nothing serious and that Mole would be better very soon. We on stage, having seen the crimson halo and witnessed Tony Bowles' fairly unambiguous gesture, were not quite as easily convinced. Being actors, of course, and while genuinely concerned, we were also probably wondering if that meant we would have the rest of the day off. But if we were indeed guilty of such callous self-interest, retribution was at hand when, about an hour later, Dickie returned from hospital, his head amply bandaged, and declared that he was eager to get back on stage for the next show.

My association with *Toad of Toad Hall* which carried over to the following year with much the same cast, and continued, allowing for a substantial gap, until the year that Richard Goolden died at the age of 86, led me to a more mature appreciation of him, both as an actor and as a man. The fact that he went on cavorting around the stage in his ancient costume as Mole with the same degree of childlike enthusiasm until only two years before his death, was reason enough in itself to admire his dedication, not to mention his amazing fortitude. He obviously approved of my Ratty, which helped of course, and in later years depended on me to some extent to help him negotiate his way through the play. In fact, and despite occasional bouts of irritation and impatience, possibly mutual, I think we both became rather fond of each other; which, I imagine, is what Kenneth Grahame had in mind when he first explored the relationship between Ratty and Mole.

oOoOo

Thirteen

There's a photograph of us all arriving at Chicago's O'Hare Airport in the early summer of 1964, looking like a bunch of happy Evangelists. Had there been another photograph of us all leaving three months later, it would have given the distinct impression that our mission had failed. There was no such photograph, however, as several members of the company had already left for an extended stay elsewhere in the U.S. while the rest of us, eager to get home, were in no mood to record our departure. It was, I recall, a pretty silent flight back to Heathrow, a silence fuelled by disappointment, strained relationships, and the presence of one man, previously held in high esteem, whose reputation now lay in tatters.

1964 Peter Dews' company arrive in Chicago (TW fifth from right)

Such a dénouement would have been unthinkable when we first assembled for rehearsals some five months earlier at a hall in Westminster, the property of the Westminster City Council Refuse Department. We were the lucky few, the ones who had been chosen to share Peter Dews' latest adventure, and if that wasn't reason enough to feel optimistic, we were being paid by our American sponsors the equivalent of $400 a week, and that was during the rehearsal period in London. On top of this, and from an entirely personal point of view, more manna had been showered on me when Dawn was invited to design the costumes for two of the three productions we were to stage at the Ravinia Festival in Highland Park, an extremely wealthy suburb some 30 miles north of Chicago and a mere stone's throw from Lake Michigan. Could such a prospect have looked any brighter?

Peter was in good form and more relaxed than I had known him to be before in a rehearsal situation. In fact, as time went on, rehearsals became more and more like social occasions, perhaps because we all knew each other so well by then and were linked, in many cases, by friendship and respect as well as by familiarity. The day would almost always begin with a game of cricket played up against the wall of the rehearsal room, for Peter had decided that, aside from taking Shakespeare to the Yanks, we would reveal to them the wonders and the mysteries of that inherently English game. Following this, we would be reunited with those members of the company who, for some bizarre reason, had chosen not to play cricket, for choir practice. Peter was in his element here, ex-schoolmaster and Methodist lay-preacher that he was, taking us through our paces with a medieval setting of the *Te Deum* and *The Agincourt Song*, both to be sung in *Henry V* which, along with *Hamlet* and *Twelfth Night*, made up the repertoire for our three month stay in Ravinia Park.

A hand-picked company of actors, as delighted to be working with Peter as he clearly was that they had joyfully accepted his invitation, was led by Robert Hardy, assigned to play the title roles in both *Hamlet* and *Henry V*, and by Eileen Atkins as Ophelia and as Viola in *Twelfth Night*. The rest of the company, fairly predictably, read like a cast list from *An Age of Kings* and *The Spread of the Eagle*, and included such stalwarts as Geoffrey Bayldon, George Selway, Jerome Willis, Jill Dixon, Yvonne Bonnamy, Bernard Lloyd, Terry Scully, Alan Rowe, Hilda Braid and me, repeating by popular demand, and definitely for the last time, my triumphant portrayal of the Player Queen in *Hamlet*, together with the Boy in *Henry V*, and Viola's twin brother, Sebastian, in *Twelfth Night*.

I often thought, in those days, of Peter Dews and David William, not only as my earliest mentors, which indeed they both were, but also as two sides of the same coin in many ways, and nothing could better illustrate this comparison than their respective passions throughout the rehearsal process. During rehearsals for *Love's Labour's Lost* in Regent's

Park, for instance, while David had completely immersed himself in the scenes between the lovers, he had virtually ignored me as I struggled to come to terms with the part of Costard the clown. Peter, on the other hand, during rehearsals for *Twelfth Night*, clearly revelled in the scenes between Sir Toby, Sir Andrew, Maria and Malvolio, while Viola, Orsino, Olivia and Sebastian were more or less left to get on with it whilst he, more often than not, would disappear behind a copy of *The Guardian* until all of the lovey-dovey stuff was over and done with. Had I not made this journey before, albeit the other way around, I might well have been unsettled by the absence of any detailed direction. But then again, had I not been fortunate enough to see Ian Holm in the same role at Stratford several years earlier, I might well have gone on thinking of Sebastian as a pretty thankless part anyway. As it was, I knew I was on pretty firm ground and, given that we were obviously not going to get a lot of help from Peter, I was able to reassure myself and my colleagues that it was obviously the reason he had entrusted those particular roles to us in the first place.

We didn't see a great deal of Chicago on our journey between O'Hare airport and Highland Park, although it didn't take some of us long to make up for this omission. Due to a misapprehension about our status, or so I believed at the time, we were allocated accommodation in the Halls of Residence within the campus of Northwestern University, although we didn't stay there long enough even to unpack our bags. Courtesy of our leading man, who interceded on the company's behalf, we were quickly and apologetically transferred to more suitable and certainly more salubrious quarters in the Hotel Moraine-on-the-Lake, although Dawn and I didn't stay *there* for long either. This came about because Mrs Dews, for reasons of her own, decided she didn't like the charming little clap-board house on County Line Road that had been set aside for her and her husband, and suggested that Dawn and I, being the only other married couple in the company, and tacitly inferring that our expectations were bound to be more modest than hers, might like to take over the tenancy. Having inspected it, we were only too delighted to move in, taking along with us our old friend, and Dawn's erstwhile flat-mate, Penny McVitie, who had been engaged as her one and only assistant in the wardrobe department. The only drawback was that County Line Road, being situated some considerable distance further from Ravinia Park than the hotel, meant that I was obliged to rent a car. But as I had already been toying with this idea anyway, restrained only by economic considerations, I saw it not so much as a drawback as the perfect excuse.

I had passed my driving test some months earlier at the first attempt, and after only a dozen or so lessons. The comparative ease with which I had achieved this had, admittedly, something to do with my previous driving experience, albeit on two wheels, and also owed more than a little to the relatively peaceful and driver-friendly roads of rural Buckinghamshire upon which I was nursed along by my driving instructor. It has to be said, however, that after forty-odd lessons on those same roads, Dawn not only comprehensively failed her test, but said good bye for ever to her brief, and far from sympathetic, acquaintance with the internal combustion engine. My first car, purchased shortly after acquiring my licence, was a cream-coloured Morris Minor Convertible, a sturdy vehicle, of which I was justly proud, although there had been times during the Arctic winter of '63/'64 when I wished I had opted for the hard-top version. It was a mere jalopy, however, when compared with the sleek automatic Ford Falcon that I rented in Highland Park and which boasted, not only an air-conditioning system, but tinted windows! Possessing such a vehicle not only gave us a sense of freedom and contributed in no small measure to my happier memories of that season, it also ensured my lasting popularity amongst the company, many of whom shared with us those mainly nocturnal trips to down-town Chicago.

Having been Hollywood educated from an early age, the American experience was more familiar than foreign to me. I had, after all, driven along those highways before, *and* on the wrong side of the road, albeit from a stalls seat in many a cinema, and from which, by the same token, I had eaten in those same restaurants, knew all about American cuisine, and had even partaken of it in my imagination whilst being entertained by the likes of Les McCann and the Red Norvo Quintet, as we were now in reality being entertained by them on our occasional weekend visits to *The London House*. a fashionable Chicago eatery at that time. Similarly, I'd visited bars and night-clubs where crooners and torch-singers had provided the background to scenes played out in numerous films and where now, in a club called *Mister Kelly's*, Dawn and I found ourselves being sung to by a young Jack Jones, whose style, tone and repertoire were deliciously reminiscent of Sinatra's, and who iced the cake for me when he coolly reprimanded a group of particularly noisy patrons sitting just below him by saying, "Gee, I wish I was down there with you. You seem to be having so much more fun than the rest of us," which could so easily have been a line from one of those myriad films that had shaped my young life.

And that was it really; fantasy and reality came together for me in Chicago, 'The town that Billy Sunday could not shut down' and where,

'On State Street, that great street, I just want to say
They do things they don't do on Broadway'.

It was also the city in which the St.Valentine's Day Massacre had actually taken place, memorialised so often on celluloid that I felt as if I had been there myself and witnessed it, along with the violent lives and frequently violent deaths of some of the world's most notorious gangsters who all bore an uncanny resemblance to James Cagney, Humphrey Bogart and Edward G. Robinson. And then, of course, there was jazz. Chicago, as it happened, was the first northern city to provide a platform for the Afro-American musicians who arrived there in their thousands from New Orleans during the early years of the 20th century in what became known as the Great Migration, bringing with them their own kind of music which, in no time at all, itself migrated across the ethnic borders, giving birth to what became known as the Jazz Age, again represented on the Silver Screen in dozens of Hollywood movies, all hungrily devoured by yours truly during my most impressionable years.

On one of our after-dark excursions to down-town Chicago, five or six of us, including Bernard Lloyd, a genuine aficionado, visited a Jazz Club called *The Plugged Nickel*, which had come highly recommended. We were all a bit surprised to find that it amounted to little more than a shack with a corrugated tin roof, and even more surprised when we were told that the $1.50 entrance fee included a first drink. Inside was a long narrow room with tables down one side, all of them empty, and a small dais about halfway down the other side on which a lone trumpeter was playing, presumably for his own benefit because, until we came along, there was nobody else around to listen to him – which was again surprising as, even to my untrained ear, he sounded pretty good. Having been served with our first drink, conversation faltered and a kind of reverential silence took its place as, led by Bernard, we all turned our undivided attention to the extraordinary virtuosity of the man's performance. When the waiter arrived to take our orders for the second drink, Bernard asked him who the trumpeter was. The waiter said, "Oh, that's Roy Eldridge." Had I known, as I was soon to be informed, that Roy Eldridge was acknowledged to be one of the greatest jazz trumpeters of the age, regarded as the stylistic link between Louis Armstrong and Dizzie Gillespie, and that, as well as enjoying a distinguished solo career, he'd played with Gene Krupa's band back in the thirties, and with Artie

Shaw and the Benny Goodman orchestra, I would have been as astonished as Bernard clearly was by his presence amongst us. My knowledge of jazz, however, was pretty elementary at the time and, while I was perfectly willing to admit that I was listening to a legend, I could only fully appreciate the experience and replicate Bernard's awed reaction to it by comparing it with how I would have felt had I stumbled across Frank Sinatra in a deserted piano bar singing *One For My Baby*, which was inconceivable except as a fantasy or, indeed, as a scene from a movie. What intrigued me more was the economic viability of the situation. Was Roy Eldridge simply playing for fun? And if not, who was paying him? In the more formalised world we had left behind on the other side of the 'pond', a venue would have been booked, a fee negotiated, and ticket prices fixed at a level to allow for all that, as well as to ensure a healthy profit for the promoter. There could be no escaping the fact that if Roy Eldridge had been depending on a slice of the takings that night at *The Plugged Nickel*, even after we'd ordered our third drink, he would have been better off playing on the sidewalk with a hat beside him.

As I have already discovered, the very process of writing a memoir brings back memories of incidents, places and people that I had all but forgotten; dimly recalled at first but with increasing clarity. If I had been asked, for instance, to name every single member of the company that had so enthusiastically and optimistically embarked on that ill-fated enterprise in the summer of 1964, I would have failed. Certainly, Arthur Skinner would have slipped through the net had it not been for one particular episode in which we became involved, making an indelible mark on my memory. Arthur paddled his own canoe, distancing himself from the rest of us, avoiding the traumas that were to come, and taking no part in the rancour that followed hard upon them. In fact, it was his very isolation from the rest of the company that was his strength. Far from being a loner, as we had thought, Arthur seized every opportunity, mostly at weekends, to venture alone into the no-go areas of Chicago, situated on the south side of the city where, armed with nothing more than a small tape recorder, he indulged his passion for Afro-American music, recording and interviewing every exponent of the Blues and its Creole variations on every street corner, and in every backyard and smoky bar-room that he could find. That he was apparently assisted in his quest by the inhabitants of that notoriously insular black ghetto and met with nothing but willing co-operation from them, astounded our American hosts and did nothing to change our preconceived opinion of him as either an intrepid explorer or totally demented. We too had visited the south side of Chicago, you see, albeit in the hermetically sealed environs of a hired coach, from which we were forbidden to alight lest our numbers for the return journey be savagely reduced, or so we were given to understand. It was certainly an uncomfortable experience, even when viewed through a moving window. The poverty, and the squalor that invariably accompanied it, seemed almost intentional, as though it had been deliberately preserved in that state as an alternative tourist attraction, a part of Chicago that bore no resemblance whatsoever to any of the other parts, and certainly not to the fantastically affluent settlements on the North Shore with which we had become familiar. Proud of its diversity, or so it appeared, there was no hint of regret or shame from anyone we spoke to that such conditions should be allowed to prevail in a thoroughly modern city, the third largest in the U.S. that was also proud to be known as the financial, economic and cultural capital of the Midwest.

But, of course, racial discrimination was part of that culture, not confined to the Deep South any more than it was contained within the ranks of the Ku Klux Klan, but deeply entrenched right across the country. The fact that it was largely taken for granted, and on both sides of the ethnic divide, was probably the most disturbing aspect of it – like the occasion when Dawn took a drink from the huge, multi-fauceted water fountain in Ravinia Park, and shrieked when the water came out faster than she'd expected, hitting her in the face, and a young black guy who had approached the tap next to her, leapt back, and said, "Sorry, sorry", before scurrying away without taking a drink at all. It took us some while to realise, and even longer to fathom, that he had actually thought she was objecting to his proximity. On another occasion, as the guests of a very nice, ordinary family, whose names and their connection with the Ravinia Festival now escape me, I was asked by the lady of the house why I had chosen to buy a long-playing record for my brother, featuring the voice of Mary Wells, who had only recently enjoyed chart success at home with a song called *My Guy*. The lady was puzzled, and I was all set to agree with her that, as far as I was concerned, Mary Wells was not a singer I would personally rate very highly, when she said with disarming simplicity, "But she's black". I was naturally rendered speechless, and only later did I consider the implications of that simple sentence, delivered without anger or outrage, but with genuine bewilderment. Obviously, there was nothing more to be said.

At Arthur Skinner's invitation, issued, I imagine, largely because we had a car and were in a position to give him a lift, we attended a party one weekend, hosted by his new-found friends in the neighbouring state of Indiana. As far as I can remember, it was a pleasant evening, spent in congenial company and the conversation, as well as the music, was free and easy. On our journey back to Highland Park in the small hours of the following morning, we were accompanied by a couple of young black guys who had begged a lift to Chicago. As we drove along what I believe was called Eden's Expressway, I caught a glimpse in my rear-view mirror of a flashing blue light. I glanced down and saw that the speedometer was registering something in excess of 70 miles an hour. I knew perfectly well, of course, that the limit on that road was 60, and as I'd already been pulled over and warned for travelling at 25.5 miles an hour in a 25 miles an hour zone, I should have known better. "It looks like the cops", I said; whereupon our two passengers, riding in the back seat, promptly disappeared into the well between us, and as close to the floor as they could possibly get. My first thought was that they must have had something to hide; either that or they were breaking a curfew imposed on all Afro-Americans after dark and outside their own territory, which wouldn't have surprised me at all. As the police car drew level with me, I began to suspect that their reasons for burying themselves in the darkest recesses of the car were more likely to be of an altruistic nature. They probably knew, and had good reason to know, that things would go easier for me if I didn't have to explain the presence of a couple of black guys in my car. For some reason, this was infinitely more shocking than either of the other two possibilities. The cop, whose face bore a striking resemblance to Rod Steiger's, wound his window down, and motioned me to do the same. When I had complied, he yelled out, "Pull over to the hard shoulder!" Not being familiar at that time with Motorway jargon, I simply stopped where I was, right in the middle of the inside lane. "What's a hard shoulder?", I remember saying, but nobody answered. Meanwhile, the cop had pulled up some distance in front of me, got out of his car and began to amble ominously back towards me, gun holstered (for the moment) on his hip.

"You know you were travelling at more than 70 miles an hour?" he growled.

"I hadn't realised, officer", I said, adding, "I'm sorry" on the off-chance that he might just pick up on the fact that I was, at least, sober and polite.

"Do you have a driving licence?" he demanded, obviously

unimpressed.

"I have an international driving licence" I replied, delving for it in my pocket.

"Is that so?" he rejoined; "well, I'm gonna give you an international ticket".

He took the proffered licence, opened it, and looked at the photograph inside before looking back at me, then at the photograph again, for all the world like he'd seen my likeness on a 'WANTED' poster.

"Say", he said, with more than a hint of suspicion in his tone, "are you a Beatle?"

"No" I replied, adding quickly and with an eye to the main chance, "but I come from the same country".

"No kidding?" he said, genuinely impressed now. "You come from England?" I smiled and nodded, grateful that he was not *au fait* enough with either the pop music scene or with geography to ask if I came from Liverpool. After a long silence, he said, "My daughter'd kill me if I gave you a ticket. So this is your lucky day. But don't do it again. And remember – I own this Highway!" With which he ambled slowly away, back to his own car, just like he was in a Hollywood movie.

History, for what it's worth in the absence of documentary evidence, records that Peter Dews, accompanied by his wife, paid a visit to Ravinia the previous year to finalise arrangements for a season, comprising three plays by Shakespeare, to be presented at the Ravinia Festival. During his visit, he had been offered a choice between the Murray Theatre and the Ravinia Festival Theatre in which to present them. Both theatres were on the same site, namely Ravinia Park, but while the Murray Theatre was a more conventional proscenium-arch theatre with a seating capacity of something in the region of 800, the Ravinia Festival auditorium seated approximately 3,000. The fact that, although roofed, its sides were open, not only to the elements, but to passing traffic, including the Chicago and Northwestern railway line which ran only a few hundred yards away, did not persuade Peter to abandon his grandiose ambitions in favour of the understandably less exciting alternative. He had already been told, however, that the Ravinia Festival Theatre had, up until that time, hosted only musical events, such as orchestral concerts and the occasional dance performance, but it had never before been used for the spoken word and, consequently, no guarantee could be given about the acoustics. Undeterred, Peter put it to the test by going up onto the stage and addressing his wife, who was standing at the back of the auditorium, thus, or more or less thus, "Can you hear what I'm saying, luvvie?" To which she replied, "Yes,

Peter", or something along those lines. History does not record whether Peter asked her to repeat what he'd said, so it could well have been that she'd heard something quite different and, in view of what lay in store for the company over the next three months, it might well have been.

Putting to one side the gift of hindsight, bestowed for the most part on those who don't have to make the important decisions, I don't think there were many members of the company, if any, who would have been able to resist the lure of the Ravinia Festival Theatre for its sheer size and scale, not to mention the possibility of attracting larger audiences than we would have been able to in the smaller theatre. Why else would we have come 4,000 miles except to make a big impression? Besides, the plays – or, at least, two of them – demanded the kind of space afforded by the Festival Theatre's stage. No, it was not Peter's decision, nor even the price we had to pay for it, that brought about the rift, but the manner in which he dealt with the problems that arose as a result of that decision.

During the rehearsals that led up to the opening of *Henry V*, our first production, we sat in the auditorium often enough when we weren't actually on stage to become aware of an audibility problem, but as Peter didn't seem to be at all perturbed, we must have assumed that it would be resolved by the time we opened, possibly with a few strategically placed microphones, or even by the presence of a large audience which, as everyone knows, can significantly affect the acoustics in any space. His mood, however, was not nearly as buoyant as it had been in the past, nor his temper as even. His peremptory dismissal of Dawn's objections to the employment of the hideous Odeon-red house curtains on the grounds that they clashed horribly with the heraldic red which figured prominently in her costumes was, perhaps, a sign of things to come, but while Dawn seethed, no banners were raised, and no other rumblings were heard. On the contrary, at about that time, our director was selected, along with ten others, to meet the challenge thrown down by a team of local cricketers in Winnetka and, having been appointed captain of our team, I suppose I must have had something to do with selecting the players although, to be honest, I don't think we would have been able to field 11 men from amongst us without Peter.

And so it was that we set out one Saturday afternoon in a minibus bound for Winnetka, about ten miles further south on the road to Chicago, apparelled in a motley array of pastel shades, having eschewed or, more accurately, having forgotten to bring any cricketing 'whites' – although in possession of bats, stumps and a number of balls, none of which the Americans were likely to possess any more than they would, in all probability, have anything more than a rudimentary knowledge of the game. We were in ominously high spirits when we arrived at the ground on which we were to play, and it was there that we received our first shock. Far from being the overgrown and untended field of our imaginings, suitable perhaps for grazing cattle, it was immaculate, an impeccably shaved carpet of grass at the centre of which lay the wicket, paler than the rest by virtue of the heavy rolling it must have undergone in preparation for our visit. On the far side of the field stood a small pavilion, from which there emerged the figure of a man, dressed all in white and with a peaked red cap on his head. "Hello!" he called out as he approached us, "Ruddy good to see you fellers!" If we had been somewhat taken aback by our surroundings, we were open-mouthed with astonishment at this apparition in white whose accent was neither American nor English and, although it bore a vague resemblance to Australian, was like nothing I had ever heard before. It turned out, after greetings and introductions had been exchanged, that he was the captain of a team made up entirely of English expatriates who played cricket regularly, and presumably against other teams similarly constituted. So, instead of teaching the Yanks how to play cricket, it looked as though we were in for a few lessons ourselves. In one of only two press cuttings that I kept (for obvious reasons) from that particular episode in my life, the headline reads: 'They Swing a 'Wicket' Bat,' whatever that means, and goes on to quote an anonymous spectator who apparently said that cricket 'is very similar to baseball in that it is played by humans.' 'The last to deny it,' the reporter continues, 'would be the feminine members of the Terry Wale Fan Club, who were watching their handsome young actor hero disport himself on the greenswards of Winnetka ... Mr Wale, a clean-cut if amply coiffured teen heart flutterer, was the captain of the Shakespearean 11.' Heady stuff that, undermined to a certain extent by the final score which would have left no one in any doubt, not even the members of my Fan Club, feminine or otherwise, that we had been thoroughly humiliated by the local opposition. And if we still entertained the notion of conquest in that other, more familiar arena, we were about to be frustrated there too.

It would be wrong to suggest that our season at the Ravinia Festival was a complete disaster. It would be equally untrue to suggest that a company, made up of so many splendid actors, somehow failed to do justice to those three wonderful plays. There were several reasons why we did not achieve the success we might otherwise have enjoyed. First and foremost, of course, there was the ongoing problem of audibility. We had opened with *Henry V*, arguably the loudest of the plays, and yet for an audience unfamiliar with Shakespeare's language, spoken in alien accents, it was going to be difficult enough for them to follow in the best of circumstances. On top of which, having to contend with the regular to-ing and fro-ing of the Chicago and Northwestern line trains was not making the task any easier. A few microphones had been installed, but certainly not enough to cover every inch of that huge acting area, so they added a few more, and then a few more until, by the time all three plays were up and running, dozens of little microphones were suspended above the stage, like an army of spiders hovering over us, giving the impression that they were part of some mysterious and obscure design concept. The problem of amplification was never solved either, and performances were regularly accompanied throughout the season by a succession of huge sound engineers placing equally huge amplifiers in strategically chosen places throughout the auditorium, adding yet another distraction, and utterly failing to provide cover for the entire audience at any one time.

Peter's *folie de grandeur* in choosing the larger of the two theatres had its artistic downside too. Adept at creating the illusion of crowds on the small screen, he was no Tyrone Guthrie when it came to populating a big stage. Too often the staging lacked depth, while the supernumeraries, enlisted from amongst the students at Northwestern University to become the English army at Harfleur and Agincourt, as well as various courtiers, pall-bearers and soldiers in *Hamlet,* stood around as though they had been hastily imposed on the production at the last minute rather than integrated into the scenes, which was pretty well what had happened. *Twelfth Night* did not suffer in quite the same way. It was beautifully costumed from designs by a colleague of Dawn's, Mark Haddon, reminiscent, both in period and style, of those exquisite creations by Lila di Nobile in that most perfect of all *Twelfth Nights* at Stratford back in1958. But the set, designed by Henry Bardon, who was unable to supervise its construction because he wasn't there, suffered cruelly in his absence.

The box trees, for instance, a familiar and well-loved part of English garden landscapes, as interpreted by the scenic department in Ravinia, placed more emphasis on the box than the tree, so that we ended up with a lot of two-dimensional wooden cut-outs which were then painted in a shade of green that bore more resemblance to the colour of a hangover than to any foliage known to man.

But it was in the run-up to the opening of *Twelfth Night* that the relationship between director and actors became strained. Peter was obviously aware of the problems we were facing, but instead of trying to resolve them, he was distancing himself from us. It was a process that would accelerate over the next few weeks until he withdrew almost entirely, as though it was somehow our fault that things hadn't gone the way he'd planned. It is impossible now, so many years later, to chart with complete accuracy, or in any great detail, the individual events that led to the rift. But I do remember quite clearly one of the first occasions, if only because it brought the company to the brink of mutiny. For some reason, during the technical rehearsal and the dress rehearsal of *Twelfth Night*, Peter decided to use Terry Scully as a whipping boy. I was not, of course, unfamiliar with this odious trait in some directors, but Peter had never been one of them. Yes, he was subject to rages, often apoplectic, but they had always been indiscriminate, and more often than not turned on people who were more than capable of looking after themselves. But Terry Scully was a gentle soul whose temperament admitted not an ounce of malice. There was something strangely fragile about him too, something that went beyond vulnerability, and which was eventually to prove debilitating. But that was some way down the line and, for the moment, it was enough to see him as an innocent victim of Peter's own inadequacies. Besides, his performance as Feste in *Twelfth Night* was perfectly good and in no way deserving the vitriol that was being heaped on it. There came a point when, almost by tacit consent, we all agreed that enough was enough and a fairly significant number of us, led by Alan Rowe, a senior member of the company, moved into the row behind where Peter was sitting in the auditorium, as if to say, "Just you do that one more time ..." In fact, I'm not entirely sure that Alan didn't actually say it. In any case, Peter obviously got the message, and he curbed his tongue. But it proved to be the watershed in our relationship with him. On a more personal level, and only a short time later, whilst in the final stages of transferring *Hamlet* to the stage, Peter visited the wardrobe department, where I was enjoying a brief respite from rehearsals, and demanded of Dawn half a dozen more costumes, presumably having underestimated the number of pall-bearers required to carry off the bodies of Claudius, Gertrude and Laertes as well as Hamlet himself. Dawn replied, quite reasonably, that it wouldn't be possible, given the length of time at her disposal, the lack of essential fabric, and the shortage of helpers available to her. Several local ladies and, indeed, for a short spell, Mrs Dews herself, had kindly lent their services as occasional seamstresses, but with the three productions all but up and running, they had departed, leaving only Dawn and Penny to put the finishing touches to the remaining costumes. But Peter wasn't having any of this. He demanded the extra costumes and then, when faced with Dawn's refusal to be brow-beaten, absurdly threatened her with legal action at the hands of the Ravinia Festival lawyers. It was at that point that I suggested he should leave. To be honest, I think it was probably more than a mere suggestion, and although I was too angry at that particular moment to consider the consequences, the icy look we exchanged before Peter turned on his heel and walked out, marked the end of an era.

It would be more than ten years, and in very different personal circumstances, before Peter and I were reconciled, and while I had cause, from time to time, to regret the terminal effects of that one brief moment, I never for an instant regretted my part in it. Our relationship, over five years, had been predominantly that of teacher and pupil, albeit a favoured pupil. I had every reason to admire and respect him; I also had a great affection for him. Moreover, he had inspired a degree of loyalty, not only from me, but from a whole host of talented and reputable actors, many of them older and more experienced than I was, that marked him out of the ordinary, to say the least. These priceless attributes, however, have to be valued by the recipient, and they have to be reciprocated up to a point, especially in adversity. It was all too easy to lay at least some of the blame for Peter's dereliction on the influence of his wife, and while she was not entirely above suspicion, it was Peter's own weakness and untrustworthiness in the face of problems he had himself engendered that brought him so low in the esteem of his colleagues.

After the opening of *Hamlet,* we saw little of Mr and Mrs Dews (aka Lord and Lady Bradford, courtesy of one particularly scurrilous member of the company), and then almost exclusively at essential social gatherings where they would maintain a distant politeness, best described as the kind of *froideur* usually reserved for those who have badly let you down. Peter was seldom seen at the theatre where we struggled on without his support and in the wake of less than rapturous reviews for the rest of the season. We also had to make do without Robert Hardy's captaincy, so clearly demonstrated when we'd first arrived, but understandably relinquished on the grounds of self-preservation, he alone having to carry the burden of two massive roles in the certain knowledge that only two-thirds of the audience would be able to hear what he was saying. Not that this debilitating factor had any significant effect on attendance, and as far as I can remember we played to pretty near capacity audiences throughout. There was only one moment that I can recall however, when 'The idea of theatre slyly raised its banner,' and the fact that it owed more to Shakespeare and to an audience largely unfamiliar with the play than to either production or performance, only served to make it more memorable. At each and every performance of *Twelfth Night,* the meeting in the final scene between Eileen Atkins and myself, as Viola and her brother, Sebastian, both wearing identical costumes, and each having thought the other was dead, provoked an audible gasp from the audience. It was a magical moment, made all the more remarkable in the certain knowledge that, in order to replicate that kind of response at home, the characters would have had to appear stark naked at the very least. We were, of course, well aware that we were celebrating in that year of 1964 William Shakespeare's quatercentenary, and nothing, at least as far as I was concerned, could have bridged that 400 year gap more tangibly than that delightful and somewhat surprising reaction. If for no other reason, it also made our trip to Chicago seem worthwhile.

But there were, of course, other reasons, some of which I have already touched upon, and many of which are best left to the imagination. That familiar virus, long associated with the 'time out' syndrome, and familiar to people from all walks of life who spend long periods away from the responsibilities of home, and in close proximity to each other, be it on a world cruise, at a party political conference or, for all I know, a meeting of the General Synod, struck at the heart of our company in the Hotel Moraine-on-the-Lake, and very few remained entirely immune. We were, after all, a company of actors from England, emissaries of that most illustrious of all English playwrights in whose fame we naturally basked, attracting by association the attention of numerous members of the opposite sex – and indeed, where applicable, members of the same sex too. Shortly before we had left England, one of our company, whose identity I have chosen for gentlemanly reasons not to reveal, had reacted very badly to her husband's suggestion that she should perhaps consider taking with her some form of contraception. No doubt, as an actor, he too had travelled the world, and was familiar with its temptations. But far from being touched by his wisdom and warmed by his generosity, she was outraged that such a thought should have even entered his head, and was at pains to share with us her shock/horror at the very idea. Needless to say, and as you have probably already guessed, the lady's feet had scarce made contact with the tarmac at O'Hare before she embarked on a series of adventures that left everyone else, including Bernard Lloyd, who was by no means idle, looking decidedly celibate by comparison. The enviable object of much female attention, from within as well as from outside the company, Bernard was pursued for some time by Donna, the hotel manager's daughter who, when she was not selling ice-cream in the hotel lobby, was desperately trying to lure him into her embrace, a mission that grew ever more obsessive, until she burst into his room late one night, and cried out, "Oh Ber*nard*, Ber*nard*, you make me feel like a queen!" Bernard apparently dealt quite ruthlessly with her, threatening to tell her father unless she left his room immediately and closed the door behind her. Whether he was motivated by a sense of propriety, by the fact that he didn't find her attractive, or because his dance-card was already full and he was in need of a good night's sleep, I was never able to discover. Dawn, Penny and I, removed as we were from the perfumed chambers of the Hotel Moraine-on-the-Lake, lived an altogether quieter life on County Line Road, although the rest of the company probably thought we were involved in a *ménage à trois.*

Drawing a veil over all this unseemliness, and by way of raising the tone, I cannot bring this chapter to a close without referring to a particularly memorable occasion towards the end of the season, when the company was invited to a party given by Mrs Douglas, a leading member of the Ravinia Festival Committee, in her lovely lakeside villa. A charming and gracious hostess, she was also the widow of James Henderson Douglas, former Secretary of the Air Force in the Eisenhower administration. She was most attentive, and personally supervised the large staff she had presumably engaged for the occasion to wait on us at the host of candle-lit tables set out on the spacious verandah. Food and drink were both delicious and abundant. She also took it upon herself to conduct a small group of us on a tour of the house, each of its graceful rooms hung with Thai silk curtains, as well as Thai silk wall-hangings and drapes of one kind or another. This ubiquitous feature she explained as being the result of her son's visit to Thailand some years earlier when he had managed to persuade the powers-that-were in that country that, with a few simple changes, they would be able to transform what had been essentially a domestic concern into an international industry; the preponderance of Thai silk in her décor was evidence of his success. Mrs Douglas then threw open a door and ushered us into a room that was simply breathtaking, both in its dimensions and in its elegance. We were obviously overawed by the sheer scale of it, and by the fact that it succeeded in being both palatial and luxurious, yet welcoming and homely at the same time. Mrs Douglas smiled and said, "That was my reaction when my husband showed it to me for the first time; I fell in love with this room." She then went on to tell us the history of her marriage to James Henderson Douglas. They had been childhood sweethearts, she said, before they went their separate ways, and were married to other people. His first wife had died and Mrs Douglas was divorced by the time they met again, both of them by then middle-aged. They had fallen in love all over again and, having decided to marry, he had brought her to this house which he already owned. "I simply adored it," she said. "And especially this room. I was disappointed, of course, that it didn't overlook the lake. Of all the rooms in the house, this is the one from which you should be able to see the lake, and you couldn't. I didn't make a fuss about it. How could I? But I guess he knew. Well, after we were married, he brought me back to the house and into this room .... " At which point, Mrs Douglas walked across to the windows, which took up all but the length of one wall, and she drew back the Thai silk curtains. "You see," she said, beckoning us over. We obeyed, and were greeted by a stunning view, right out across Lake Michigan. "He had the house picked up and turned around," she said, her voice and her eyes reflecting, even after so many years, the joy and the love she had obviously felt for that very rich and wonderfully romantic man, as she added, with some difficulty, "It was his wedding present to me." Another scene from yet another movie, and the perfect memory to bring back with us from a less than perfect theatrical venture.

The first thing Dawn and I did when we got back home was to go and pick up our cat from the farm on which we had billeted him, rather than in the enclosed spaces of a cattery which might well have cramped his style. As we climbed out of the car, we were greeted by the lady to whom we had entrusted the well-being of our beloved pet, and as she led us towards the house, she told us that for the past two days Bosie had sat in the hall, staring at the front door, something he had never done before in all the weeks we had been away. We were already excited by the prospect of seeing him again, and now we were tingling with expectation, sensing the existence of a psychic bond between us of which, until that moment, we had been unaware. The lady opened the door and, sure enough, there he sat, looking up at us with those impenetrable blue eyes. "Hello, Bosie," I said, beaming with pleasure to see him looking so sleek. He rose to his feet at that point, and with a look reminiscent of the basilisk glare I had received from Peter Dews, he turned on his figurative heel, and walked away. It took us some time to capture him and confine him in his basket before we were able to get him into the car and drive him, protesting, all the way home, from which safe haven he then disappeared for two whole days before returning, his protest made, to pick up the threads of his life in rural Buckinghamshire. And so, give or take a bit of jet-lag, and the odd twinge of regret and disappointment, things slowly returned to normal, although not for very long.

oOoOo

Fourteen

I have good reason to remember Derek and Julia Parker; they were our near neighbours when we lived in Notting Hill Gate, and are best known for their innumerable books on astrology and the interpretation of dreams. But while these gifts played no part in predicting the future of a Libran and Piscean conjunction in relation to the planets, they were indirectly responsible for realising our dreams in an altogether more terrestrial way.

At the time we met them, early in 1962, Julia was teaching art in Hammersmith while Derek was doing the odd bit of journalism together with some radio work and other bits and pieces which included some casual employment for ABC Television. This involved reading and reporting on scripts submitted for *Armchair Theatre,* their prime drama slot at that time. In fact, such was the popularity of *Armchair Theatre* that the production office was unable to cope with the number of unsolicited manuscripts which, in one form or another, were landing on its doormat every day. In the end, they had no alternative but to engage the services of outside readers. Nowadays, of course, these kind of random submissions would simply never be acknowledged, let alone read and, at the very least, politely rejected. Not for nothing are the '60s regarded, by those of us who were around at the time, as the Golden Age of television drama, and it was the passionate determination of those in charge not to leave a single stone unturned in their search for new and exciting writers that was in large measure responsible for that enduring reputation.

Derek Parker, having been one of *Armchair Theatre's* outside readers, was aware that they were still understaffed in that particular area and he suggested I might like to augment my income by offering them my services. And so, following a meeting at Teddington studios with producer, Leonard White, I was given a bundle of scripts and asked to report on them. This involved reading them, writing synopses, assessing the quality of the writing and, where appropriate, offering constructive criticism. I can't remember how much I was paid per script, but it must have been worth having as, for the next two years, even after we'd moved to Great Missenden, I made regular trips to Hanover Square, ABC Television's London office, to deliver my completed assignment and to pick up another batch of scripts. By the time I went to Chicago and was obliged to give it up, I must have read somewhere in the region of 400 submissions, only two of which I recommended for production, and only one of which was actually televised – a play entitled *The Pretty English Girls* by John Hopkins, a writer already well established as one of the leading contributors to that most seminal of all police series, *Z Cars,* for which he wrote an amazing 57 episodes. The other play was written by my old friend, Paul Bailey, a beautiful piece of work set in an old people's home which, for some undisclosed reason, was considered unsuitable for *Armchair Theatre.* This strange decision, however, turned out to be a blessing in disguise as far as Paul was concerned for, having been spurned by television, he decided to turn his play into a novel. It was called, as it was in the original version, *At the Jerusalem*, and it went on to win a Somerset Maugham Award, heralding his career as a novelist and biographer of considerable note, during which time he was twice short-listed for the Booker Prize. The rest of the scripts I read, in an assortment of formats and of varying lengths, were made up of a small number of worthy attempts deserving encouragement, and an equally small number of plays inspired by insanity which were great fun to read but whose authors, if not already incarcerated, clearly should have been, plus a huge number of unutterably boring plays. The dogged determination of those deluded people to pursue their mind-numbingly tedious ideas to the bitter end was the bane of my life as a reader, but it taught me a great deal about writing. Arguably, it taught me more than I would have learned from an exclusive diet made up of the greatest and the best. It certainly taught me how *not* to write a play for *Armchair Theatre* and consequently, or so I thought, how best to write one.

Dawn and I had already toyed with the idea of writing a play about the thief in the basement at 29 Luna Street, but we'd abandoned it for reasons I can no longer remember, but which possibly had something to do with our own close association with the central character. What we were looking for was something entirely of the imagination, and we finally came up with an idea that, for some now mysterious reason, we were both equally enthusiastic about. It was set on a modern housing estate serviced by a small sub-post-office-cum-sweetie shop, run by a seemingly cosy middle-aged lady whose interest in the local residents went beyond the bounds of good customer relations and, aided by confidential information gleaned from the various letters and parcels that passed through her hands, strayed into the murky world of blackmail. When this sideline began to take up more and more of her time, she was obliged to take on an assistant to deal with the more mundane aspects of the confectionery business and she chose to offer the job, for entirely devious reasons, to a none-too-bright down-and-out called Arthur Potts, a character conceived and written for that wonderfully eccentric actor, Freddie Jones. For some strange reason, however, the shopkeeper had not only underestimated his intelligence, but had also failed to detect the lurking psychotic concealed beneath his servile manner and, to cut a long story short, motivated by no other reason than resentment of her contemptuous attitude towards him, he ended up killing her with a toffee-hammer.

An Interest in People, as it was called, was politely rejected by *Armchair Theatre* on the grounds that it required too much film for what was essentially a studio-based drama series. Looking back from such a great distance, and cringing somewhat, I can think of at least half a dozen other reasons they could well have cited for turning it down, but at the time, both Dawn and I were astonished. In fact, so convinced were we that *Armchair Theatre* had got it badly wrong that, instead of consigning our play to the dustbin and giving up any ideas we were entertaining about our future as writers, we sent it to Tony Garnett. Tony and I had shared the distinction, four years earlier, of being members of the permanent company of *An Age of Kings*. Memorably, we had shared a scene with Frank Windsor when, as three soldiers in the army of Henry V, we had sat around a camp fire and contemplated death on the eve of Agincourt. On that occasion Tony had been allowed to indulge his native Birmingham accent which, with some difficulty, he had been obliged to suppress in various other roles throughout the series. I remember him as a congenial company member, extremely popular, and never more so than when he brought his long-time girl-friend to meet us all at rehearsals one day. She was, on the face of it, a sweet and innocent young girl whose name was Topsy Jane, and whose Birmingham accent was, if anything, even denser than Tony's. They also shared a total absence of fat on their frames, and when someone remarked on this, Topsy Jane said quite matter-of-factly, "Yeah, we're so skinny when we fook our bones rattle together."

Tony subsequently gave up acting for a living, put on a bit of weight, and became script editor on BBC 1's *The Wednesday Play,* which became in its later years *Play for Today* simply so they could screen it on a night other than on a Wednesday. But it was in its earlier manifestation, between 1964 and 1970 that it laid down the foundations of what is now looked back upon as the most prestigious and influential single play series in the history of television. As with *Armchair Theatre, The Wednesday Play* was inaugurated by Canadian émigré, Sydney Newman, who brought with him from the other side of the Atlantic the singular gift of objectivity, viewing British society, its strengths and its foibles as well as its deeply-rooted class structure, from the outside, and seeing much therein to be exploited in dramatic terms. Truth to tell, he had already eschewed adaptations of stage plays and middle-class drawing-room dramas in much of his programming for *Armchair Theatre*, opting instead for the gritty realism of the 'kitchen sink'. But, in migrating from ABC Television to the BBC, he was given a larger canvas, a 75 minute prime-time slot, uninterrupted by commercial breaks. He had also arrived at a time when, following an eight-year decline, viewing figures were making it clear that there was no longer any appetite for the single play. But it was Sydney Newman, together with his newly-appointed producer, James MacTaggart who, over the next couple of years, were to prove otherwise.

In the annals of British television no plays would make a greater impact nor leave a more permanent legacy than Nell Dunn's *Up the Junction* and Jeremy Sandford's *Cathy Come Home,* abrasive working-class plays with more than a hint of the documentary about them, as was James O'Connor's death-row drama, *Three Clear Sundays,* broadcast to coincide with parliament's debate on the abolition of capital punishment. Unforgettable too were Dennis Potter's politically motivated *Nigel Barton* plays, not to mention his take on the last hours of Jesus, *Son of Man,* hugely controversial as were many of *The Wednesday Play* offerings which saw the emergence, for better or for worse, of the Clean Up Television Campaign, led by Mary Whitehouse. David Mercer's reputation as one of Britain's most insightful television dramatists was confirmed by several *Wednesday Play* productions, including *A Suitable Case for Treatment* and *In Two Minds*, whilst Hugh Whitemore, John Hopkins, Alun Owen, Simon Raven, Alan Plater and Charles Wood were amongst others who made their own highly individual contributions to the series which, within its first two years, was regularly attracting in the region of an astonishing 12 million viewers.

What could I possibly have been thinking of, you may well ask, by sending *An Interest in People* to Tony Garnett? Surely I didn't think it was a potential *Wednesday Play?* Well, no, I don't think I did, although, to be honest, I can't remember what I did have in mind. Having worked alongside Tony in *An Age of Kings*, I suppose I could have been seeking a bit of encouragement; a second opinion perhaps. Obviously, our own opinion of the play must have been higher at that time than memories of it would seem to suggest. In fact, we may well have been incensed by *Armchair Theatre's* negative response, and were looking for some kind of vindication. I don't even know if I expected Tony Garnett to read it, let alone respond. But he did; and in the absence of a verbatim record, I will attempt to recall the substance of our telephone conversation ...

Tony *(in a Birmingham accent)* I liked your play a lot. It's not for us, though.

Me   No, we realised that. Just wanted a bit of advice, I suppose.

Tony Send it to *Armchair Theatre*. Perfect for that slot.

Me   We did. They said, "No thank you."

Tony You've been done.

Me   Well, nice of you to say so.

Tony Listen, have you two got anything else up your sleeves – something you and Dawn really want to write?

Me: Well, as a matter of fact, we've been making a few notes on a play about marriage.

Tony That's it then - that's your working title. *Marriage*. Just get on with it. Write the play you want to write. Let me have a draft in – what shall we say – two months time? And we'll take it from there.

Me   Are you commissioning us?

Tony Didn't I say? Yes, the money's yours. The only proviso is we might not do it. I've got 19 slots and I'm commissioning 23 writers, so four plays won't get done. One of those could be yours. As long as you're prepared to take that risk, I'll put a contract in the post.

It was as simple as that; and the only reason I have recorded the conversation, or as nearly as I can remember it, is to demonstrate how times have changed. For a start, there is little or no space in television schedules these days for the single play, and those that slip through the net are invariably written by established writers as star vehicles for famous actors. Can you imagine, for instance, a mere script editor being empowered nowadays to offer a commission to two unknown writers for such a prestigious drama series as *The Wednesday Play*? It was pretty incredible even at that time I must admit, and it took Dawn and me several eye-blinking hours to convince ourselves that it wasn't a dream, and although a cheque for £450 arrived in the post a couple of days later, it was certainly a dream come true.

We had indeed been discussing an idea about marriage, so I wasn't exactly shooting in the dark when Tony had asked that question. In fact, we had a pretty good idea what the theme would be, although the mechanics were still relatively new to us. It didn't take us long, however, to discover that it was Dawn who had the ideas and I who would write the dialogue. These boundaries became blurred, of course, as time went by, but it proved to be a good, and extremely practical, point of departure. For starters, it meant that we didn't have to spend all of our time huddled together over one portable typewriter. Dawn had the idea, and then went away to get lunch ready while I wrote the words. Well, maybe it wasn't quite as simple or, indeed, as sexist as that, and there were times, as weeks turned into months, when Dawn carried the burden alone while I, having tired of the whole damn business, went off to graze in pastures new. Looking back from this great distance, and while *The Bond*, as our play came to be called, was the single most important event of 1965, there were other happenings, most of them transient, but one in particular that was to have a far-reaching effect on my life, both professionally and personally.

I'm not at all sure now whether Joan Knight wanted to meet me before she offered me a couple of parts in her forthcoming season at the Castle Theatre in Farnham, or whether she took James Culliford's word for it that I would be right for them and simply booked me on his recommendation.

What's certain is that, had Jimmy not mentioned me to Joan, it is unlikely she would have offered me the parts of Lorenzo in *The Merchant of Venice* and Richard in Christopher Fry's *The Lady's Not For Burning* for the simple reason that she didn't know me. Jimmy and Alfie Lynch, on the other hand, had known Joan for some considerable time and had both worked with her on a number of occasions, so she obviously trusted their judgement, not to mention the fact that Jimmy was to be playing Shylock and would therefore have a vested interest in who would be sharing the stage with him.

Joan Knight was a mountain of a woman even then and, with a personality that matched her girth, she all but burst out of that tiny theatre in Castle Street. She was also distinguished in her post of Artistic Director for having graduated by way of stage management rather than from university, an unfamiliar route to hierarchical ascendancy in the theatre even then, and all but unheard of nowadays. It would be another nine years before she and I were to work together again when I was to become more familiar with her multi-faceted persona, but I was immediately struck by the genuine warmth of her welcome, and by the equally genuine respect in which she was held by actors and stage management alike. I, of course, had no idea at that time of the immensely important part she was eventually to play in my life, and at the end of six very enjoyable weeks in the spring of 1965, I left Farnham with no intention of returning to that, or indeed, to any other repertory theatre again.

It was during the two-week run of *The Merchant of Venice*, directed by Joan's associate, Anthony Tuckey, that I became aware of being on the receiving end of the kind of adulation normally reserved for matinée idols. In fact, it was at the schools' matinées that it first manifested itself, although it was not long before the female element of that audience, having persuaded their friends to join them, began to infiltrate the evening performances where, unchaperoned by their teachers, screams greeted my first and every subsequent entrance as Lorenzo, loud sighs accompanied my performance, hysterical tears bade me farewell at the curtain-call and hordes of young girls, having exchanged their school uniforms for more sophisticated evening wear, waited outside the theatre for my autograph. The passage of time being apt to lend a gloss to such things, and possibly even lead to gross exaggeration, it would be in the best interests of historical accuracy to point out that the aforementioned 'hordes' probably amounted to 20 or 30 at most, and that in the light of this retreat from fantasy it would be advisable to make similar adjustments to the other claims made in this paragraph. That it happened at all is beyond dispute, however. Bob Harris, leaving the theatre on one occasion after playing Launcelot Gobbo, announced to the assembled 'hordes', "He'll be out in minute, just as soon as he's put his teeth in!" The effect this experience had on me was galvanising and, remembering the fan base I had gathered in Chicago, not to mention the policeman who had mistaken me for a Beatle, I determined that, instead of working my socks off for a measly £11 a week in Rep, I was going to make my fortune as a pop star.

There's a scene in *The Adventures of Barry Mackenzie*, Barry Humphries' 1972 film about a sex-hungry Australian on a rampaging visit to the old country, in which the eponymous hero, seeking somewhere to live, is told by a fellow countryman to check out Michael Baldwin because he'll always let you stay even if he hasn't got any room. Dawn and I were the only two people in the audience who laughed out loud when we saw it for the simple reason that Michael Baldwin was a close friend of ours, and that Barry Humphries, whether or not from any personal experience, had got him absolutely right. Michael's reasonably spacious flat near Clapham Common was invariably awash with waifs and strays, not exclusively of antipodean origin although there always seemed to be at least one Australian in residence, usually waiting on a vacancy in somebody's flat in Earl's

Court. The others, more or less itinerant, seemed to come and go as it suited them, from overnight acquaintances en route to somewhere or other, to friends whose marriages had split up or who had illicit reasons for wanting to spend a night away from home, and to homeless pop singers, desperate to remain in the Big City while there was still a chance that their luck might change, and especially in rent-free accommodation. At that time Michael was a costume designer with Associated-Rediffusion, the major ITV company in the capital, and as such came into regular contact with the pop scene and its proponents through the medium of *Ready, Steady, Go!*, ITV's more streetwise version of the BBC's *Top of the Pops*. And it was, indeed, because of Michael's involvement that Dawn and I visited the studios in Kingsway to witness Tom Jones singing *It's Not Unusual*, his first number one hit. We were, I recall, given privileged treatment and were not required to jig around with *hoi polloi* in the pit, thanks to another of Michael's occasional lodgers, Paul Raven, a rock singer whose day had apparently come and gone, and who had ended up as official 'chucker-out' and 'warmer-up' on the programme. That was the first time we met Paul, and over the next couple of years, not having a base in London ourselves and therefore being fairly frequent visitors to Michael's flat, we got to know him pretty well. Paul's sad tale – and every failed pop singer had a tale to tell – was that, having recorded a song called *Tower of Strength* which looked all set to reach the charts, his agent did a deal with Frankie Vaughan's agent whose client then went on to record it himself, thereby nobbling Paul's effort and landing up in the number one spot for four consecutive weeks in 1961. Whether there was any truth in this story we never discovered, but it was pretty convincing the way Paul told it.

In the summer of 1966, having been invited to the wedding of one of my fellow actors from our Chicago trip, Leonard Cracknell, to his long-time girl-friend, Rosemary, and having been encouraged to bring a friend with us, we had no hesitation, for some reason, in taking Paul along. The wedding reception took place within the confines of a spacious marquee in the grounds of a large house somewhere in Brentwood, Essex. We were, I confess, taken aback, not only by the lavishness of the setting, but also by the preponderance of well-heeled chinless wonders who inhabited it. Having known Len and Rosemary for some considerable time, we had no idea that either of them came from such a background, although we were pretty sure it wasn't Len. The atmosphere was oppressively exclusive, to say the least, with tight little clutches of loud-voiced young men, morning-suited for the most part, and giggling gaggles of shrill-voiced young women in a variety of pastel shifts, all of them drinking champagne, and none of them paying any attention to the new arrivals, namely us, or giving even half an ear to the four-piece pop group who were playing, none too badly, on a dais at the far end of the marquee. For want of anything better to do and, in the absence of any invitation to join the party, we formed our own little group and listened to the music. It was partly out of sympathy for the musicians, playing for nobody but themselves and we three, and partly because we'd never heard Paul sing, that we suggested he should go and liven up the proceedings by joining them. He demurred at first, but when we persisted he finally caved in and approached the dais at the end of one of their numbers. They were naturally sceptical, given the general level of musical appreciation amongst their audience, but having assured them that he was a professional, they agreed and asked him what he wanted to sing. He asked if they knew *In the Midnight Hour*, a recent Top Twenty hit by Wilson Pickett. They obviously did, so Paul mounted the dais, and said, "Okay, Key of G and vamp 'til I'm ready." After exchanging anxious looks, they began to play and Paul went into an improvised intro in the rhythm of the song, demanding that everyone shut up and listen. By the time he started to sing it with the proper lyrics, he had certainly claimed their attention. Not that he would have held onto it for long had he not been able to deliver the goods. But he did, and it was an extraordinary demonstration, not only of his ability to sing, but to sing a song so recently associated with someone else, and yet to make it his own. What was even more impressive was his showmanship. In under a minute he had transformed a bunch of indifferent yuppies into just so many willing slaves. Having reached the end of the refrain he went back to the beginning, changing the lyrics yet again, exhorting his audience to turn around, kneel down, stand on one leg, jump up and down, and to perform all sorts of other silly antics, every one of which they willingly, even gleefully, carried out, hypnotised by the spell he seemed to have cast over them. Dawn and I, while remaining aloof from the proceedings, could only stand there and marvel at his power and his animal magnetism, neither of which, even in our wildest dreams, could we have imagined he possessed during our brief friendship with him. I have since wondered from time to time if any of those young people, whose evening had been transformed by his presence, have ever realised that they were being entertained, and mildly humiliated, by the future Gary Glitter.

This story would, of course, have been seen in a very different light had it not been for the unfortunate turn of events that led, eventually, to his fall from grace. But Paul was a gentle soul when we knew him, far removed from the 'glam-rock' image he was to assume and not given to the extravagant displays of his alter-ego. Yes, he was certainly promiscuous, and maybe a little jaded in his sexual preferences, but no more so than many another rock singer who had had it handed to him on a plate from an early age. At that time, however, those preferences expressed themselves in terms of 'how many' rather than 'how old.' How sad that, in his continued search for stimulus, he ultimately found himself inhabiting the despicable and heinous world of pædophilia. As it is something I have never had the misfortune to come into contact with, I can only say that I'm glad I knew him before all that happened, and I'm glad I was there when he sang *In the Midnight Hour* at that wedding reception in Brentwood because, to my way of thinking, Gary Glitter was never as good as Paul Raven was that evening.

Although this story was essentially a digression, since my career as a pop singer had nothing to do with Paul Raven, it was related to it, and in a very literal sense too, as it was with his brother that I took my first faltering steps down that road. Tony – who was neither Raven nor Gadd, which was their family name but, for some obscure reason, Russell – was younger than Paul, and a very competent guitarist. He was also a lazy bugger with the unfortunate habit of spiking his cigarette, between puffs, onto the loose end of a guitar string. These drawbacks did not augur well for our longevity as a pop duo, but for a while I was content to meet up with him and practise a few songs, finding my pop voice, as it were, and desultorily planning our future. In any case, I needed him at that stage as he was the only guitarist I knew and I didn't play any instrument at all. Against all the odds, however, we did manage to get one gig before we went our separate ways. It came about after I bumped into another old friend from *An Age of Kings,* Leon Shepperdson, with whom I had jointly auditioned for the Marlowe Theatre in Canterbury five years earlier. He was living in Islington at the time and, returning home one evening, had paused to listen to the alluring sounds of a pop group practising in the front room of a house on the other side of the road. He was obviously very taken with what he heard and also having a head for business, he crossed the road and knocked on the door, only to emerge some time later as the manager of a multi-racial group called *The Equals,* who eventually went on to record a number of chart successes, including their No 1 hit, *Baby Come Back* in 1968. For the time being, they were to act as my backing group when we were booked to make an appearance at the Whittington Hospital in Highgate at a doctors' and nurses' social gathering. Truth to tell, they were the top-liners, and Tony and I were there merely to fill in, although they did back me on several numbers, none of which I can recall now. My big moment, however, came later in the evening when, between two of their sets, I launched into a medley of songs from *West Side Story*, accompanied solely by Tony on bongos, the very recollection of which freezes the blood in my veins even now. The fact that the audience stood quietly and listened all the way through to the end was probably because they had danced themselves to a standstill by then and were happy to take a break, while the polite applause that followed, instead of a volley of bedpans, clearly said more about the kindness and the forbearance of NHS staff, not to mention the absence of handy bedpans, than it did about my performance, over which I intend to draw an immediate veil.

While Tony Russell and I remained friends thereafter, our musical partnership came to an end that night, precipitated by an offer to become the third voice in an already established duo. It was again through Michael Baldwin's contacts that I met Glen Stuart who, along with Nola York, had already proved themselves to be no mean songwriters. Their performances, however, while proficient enough, and especially where they featured Nola's marvellously powerful voice, lacked a sufficiently strong male counterpoint. So, having demonstrated my vocal prowess, I was invited to join them, and was immediately caught up in a working schedule that only served to highlight the lackadaisical way Tony and I had approached the job. The downside was that it also imposed a degree of stress on my working relationship with Dawn as we struggled to sustain our focus on *The Bond*. We had delivered the first draft to Tony Garnett, and over the next few months were involved in a series of meetings with him at the Television Centre, the outcome of each being a seemingly endless list of rewrites which, once accomplished, were superseded by others, none of which appeared to bring us any closer to a commitment from the BBC to produce the play. But, to be fair, Tony never suggested at any of these meetings that we were any nearer to getting the play accepted, and while he insisted that he was perfectly happy to work on it with us for as long as we wanted to, he made it clear that we were free to throw in the towel whenever we felt we'd had enough. I have to say that, had it not been for Dawn, there were times when I might well have taken him up on the invitation. I was obviously busy elsewhere and, having joined up with Glen and Nola, entertained high hopes for a while that fame and fortune were beckoning, so I was in no mood to put up with the element of drudgery that went hand-in-hand with constant re-writing. But Dawn stubbornly refused to give up and, while there were periods when she found herself working entirely alone on the script, I never strayed too far or too long from her side. Besides, she was pretty much in favour of my excursion into the pop world, having accompanied Tony Russell and me to Carnaby Street where we were outfitted, under her supervision, in a variety of trendy garments, most of which we never had the opportunity to wear. She was also responsible for giving a name to the newly-formed trio, and it was consequently as *The Bow Bells* that we were launched upon an unsuspecting world.

There was no doubt that Glen Stuart was the driving force behind the group, and it was at his Soho flat that plans were made and songs were rehearsed to a well organised schedule. He was an entirely affable carrot-haired Pinocchio look-alike, although even in the early days there were hints that he and Nola had personality issues. Nola was a Liverpudlian girl whose voice was at least as good as any of the other young vocalists around at that time, and better than most, equally at home with rock and soul songs as she was with ballads. The trouble was that Nola wasn't exceptionally pretty except when she was singing, when her talent more than made up for her lack of superficial glamour and, as I have found throughout my life, genuine talent is the most powerful of all aphrodisiacs. The commercial world, however, was essentially immune to such subtleties and, as time went by, it became clear that the kind of exposure we needed, and particularly on television, was going to be hard to achieve.

The Bow Bells reached their apogee, somewhat surprisingly, within a few months of their début and, for a short while afterwards, enjoyed some exposure in a few London venues, including the 100 Club in Oxford Street, not to mention a television appearance, albeit as guests on an afternoon show. This all came about when we were invited to record two of Glen and Nola's songs, and if *The Bow Bells* achieved a place, however marginal, in the history of pop music, it was because we were the first pop group ever to be recorded on the Polydor label. I have no idea what led us to be so distinguished, but I have almost total recall of that day in the studio, situated somewhere in the Holland Park area of West London, when we arrived to find the musicians already assembled and waiting on the appearance of the musical arranger whose tardiness was due, no doubt, to the fact that he was probably the most overworked musical arranger in the business. I won't even begin to catalogue Les Reed's credits as an arranger, conductor, composer and multi-instrumentalist, except to say that his services had been eagerly employed by many of the biggest names in the recording industry, from Tom Jones to Johnny Mathis, from Bing Crosby to Roy Orbison, and from the Glenn Miller Orchestra to the London Philharmonic. As a songwriter he had also collaborated with, among others, John Barry and Sammy Cahn. Needless to say, Glen, Nola and I were flattered, if a little puzzled, by his interest in us although, no doubt, Polydor were anxious to have at least one big name on the label, and made it worth his while. But then again, maybe he just liked the songs. His eventual arrival, obviously crammed in between half a dozen other recording sessions, was brisk and incredibly efficient. Having greeted us rather perfunctorily, as if we were only of peripheral interest, he laid out his sheets of manuscript paper on the top of a grand piano, and with no more effort than he would have expended on a shopping-list, he scribbled down the parts for each instrument, handing each one to the relevant musician while scribbling out the next one without a moment's hesitation or a pause for reflection. His energy galvanised the studio into action and, within a matter of only a few minutes, he was conducting them as they played the accompaniment to the first song, which was called *Not To Be Taken,* and which began thus:

'Someone should take you and put you in a bottle of blue,
Then tie a great big 'danger' label on you;
It should say 'Not to be taken',
No, no, no, not to be taken,
You're not to be taken – seriously.'

I remember thinking at the time that Les Reed's arrangement was incredibly imaginative given the fairly conventional structure of the song, and even listening to it now – although it is in many ways an archetypal product of the '60s – I am still struck by its originality, and it was, without question, Les Reed's contribution to the recording that made it the obvious choice for the 'A' side of our record. The other song, called (believe it or not) *I'm Gonna Try Not To Hold It Against You,* was a very catchy jazz waltz, and while Nola sang the middle-eight, I had a solo line in each of the verses.

For two glorious weeks we revelled in being Radio London's Tip for the Top. But the limelight somehow eluded us and, without the power of Polydor's later publicity machine behind us, the record didn't get enough air time to make Radio London's prediction come true. I still have, and treasure, the original 45 rpm recording in my collection and even play it occasionally, relishing the nostalgia it provokes, still enjoying Les Reed's ingenious arrangement, and drawing the attention of anyone in the immediate vicinity to my solo contribution on the 'B' side.

It had been on the cards for some considerable time, but when Glen and Nola finally fell out in the wake of the record's release, together with the dawning realisation that it wasn't going to make it into the charts, it became clear that *The Bow Bells*, without their song-writing team, would cease to exist.

1965 The Bow Bells. TW, Nola York and Glen Stuart.

Glen went on to co-found a group called *Magna Carta,* and Nola joined a girl group called *The Chantelles.* Meanwhile, Nola and I said a protracted goodbye to each other in the *Pink Elephant,* a rather shabby night-club just off Shaftesbury Avenue where, as a duo, we supported for a short season a fairly outrageous drag-act, Rogers & Starr (window-dressers by day), whose first entrance, carrying trays around their necks, attached to which was the slogan, TO SAVE OUR SAILORS FROM GOING DOWN, set the tone for the evening and, given that most of the audience were of a similar persuasion, made Nola and I very glad that we occupied the first half of the bill.

I was not sorry that it had all come to an end, although I look back on my brief career as a pop singer with a kind of affectionate nostalgia. But having dreamed of a meteoric rise to stardom, I was not prepared to settle for anything less, and decidedly not the prospect of trailing around the country from one dingy club to another trying to make a living, which was the only realistic future I could foresee. Besides, I was suddenly free to give my entire attention to the equally uncertain prospects of my career as a writer.

Our meetings with Tony Garnett had continued unabated, although occasionally without my presence, and the subsequent rewrites had been diligently undertaken by Dawn and, somewhat less diligently, by me too. At one such meeting I remember marvelling at the amount of time Tony was prepared to lavish on this one project when he had 22 other plays to consider, presumably bestowing on their authors the same degree of care and attention. Both Dawn and I had the most enormous respect for him and we could not help feeling as cheated on his behalf as he obviously did himself when, at yet another meeting, the door opened and in came James MacTaggart, producer of *The Wednesday Play,* who threw an envelope onto Tony's desk, turned round to see us sitting there, and said, "Well, congratulations! We're doing your play." The door closed behind him, and Tony, clearly seething, said, "Coont!", with which sentiment we could not but agree, for if anyone had earned the right to impart that news, and to enjoy in private our euphoric response to it, it was unquestionably Tony Garnett.

The Bond was transmitted on December 5th, 1965 and Tony's summary of the play, printed in the *Radio Times,* pretty well tells you all you need to know: 'Chris and Sally have everything. They are young, attractive, and about to be married. But more than that, they are the new Britain. Every politician woos them. Anyone with something to sell tries to seduce them. They are the new middle-class. Their future is rosy. This is *their* world. Most other people are thought to envy them – the Joneses we are invited to keep up with. A white wedding, a Paris honeymoon, and a beautiful London home. They have glamorous careers. Their friends are smart and successful. They are full of good taste. They know where they are going. They love each other. Tonight we look at these people, not as the advertisers and politicians do, but as they are. This is a play by a young married couple about a young married couple and it is important to all of us. Because most of us have either fallen in love and married – or will do. And trying to make marriage work is a moving, difficult, and hysterically funny experience. This is Dawn Pavitt and Terry Wale's first play and it is directed by Mary Ridge.'

1965 BBC The Wednesday Play - The Bond, starring Hannah Gordon.

Mary Ridge was a joy to work with from start to finish. Having established an immediate rapport with her which was based, although not exclusively, on her empathy with the play, we both found the experience hugely rewarding, especially since the policy of *The Wednesday Play* team was to require the presence of the writers throughout the entire process. Casting the play came, of course, pretty high on the list of priorities and, because of our background, Mary was prepared to listen sympathetically, and often positively, to our suggestions. Thus it was that several actors we'd had in mind while we were writing it, ended up playing the parts. I cannot recall now who it was we suggested for the main part of Sally, but it certainly wasn't Hannah Gordon, as neither of us had even heard of her. But Mary insisted that we meet her before considering anyone else, and one meeting was all it took. Sally was Hannah's first major television role and it marked the beginning of a long-standing love affair between her and the camera. She was perfect for the part, her essentially feminine allure concealing a fierce intelligence which were exactly the right ingredients for a character who bore a striking resemblance to Nora in *A Doll's House* although, to be honest, I don't think that particular analogy occurred to us at the time.

Shortly after the play was transmitted, however, Tony Garnett told us of a letter he had received from a clergyman saying that *The Bond* was the first female existentialist drama that had been written since Ibsen, which was extremely flattering, of course, but hardly credible. On the other hand, the observation having been made by a man of the cloth who was doubtless encouraged to make it by a 'higher authority', who were we to disagree? Truth to tell, the plot was not a million light years away. A young couple, enjoying separate professional careers in television, fall in love and get married, both of them prey to the 'happily-ever-after' syndrome. In fact, I think that *Happily Ever After* was, for a while, an alternative title. If not, it should have been! Her working-class family naturally assume that she will give up her job, have a family and embrace domesticity. Rather more surprisingly her husband, coming as he does from a new and supposedly more enlightened generation, is of the same mind. She, on the other hand, has no intention of sacrificing her career on the altar of matrimony and will only consider having children when she is good and ready. She stands her ground against formidable opposition until her marriage is all but on the rocks. Unlike Nora, however, she doesn't walk away. Being nothing if not an optimist, Sally decides to fight for her marriage as well as for her independence and the closing shot sees her at Heathrow Airport waiting to welcome her husband home from a trip abroad, hopefully to effect some kind of reconciliation.

All this must seem quite old-fashioned now, and without Ibsen's genius, which made most of his plays pretty well timeless, this is just what it is. But almost everything depends on timing, and I would remind you that by 1965, not a single bra had been burnt in the name of feminism nor would it be for another three years, except by accident or in the heat of the moment.

Not that *The Bond* set the world on fire, although it was well enough received. What it did achieve was a degree of recognition for its authors, who were immediately signed up by a literary agent, offered several commissions, both for television and radio, and who greeted the arrival of 1966 under the impression that maybe, just maybe, they had become playwrights.

oOoOo

Fifteen

There are periods in one's life which could well be looked back upon as watersheds, and whether I knew it or not at the time – and I don't think I did – this was one of them. My brief stay in Tin Pan Alley was obviously symptomatic, albeit a passing fancy; similarly with my desire to write. Oh, I may have toyed with one or two ideas en route, but the notion of earning a living as a playwright remained firmly rooted in the realms of fantasy. I do believe, however, that nothing happens entirely by accident, a belief given some substance, I admit, when you have the opportunity to view things retrospectively.

My feelings about being an actor were beginning to undergo something of a sea-change which, I suppose, was not entirely surprising given that, at the age of 28, I had already been doing it for 15 years, had never considered doing anything else, and had somehow managed to preserve my early dreams and ambitions, more or less intact, until now. True, I had toyed with the idea of giving it up at the end of my season with the Royal Shakespeare Company, but even had I not been pulled back from the brink by Sir John Gielgud, I doubt if I really would have re-enlisted in the RAF which I half jokingly considered to be my only other option at that time. In any case, I went on to enjoy two of the happiest and most fulfilling years of my professional life at the Open Air Theatre, Regent's Park, where my doubts were well and truly shelved. And then, of course, came the Ravinia Festival, when a keenly anticipated visit to the USA with a much admired director of Shakespeare's plays – well, at least some of them – had turned out to be chimeric and, in the wake of which, I had begun to feel, if not disillusioned, certainly disenchanted.

It had, of course, been drummed into me over the years that the transition from child actor to the grown-up variety, far from being a rite of passage, is like entering an entirely different, more densely populated, and infinitely more competitive world, a world in which none of your childhood achievements count for anything more than acquired experience and fond memories; and it has to be said that very few fledgling careers survived that transition. I myself had been protected to some extent from this blast of cold air by the fact that I looked younger than my years and remained relatively small and slightly built so that, by my mid-twenties, I was still playing the kind of parts, and occasionally exactly the same parts, that I had played during my adolescence. By 1966, however, one thing was certain. I wasn't going to grow any more, and all my cherished dreams of playing the great

Shakespearian roles would probably come to nothing for the simple reason, if for no other, that I wasn't physically built to play them. Was I then prepared to settle for anything less? I really didn't know and, to tell the truth, these uncertainties were hardly critical at that time, being newly born and only occasionally dwelt upon. It would take another couple of years before I had to face now-or-never decisions about my future. I certainly hadn't consciously chosen to write as an alternative to acting; it was simply a new and exciting challenge. In fact, I had every hope that I could do both, with the writing filling up those parts of me that were left empty by the spasmodic and essentially piecemeal nature of television work which was all, or very nearly all, that I was being offered at the time. Not that I didn't enjoy it and, indeed, one of the highlights of 1966 was renewing my acquaintance with Richard Martin, who I had worked with at the Belgrade Theatre in Coventry back in 1959. Clearly, in the interim, he too had faced that critical decision and had chosen to give up acting in favour of a career as a television director. We were to work together on several occasions over the next few years, the first being a six-part serial for BBC 2 called *Ransom for a Pretty Girl* in which Leon Thau and I played key roles as the villains of the piece, albeit we were only known as the Driver and the Passenger. The serial involved, I recall, several delightful trips to Loch Lomond where we stayed in a very nice lochside hotel on the banks of which, in Episode 6, I met my demise, at the hands of a very young James Cosmo, face down for what seemed like an eternity in a freezing stream, or 'burn' as the Scots call it. I was subsequently resurrected by Richard to play another baddie in an episode of the Edgar Lustgarten series, *Scales of Justice*, which was shown in cinemas as well as on TV, and which enjoyed the special distinction of being the series that closed down Merton Park Studios. My abiding memory of *Infamous Conduct*, as that particular episode was called, was standing on a box in the studio so that I could play head-to-head with the exceedingly tall star of the film, Dermot Walsh, and then being captured in long-shot as, boxless, and clearly incapable of having an intimate conversation with anything higher than his armpit, I walked down the road beside him.

I made several other television appearances around that time and, while short-lived, were at least periods of employment. The need to diversify was therefore not predominantly an economic one. Dawn was still kept relatively busy cutting costumes on a freelance basis, although her career as a designer had all but come to an end. Skimpy budgets together with cost-cutting exploitation of her other skills in

Regent's Park, plus her unhappy experience with Peter Dews at the Ravinia Festival had obviously precipitated that decision. Far from putting all our eggs in one basket, then, it was against this background that we embarked upon our joint career as writers. In the immediate aftermath of *The Bond*, we were invited to write a play for the BBC2 series, *Thirty Minute Theatre*, the mandatory requirement for which was not only its length but that it had to be written for live transmission. Looking back, it seems odd that live television drama should have been celebrated with more than a hint of nostalgia so soon after they had happily embraced the new technology, but it obviously had its appeal, and it was certainly a challenging exercise. Not nearly as challenging, I might add, as the 30 minute format which, for a chronic over-writer, was a task bordering on the Herculean.

A Girl's Best Friend was the first of three plays we were commissioned to write for *Thirty Minute Theatre*. It starred Faith Brook as a single mother and shopkeeper, only too happy to flirt with a salesman (Ray Brooks), until she discovers that he is using her as a means to an end, the end being her teenage daughter, played by Tessa Wyatt. We then went on to write *Play To Win*, in which a young wife, played by Alethea Charlton, married to a feckless husband (Mark Eden), determines to carve out a career for herself in the commercial world. Our third and last play for *Thirty Minute Theatre* came about as a direct result of my one and only theatrical venture in 1966.

I was invited by Jerome Willis, a fellow member – or ex-member – of the 'Peter Dews Repertory Company', to play the part of Maurice in his production of Pauline Macauley's play, *The Creeper*, at the Churchill Theatre in Bromley. During the run, my opposite number in the play and with whom I shared a dressing-room, told me of an idea he had had for a *Thirty Minute Theatre* play which he was sure he would never get around to writing. I liked the idea, as did Dawn when I told her about it, and so we bought it, subject to its acceptance by the BBC, for what I recall was 10% of the fee plus an on-screen credit – 'From an idea by Tony Holland.' He obviously made a good deal more money over the next few years than the measly £30 I think we paid him, firstly as script editor on *Z Cars* in the early '70s, and than as co-creator, with Julia Smith, of *EastEnders*, the BBC's flagship soap-opera for which he also received, and has gone on receiving, more on-screen credits than he could have imagined, even in his wildest dreams, 20 years earlier. *The Isle is Full of Noises* was about a mature, responsible and, on the face of it, well-adjusted business-woman who conducts what appears to be a perfectly reasonable campaign against excessive noise levels. Her personal crusade, however, becomes an increasingly irrational obsession, and she ends up, having suffered a mental breakdown, living in a world of total silence. The part was played, quite beautifully, by Nancie Jackson, who had also appeared in *The Bond* and in *Play To Win,* and whose work I had admired in *An Age of Kings*. She was also a favourite with Mary Ridge who was, happily, once again our director.

We were also commissioned to write several plays for radio at around about the same time, and found ourselves facing a future in which writing was apparently going to play a more dominant part in our lives. What had been little more than a fantasy only a year earlier had become a reality, encouraged as we were by a demand for our services and, not least, by the positive input of our literary agent, Roger Hancock, a delightful man whose energy and enthusiasm spurred us on and opened doors for us. While being recognisably the brother of comedian, Tony Hancock, Roger was an altogether different man; the other side of the same coin if you like, blessed with a sunnier nature than his brother, and a stranger to those demons that hounded Tony to his death in 1968. There's a story I first heard many years ago that perfectly illustrates the bewildering dichotomy between those who make us laugh and the depression that so often besets them. It takes place in the taproom of a London tavern early in the 19th century where a man, taking a drink before going to the theatre, sees another man, sitting close by, nursing a pint and looking positively suicidal. He takes it upon himself to approach the man and suggest that he accompanies him to the theatre to see the comedian Joseph Grimaldi, who's so funny he'll be bound to cheer him up. The other man, without even looking up, says, "I *am* Joseph Grimaldi." Roger Hancock was, it must be said, a very entertaining man, and laughter played a significant part in our relationship with him, but I don't imagine he ever envied his brother's extraordinary talent or the fame and the torment that went with it.

It was Roger who arranged a meeting for us with another of his clients, John Frankau, a producer/director with BBC Television at that time who was in the process of setting up a new television series. Having seen something of our work, he wondered if we might be interested in contributing an episode to it; whereupon, he presented us with the outline and left us to come up with a synopsis. What on earth it was, apart from inspired intuition, that suggested to John we might be suitable writers for *Mickey Dunne* I have no way of knowing, but somehow he got it absolutely right, and as well as deriving enormous pleasure from the experience, I can now say – without undue modesty – that we succeeded in writing the two most successful episodes of that short-lived series. I have since read that the reason *Mickey Dunne* only survived for 14 episodes was because audiences failed to respond to it in sufficient numbers. I have no idea what the viewing figures were; I'm not even sure we thought much about things like that in those far-off days. In any case, I still believe that the main reason for its premature demise lay in its format, which demanded too much of its eponymous hero, played with great charm and humour by Dinsdale Landen. Mickey Dunne was a Londoner on the make. His only objective was to be a success, in love as well as in business, in both of which he was doomed to fail because, although superficially streetwise, he was essentially naïve and soft-hearted, successful only in creating opportunities for others less endearing and more ruthless to elbow him aside. The problem was that, having borrowed certain aspects of the character from Bill Naughton's play, *Alfie*, Mickey was not provided with a sidekick and, consequently, instead of sharing his innermost thoughts with an on-screen companion, he was obliged to confide in his audience who, for obvious reasons, were unable to engage him in conversation. The long and the short of it was that, after 14 episodes, Dinsdale was understandably too exhausted to continue. But it was great fun while it lasted.

Our first episode, cheekily entitled *Are There Any More At Home Like You?*, showed Mickey in gallant mode, riding to the rescue of a young Italian maiden, seemingly in distress, and taking up the cudgels on her behalf with her family, Italian restaurateurs with more than a hint of *La Cosa Nostra* in their demeanour. It transpired, however, that the young girl (delightfully played by Nike Arrighi who had also played the heroine in *Ransom for a Pretty Girl*) was the real Mafiosa, twisting Mickey around her little finger in her efforts to extract money from her blameless family. The only memorable audience reaction to this episode came in the form of a protest letter to *The Times* from the Italian Ambassador! John Frankau's reaction, however, was a bit more positive in that he commissioned us to write a second episode which, retaining the interrogative as a kind of trade mark, we called *Yes – But Can He Go the Distance?* As the title suggests, the plot revolved around the world of prize-fighting which Mickey, in an excess of enthusiasm, decides to enter having watched a young lad work out with a sparring partner in a local gymnasium from which Mickey, with no previous experience, eventually emerges as his manager. But Mickey is nothing if not an incurable optimist and, given the lad's obvious qualities in the ring, he sees it as an opportunity not to be missed. His protégé certainly inspires confidence. He is tall, muscular, fast on his feet and long of reach. He is also stunningly good-looking, black as ebony and, being a second-generation Londoner, speaks the same language as Mickey, without a trace of his Afro-Caribbean origins. What Mickey chooses to ignore is the boy's reluctance to become a boxer, having been pushed into it by his father, instead of being able to realise his own ambitions as a pop singer. At a pub party following his first successful bout under Mickey's management he gets up to sing and is immediately snapped up by a musical entrepreneur, thus bringing a welcome end to his boxing career and, not so happily, to Mickey's dreams and aspirations.

I don't recall Dawn and I having any serious misgivings about the casting of this role when we created the character, and maybe we even thought there would be a queue of young black contenders for it. If so, we were about to be disillusioned. John Frankau told us that, after an exhaustive search had been made for an actor with all the necessary qualifications, the best suggestion they could come up with was Kenny Lynch. Not that we had anything against Kenny Lynch who was a notable performer at the time, both as a comedian and as a singer, but besides being too familiar to audiences, too distantly related to his Caribbean forbears and too comfortable with his own Englishness, he was also ten years too old for the part. Nevertheless, there appeared to be no alternative, and we left the BBC Television Centre that day with heavy hearts, possibly even toying with the idea of 'blacking-up' a white actor which, believe it or not, would not have been deemed politically incorrect as no such crime existed in 1967. Goodness, white actors even got to play Othello in those days, and *The Black and White Minstrel Show* was still flourishing on the nation's TV screens. Nevertheless, I don't think we seriously considered it as an option, and it was with a degree of despondency that we left the Television Centre and went to visit my parents in nearby Kensal Rise.

Fortuitously, my brother, Peter, was home from work and enjoying his tea when we arrived, and so I asked him, somewhat idly, if he knew of anyone who might be right for the part. I had no real expectations, but at least he was ten years younger than I was and consequently better acquainted with that generation of performers from amongst whose ranks lay our only hope. He pondered the question for a while before saying, "Only Spence". "Spence? Who's Spence?" I asked. He told me that Spence, whose full name was Linbert Spencer, was his best friend at Rolls-Royce where they both worked in the accounts department. I was about to point out that we were looking for someone with a bit of professional experience when he rather grudgingly elaborated, "He does a lot of amateur acting. He's good." So I decided, more out of politeness than anything else, to pursue it. "Could he play a boxer, do you think?" "Well," said Pete, still without any marked enthusiasm, "he was Light-Middleweight Champion of Willesden last year." My pulse began to quicken, although I made a determined effort to remain sceptical. "But can he sing?" I countered, in a tone that suggested it was obviously too much to ask for, "Oh, he sings all the time. He's with the Salvation Army. He's got a good voice." Still searching for a caveat, I probed further. "And he's black? I mean, really black, is he?" With more emphasis than he had hitherto employed, Pete said, "Oh yeah, he's black all right." "And he speaks with a London accent?" I asked, by now fully expecting another positive answer. But Pete became thoughtful again, and I felt the adrenalin slow to a crawl as I waited for the inevitable stumbling block. "Well, no ...," he finally conceded, and after another pause, he said, "He speaks the same as what I do." Well, no one even vaguely acquainted with my brother (except himself, or so it seemed) would have had any doubts about his origins. "Is he on the 'phone?" was the only question left to ask, and within half an hour Linbert Spencer, the 19 year-old black Adonis of our dreams, was standing on the front door-step. I took him into another room, got him to read a few extracts from the script, asked him if he was up for it which he clearly was, and telephoned John Frankau. "We've found him!" I said, and after a hastily arranged meeting, he was offered the part. I don't think John ever entirely believed our story, so perfect was Spence in every way that he was convinced we had long been acquainted with him and had written the part with him in mind from the very beginning. I am reminded, however, that while he was indeed perfectly cast and turned in an excellent performance, nervous tension robbed him of his voice in the final scene and he was unable to sing the song that launched his chosen career, although he successfully mimed it to a vocal provided by none other than Kenny Lynch who just happened to be in the building at the same time.

Unsurprisingly, Linbert Spencer gave up his job at Rolls-Royce and, for a while at any rate, became a professional actor, enjoying considerable success, both in theatre and on film, and finally meeting his Waterloo in the long-running musical, *Hair*, a show for which I myself had auditioned. I was, in fact, recalled four times, having competently sung my way, unaccompanied, through the first three, until they decided on the fourth occasion, probably as a result of my relatively conservative approach to expressive movement, that I was a little too set in my ways to truly belong to the *Age of Aquarius*. As far as Spence was concerned, flying in the face of most actors' dreams of a long West End run, the daily repetition over a long period of time successfully and permanently killed off his interest in acting as a career, and he went on to become a leading figure in Social Services in the Midlands, finally making a name for himself in the world of politics, fighting for equal opportunities on behalf of various ethnic groups, and ultimately being awarded an OBE. So much for the smell of the greasepaint!

Not for nothing, as we were beginning to discover, was John Frankau described by our mutual agent as 'The runaway horse', and an uncanny foresight about our immediate future in his company may well have played a part in our decision to leave Great Missenden and return to London had we not, in truth, been planning it for some time. Our cat had already made his feelings known shortly before when he absconded in a removal lorry and ended up in Brentwood, Essex. This destination was entirely random as far as he was concerned, having climbed into the back of the lorry while it was being loaded and fallen asleep, and it was not until our erstwhile neighbours telephoned us from Brentwood to say that upon opening up the lorry the removal men had been confronted briefly by the sight of a demented Siamese cat, tail up and fur standing on end, that we had any idea where he had gone. Apparently he had fled from his enforced confinement and disappeared down the road before anyone could stop him. Without holding out any great hope we advertised his disappearance in the local Brentwood paper and, as luck would have it, we learned that he had managed to avoid a confrontation with foxes and was now living with a family on a housing estate where his haughty demeanour stood out like a sore thumb. It wasn't long before I was informed of his whereabouts and drove down to Brentwood, armed with a small reward, to retrieve the miscreant. In a scene reminiscent of the one that was played out on our return from Chicago, Bosie was sitting looking up at me with something akin to disdain when I arrived at the door. From the back of the house a couple of kids suddenly appeared, and yelled out, "Run, Simmy! Run, run!" Whereupon 'Simmy' turned tail and ran. I was half inclined to shout, "You'll get no pheasant here" and leave him where he was, but I didn't. Instead I cornered him and was soon driving back to Great Missenden, some 60 miles away on the other side of London, listening to his screams of protest from inside his cat basket every inch of the way.

Our decision to move back to London, however, had nothing to do with Bosie. Nor had we tired of our rural abode. We had simply had enough of the increasingly frequent journeys we were having to make to the Television Centre at the behest of John Frankau. On top of this, Dawn had an ongoing working relationship with another freelance costume-maker, Natasha Kornilof, which involved regular visits to her home in Greenwich, even further away than White City. Having been born and brought up in North London, the idea of living south of the river had never entered my head. But we were both immediately attracted to Greenwich and, in time, grew to love it. In fact, it became my home for the next ten years and, should I ever decide to live in London again, only financial considerations would induce me to look elsewhere. Besides its obvious appeal – the wide open spaces of Blackheath and the stunning views from Greenwich Park of London's dockland area – more of our friends lived there than in any other part of London. There was also the added bonus of the number 53 bus route, surely one of the most user-friendly services in the city, running from Woolwich to Camden Town via Blackheath, and transporting you to the heart of London's West End in little more than 30 minutes – or at least it did in those days. So we found a relatively spacious first-floor flat in a fairly substantial Victorian house at the very top of Blackheath Hill, bordering on Blackheath itself, set back from the busy road, and further protected by a couple of tall trees and a garden so overgrown that Bosie happily adopted it as his own private jungle, became fiercely territorial, and never showed any desire to leave home again.

The move was indeed timely for no sooner had we said farewell to *Mickey Dunne* than we were asked by John Frankau to come up with an idea for a series of our own, and no sooner had we done that than we were commissioned to write a pilot episode. It was then that we experienced the full impact of John's unbridled enthusiasm, and a work ethic that took no account of time, distance or expense. Certainly, the leisurely journey we had enjoyed with Tony Garnett on *The Bond*, although fairly recent, seemed to have belonged to an entirely different age in the face of John Frankau's determination to meet impossible deadlines that, as far as we knew, no one but he himself had set. We had already glimpsed this aspect of John's character on *Mickey Dunne*, but then we had merely contributed to a series created by someone else, whereas on this occasion, as co-creators, we were to experience the full blast of his single-minded dynamism. A regular feature of our working injunction was to accomplish the required rewrites as soon as inhumanly possible. Meanwhile, he would return to his own home, grab a few hours sleep, and await a call from us as soon as we had finished, usually in the early hours of the morning, to say that we had put the rewrites in a taxi which was on its way to him in Kingston-on-Thames. We would then grab a few hours sleep ourselves and await his call to arrange a further meeting, at the end of which the whole process would begin again. It was a kind of madness and yet, despite our doubts about the need for such a degree of urgency, we got caught up in it and responded enthusiastically to all, or nearly all, of John's demands. I suppose it made us feel that we were involved in something of great importance.

If I remember rightly we were enjoying a meal at a restaurant in nearby Lewisham when the vague outline of what was to become *Flashpoint* took shape. Looking back, it is hardly surprising that it was inspired by political events, for while the '60s are probably best remembered for the *Beatles* and the mini-skirt, the second half of that decade saw more political and social upheaval than at any time since the end of World War II. Perhaps even more significantly, a younger generation than ever before was beginning to play a more proactive role in many of these events, their awakening consciences swelling the ranks of the already well-established Campaign for Nuclear Disarmament: leading the protests against the Vietnam War outside the U.S. Embassy in Grosvenor Square, demonstrating against U.S. attempts to overthrow the Cuban dictator, Fidel Castro and marching and crusading on behalf of a variety of causes, none of which were motivated by self-interest. Nor were these manifestations of unrest confined to Britain. The younger generation of Americans had, in any case, never been known for their indifference to politics, and they had more cause to protest against the Vietnam War than anyone else apart, that is, from the Vietnamese. But all over Europe young people were making their feelings known on a wide range of issues, none of them more widespread and more violent than the Paris student riots of May 1968 in which my old friend from *An Age of Kings*, Patrick Garland, became inadvertently involved. Several years later he told me that he had been caught up in a crowd of students who were having seven bells knocked out of them by baton-wielding gendarmes. Approached by one of these, and in imminent danger of being walloped himself, he cried out, *"Je suis Anglais, je suis Anglais!"* The gendarme paused only briefly before bringing his baton down heavily on Patrick's shoulder. *"Ça c'est pour Jeanne d'Arc!"* he growled before stomping off in search of other victims.

Neither Dawn nor I had ever voted for anything other then the Labour Party since we were old enough to vote, but while my own allegiance was pretty well in-bred, my father having been a union man all his working life, Dawn's was of a more intellectual persuasion, doubtless conditioned by her student days at the Old Vic School, since her parents, having achieved *petit bourgeois* status, were Tories both; Rose less so by conviction than by convention, I think, and Jack because his managerial job demanded it, as did his membership of the Freemasons, I imagine, or else he would never have been persuaded to wear an apron. Until the late '60s, however, my own left-wing bias was entirely theoretical. I was, of course, emotionally involved in politics by the numerous films that made a lasting impression on me at that time and, in particular, by *Z,* the brainchild of the Greek director, Costa Gavras, fictionalising (only just) events leading up to the Colonels' coup in Greece in 1967. Besides being a gripping thriller, enhanced by some superb performances and by the wonderfully evocative music of Mikis Theodorakis, it was overtly and subjectively political, and bravely – given that the military junta was still in power in Athens – announcing in the opening credits that 'any similarity to real people and events in this picture is entirely intentional.' Some years later, Costa-Gavras was unsuccessfully sued for libel by the US Ambassador to Chile following the release of his film, *Missing,* a somewhat glossier, more fictitious, yet none the less compelling, account of American involvement in the Chilean coup d'état of 1973, which saw the death of the democratically elected President, Salvador Allende, and the rise to power of the military dictator, General Pinochet. Shortly after these events took place, I remember being held up in traffic somewhere in Central London and becoming more and more irritated by the delay which was lasting beyond all reasonable expectations. It was then that I saw the cause. A column of marchers appeared, holding aloft a variety of banners, all proclaiming their outrage at events in Chile, and their solidarity with the suddenly disenfranchised people of that country some eight thousand miles away. My irritation evaporated in the face of such an awe-inspiring demonstration of political commitment that, at that time, knew no boundaries.

But our main inspiration for *Flashpoint* came from the written word. A collection of articles written by that definitive foreign correspondent, James Cameron, was published in a book, *Point of Departure*, which played a significant part in our early thoughts on the subject. I remember particularly his eye-witness account of the test explosion by the US of a hydrogen bomb on Bikini Atoll in 1954. His prose was always vivid, his emotions always engaged. In the early '50s he had reported, along with photographer, Bert Hardy, on the Korean war, and the idea of a similar partnership took root and eventually became the core at the centre of *Flashpoint*. We had also been struck more recently by the power of Donald McCullin's photography in a host of different war situations, in Cyprus, and in Jerusalem during the Six Day War. These photographs, along with the prose that accompanied them, were clearly not taken or recorded with a cold, objective eye. How could they have been, except by an automaton? Objectivity, as I had understood it, was held to be the imperative of good journalism, but the nature of journalism had changed, and particularly in war situations which put the journalist and especially the photographer in the front line. As James Cameron recollected of their joint assignment in the Korean War: 'There was one signal difference in our roles; he (Bert Hardy) had to take the pictures, and it was long ago established that one way you cannot take pictures is lying face down in a hole ... His art can never be emotion recalled in tranquillity. Ours can – or could be.'

And it wasn't just the fighting that was now being recorded with such immediacy, but thousands of unposed and spontaneous moments before and after the battle; the fear, the pain, the grief. Who could forget, having seen it, Donald McCullin's picture of the woman whose husband had just been killed in Cyprus, the power of which lies, not only in the situation, but in the photographer's art, capturing its immediacy and at the same time, by virtue of its skilful composition, embodying the nature of grief itself? That this was the voice of the correspondent was unquestionable. It was – still is, I believe – powerful stuff. It certainly made up our minds for us and, by the time we'd finished our meal in that Lewisham restaurant, we knew what *Flashpoint* was going to be all about.

At the centre of the series, our freelance journalist/ photographer team would respond to commissions from newspapers or magazines, even occasionally following their own instincts, to cover a variety of stories across a wide range of subjects, personal as well as political, and as geographically far-reaching as the budget would allow. But it was to be a series essentially about them and their responses to the situations in which they find themselves and the people who, in the pursuit of investigative journalism, they are obliged to confront. Above all, their occasionally conflicting views on the dichotomy between objectivity and subjectivity would ensure that their relationship was never allowed to become too cosy, nor their characters too peripheral. They would also have a great deal in common, of course, not least their broad political leanings – to the Left, it goes without saying, although their backgrounds would be very different. Upper middle-class Rupert, our foreign correspondent, having enjoyed the benefits of a private education and three years at Oxbridge, bringing his intellectual commitment to bear on a story, was nonetheless subject to an emotional response when faced with stark reality. Neville, however, our photographer, would be altogether less complex. A Londoner, the son of working-class Tory parents – hence his Christian name – and only too familiar with poverty and deprivation, crime and gratuitous violence, he would appear to be, on the surface at least, less impressionable. However, with one picture (according to the popular proverb) being worth 1,000 words, he is only too aware of his overriding imperative – to get it absolutely right first time.

John Frankau was enthusiastic about the idea, and immediately arranged a meeting with the Head of Drama Series at the BBC, Andrew Osborne, a nice enough man to be sure, although he gave us fair warning of at least one of his shortcomings at that very meeting. Having read and presumably understood the outline for the series, and inspired, no doubt, by the boundless opportunities afforded by it, he gleefully came up with a plot about an aeroplane crashing for no obvious reason, a mystery only solved when photos taken from a window in the aircraft on a previous flight reveal metal fatigue in one of the wings, inadvertently caught in the frame by our otherwise totally professional photographer. No kidding, that was the plot and, had we not caught a conspiratorial wink from John Frankau at that moment, we would have been tempted to throw in the towel there and then. As it was, we smiled sycophantically, murmured something like 'great idea' and left the Television Centre with Andrew Osborne's blessing on the series and a commission from John to write the pilot episode.

I do not remember much about the storyline of *In Memoriam*, which is hardly surprising as it was never produced, but I do recall that it had something to do with neo-Nazi activity in the Alto Adige on the border between Austria and Italy. I have vivid memories, however, of the familiar frenetic activity that was part and parcel of writing a script for John Frankau. I also recollect the problems we had with casting our two main characters, a process made all the more difficult by the fact that we were casting them for an entire series instead of a one-off drama where you didn't have to live with your mistakes for too long. We were perfectly happy when John suggested Julian Glover for the part of the journalist. We both knew him well and I had worked with him on *An Age of Kings*. He had all the right qualities for Rupert. But we were less enthusiastic about his choice of Patrick Mower for the part of the photographer. He had none of the rough edges we'd envisaged and was far too 'pretty' in a matinée idol kind of way to suggest a working-class background or, indeed, to provide a sharp enough contrast with Julian's journalist. But John rejected our alternative suggestions, and we had no choice but to go along with him, albeit with serious reservations.

The script was finished, the two main actors contracted, a crew booked and location filming in the Alto Adige already scheduled when the bomb dropped. Andrew Osborne called John's office to say, "Oh, by the way, I did tell you, didn't I, that the pilot episode, for economic reasons, has to take place in the sterling area?" Well, clearly he hadn't, but as legal proceedings were out of the question there was no point arguing about it. "Can you write a script set in the sterling area in the next two weeks?", John asked us, although he must have suspected what the answer would be as he already had another writer up his sleeve who, he assured us, would be equal to the task. "Would you mind?" Knowing full well that we'd be hard-pushed to come up with a decent storyline let alone a finished script in two weeks, we were obliged to go along with him. It was a decision we came to regret and would have been better advised to let it go; a good idea wrecked by mismanagement. As it turned out, John Gould's script, set in Gibraltar, bore little or no resemblance to our original outline, marginalised the two main characters in a plot that was at best routine, and the end product, when shown, made no impact whatsoever. Not surprisingly, the pilot episode was the first and last that was screened, and so that was the end of *Flashpoint*. Even now, however, about fifty years later, and taking on board the many earth-shaking and headline-grabbing events of today, I think *Flashpoint* is still a TV drama series just waiting to be made; all the more compelling now for featuring, as it surely must, a *female* journalist, and upon which, for 10% of the fee per episode plus an on-screen credit, I would happily bestow my blessing.

As it was, and with no intention of allowing ourselves to be railroaded by the likes of John Frankau onto a conveyor-belt, turning out scripts which, more often than not, would be based on someone else's format, simply in order to make a living, was not on the cards. We wanted to go on writing, of course, but only what we chose to write, and only at our own pace which, compared with the slavish dedication of John Gould, was pretty leisurely.

But in order to pursue this course, we had to have an income. Acting wasn't an option for several reasons, the first being that theatre work was just as demanding and time-consuming as writing, and besides no one was asking. I'd made several recent television appearances, but none of them came with a guarantee of future employment. What on earth led me to think that becoming an actors' agent would provide the answer I have no way of knowing, at least not at this distance, although it must have seemed like an attractive proposition at the time because in the late summer of 1968, that is what I became.

oOoOo

Sixteen

Sitting at the traffic lights in Lewisham Vale during a heavy downpour, I happened to glance down and saw that my feet were under water. Obviously, the red Mini I had acquired in part exchange for my Morris Minor in Farnham some three years earlier was in a terminal condition and, to make matters worse, was unlikely to realise much in the way of a deposit on a replacement vehicle. Although I was not exactly living in straitened circumstances at the time, my bank balance would have suggested otherwise, and there was no conceivable way I was going to be able to lay my hands on anything beyond the value of the car in which I was slowly drowning from the feet up. A showroom was obviously out of the question, so I made my way to a yard in Greenwich which I'd been told provided little more than a temporary reprieve for the last chance saloons thronging the forecourt. After receiving a pretty damning review from the overalled manager, which was not entirely unexpected, he conceded that the tyres were still serviceable and offered me £40. I asked, without having any grounds for optimism, if £40 would provide a deposit on anything he had in stock. He made a lot of negative noises accompanied by much shaking of the head, before finally pointing towards some indeterminate vehicle at the far end of the yard. "Only that," he said, leading the way past rows of sad-looking cars and vans, all of which were obviously way beyond my means, and finally stopping in front of a huge and extremely ostentatious vehicle which I took to be his prize possession. "You can have this for £150", he said, "and I'll accept £40 as a deposit." Having finally realised that he wasn't taking the mickey, I accepted the offer and drove out of his yard behind the wheel of a Mark IX Jaguar automatic with cream leather upholstery, walnut fascia and trimmings, and cocktail tables of the same finish in the back. The fact that it was the only car I ever owned in which you could actually witness the fuel gauge moving down while you were driving did explain, to some extent, the dearth of potential buyers in downtown Greenwich, but it became from that very first moment my pride and joy, and what was more, entirely appropriate in my new role as a Theatrical Agent.

When, over a drink or two during my brief sojourn at the Churchill Theatre in Bromley, I told Jerome Willis of my doubts about pursuing an acting career, he told me that Donald Bradley, his own agent, was looking for an assistant, the end result being that I went to meet him and was subsequently offered the job. It helped that I already knew Donald as he had been associate to John Penrose when I had been briefly represented by him several years earlier. As with John Penrose, Donald had also been an actor in his younger days and had achieved a degree of fame in Ludovic Kennedy's *Murder Story* for which he received marvellous reviews and, as some might say, the kiss of death by being featured as 'Tomorrow's Lead' in the September 1954 edition of the magazine, *Plays and Players* What it all goes to show, however, is that the transition from actor to agent was far from being unprecedented.

Donald was one of four actors' agents who, together with two literary agents, made up the combined operation known as Richard Hatton Limited, whose sumptuous offices were in Curzon Street, right in the heart of Mayfair. In 1968 it was already something of an anachronism, being one of the few remaining big-time agencies, if not the only one, that was entirely home-grown, the other major players in the league being either off-shoots of American agencies or largely dependent on American money. I didn't know it at the time, of course, but the days of Richard Hatton Ltd were already numbered, although I might have guessed, had I been more familiar with that particular world, that there was a degree of profligacy in the day-to-day running of a business that was probably unsustainable, even given that their clientèle at that time included such names as Sean Connery, Robert Shaw, Sheila Hancock, Leo McKern, Romy Schneider, Leonard Rossiter, Alan Bates and that brightest of celestial bodies, Ingrid Pitt. As far as I was concerned, it was life in the fast lane, and that wasn't just because I could drive my Jag to see some of the less well-heeled clients at work in various parts of the country before driving them in comparative luxury back to their digs. There was a story circulating at the time and, for all I know, I could have been the one who circulated it, that nobody ever went out to post a letter at Richard Hatton's without taking a taxi. It was a joke, of course, but only just.

There was a very exclusive restaurant just across the road, with prices to match, where clients – even mine – were occasionally treated to lunch, and it was not uncommon for lunches of this nature to last until 3pm after which there was little point in taking on anything of a serious nature. That same restaurant, *The White Elephant*, also supplied us with a hamper full of goodies every Friday to help make our weekly staff meeting a more convivial affair. This is not to say that business was neglected. In fact, a good deal was accomplished between these lunch breaks, although it was common knowledge that Donald was seldom without a glass of whisky on his desk after 11am. But as I didn't have to spend a good deal of my time closeted with Robert Shaw or attempting to negotiate over the phone with elusive movie moguls such as Harry Saltzman, I was in no position to disapprove. On one occasion, fortified no doubt by a glass or two, and after having spent a couple of frustrating days trying to make contact with Mr. Saltzman in order to discuss a vitally important contractual detail, and having been fobbed off on each occasion by his minions, my intrepid boss called him at home. "You bastard, Bradley", Saltzman yelled down the line, "calling me at home when there's been a death in the family!" Chastened and apologetic, his Scotch courage having deserted him, Donald hung up without addressing the issue, only to discover some time later that Mr. Saltzman's outburst had been a total fabrication. While feeling a good deal of sympathy for Donald, I couldn't help thinking that the contractual detail in question, relating as it no doubt did, to Robert Shaw, was probably preposterous and that therefore Harry Saltzman had good reason to lie. Some time later, I was given a contract to peruse relating to Mr. Shaw's engagement in the New York production of the musical version of *Elmer Gantry*. The document in question ran to forty pages and included a clause stipulating the wattage of light-bulbs round his dressing-room mirror. It was one of life's most delicious little ironies that *Elmer Gantry* closed after only one performance.

Richard Hatton Limited was a bit like a doctors' practice in that, while each agent looked after his or her own particular clients, ultimate responsibility devolved on the agency as a whole, which was why sharing information was vital, and was as good an excuse as any for the weekly chicken-and-wine-fest. While a disproportionate amount of Donald's time was taken up with Robert Shaw, I inherited, to all intents and purposes, some of his less demanding and certainly less profitable clients. By and large, this was a very satisfactory arrangement and, with one or two exceptions, I enjoyed forging relationships with the sort of actors whose concerns I understood and with whom I had a good deal in common. Richard Hatton also had an assistant whose function was much the same as mine, Richard's time being taken up with a handful of big-time players, chief amongst whom was Sean Connery. I had been acquainted with Sean, of course, during *An Age of Kings*, following which his star had been well and truly in the ascendant. Not being an exceptionally gifted actor, he was blessed with the physique and the rugged good looks that landed him the part of James Bond, after which – and despite his unyielding Scots accent – nothing could hold him back. I was not privy to the business conducted behind closed doors between Richard and Sean as I had been to some extent with Donald and Robert Shaw, but Sean was always a welcome visitor to the office where his friendliness and good-natured banter was greeted by everybody's undivided attention and his jokes with more laughter than they generally merited.

Apart from Judy Scott-Fox, who joined the agency some time after I had been installed, and who brought with her Alan Bates amongst others, there was Norman Boyack, the one remaining actors' agent. Norman, with whom I went on to enjoy a long business association and an even longer friendship, and who had also very briefly been an actor, was the kind of person to whom you turned when you were in danger of being overwhelmed by the enormity of it all: the big names, the big money, the big egos and the even bigger pretensions. Norman was a stranger to toadyism and, without short-changing his clients in any way, he managed to stand back and view it all with humour, sometimes wicked, but never cynical. Norman was a tonic, as was Camille Marchetta, a delightfully effervescent New Yorker who was attached to the literary department which was under the virtually autonomous rule of the bull-like Terence Baker. Norman and Camille enjoyed a wonderful rapport which I like to think I shared to a degree, although for some peculiar reason the occasion I remember most vividly was lunching with Camille at another restaurant just across the road, *The Day and Night of the Chimera*, where we ordered omelettes. When they arrived, she decided that hers was not well done enough and she sent it back. Shortly afterwards, the manager arrived at our table and told us that not only had the chef flatly refused to 'overcook' the omelette but that he, the manager, would be obliged if we would now leave his restaurant, never to return. Camille must have told Richard Hatton who, unbeknownst to me at the time, wrote a letter of complaint to the restaurant manager, who claimed, by way of reply, that his chef was one of the best chefs in Madrid. Richard wasted no time before responding, 'There are no good chefs in Madrid,' bringing the correspondence to an end.

The highlight of my relatively short stay with Richard Hatton Limited was, without question, the transfer to the West End of the Glasgow Citizens Theatre production of Brecht's *The Resistible Rise of Arturo Ui*. The reason for my involvement, however peripheral, was because Leonard Rossiter, who played the title role, was one of our clients, and it was in this capacity that I was present on its first night at the Saville Theatre in July 1969 and, by choice, on several occasions thereafter. *The Resistible Rise of Arturo Ui* is Bertolt Brecht's take on the rise to power of Adolf Hitler, from which he fled in 1933 to take up residence in America which is where, in the Chicago of Al Capone, the play is set. Ui is a small-time gangster whose overweening ambition, rooted in his determination to take over the ailing cauliflower trade, employing to this end, bribery, coercion and assassination, sets him on the all-too-familiar road to absolute power. It is a chillingly funny satire on the events which led to the Nazi take-over in Germany, peopled by characters whose names and personalities bear an uncanny resemblance to Hitler's own henchmen, and which contains at its centre a character of such complexity that it would be unrealistic to expect any actor, no matter how accomplished, to fully embrace, let alone bring to it something of himself, namely an obsessive desire to make the part his own.

To those who, for whatever reason, didn't manage to see Michael Blakemore's impeccable production, and whose memories of Leonard Rossiter are confined to his admittedly superb television appearances in *The Fall and Rise of Reginald Perrin,* or in *Rising Damp,* I can only say that you were sadly either born too late or you were in the wrong place at the right time, for there can be no doubt that you missed one of the greatest performances by a British actor it has ever been my privilege to see, and I was far from being alone in that opinion. Frank Marcus wrote in the *Sunday Telegraph,* 'This is the most vivid, compelling and hilarious acting currently on view on the London stage. It can best be described as volcanic: it alternates between menacing, brooding inertia and eruptions of hysterical violence. The loathsome obsequiousness, the foxy charm, the startled backing into furniture, the ever-present awareness of himself as an actor calculating effects, make up not only a great performance but a great Brechtian performance.' Martin Esslin in *Plays and Players* wrote, 'Leonard Rossiter is, in my opinion, better than even the Berliner Ensemble's Ekkehard Schall in the part ... Rossiter's performance is Chaplinesque in the best sense of the word – it is grotesquely comic and yet displays the control of movement one associates with ballet.' Irving Wardle, *The Times* critic, wrote that it was '...one of the most staggering examples of grotesque comedy I have ever seen', and finally, for good measure, an unqualified paean from Clive Barnes of the *New York Times:* 'Mr Rossiter is perfect – a trampled paranoid, comically mean-minded with the timing of a comedian and, stealthily developing, the arrogance of a madman. Even at his funniest, Mr. Rossiter never lets us forget the gas chambers, the bombs, the slaughter.'

There was a particularly memorable scene in which Ui, mindful of the need to improve his image, employs the services of an actor of the old school to give him lessons in deportment and the use of gestures, urging him to walk more gracefully, and to use the full length of his arms, gesturing from the shoulder rather than the elbow. Ui's ineptitude, and his subsequent frustration were utterly hilarious until suddenly, and by some uncanny process, entirely unforeseen, he managed to translate all this tuition – to the dismay of his tutor but to his own obvious satisfaction – into the goose-step and the Nazi salute. Not for the first or last time during that amazing performance, the smile was wiped off my face and I gasped with astonishment. I saw Leonard perform on a number of occasions thereafter, notably in Pinter's *The Caretaker* and in *Tartuffe*, and whilst he was never less than impressive, his obvious empathy with the character of *Arturo Ui* provided him with a unique opportunity to demonstrate all of his considerable skills in one role. His sudden death at the age of 57 in 1984 was not only horribly premature, but it was also a huge loss to the acting profession, and although his lasting fame resides in the world of television, I shall remember him chiefly for that riveting theatrical performance.

I was bound, however, in my capacity as Donald Bradley's assistant, to represent the interests of lesser mortals. Not that all of the clients who came within my limited sphere of influence necessarily belonged in that category. There were those amongst them who, but for fortune, might have gone on to achieve greater success, in which case Donald would undoubtedly have taken them under his own wing, and I would have been deprived of the pleasure of representing them myself and of treating them to the occasional lunch at *The White Elephant*. There were those, on the other hand, with whom I found it difficult to communicate on any level whatsoever let alone over a convivial lunch, although not having had any say as to whether we should have represented them in the first place, I was obliged to treat with a degree of respect. To this day I haven't the remotest idea, for instance, why such a prestigious agent as Richard Hatton should have decided to represent Keith Bell who, aside from being Tom Bell's younger brother, had nothing to recommend him, apart from his boyish good looks and a degree of self-confidence that was founded on very little, apart from being Tom Bell's younger brother. Anyway, whatever it was that had persuaded Donald Bradley to take him on, it was I who was given the job of representing him – clever old Donald! Following an interview, which I don't remember arranging for him, and obviously because of his boyish good looks, and the fact that he was

Tom Bell's younger brother, he was offered a nice little cameo role in *The Last Valley*, a feature film starring Michael Caine and Omar Sharif. My only input (Donald having negotiated his fee) was to assure the film's production office that Keith was perfectly at home on the back of a horse. I had, of course, taken the precaution of checking this out with Keith beforehand, when he told me that he intended to take a few refresher lessons as it had been some while since he'd last been in the saddle. It was only a week or two later that I received a telephone call from Austria where *The Last Valley* was being shot. It was the production manager, and I gathered quite quickly that he was not best pleased and that, from the tone of his voice, I was not entirely exempted from his displeasure. It seemed that Keith had not only experienced considerable problems mounting the horse assigned to him, but was incapable of remaining mounted at a mere canter and had fallen off, incurring only a minor injury but successfully putting the brakes on filming for some considerable time. After which, he was put on a plane and sent home in disgrace, and while it was never suggested that I had taken liberties with the truth in order to get my client a job, the inference was there, for which I could never find it in my heart to forgive Tom Bell's younger brother.

This was small beer, however, when set against the antics of Alexis Kanner, a young Canadian actor whose arrogance apparently knew no bounds. Once again I was on the receiving end of a call from the production office at Elstree Studios where a film called *The Anniversary* was being made. The voice at the other end made it clear that they were anxious to trace the whereabouts of our client who had been due half an hour ago on the set where the star of the picture, Miss Bette Davis, was even now waiting for him. My God, I thought, what could possibly have happened? I checked at the switchboard to see if there had been any messages, went through to Donald's office, just in case he'd heard something and forgotten to pass it on to me, and then, as a last resort, dialled Alexis's home number. I was on the point of hanging up when the receiver at the other end was lifted and a sleepy Canadian voice answered, somewhat put out at being disturbed. "Oh, God," he drawled, "I must have overslept. Just give them a call and tell them I'll get there as soon as I can," Had I been on the other end of the phone, I might well have considered suicide, but this guy obviously didn't give a damn that he had kept Bette Davis hanging around on a film set waiting for him to turn up. There followed the mortifying task of calling the production office to explain the inexplicable and to offer apologies on behalf of a client who, far from expressing remorse, had reacted with scarcely concealed irritation. Unbelievable! It came to my ears, some little time later, that he had joined the cast of the BBC Television series, *Softly, Softly,* playing the part of a newly enlisted Detective Constable. Apparently, Alexis held very strong views on the disparity between television cops and the real thing, and was consequently determined to inject a degree of authenticity into the series. This consisted, in the main, of unilaterally re-writing the scripts, so that he was able to question the orders given to him by his superiors, Detective-Superintendent Barlow and Detective-Sergeant Watt. In the main this involved long pauses as he mulled over the efficacy and/or the practicality of the orders he'd been given, taking time to light a cheroot before accepting the orders, either enthusiastically or grudgingly, as he saw fit. This obviously well-researched authenticity had the effect, not only of adding minutes to the running-time of each episode, but of leaving Barlow and Watt with a considerable amount of egg on their faces. I was given to understand that it did not take long – a few episodes at most – before Stratford Johns and Frank Windsor issued a joint ultimatum to the producer of the series which, in the absence of anything more detailed, can be summed up in the following words, 'either he goes or we go.' History records that Stratford Johns left the series of his own accord in 1972 and that Frank Windsor was promoted and went on playing the role he had originally created in *Z Cars* right up to, and including, the very last episode of *Softly Softly* in 1976. For all that I never heard of Alexis Kanner again, having been denied the stardom he so obviously craved, he remains, if memory serves me right, one of the reasons I decided to give up being an actors' agent.

Dawn and I had both taken on full time jobs in London to give us the financial security to be able to write together at home. But, for some peculiar reason, it had never occurred to us that the demands of our separate jobs, both in terms of time and energy, would make writing anything at all virtually impossible. Not that we hadn't had a few ideas, one of which we were particularly keen to pursue, but it was beginning to look increasingly unlikely that unless we could find jobs that paid a reasonable amount of money for doing virtually nothing, we were going to lose any kind of momentum, swiftly followed by the urge to write nothing at all. However, no immediate decisions were made, except to avail ourselves of one of the most enticing benefits of full-time employment – the paid holiday!

Apart from a short honeymoon visit to Paris and a working trip to Chicago, Dawn and I had never been abroad together and, as far as

I can recall, we had never entertained notions of sun-soaked holidays in the Mediterranean. In fact, so ignorant were we of the burgeoning trade in package holidays, that we didn't have a clue how to go about it and where to choose as a destination. In the end we shut our eyes and stuck a pin in a map of Europe. We then went to the nearest travel agent and booked a fortnight's half-board accommodation at the Adriatic Hotel in what was then the Yugoslav resort of Opatija. Had we known that what we were about to enjoy was not so much a therapeutic break as a cathartic experience we might well have played it safe and opted for somewhere less exotic. Somehow I doubt it though, and in any case, by the time I discovered exactly where we were in geographical and literary terms, it was too late and its magic had already worked on me. True, we hadn't been shipwrecked and washed up on a strange shore, but we soon discovered, as much by happenstance as Viola in *Twelfth Night*, that we had booked a holiday in Illyria (the old name, and the name used by Shakespeare for this part of the Croatian coast). Two weeks later we arrived back in London, handed in our respective notices, and made plans to return as soon as possible. Looking back on it now, it's easy to see it as a kind of sabbatical, a period of adjustment, or simply as a totally irresponsible adventure, but we certainly weren't thinking of it in any of those terms when, in the autumn of 1969, we hired a car and drove back to the Adriatic coast.

'And what should we do in Illyria?' We had enjoyed a wonderful fortnight's holiday, absorbed about as much of the ambience, the sun and the sea, the local food and drink, the music and the art, as it's possible to absorb in two weeks. We had also made a few friends amongst the local population, several of whom had taken it upon themselves to introduce us to a way of life so far removed from our own, and yet so utterly beguiling that a curious affinity had sprung up. Had we been seasoned travellers we might well have enjoyed it just as much, promised ourselves a return visit at some point in the future, and left it at that. After all, I have since frequently fantasised about emigrating to any one of a number of Greek islands, although now I know – at least I think I do – that these flights of fancy amount to no more than that. But, oddly enough, it wasn't fantasy that prompted our hasty return to Opatija so much as the possibility of living and working there, certainly as writers, but with some kind of paid employment to provide the financial back-up we would obviously need. The journey by road, following a route with which I was to become only too familiar, was undertaken in a Mini owned by Anne Bargeman, a friend of Dawn's who had her own reasons for wanting to visit Yugoslavia, and who was quite happy to share the driving with me. It was largely due to her feats of endurance and expert skills, however, that we managed to accomplish it, travelling through France, Switzerland and Italy, a distance of around 1,100 miles, in two days (and nights!), and it was with no mean sense of achievement that we finally found ourselves gliding down the hill from Matulji, site of the nearest railway station, and onto the Ulica Maršala Tita, Opatija's main street. There was something even more magical about arriving that way rather than by air, a sense of its real distance from home, the variety of landscapes traversed on the way, from the long, straight, poplar-lined roads of France to the snow-capped mountain passes of Switzerland and then down to the plains of northern Italy with the Italian lakes passing by on one side while, on the other, towns and cities such as Verona, Padua, Mantua and Venice, only previously encountered in an imagination fired by the plays of William Shakespeare who had almost certainly, and quite incredibly, conjured them up from his imagination too. I was to undertake that same journey on several occasions in the future, the gaps between visits, both for personal and political reasons, growing wider in the course of time. But never did it pall and never on any of my subsequent visits to Opatija did I experience anything less than the wonder and delight that I imagine Tommy Albright would have felt if, on his return to Scotland, he found that Brigadoon was still there.

Shortly after our arrival, Anne Bargeman headed off to Belgrade to meet up with her friend, Boris, and we paid a visit to the British Consul in Zagreb, the capital of Croatia. There, we were told in no uncertain terms that in Yugoslavia, a communist country, no kind of business venture sponsored by foreign nationals would be allowed unless – unofficially, of course – we were to enter into a partnership with a native Yugoslav who would be legally responsible for the conduct of the business. Nothing daunted, we returned to Opatija where we met up again with Stefan Đukić, one of those who had taken it upon himself for reasons that were not entirely selfless, to introduce us to a world beyond the one described in the Thomas Cook brochure. Stevo not only played drums in the band which provided the evening's entertainment at the Adriatic Hotel, but by day he also ran the hotel's beach bar, and was well acquainted with just about everybody who was anybody in Opatija and, doubtless, throughout the entire Yugoslav Republic. It was he who arranged a meeting for us with Marinko Nikolac, the landlord of a sea-front boutique long since abandoned by its dilettante proprietor who, according to Stevo, would have liked nothing better than to have his business up and running, as long as he didn't have to get up and run it himself. What moonstruck notion it was that persuaded us to believe that running a boutique in a foreign country would be less time consuming than the two jobs we had just quit I cannot begin to comprehend, but since neither of us demurred, it must have made some sense at the time. It was not long, however, before we realised that any arrangements made to meet with Marinko were guaranteed not to take place at the appointed time. Not that Marinko, or Piko as he preferred to be called, was anything other than charming and apologetic when we did eventually meet, as he was to be on every occasion thereafter. In appearance and manners, Piko was more like a relic of Croatia's Austro-Hungarian past than a true Slav, left behind along with many of the handsome edifices of that now extinct empire when Opatija was known as Abbazia, the Italian word for 'Abbey', deriving from an even earlier period in its chequered history. Indulgently proportioned, fair-haired and generously moustached, Piko would rise to greet us, incline his head and all but click his heels together before returning to his glass of šljivovica (plum brandy) and settle in for a long and bibulous morning, afternoon or evening of discourse. His English was quite good, if somewhat quirky. "Why you want to live here?" he asked on one occasion, "You are in love with noble savage?" I remember we thought that was a bit extreme at the time, but on reflection, he wasn't too wide of the mark. I remember too that it took three such virtually random meetings before we managed to persuade him to let us see his little shop, by which time we had, of course, come to the conclusion that a business partnership with him would be nothing short of disastrous. The fact that we became good friends and went on to enjoy many similar encounters with him was a perfect example of the wisdom of not mixing business with pleasure.

Meanwhile, it was Stevo who organised the remainder of our stay, persuaded us to check out of the Hotel Kristal, and installed us very comfortably in the bosom of his family and, by so doing, introduced us to the small fishing village of Volosko, two kilometres from Opatija, with a seafront walk connecting the two. A maze of tiny streets led steeply upwards from the small harbour, flanked by innumerable compact dwellings, all dating back to a time when Volosko had been entirely dedicated to fishing, populated pretty-well exclusively by fisher folk. More recently, it had become something of a haven for those who knew their way around, the perfect retreat from

Opatija's busy beaches and bustling night-life, and boasting a very attractive restaurant called the *Plavi Podrom* whose tables spilled out enticingly onto the waterfront. But Volosko had no hotels, and although the rabbit-warren of dwelling-places that rose up behind it had been transformed from its humble origins into a picturesque backdrop, it was still inhabited by an entirely indigenous population. Amongst them, in two adjoining apartments, the Đukić family had their home, and it was here that we were invited to spend what was left of our brief stay.

Stevo, in his twenties and a bachelor still, shared a small flat with his mother, Milka, the revered matriarch of a tightly-knit family which included Bata, Stevo's elder brother, together with his wife, Sofija, and their ten year-old daughter, Draga, who occupied a relatively spacious apartment, although how they managed to accommodate us in an extremely comfortable double-room of our own remains a mystery.

The Đukić family, we soon learned, had come originally from Serbia, a fact that had little significance for us at the time, and even when Stevo told us, with an expressive gesture of contempt, that he had little regard for his sister-in-law, Sofija, because she was a Bosnian, we chose to make light of it, equating it in our innocence to the traditional antagonism between the Scots and the English. Little did we know. But then we knew virtually nothing about the Federal Republic of Yugoslavia beyond the fact that it was made up of six previously separate regions of which Serbia was the largest and politically the most important, containing as it did the capital city of the Republic, Belgrade. We also knew that, along with the other five: Croatia, Slovenia, Bosnia-Herzegovina, Montenegro and Macedonia, it had been forged into a seemingly indissoluble unit at the end of the Second World War by one man, Josip Broz, known as Tito, who had led the resistance against Nazi occupation at the head of his Partisan army and who was now installed as the much-loved President of a determinedly independent communist country.

Of course, we knew a little more about Croatia than any of the other regions because that's where we were but, aside from Stevo's apparent aversion to Bosnians, we were entirely ignorant of the underlying political, racial and religious divisions that would ultimately, and with the charismatic Tito scarce cold in his grave, tear the country apart. But in any case, as far as we could see, Stevo was hardly a typical Yugoslav anyway, and neither was he a communist in any way, shape or form. In fact, Stevo nursed entrepreneurial and capitalistic ambitions that, had it been ten years later, would have found a more sympathetic home in Margaret Thatcher's Britain. His dreams at that time, however, were entirely focused on a future in the USA. He was captivated by all things American, its popular culture as well as its economics, and one of his oft-repeated boasts was that he shared a name with Steve McQueen. We were given no reason to believe that any of the Đukić family, having made their home in Croatia, felt nostalgic or in any way nationalistic about their origins. It has to be said, though, that there was an underlying arrogance in Stevo's make-up that could now be interpreted, with the benefit of historical perspective, as a reflection of more recent Serbian intransigence. But all we had to go on at the time was that he didn't like Sofija which was strange because, no matter where she came from, she was a very nice lady.

The contrast between Stevo and his elder brother, Bata, could not have been more marked had they been sired by different fathers. Neither of them was tall, but that was about the only thing they had in common, and while Stevo could conceivably have come from any one of a number of European regions, Bata was Balkan through and through. He was swarthier than his younger brother and bore all the characteristics that, in an immigrant population, would surely have ghettoised him, while Stevo bore no such marks and could easily have been assimilated into the mainstream of any society that he set his sights on. The fact that he didn't and, in the long run, settled for a life in his own community was a subject I never had the opportunity to discuss with him, but it probably had at least something to do with remaining a big fish in a small pond. It was in the bosom of this congenial family that we spent most of the time that we had left to us before Anne Bargeman returned from her trip to Belgrade and we set off for home, no closer to resolving our dilemma but no less determined to pursue our dream.

Three years earlier, in August 1966, somewhat overshadowing London's celebrations following England's World Cup victory, the horrific murder of three policemen took place in Braybrook Street, close to Wormwood Scrubs prison. There was an understandably extreme reaction from press and public alike and, in particular, an impassioned call for the restoration of the recently abolished death penalty for the convicted killers. I particularly remember, and with good reason, a photograph taken on the occasion of the then Home Secretary, Roy Jenkins' visit to Shepherd's Bush police station, where the three policemen had been based. It appeared in one of the tabloid newspapers and showed a crowd gathered on the pavement outside the station, most of them carrying placards and banners demanding the return of capital punishment. This was hardly surprising in itself, but the fact that the crowd was made up predominantly, if not exclusively, of women was something of a shock to the system, and all the more so because the faces of those women, contorted as they all were by hatred, spoke more of vengeance than of justice.

A photograph of the killers themselves could not have been more chilling. It did, in time however, give rise to an idea for a screenplay, very much inspired by that photograph, but also owing something to *The Bacchae* of Euripides. This was, in fact, the project we were engaged on when we realised that full-time employment in London or, indeed, running a business in Croatia, was not going to provide us with the time we needed to write it. But the die was already cast and, not being gifted with foresight, had we known that all it would finally take was a fortnight's solid rainfall to interrupt our lotus-eating existence or, indeed, that the completed screenplay would, apart from Deborah Kerr's outraged sensibilities when she read the castration scene, arouse little or no interest, things might have turned out very differently, but we were stubbornly convinced that six months in the sun was an essential requirement. This delusion was sustained by Roger Hancock and Brian Codd, our literary agents, who offered us £500 by way of a commission, suggested that our leading male character, an immigrant worker on a new stretch of motorway, might just as well be a Yugoslav as anything else, providing us with, at least, a tax-deductible reason for being there, and – the icing on the cake – secured a further commission for us from the *Mirror Magazine* to write a feature on the Pula Film Festival, for which we received a further £150. That we barely had time for more than a fleeting visit to Pula before the *Mirror Magazine* collapsed and that we were not asked to return the fee, was an added bonus. We must, I suppose, have had a few quid of our own tucked away, but it couldn't have been much, and since we scarcely worked between November, 1969 and April, 1970 when we set off once again on a journey that had acquired, quite suddenly, a bizarre inevitability, like a Date with Destiny or some such nonsense, we embarked upon it with just £650 and, with little or no hope of augmenting it, decided that we would return home once it had run out. The fact that it lasted us until the end of September was a remarkable achievement, even in 1970, as I don't recall that we denied ourselves too much in the way of food and drink, enjoyed comfortable lodgings, and travelled a good deal. It goes without saying, of course, that the cost of living in Yugoslavia was considerably lower than it was in the UK, and it cannot be denied that we enjoyed a fair amount of hospitality, mainly courtesy of the Đukić family, but even so ... six months! The most urgent economy, of course, was getting rid of the Jaguar which would have cost us the best part of £650 in petrol alone; not only that, but it would have raised a good many Slavic eyebrows, not to mention expectations of its owner's wealth. So I managed to swap it without money changing hands, as far as I can remember, for a Renault 4, one of those funny little cars that seemed to have been made of tin and which had its gear-stick protruding from the dashboard, so it was a case of 'from the proverbial to the proverbial', but while I did lament the loss of luxury, it proved to be an extremely hardy and reliable little car whose performance, although scarcely spectacular, was impressively resilient.

Having parked our Siamese cat in temporary accommodation once again, evincing little more than a feline shrug this time, we set off on what was fast becoming a familiar journey, although at a more leisurely pace on this occasion, mainly because there was no reason to hurry and so we stopped off overnight on several occasions in France and Switzerland, but also partly due to an inadvertent diversion which took us on a hair-raising precipitous detour through the Apennines and eventually landed us, by luck rather than by judgement, in Mantua, way off our route in any case which should have been by way of Verona, but no more than half a day's fast gallop away as Romeo would have known only too well. There we booked into an hotel, clearly suffering the after-effects of our ordeal, and although it was long past dinner-time, we were served up with an enormous pasta dish by the motherly *proprietaria*, whose concern for our welfare seemed to outweigh any other considerations. The next morning, having expressed our gratitude, and having been waved off, for all the world like departing family, we embarked on the final leg of our journey and, with a peculiar sense of homecoming mingled with excitement at the prospect of a new challenge, we arrived in Opatija the following afternoon.

The excitement was, in part, due to my efforts throughout the long winter months to master the Serbo-Croatian language. This was accomplished at home and alone, there not being too many opportunities to pass the time of day with Croatian speakers on the streets of London, although I admit to visiting the Yugoslav Club in Ladbroke Grove on a couple of occasions which, together with my two previous visits to the country, gave me a pretty good idea of how it was supposed to sound, and with my Thespian pride at stake, I was determined above all things not to sound like a foreigner. From my very first encounter with the guard at the Croatian border post who, following a brief exchange, expressed some surprise when I presented him with my British passport, I had every reason to believe that I had achieved my goal. As time went by, however, my accomplishment turned out to be double-edged, finding it relatively easy to assume a cloak of ethnicity when talking, but utterly confounded by my limited vocabulary so that, when it came to holding a conversation, I probably sounded like a Croat with learning difficulties. This debility became less acute over the following weeks and months as I learned to listen as well as talk, and by the time we left for home in October, I was able to converse quite fluently. I should point out, for the benefit of anyone remotely interested, that the main difference between the Serbian and the Croatian aspects of the Serbo-Croatian language, aside from dialect and spelling, is that Serbian employs the Cyrillic alphabet while Croatian uses the Latin, so it's just as well that we ended up in Opatija rather than in Опатия or I probably wouldn't have taken it on in the first place.

We had already decided to make our home in Volosko, rather than in Opatija, and not only for economic reasons, but because we found the relative absence of tourists and all the trappings that went hand-in-hand with them, a distinct advantage, especially so since it was our ambition to live alongside the local community and, as far as possible, come to be accepted as part of it. The Đukić family were, of course, at the heart of this plan, although Stevo was away from home when we arrived, playing his drums on board a cruise liner somewhere in the Atlantic Ocean and was not due back until the beginning of May, and so we had to make do without his entrepreneurial skills for the time being. In his absence we managed to find ourselves a small room beside the harbour, lacking in anything but the most basic facilities. Obviously, we couldn't contemplate spending the next six months penned up in what amounted to little more than a large cupboard, so we decided, after having put the rigours of our journey behind us, to set off again in our intrepid Renault 4, see something of the country beyond our chosen horizons and, ultimately, arrive in Dubrovnik in time to pick up Stevo from his ship, drive him home and let him sort it out.

The most direct route to Dubrovnik would have taken us no more than a day and a half, a mere 400 miles along the Dalmatian coast, an alluring prospect what with the Adriatic on one side and its many picturesque resorts on the other, not to mention the beautiful city of Split, the second largest in Croatia, which grew up around the palace built for the Roman Emperor, Diocletian. It was a journey we would undertake later on, but on this occasion, time not being of the essence, and knowing we would be making our eventual home by the sea, we decided to travel inland to see something of the real Yugoslavia. We went by way of Zagreb and, as cars gradually gave way to horses and carts, headed for the border that separated Croatia from Bosnia-Herzegovina, our initial goal being the capital city of Sarajevo. We passed through several towns on the way, notably Banja Luka and Jajce, and only a short distance from Srebrenica, all names with a chilling resonance now, as was Sarajevo itself, the main target for the Serbian army's indiscriminate bombardment some 20 or so years later.

But then Sarajevo already had a pretty chilling history of its own, and one of my most abiding memories of that trip was when we stood on the very corner of the street from where Gavrilo Princip had fired the shots that killed the Archduke Franz Ferdinand, heir to the Austro-Hungarian throne, and his wife, Sophie, in 1914, sparking off events that led to the Great War. It was, nonetheless, a very beautiful city, bursting with vitality, a meeting place between East and West, where church spires shared the landscape with minarets, and bells vied for attention with the muezzins' calls. Somewhat reluctantly, I recall, what with Dawn being addicted to bustling market-places, we left Sarajevo after a couple of days on what was meant to be the last leg of our journey to Dubrovnik, crossing the Neretva Valley and by-passing the city of Mostar before stopping for a meal at a roadside *gostionica*. We had scarcely finished our carafe of wine when the waitress arrived with another which we had not ordered. She told us that it was the gift of a fellow customer, and indicated a table some distance away from us at which several men were sitting, one of whom smiled across in our direction. We, of course, smiled back, nodded our acceptance and raised our glasses to him. Shortly afterwards, the same waitress returned and, on behalf of our benefactor, issued an invitation to join him and his colleagues at their table. It was with a degree of reserve, bearing in mind that we still had some distance to cover, that we accepted the invitation and, with much shifting of chairs, were welcomed at their table where we were greeted with yet another carafe of wine. They seemed a nice enough bunch and, having about as much English as I had Serbo-Croatian, we were able to converse quite happily for a while until I suggested that it was time we left if we wanted to reach Dubrovnik that evening, whereupon they all laughed, and our host pointed out that we had drunk far too much to attempt such a difficult journey. He then went on to suggest that we should stay at his house overnight, an invitation we were loath to accept, partly out of native politeness, but largely from an equally native suspicion that such an offer would be bound to come at a price. I had to admit, however, that I was in no condition by then to drive anywhere, let alone through mountain passes, and that we had no alternative but to accept the invitation, albeit with a sense of foreboding as we slowly followed his car back into Mostar.

As it turned out, Mithat and his wife, Emira, both of them schoolteachers, were two of the nicest, kindest and most trusting people we were to meet during our stay in Yugoslavia. There was no way, prior to the invention of the mobile 'phone, that Emira's husband could have prepared her for the arrival on her doorstep of two stray, and slightly drunken foreigners, but she welcomed us into her house with genuine warmth, as though we had been eagerly expected, and ushered us into a large room which boasted a comfortable double bed, told us that she and her husband would have to leave for work early the following morning, but that we were not to disturb ourselves. She then handed us the key to their house, said we were to help ourselves to breakfast, were free to come and go as we pleased and were welcome to stay as long as we liked. As if all this overwhelming hospitality was not enough in itself, it obliged us to pause in our journey and to take in some of the delights of the beautiful city of Mostar which we had passed the previous day without a second glance and, quite possibly, would never have seen.

Mostar was the capital of the Herzegovina region, a city that dated back to the 15th century and which owed its status in terms of growth and development to a time when Ottoman rule prevailed in much of that area. Like Sarajevo, its population was pretty evenly divided between Muslims and Christians, largely of the Orthodox persuasion, but with a Croatian element in some areas that leant towards Rome. Without doubt, in a city of eye-catching beauty, its most outstanding feature was its old bridge, the *Stari Most*, after which the city was named. Designed and built by the Turks 500 years earlier, it arched its back high over the River Neretva and provided an unmissable experience, not only for anyone venturing to cross it, but also for those down below who were able to watch a seemingly endless stream of local lads dive into the fast-flowing and rock-strewn river 400 metres below them, a breathtaking spectacle which cost passers-by a measly 5 dinars per dive.

Amongst the many tragedies that befell that region in the early 1990's, nothing was more poignant in symbolic terms than the wanton destruction of that iconic landmark. All the more so in that it was inflicted, not by the Bosnian Serbs, but by the Croats, barely disguising self-interest under the cloak of national unity when Bosnia-Herzegovina sought independence from the Yugoslav Republic in the early '90s. I still have a photograph of the *Stari Most*, taken at some point during those few days we spent there, which serves to remind me of how naïve we were at that time in our appreciation of the country we had chosen as a second home. We knew a little of its turbulent past, its struggles against domineering neighbours and, of course, of its heroic partisan army in the Second World War when, under Tito's command, they had tied down three German divisions in that very area we were visiting; the Neretva Valley. What we didn't really appreciate, masked as they were by the essential conviviality of the Slavic people in general, were the deep divisions, both ethnic and religious, that had always existed between the six regions that made up the Republic, and which were destined to open up again once the adhesive influence of President Tito had been removed by his death in 1980. But at that time, leaving aside our friend Stevo's antipathy towards his Bosnian sister-in-law, which we attributed to a personality clash in any case, we were essentially innocents abroad, and happily so. We have no way of knowing what became of Mithat and Emira. We had so little time together we barely got to know them at all, any more than they got to know us. And yet their hospitality and their generosity assumed a familiarity, so that when we drove off the following morning, it was like the parting of old friends.

As a result of our unscheduled two-day stay in Mostar, we caught little more than a tantalising glimpse of Dubrovnik before Stevo disembarked from his cruise ship and we headed back to Volosko by way of the coast road, Stevo sharing the back seat with a huge duty-free hi-fi system. It was only a couple of weeks later that we moved into a spacious and comfortably furnished room with use of a kitchen and bathroom on the first floor of a house situated on the road leading from the harbour onto the main road, and owned by a very nice lady called Dubravka who was, of course, a friend of Stevo's. Best of all, our room had a balcony which overlooked the Kvarner Bay, a delightful little promontory upon which, as I recall, we spent most of our early evenings, glass in hand, before venturing out to face the rigours of Opatija's nightlife. There's no point in pretending that our sojourn, apart from those two rainy weeks during which we wrote our doomed screenplay, was anything other than a hedonistic indulgence, punctuated at times by various insights, a few revelations and other more or less meaningful moments, like the time I was summoned out onto the balcony by Stevo's voice calling up to me from the street below, "Terry, I have sin! I have sin!" Until that moment, I had no idea that Stevo regarded me in any way as a confessor, nor did I think the situation, lacking the privacy of the confessional, was entirely appropriate for the unburdening of the soul. It was only when I looked down and saw the rapturous smile on his upturned face that I remembered the word 'sin' in Serbo-Croatian means 'son'. On our previous visit we had been invited by the Đukić family to celebrate the marriage of Stevo and his bride, Anica. This had come as something of a surprise to us, and not only because we knew Stevo to be a serial womaniser for whom wedding-bells, were they ever to ring, certainly played no part in his plans for the future at that time, but also because Anica, who had a very pleasant smile and not a word of English, was neither pretty nor shapely, essential requirements in all of his casual encounters. In fact, she was rather plain and inclined to fat, and had we been told that Stevo had hired her services to help stack crates in his beach bar or that she had been employed to carry his drums for him we would not have been at all surprised. But marriage came as something of a shock, a shock we had barely come to terms with when, from his seat beside her, he said, "You like my wife?" We smiled and nodded. "She seems very nice," I mumbled, and Stevo grinned. "The next one will be better," he said, and a good deal less than nine months later there he was, joyfully celebrating the birth of his son, which explained everything, except that it didn't really explain anything at all.

Forty years on, and in entirely different circumstances, I visited Opatija again, and probably for the last time, only to discover from his grieving widow that Stevo had recently died of testicular cancer. She was not 'The next one' or indeed the one after that, but none other than Anica, scarcely transformed over the years into anything approaching Stevo's youthful ideal, but simply older and, if anything, more corpulent than she had been on her wedding day.

Our contacts with the cultural life of Croatia were, to be honest, spasmodic, our pleasures being largely pursued on the beach and at the table, although we did take more than a passing interest in the naïve paintings which were more or less indigenous, exemplified by the works of Ivan Generalič and Ivan Lacković and, in fact, we did purchase three such paintings, and I am still at a loss to know how we managed to afford them. We also paid a visit to the Croatian National Theatre in the nearby port of Rijeka where we saw an excellent production of Ostrovsky's *Wolves and Sheep* which contained a remarkable drunken performance by an actor whose name has gone the way of a great many people's names lately, although we did become friends for a while, and with whom, along with other members of the company, we enjoyed several social occasions. Along the way, we became acquainted with the theatre's box office manageress, a lady whose name I do remember for obvious reasons. Lina Ilić had worked at the same theatre since before the war when she must have been very young indeed. Her husband had been one of a number of young men in the nearby village where they lived who had been taken from their homes, lined up and shot by German soldiers, two of whom had been billeted with her on the very same day. She also told us of evenings when, on leaving the theatre, she had walked along the tree-lined road that led to the bus station, the branches of the trees bearing the bodies of other young men, suspected partisans hanged as a warning to others, or simply for the hell of it. We were neither of us entirely ignorant, of course, of the brutality that went hand-in-hand with Nazi occupation, but being there, and meeting someone whose life had been so personally and profoundly affected by it, was a chilling experience, and all the more so as we had not only chosen it as a holiday destination but were also obliged to share it with a disproportionate number of pleasure-bent Germans. In one of my many halting conversations in the native tongue, I remember asking a young man how they were able to tolerate this latter-day invasion, and although I don't think I managed to summon up the Croatian word for 'inappropriate', he got the message anyway, and said, "All are free to come here, but few are welcome."

We were not sorry to leave when October came around. It had been, for the most part, a glorious once-in-a-lifetime adventure, and one that I look back upon, even now, with unreserved pleasure and the fondest of memories, but the occupations we had so blithely walked away from were beckoning again, if only because we had a living to make. Not that we entirely turned our backs on Yugoslavia, nor on the friends we had made there. In fact, we returned the following year for a short holiday and, as a way of saying thank you for all the hospitality we had enjoyed, we took Sofija and little Draga back with us for a holiday in London.

With no writing projects lined up, Dawn had little choice but to take up her cutting scissors and her needle again, while I had no option, given that I had no desire to represent anyone but myself in future, but to resume my career as an actor, destined – at least in the short-term – to become once more a familiar face at the Chadwick Street Labour Exchange.

oOoOo

Seventeen

While we had been away from home, the Conservatives had come to power, and at their helm that great advocate of the Common Market, Edward Heath, whose first move in that direction was the decimalisation of our currency which took place in February 1971. So, had we got back from Croatia four months later than we did, the tuppence we had left over when we arrived at Blackheath where our Renault 4 breathed its last breath, would have been worth £0.0833. There were, of course, other momentous things that happened during our absence, although nothing of greater import as far as I was concerned than Norman Boyack's defection from Richard Hatton Limited to join forces with Jeremy Conway. It was, and I think I knew it at the time, a gesture of friendship rather than any great expectation on Norman's part, that led to me becoming a client of Boyack & Conway Limited. The only reason I know exactly when this happened is that I remember leaving their offices clutching a copy of *Tea for the Tillerman*, the first album by Cat Stevens, another of their clients, and which I still possess, much played, in my increasingly archaic vinyl collection.

If our sabbatical in Yugoslavia could be looked upon as a kind of interval in my career, critics would have been entirely justified in saying that Act Two got off to a painfully slow start. I made a couple of television appearances, so insignificant that I have no recollection of them whatsoever, except that they were provided by friends who, like Norman, were anxious to give me a helping hand back into the profession. But it was a return to acting in the theatre that I had set my sights on and I was going to have to wait until the following year for anything to materialise on that front. Dawn's skills, however, being in greater demand than mine, were very soon employed in making costumes alongside her partner-of-old and near-neighbour, Natasha Kornilof. The fact that, for the time being at any rate, we seemed to have lost our way as writers, which she obviously found frustrating, at least she was able to make a living which was more than I was capable of doing. Meanwhile, we settled back into our comfortable flat on Blackheath Hill, as did Bosie who, incarcerated in a cattery for the last six months, seized possession of the jungle that was our garden, re-establishing his territorial rights with renewed fervour. On one occasion I came across him, ears flattened, back arched and tail erect, confronting a huge black tom-cat who, in Bosie's absence, had obviously taken trespass as his right. Pound for pound he could have made mincemeat of our little Siamese, but when I tried to intervene, Bosie nearly had my hand off and I was obliged to mind my own business. The confrontation finally ended when the big black cat, outfaced and clearly as intimidated as I had been, backed off and scuttled away, never to be seen again, leaving Bosie the undisputed lord of his demesne.

Our circumstances during that time led us to take a more than passing interest in local matters and, somehow or other, we became involved with the south-east London branch of the National Council for Civil Liberties. I even became its secretary for a while, and as well as espousing many of its causes it enabled us to employ our otherwise dormant creative urges by setting up fundraising events, notably a compilation of prose, poetry and song which, under the title of *Trials and Errors*, we took to a variety of venues, culminating somewhat later in a performance at the Mermaid Theatre where I managed to persuade Eileen Atkins to take the female role, thus ensuring reasonable box-office returns. For the most part, however, it fell to a changeable feast of old chums, depending upon their availability, but always including yours truly, so that I was able to hone my rusty acting skills and, at least to some extent, assuage my yearning to tread the boards again.

In *Trials and Errors* we attempted to encompass the concept of justice in general terms, its natural course as well as its miscarriages. We also got involved with the gypsy community, faced at that time with even greater prejudice than usual, and threatened with large-scale closures of caravan sites up and down the country. In the course of researching the subject, prior to putting together another richly documented compilation, we paid several visits to a caravan site, known at that time as Folly Lane, in Walthamstow. I remember approaching it for the first time, not entirely free myself from the preconceptions and prejudices surrounding that rootless tribe. But instead of being set upon by lurchers, beaten with sticks, accosted by lavender-sellers or threatened with curses, we were warmly welcomed and, not only that, discovered when we left that the tyres were still on my car – which, incidentally, was by now a very smart-looking Humber Sceptre! On the gypsy encampment, we were entertained by the leader of the community, a genuine Romany, whose caravan was richly decorated and incredibly ornate, surely designed to stay in one place rather than trail around a country with a climate such as ours. On a tour of the site, we were introduced to various characters, watched children play, and allowed to take as many photographs as I wanted to with my recently acquired Pentax Spotmatic, our host generally going out of his way to disprove the popular view of travelling people as inhospitable. He went even further when he invited us to visit a horse-fair out in Essex, a wild occasion at which horses were galloped, sold, exchanged and bartered for, and at which my camera was constantly employed, providing us with some wonderful photographs (although I say it myself) with which to enhance our own travelling show called, for want of anything more to the point, *Gypsies.*

These, and other activities on behalf of the NCCL, which included taking part in marches and demonstrations and organising seminars, one with the local police to answer charges of racism and, on another occasion, with two representatives of the Gay Rights movement who did their level best to alienate opinion by cuddling up to each other throughout the meeting, were extremely time-consuming. But since we had little else to consume it with, affiliation to a worthwhile cause proved to be a more than justifiable diversion from the main event. It also gave us the opportunity to meet James McGoldrick, one of the leading lights of the south-east London group and a formidable advocate of equal rights whose income, or a substantial part of it, in his professional capacity as a solicitor, derived from legal aid. The fact that Jim McGoldrick was considerably overweight, drank too much and looked like an unmade bed with features barely discernible beneath a forest of facial hair and a pair of thick-lensed glasses, did nothing to obviate his animal magnetism; or so I was led to believe. My own relationship with him was to go through several highs and lows over the next few years, placing him for a time at the centre of my life, and effectively changing it for ever. But that was in the future, and for the time being I shared with Dawn, as well as a new and valued friendship, a great respect for him and for his championship of the under-dog.

With time on my hands, and few prospects of work, I spent at least some of my leisure hours trying to write something of my own, toying with several ideas, painfully aware, for the very first time, of the solitude that most writers regard as a way of life. Having recognised long since that our partnership had largely, although not exclusively, derived from Dawn's original ideas, I turned to history for my inspiration, and was in the process of researching material for a television dramatisation of the French Revolution, nothing if not ambitious, when Roger Hancock called, and asked if we would be interested in working alongside another client of his, a producer with London Weekend Television, on a projected series about Charles II, provisionally entitled *The Merry Monarch*. In spite of the fact that we had been working together on and off for the past few years on a play about a 17th century Quaker called James Nayler, a subject close to Dawn's heart, she was not generally inspired to write historical dramas, and especially not those with titles like *The Merry Monarch*. So I went alone to meet the producer, whose name escapes me, and from whose office I emerged some time later with a list of books on the subject, together with an invitation to collaborate with him on a projected drama series which would be based on the legendary sex-life of that randiest of monarchs. It didn't take me long to discover that, while the sexual antics of Charles Stuart undoubtedly played a significant part in his life, there was a much more exciting story to tell.

Following the final defeat of the Royalists by Parliamentary forces under the command of Oliver Cromwell in 1646, Charles, Prince of Wales as he was then, managed to escape to Jersey, from where he began his long exile, moving from country to country throughout Europe as necessity and his diminishing resources dictated. Countries that had initially welcomed and even feted him, became increasingly embarrassed by his presence when, after the execution of his father, and the establishment of the Commonwealth, they realised they would have to get rid of him if they wanted to do business with Cromwell. The fact that Charles not only survived this humiliation, together with attempts on his life, betrayal from within his own party, and a vagabond existence not far removed at times from penury, only to be invited to return to London in triumph at the age of 30 and crowned King in 1660 was a truly riveting story that was simply begging to be dramatised. Unfortunately, my prospective collaborator, having set his heart on a bawdy romp, didn't agree and, whilst generously giving my slant on the story his blessing, he withdrew from the project. In all honesty, I think he had tired of the whole notion and was, in any case, far too busy producing popular television programmes to embark on the search for a more compatible partner. So I immediately set to work on preparing an outline for the series, provisionally entitled *The Exile*, sent it to Roger Hancock and promptly forgot all about it which was not entirely surprising as at long last, in the early summer of 1972, the theatre beckoned.

It was almost 17 years earlier, when I'd been a member of the Midland Theatre Company in Coventry, that I had worked alongside an actor called Colin George. He had been one of the two Antipholuses, playing opposite Alan Bates when I had played Dromio of Ephesus (or was it Syracuse?) in *The Comedy of Errors*, and later in that same season, when I had given my Jim Hawkins in *Treasure Island*, he had been Doctor Livesey (or was it Squire Trelawney?). Anyway, it was quite a long time ago and our paths had not crossed since then, so I can only think that it was at the behest of my agent that Colin, founder and artistic director of the newly-opened Crucible Theatre in Sheffield, agreed to meet me. He was, as I recalled from earlier days, an extremely pleasant man although, I now discovered, somewhat blinkered in his perceptions. After the usual pleasantries, he made it clear that he suspected the reason behind my protracted absence from the stage was more sinister than I was prepared to reveal. Not having suffered any physical incapacity or illness, could it possibly have been brought about by a drink or drug-related problem? It was not so much an accusation as a sympathetic enquiry, but I was taken aback all the same. Had I known at the time that Colin's career as an actor had been cruelly terminated by the debilitating side-effects of a collapsed lung, I might have understood why he found my reasons, amounting to little more than the desire for a change of scene, difficult to believe. He was, however, prepared to give me the benefit of the doubt, although his caution was reflected in the parts I was initially offered in his forthcoming season. To be perfectly honest, after 18 months in the theatrical wilderness, I had reached the stage where I would have accepted virtually anything.

The Crucible Theatre, which opened its doors for the first time in 1971, was a very special theatre, having been designed by Tanya Moiseiwitsch, with whom I had been privileged to work along with Tyrone Guthrie back at the Old Vic some 20 years earlier. That illustrious partnership had subsequently been extended to the other side of the Atlantic where she worked alongside Guthrie in Minneapolis and at Stratford, Ontario, playing an important part in designing the new theatre which opened there in 1957. Taking her inspiration from this, the Crucible Theatre not only boasted a remarkably intimate 1,000 seat semi-circular auditorium and an elegant and welcoming foyer but also, due to the fact that Tanya was a professional practitioner rather than a disinterested architect, a great deal of care had been lavished on the backstage area where conditions, usually cramped, windowless and occasionally underground, were both spacious and bright, the dressing-rooms boasting windows that actually provided views of the outside world. The greatest irony surrounding the existence of the Crucible Theatre half a century or so later is that, while it continues to provide stimulating drama to an appreciative audience, its fame derives almost entirely from its reputation as the home of snooker, its splendid auditorium given over every year to a game which used to be confined to the back-rooms of pubs and which, although now regarded as a spectator sport, is only marginally more watchable than darts in my opinion. Still, I imagine it makes a great deal of economic sense as far as the theatre is concerned. In fact, the Crucible re-opened in 2009, following refurbishments costing £1.5m, a sum of money that almost certainly didn't come from putting on plays, no matter how successful at the box-office.

I knew little of the history of the Sheffield Playhouse which, until the Crucible came along, had been the home of repertory theatre in that city, renowned for its silver-plated cutlery and very little else as far I was aware, but it must have been able to rely on a regular and surprisingly sophisticated audience, or Colin George would surely have baulked at the idea of opening his 1972 season with *The Persians* by Aeschylus, followed by productions of *The Taming of the Shrew* and a new play by John Spurling called *Peace in our Time*, charting the events which led to the Second World War. With not an Agatha Christie in sight and clearly not too many laughs in store, my preconceptions about the Industrial North were obviously well wide of the mark. Colin himself was to direct the Greek play with sets and costumes by Tanya Moiseiwitsch and a company that owed much to the theatre's Canadian connections. Douglas Campbell, another Guthrie protégé with whom I had last worked at the Old Vic in *Julius Cæsar*, was to play the Ghost of Darius, with his wife, Ann Casson, daughter of Sybil Thorndyke and Lewis Casson, as his widow and mother of Xerxes, the present King of Persia. There was only one other named part in the play, that of the Messenger, and I might well have made a decent stab at that, but obviously I was not entirely trusted to remain sober or free from whatever other addiction had forced me to take refuge in a rehabilitation centre for the last three years, and so I was consigned to the Chorus. Not that the Chorus is a minor role in Greek tragedy, far from it, but it is a part that is generally shared with a number of other actors who would, no doubt, be able to cover up for me in the event of my incapacity for whatever reason. Colin's real mistake, however, which had nothing at all to do with me, lay in inviting an actor called Paul Angelis to play the part of Xerxes and, even more incomprehensibly, Petruchio in *The Taming of the Shrew*. Were it not for the fact that, some years later, I became more personally exposed to what I saw as Colin's congenital naivety, I would still be at a loss to understand how he came to make such a hash of casting those two key roles. I suppose it's just about conceivable that he might have been influenced, at least as far as Xerxes was concerned, by Paul's claim to his family's Greek ancestry, a confidence he shared with me in the few short days before we stopped talking to each other, but it's hard to credit even Colin with that degree of unworldliness. To some extent, the reason for his presence was later explained when, in *Peace in our Time,* he played Heinrich Himmler, a part that could have been written for him had the author conceived the character as a Liverpudlian thug, rather than a German one. But the really positive influence he exerted, although inadvertently, was that within a very short time he managed, by virtue of his indiscriminate malevolence, to transform a disparate bunch of actors into a genuinely united company. During my time in Sheffield, I was able to renew my acquaintance, not only with Douglas Campbell, but with the delightful Ronald Cunliffe, with whom I had worked in Regent's Park, as well as forging new friendships, mostly temporary, but two of a lifelong nature. Michael Tudor Barnes, whilst being every bit as good at the Messenger as I would have been, went on to give a truly memorable performance as Adolf Hitler in the John Spurling play, inspiring me to create Bosworth Productions, a company whose sole aim was to raise enough money to stage Shakespeare's *Richard III,* with me as director and Michael in the title role. Needless to say, nothing ever came of this, although there is to this day an account buried somewhere in the vaults of Barclay's Bank with a balance of about £80 plus interest which no one person involved with Bosworth Productions was ever given the authority to withdraw. Also in the company, along with her boy-friend, Neil Phillips, was the gorgeous Jill Baker whose unavailability was probably a blessing in disguise as we remained close friends for a good many years.

Rehearsals for *The Persians,* when not contained within the walls of the generously proportioned rehearsal room, were conducted in the even more commodious surroundings of the nearby moors, where we members of the Chorus, wielding long wooden staves, were drilled both vocally and physically, whilst at the same time being totally mesmerised by our director's grim determination to outdo us all in every department. In fact, there were occasions when Colin became so focused on himself, locked in mortal combat (or so it seemed) with his own infirmity, that we could have tiptoed away, and he probably wouldn't have noticed. As it happened, and contrary to expectations, *The Persians* became the highlight of the season and, but for the one glaringly obvious exception, all the members of the cast acquitted themselves well in what turned out to be an extremely good production. Of course, a great deal of this was due to Tanya's magnificent set and costumes. Douglas Campbell, not what you'd call a small man in any case, towered above the action as the old king's ghost, hugely helmeted and lifted another four inches above the rest of us by built-up shoes concealed beneath his robes so that his presence, intimidating enough in the pub across the road, was truly awe-inspiring, whilst the Chorus were classically masked and wore robes that looked, and indeed felt, as if they had been sculpted in stone. We had, of course, used practice masks during rehearsals, and they took some getting used to, but I don't think any of us had anticipated the benefits that they bestowed until after the play had opened. There was no need to use make-up, for instance, a definite bonus, and particularly at the end of the evening when a quick exit from the theatre meant an extra drink before closing-time. It also meant that we could enjoy a degree of anonymity so that when Xerxes entered, following the catastrophic defeat of the Persians by the Greeks at Salamis, and began his lament with the words, "Twice have I failed," the voice that said "three times" could have come from any one of us. In fact, the only thing I can say with any certainty even now, is that it wasn't me, although I confess to experiencing both astonishment and delight, an entirely inappropriate response, which was happily masked from the audience. But by far the most amusing story I have hung on to from that production is the weekly appointment we kept in the Green Room where, conveniently coinciding with a lengthy absence from the stage, the Chorus gathered to watch *Monty Python's Flying Circus* on TV, a great favourite with us all at that time. So there we sat, a group of ancient Persian elders, gravely masked, falling about with laughter beneath expressionless faces, at the zany and surreal antics of John Cleese, Eric Idle, Michael Palin et al, and providing a mirror-image, in fact, of the very show we were watching. I don't know how long it took us to see ourselves as others might have seen us, but it remains a memory worth cherishing and especially in a season that was otherwise more or less unmemorable.

The last time I had appeared in *The Taming of the Shrew* was when I played Katharina at Kilburn Grammar School 19 years earlier, and I was not, on this occasion, destined to feature quite so strongly. My major contribution to the production, directed with a good deal of bombast by Douglas Campbell, was my portrayal of the Pedant, who makes his first appearance in Act IV and is only on stage at the end of the play to swell the numbers. Hence my memories are hazy, and relate almost entirely to the insufferable problems experienced by the actress who inherited my former role. Jane Casson was another member of the Thorndyke/Casson dynasty, a very nice lady who may, or may not, have succeeded in realising the wonderful opportunities on offer with Katharina, but who was prevented from achieving much of anything beyond her survival, partnered as she was by Paul Angelis as Petruchio. I remember seeing a production of *Much Ado About Nothing* at the RSC several years later in which Judi Dench, as Beatrice, appeared to be similarly marginalised by Donald Sinden's Benedick, a self-centred, front-cloth performance, seemingly reluctant to share the stage with Beatrice, let alone fall in love with her. But at least it had the virtue of being audience-friendly, while Paul Angelis made no friends on either side of the footlights.

It was in November of that year that Bosie, our beloved cat, died. Dawn told me on the telephone that she had found him in the basement area of our flat, a place we used for storage and nothing much else, into which he had obviously crept for the sole purpose of expiring as he had never, to our knowledge, been down there before. It had, apparently, been the result of kidney failure, a weakness to which Siamese cats were particularly prone, or so we were told. He was 11 years old, and would be very much missed by both of us. I knew, in fact, that no other cat could satisfactorily replace him, which was why, having sought out a local breeder in Sheffield, I bought two Siamese kittens, and took them down with me on my next trip to London. They were brothers, but quite unalike in personality as well as in appearance, one being a haughty lilac-point while the other, a seal-point like Bosie, was altogether rounder and more susceptible to human contact. We called him, for some obscure reason, Ali, while the lilac-point was named Piko, after our Croatian friend, Marinko. Dawn was delighted when I arrived home with them which was just as well, having had the sad task only the day before of burying Bosie's remains in the garden over which he had reigned supreme for the past two years.

Meanwhile, with the autumn season drawing to a close, and having obviously and demonstrably overcome whatever it was that had afflicted me, Colin rewarded me with a major role in the Christmas production of *Pinocchio*. Not that I welcomed the part of Gepetto wholeheartedly as it entailed a good deal of make-up as well as a wig and a moustache, an irksome exercise, and particularly so when undertaken at 9 o'clock in the morning so that I could join the rest of the cast in the foyer where we had been required by our director, Caroline Smith, to extend a warm welcome to the tiny-tots who had come, along with their teachers, to see the 10 o'clock show. It was pay back time with a vengeance for the peachy days of ancient Greece, or so it seemed at the time. We gave two performances a day of *Pinocchio*, one at 10am and the other at 2.30pm, the evening slot given over to the altogether more elegant, and slightly more sophisticated charms of Sandy Wilson's *The Boy Friend* in which, had I been given the choice, I would have preferred to appear. What made *Pinocchio* tolerable was having to share the stage with Michael Tudor Barnes as the eponymous puppet, and with Jill Baker as a mute clown whose function in the play only became clear when, as a result of one of our director's dotty ideas, Michael and I had been left to sleep on stage during the interval. Not only was this an extremely inconsiderate notion, depriving us of a refreshing cup of tea, but also exposing us to the unwelcome attentions of a number of children who climbed up onto the all too accessible stage and interfered with us in a variety of ways. We were probably in the middle of our third or fourth performance when I had my 'sleep' interrupted, not by some importunate infant, but by the silent clown who, for some reason, kept us company throughout the play. On this occasion, she prodded me, and when I opened my eyes, expecting the worst, she pointed in the direction of Pinocchio's truckle- bed. I looked round and, to my astonishment, saw Michael sitting on the edge of it, eyes closed and arms outstretched prior to sleep-walking off the stage and all the way to the Green Room whither Gepetto and the Clown, naturally concerned for his welfare, followed him. I don't know if Caroline ever returned to see her production again but if she did she never mentioned it, whilst Jill and I, brimming over with gratitude and admiration, followed our rebellious puppet to the Green Room at the interval of every performance thereafter.

The Crucible's Canadian connection, however, had nothing whatsoever to do with the irresistible offer I received during the run of *Pinocchio*, which was to play Guildenstern in *Hamlet* and in Tom Stoppard's *Rosencrantz and Guildenstern are Dead* at the Manitoba Theatre Centre (MTC) in Winnipeg. The invitation came, in fact, by way of David William with whom I had not worked since the summer of 1963 and, even more surprisingly, it had been confirmed by Douglas Rain, a Canadian actor with whom I had not worked for a good deal longer than that when, for a brief spell, we trod the same boards at the Old Vic in Guthrie's production of *A Midsummer Night's Dream*. Douglas was to be directing the Tom Stoppard play which, along with *Hamlet*, was all but cast except that he was unable to find a young Canadian actor with enough classical experience to play Guildenstern opposite Bernard Hopkins, who was to play Rosencrantz. Well, it so happened that Bernard was David William's long-term partner, and when Douglas sought his advice, David came up with my name, happily a familiar one as far as Douglas was concerned, although it undoubtedly owed more to his faith in David's judgement than to any fond memories he may have had of our time together in the Waterloo Road, that he was persuaded to offer me the part. As far as I was concerned, the whys and wherefores were of little consequence. I had seldom been as excited about a new play as I had been when I saw the original National Theatre production at the Old Vic in 1967, and that such an undreamed-of opportunity to play one of the two leading roles should simply fall into my lap without so much as an audition, and at a time when all that faced me was another indeterminate period of unemployment, was a cause for nothing but rejoicing. Well, almost nothing.

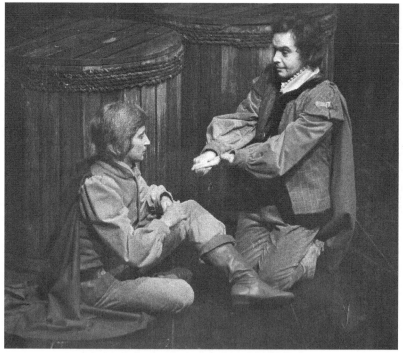

1973 Rosencrantz and Guildenstern are Dead - Manitoba Theatre Centre in Canada, with Bernard Hopkins.

I had all but forgotten *The Exile* by this time, but a telephone call from Roger Hancock brought it sharply back into focus. The BBC TV drama department had liked my outline for the series and were prepared to commission a pilot episode. This was, of course, wonderful news, but coming when it did, my joy was not exactly unconfined. In less than a month I would be on my way to Canada where I would be heavily involved rehearsing, not to mention learning, a major role in unfamiliar surroundings alongside a company of actors, largely unknown to me and with whom I would be expected to forge some kind of a relationship outside of the rehearsal room. On the plus side, my involvement in rehearsals for *Hamlet* would be less demanding than in the Stoppard play. But more to the point, it felt good to be in demand suddenly and unexpectedly and, afflicted as I was with incurable optimism, I saw no reason why I shouldn't be able to fulfil all my professional obligations. The BBC had, after all, given me six weeks to deliver, so I could make a start on *The Exile* before I had to leave home.

It was not without a backward glance that I made my way to Heathrow in early February, 1973. After all, I had been away from home, but for the occasional weekend visit, for the best part of five months and here I was, barely three weeks later, putting even more distance between us; non-commutable distance this time, and for the next three months. It wasn't that I entertained any serious misgivings about the future of our marriage, although I was obviously, and perhaps understandably, apprehensive about being apart from Dawn for such a long time. We had lived in each other's pockets for so many years, sharing a professional as well as a private life, and had recently embarked upon a foreign adventure that had, if anything, made us even more interdependent. The resilience of our marriage had never been tested beyond the usual ups and downs of any intimate relationship, invariably resolved in the good old 'kiss-and-make-up' tradition, and certainly always before going to sleep. The effects of a lengthy separation, however, were all unknown and, to mitigate this to some extent, Dawn and I agreed that she should fly to Canada in time to see the opening night, and to hell with the expense!

Winnipeg was as cold as I had been told it would be, and a good deal colder than I could possibly have imagined. The snow lay deeper than I had ever seen it except in *Scott of the Antarctic*, although I don't remember ever seeing it fall. Somehow or other it contrived to fall at night, so that you were greeted every morning by a pristine landscape of the purest white under a sky which emphatically denied responsibility for it by being always cloudless and blue. I'm sure there were occasions when this was not entirely true, but it is certainly the way I remember it. I also remember the junction of Portage Avenue and Main Street, famed for being the coldest and windiest location in Canada, an unsubstantiated claim it has to be said, but if there is anywhere colder and windier I certainly wouldn't choose to stand there as I did once and once only at Portage and Main, barely surviving to tell the tale. For anyone not too familiar with the geographical regions of Canada, as I wasn't at the time, I should perhaps point out that Winnipeg is the capital of Manitoba, Canada's prairie province, situated right in the middle of the country and just a few miles north of the US border. Another thing worth taking on board before you embark on your first trip across the Atlantic, and on every occasion thereafter, is the sheer size of the country you are heading for and the distances between one place and another. I had scarcely checked into my little apartment at the Delaware Motor Lodge when I decided to put a call through to my old friend from drama school days, Sandy Black, who had recently returned home to Canada to become Technical Director at Ryerson University's Theatre School in Toronto. He was pleased to hear from me, of course, but when I suggested that he might care to pop across to Winnipeg, he tactfully informed me that 'popping across' was not really an option as the distance between Toronto and Winnipeg was just about the same as it was from London to Rome. Being close friends, however, we did come to an accommodation and Sandy agreed to pop over on condition that I popped in to see him in Toronto on my way back home at the end of the season. As it happened, as soon as rehearsals began, the topography was neither here nor there as, apart from the occasional diversion to a restaurant or a bar, the only road I travelled until the end of April was between the Delaware Motor Lodge and the Manitoba Theatre Centre on Market Street.

What I hadn't taken into account when I had been offered the job, beyond the daunting prospect of playing my first major role in the theatre since ... well, since playing Puck in Regent's Park, was the resentment we might have to face from young Canadian actors who thought they should be playing the parts and who, with post-colonial axes to grind, were determined to make us feel like the intruders we undoubtedly were. Indeed, the very notion of inviting relatively unknown English actors to play leading roles which their Canadian counterparts were perfectly capable of playing themselves, was already becoming something of an anachronism, and in a few short years, outside of being a member of an English touring company, I wouldn't have stood a chance of being invited to work in Canada. If I was, as I say, blissfully unaware of this chink in my armour during the run-up to rehearsals, I was left in little doubt when, as we started to work on the opening scene, I began to feel the sting of slings and arrows. *Rosencrantz and Guildenstern are Dead* begins with our two eponymous heroes in a kind of limbo, on their way to the Danish court at the behest of the new king, Claudius, in order to keep an eye on his nephew, Hamlet, with whom they were at University in Wittenberg, and who is now mourning the death of his father. The fact that they were never what you would call Hamlet's bosom-buddies suggests that there is more to this invitation than meets the eye, or indeed less. But a summons is a summons and, who knows, perhaps an opportunity for advancement. Nevertheless, their uncertainty is compounded as they sit there playing *heads or tails* in no-man's-land, one tossing coins and the other catching them, Rosencrantz happily and unquestioningly proclaiming 92 'heads' in a row and Guildenstern speculating on the odds against this extraordinary occurrence which, at the very least, suggests that the law of averages no longer applies or, to cut to the quick, that the time is out of joint and that something is definitely rotten in the state of Denmark. This scene, as you might imagine, represents something of a challenge, especially coming as it does right at the beginning of the play. I am quite sure that I must have tossed a coin or two during the course of my life, but never before had I been required to toss a bagful of them, one after the other, across a considerable distance and from a variety of different angles, culminating in a backwards flip over the shoulder as I moved upstage, all of them having to be accurately directed so that Rosencrantz could easily catch them without moving from his seat. Whether Bernard Hopkins or I had the more difficult task is open to debate, but between us we made a complete mess of it, with coins flying off in all directions, and Bernard managing to drop the odd one that came within reach. Our ineptitude was made all the more humiliating by the presence of our two Canadian understudies who, sitting on the sidelines, repeatedly and unerringly tossed a coin to each other without ever taking their eyes off us. That very evening in my apartment, having provided myself with a couple of dozen old twopenny coins from the theatre, the ones we would be using in the show, I placed my upturned fur hat on the sofa, went to the other side of the room and began tossing them in the general direction of my hat, having vowed that I would not go to bed until all 24 had consecutively landed inside it. By 2am the following morning, utterly exhausted, I had fallen asleep next to my fur hat. But I had succeeded, and was subsequently rewarded by the conspicuous absence of our gimlet-eyed understudies and their gratuitous exhibitionism as all, or nearly all, of my coins landed in Bernard's hand, or close enough for him to catch them, which he did; well, most of the time he did.

Bernard Hopkins and I weren't the only two English actors in the company, but whether Alan Dobie or Edgar Wreford suffered similarly I have no idea. Somehow, I don't think so; Edgar, after all, who had been cast as Polonius in both plays, was an actor of great experience and maturity which would undoubtedly have generated a degree of respect amongst the natives from the word go, whilst Alan Dobie, headlining the company as Hamlet, had only recently enjoyed considerable success, abroad as well as at home, as Andrei Bolkonsky in the BBC Television adaptation of Tolstoy's *War and Peace.* I already knew them both, of course; Edgar having been a colleague in *An Age of Kings* and Alan from way, way back. There was also an actor called Maurice Good, playing Claudius, but he was a Dubliner in any case who went on to take up Canadian citizenship, so he didn't really count. But it was a comfort of sorts that Bernard and I weren't the only foreigners in the company for, to tell the truth, I never did feel entirely at ease there. Playing Guildenstern in the Stoppard play would have been enough of a challenge wherever it took place but it was made all the more so, feeling as I did, that I not only had to be good, but that my performance had to be good enough to justify my very presence in Canada. Against that somewhat nerve-wracking backdrop, I managed not only to survive, but somehow or other I began to enjoy the situation, and having something to prove beyond my ability to handle the part became a stimulus rather than an obstacle. I enjoyed rehearsals enormously. Bernard and I, never having met each other before, were happily in tune both on stage and off, while Douglas Rain, an actor himself, proved to be an extremely actor-friendly director, sharing the experience with us rather than handing down edicts as so many of them did – and may still do! When we were joined, as Rosencrantz and Guildenstern often are in a number of scenes, by the Player, another dimension was added by the presence of Roland Hewgill, a tall and rather gaunt Canadian actor with whom we both had an immediate rapport. Roly was certainly eccentric, even possibly a little unstable, a condition which would eventually be employed against me, but for the time being we all enjoyed each other's company, not only in the rehearsal room but socially too. It would be impossible now – and difficult even to imagine – that there was a time when smoking was allowed in a rehearsal room – 'and a good thing too' says my conscience, although the fiend at my elbow still says 'those were the days'. Of course, the director could, and very often did in those days, impose an embargo but, as it happened, our director smoked more than we did, probably because he had less to say, but there were occasions I recall when the four of us were at it together that the atmosphere in the rehearsal room resembled a London Particular. They were nonetheless productive days, and if I had admired the play when I first saw it, my enthusiasm grew with familiarity. Tom Stoppard's love of the English language obviously sprang from discovery rather than heritage, having spent his early years as Tomâs Straussler, whose family had fled their native Czechoslovakia with the Nazi invasion in 1939, and whilst my own background couldn't have been more different, and certainly a good deal less exotic, my passion for our language was not inherited either. In common with many other natives, I regarded it as little more than a means of communication until I discovered Shakespeare, courtesy of Peter Wright at Kilburn Grammar School, and subsequently at the hands of mentors such as Peter Dews and David William. Certainly I shared Stoppard's relish in its use, the intellectual conceits, the word-play, the double meanings. I envied him his skill. But, most of all, I looked forward to the opportunity of pretending, for a couple of hours every night, that the words he had put into Guildenstern's mouth were mine.

Rehearsals for *Hamlet*, under the direction of the MTC's artistic director, Ed Gilbert, barely made an impression, partly because Rosenscrantz and Guildenstern are surplus to requirements for much of the time, plus the fact that most of their scenes in *Hamlet* are included in the Stoppard play. What I remember mostly is that they afforded me the time to learn my lines for 'R & G', no mean feat, and to get on with writing my pilot episode of *The Exile*. No, I hadn't forgotten all about it, for the good reason – if for no other – that if I failed to meet the deadline imposed by the BBC, I would forfeit my fee. There was more to it than that, of course, but it was as good an incentive as any to get it finished before we embarked on technical and dress-rehearsals for the double bill. I had made a start before leaving home and, somehow or other, had managed to bring it tantalisingly close to a conclusion when I received a telegram from Roger Hancock, briefly reminding me that the completed script had to be in their hands within the next six days which meant, back in 1973, that I would have to post it within the next two. Fortunately, this gave me the best part of a weekend to wrap it up. The pilot episode, which was set on the island of Jersey where Prince Charles had taken refuge following the defeat of the Royalist forces and the execution of his father, dealt mainly with the politics of the time and also served as a prelude to his 11 year exile. Although I had earlier scorned the idea of a series called *The Merry Monarch*, based exclusively on his legendary love-life, I obviously couldn't ignore the fact that Charles Stuart had well earned his music-hall reputation as a bit of a lad for the ladies, and Jersey was obviously the place to sew the seeds, as it were. The problem that faced me was that, while many of his later affairs were pretty well documented, there was no evidence of a sexual encounter at that time or in that place, so I had to invent one. I cannot begin to describe the agonies I suffered in the process, cringing with embarrassment at the very thought of it, knowing that whatever scenario I eventually came up with was bound to appear contrived. It was in the early hours of Monday morning, with a gaping hole in the middle of an otherwise completed script, that I finally faced my demon. I thought, 'what the hell, at least I'll get paid!' and so, eyes propped open with the proverbial matchsticks, I wrote the scene which, in outline at least, was relatively simple: 'Mother of a young girl seeks an audience with Charles, fully intending to castigate him for attempting to seduce her daughter, and ends up seducing him herself instead'. I posted it off to London that morning, only hazily aware of what I had written, but simply relieved that I had managed to write it at all. A week later, I received a letter from Brian Codd, Roger Hancock's associate, informing me that the script had arrived and been sent to the BBC. He went on to say how much he had enjoyed reading it, and how he had been particularly taken with the seduction scene which, he proclaimed, was one of the most erotic scenes he had ever read. Unfortunately, as it happened, *The Exile* never saw the light of day. There were discussions about it when I returned home, and I was urged by the head of the series department to begin it earlier, incorporating the tail-end of the Civil War; but just how far back was I supposed to go? I also believed, rightly or wrongly, that events in England, which had in any case, been pretty well explored on screen over the years, and most recently in the film *Cromwell*, ought to be held at arm's length, seen through the eyes of Prince Charles who wasn't there but whose future depended on the outcome. In any case, I had no desire to get bogged down in the world of Cavaliers and Roundheads from which it would be difficult to escape, and so the enterprise foundered. I suspected at the time, and still do, that the BBC's enthusiasm for historical series had begun to wane anyway in the wake of *The Six Wives of Henry VIII* (1970), *Elizabeth R* (1971) and the story of Henry VII's reign called *The Shadow of the Tower* in which I had made a brief appearance in 1972. I still believe *The Exile* had great television potential and, but for poor timing, who knows but it might well have been given the green light. It was a disappointing outcome but, bearing in mind that I had other priorities at the time, one I didn't dwell upon.

Meanwhile, we had successfully opened our season at the Manitoba Theatre Centre with *Rosencrantz and Guildenstern Are Dead.* It should, of course, have been *Hamlet,* but the MTC's subscription system had, for reasons unknown, got it wrong, so that subscribers came to see the Stoppard play first when it ought to have been Shakespeare's. Bernard and I had no reason to complain, however, as we must surely have been the first and only Rosencrantz and Guildenstern in history to have been greeted with a regular entrance round of applause on making our first appearance in Act 2 Scene 2 of *Hamlet,* a pleasurable experience which, I need hardly say, was not shared by Claudius and Gertrude.

I was in the middle of a dress-rehearsal when Dawn arrived at the airport and so I had provided her with a chauffeur-driven car to take her to the Delaware Motor Lodge where she was greeted by a profusion of flowers. I might well have gone to these lengths in any case as I had missed her desperately and, being unable to greet her myself, wanted her to be in no doubt about the intensity of her welcome. There was, however, an added dimension to it now as I had learned over the past few weeks in a series of telephone calls that, shortly after I left home, she had embarked on a relationship with Jim McGoldrick. My use of the word 'relationship' is deliberate, although chosen retrospectively, as my emotions at the time allowed little room for semantics. But I believe – indeed have every reason to believe – that had she admitted to a night of passion, or even two nights, I would have been able to deal with it. True, I would have been upset and, more to the point, bewildered that she could have found such an unprepossessing man attractive enough to share with him the kind of intimacy we had shared, but as I have never set a high price on purely physical fidelity, having myself been guilty of the odd peccadillo, I wouldn't have seen it as a crisis had it not been for her expressed intention to carry on with it. I was thus faced with a dilemma and, it has to be said, a painful one. Looking back on it all now and knowing what the consequences would be, it is relatively easy to pass judgement on myself, but that old devil 'hindsight' remained as usual hidden, and doubtless grinning, somewhere in the future. I know now that I ought to have issued some kind of ultimatum: 'End it now or else ...' or even 'End it by the time I get home or else ...' But I did neither. The trouble was that I was guided at the time, not by any rational considerations, but by emotional turmoil. I had fallen in love with Dawn when I was 17 and she was 21, a love that had survived many separations and upheavals and had led, albeit by dint of at least a degree of dogged determination on my part, to marriage. We went on to share, over the next ten years, much more than a bed but a partnership, both personal and professional, and I had every reason to believe that my feelings were reciprocated. In short, life without Dawn was unimaginable and I was afraid of losing her. And so I let it rest, although 'rest' was the last thing I was able to enjoy, putting my faith in the passage of time to resolve the situation, and fondly believing that no affair, however passionately conceived in my absence, could possibly outlive my return. I have to say, in my defence, that Dawn said and did nothing to suggest that her feelings towards me had changed. She had, after all, come all the way to Canada to be with me and, apart from her confession and the soul-searching sessions that went with it, we enjoyed each other's company in much the same way as we always had, danced together at the first night party, and made love with genuine affection. There is no doubt that I had been badly wounded but, as she left to return home, I had no reason to believe that it might prove fatal.

I was left, for obvious reasons, feeling somewhat vulnerable so that, during the interval of a performance of 'R & G', when I was presented with a bottle of vodka by a member of the stage management team who had been asked to deliver it to me by a lady in the audience, and I read in the accompanying card the words 'Thank you for a most stimulating performance!', I enquired of the messenger the nature of the donor. He said she was a very attractive young woman who had been to a previous matinée performance with her school children charges and had returned on her own because she had enjoyed it so much. I asked if he would convey my thanks to her and scribbled a hasty note suggesting that if she would care to join me in Room 111 of the Delaware Motor Lodge at 11pm that night we could, perhaps, open the bottle of vodka together. Somewhat to my surprise she arrived on the dot although, maybe not so surprisingly in the circumstances, the bottle of vodka remained unopened. Our relationship, for want of a better word, continued on a happily casual basis until she revealed that her husband, a fervent Christian of fundamentalist convictions, might find out, and with dire consequences. It was at that point, my self-confidence having been to some extent restored, I decided that discretion was the better part of valour.

Luckily, my daytimes were full of distractions. I was commissioned by the Canadian Broadcasting Corporation to do a radio adaptation of Alexei Arbozov's play, *The Promise*. I have no idea now how this came about, but I was thankful for it as it kept me fully occupied for a couple of weeks. Of course, performances of 'R & G' provided the pivotal point of my existence and, with full and enthusiastic houses, I went on enjoying it. *Hamlet* enjoyed some success too, although it didn't have quite the same impact. True, it was familiar territory, even for Canadian audiences, and it certainly didn't provide as many laughs as the Stoppard play, but there was something else that was lacking, namely an engaging central performance. Having admired Alan Dobie's Macbeth at Ludlow Castle back in 1961, which was the last time I had seen him on stage, I was at a loss to understand his apparent detachment from the character of Hamlet. It certainly wasn't true of his performance in *Rosencrantz and Guildenstern Are Dead* where, freed from the many complexities inherent in Shakespeare's play, he succeeded in creating a character which, although on the fringes of the action for much of the time, was both multi-faceted and unpredictable. Moreover, he appeared to enjoy inhabiting the role, a process of assimilation that he had clearly resisted in his approach to the same part in *Hamlet*. One evening, inspired by drink no doubt, I asked him why he had chosen objectivity rather than involvement. Far from being offended or asking me what the hell I was talking about, he told me, quite seriously, that he didn't want to impose his interpretation of Hamlet on the audience but allow it to speak for itself. When I ventured to suggest that it was his interpretation of the role that audiences came to see, he said that his responsibility was to present Shakespeare's *Hamlet*, and not some actor's version of it. I could scarcely believe what I was hearing, although I'm sure that I thought, rather than gave voice to my suggestion, that in that case he would be better employed handing out copies of the text. It was then that I remembered hearing about a confrontation between Alan and David William when, in rehearsals for the Ludlow *Macbeth*, Alan had stubbornly refused to give credence to the supernatural, citing all kinds of rational explanations for the otherwise inexplicable. Alan's impressive performance, however, which I did see, gave not the slightest hint of scepticism which led me to believe that David William, for all his occasional silliness, must have been a more persuasive director than Ed Gilbert. Alan had been a wonderfully instinctive actor when I first knew him, but somewhere along the line he must have allowed himself, or been led to believe, that he was an intellectual, a pretension no doubt nourished by the undeniable effect he had on the opposite sex, many of whom attributed his usual uncommunicative and somewhat sullen demeanour, not to a lack of social skills, but to depth of character. In Alan's case, however, still waters did not run very deep.

On an altogether lighter note I remember, towards the end of one particular performance, standing on the stage next to Rosencrantz as the play came to an end, both of us having been sent to our deaths in England in lieu of Hamlet, and pondering the arbitrary events that had led to our demise when Rosencrantz suddenly disappears, swallowed up by the darkness, leaving me to wind up my little speech with the words, 'Now you see me, now you …' before being swallowed up myself. On this occasion, the spotlight went out on me and, as I turned to make my way quickly to the nearest exit, I misjudged the angle of my turn, walked off the stage and fell into the auditorium. When the lights came up on the final scene, which is in fact the last scene from *Hamlet,* the audience was greeted by the sight of Guildenstern, having obviously escaped death and swum all the way back to Denmark, clambering onto the stage just in time to miss being in at the kill. The rest is silence!

Winter became spring overnight, or so it seemed to someone who came from a country whose climate was more sluggish, dragging its heels from one season to another. Our season at the theatre came to a close just as suddenly at the end of April and, while I had enjoyed the challenge of playing a major role in such an exciting play so soon after my 'comeback', and was happy enough that Bernard and I had succeeded in justifying our presence in Winnipeg, even to the extent of becoming fairly adept at tossing coins, I was not sorry to be going home despite the uncertainties that awaited me there. As promised, I broke my journey and popped into Toronto to spend a little time with Sandy, and then flew on to London where I was not only greeted with great warmth and affection, but with a surprise 'welcome home' party; walking into a Greenwich club for what I had been led to believe would be a quiet reunion with Dawn, only to find it thronged with friends. I could not have imagined a happier homecoming although, had I been consulted, and quite naturally I wasn't, I wouldn't have included Jim McGoldrick on the guest list.

oOoOo

Eighteen

I couldn't have been back from Canada for more than a few weeks when I was offered a part in a new play by Nicholas Salaman called *Mad Dog* at the Hampstead Theatre Club. There were several reasons I decided to do it, money obviously not being one of them at Hampstead, so there had to be strong inducements. I was naturally anxious to consolidate my recent spell of employment with something in London, but what proved even more tempting was that the offer had been made by yet one more friend from *An Age of Kings,* Patrick Garland, by now a director of some standing both in the theatre and on television. Not only that, but also because the play would star one of my favourite British film actors, Denholm Elliott, and feature as his daughter, '60s pop idol Marianne Faithfull, currently better known for her addiction to cocaine and her outrageous doings with *The Rolling Stones,* culminating in the notorious Mars bar episode! And then again, there was the undeniable lure of a West End transfer, which must have been on the cards, or why else would Denholm Elliott and Marianne Faithfull have been tempted? I was also looking forward to meeting up again with Terry Scully. We hadn't met since returning from Chicago in 1964, although I had heard on the grapevine that only recently he had suffered a major blow when, on returning to his flat in London after spending Christmas Day with his family up north, he found that his partner had taken his life. Terry was known to be a fairly fragile creature anyway or why would the company have reacted so strongly to the treatment meted out to him by Peter Dews in Ravinia? It was likely, I thought, that Patrick had responded to this latest crisis in his life by offering him a major role in *Mad Dog.* I was less enthused, it has to be said, by the prospect of meeting up again with Georgina Ward, from whom I had last parted without a word of farewell at the end of that gruesome season in Stratford-upon-Avon 12 years earlier. Within a week, however, we had again become fast friends, both of us now seeking out each other's company in the turbulent days to come as if the bad blood between us had never existed.

To be perfectly honest, I remember very little about the play itself, the rehearsal period producing more drama than the author or the director could possibly have imagined or, indeed, wished for. It was, I believe, a satire on the decline and disintegration of the aristocracy with Denholm Elliott as the mad dog Lord something-or-other of the title. Together with Tom Georgeson and John Forgeham,

I played one of his Lordship's intimidating minders whose function was enigmatic, to say the least, hovering somewhere between bodyguards and warders. Very early on in rehearsals, a relationship sprang up between Terry Scully, who had been cast in the role of the butler, and Marianne Faithfull, a relationship partly based, I thought, on mutual dependency. Not surprisingly, given her lifestyle to date, Marianne was pretty wobbly, but next to Terry Scully she proved to be the Rock of Gibraltar. In fact, the only thing I really remember about her was her apparent inability to straighten her arms, a condition that I eventually, and not alone, diagnosed as muscle contraction, the cause of which I will leave to your imagination. Terry's problems were more immediate, however, and it soon became obvious that the remedy prescribed by Patrick had not met his needs. He was clearly unable to focus, neither on the job-in-hand nor on the people with whom he was working. He was certainly in no condition to take direction, to learn lines or to relate to his fellow actors, and for anyone who had worked alongside him before, as I had, and known him to be an entirely affable and professional company man, this was alarming. Things came to a head one day when, late for rehearsals, he arrived in the middle of a scene in which he was not involved and, apparently oblivious, wandered into the acting area, looking from face to face without a glimmer of recognition until he turned away and saw Marianne, sitting out front. Rehearsals had come to a grinding halt as everyone waited in silence, breaths bated, for the outcome. Suddenly, on seeing Marianne, the storm broke as, with a cry, he rushed across the rehearsal room and flung himself onto the floor in front of her, burying his head in her lap and howling. She was the only one present, it seemed, who was not transfixed as she responded calmly, and with what seemed like familiar tenderness, by stroking his head. It was at that point that Patrick, anxious to reassert his authority and, incidentally, to get rehearsals back on track, gently intervened, only to be met with an eruption of hostility from Terry who, quite simply, went berserk. It took four of us to hold him down on the floor, and when Patrick knelt down and tried to reassure him, Terry quite venomously spat in his face. An ambulance was quickly summoned and eventually, still struggling and completely out of control, Terry was straitjacketed and taken away. It was a horrifying moment, and one from which the company did well to recover, although the play, dealing as it did with madness, was never able to match it.

Even taking into account what had happened, I don't believe that Patrick ever looked back on his choice of Terry Scully as a mistake, although I am sure he positively regretted his decision to employ John Forgeham, whose behaviour throughout rehearsals and the run of the play, as Tom Georgeson and I had better reason to know than most, was thoroughly objectionable. He was a belligerent bully, self-opinionated and disruptive and, I thought at the time, possibly teetering on the edge of madness himself. On one occasion, during a dress-rehearsal, Patrick interrupted one of Forgeham's all-too-familiar diatribes by inviting him to come down into the auditorium for a private chat. Forgeham replied, with all the menace of an East End mobster, "You wanna speak to me, you come up here!" Patrick, very wisely in my opinion, backed off.

1973 Mad Dog - Hampstead Theatre Club - Georgina Ward

Let it be noted, however (and for what it's worth), that John Forgeham's name was forthwith added to my blessedly short list of actors I would go out of my way to avoid working with ever again; nor did I, but for very different reasons, ever work with Terry Scully again, and the part of the butler was taken over by Ken Wynne. I later heard, however that, following his recovery, he decided to give up acting and went on to become a market gardener somewhere up north. He was a dear man, and I do hope he found peace and a degree of contentment wherever he went and whatever he chose to do with the rest of his life.

The main reason I set such store by my rekindled friendship with Georgina was largely to do with what was happening at home. I had returned from Canada to find Jim McGoldrick still in place as Dawn's lover with no intention on her part of putting an end to the relationship. I had also learned that while I was away they had spent a weekend together in Paris which is the city we had chosen for our honeymoon. Sentimental nonsense, of course, but I can't deny that I would have borne it a little easier had they chosen Stuttgart. The pain I felt was indescribable, and happily impossible to recapture all these years later, but it was why I figuratively fell into Georgina's arms which she, equally figuratively, opened for me. She was a very special lady, and enormously attractive which, while it had no bearing on our relationship, certainly enhanced it. That she had chosen me to be her bosom buddy did wonders for my self-esteem at that time, and although I would gladly have taken it further, I was in no fit state to take rejection on the chin and left the ball firmly in her court which is where it remained. I don't know quite what I was looking for, except distraction, but it obviously wasn't a lasting relationship because I already had one of those, or so I believed; which brings me, kicking and screaming, to the point. The time has come for a little soul-searching, I think. As a self-appointed critic, firing off in all directions, it would be grossly unfair if I didn't have the courage to turn the gun on myself from time to time. I was faced with several options, so the situation wasn't entirely out of my control. I could pack my bags and leave home; I could ask Dawn to leave, or I could simply turn my back, using my actor's skills to feign indifference until she came to her senses. I did none of these things, or to be brutally frank, I was too weak to commit myself to any of them. When Dawn decided that the time had come to move house, I could have told her that I was happy to stay where I was, but I moved with her, and I was given every reason to believe that she wanted me to. In any case, I clearly wasn't prepared to test the water. A dichotomy existed in our relationship, and on one level nothing much had changed. We still enjoyed each other's company and shared the same opinions about most things. For much of the time it was relatively easy to sideline the issue but when it came back into focus again, as it did all too frequently, I was unable to dissemble; all rational decisions were swept away in the emotional turmoil. The very notion of giving it my blessing in the certain knowledge that it was bound to come to an end in time I was unable to act upon. Clearly my skills as an actor, however refined, did not apply to real life. Vacillation, petulance and an unbridled temper were all that I could fall back on in the circumstances, and while it is easy now to dissect it all and find little evidence of a spine in my conduct, I was at the mercy of passion during that period of my life which I now look back upon with some regret, if only because it affected someone else who was to become very dear to me and it hindered me from moving on.

We moved from Blackheath Hill to Kidbrooke Park Road on the other side of Blackheath for no other reason, or so it seemed, than to exchange rent for mortgage repayments. The flat we were leaving was larger and more characterful even if it did contain a tiny kitchen and involved a bit of a trek down two flights of stairs to reach the bathroom. It also boasted two bedrooms while the new flat, a ground-floor conversion, had only one. It was certainly very pleasant and, besides being equipped with more up-to-the-minute fixtures and fittings, it afforded a view from the living-room window of an attractive shared garden, into which I can't remember ever venturing. It also boasted an off-street parking area. But only a few weeks later, on an ill-starred journey to Devon, my Humber Sceptre was written off following a collision with a lamp-post in Aldershot (*non mea culpa*, having swerved to avoid a speeding car crossing my path), so the parking space remained just that. But the most significant thing about the move, besides changing from tenants to home-owners, was that we took out a joint mortgage, confirming our status as a married couple which, taking into account the helter-skelter ride of recent months, was a confirmation devoutly to be wished. The icing on the cake was applied some little time later when, for unexplained and unsolicited reasons, 'Darling Jim' became 'that unprincipled shit' and never darkened our doorway or my spirits again.

In the words of Stephen Sondheim, 'The end doesn't mean that it's over', but for the time being at any rate my pulse rate returned to something approaching normal, and life resumed its barely remembered tranquillity.

On the work front, as with my pulse rate, things had slowed down of late and, faced with the challenge of making mortgage repayments which were considerably larger than the rent we had paid on Blackheath Hill, I was obliged to take a job at the local branch of Augustus Barnett, the wine merchants. I was there for a good deal longer than I had hoped, and even began to enjoy it, particularly on a Saturday evening as I walked home with a case of very decent French claret for which I had paid 49p a bottle. I also had the pleasure of sharing the workspace with a very nice, quiet young man called Charles whom I invited back on several occasions to help us drink it. Owing to the temporary nature of the job, it was essentially a casual acquaintance, and indeed I hardly ever saw him again after I left Augustus Barnett's, which is why it's so difficult, all these years later, to describe him; but describe him I must to the best of my ability, for it was Charles who turned out to be the unlikely catalyst in my marriage and, indeed, in the shape of my life to come.

There was something ethereal about Charles, not exactly wraith-like, but certainly other-worldly and soft-footed. For instance, I would suddenly turn around at work to find him standing behind me although I had neither heard nor sensed his approach which was almost deferential, as though he were apologising for invading my space. Received wisdom prompts me to suggest that he was apologising for his very existence, although of course I didn't entertain any such thoughts at the time. As far as I was concerned, he was simply a bit of an introvert, a lost soul living away from his home in Bristol and in need of friendship which I was only too happy to offer him. He was, it has to be said, an attractive young man, possibly ten years younger than me which meant he was 15 or so years younger than Dawn. He was also good-looking in a fairly androgynous way which led me to suspect that if he leaned in any direction at all, which was open to question, it would be towards his own gender. But he was an extremely personable young man, and we enjoyed his company.

At some point during the spring of 1974, I was approached by Robin Midgeley, the Artistic Director of the recently opened Haymarket Theatre in Leicester, with an offer which, if not on the face of it exactly what dreams are made on, would have provided me with the opportunity to work in a new theatre and with a director previously unknown to me. There are many such reasons trotted out by actors as justifications for accepting the unacceptable, but desperation is not usually admitted to be one of them. The naked truth was that only a year earlier I had been flown over to Canada to play a massively demanding role in which I had achieved a considerable degree of success, and here I was, on the verge of accepting an offer from a provincial repertory theatre to take over the part of one of Joseph's brothers in *Joseph and the Amazing Technicolor Dreamcoat*. And I would have accepted it too had Robin Midgeley not urged me to come and see the show which was already up and running before committing myself. The long and the short of it was that I travelled to Leicester, saw the show, hated every minute of it, and was on my way out of the auditorium when I was confronted by Robin who must have read my mind, probably writ large on my face, as I tried to decide what I was going to say to him. "You didn't like it, did you?" he surmised. "No, I'm afraid I didn't", I said, and left it at that. He didn't seem to mind. He didn't even bother to ask me why. We said goodbye quite amicably, although I suspected he would never ask me to work with him again, and he never did. Well, I mused as I returned to London, obviously I wasn't as desperate as all that.

It couldn't have been more than a month or so later that I received a telephone call from Joan Knight. I hadn't worked with Joan or indeed spoken to her since 1965 when she ran the Castle Theatre in Farnham although I knew, of course, that she was now artistic director at Perth Theatre in faraway Scotland from where she was now calling to offer me the part of Naphtali, one of the brothers in *Joseph and the Amazing Technicolor Dreamcoat*. As luck would have it, she didn't pause long enough to allow me to open my mouth, changing forever the course of my life, before adding, "… and Sir Andrew Aguecheek in *Twelfth Night*".

It was hardly surprising, given that my departure for Scotland was imminent, that I should ask Charles to take my place and accompany Dawn to the Mermaid Theatre for a performance of *Cole*, a musical tribute to Cole Porter written by our friend, Benny Green, for which we had already booked tickets. As I set off in Bernard Lloyd's Datsun, kindly lent to me while its owner was with the Royal Shakespeare Company in New York, I was blithely unaware, and would in fact have derided the possibility that Cole Porter's songs were about to provide the prelude to a relationship that not only appeared to resolve any ambiguity there might have been about Charles's sexual orientation, but which effectively put a nail in the coffin of our marriage, a nail that wasn't finally hammered home for another two largely torturous years.

On a more positive note, it was a joy to find myself back inside a traditional, proscenium-arch theatre again after working in a variety of hybrids for so long. Perth Theatre, which opened its doors for the first time in 1900, had undergone a great many changes in its chequered history, but it remained not only a rare and beautiful example of its kind, but also at the very centre of the community it served. The partnership of Marjorie Dence and David Steuart had laid the foundations of the first ever repertory theatre in Scotland in 1935 which, in its first three years, had staged 144 plays. Marjorie Dence died in 1966 and, following a brief hiccough under the leadership of actor, Iain Cuthbertson, Perth Theatre was fortunate indeed to acquire the services of Joan Knight, a formidable lady of great insight and determination, as its Artistic Director. I also learned very early on in my association with her that Joan Knight was a good person to have on your side, the reverse being equally true. She was not, however, to direct either of the two productions in which I was to appear, although she presided over the company meeting on stage that launched the Autumn Season of 1974. I was surprised that I didn't know anybody in the company. Crossing paths with actors from the past had been a regular and reassuring feature of my life in the theatre, even as far away from home as Winnipeg. Making new friends is, of course, one of the most attractive aspects of our peripatetic profession, but a familiar face or two help to ease the way, especially when you have just arrived in a new town. Even more disquieting was that I found myself surrounded by people who were, almost without exception, younger than me and most of them considerably so. It was certainly the first time I had consciously seen myself, still a child actor at heart, superseded by a new generation. Of course, any cast assembled for a production of *Joseph* was bound to be youthful and I thought I might have very little in common with them. I found myself, almost by default, talking to a very attractive lady who turned out to be Joan Knight's secretary. Not that Jenny was nearly as old as I was, but she had about her an air of sophistication that obviously went hand-in-hand with her job and which I found more compatible with my senior status! She would also be the only one equipped to tell me who everyone else was, and she was in the process of pointing out people and naming names when I became aware of some activity behind me. I turned and saw, sitting on a set of steps upstage, and very much the focus of several photographers' lenses, a pert and petite raven-haired creature who was clearly very much at home in the limelight. "That's Lesley Mackie," Jenny said, following my gaze. "Local girl, is she?" I asked, somewhat condescendingly assuming that the photographers were not there on behalf of any national newspapers. "Yes", said Jenny, "she's from Dundee", which I supposed, not knowing exactly where Dundee was, meant that it was quite close to Perth. "She's working here at the moment, taking part in our summer season". Cute, I thought, although I didn't say so. I might also have thought that, had she been a good deal older, and had I been better acquainted with the poetry of Robert Burns, she might well have inspired him to write *Bonnie Lesley;* but I wasn't, and in any case she was far too young for *me*, never mind Rabbie Burns!

One of the most intriguing aspects of our business is that things seldom, if ever, turn out the way you expect them to. I had not exactly been looking forward to rehearsing *Joseph* and had steeled myself to endure the experience stoically with the happier expectations of *Twelfth Night* only a couple of weeks away. That the reverse turned out to be the case is something of an exaggeration as not even a disappointing production can entirely erase the pleasure of playing in that most delightful of Shakespeare's comedies. But working on *Joseph and the Amazing Technicolor Dreamcoat* was, against all the odds, a complete delight. This was due in no small measure to the director's vision which, disarmingly self-effacing for a director, relied on simplicity. Christopher Dunham, besides being an old colleague of Joan's, was also the artistic director at the Palace Theatre, Westcliff-on-Sea. Not only was he reassuringly in the same age bracket as myself, but we shared many points of reference and spoke the same kind of language in theatrical terms, so we got on very well together. It also turned out that I'd worked alongside his wife, June Watson, when she'd played Portia in *The Merchant of Venice* in Farnham.

I don't know if I was consciously aware of it at the time but, despite my long cherished passion for musicals, I had never appeared in one myself, and the prospect of making my musical début in a show that I had positively disliked when I saw it in Leicester, was both uninspiring and nerve-wracking in about equal measure. That it finally became merely nerve-wracking was due almost entirely to Chris Dunham's inspirational leadership. In Robin Midgeley's production, you couldn't see the wood for the trees, so cluttered was it with gratuitous effects, with lavish costumes and magnificent sets, not to mention ingratiating pantomime jokes and, finally, the appearance of a modern limousine bearing the successful Joseph back to his family; the whole thing masquerading as a large scale musical when it is nothing of the sort. The charm of Andrew Lloyd Webber's music and the wit and poignancy of Tim Rice's lyrics were quite lost on me in the Leicester production, as was the essential simplicity of the biblical story in which Joseph's coat of many colours is meant to stand out. Whether Perth Theatre could or could not have come up with a comparable budget was beside the point; their production was truer to the spirit of the piece and, in my opinion, served the interests of its creators far more faithfully. One of the reasons I remained nerve-wracked was that I had never danced on stage before, and only very rarely off it. I mentioned earlier that the only dance I had ever mastered was the Twist, which was not really a dance at all. It's not that I lacked a sense of rhythm or, indeed, that I was unable to move in time with the music. Dancing lessons would probably have resolved this dilemma, but the waltz, the foxtrot and the tango never appealed to me while the altogether more thrilling manifestations of the art by the likes of Bob Fosse and Jerome Robbins were way beyond my capabilities, even in my dreams. Fortunately for me and, let it be said, for one or two others in the company, Chris Dunham had cast himself as choreographer as well as director and, being extremely actor-friendly, he devised routines that even I could execute with a degree of panache.

Despite my earlier reservations about the youthfulness of the company, we all got along happily together. Several, like me, were London-based, thrown together with a handful of native Scots plus a few others from various points of the compass, and one from as far afield as Athens. I took a particular liking to Kevin Williams who distinguished himself very early on with his musicianship and with his keenly observed burlesque of Elvis Presley in the role of the Pharaoh. Kevin was everything I was not and so, I suppose, it was the attraction of opposites that drew us together. He reminded me a little of people I'd met on my brief excursion into the world of pop music nearly ten years earlier, and indeed he was part of that world. He was a born hustler, and whilst I would pay over the odds for something sooner than enter into negotiations, Kevin was compelled to bargain, even over the price of a plectrum. He paid little heed to rules, regulations or conventions so that while being in his company was often an unpredictable experience, it was certainly never dull. Fortunately, he had his lady-friend, Christine, in the company with him which, to some extent, reined him in. Campbell Morrison, 'Billy' as he was known, had no such restraining influence and was liable to go off like a fire-cracker on any pretext. Billy was a Glaswegian who enjoyed nothing more than reverting to type, parodying his origins and playing the hard man, inventing (or presumably inventing) stories that were intended to inspire caution in other men and lust in the opposite sex, but left you wondering why, if they were true, he was not serving an indeterminate prison sentence in Barlinnie. But there was another side to Billy which, while never admitting vulnerability, revealed him to be both warm and affectionate and, when it suited his image, quite chivalrous. As well as playing two of Joseph's brothers, Billy and I were paired as Pharaoh's butler and baker, so we got to know each other pretty well and, along with Kevin, I went on to work with him on a number of future occasions while the rest of the guys were, with one or two exceptions, but fleeting acquaintances. They were a convivial bunch nonetheless and we had a lot of fun together, both at work and at play, largely given over to poker schools, organised by Kevin Williams, of course, and flavoured by Campbell Morrison's 'Wild West' approach to the game.

Amongst the girls, nice enough though they all were, only one made any real impression on me, and that was the aforementioned Lesley Mackie who, I learned with some surprise, was the only member of the company whose face I had seen before and should have remembered. Less than a year earlier, Dawn and I had been to see Nicholas Roeg's acclaimed film adaptation of Daphne du Maurier's short story, *Don't Look Now*, at a cinema in Bromley and were treated, if that's the right word, to a supporting feature called *The Wicker Man*. There is a scene from it in which Edward Woodward as a po-faced police sergeant, investigating the disappearance of a young girl on a remote Scottish island, visits the local schoolroom, brusquely interrupting a lesson about the phallus, to enquire of the teacher the whereabouts of the missing child whose very existence she refuses even to acknowledge. He then takes note of an empty desk and makes his way towards it, stopping at an adjacent desk where sits a distinctly chubby schoolgirl who is clearly concealing something. He opens her desk and discovers, to his horror, a beetle tethered to a thread attached at the other end to a nail and walking round and round in a circle, slowly and ineluctably drawing closer to the nail against which it will eventually strangle itself, a process described by the girl, with a mixture of childlike guilt and precocious relish, the latter underlined with a tongue planted firmly and unambiguously in her cheek. Lesley was by no means chubby any longer; cuddly perhaps, and certainly curvaceous rather than angular, but the other two facets on display in that scene were there for all to see, the girl and the woman, constantly vying with each other so that you never quite knew with which one you were dealing, an ambivalence made all the more unsettling by the fact that she was barely five feet tall. She wasn't exactly pretty, at least not in the picture postcard sense, but her large brown eyes conveyed much more than conventional prettiness and found their perfect setting in a face that was both delightfully feminine and full of character. Another thing I discovered was that she had sung the Highland lament that accompanied the opening sequence in *The Wicker Man*, a hauntingly beautiful backing to one of the few memorable scenes in that picture, and from a voice that I now had the pleasure of hearing every day in her role as one of the narrators in *Joseph*.

The opportunity to discover so much about Lesley in such a comparatively short time was made possible by the fact that on my daily journey from Methven, a little village just outside Perth where I had mysteriously chosen to live, I passed the house which she shared with several other members of the company and, more often than not, stopped to give her a lift into the theatre. The return journey, depending on the time of night and any prior commitment I might have made to a poker session, occasionally led to an invitation to join her and her housemates for a late night drink; Cinzano, if my memory serves me right, or was it sweet martini? We certainly appeared to enjoy each other's company, but if my feelings about her were becoming more ambivalent by the day, as they surely were, they were tempered by the existence of a boy-friend who, while not actually living in Perth, had his home in Dundee, although at that particular time he was in the army and stationed in Loughborough, a long, long way from home. It was, quite literally, a boy-next-door romance which began after she had returned home following graduation from the Royal Scottish Academy of Music and Drama in Glasgow two years earlier, and it might well have worked out in the long term had Lesley been a typical girl-next-door instead of an actress, and a particularly flirtatious one to boot. She certainly took the relationship seriously, so I was duly circumspect. Jack was, after all, the right age for her, and neither was he already married. If I was tempted at times to disregard these reservations, it was largely due to a suspicion I harboured that the attraction I felt was mutual. Why else were we spending so much time together, and not just at work but during our leisure hours too? I discovered the answer to this when she invited me round for a meal one Thursday evening towards the end of the rehearsal period. I was leaning against the door-jamb in her kitchen, watching her as she concocted a steak pie, ostensibly making sure that she didn't leave the plastic-handled knife in the dish before she covered it with pastry which she confessed she had done on a previous occasion, but in truth because I liked watching her whatever she was doing, and being busily engaged in the kitchen was new to me, and apparently fairly new to her too. Quite spontaneously, as she passed me, I took her arm, pulled her towards me and kissed her. She didn't exactly push me away, but she took a couple of steps back when I released her and, her brown eyes even larger than usual, she gasped, "But I thought you were gay!" So *that* was it! I'd been cast in the role of 'gay friend'. Suddenly it all fell into place. Lesley was a very attractive young lady whose outgoing personality and essential warmth hinted at intimacy which, given her lack of height, made her vulnerable to predators. What she was looking for was someone who enjoyed her company and with whom she could be entirely herself, safe in the knowledge that he wouldn't be remotely interested in any of the other goods that were on display. The irony of the situation was not lost on me, for had I not cast Charles in that very role when I introduced him to Dawn? I believed that Charles had been engaged in homosexual practices until he met Dawn, whilst I merely gave that impression, and even then only to Lesley Mackie as far as I could tell. To give her her due, I suppose she had good reason to suspect, in her delightful naivety, that I might have leant in that direction. For instance, I hadn't mentioned my marriage at that time which I may well have concealed for predatory reasons of my own, although I don't recall any deliberate omission on my part, and in any case, getting a word in edgeways with Lesley, who talked incessantly and faster than anyone I had ever met, meant that you had to be fairly economical with words. But even putting the question of my marital status aside, I had to acknowledge the impression I must have made on her, conditioned as she obviously was by her upbringing alongside the legs-wide-apart machismo of the average Scottish male. My hair, for instance, which I always wore fairly long in any case, was shoulder-length now, grown on purpose to avoid the inconvenience of wearing a wig as Andrew Aguecheek, and highlighted as it was by the odd glint of grey, natural although premature, not to mention my predilection for pink shirts, I could well understand that it may have given rise, at the very least, to a question mark. "Well, I'm not", I said and kissed her again.

Joseph and the Amazing Technicolor Dreamcoat was if anything, more fun to play than it had been to rehearse. For my part, this was largely due to the fact that it was an entirely unexpected pleasure. Full and enthusiastic audiences greeted every performance and standing ovations invariably brought each of them to a close. Not only was this a phenomenon unfamiliar to me, except at the Royal Opera House, Covent Garden, where it was taken for granted, but I was given to understand that, as far as Perth was concerned, it had been an entirely alien concept until now. Audiences for 'Joseph' contained a large number of young people, of course, whose responses were bound to be less inhibited than those of the older, more reserved element that made up the vast majority of Perth's regular theatregoers, but as far as

I could make out, no such distinction existed at the end of 'Joseph' when not one bum, neither firm nor wizened, remained seated as we took our curtain calls. My enjoyment was further enhanced by the contrasting disappointment I felt as we embarked upon rehearsals for *Twelfth Night*. Not that I was anything but delighted to be playing Aguecheek, a part for which I would not normally have considered myself suitable, at least not physically, the character being traditionally seen as tall and willowy. But that was one of the great joys of working in a repertory theatre back in those days, and particularly in a repertory theatre whose policy was dictated by such a formidable woman as Joan Knight. The actual production of *Twelfth Night*, however, was presided over, not by Joan herself, but by her Assistant Director.

Andrew McKinnon was an admirable man in many ways, and one of the most intellectually challenging people I had worked with since my time with David William in Regent's Park. Unfortunately, however, Andrew was at his most challenging outside of the rehearsal room in which he soon established himself as a bit of an onlooker. Not that directors who have a lot to say for themselves are necessarily good directors. There are, indeed, times when as an actor you might wish they would simply shut up and let you get on with it, an implausible scenario made all the more improbable by virtue of the very word 'director' and the authority bestowed along with it, giving them *idées au dessus de ses gares*. There are those, of course, who have earned their stripes and with whom it is a privilege to work. Very occasionally, you might be persuaded to jump through hoops to satisfy the demands of a director who inspires unquestioning confidence. But these are rare creatures with whom my only quarrel is that they have tacitly allowed lesser beings to share their job title. I should immediately point out that not one word of this polemic, which is nothing but a quick diversionary canter on an old hobby-horse, is meant to refer to Andrew McKinnon. Whilst I felt that Andrew was no great shakes as a director, he was a perfectly charming and erudite facilitator. Now there's a word! Can you imagine it? 'The production was facilitated by ...' Time to dismount, I think! Anyway, Andrew had a perfect understanding of the text and the skill to communicate it. What he didn't have in any great measure was theatrical flair, and what he lacked entirely was the common touch. He was a scholar whose natural habitat, I thought, lay in the olive grove of Academe rather than in the circle bar. But he had certainly done his homework, and he had an intriguing concept for the production which he enthusiastically imparted to us on the very first day; it was to be 'Hogarthian'. We were suitably intrigued and waited, in vain as it turned out, for Hogarth's name to be mentioned again. Beyond the fact that the costume designs placed it in the early 18th century, no other reference was made to that particular artist that threw any light on Andrew's inspiration. His name, however, did come up a few times in whispered asides during performance and, on one occasion towards the end of the run, with a triumphant cry of "Hogarth!" from Sir Toby and company as they staggered drunkenly off the stage.

Quite a few members of the 'Joseph' company stayed on for *Twelfth Night,* amongst whom both Kevin Williams and Campbell Morrison featured in relatively minor roles while Nigel Williams, an impressive Joseph, made a valiant stab at Sir Toby although he lacked the weight of years. He was more than ably abetted, however, as was I, by Lesley Mackie's delightfully mischievous Maria. A somewhat surprising newcomer to the company was Leonard Whiting who played Feste. Leonard had achieved something approaching stardom when he had played Romeo in Franco Zeffirelli's filmed version of Shakespeare's play a decade earlier, but obviously his star was no longer in the ascendant, else why had he come to Perth? He was a pleasant, good-looking young man, which is nearly all that I can remember about him, except that he took a fancy to Lesley and that I was obliged to take a corner rather too sharply to throw them apart whilst sharing the back seat of my car. This was, startlingly, the first time I had felt possessive about someone who wasn't Dawn. We both knew, of course, that our relationship would come to an end when I returned to London. I had come clean about my wedded state as soon as we had dealt with the question of mistaken proclivities. She was also well aware of the precarious state my marriage was in, if only because our time together was punctuated by telephone calls which invariably left me unfit for company, even hers. But if Lesley wasn't the cure for what ailed me, I could not have wished for a more effective palliative. She was a fun-loving girl, uncomplicated in her outlook, and seemingly reconciled to the problems that inevitably accompanied our being together, and which she handled with a stoicism that belied her overt girlishness; but then she was a mass of contradictions. In our short time together I had witnessed her genuine vulnerability as well as her defiant independence which was no mere show either but deep-rooted in a personality that desired attention but only on her own terms. She delighted in being cast as a flibbertigibbet and was capable of playing it up to the hilt. But her essential femininity was strongly laced with a no-nonsense egalitarian approach to life which insisted on standing her round in the pub or the theatre bar while many others of her sex were only too happy to smile and say, "Thank you very much." How she managed to do this on a regular basis and make her wages last until Friday while the rest of us were asking for a sub by Wednesday remains an unsolved mystery. She was, let it be said, quite capable of annoying me too. On a number of occasions we were invited with a few other members of the company to Andrew McKinnon's flat in York Place where we were expected to participate in a game called 'Botticelli'. These evenings were patently designed to demonstrate Andrew's encyclopaedic knowledge at the expense of his guests' self-esteem, selecting as his subjects the most obscurely celebrated painters from the 15th century and composers whose names were all but unpronounceable. Being the most senior contestant and something of an intellectual snob, I took it all very seriously and keenly resented my own shortcomings. Lesley, on the other hand, was perfectly happy to play the dumb brunette, clearly deriving more pleasure from the laughter her answers inspired than I did from my very occasional success. Taking her to task for playing to the gallery, which I did from time to time, was liable to evoke a response which had nothing to do with self-reproach and everything to do with a childlike obduracy, as if to say, "if you don't like me the way I am, see if I care", and underlining it by making sure the next time I saw her she would be engaged in some other activity she knew wouldn't meet with my approval, like walking down the street in her least alluring garb, and munching pickled onions out of a paper bag. The trouble was, of course, that I did like her the way she was because whatever she did, she made me smile. Towards the end of the season we spent an enjoyable couple of days, accompanied by Kevin and Christine, in Oban on the west coast of Scotland, and I remember telling Lesley, as we walked along the seafront, that I was 35 years old when I was, in fact, 36. How pathetic was that? Did I really think that one year was going to make a jot of difference to the perceptions of a 23 year old? And what did it matter anyway, since we were about to say goodbye to each other?

Notwithstanding a tinge of sadness, I experienced a great sense of relief when the season came to an end. I simply couldn't get back to London quickly enough. When it came down to it, Lesley too, had her own life to live and her own future to determine without me around to muddy the waters. Whether I had played the role of catalyst in her relationship with Jack I had no way of knowing, and the fact that I couldn't see a way ahead for them as a couple was beside the point.

What was entirely the point, as far as I was concerned, was that I had a broken marriage to mend and, quite unintentionally, Lesley had played a large part in equipping me to deal with it, whatever the outcome. For all manner of reasons she and I certainly didn't have a future together; not only was she far too young for me, it was also unlikely I would ever return to Perth. As I began the drive home on that Sunday morning in mid-October, I also recollected a few other instances that may well have contributed to a fondly remembered interlude, but were hardly the stuff upon which long-term relationships were founded. Her literary tastes, for instance, were pretty well confined to *Good Housekeeping,* although I suspected that, along with eating pickled onions in the street and seeking new acquaintances from amongst the Young Conservatives of Perth, this was as much an act of defiance as a chosen path.

Nothing however, not even these fond memories, could have prepared me for the reality of my homecoming. Having known Dawn for almost 20 years, and having been married to her for 13 of them, enjoying along the way a professional partnership that brought us together and tested our compatibility in a variety of ways untried in most other marriages, I had every reason to believe that our bond was indissoluble. I also knew better than anyone else, although I never once seriously considered it might apply to our relationship, how intransigent she could be when it came to burning bridges. I was there, after all, when she told Frank Dunlop what he could do with his job when she was wardrobe mistress in Coventry back in 1955. I had been only too aware of her whittling away at her career as a stage designer as, one by one, her employers failed to live up to her expectations, and I had witnessed her icy dismissal of Peter Dews at the Ravinia Festival in Chicago, pre-empting a more general disillusionment with him amongst the company. More recently, of course, there was the case of Jim McGoldrick who had, for reasons unknown to me, been banished forever from her presence, let alone from her affections. Why then had I not even imagined that it could happen to me too? Not that she was insensitive to my feelings or in any way deliberately cruel. But she had made up her mind. She had reached a turning-point in her life, she said, and it was time for a new broom. The fact that my return had pretty-well coincided with her 41st birthday and that our relationship had been foundering for much of the past year, led me to consider the possibility that she had reached a psychological watershed of some kind. Not that such a consideration provided any kind of balm for the pain I felt. Clichés and metaphors abound, none of which capture the rawness of the wound, and amongst which 'broken-hearted' is undoubtedly the most euphemistic. There was nothing remotely romantic or poetic about the state I was in, and while it is an agony not easily recollected, like childbirth (or so I am given to understand), it is also an experience that alienates you from society.

There was no question that we could go on living under the same roof, for even had it been a two-bedroom flat, which it wasn't, Dawn made it quite clear that she was prepared to move out if I insisted on staying and, as far as I was concerned, the very notion of living alone in Kidbrooke Park Road, the move there having been her idea in the first place, and which she had occupied more constantly than I had, was inappropriate to say the least. As luck would have it, and I was in sore need of a bit of that, Bernard Lloyd had not only left me the keys to his car but also the keys to his flat, asking me to keep an eye on the place during his absence. So I took up residence there for the time being, returning to Kidbrooke Park Road, only a ten minute walk away, to pick up my belongings in a piecemeal kind of way which, although convenient, effectively prevented me from making a clean break, allowing me to go on believing, from day to day, in the possibility of some kind of reconciliation. It was only with the approach of Christmas that the axe fell. It was not that we had ever celebrated Christmas in a traditional way but simply because Dawn and I had never spent it apart, that I somehow believed there would be a sentimental rapprochement of sorts, if only for that season. I was consequently devastated when, on one of my more or less frequent visits, she told me that she intended to spend Christmas with Charles at his home in Bristol.

It was only when considering the alternatives to being alone at that time, that I lighted upon the only one that held the kind of solace and unquestioning companionship that I craved. And so it was that I arrived at Euston station early one morning in mid-December 1974 where, a little the worse for wear and decidedly thinner, I caught the through-train back to Perth.

oOoOo

Nineteen

There are years I would not care to live through again, and 1975 was the worst of them. Not that it was without its lighter moments or, indeed, its professionally challenging ones. Again, with the benefit of hindsight, it is only too easy to attribute my overriding sense of desolation and the mood swings that accompanied it, not to mention my questionable behaviour at times, to my own weakness and irresolution. Had I known at the time that my separation from Dawn was a blessing in disguise, and that it marked the beginning of a new chapter in my life instead of an end to all that I held dear, I would obviously have dealt with it in a very different way. But life simply isn't like that; and whilst on the subject, it's worth mentioning that when a marriage guidance counsellor I just happened to be sitting next to at a dinner-party one evening, and to whom I was obviously unburdening myself, told me that what I was suffering was akin to grief from which, like grief, it would probably take two years, more or less, to recover, I all but laughed in her face. The very idea that the curtain which had fallen so precipitately on my life would rise again to reveal a brand new landscape was, given my state of mind at the time, a ludicrous prediction, bordering on the psychic. I never met that lady again, but had I done so two years later, I would have hailed her as a seer.

Whether my brief visit to Perth at Christmas had anything to do with it or not, I readily accepted Joan Knight's offer to return in February, initially to swell the ranks of the company in a production of Brecht's *Mother Courage*, but principally to play the title role in a Scottish adaptation of Nikolai Gogol's *The Government Inspector* which, following the run of *Mother Courage*, was scheduled to embark upon a tour of obscure provincial towns with exotic-sounding names like Beith and Troon. The only thing I can clearly remember about *Mother Courage*, aside from Jan Wilson's plucky performance as the mother, is Lesley Mackie as her daughter, Kattrin. There are several reasons, besides the quality of her performance, that I remember it so clearly. Having been worked off her feet for the previous eight or nine months, Lesley had had the temerity, born of ingenuousness I think, to ask Joan for a 'play out' to which Joan had responded with apparent largesse by casting her as Kattrin which she said would be as good as a 'play out' since Kattrin was dumb and therefore Lesley wouldn't have any lines to learn. The fact that she was barely off-stage throughout the entire play, together with the physical demands the part made on her, not only in compensating for her inability to express herself in any other way, but finally in a death-defying fall from a ten-foot high roof, albeit onto a well-placed mattress out of sight of the audience, would have made learning George Bernard Shaw's *St Joan* a comparably alternative 'play out.' To illustrate the point, Christopher Small from the Glasgow Herald wrote: 'There is a breathtaking moment at the end when dumb Kattrin is drumming to rouse the sleeping town as the soldiers who were to surprise and sack it raise their weapons to shoot her down; she defies them with a smile of beatific triumph, they fire, and without a sound in one swift motion, she turns and falls off the roof, diving out of her life and theirs. How Lesley Mackie manages this without severe injury is a mystery, but it is the fitting climax to a beautiful performance which, without a word spoken, puts dumb, homely, simple Kattrin with her grotesque gestures and her inarticulate animal cries, where she belongs, at the moral heart of the play, emblem of the real goodness that only speaks in deeds.'

It will be all too clear by now that Lesley and I had grown closer, although I was in no condition to measure the distance nor to consider the implications. That she lifted me out of my emotional quagmire for long periods at a time was unquestionable. That she made me laugh more often than I would have thought possible was surprisingly true, and that we enjoyed moments of genuine tenderness, while it was strange to me, was undeniable. Not that either of us had any degree of permanency in mind although, to be perfectly honest, I had no real idea what Lesley might have felt had I been free of the ties that bound me.

Andrew McKinnon did a very good adaptation of *The Government Inspector*, which turned out to be an enjoyable experience. A fault-line, however, ran through the project that made its basic premise difficult to believe in at times. Gogol's play had been set amongst a peasant community in rural Russia where the leading character, bringing with him all the sophistication of an urban background, finds it all too easy to exploit his mistaken identity. It was hardly surprising, I suppose, that a Scottish version of the play was going to be set in Scotland, but it's a well-known and well-documented fact that Scots are not noted for their gullibility whatever their background or however remote their habitat. Not for nothing are they known as a canny race, and whilst I am aware that I'm talking about stereotypes here, and that every village anywhere will probably harbour its idiot, the Scottish character does not easily lend itself to being duped, so that their ready acceptance of this stranger in their midst as a Government Inspector, and not only that but an English Government Inspector, undoubtedly raised a few Scottish eyebrows in the audience.

I returned briefly to Perth at the end of the tour before heading back to London, taking with me fond memories of a blonde-bewigged Lesley sitting on a swing and singing *Someone to Watch Over Me* in a delightfully vivacious performance as Kay in the 1927 Gershwin musical *Oh, Kay!* Far removed from the shapeless bundle of inarticulate energy she presented as Kattrin, but just as believable, it was becoming easier to understand why Joan Knight was reluctant to give her a break.

Parting with Lesley was comparatively easy if only because Joan had already invited me back for the summer season, an offer I was not about to refuse, particularly as it included the chance to direct my first professional production. There were other reasons, of course, for wanting to put as many miles as possible between myself and London. In the course of a series of depressing telephone calls whilst in Perth, I had been left in no doubt as to the terminal nature of my marriage. Dawn had decided to move down to Bristol and set up home with Charles. This meant selling the flat in Kidbrooke Park Road unless I wanted to buy her out and go on living there myself. But as I neither wanted, nor could afford, to take her up on that offer, the flat went on the market and we proceeded to lay claim to the innumerable objects we had gathered around us during the 13 years we had lived together. This went surprisingly smoothly and, apart from the odd emotional outburst and the occasional tear, we both of us dealt with the distasteful task in a remarkably civilised manner. There was, thankfully, no dispute over the ownership of our record collection since, apart from a few classical pieces, she showed little or no interest in inheriting any of the numerous Frank Sinatra, Ella Fitzgerald or Judy Garland albums we had accumulated. I thought this was surprisingly generous of her until I realised that Dawn's taste in popular music was strongly influenced by the person with whom she was sharing her life and that, since her affair with Charles had begun, she had been almost exclusively hooked on *The Grateful Dead*.

There were compensations, however. Her departure from London meant that I was not continually haunted by her presence only a few streets away, although on her occasional visits I was almost always sure to be there at Victoria coach station to meet her, to accompany her on her errands and to see her off on the bus back to Bristol at the end of the day. I looked forward to those occasions which were always companionable and very often affectionate. No man, no matter how intimately involved with her, knew her as well as I did, and no woman could have been better acquainted with me. It was Dawn, after all, who had moulded me and imbued me with tastes and opinions which, in time, had become mine. We had shared too much to be able to turn our backs on each other so peremptorily, although I do wonder from time to time whether she would have gone to the same lengths as I did to stay in touch, or simply have allowed us to drift apart. Whatever our motives, they sadly differed in one respect; she obviously had no desire to turn the clock back, whilst I looked forward to every meeting with an optimism that owed more to romantic fiction than reality, with the result that I was left feeling lonely and abandoned at the parting of our ways. It certainly improved with time but whether this had anything to do with the *Ativan* tablets I had been prescribed to combat my anxiety problems or whether I simply came to accept the situation for what it was, I have no way of knowing. It could also have had something to do with other distractions, including a television job I walked into shortly after returning from Perth. It was called *One of the Family*, written by Charlotte Bingham and Terence Brady, the third in a trilogy of plays about marriage, and it was directed by my old friend, Richard Martin, with whom I had last worked all but ten years earlier on the BBC2 serial, *Ransom for a Pretty Girl*. This one featured Polly Adams alongside Alec Guinness's son, Matthew, and a very diverting episode it turned out to be, not only because in the main it was fun to do – working with Dickie Martin was always fun. In the middle of rehearsals, however, Joanna Van Gyseghem, who was playing one of the leading characters, collapsed and was rushed to hospital suffering from what I understood to be 'fallopian tube problems'. Having been married to a woman for 13 years without once broaching the subject of childbirth, I was astonishingly ignorant about those parts of the female anatomy that couldn't be seen or touched. When she didn't return the following day, however, and was immediately replaced by Phillipa Gail, I gathered that her condition was of a serious nature, and totally unrelated to indigestion, which had been my initial diagnosis.

I was also singularly fortunate in having somewhere to live in what had become over the years my favourite part of London. Having informed Bernard Lloyd of my enforced migration to his flat, he had let me know that not only was he happy to have it occupied during his protracted absence, but that I was to regard it as my home for as long as I wanted. It was a spacious flat which, even with Bernard's return, would comfortably accommodate two people in a virtually self-contained environment, and so I was perfectly happy to accept

Bernard's generous offer and, for the next two years, 23 Vanbrugh Park, on the fringes of Blackheath and but a stone's throw from glorious Greenwich Park, became my home. It was there that my life, or what passed for it at that time, took on a somewhat surreal quality, no doubt exacerbated by the *Ativan*, but which had its roots in the problems faced by a 37 year old married man having to make unilateral decisions – decisions that affected no one else in the entire world – for the first time in his adult life. Much of it was like a strange dream in which I drifted from moment to moment without any real sense of purpose, but just occasionally it took on the more disturbing characteristics of a nightmare, like the time I returned from an assignation in Putney, took my tablet and almost immediately fell asleep, only to be woken shortly afterwards by the front-door bell ringing with a bad-tempered persistency that I could scarcely ignore. I staggered to the door which I barely had time to open before two uniformed policemen, an officer and a sergeant, pushed their way past me and into the flat where the officer made straight for the telephone, situated on a small table at the far end of the hall, while the sergeant, altogether burlier and more aggressive than his superior, pinned me against the wall and accused me of making 'bomb hoax calls'. In my soporific state, I remember trying to make sense of the accusation. What the hell was a bomb hoax call, and how did they know it was a hoax? Maybe the bomb hadn't gone off yet, or were they still looking for it? I was utterly bewildered. "I've only just got in", I managed to say; "I went straight to bed". The sergeant wasn't having any of that. "Yeah? Where have you been then?" Without considering the implications, I said, "I spent the evening with a friend in Putney". "What's this friend's telephone number then?" he demanded. The thought of a friend being woken up in the middle of the night and quizzed by the police pulled me up short, banishing the last remnants of my drug-induced drowsiness. "I haven't a clue", I lied. But he hadn't given up yet. "How did you get there?" he persisted. "I drove there", I replied. He obviously thought he'd caught me out. "And you say you only just got back? So the engine'll still be hot, won't it?" I ventured to suggest that it probably would be, and pointed him in the direction of my car. All this while the officer had been engaged in a muted conversation on the phone which drew to a close as the sergeant returned. "Well", I said, "was the engine still hot?" "Warm", he said grudgingly. He was then taken aside by the officer who murmured something about a mistaken digit and left without a word. The sergeant followed him, turning at the door and glowering at me before making his final exit. "We'll never know the real truth, will we?" was his parting shot. I wondered for a while afterwards whether their visit had been prompted by my relatively recent involvement with the National Council for Civil Liberties which, on several occasions, had taken the Lewisham police force to task, mainly for its cavalier attitude towards the local immigrant population. But having moved home twice since then and currently living as a guest in someone else's, it seemed an unlikely motive, although their attitude and general behaviour certainly vindicated our campaign, and left me thinking how much worse it might have been if I'd been born a different colour. The following morning I woke up wondering if it had actually happened at all, or if I'd simply dreamed it up under the influence of *Ativan*.

The 1975 summer season in Perth opened on July 29th with yet another Ray Cooney/John Chapman farce called *Move Over, Mrs. Markham!* This was followed by *Cowardy Custard*, and finally by *The Day After The Fair*, Frank Harvey's adaptation of the Thomas Hardy short story, *On The Western Circuit*, remembered by me now for many reasons, not the least being that it marked my professional début as a director, and that I was fortunate to have been given a play devoid of any challenging theatrical effects to cut my teeth on. The leading character, a very English Emma Bovary called Edith Harnham, trapped in a loveless and childless marriage, is prevailed upon by her unlettered maid, Anna, to reply on her behalf to a series of love-letters from a young London-based lawyer whom she had met and fallen in love with at a country fair. Deceived into believing that the beautifully expressive letters he receives were indeed written by the maid, and finally learning from one of them that she is pregnant, he has no hesitation in proposing marriage to her. Too late, he discovers the deception, realising that he has given his heart to the writer of the letters and that she too, in opening her heart to him, albeit by proxy, has experienced an awakening of love hitherto unknown to her.

It was predictable in the circumstances, I suppose, that Joan had already made up her mind to give the part of Edith to Janet Michael, a local actress with whose work I was not familiar at that time. There was no arguing with Joan, however – there seldom was – and as it turned out, although not in possession of Edith's fragile beauty, Janet was certainly an accomplished actress, and so I had very little reason to complain.

It was surprising, however – and all the more so retrospectively – that the bubble I had inhabited for such a long time burst so suddenly and so peremptorily. But burst it did, and the very first thing I did was to seek out Lesley Mackie, and suggest we should make a commitment to each other by choosing to live together. Lesley, being Lesley, topped all other surprises by actually agreeing, and shortly afterwards we moved into a little flat in Victoria Street, procured for us by the landlord of the pub across the road. The flat was pretty basic, lacking in all but the most essential amenities, but it did give us the chance to experience the kind of privacy it is impossible to achieve in shared accommodation and which, in any case, only a week earlier, neither of us had dreamed was even remotely on the cards. In fact, I have very happy memories of our time in Victoria Street. There were times, in fact, when I genuinely believed I had found the answer, when thoughts of a future with Dawn were sidelined, as Lesley and I grew closer together, took more pleasure in each other's company and enjoyed a greater degree of intimacy than we had hitherto known. But while this new arrangement suited us, it certainly didn't meet with universal approval, and was decidedly frowned upon by Lesley's parents and, in particular, by her father who wrote to her that she would never now walk down the aisle on his arm. With half of her family, as well as her mother and father, living only 20 miles down the road in Dundee, his reaction to the news that his only daughter was living with a married man was perfectly justified, although at the time I was more concerned by the distress it caused Lesley. Then there was Joan Knight, apparently happy for us, and promising to intercede on Lesley's behalf with her parents, but who also on one memorable occasion told her that she was 'never to think of marrying Terry Wale', an edict delivered from a toilet seat in the Ladies' Room at the theatre, with the door wide open, which did nothing – according to Lesley, who had only come in to wash her hands – to undermine Joan's authority.

Meanwhile, the summer season continued to unfold, most enjoyably with that delightful celebration of Noël Coward's music, *Cowardy Custard*, in which I was allocated several solos, including the opening number, *Where Are the Songs We Sung?* and, even more challengingly, *Nina (from Argentina)*, if only because I was all too familiar with Coward's own definitive version of it. I also joined with the other male members of the company in a variety of upper-class guises in that classic, *The Stately Homes of England*, as well as partnering a terpsichorean Lesley Mackie in *I Like America*. She was mostly partnered throughout the rest of the show and, somewhat irksomely, in the more romantic duets, by a considerably younger man, a relative newcomer named Kevin Whately. Kevin and I shared a dressing-room alongside our Musical Director and accompanist, John Scrimger, whose name and reputation were already well-established in Perth and who was just as much at home occupying centre stage, which he did throughout *Cowardy Custard*, as he was in the orchestra pit. It was John who recommended a glass of port as a suitable lubricant for the vocal chords, referred to in musical circles as 'P for the V', and as neither Kevin nor I had ever experienced the kind of demands made on the vocal chords by a show like *Cowardy Custard*, we were more than happy to take his professional advice. I do not recall now what dosage was prescribed, but I do have vivid memories of asking, quite frequently, whose turn it was to buy the port. Whether or not it improved the quality of our voices it certainly enhanced our camaraderie.

1975 Cowardy Custard - Perth Theatre with Martyn James, Kevin Whately and Roy Boutcher.

At an earlier meeting with the wardrobe department to discuss costume requirements for *The Day After the Fair*, it soon became clear that, while their stock of late Victorian costumes was perfectly adequate and, with minor alterations here and there, would easily meet the requirements of the play, there was one dress they would not be able to supply nor, in the absence of a costume designer, could it be created on the premises. I wanted a dress that was an outward expression of Edith's transformation, a spring-awakening as she begins to experience the power of love for the first time in her life, and as far as I was concerned there was only one person capable of interpreting that vision. The wardrobe department raised no objections and the budget allowed for it, so I invited Dawn to design and make the dress. She was happy to accept the offer, if only to renew her acquaintance with a theatre she had worked in long before even she and I had met.

The Day After the Fair was the first play I had directed since 1958, and that had been an amateur production presented by RAF Cardington's Dramatic Society. A lot of water had flowed under the bridge since then and most notably in my encounter with – or growing awareness of – 'directors' theatre'. It was in 1973 that Peter Hall had, in his own words, 'ascended the throne' as director of the National Theatre and, while by no means alone in his pretensions, by his own admission became the first crowned king of a regime over which the director now reigned supreme. I had, of course, been no more than a child when I made my first professional appearance, and my formative years had been spent under the baton of singularly gifted directors such as Tyrone Guthrie, a giant in more ways than one, and whose hierarchical supremacy went unchallenged for the simple reason that he was brilliant at his job. I had no way of knowing at that time, of course – and in all probability they had not clawed their way to the surface by then – that there were others whose variable talents were not reflected in the degree of power they enjoyed. But somewhere along the line, a gradual usurpation had taken place which allowed them the unquestioned authority to dictate, not only decisions taken in the rehearsal room, but the future of theatre itself. Only a couple of years earlier an attempt was made by a group of actors, led by Ian McKellen and Edward Petherbridge, to correct this imbalance and to restore the actor's historic pre-eminence with the formation of The Actors' Company. They and their colleagues, all actors, would choose the plays, cast them and engage the services of a sympathetic director to oversee the production, their inspiration being Harley Granville Barker, one of the most influential actor/director/playwrights of the 20th century, who said that 'the art of the theatre is the art of the actor, first, last, and all of the time'. It's worth pointing out, I think, that it was David William, an actor/director of considerable stature in our own time, who urged them to turn their dream into reality. But, sad to say, The Actors' Company was destined not to survive for a variety of reasons, one of which was that its leading members were lured away by offers they couldn't refuse.

I cannot truthfully say that I was unduly troubled by any of these considerations as I took my place before the assembled cast and backstage team on the first day of rehearsals for *The Day After the Fair*. For a start, I had never entertained dreams of power, not even in my sleep, and even if I had they would have been totally eclipsed at that time by concerns about my own competence. I was only thankful that, in an amateur capacity or not, I had been responsible for staging several plays in the past and was well aware – if only due to the lowliness of my rank in the RAF – that the only way to achieve authority is to earn respect.

I was singularly fortunate in that my task was made less intimidating by the absence in the play of any great technical demands, and more rewarding by the fact that, having worked alongside them in the previous two productions, the actors were only too happy, at least for starters, to hand me the reins. They, in their turn, seasoned players that they mostly were, made my job entirely pleasurable – well almost entirely. My only real challenge was in using every means at my disposal to get a credible performance out of Kevin Whately. Now Kevin, as I have already said, was an affable young man, an unaffected Tynesider, whose company I had enjoyed in the dressing-room, but whose limitations as a stage actor, seemed to be confined to those very same characteristics. He was called upon in *The Day After the Fair* to portray Charles, a budding young barrister from London on a tour of the Western Circuit in the late nineteenth century whose looks and charm bewitch an ill-educated servant girl. It was surprising and frustrating to discover that Kevin appeared to neither understand the style of the period in which the play was set, nor the essentially charismatic qualities of a man who was capable of engendering such extreme emotions in two vastly different women, separated not only by age but by birth and education. It soon became clear that with Kevin what you saw and heard was what you got, so that when the final curtain fell you were left in no doubt that he had made the right decision by marrying the servant-girl! As you'll probably know, Kevin found his métier and went on to achieve television stardom.

In all other respects the production fared well and was favourably received, the honours being shared by Lesley, of course, as the deliciously gullible maid, and by Janet Michael on her journey from respectable maturity to love-stricken adolescence, her transformation perfectly captured by Dawn's beautifully designed apple-green dress. It goes without saying that there were lessons to be learned if I wished to go on directing, although there was only one that I consciously took note of at the time. There is a scene, fairly early on in the play when Anna, hopelessly struggling to reply to Charles' first letter before enlisting Edith's help, is interrupted by the arrival of Sara, the other household maid, whereupon Anna panics and quickly hides her scribblings. At first, I was only vaguely aware that she was alone on stage for longer than she had been in rehearsal, and it was only when she glanced over her shoulder for the third time that I realised something had gone wrong. Where the hell was Sara? Naturally, I panicked and rushed backstage where I encountered Judi Maynard in the middle of changing into her next costume, having totally forgotten the scene she was supposed to be playing. Looking back, I somehow doubt that my headlong approach, heralded by words similar to those that had gone through my head when I was sitting out front, was the ideal way to handle the situation. But the real lesson, and the one I took to heart, was that if a director feels the need to sit down during a first night – and I seldom did thereafter – it has to be on a seat adjacent to an exit sign right up at the back of the auditorium, and certainly not ever in the middle of the stalls surrounded by paying customers!

The extraordinary success of *Joseph and the Amazing Technicolor Dreamcoat* the previous year had encouraged Joan Knight to adopt the policy, at least for the time being, of opening the autumn season with a musical. I can only hazard a guess at the sequence of events that led to *Cloud Nine* being that musical, although I'm pretty sure that I played a significant part in getting it staged at Perth Theatre. My not entirely infallible memory suggests that, after our return to London the previous year, Kevin Williams and I met and he asked me if I would care to listen to a tape-recording of the score he had written for a musical called *Cloud Nine*. It was essentially a rock musical and consequently not exactly my cup of tea, although I enjoyed listening to it and, in fact, found several of the musical numbers quite appealing. Well, I suppose I must have done or I wouldn't have given it to Andrew McKinnon when I returned to Perth the following spring to start rehearsals for *The Government Inspector*, and the rest, as they say, is history, which has a habit of repeating itself. The previous year I had only agreed to appear in 'Joseph' because the offer had been coupled with the chance to play Sir Andrew Aguecheek in *Twelfth Night*. On this occasion, the irresistible lure turned out to be Lucio in *Measure for Measure*, and thus I found myself, not nearly so reluctantly it has to be said, agreeing to play a character called Nob in *Cloud Nine*.

Remembering now that only a year earlier I had left Perth with no intention of ever returning, it would be only too easy to claim that Destiny had been responsible for the sequence of events that kept taking me back there. But it makes a lot more sense to cast Joan Knight in that role since she was the only person offering me any work at the time. I do, however, occasionally wonder what course my life might have taken had Perth not played such a significant part in it, and none of the options I come up with, even when omitting the most pessimistic of them, could have led to a happier and, in career terms, a more auspicious outcome. Not that I had any great affection for the place at that time. Despite the beauty of its surroundings and its regal status in the history of Scotland, back in the mid-seventies Perth was bereft of all but the most basic of amenities. At the heart of a farming community it boasted a respectable, if somewhat dour, population during the hours of daylight. But after dark, although some of the more adventurous amongst them could be found occupying the theatre's auditorium, out on the streets it was a different matter. A sense of danger lurked around every corner as drunks, many of them clutching their bottles, emerged seemingly from out of nowhere to populate all the alleyways, or vennels as they are known in Scotland. In Cutlog Vennel, for instance, where the theatre's stage door was once situated, you would be lucky indeed not to run into, or stumble over, Jean Rattray, the uncrowned queen of Perth's vagrant population, and whose death at the age of 55 in 2006 was commemorated at the Salvation Army Hall in South Street where she was hailed as a Perth Legend. Legendary too were the parks that flanked the town to the north and south. The North Inch, situated on the banks of the River Tay, had witnessed the *Battle of the Clans* back in 1396, while the South Inch was the venue for seasonal fun-fairs and for the annual Guy Fawkes night celebrations. The number of decent restaurants in Perth back then could be counted on the fingers of – well, one finger, to be perfectly honest. There were a handful of passable eateries if you were looking for lunch or high-tea, another Scottish favourite which effectively did away with the need for dinner and allowed you to get home in time to avoid the drunks. But if you wanted to eat after the show without risking salmonella in one of the worst Chinese restaurants I have ever encountered, there was only one option, and even *Timothy's* would only stay open late enough if you made a special request, and only then if there were enough of you to make it worth their while. Nevertheless, it was an experience not to be missed. *Timothy's* was not only good value, but delightfully idiosyncratic both in its furnishings and its menu which consisted of a variety of smorgasbord dishes given the Scottish treatment and served as main courses by Atholl, invariably kilted, at individual and genuine antique tables. The occasional visit to *Timothy's* with members of the company plus numerous Sunday evenings spent with Lesley at the Isle of Skye hotel just across the river where we ate, drank and danced – yes, danced the night away before tottering back across the bridge to our little haven in Victoria Street are pleasant memories of a town which, at least, I was growing accustomed to, and given that for the foreseeable future my fate was to be bound up in one way or another with Perth Theatre, this was no bad thing.

During the course of the autumn season I was commissioned by Joan Knight to write a play for Perth Theatre based on Jessica Mitford's autobiography, *Hons and Rebels*. It's difficult now, of course, to recapture the inspirational effect it had upon me that led me to write to the author who at that time was working as a university lecturer in Berkeley, California, asking for her permission to go ahead with it. It was only after she enthusiastically endorsed the idea, that I informed Joan, and so for the best part of what must have been the next seven or eight months I became increasingly preoccupied with Jessica Mitford's world, and with writing my first play for the theatre.

Meanwhile, *Cloud Nine* gave way to *Measure for Measure*, and finally – at least as far as I was concerned – to Alan Bennett's *Habeas Corpus*, in which I played Sir Percy Shorter, whose recollections of an under-the-table liaison with Lady Rumpers during an air-raid contain the unforgettable memory of 'admiring her face in the light of a post-coital Craven A.' *Cloud Nine* turned out to be a bit of a disappointment, although it did well at the box-office and managed to attract a younger audience than usual into the theatre. But the book, written by Kevin Williams and his long-time partner, Christine Kimberley, was daffy to say the least, involving a power-struggle between Father Time and Mother Nature's Child, whose obvious resemblance to Oberon and Titania, reinforced by a decidedly Puckish Cupid was, as far as I can recall, never acknowledged. For some quite arbitrary reason, their chosen battleground was Milton Street and its inhabitants, over whose lives they sought to exert conflicting influence. There were six of us living in Milton Street, Petra Siniawski and I representing the upper-crust, hence the names 'Nob' and 'Deb', whilst Lesley and Nigel Hughes, as 'Me' and 'Head', reflected the 'way-out' modern generation, searching for the meaning of everything, and finally 'Girl' and 'Boy' who were meant to be, as their names suggest, a very undistinguished and ordinary couple. They were played by Jane Egan and Kevin Whately, who was, on this occasion, perfectly cast. The music, played by a talented group of rock musicians led by Simon Webb, lifted the show above the banal, but it was good fun to be in nevertheless and it did manage to mark one milestone in the history of Perth Theatre when the stage collapsed under Mother Nature's Child, played by Dutch actress, Thea Ranft, and the audience was treated to the 'F' word for the very first time.

Memories of *Measure for Measure* pale by comparison, if only because it was very ably directed by Joan herself, and was comparatively accident-free, although the casting of Lesley Mackie as Isabella did raise the odd eyebrow, most notably the one belonging to Martyn James. Martyn was, like Janet Michael, a Perth resident and consequently a familiar face on that particular stage. He must have been in his late-twenties back then but he was a big man, heavily built, and tended to be cast in more mature roles. He'd recently played the dull, autocratic 40 year-old husband in *The Day After the Fair*, for instance. In fact, in repertory terms, he was a very useful man to have around. Martyn was known to be a gossip, but as a comparative newcomer at that time I had no reason to pass judgement on the subject, until one evening, in the run-up to rehearsals for *Measure for Measure*, Lesley and I left the overcrowded circle-bar and adjourned to one of the boxes in the auditorium with our drinks where we overheard Martyn in the corridor behind us vehemently holding forth on the ridiculous casting of Lesley Mackie as a novice nun – "and a virgin, for God's sake!" On leaving the theatre she crossed paths with Martin and expressed her dismay that he would speak of her in that way – loudly and in a public place. Now most people would have either offered their apologies or, at the very least, laughed it off. But Martyn immediately turned the tables on her and became the injured party. Deeply affronted by Lesley's remarks he took his complaint to Joan, threatening to leave the company if Lesley didn't apologise. Joan subsequently summoned Lesley to her office where she said she was perfectly aware that Martyn was a loose cannon, not to be taken seriously, and that Lesley should forget all about it; in fact she found it hilarious. But then Joan, as I was beginning to discover, was bound by fierce loyalties which knew no limits just so long as you were in favour. I have often speculated on the reasons I enjoyed her approbation at that time. That we'd worked together in the past was, of course, a plus, together with the fact that I was going through a period of inner turmoil which always brought out the mother in her. But my ruminations always lead me to the same conclusion: I was Lesley Mackie's chosen companion, and Lesley Mackie was Joan's prodigy, else why would she have cast her in the unlikely role of a novice nun – and a virgin, for God's sake? When Joan allowed her to record a radio play in Glasgow during the run of *Measure for Measure* and her train back to Perth was delayed, Joan herself drove to the railway station to meet her, leaving instructions that the curtain was to be held until she arrived, which she did half an hour later. She also went on to release her from her contract so that she could accept the offer of a television play in London, which meant that I was deprived of her company in *Habeas Corpus*, although her legacy stood me in good stead when I turned down the offer to stay on at Perth for the pantomime on the grounds that the part of Idle Jack in *Mother Goose* should by rights – given the character's interaction with the audience – be played by a Scotsman, a decision that Joan accepted with good grace, and which, quite incidentally, left me free to join the company at Birmingham Rep for their Christmas show which was, happily, not a pantomime!

oOoOo

Twenty

I was not alone, it seemed, in suffering the 'pangs of dispriz'd love', although in Peter Dews' case I found it difficult to imagine a downside. Along with a good many members of the company who fell out with Peter during the Ravinia Festival in Chicago back in 1964, I believed that his behaviour had been unduly influenced by his wife, whose background and experience did not qualify her to have any opinions on theatrical matters, let alone to air them. Moreover, those amongst us who had already had a first taste of Ann's overweening presence during *The Spread of the Eagle* found it hard to understand how Peter could have allowed her that kind of leeway. Nevertheless, her departure to work alongside an actor whose name I cannot recall, together with my own enforced separation from Dawn, made the prospect of a reconciliation between Peter and myself not only possible but, from my point of view, well worth pursuing. Not that I was motivated in any way, or at least not consciously, by the prospect of future work with him even although, at that time, Peter's star had been in the ascendant for several years as a theatre director, most notably with Peter Luke's *Hadrian VII* which won him a Tony Award on Broadway, and with a hugely successful production of Robert Bolt's *Vivat! Vivat Regina!* both in London and in New York. But even as we flew back from Chicago more than ten years earlier, the rift between us already established, I knew I would miss his friendship. Unlike Dawn, whose quarrel with Peter was certainly more substantial than mine, I found it harder to sever the ties. I had always known, of course, how adept Dawn was at walking away from those she had previously admired or respected when they failed to live up to her exacting standards, and a part of me still saw that as a strength; but it was not one that I shared. As far as my chequered relationship with Peter Dews was concerned, the happy memories far outweighed the bad and, given that there were no longer any flies in the ointment, it seemed like a good time for building bridges.

So, in the spring of 1975, behind the wheel of my newly-acquired Triumph Herald Estate, I stopped off in Birmingham on my journey to Perth and met up with Peter who made it quite clear that he was as keen to bury the hatchet as I was, and without exchanging – as far as I can remember – a single word about our respective spouses, or indeed about the Ravinia Festival, we parted the best of friends again. It didn't come as a complete surprise, therefore, when he asked me to join the company at Birmingham Rep for the 1975 Christmas show,

Toad of Toad Hall. What did come as a surprise – although 'shock' would more accurately describe my reaction – was that he was offering me the part of Mole! Having played Ratty alongside the legendary Richard Goolden as Mole on two previous occasions, I was not inclined to step into his shoes and, in any case, the essentially shy, reclusive and unworldly nature of that small burrowing animal was utterly alien to me. The fact that one of the local critics described my performance as 'dismally charmless' was perhaps a little unkind, but at least I knew where he was coming from. On the other hand, I was not about to turn down the opportunity, however inappropriate, of working with Peter again; and, in any case, that review hadn't been written yet!

The old Birmingham Rep which was founded in 1913 by Barry Jackson became one of the most influential companies in the history of English theatre, playing host to the early pre-war careers of Laurence Olivier, Edith Evans and Ralph Richardson amongst others, and throughout the '50s and '60s the beginnings of a host of relative newcomers, including Albert Finney, Ian Richardson and Derek Jacobi. The old Rep in Station Road had finally given way in 1971 to a brand new 901 seat theatre on Broad Street in an area now known as Centenary Square. As I walked into its spacious and all but deserted foyer on that morning in early November 1975, the only person I saw was Ann Dews. I had heard some weeks earlier that there had been a rapprochement, but running into her before I'd had the chance to find my feet in these new surroundings did not augur well. She was sitting at a table by the window nursing a cup of coffee, and I had no alternative but to join her although, even as I approached, serious doubts entered my mind as to her identity. Could I have been mistaken? If this was indeed Ann Dews, what had happened to the twin-set and the schoolmarmish hair-do? What had become of the well-upholstered bosom and the sturdy hips? And where had that sparkle in her eyes come from? After the customary courtesies, I paid her the compliment of remarking upon her appearance, whereupon that all too familiar smirk returned to her lips, and she said, "What do you want from Peter?" Clearly, her transformation had been entirely cosmetic.

Blessedly free from her irksome presence, which was doubtless focused on more eminent personages than we poor players, the rehearsal period was decidedly, and somewhat surprisingly, calmer than I had reason to expect. I knew that Peter had suffered a heart-attack several years earlier, which was not surprising at all; his frequent volcanic eruptions, raising his blood-pressure alarmingly, provided a clear indication of what lay in store. But he was altogether quieter now, not nearly so volatile, except for occasional flashes, usually directed at Roger Milner, who was obviously not authoritative enough as Badger, but whose pleasantly quiescent personality rendered him all but immune to Peter's barbs. For the most part, however, good humour reigned supreme, and the rehearsal period, if my memory serves me right, was hugely enjoyable. Not only that but, wonder of wonders, I even began to feel reasonably comfortable as Mole.

1975 Toad of Toad Hall - Birmingham
a 'dismally charmless' TW with Ellis Jones and Hywel Bennett.

There was only one 'star' in the proceedings and, appropriately enough, he came in the shape of Mr. Toad, a thinly disguised version of the actor himself, whose name was Hywel Bennett. I have only twice worked alongside an actor hell-bent on self-destruction, and for some strange reason they were both Welsh; something to do with choosing Dylan Thomas as a role model, perhaps, or maybe Richard Burton? In any event, I had no recourse at that time to historical perspective, so as far as I was concerned, Hywel was simply riding high – possibly too high – on an enviably high-flying career, appearing in a string of movies which included *The Family Way* in which he starred alongside John Mills and his daughter, Hayley. There was no good reason, at least in my book, why he shouldn't be enjoying life to the full and, for all I knew, he was. He certainly lived it at a faster pace than I was accustomed to, but then I have never been attracted to perilous fun-fair rides, preferring instead the more sedate journey of the merry-go-round. But Hywel was nothing if not seductive and, my preferences notwithstanding, I frequently found myself adopting his life-style on the grounds that I would be causing him untold misery if I demurred; and I was not alone. On a number of occasions, he managed to persuade a good few of us to accompany him to *Barbarellas,* one of Birmingham's noisier and more heavily populated night-spots, from which only to disappear shortly afterwards, leaving us all in the lurch. We never knew where he went, but increasing familiarity with Hywel's propensities suggested it was either to enjoy a 'naughty ciggie' in some back room or a sexual liaison with one of the many women who seemed only too happy to fall at his feet, if you see what I mean! At that time, Hywel was married, and went on being married for some years after, to Cathy McGowan, the well-known presenter of ITV's pop programme, *Ready, Steady, Go,* but who never, to my knowledge, visited her husband at the Birmingham Rep. A string of other young ladies, however, one or two of them bearing familiar names and faces, did turn up at the stage door from time to time, carrying overnight bags, a tribute to Hywel's undoubtedly charismatic appeal, but one which also posed a few questions about his marriage, and how it managed to last for as long as it did. To be fair, however, Hywel was not alone in his profligacy at that time; he merely led the way. Never having appeared in a pantomime, I was not as familiar as many were with the 'two performances a day' syndrome which applies to nearly all Christmas shows, and which effectively throws a company together in a more intimate way, for no other reason than there's little or no time for socialising in the outside world, and especially when you're living away from home. Nevertheless, the licentious conduct of many of the animals along the River Bank: Weasels, Stoats, Ferrets and, appropriately enough, the entire Rabbit family, while true to nature, was not necessarily what Kenneth Grahame had in mind when he wrote *The Wind in the Willows*, nor I think did A.A.Milne, or he might have considered changing the title of his play to *Up Tails All!*

It surprises me even now to claim that I had already made some progress on my Jessica Mitford play. But I surely must have done, although my recollections of doing anything about it in Birmingham are restricted to one, and that was tangential, to say the least. I was neither exalted enough, nor had I any of the right connections, to lay claim to a flat within the precincts of the theatre, and so I was obliged to find 'digs', which I did with the help of a published list, and which turned out to be comfortable enough, and close enough to the theatre not to cause me too much inconvenience. The landlady was an elderly widow called Doris, who made me welcome although, in the manner of traditional theatrical landladies, she was also quick to make known to me 'The rules of the house', foremost amongst which being the strict edict – non-adherence to which would result in immediate eviction – not to bring members of the opposite sex back at night. Several had tried it, she expostulated, but being a light sleeper, she had heard their multiple tread on the stairs. Even when one had tried to evade detection by carrying the object of his desire up to his room on his back, she had been woken by the unfamiliar creak of the floorboards. Duly warned, I promised to confine these activities to my dressing-room at the theatre and to the back of my car, although I didn't share this private vow with Doris. The only other disadvantage was that, comfortable and convenient though my lodgings were, there was nowhere I could set up my typewriter, which brings me back to the starting-point of this story. So I took it into the theatre one morning and set it up in my dressing-room, knowing that I would have a good three or four hours before I had to start preparing for the matinée performance. Had I known that the natural urge to fortify myself with a cup of coffee before starting work was to have such dire consequences, I would have given the Green Room a wide berth, and made do with a glass of water. It was only about 10 o'clock in the morning, but Hywel was already ensconced there alongside John Sharp, a well-known actor of Falstaffian proportions and similar appetites which he was already imbibing as I walked in. I was invited to join them, and after feebly protesting that it was a bit early in the day for that sort of thing, I finally succumbed and accepted the offer – but just the one, mind you! Three hours later I had to be all but carried up to Hywel's flat and plied with large quantities of black coffee without which Mole would have been quite incapable of emerging from his hole that day. It is hardly surprising, I suppose, that my memories of the actual production of *Toad of Toad Hall* in Birmingham are overshadowed by memories of the twilight world I inhabited for much of the time.

I do recall that Hywel Bennett's performance as Toad, which never quite measured up to the promise it held out in real life, nevertheless left an indelible impression, especially when his foot suddenly swelled up with blood poisoning – derived from which of his many indulgences is anybody's guess – and he was consequently obliged to play a number of performances with a walking-stick. Hywel subsequently went on to star in a television series called *Shelley,* for which he will probably be best remembered. He retired from the business in 2007, suffering from a congenital heart disease, although it's hard to believe that his lifestyle had nothing whatsoever to do with that either. Then there was Ellis Jones, who made a pretty good fist of Ratty – and he must have done, or I wouldn't be saying so – and who managed to keep his distance without being in any way anti-social by embarking upon a personal quest to sample and compare all the real ales in the Midlands. And finally, Brendan Price, affectionately known as 'Pricky', who became a long-term friend, and not just because he always managed to make me laugh as Chief Weasel, but because he became my more or less constant companion on all of those Hywel Bennett inspired outings. Brendan had his own agenda; not all that different from Hywel's, except that self-preservation was high on the list of his priorities, even though it included an extravagant fondness for Lanson Black Label champagne. I clearly remember, however, that the relationship between actor and audience was not nearly as comfortable in Birmingham as it had been at the Crucible Theatre in Sheffield, both of them relatively newly-built theatres. The stage was too high for a start, which distanced the action from the audience, and especially from those sitting in the front rows. On the plus side, it rendered the stage pretty well inaccessible, which was no bad thing, for had we been playing *Toad of Toad Hall* at the Crucible, there's no knowing how many young people would have invaded the River Bank or disappeared into the Wild Wood, never to be seen again.

When the final curtain fell on 31st January, 1976, I headed back to London, determined that nothing was going to prevent me from getting on with the Jessica Mitford play which Joan Knight had already pencilled in for an autumn première at Perth. A brief diversion arrived at about that time in the shape of Lesley Mackie who had been summoned to an audition in London for the part of the soubrette in a revival of Leonard Bernstein's *Candide*. Delighted as I obviously was to see her, I was thrilled by the possibility that she might be offered a major role in one of my favourite musicals, so I accompanied her to the theatre where I stood in the wings while she sang her audition piece. There was a silence when she finished, and then an American voice, probably the voice of Hal Prince, asked her if she could reach a top *E flat* which, with the aid of the pianist, she quite comfortably managed. This was followed by another pause, and then the impresario's voice again, telling her that she would be sent a copy of the aria, *Glitter and be Gay,* and if she managed to cope with it when recalled, he would very much like her to play Cunégonde, the juvenile lead. This was the part originally played on Broadway by Barbara Cook and I could hardly believe what I was hearing, which was not entirely surprising, as it turned out I wasn't there at all. It took Lesley some time to persuade me that this was the case and, in retrospect, and after a good deal of soul-searching, I had to agree that my presence in the wings of a West End theatre during the audition process for such a major project was an unlikely scenario. Why then were my memories of it so vivid? Lesley's minutely detailed description of the event obviously played its part, along with my all-too-fertile imagination. But I like to think that, for purely theatrical reasons, I believed the story would have more impact coming from a third party who had witnessed it. Sadly, and for a variety of reasons, the production never materialised, and so Lesley's immediate future was confined to working in Scotland. She had, however, managed to acquire a London agent for the first time in her working life and, following such a positive reaction from so illustrious a producer – and I'm still not a hundred per cent convinced I wasn't there to hear it – surely her horizons were well set to broaden.

Meanwhile, all my energies became focused on translating Jessica Mitford's biography into a play. In fact, having spent most of my life as a writer in partnership with a co-author, I really hadn't taken on board the degree of seclusion it demanded. At another time and in another place, this would have been an ideal subject for Dawn and I to have worked on together, being on the same wavelength, exchanging ideas, thinking the same thoughts, sharing moments of inspiration; but those days were gone. I was isolated, with no points of reference outside my own head, and virtually imprisoned within the walls of my small corner at 23 Vanbrugh Park with neither the time nor the inclination to entertain thoughts of anything but honouring my contract with Joan Knight, and delivering a script which would, at the very least, ensure I was paid the second half of my fee. But solitude, which the vast majority of writers would acknowledge as their *sine qua non*, has never been my strong point, and it was only with a kind of dogged determination that I approached the task that lay before me.

At the heart of Jessica Mitford's book is a love story which, if not unique, is unusual enough to engage an audience's imagination, as it did mine when I first read about it. The Honourable Jessica, daughter of extreme right-wing peer, Lord Redesdale, meets, falls in love with, and eventually marries Esmond Romilly, nephew of Winston Churchill; bringing together two eminent families who, unlike the Montagues and the Capulets, are not at war with each other, at least not yet. But Esmond is a rebel and Jessica a kindred spirit-in-waiting. Together, and initially under Esmond's tutelage, they scandalously espouse the political left, culminating in 1936 with their commitment to the Republican struggle against the invading Fascist forces in that tragic conflict known as the Spanish Civil War. Jessica's defection from traditional family loyalties provides the background to the story which, in my dramatisation as in Jessica's biography, takes reminiscence as its starting point. She returns to Swinbrook House, the now deserted family home in the Cotswolds, some 30 years after these events, and relives episodes from her childhood. Under the family arms with its blandly self-assured motto, *God Careth for Us,* we meet the members of her extraordinary and eccentric family; her father, the irascible Lord Redesdale, an indiscriminate racist and a shameless philistine, and her mother, whose quietly-spoken and genteel manner only thinly disguises similar prejudices, asserting in her role as her children's teacher that England and all of its dominions are unquestionably good because 'they are coloured a lovely pink on the map, whereas Germany is a hideous mud-coloured brown'. Then there are Jessica's siblings; Nancy, her eldest sister, first to suffer their father's heathenish rage when she decides to become a novelist, and who goes on to become an extremely successful one, *The Pursuit of Love* and *Love in a Cold Climate* being two of her most enduring titles. Then there is Diana, who earns her place in history by marrying Oswald Mosley, founder in 1932 of the British Union of Fascists whose support of the Nazi régime in Germany leads to him being detained by the British Government during the early years of the war. Not to be upstaged by her older sister, Unity Mitford follows her particular star all the way to Germany, where she not only becomes heavily involved with the Nazi hierarchy, but also enjoys a close personal friendship with Hitler. She attempts suicide when Britain declares war on Germany, and eventually dies as a result of the head wound she had inflicted on herself. With such a background, crammed to bursting with so many colourful characters, and not only within her family, Jessica's adventures in Spain, from where she and Esmond are finally evacuated in a British destroyer, diverted from its course on government orders lest Britain's neutrality be compromised by the participation of two such eminent members of the English establishment, made it patently clear that here was a play waiting to be written, and write it I did, grim determination gradually giving way to an overwhelming commitment. In this, I was not entirely alone, as Jessica and I communicated with each other quite regularly. At her request I sent finished scenes to California and received prompt replies expressing enthusiasm, tempered with copious constructive notes. I was in seventh heaven for a lot of the time, and especially during those periods when I was so completely inhabiting Jessica's world that the play seemed to be writing itself. Well, that was certainly the case until one day late in March when I was invited back to Birmingham.

I might have had second thoughts when I was offered a part in Guy Bolton's translation of Marcelle Maurette's play, *Anastasia*, but as soon as I knew it was to be directed by David William, choice was all but taken away from me. I had made considerable progress with the Mitford play, after all, and once *Anastasia* had opened I would have the days to myself again. So it was back to Birmingham and, incidentally, back to Doris's house.

Oddly enough, my only abiding memory of that return visit to Birmingham was a show I saw in the adjoining studio theatre called *Are You Now Or Have You Ever Been?* by Eric Bentley. It was a documentary drama culled from the actual hearings of the House Un-American Activities Committee which had its beginnings in the late 1940s and had subsequently inspired Arthur Miller's play, *The Crucible*, taking as its subject the infamous witch-hunts that took place in Salem, Massachusetts in 1692. No less infamous were the so-called witch-hunts conducted by HUAC, inspired by paranoia and megalomania in about equal measure, which were designed to root out communist sympathisers from public life, and were led by the now notorious American Senator, Joseph McCarthy, aided and abetted by two future U.S. Presidents, Richard Nixon and Ronald Reagan, who was himself in Hollywood at that time, probably blaming those subversive elements for his failure to achieve major stardom, and who, along with Walt Disney, managed to get the red spotlight turned on the film industry and other associated professions. It was these hearings that formed the substance of Eric Bentley's dramatic reconstruction, featuring screenwriters, directors and actors whose political affiliations, even if not mirrored in their work, were open to question; that question being 'Are you now, or have you ever been, a member of the Communist Party?' The consequent effect upon the lives and livelihoods of those who testified and those who remained silent, not to mention the emergence of a surprising number who, to save their own skins, were prepared to betray others, was indeed reminiscent of the hysteria that had gripped Salem 250 years earlier, and for a few short years it shook the very foundations of American democracy. Besides having other fish to fry in 1953, I was also too young to take much notice of what was going on in Washington DC, but although it was all but done and dusted by 1976, *Are You Now Or Have You Ever Been?* brought the immediate effects of McCarthyism, as it came to be known, vividly back to life. It could so easily have been written and presented as a history lesson, engaging enough to be sure, but of mainly academic interest. As it happened, however, largely due to Eric Bentley's inspired interpretation of events and some very impressive performances, the Birmingham production was so vivid and authentic a reconstruction that I was completely transported. I had no idea at the time, of course, that its legacy would serve me well before too long, although I could have wished otherwise. But that's another story.

My memories of *Anastasia* are patchy by comparison although, given its historical background, in other circumstances, I imagine I might well have become more emotionally involved. But uppermost in my mind was the pressing need to get on with the Jessica Mitford play. I have no reason to doubt, however, that I enjoyed being in *Anastasia*. Working with David William again was obviously a happy experience, and the company, led by Peter Brook's wife, Natasha Parry, as the enigmatic heroine, Anna Broun (or was she indeed the Grand Duchess Anastasia?), was entirely congenial. In fact, the only memorable, if invisible, wound I carried away from that engagement was inflicted by a local newspaper review which described my performance as 'preposterously bad'. That it was delivered by the same critic who had branded my Mole in *Toad of Toad Hall* 'dismally charmless' naturally led me to believe that our paths must have crossed at some point and that, somehow or other, I had deeply offended him. He was, of course, perfectly entitled to find my performance as Piotr Petrovski not to his taste, but I'm reasonably certain that nothing I have ever done could be described as preposterously anything – well, at least not as an actor!

When *Anastasia* left Birmingham for a week to play at the Pavilion Theatre in Bournemouth, I invited Lesley to accompany me, and if memory serves me right we enjoyed our time there. I then made the preposterous mistake of asking her to come and stay with me in Blackheath once the run had ended. I should have known by then that writing, and particularly writing under pressure, isolated me completely from any kind of human contact. As soon as *Anastasia* had come to an end, and with a deadline on the not-too-distant horizon, my days were completely consumed and, not surprisingly, Lesley began to feel more than a little *de trop*. I was behaving insensitively, to say the least, and even when she decided to cut short her visit and return to Scotland, I scarcely noticed. She was, after all (if a little earlier than planned), returning to fulfil professional obligations of her own in Perth where she was about to play Annie in Alan Ayckbourn's trilogy *The Norman Conquests*, and where I would be joining her in any case, just as soon as I had completed my first draft. Joan Knight had invited me back, principally so that we could work together on putting the final touches to the play, scheduled to open in November. There would certainly be a fair amount of rewriting to be done, not to mention some substantial cutting, none of which could be achieved without Joan's input and particularly as she was to be directing it. But she had also asked me to join the company so that I would be receiving a salary plus subsistence during the run-up to production, which was very considerate of her. Mephistophilis in Marlowe's *Doctor Faustus* was a major role, to be sure, but a silent presence for much of the play, so I was spared the time-consuming task of learning lines, or at least not too many of them. In Shaw's *Man and Superman*, which was to play in repertoire with *Doctor Faustus*, I was offered something even less demanding, although I cannot remember what it was now for the simple reason that I never got to play it.

Meanwhile, many years had passed and been glimpsed by the time we return to Swinbrook House only an hour or two after Jessica first arrived, transported back to the present following Esmond Romilly's death when, as a member of the Royal Canadian Air Force, he is killed in a bombing raid over Germany. The chauffeur who had brought her there only a short while ago has returned and so, without another backward glance, she consigns the empty house and the ghosts that have haunted it to the past, as the lights fade and the curtain falls.

The fact that I hadn't invented the story or created the characters did nothing to lessen its hold on me, so that while I was undoubtedly delighted to have reached the end of my particular journey, it was not so easy to consign it to the past. So it was back to Perth again and, somewhat ironically, back to cohabiting, or perhaps 'sharing accommodation' with Lesley would be a more apt way of describing it. Happily, on this occasion, her leisure time was fairly obsessively taken up with sun-bathing during what was turning out to be one of the hottest and most prolonged summers in living memory, and sun-bathing being an essentially solitary occupation, I was able to devote myself, qualmless, to the inevitable rewrites that followed my numerous meetings with Joan. We had even reached the stage of talking about casting, and had all but decided to offer the part of Jessica to Gemma Jones, when disaster struck. It came in the shape of a telegram from California which read as follows: 'I have decided not to allow you to do the play. My husband, who is a lawyer, tells me that if you go ahead with it we can sue you. Jessica Mitford.' I was poleaxed, of course. That entirely gratuitous threat, made by someone I felt I had come to know and whose enthusiasm and support had helped to sustain me, was quite devastating when she might at least have given me a reason. I knew perfectly well, of course, that I had no rights beyond a mutual agreement, which was undoubtedly naïve of me when I knew that she was free to change her mind at any time if she didn't approve of what I was doing. But never had she given me any reason to believe this was the case. In due course, and certainly not courtesy of Miss Mitford, I learned that the film director, Tony Richardson, had obtained those very rights I had failed to secure, probably as a vehicle for his wife, Vanessa Redgrave, and which might well have been exclusive rights. But the Jessica Mitford with whom I had become so intimately involved through the pages of her book, and who would never have treated anyone in such an insensitive way, instantly became a fictional character as far as I was concerned. The fact that the film was never made, even had I known it at the time, would have been cold comfort given the sense of desolation I felt, not to mention the acute embarrassment I suffered when I had to break the news to Joan. I had no reason to expect anything but a stern rebuke, "You mean you didn't have the rights?" It was she, after all, who had procured the commission and who would be held accountable for the money I had received. Would I have to pay it back? She listened intently as I struggled to find the right words. Then she nodded sympathetically. "Never mind, darling", she said, "There was still a lot of work to be done on the play, and I don't think you would have had the time because I want you to play John Tanner in *Man and Superman*." Of all the imagined responses I had conjured up, including the more fanciful ones like sympathy and forgiveness, this took the biscuit. And not only because it was so unexpected, but because it immediately and effectively removed the burden I had been carrying by replacing it with another one. John Tanner, after all, is one of the biggest parts ever written, and certainly the biggest George Bernard Shaw ever penned. Not only that but Tanner was meant to be somewhat taller than I was. Peter O'Toole had scored a notable success in the role at the Bristol

Old Vic back in 1958, going on to play it in the West End several years later, and was generally regarded as the modern prototype. But then again, thanks to Joan, I had recently been invited to play Sir Andrew Aguecheek, another traditionally tall character. No, it was the timing, not to mention the magnanimity of her offer that floored me, and I hope I managed to convey the gratitude I certainly ought to have felt as, from that moment, I never – until now – gave Jessica Mitford or her story another serious thought. As if this consolation wasn't enough, Joan went on to suggest that I should put all the research I had done into the Spanish Civil War to good use by devising a documentary drama on the subject for her Theatre-in-Education programme.

It's almost inconceivable to me now that I managed to do this in the time that was left to me before rehearsals began for *Man and Superman;* and not only that, but that I had also managed to make a considerable dent in the task of learning Jack Tanner's lines, a feat that would have been virtually unachievable within the three or four week rehearsal period allocated, not only to Shaw's play, but also to Marlowe's *Doctor Faustus.* All I can say, without the benefit of a journal which, in any case, I wouldn't have had the time to write, is that I not only found Shaw's impeccably structured dialogue as easy to learn as Shakespeare's blank verse, but more to the point, I was also considerably younger than I am now. Add to these obvious bonuses the powerful influence of *Are You Now Or Have You Ever Been* at Birmingham, which must have inspired me to produce something about the Spanish Civil War; a documentary which could well have a similar impact. Certainly the raw material available to me, much of it already researched and conveniently to hand, obviously made my job a good deal easier than it would otherwise have been. The only thing I am sure of, having no memory whatsoever of the process, is that *Yesterday the Struggle* was performed in a number of local schools by a small company of actors who, along with a talented guitarist, played out the history of the Spanish Civil War through the poetry of W.H.Auden, Louis MacNeice, Laurie Lee, John Cornford, Stephen Spender, and a host of others, along with the writings of George Orwell, Esmond Romilly and Ernest Hemingway, together with speeches by leading political and military figures on both sides of the fence, plus a selection of the songs that were sung during that dreadful conflict which had begun exactly 40 years earlier. Whether or not it had a powerful effect on audiences was difficult to ascertain on a schools' tour, but at its first performance in the Perth Theatre foyer, a party of eight former members of the International Brigades, who had travelled from Glasgow to see the show, said afterwards that they had been deeply moved by it, which was good enough for me.

Rehearsals finally started in mid-October for *Man and Superman*, followed a week later by *Doctor Faustus*. The rest of the season, in which I was to be fairly heavily involved, was already planned. A production of *Devil in the Fog*, based on Leon Garfield's children's novel would replace my own sadly abandoned play, following which I would start rehearsals for *Sleuth*, Anthony Shaffer's brilliantly symbiotic thriller, an exciting prospect which would take me well into the New Year. The best news of all, however, was that Lesley had been invited to play Dorothy in *The Wizard of Oz* at Birmingham Rep over the Christmas period. Only a year earlier, with Dundee Repertory Theatre planning a production of the same play themselves, she had been snubbed in favour of another young actress who, although perfectly competent, was not possessed of the diverse qualities that go to make up the character of Dorothy Gale. Joan Knight herself had suggested Lesley for the role which, given her undeniable partiality, may well have had the opposite effect on the artistic director at Dundee, Stephen MacDonald. Stephen and Lesley had last worked together in *Pygmalion* at Perth when Joan had allowed Lesley to miss two performances so that she could go to Glasgow for a brief television job, necessitating understudy rehearsals which obviously, and quite justifiably, annoyed Stephen as he was playing Professor Higgins. But that was Joan's fault, not Lesley's, and consequently I was moved to write to Stephen myself, having worked alongside him way back in 1955 with the MTC in Coventry. In no uncertain terms, I told him that Lesley was 'The nation's Dorothy' and that, in effect, he would be cutting off his nose to spite his face if he didn't offer her the part. Clearly, my own partiality cut no ice with him.

A short time later, when it was announced that the Lyceum Theatre in Edinburgh was to stage a production of *The Wizard of Oz*, Lesley auditioned for it and was offered the part by its director, Anna Barry, only to have the offer withdrawn by the Lyceum's new artistic director, who turned out to be... yes, you guessed it. Well, you can imagine my delight when, without so much as an interview, let alone an audition, she was offered the part by Clive Perry, who had recently vacated his post at the Lyceum and become the artistic director at Birmingham. Clive was, in fact, Joan's oldest – if not her first – protégé, and so it could easily be conjectured by those who didn't know him that he had been obliged to do her bidding. But Clive Perry, more of whom you will hear anon, was not the kind of man to do anybody's bidding but his own. Besides, he had worked with Lesley himself when she had stolen several scenes as Jackie Coryton in Noël Coward's *Hay Fever*, an entirely captivating performance that I was to see myself in a later production. The point being that Clive knew only too well what Lesley would bring to the part of Dorothy without a nod from Joan, whose own partiality in any case derived first and foremost from her appreciation of Lesley's qualities as an extremely versatile actress, as did mine up to a point. In fact, if I'd thought about it at the time, which I didn't, my relationship with her would hardly have survived for two on-again-off-again years had it been based solely on her feminine attraction.

With the final eclipse of that vintage summer, the run of Ayckbourn's *Norman Conquests* came to an end and Lesley returned to her family home in Dundee prior to leaving for Birmingham. Whilst I cannot lay claim to a sudden dawning of objectivity, nor indeed of conscious self-sacrifice, I must have seen her imminent departure as a kind of watershed and, given that we still appeared to be on the road to nowhere, I suggested that while she was away she should find herself a 'nice young man'. I told her there was no reason why we couldn't remain friends, but that since I was in no fit state to make a commitment, I didn't want to stand in her way. I was well aware, of course, that she was a consummate flirt, more than capable of paying me back in kind, but her determined independence didn't entirely mask her vulnerability, and I wanted (at least I think I did) to relieve her of any sense of obligation or responsibility she might feel towards me should there be the chance of a serious relationship with someone else. With characteristic stoicism she went along with all I had to say – or maybe she was just politely acknowledging the obvious!

I was about to discover, with *Man and Superman* well into rehearsal, that Joan Knight was not quite as infallible as I had believed her to be. Had I been more familiar with the inherent problems of staging a play by George Bernard Shaw, I would probably have been surprised to learn that she had chosen to hand the baton to a young trainee director. But this was my first venture into Shavian territory, and I was naturally blinkered by the mammoth task that lay ahead of me. In any case, with all of us buried in our scripts, it wasn't until we had discarded them and discovered that our director's eyes remained glued to his, that alarm bells started to ring. It began to dawn on me, and I was not alone in my dawning, that he probably didn't know what else to do and that we, the actors, were going to have to direct the play ourselves. In different circumstances the absence of a director might well have been seen as a welcome relief, but this was a play that required a director's eye if only to make sure we weren't standing in front of each other. On the odd occasion when he did lay the script aside and tried to make contact with us, he had little or nothing to say and was quick to snatch it up again. What began as distant rumblings and furtive glances at each other soon became the main topic of conversation at coffee and lunch breaks. With the inexorable approach of an opening night, and without any sign of a cohesive production, open rebellion was finally triggered during a rehearsal of the last scene in the play when Tanner, railroaded into proposing marriage to Ann Whitefield, played by Sue Carpenter, attempts to justify his decision before the entire company. It was a fiasco; no one knew where they should be standing or what their reactions to Tanner's speech ought to be, never mind how they should be expressed. Alone at the centre of this vacuum, I felt completely exposed, and suggested to our young director that maybe he ought to spend a bit of time orchestrating the scene. After a lengthy pause, he said, "I'm sorry, Terry, I don't know what you mean." Unfortunately, Joan was away in London auditioning for the following season, and so I had no alternative but to speak to her associate, Andrew McKinnon. I made it clear, speaking on behalf of the entire company, that we had grave doubts about being ready to open the following week. He listened sympathetically, but made it equally clear that he was not in a position to do anything about it except to inform Joan. To give him his due, he must have told it like it was, for Joan was on the next train back to Perth where, the following morning, she saw a run-through of the play, after which she sent us away for lunch. In the afternoon we began to work through the play again from the very beginning with Joan who, having played the part of Fletcher Christian, took command, and with all the skills in stagecraft and the technical expertise that came with her background in stage-management, she managed, in the few days that were left to us, to structure the production and restore our confidence, more than making up for her original sin. *Man and Superman* finally opened and, while it may not have been especially memorable, thanks to Joan and to a company of actors united in adversity, it was at least a committed and enthusiastic production. Audiences seemed to enjoy it, and the reviews were, by and large, complimentary; one in particular, and for obvious reasons, was worth saving. It was again from Christopher Small of the Glasgow Herald, who wrote 'a really excellent piece of work, dexterously staged … and very well acted all the way.' He then went on to say: 'Terry Wale is a fine vigorous Tanner, more Napoleonic than Shavian in appearance, but recalling Shaw's unfortunate admiration for Bonaparte, one can't think that inappropriate.' We never set eyes on our young director again whose name I have refrained from mentioning, not because I can't remember it, but for reasons associated with his later appointment to the post of Director of the Shaw Festival in Ontario. This is a joke, I hasten to add, although – let's face it – stranger things have happened!

1976 Man and Superman - Perth Theatre, with John Buick.

The journey we undertook with *Doctor Faustus* was, by contrast, luxurious. Andrew McKinnon, having adapted the play himself, was at the helm, happily in his own intellectual comfort zone, full of ideas and enthusiasm. The part of Faustus was played by Graham Padden – Octavius in *Man and Superman* – and so we found ourselves teamed again. Having been through proverbial hell in Shaw's play there was something disquietingly pleasurable in contemplating the real thing in Marlowe's. But aside from enjoying Graham's company on stage, we became close friends for all sorts of reasons, not least for sharing a kind of heritage. Graham was married to Teresa whose maiden name was Campbell, the daughter of Douglas Campbell, with whom I had worked at the Old Vic and at the Crucible Theatre in Sheffield alongside her mother, Ann Casson, herself the daughter of Lewis

Casson and Dame Sybil Thorndike. Not that I am laying claim to any kind of kinship, but simply that the connection went back a long way. Teresa, herself an actress, was with us in Perth too, and on the verge of giving birth to their first child, so we spent a good deal of our leisure time in each other's company.

I thoroughly enjoyed playing Mephistophilis, and not only because he had considerably fewer lines than Jack Tanner and that it provided me with a welcome respite, but because it gave me the perfect opportunity to put into practice a theory that had first come to my attention some years earlier. I cannot remember now who wrote about the 'powerful stillness' of the young Richard Burton's performance in Christopher Fry's *The Lady's Not For Burning* back in 1949, but I know I read about it when I was playing the same part myself in 1965 at the Castle Theatre in Farnham, in a production coincidentally directed by Joan Knight. But I didn't have to go back that far to recall, even more vividly, a shining example of it in 1973 when the National Theatre, still based at the Old Vic, staged a production of Trevor Griffiths' play, *The Party*, in which Laurence Olivier, making his last stage appearance, played an iconic Glasgow socialist, invited as guest of honour to a meeting in London of a group of intellectuals, all of them members of the Socialist Workers Party. When he failed to turn up at the pre-arranged time, they decided to go ahead with the meeting, and it wasn't until Dennis Quilley was in the middle of a lengthy speech that Olivier arrived and was deferentially offered the floor. He demurred, and urged Quilley to carry on, taking a seat opposite him where he sat, remaining perfectly still while listening to the rest of the speech, his back all but turned to the audience, his concentration entirely focused on the speaker. I knew, of course, that the arrival of Laurence Olivier onto a stage was bound to make an impact, heightening expectations, and I myself was far from immune to his mesmeric appeal. But this was different. His entrance as John Tagg, the star attraction, was calculated to achieve exactly those expectations, but it was immediately denied by the character himself who, quite literally, chose to take a back seat; and yet it was impossible to ignore him or to take his presence for granted. No matter how hard I tried, I could not stop my eyes from being drawn back to that statuesque figure who managed, without so much as raising an eyebrow which in any case I couldn't see, to demonstrate the power of stillness. Now, for an actor who was brought up to believe that if you didn't move, no one would know you were there, this was a revelation, and without in any way comparing my physical presence to God's, it sowed the seeds that I determined to reap as Mephistophilis, whose task it is to seduce Faustus into selling his soul to Lucifer without in any way revealing, beyond semantics, the price Faustus would ultimately have to pay. It was not an easy task but an immensely rewarding one, the lessons from which would inform my approach to acting from that point on. I was also given reason to believe that, up to a point, I had succeeded in what I set out to achieve: 'played with a chilly stillness ... Terry Wale's Mephistophilis, of white and bitter face, credibly pronounces the formula that, "where we are is hell, and where hell is there must we ever be" with all the gentle dignity of an angel, albeit a fallen one ... His gaze always intent on his prey, he holds the doomed Faustus with his eyes throughout the play.'

For all that we had bid each other a fond farewell, and acknowledged a kind of sea change in our relationship, Lesley and I had spoken frequently on the telephone since she left for Birmingham. Blow-by-blow descriptions of the rehearsal process for *The Wizard of Oz*, provided the substance of those largely one-sided conversations into one of which she managed to drop the news that she had found her 'nice young man'. I had no reason to complain, of course, and not being exactly bereft of similar comforts myself, I would have welcomed it had she not insisted on updating me on its progress in every subsequent call. He was an actor, of course, whose name, unfamiliar to me at the time, was Christopher Scoular, and who had been on tour with something or other playing at the Alexandra Theatre in Birmingham when they met. He had since then taken every opportunity, or so it appeared, to return as often as possible, so he was clearly smitten, which was all well and good, I suppose, but did I really need to know? More to the point, and much more entertaining, were the ongoing stories of Clive Perry's modus operandi, already the stuff of legend, whose style as a director was more in keeping with the antics of one of the dottier Roman emperors, leaving in his wake a trail of broken actors, many of them in need of psychiatric treatment. Lesley's experience at his hands was mild by comparison, but one or two incidents are still worth recording here. For instance, the occasion he stopped her from enjoying an evening out with her fellow actors, barring her way in fact, on the grounds that she would have to go home and learn the Scarecrow's lines. Norman Vaughan was a well-known comedian at that time, having achieved television fame as Bruce Forsyth's successor in *Sunday Night at the London Palladium* which was why, presumably, Clive had offered him the job. It didn't take long, however, to discover that, while comparatively adept at ad-libbing, he was all but incapable of memorising the script. I suppose Clive's injunction made some kind of sense in the circumstances, Dorothy being the only character in a position to prompt him.

A week before it opened, Lesley had been sent to the local dog pound to look for a dog to play the key part of Toto. She returned with a little white terrier, which looked the part but, at only a year old, was not quite ready for such a demanding role. It was at the Technical Dress Rehearsal that Clive came into his own. Tied by its lead onto a high farm cart as the orchestra launched into the opening bars of *Over The Rainbow*, the creature panicked, leapt off, and was left dangling by his neck until a member of the Stage Management team rushed onstage to rescue him. Lesley was obviously quite shaken and close to tears when a voice from the auditorium shouted, "Tie it up again – it won't do the same thing twice!" They eventually settled on using the dog as little as possible and found a way of tying him to an invisible pole in the wings at the beginning of each scene and collecting him each time she continued on her journey to Oz. The final episode came shortly after the show had opened when the poor little dog, exposed to an audience for the first time, urinated over Lesley's ruby slippers, went for her throat when she picked him up, and finally succumbed to canine distemper. The following day, Clive arrived at Lesley's dressing-room door with a somewhat larger dog, a baby Alsatian in fact, and all but daring her to question his choice!

The season at Perth eventually came to a whimpering end with a production of *Devil in the Fog*, about which the less said the better. It was adapted from an award-winning children's novel but its shortcomings as a piece of theatre were so obvious to virtually everyone in the cast that when Mike Ockrent, a director who was already enjoying considerable success before going on to enhance it with West End and Broadway productions of *Me and My Girl* and *Girl Crazy*, came to the dressing-room I shared with fellow company member, John Buick, and rhapsodised about the show he had just seen, John and I were so taken aback that we could hardly wait to ask his wife, Sue Carpenter, who was in the cast, if he had really enjoyed it. "Of course he didn't", she said, deeply affronted, "he's not stupid!" which begs the question, already touched upon in an earlier chapter; what do you say when you haven't liked a play, or a performance, and you are confronted by someone involved in it? There is no easy answer to this, but what you certainly don't do is seek them out and rave about it.

I enjoyed a short break before rehearsals were due to begin for *Sleuth*, so I paid a brief visit to London from where, accompanied by

Bernard Lloyd, I drove to Birmingham to see *The Wizard of Oz* which had opened only the night before. It was, I recall, a fairly lavish production in which the Munchkins were outstanding, if only because they danced their way through the evening bearing a strong resemblance to a line of chorus girls, each and every one of them a head and shoulders taller than Dorothy; not quite what I had expected, having grown up with indelible memories of MGM's Munchkinland, but which shouldn't have been surprising given Clive Perry's inability to distinguish between a small terrier and a German shepherd dog – which, incidentally, was yet to make its début. Of one thing, however, I had no doubts at all; my earlier, and somewhat extravagant, claim that Lesley Mackie was 'The nation's Dorothy' was entirely borne out. Without in any way owing anything to Judy Garland's interpretation which, in any case, she had never seen, she captured the vulnerability and the pluckiness of Dorothy Gale, not to mention the essential youthfulness of the character, albeit she was several years older than Garland was when she played the part. It was an altogether enchanting performance, and one that was to have significant personal and professional repercussions on both our lives.

Back in Perth, *Sleuth* turned out to be an absolute joy, both to rehearse and to play, although it has to be said that while Andrew McKinnon was an appreciative and supportive audience, his contribution as director was undermined by ill-health. Images of him, swathed in a blanket and clutching a hot-water bottle, dominate my memories – possibly unfairly – of a rehearsal period that owed more to the rapport I shared with my fellow actor, Roger Kemp, than to any directorial input. I had already been directed by Roger in *The Government Inspector* so we weren't exactly strangers. He had also played the part of Andrew Wyke before, and consequently brought a good deal of that experience with him. For my part, I had nursed a desire to play Milo Tindle ever since I first saw the play in London some six years earlier. It was a thrilling, if exhausting, experience, in one of the most physically demanding roles I have ever played, made all the more so by having to sacrifice the interval to a mammoth costume and make-up change involving, amongst other items, a wig, moustache and sideburns, cheek-padding and four-inch lifts, ruling out even the possibility of a cup of tea. But the rewards more than made up for the investment as audiences nightly confirmed their recognition and appreciation of a play, which not only wittily parodied an entire genre, but turned out to be one of its most brilliant examples.

Roger Kemp and I headed south shortly after *Sleuth* came to an end, stopping off en route in Birmingham to see the last night of *The Wizard of Oz* and, as pre-arranged, to drive Lesley to London where I would drop her off at Christopher Scoular's flat in Bayswater. There was, needless to say, a farewell party in the Green Room, so we didn't leave Birmingham until after midnight and, having deposited Roger at his home in Islington, I was on the point of heading for Bayswater when Lesley said she thought that it was too late to disturb Christopher and that it would probably be better if she came back to Blackheath with me if I didn't mind taking her to his flat the following morning. I confess I found it difficult to believe that Christopher would not have welcomed her with open arms whatever the time of day or night. The next day I carried her suitcases up to the front door of his flat, asked her not to ring the bell until I had departed, kissed her and went on my way. I don't think I had even crossed the river on my way back to Blackheath when it struck me, quite out of the blue, and without any kind of presentiment, that I had just shot myself in the foot.

It is all but impossible to describe what I felt at that moment without resorting to clichés, or to theatrical images of curtains rising on brand new landscapes. Come to think of it, as I did right there and then, that was precisely the way I had seen it, albeit in derisory terms, when I had been advised two years earlier that it would take me two years to recover from my broken marriage. Obviously there had been a process, during which I had pined less, and indeed thought less about Dawn, but I had never entertained any serious doubt that, had she sought a reconciliation, I would have returned to her. Sitting in the traffic somewhere south of the river by that time, I knew with absolute certainty that I no longer had any desire to go back, that a curtain had indeed lifted, and that what I wanted, more than anything else in the world, was to have Lesley back with me. I also knew, with equal certainty, that there was only one way I had any chance of achieving this.

oOoOo

Twenty one

It didn't take a great deal of imagination to anticipate Lesley's reaction to yet another *volte-face* on my part, so as soon as I returned to 23 Vanbrugh Park that morning, and before time had eroded the impact of the revelation I had just experienced, I put it all down on paper, the better to convince her that it was not a sudden whim, brought about by jealousy, possessiveness or whatever, but a fundamental change of heart. I met her for lunch the following day, and presented it to her together with a spoken postscript proposing marriage. Not surprisingly, she was somewhat taken aback. Having embarked on a new and untried relationship, I could hardly have expected her to return with open arms to one that had been tried, tested and found wanting. I alone knew, and with absolute certainty now, that we belonged together, and I was not about to step aside, as she (and somewhat later Christopher) suggested I should do, the better to allow her new-found love to either blossom or wither. Fortuitously, she achieved a degree of independence when she left Christopher's flat, as she had always intended to do, and moved into another in Golders Green, temporarily vacated by Ursula Smith with whom she had shared a dressing-room in Birmingham. Just as fortuitously, this meant that her journeys to and from her new home were more complicated than they otherwise would have been, and only made less so by the availability of a car which Christopher did not possess, but which I did, although it wasn't exactly mine but Bernard's who was in Ottawa at the time, somewhat coincidentally playing Jack Tanner in Peter Dews' production of *Man and Superman*. Nevertheless, courtesy of Bernard's car and my own dogged determination, I made myself available to take Lesley everywhere she wished to go, and even to the occasional rendezvous with Christopher. My sole purpose at that time was to convince her of my resolve, and at the very least to sow the seeds of doubt in her mind, after which – and on more or less equal terms – she would be free to choose between us. I only began to suspect that I had made some progress in that direction when Mary MacGregor's recording of *Torn Between Two Lovers* entered the charts and became, for a while at any rate, very personal to Lesley.

The final episode in this potted version of a much more complex story came about one evening when Lesley was invited by a couple of old friends from Scotland to join them for dinner at their flat in Hackney. I went to collect her later in the evening and spent a bit of time with them all, only to find as we left, that a dozen or so tickets claiming that parking was forbidden had been stuck to all the windows of the car. It was annoying to say the least, and particularly so as the car park attached to the flats was vast and all but empty. A degree of stoicism was required, however, so we returned to the flat where our hosts, having provided me with sympathy together with a bucket of water and a scraper, suggested Lesley should remain while I went back to remove the stickers. 20 minutes or so later, mission accomplished, I returned the bucket, collected Lesley and went back to the car only to find that, during my brief absence, the windows had been covered with even more stickers than before. I didn't know whether to laugh or cry, and as I stood there, trying to make up my mind, I heard Lesley say, "Well, all right then." I looked at her, uncomprehendingly, and said something like, "What's all right?", to which she replied, "I will marry you." I confess that I don't remember what happened next or, indeed, how I managed to get her home, but then why should I? What I do remember is that some little while later it occurred to me that pity may have played some part in her decision; but what if it had? 'Pity should be cherished, lest you drive an angel from your door', wrote William Blake. In the end, however, I managed to convince myself that while a degree of pity may well have prompted her timing, she had probably already made up her mind!

Not that it was all plain sailing from that moment on. For a start there were divorce proceedings to consider, a subject which neither Dawn nor I had broached before, but to which she readily agreed. As far as Lesley was concerned, the approval of her parents topped the list of her priorities and, while I had enjoyed of late a good relationship with them, and especially with Violet, her mother, I doubted that either of them would revel in the prospect of their 25 year-old daughter's marriage to a 39 year-old divorcee. She was faced, however, with other more immediate problems to resolve.

When Clive Perry's plans to take his production of *The Wizard of Oz* into London had failed to materialise, thwarting Lesley of her West End début once again, she had auditioned for a touring production of Julian Slade's musical version of Sheridan's *The Duenna* and was offered the part of Donna Louisa, the juvenile lead, which she had happily accepted. Christopher Scoular, on the other hand, who had himself been offered a part in the same production, had only agreed to do it so that he and Lesley could be together. Knowing that Lesley was, in any case, finding it difficult to break the news to Christopher, I took the problem out of her hands by insisting that we should become officially engaged before the tour began. That my Access credit card was rejected and that I had to borrow the money from her to pay for what was a very modestly priced engagement ring speaks volumes, not only about the state of my finances at the time, but also about the strength of Lesley's commitment to our future together.

Having been more or less constantly employed in the provinces for the last two-and-a-half years, returning to a wholly indifferent London was a chastening experience. That this was offset to some extent by the change in my personal circumstances, and by the euphoric mood that accompanied it, did not alter the fact that I needed to make a living, if only to avoid the prospect of arriving at the altar direct from the dole queue, and probably having to borrow more from Lesley to purchase the wedding-ring! Thanks to my dear friend from Sheffield days, Jill Baker, I was employed for a short season as a member of Michael Croft's company at the Shaw Theatre in Euston Road, playing the Earl of Worcester in a modern-dress production of Shakespeare's *Henry IV pt 1,* notable only for the fact that it contained a number of actors who had graduated from the National Youth Theatre of which Croft had been the founder. Once it was over, Jill went on to procure for me another job, this time as barman at *The Alibi* club in Chelsea to which she herself returned as a waitress following her performance as Lady Hotspur. I had my doubts about that particular gift, but with nothing else on the horizon, my options were somewhat limited. *The Alibi* club provided me with a living of sorts, and although the hours were uncongenial to say the least, it turned out to be a challenging experience, if only for introducing me to the art of cocktail making. *The Alibi,* as it happened, was a fairly exclusive establishment, catering to the requirements of a largely theatrical clientèle, mainly from the upper echelons, whose tastes and pocketbooks disdained the mundane in favour of exotic concoctions I had never even heard of let alone concocted. I pride myself, nonetheless, that before long I was able to take orders for such drinks as *Brandy Alexanders, Harvey Wallbangers, Manhattans, White Ladys* and *Tequila Sunrises* without turning a hair, or at least not in front of the customers from whom my endeavours, once I had located the required ingredients in my well-thumbed cocktail book, were well and truly hidden. The only other memory I have of my time at *The Alibi* – save for the sound of *The Eagles'* recording of *Hotel California,* and Peter Gabriel singing *Solsbury Hill* – was the occasion when I became aware of the actress, Jill Bennett, who was apparently enjoying a congenial cocktail with her male companion, when she suddenly threw the contents of her glass into his face and stormed out. Had I known at the time that her marriage to playwright, John Osborne, was nearing its acrimonious end, I would likely have put two and two together, claiming some personal involvement in that whatever it was I had concocted for Miss Bennett was now running down the face of the illustrious author of *Look Back in Anger*. But since I never got to see his sodden features I cannot, hand-on-heart, swear that it was him.

The Duenna opened at the Yvonne Arnaud Theatre in Guildford at the end of March, and toured for the next six weeks. Somehow or other, I managed to see it several times en route, although once would have been enough for me had Lesley not been in it, singing very prettily, and looking quite lovely. When the show went on to play at the Alexandra Theatre in Birmingham, the local newspaper celebrated her return to the city in the wake of her memorable performance as Dorothy in *The Wizard of Oz*, with an article under the witty headline: MACKIE'S BACK IN TOWN. For undisclosed editorial reasons, however, they chose to illustrate it with a picture of Lesley, not in one of her lovely 18th century dresses, but disguised as she was required to be in just one scene, black-cloaked and hooded, her face all but hidden, so that anyone reading that headline, and seeing that picture, would have been more likely to rush home and lock their door than welcome Mackie back!

I was at home in Blackheath when I received a telephone call from Peter Dews. "Hello, luvvie", he said, "How d'you fancy coming down to Chich?" I already knew that Peter was due to take up the post of Artistic Director at the Chichester Festival Theatre the following year and that, in preparation for this, and under the present stewardship of Keith Michell, he was going to mount a production of Shakespeare's *Julius Caesar* as part of the current season. "I'd love to, Peter", I said, doing my best to conceal the sigh of relief. "What do you have in mind?" After suggesting that if I wasn't already sitting down I should maybe do so, he went on to say "I'd like you to play Calpurnia". Following a lengthy pause, and having failed to come up with anything more apropos, I asked, "Why?" to which he quickly replied, "Well, you were a wonderful Player Queen in *Hamlet*". "But that was years ago, Peter!" I protested. "I know luvvie, I know, but Calpurnia is a middle-aged woman!" He went on to reassure me – well, up to a point – by explaining that it was to be an all-male cast. But when I asked him what else was on offer for the rest of the season, he said he didn't know, and that I would have to ask Keith, who was in charge of casting the other plays. Keith Michell and I hadn't met since we had acted opposite each other, as Marc Antony and Eros, in *The Spread of the Eagle*, back in

1963, and given that I had played a significant part in the 'end-of-term' show which brought the series to a close, and in which Keith's approach to acting had been pitilessly satirised, I had no reason to expect a warm reception. I couldn't have been more wrong, however, so he had obviously either forgotten or forgiven the offence. But then again, maybe he hadn't, since it transpired in our subsequent conversation that there was not a single part he could offer me. *Waters of the Moon* and *The Apple Cart* were already cast and there was nothing suitable in his own show, a musical celebration of the Queen's Silver Jubilee called *In Order of Appearance*. In the face of my obvious reluctance to take it any further, he went on to express what I took to be genuine regret, adding that, while Peter was bound to be very disappointed, he would perfectly understand if I found it difficult to justify a season in Chichester playing Calpurnia and nothing else. So, as far as I was concerned, that was the end of the matter, and all I had to do was to convince myself that, with nothing else in the pipeline, I had made the right decision. It was only a couple of days later that I received a phone call from Patrick Garland, who began where Keith had left off by telling me how disappointed Peter was that I had turned down his offer. I was girding my loins to resist an attempt to persuade me to change my mind, when he said, "As well as *The Apple Cart*, I'm going to be directing a promenade production of *Murder in the Cathedral*, in Chichester Cathedral. Keith will be playing Becket. What would *you* like to play?" After only the briefest of hesitations, I said, "How about First Tempter?" Patrick was equally concise. "It's yours", he said. "Now will you come?"

My season at Chichester couldn't have got off to a better start. At the wheel of my recently-acquired Rover 100, I had extended my search for accommodation beyond the city limits and closer to the sea. I had heard that a man called Roger Bunn, owner of several large caravan sites on the nearby West Sussex coast, was looking for a temporary tenant at his home in Selsey, a seaside town that not only boasted several extensive beaches, but also the celebrated astronomer, Patrick Moore, as a near neighbour. Moreover, it was only seven miles from Chichester, which made it a very attractive proposition. Even so, as I drove up the gravelled driveway to the porticoed front door of Roger Bunn's newly-built neo-Georgian mansion, I couldn't help thinking that what he probably had in mind was the servants' quarters; and even as the affable young man led me round to the side of his house, I was already trying to come to terms with the distinct possibility that it might even be a written off caravan in his back garden. But when he opened a side door and ushered me in, I found myself in a self-contained flat into which we had gained access through what he said would be my very own front door. He went on to explain that his long-term plan for this wing of the house was to convert it into a leisure suite, featuring a sauna, steam-room and a small gymnasium, but meanwhile he wanted it to be lived in, and had it furnished accordingly. It wasn't a spacious flat but it was well laid out, with a fully equipped galley-type kitchen, bathroom and a comfortable bed-sitter with a retractable double-bed, a television set, a telephone and – wait for it – French windows leading to an open-air swimming pool. This, of course, made perfect sense as an extension to the planned leisure suite, but it wasn't exactly on the wish-list when it came to theatrical digs. Needless to say, I was only too happy to take Roger Bunn up on his generous offer, although the summer of 1977 bore little or no resemblance to its predecessor, so that while I may well have sat by the pool on the occasional balmy day, I don't recall ever venturing into it. Nevertheless, Selsey provided me with the perfect location and a flat to which I enjoyed returning at the end of every day.

It strikes me now, even if it didn't at the time, that my reason for finally accepting the season at Chichester bore a striking similarity – if not with such life-changing consequences – to Joan Knight's offer, three years earlier, to appear in *Joseph and the Amazing Technicolor Dreamcoat* at Perth, which I had all but turned down until she coupled it with the chance to play Sir Andrew Aguecheek in *Twelfth Night*, the entirely unlooked-for outcome being that I enjoyed *Joseph* a good deal more than *Twelfth Night*. Not that I didn't enjoy playing the First Tempter in *Murder in the Cathedral*. Perched high on the transept above the nave of that beautiful cathedral was a thrilling experience made all the more poignant knowing that those very stones had been standing there 800 years earlier when Thomas Becket had actually been murdered less than a 100 miles away. But the promenade concept, while it provided a fascinating tour of the cathedral, only served to dissipate the dramatic impact of the play as scene after scene, played in a variety of locations, had to be put on hold, waiting for the audience to catch up. This handicap was compounded by Keith Michell's performance as Becket, self-regarding as usual, and all but begging to be martyred from the outset to ensure his place in history. It was as Calpurnia in *Julius Caesar*, however, that I derived the greatest pleasure. Peter Dews had long since decided to set the play in the Jacobean period, a decision based entirely on the congruity between the meeting of the conspirators in Act 2 Scene 1, and the famous picture of a similar gathering in 1605 of those involved in the Gunpowder Plot. The fact that the rest of the play, devoid of similar analogous moments, was somewhat gratuitously compromised by this decision did, I suppose, at least provide a good excuse for an all-male cast. More to the point, as far as I was concerned anyway, was that it allowed me to swan around, bearing a striking resemblance to Queen Elizabeth I, an image I was only too happy to promote, both on-stage and off, where people deferentially stood aside to allow me to pass, although it might well have had something to do with the size of my frock!

1977 The Chichester cricket team.

My experience was further enhanced by the fact that I couldn't have had a nicer and more considerate 'husband' than Nigel Stock as Julius Caesar, that Cassius was being played by my old friend, Charles Kay, with whom I hadn't worked since that 'memorable' season at the Belgrade Theatre in 1959, and that the company contained a host of easy-going and companionable people, amongst whom was the charming Gary Bond as Brutus, whilst that most ubiquitous of all actors, Vernon Dobtcheff, whom Patrick Garland had last bumped into whilst changing trains at Avignon, lived up to expectations simply by being there, as was his Soothsayer when Caesar just happened to pass by on his way to the Forum. Oz Clarke featured strongly too, although it was not so much as an actor as in his role as a lover, and generous sharer, of vintage wines that he was truly appreciated, and who later went on to indulge his passion in several television series, while Tony Robinson confounded Peter Dews' description of him as a 'poison dwarf' by becoming the much-loved Munchkin, Baldrick in that hugely successful television series, *Blackadder*, as well as eventually acquiring for himself a more prestigious reputation, and a knighthood, as the Presenter of the long-running archaeological series, *Timewatch*.

The season was well under way by the time rehearsals began for *Julius Caesar,* and once we'd opened, in repertoire with the other productions, we played on average about three performances a week, so those of us who weren't appearing in anything else were able to enjoy a great deal of spare time, allowing me to take advantage of my idyllic seaside accommodation, to play the occasional game of cricket and, of course, to entertain Lesley who was able to come down for a while before heading back to Scotland and a Perth Theatre tour of *The Matchmaker* and Molière's *The Hypochondriac*. Meanwhile, she'd moved into the Blackheath flat as soon as the tour of *The Duenna* had come to an end and together we'd taken a trip to Dundee where I happily discovered that, while her parents may well have wished otherwise for their daughter, they were clearly in favour of her getting married to someone. Wedding plans were discussed and, undeterred by my current marital status, a church wedding was decided upon. I had no objection to this, although I suspected that the church might have had, and probably would have if it had been the Church of England. The Church of Scotland, however, had no such qualms, or at least not in the person of Duncan Darroch who, having made a few courteous enquiries about the sincerity and gravity of my commitment, and having ascertained that divorce proceedings were well and truly under way, expressed himself more than happy, not only to sanction a church wedding, but to return from his retirement as a Minister of the Church, in order to conduct the ceremony himself.

We had scarcely begun rehearsals in Chichester when I heard from Lesley that Clive Perry had been in touch with an urgent request for her to take over a couple of roles in *Measure for Measure* and in Ben Jonson's *The Devil Is An Ass* for an imminent European tour, due to the sudden illness of Janet Maw who had been playing the parts in the UK. Bernard Lloyd, recently returned from Canada, was playing the Duke, and was now fleetingly in residence at 23 Vanbrugh Park before flying off to Zurich on the first leg of the tour. So it was together with Lesley that he left for Heathrow, using the journey to familiarise her with the Ben Jonson play and help her with the lines. They then joined the rest of the company, assembled in the departure lounge at Heathrow, only minutes before boarding their flight, when the Company Manager, having been summoned to take a telephone call, returned to inform Lesley that, instead of facing surgery for suspected appendicitis, Janet Maw had been diagnosed with a stomach bug from which she was all but recovered, and would therefore be able to join the company in time for their opening performance. He went on to say that, regrettably, he had no alternative but to thank Lesley, and to bid her adieu. And so it was that, with one sad suitcase on the ground beside her, she was left to wave goodbye to a bunch of demonstratively sympathetic actors with whom she was destined not to work, never mind being deprived of the exciting prospect of acting in a foreign country for the first time. Clive Perry was obviously well aware of the disappointment and inconvenience she must have suffered by giving her a bunch of flowers, a book-token, and the taxi fare from Heathrow to Chadwick Street Labour Exchange!

It was no ill wind, however, as it meant that Lesley and I would be able to spend more time together before she had to go back to Scotland, and there was a great deal to talk about, given that I wouldn't be seeing her again until I joined her there at the end of the Chichester season and just prior to the wedding. There was the guest-list, for instance, traditionally the responsibility of the bride's mother, and which therefore consisted of a large number of uncles, aunts, cousins and friends of the bride's family. Lesley and I were permitted, of course, to invite a few friends of our own, an arrangement that was bound to favour Lesley, her choice being largely of Scottish origin. This seemed to me to be an entirely reasonable proposition since it fell to Violet to organise the entire occasion and to pay for virtually all of it. Then there was the question of the divorce proceedings which, for obvious, if not entirely ingenuous reasons, I had placed in the hands of James McGoldrick, implicitly daring him to charge me for it which, to give him his due, he never did. But Lesley was understandably nervous about the timing of it. The banns had to be read on three successive Sundays prior to the wedding, by which time the *decree absolute,* the final termination of my previous marriage, had to be legally authorised, or I would lay myself open to a charge of bigamy. I had no good reason to doubt McGoldrick's professionalism, nor his desire to make some kind of personal reparation, but Lesley had no reason at all to put her trust in him following a wine-soaked evening we had spent with him and his new wife at their luxurious home in South-East London, during which he managed to consume the best part of five bottles and, while attempting to bestow on Lesley a farewell kiss, fell backwards in their hall and dragged her down on top of him!

There were, of course, decisions to be made on a variety of other subjects, none of which involved me more directly than the choice of a wedding-dress. Being somewhat petite, her options were limited when it came to buying something 'off-the-peg' while the cost of having one designed and made especially for her was likely to be prohibitive. It came to me then that there was only one person I could entrust with such a sensitive commission, and so it came to pass, somewhat bizarrely, that Lesley's wedding-dress was designed and made for her by the woman to whom, at that time, I was still legally married. Needless to say, no one in her family, with the exception of her mother and father, knew of this, nor that Dawn had charged her a mere £50 for it, including the cost of materials. This had, of course, involved a trip to Bristol, and included a meal out with Dawn and Charles, a perfectly relaxed and affable affair which finally laid to rest any lingering unease between us, and provided one more respite in what was turning out to be a fairly leisurely and sociable season. On one such social occasion, we invited Peter and Ann Dews to have dinner with us at my flat in Selsey, during the course of which Ann, a stranger to subtlety, made a point of taking Lesley under her wing, fondly bestowing upon her the patronage and approval that was in her gift, together with friendly tips on cooking, and other familiarities, making it crystal clear that she thought my future wife was a vast improvement on my previous one. She had, of course, completely misjudged Lesley, mistaking the girlishness that was certainly a feature, for gullibility, which it never was. Besides, Lesley was already well acquainted with the resistible rise of Ann Dews, and was happily immune to her blandishments. Thankfully, Ann had at least learned to keep her distance from the rehearsal room and other working environments, and might well have been fondly regarded by those who hadn't crossed her path before. Peter was a pleasure to work with, as he had been a couple of years earlier at Birmingham; not as inspirational as he had once been, but then again not nearly as volatile. Only once, during rehearsals, do I remember him erupting, and that was when a party of tourists, obviously keen to visit whatever Chichester had to offer, chose to come into the theatre's auditorium during a dress rehearsal and swiftly backed out again in the wake of one of Peter's now fondly remembered tirades. Sadly, this was the last time I was destined to work with him, and although our relationship over the years had suffered a few set-backs, one of them verging on the terminal, we were both obviously prepared to forgive and forget, and he remains, to this day, one of a mere handful of directors with whom I count it a privilege to have worked, and to whom I am indebted, along with David William and Peter Wright, of Kilburn Grammar School, for inculcating in me a knowledge and a love of Shakespeare that I prize beyond measure. Later in the season, Peter even allowed me to reassert my masculinity when he cast me as Cassius in John Bowen's *Heil Caesar*, an updated version of Shakespeare's play, staged at the *Dolphin & Anchor*, a pub venue in Chichester which foreshadowed the creation, in 1989, of the Minerva Theatre, and where a number of other 'alternative' productions were staged back in 1977. These included a revival of my Spanish Civil War documentary, *Yesterday the Struggle,* featuring, amongst others, Tony Robinson and Gordon Griffin, a member of the company with whom I shared an immediate rapport as well as a number of 'legendary' Sunday lunches at the *George & Dragon* or, alternatively, *chez moi* in Selsey where, according to Gordon, my Sunday roasts fared extremely well by comparison – hence our long-term friendship!

It was with Gordon that Lesley and I went to see a production of N.C.Hunter's play, *Waters of the Moon,* at the Festival Theatre, starring Ingrid Bergman. Lesley might well have enjoyed it more had she not been suffering a bout of hay fever at the time, but I very much doubt it. It was early on in the proceedings that I experienced a sense of *déja vu.* It suddenly struck me that I had once, many years ago, appeared in a production of N.C. Hunter's *A Day By the Sea* in a long-forgotten venue on the fringes of Manchester. I was obviously pretty wet behind the ears at that time, but my long-term memory being what it is, I knew that the only reason I could have so entirely forgotten it was that it was entirely forgettable, and it only struck me at that moment because I knew I was living through a similar experience. In the early '50s N.C. Hunter had been described as the 'English Chekhov', blithely ignoring or, indeed, ignorant of the fact that the sombre and sentimental English translations of Chekhov's plays at that time, and hence our perception of them, was well wide of the mark. For anyone who witnessed the Moscow Art's season at Sadler's Wells in 1958, as I did, it will have come as a revelation that the plays were funnier and more robust than we had any reason to expect. There can be very little doubt that Hunter's early successes were due in no small measure to the quality of the stars who were persuaded to appear in them. The presence of Ingrid Bergman on stage at Chichester did little to enhance the overall vacuity of *Waters of the Moon*, although on the plus side, it did nothing to dim my star-struck pride at being a member of the same company, or from the thrill of actually meeting and shaking hands with the star of *Casablanca*.

Lesley left Chichester for Scotland some time before we did *Murder in the Cathedral*, or indeed *Heil Caesar*, and so it was an image of her husband-to-be as a female impersonator that she carried with her on her journey north! My anxieties regarding the divorce, on hold while she was around, came to haunt me with a vengeance after she left. Bearing in mind that six weeks and a day have to elapse after the issue of a *decree nisi* before the *decree absolute* can be authorised, followed by three successive weeks for the banns to be called, here we were, the clock ticking away, facing the prospect of having to postpone the wedding, an unthinkable scenario given the preparations that were already well in hand, and the embarrassment Lesley's mum would have to suffer should the plans go awry. I spoke to McGoldrick, doing my best to conceal my anxieties, but suspecting all the while that maybe Lesley had been right about him and that, somewhere along the line, he had either contrived to put the whole thing on a back burner or that he had simply forgotten all about it. But he was imperturbable. Time was still on our side, he assured me, and whether or not his confidence was founded on professional expertise or professional gloss, I had no way of knowing. Suffice it to say that the first decree was issued the following week which, allowing for the subsequent nine weeks and a day would permit me to enjoy the prospect of being a single man for two whole weeks! Meanwhile, Lesley and I were in constant touch, finalising guest-lists, choosing music, and deciding where to spend our honeymoon which would last for all of one night, and in a nearby hotel, as rehearsals were due to begin the following day for a production of *Blithe Spirit* at Perth Theatre, in which we were both to feature.

Had I not been looking forward to a momentous and imminent change in my private life, I would have felt sadder than I did when I said goodbye to Chichester, and more especially to my little flat in Selsey. But I took away with me many happy memories, both professional and personal, together with the indelible memory of a review of *Julius Caesar* from the *Guardian* theatre critic, Victoria Radin, who accused me, for the first and only time in my life, of being too tall for the part! Lesley and I were married in Dundee on October 9th, just seven months after she had accepted my proposal.

There was a degree of controversy about our choice of a Sunday wedding. In fact, her grandmother had to be persuaded to come; but given that Lesley had two shows on Saturday and was in rehearsal for the rest of the week, we had little or no alternative. In any case, she looked lovely in her wedding-dress, as evidenced, not only by the approving crowd that had gathered outside the church, but by her father, looking proud as a peacock as he 'gave her away', clearly reconciled by now to her fate; and by me, of course, whose happiness was replete as she walked down the aisle to the strains of Haydn's *St Anthony Chorale*, played on the church organ by Perth Theatre's John Scrimger. Standing beside me was Andrew McKinnon, whose role as Best Man had come about for largely logistical reasons, my brother being unable to make the journey due to his wife's burgeoning pregnancy, and with Bernard Lloyd yet again out of the country. I had no reason, however, to regard Andrew as any kind of an understudy. He was both charming and attentive, bringing a touch of his familiar erudition to the proceedings by wishing us "the wisdom of Solomon, the riches of Croesus and the children of Israel!" I had few personal friends in attendance, largely because of the distance from London, although Norman Boyack, who was still my agent, together with his wife, Althea, managed to make the trip, as did Brendan Price who, enjoying a bit of television fame at the time, and with the aid of a bottle of Lansen Black Label, managed to seduce one of Lesley's cousins later in the day!

Happily, my mother and father were there, although I have since suffered occasional pangs of guilt that, having travelled so far, I may not have paid them enough attention. I hope that wasn't the case, and neither of them ever complained about it, so it's probably safe to assume that my uneasy conscience was, and remains, the work of one of those all too familiar demons from the past that are sent to torment us. What I have good reason to remember, although I cannot swear that the subject came up during our nuptials, is the story my father told me about his purchase of 137 Purves Road, the house in which they had lived as co-tenants with Mr and Mrs Smith since the beginning of World War II, and with whom we had shared an Anderson shelter in the back garden during the air-raids on London. He had been surprised to see in a local estate agent's window that the house was up for sale, and on an impulse had gone in and expressed a casual interest in buying it, although he thought the asking price of £2,000 was too high, bearing in mind the work that was needed to repair the back garden wall. He could not have been more surprised when they immediately reduced it to £1,800, an offer he could hardly refuse. The upshot was that, for undisclosed reasons, Mr. and Mrs Smith decided to move away, probably because they could not countenance sharing the house with their erstwhile co-tenants, now about to become their landlords.

My father, having had no intention of occupying the upstairs flat, suggested that Lesley and I might like to live there, rent-free, should we be looking for a London home, a gift we happily accepted. My mother, however, and for some mysterious reason, was less enthusiastic, even somewhat hostile to the idea, although what objections she had were never entirely clear. It transpired in time that she was in the very early stages of Alzheimer's, our first acquaintance with that awful disease, during the course of which my father was to suffer terribly.

While promising ourselves a more exotic, if belated, honeymoon, our brief stay at the Ballathie House hotel just outside Perth provided a welcome pause before rehearsals began for Noël Coward's *Blithe Spirit* in which I was to be playing the relatively undemanding role of Dr. Bradman while Lesley was in her characterful element as Edith, the somewhat frowzy household maid, her delightful bridal persona but a memory. Perth Theatre had pushed out the boat on this occasion to secure the services of the popular Scottish comedian, Rikki Fulton, to play the part of Charles Condomine, which seemed unlikely casting, considering that the part had originally been played by Noël Coward himself. Rikki was accompanied by his wife, Kate Matheson, who had been cast as Condomine's late wife, Elvira. Kate was a charming lady to have around. Would that Rikki Fulton's two little dogs, who he also insisted on bringing to rehearsals with him, had been as appealing! They growled their approval every time he spoke, made unscripted entrances during other people's scenes in order to be closer to him, and farted constantly, filling the rehearsal room with a stink to which he alone was immune. Whether or not Andrew McKinnon, as director, had been instrumental in casting the part I had no way of knowing, although it was much more likely that Joan made the decisions when it came to dealing with celebrities, as evidenced by Andrew's ready compliance with anything and everything Rikki Fulton did, suggested, or insisted upon. There were the relatively minor incidents like pitting himself against Noël Coward's razor-sharp wit, by remarking as he took a bite from his toast and marmalade, "Mmmm, Golden Shred – delicious!" But he broke entirely new ground when he insisted on opening the play by sitting at the piano and playing, in its entirety, Irving Berlin's *Always*, a song associated in Charles Condomine's mind with his deceased wife, and consequently anathema to him in any way, shape or form, let alone choosing to play it himself. Worse still, he played it throughout the opening scene in which his current wife, played by Anne Kidd, and my current wife were trying to serve the author's intentions by setting the scene. Not only that, but he deliberately courted and received a round of applause at the end of it. It so happened that Lesley and I were renting a flat in a nearby block next door to the one in which Rikki and Kate were installed and, early on in rehearsals, we joined them for supper, during the course of which I played with fire by saying that I thought it was not a good idea of Andrew's to ask him to play *Always* for the aforementioned reasons. There was a pause, during which he studied my face, before saying, "It wasn't Andrew's idea, it was mine". "Oh", I said, feigning surprise, "I'm sorry I mentioned it".

It was also during rehearsals that I received a telegram from Dawn asking me to call her. Telegrams were the only means of urgent communication in those days, before the coming of the mobile phone, and more particularly if the addressee was away from home and didn't have a personal telephone number. Nevertheless, I had a premonition about it, if only because I couldn't imagine what else would prompt that kind of urgency. I was right, in a sense, although I could hardly have predicted the nightmare scenario that unfolded when I called her; Charles was dead. He had thrown himself from the Clifton suspension bridge in Bristol, and Dawn had only heard about it on a television news programme later the same day. I could hardly begin to imagine the shock and the horror she must have experienced, and my heart went out to her. I had long known, of course, having been acquainted with Charles before they met each other, that he suffered from depression, which I had put down to his sexual ambiguity, a problem that I thought had been resolved when he and Dawn got together. But for those of us who don't suffer from it, or who use the word to describe being a bit down in the mouth, it's difficult to comprehend the severity of such a condition. I knew from Dawn that it was ongoing and that he usually dealt with it, as with migraine, by lying in a darkened room until it lifted. But that it could descend so suddenly, and seemingly without warning, and that it could so peremptorily lead you to take your life, was beyond my imagination. Dawn told me that she had left him that afternoon in charge of the clothing boutique they had recently established so that she could do some shopping, and that when she'd called him later as he was about to close up for the day, he seemed in good spirits and looking forward to seeing the pair of vintage shoes she had just bought. At the inquest, a schoolboy, on his way home, told how he had been walking behind Charles as he strode purposefully across the bridge before placing a hand on the rail and, without a moment's hesitation, leaped over it.

For reasons that I perfectly understood, Dawn had turned to me, for the simple reason that I was the only person she could have turned to at such a time. I likewise felt that I wanted to support her if only by way of the telephone. Had I turned my back on her at such a time, who knows but I could well have yet one more demon to haunt me.

On a happier note, and with Christmas fast approaching, Lesley was due to take up Clive Perry's offer of a couple of decent parts in *A Christmas Carol* at Birmingham. That he went on to offer me a small part in the same production simply because he thought we might be happier spending our first Christmas as a married couple together rather than apart, was surprising to say the least, Clive not being famed for his largesse. He knew, of course, that I had been invited by Joan Knight to embark upon my second outing as director at Perth Theatre, and that I would regretfully have to say no to his offer, a caveat he anticipated by telling me that I would not be required for the first week of rehearsal, by which time, as he also knew, I would be free to join the company in Birmingham. I was, of course, happy to accept Clive's generous offer, and grateful to him too for providing me with the happy prospect, whatever the outcome of the daunting journey I was about to embark upon in Perth, of playing George the Bystander alongside Lesley for Christmas.

oOoOo

Twenty two

I was never in two minds about taking up Joan Knight's invitation to direct Samuel Beckett's *Waiting for Godot*, but it troubled me nonetheless. It was, after all, only my second professional production, the first having been a relatively simple proposition, if only because it had a plot, a climax, a dénouement, a beginning, middle and an end. The storyline was also peopled with characters who made choices, and who developed them accordingly, while *Godot* was as bereft of these guidelines as it was of a recognisable location or setting. I was also puzzled, not only by Joan's decision to do the play at all, and in Perth of all places, but to entrust me, a relative débutant, with the task of staging it. Had I not already been well acquainted with Joan, I might have suspected she was preparing herself for its inevitable failure at the box-office by distancing herself from it – "nothing to do with me, darling!" But that wasn't like Joan at all, for only a year earlier, having delegated Shaw's *Man and Superman* to a young and totally inexperienced director, had she not returned post-haste from London to effect a last minute rescue? So I could only surmise that, for reasons best known to herself, she thought I could handle it or, at the very worst, she would be on hand should she be required to pull the fat out of the fire.

It was in 1955, just before I left the Webber-Douglas Academy that I went to see the first London production of *Waiting for Godot* at the Criterion Theatre, a bewildering experience, and one that I wouldn't have wanted to live through again. Not that I recall feeling any degree of fervour about it, either one way or the other, unlike a significant number of playgoers during its run who were reported to have raised their voices in boisterous protest more typical of 18th century audiences than their relatively polite modern counterparts whose objections are generally expressed by not coming back after the interval. Very few, I venture to suggest, myself included, could have predicted its future status as a modern classic, inspiring many others, Harold Pinter for one, to carry the flag for what came to be known as the *Theatre of the Absurd*. My original thoughts on the play are nowhere recorded, but had I been acquainted with Kenneth Tynan's review of that first production, I would surely have shared his opinion, although I doubt I would have been equipped to express it as articulately as Mr Tynan: 'By all the known criteria, Samuel Beckett's *Waiting for Godot* is a dramatic vacuum. Pity the critic who seeks a chink in its armour for it is all chink ... Unavoidably, it has a situation, and it might be accused of having suspense, since it deals with the impatience of two tramps waiting beneath a tree for a cryptic Mr. Godot to keep his appointment with them; but the situation is never developed, and a glance at the programme shows that Mr. Godot is not going to arrive. *Waiting for Godot* frankly jettisons everything by which we recognise theatre. It arrives at the custom-house, as it were, with no luggage, no passport, and nothing to declare; yet it gets through, as might a pilgrim from Mars. It does this, I believe, by appealing to a definition of drama much more fundamental than any in the books. A play, it asserts and proves, is basically a means of spending two hours in the dark without being bored'.

Rumour had it, and it was quite feasible, given that Joan had her faults as well as her many strengths, that she had asked Rikki Fulton to appear in it at Perth, but that he, equally feasibly, had turned it down; whether because he thought it was a load of shite, or because I was to be directing it, is anybody's guess. Whatever the reason, I could only be grateful, as he would very likely have insisted on meeting Godot at the end of the play, probably in the shape of his old comedy partner, Jack Milroy, with whom he could have rounded off the evening with some couthy Scottish humour, leaving audiences to go home with smiles on their faces. There was little doubt, on the other hand, that his presence would have lured more people in to see *Godot* than it otherwise did. The play, however, together with its director, could not have been better served than by the cast Joan finally assembled. Roger Kemp was to play Vladimir, and by so doing he and I were united once again. Two other familiar faces, neither of whom I had worked with before, were Jake D'Arcy who was to play Estragon, and Alec Heggie as Pozzo. Allowing me some token input, Joan had suggested I might like to cast Lucky, the remaining character, myself, and I had no hesitation in offering the part to Christopher Selbie, a former colleague from Chichester, whose company I had enjoyed there, both backstage and on the cricket pitch! The fact that I enjoyed directing *Godot* more than I could possibly have imagined was due in no small measure to the quality of those actors, and to the positive atmosphere they generated in the rehearsal room where we became a team, each of us sharing a journey dedicated to serving the interests of a play which, without a beginning, middle, or end, we all came to acknowledge, if not as a masterpiece, certainly as an exceptional piece of theatre, and one which would enjoy a great many more revivals in the years to come.

Staging Beckett in Great Britain, edited by David Tucker, is a book in which the author goes to considerable lengths documenting the growth of Samuel Beckett's influence here at home, and not only on the legacy inherited by our own playwrights, but with a string of plays written by the man himself, including *Endgame, Krapp's Last Tape, Happy Days* and, of course, *Waiting for Godot.*

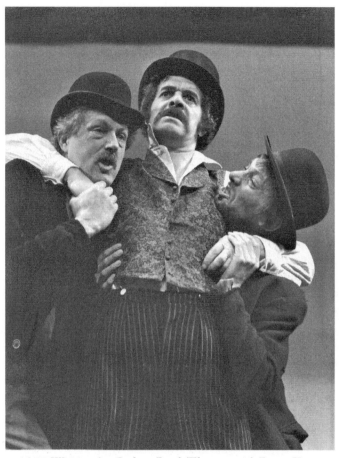

1977 Waiting for Godot - Perth Theatre, with Roger Kemp, Alec Heggie and Jake D'Arcy

Waiting for Godot opened at the Arts Theatre in 1955 to a fairly hostile reception, could well have been the beginning and the end of his influence, which would certainly have meant that David Tucker's book wouldn't have been written, and I wouldn't have been able to read, 39 years later, the following review: 'It would not be until Terry Wale's production of *Godot* at Perth Theatre that Scotland finally produced a reading that lived up not only to the author's description of it as a tragicomedy but also to his stage directions. This production's main strength is that it did not labour the text; neither did it indulge in fanciful elaborate settings. Instead it offered all the simplicity and heart-wrenching tragicomedy that is inherent in the play, making it one of the most respectful and memorable treatments of Beckett's writing in Scotland for a long while'.

Shortly after my arrival in Birmingham, and at Dawn's request, I drove down to Bristol, simply to be there while she scattered Charles's ashes on Glastonbury Tor, a Somerset hill famed not only for being at the heart of the Arthurian legend, but also for its music festival. It was an altogether strange experience, witnessing a grief I could not share while, at the same time, wanting to provide comfort and support for the person who had left me for him. Thankfully, the proceedings came to a more bizarre conclusion when, having driven Dawn back to her Bristol flat, she handed me the Co-op funeral urn which had contained Charles's ashes, and asked me to dispose of it. I suppose it was the least I could do in the circumstances, but having arrived back in Birmingham still clutching it, and reluctant for obvious reasons to take it with me into our Edgbaston flat, I was left with no alternative but to dispose of it in a waste-bin on the street. As it was, a good deal of forbearance was required on Lesley's part to cope with my visit to Bristol, and in the months that followed with the numerous phone calls I felt obliged to make as I sensed that Dawn was teetering on the edge of a precipice. But Lesley took it all in her stride, exhibiting a degree of stoicism that effectively masked the pain she undoubtedly felt.

But we all have our crosses to bear, however light by comparison, and mine came very shortly after rehearsals for *A Christmas Carol* began, when I learned that the actress who was to play the part of Caroline, George the Bystander's wife, was a lady by the name of Lesley Joseph, who had played Glinda, the Good Witch in the previous Christmas production of *The Wizard of Oz*, and who had allegedly been lured back by Clive Perry on his assurance that Caroline was a substantial role. The fact that I had happily, and gratefully, accepted his offer to play George for exactly the opposite reason, and that I was looking forward to a relatively undemanding season, did not even allow me a voice in the 'debate' that obviously followed, as the parts of George the Bystander and Caroline Bystander grew larger by the day. But it was Clive's apparently willing compliance with her suggestions that puzzled me more than anything else. Clive was not famed for his kindly disposition when it came to professional matters, as I had been given good reason to believe from a number of people.

But what was even more puzzling was that, in rehearsals for *A Christmas Carol*, contrary to expectations, his conduct was all but seraphic. He never once raised his voice and, indeed, for long periods of time, scarcely used it at all. Having briefly entertained the unlikely notion that he had undergone a Scrooge-like transformation, it finally transpired that he had become involved in a training programme called 'est' which, incorporating the Socratic method, 'aimed at enabling participants to shift their contextual state of mind, around which their life was organised, from the attempt to get satisfaction or to survive, to an experience of actually being satisfied and experiencing oneself as whole and complete in the present moment, offering people the opportunity to free themselves from the past, rather than living a life enmeshed by their past'. So ... maybe the Scrooge analogy wasn't so wide of the mark, after all, and whatever the treatment, and however long its effects were likely to last, there is no doubt that we all benefited from it at the time, so 'God bless us, every one!'

My memories of the production itself are pretty sketchy, although it turned out to be more fun than I had expected it to be. The acting company, led by Bob Grant (of *On the Buses* fame) as Scrooge, was largely convivial, and while the less and less peripheral role of George the Bystander was memorable for all the wrong reasons, I more happily recall *my* Lesley's effervescent performance as Belinda Cratchit. Meanwhile, she and I enjoyed our first Christmas together as man and wife, which was indeed a memorable occasion, and not only because our fellow tenants in Edgbaston had chosen to spend it elsewhere, but also because Andrew McKinnon trumped Clive Perry's wedding gift by offering us, as a Christmas present, a season together at the Pitlochry Festival Theatre. I had no idea, of course, back in 1951, the year in which I made my professional début as an actor at the newly-opened Mermaid Theatre in St. John's Wood, that another theatre had also opened its doors for the very first time some 400 miles away in Pitlochry. But then I was only 13 years old at the time and knew very little about anything, let alone where Pitlochry was, or even that it existed. I was to learn in time that the only other thing these two theatres had in common was that the Mermaid, conceived and exquisitely designed to resemble an Elizabethan playhouse, was built at the back of Duff House, the home of Bernard Miles, while the Pitlochry Festival Theatre, a somewhat inferior tented structure, was erected in the grounds of the decidedly more stately Knockendarroch House, home to the Festival's founder, John Stewart.

Although I had never had the opportunity to visit it, let alone see a play there, Pitlochry was only about 30 miles north of Perth, best known as a popular stopping-off point for tourists on their way to the Highlands; its outstanding feature, aside from its beautiful setting amongst the Perthshire hills, was the Scottish Hydro-Electric plant with its specially constructed dam and the fish ladder up which, on a lucky day, you could watch the salmon climb from the River Tummel into Loch Faskally. But it was pretty much a one-street town, and there was little else to prolong a visit until the Pitlochry Festival Theatre, with its slogan of 'Stay Six Days and See Six Plays' came into being. Even then, the theatre was somewhat tucked away in a side street, and you would have been unlikely to stumble across it unless you'd been there before! It would take 30 years for the wise burghers of Pitlochry to fully grasp its cultural, not to mention its economic potential, when the doors finally opened on a brand new contemporary theatre situated in Port-na-Craig, high above the town on the other side of the river, affording wonderful views over the Tummel Valley. But that was still three years away when Lesley and I first arrived at the beginning of March 1978 to begin rehearsals for the Festival Theatre's 28th annual season, now under the direction of Kenneth Ireland, who had not only inherited the old theatre upon John Stewart's demise some 20 years earlier, but also the tenancy of Knockendarroch House, although we were later given to understand it had been intended as a legacy to provide accommodation for the actors. Not that Lesley or I had any reason to complain as we moved into our delightful two-bedroom cottage, situated a mere 100 yards from the stage door, as long as you were prepared to climb over the fence to reach it!

My memories of our season at Pitlochry are largely anecdotal, and were it not for the fact that Lesley, unlike me, has maintained a diary of events, I wouldn't even be able to remember which of the six plays opened first. I do recall, however, and for very obvious reasons, that the most daunting prospect I faced was a return visit to the role of Ariel in *The Tempest*, the part I'd first played at the age of 12 at Kilburn Grammar School when my own unworldliness was more in accord with that spirit's ethereal nature. Having just celebrated my 40th birthday, 27 wagons full of personal baggage later, I knew I was going to have to dig deep if I was to rediscover that kind of unworldliness. But *The Tempest*, as it turns out, did not open the season as I had thought, although we were rehearsing the first three plays at the same time, and it could well have been any one of them had I not been able to refer to Lesley's diary, which states, unequivocally, that on April 10th the season was launched with a production of Ben Travers' farce, *A*

Cup of Kindness, followed five days later by the opening of Terence Rattigan's *While the Sun Shines,* and only then, on April 28th, by *The Tempest.* The very idea of embarking on such a mind-boggling schedule now is beyond imagining, although I obviously took it in my stride at the time, and given that the theatre had to make good its commitment to staging six different plays in as many days, then obviously all six had to be up and running in time for the tourist season. On the plus side, however, Lesley and I appeared in only five of the six and so, on paper at least, there was some respite. The next two productions, scheduled to open in May and in June, were a relatively obscure 18th century piece, entitled *Know Your Own Mind,* by Arthur Murphy, and Brecht's *The Caucasian Chalk Circle.* But it was with the Ben Travers play that rehearsals began, under the direction of Andrew McKinnon, and alongside a company of actors, most of them unknown to me at the time, but with whom I was destined to spend the next eight months in a variety of unpredictable situations, personal as well as professional, while closeted in what was little more than a village, from which it was all but impossible to escape without the assistance of four wheels and an engine, giving rise to a condition known, I believe, as 'cabin fever'. I remember suffering from something very like it back in 1961 when, driven by desperation, I strove to master my Lambretta, upon the two wheels of which I was able to put Stratford-upon-Avon behind me from time to time. But, as far as Pitlochry was concerned, while I recognised the symptoms in others, living and working alongside my dear wife, and being able to talk with her about the ups and downs of a shared experience, knowing that at the end of the day we would inevitably wind up sharing the same bed, was little short of beatific. Besides which, I had my trusty Rover 100 to hand, not to mention our lovely little cottage which provided something of a haven, and a temporary remission for the chosen few company members who were less fortunate than we were.

The mulled-over problems we encountered with *A Cup of Kindness* were, however, entirely due to the play which, coming from the pen of the man who invented the 'Aldwych Farce', providing sure-fire laughs for a whole generation of playgoers back in the 1920s, simply wasn't funny enough; and before anyone leaps to the conclusion that its failure was due to the absence of those legendary comic actors for whom it was written, I should point out that when the 91 year-old Ben Travers was leaving the theatre after seeing the show, he was heard to say, "Not one of my best!" On the plus side, it allowed me to renew my on-stage relationship with Moira Lamb, with whom I had enjoyed a post-coital 'Craven A' in Alan Bennett's *Habeas Corpus* a couple of years earlier in Perth. We were husband and wife on this occasion, an equally unlikely coupling given that she was at least twice as large as me in all directions, but obviously one with comic potential. Moira was a very sweet lady, but no great shakes as an actress, her numerous seasons at Pitlochry all but inexplicable were it not for the fact that she was married to Kenneth Ireland, the Festival Theatre's director, whose determination to go on employing her at all costs clearly established a precedent for at least one future artistic director at Pitlochry. But Kenneth was an unusual man in many respects, and he certainly wasn't perfectly cast himself as a theatre director, bearing more than a passing resemblance to one of Dickens' eccentric businessmen; a lawyer, perhaps, or a funeral director.

1978 Know Your Own Mind - Pitlochry Festival Theatre, with Graham Pountney.

A couple of years later, Lesley and I paid a visit to Pitlochry, where we saw a production of *The Importance of Being Earnest* in which Moira had been cast as Lady Bracknell. On our way into the auditorium, Kenneth had suddenly appeared beside us and, in hushed and excited tones, told us to listen out for Moira's delivery of 'A handbag?', two words most memorably associated with Dame Edith Evans' outraged hauteur in the 1952 film version of the play, but which Moira had obviously made her own. That Kenneth's opinion of his wife's talent, although undoubtedly genuine, was well wide of the mark was clearly demonstrated when the moment came and went without anything more arresting than the delivery of a somewhat bland enquiry, leaving me to wonder if she'd said those famous words at all. I was only grateful that we were spared another encounter with Kenneth on our way out.

To redress the balance a little, it's worth pointing out that in 1981, only a year after that visit, the new theatre on the other side of the river opened its doors for the very first time, the culmination of a project that had taken 30 years to come to fruition against a background of post-war austerity, periods of recession and lengthy debates about its economic viability. It was clearly no easy task, and it was led over the years, following the death of John Stewart in 1957, by the guiding spirit of Kenneth Ireland without whose commitment and expertise in a variety of areas, of which we mere transitory actors were largely unaware, it may well never have come to pass. It was all too easy for us to cast him as an Aunt Sally, and in the circumstances we could probably be forgiven for that. History, on the other hand, and those who wrote it, had no such excuse. After only two seasons in the new theatre, the 'powers that were to be' cast him adrift without fanfare; since when, his enormous contribution to the existence of the Pitlochry Festival Theatre has scarcely been acknowledged, let alone celebrated. That Kenneth's departure also brought to an end Moira Lamb's perennial appearances on the Pitlochry stage was unlikely to have been coincidental.

Moira, in fact, did not appear in *While the Sun Shines,* the second play of the 1978 season, and neither did the other two actresses with whom we were previously acquainted, Ursula Smith and Helen Lloyd, both of whom had gone on to begin rehearsals for a new play called *The Shooting Range* by Eric MacDonald, in which neither Lesley nor I were involved, and which was embraced by its cast at the beginning of rehearsals with something less than enthusiasm. By the time the play opened, however, their journey had apparently been rewarded, and at least some, if not all of them, were confident of its success. Lesley, having fortuitously contracted some minor ailment, was unable to attend the first night, an occasion I was to share with our latest guest, Bernard Lloyd, whose visit to Pitlochry, following yet another overseas engagement, had been heralded with keen anticipation, together with a degree of trepidation. We had not, of course, been secretive about his imminent arrival, news of which led Ursula Smith to suggest, somewhat snippily, that we remind him of her name. They had, it transpired, recently worked together, during which time he had persisted in calling her 'Liz', no matter how often she corrected him. There was not a trace of humour in her voice as she gave vent to her feelings, which suggested that she may well have had to deal with other of Bernie's fabled foibles along the way. In any case, we told him very shortly after his arrival of Ursula's complaint, about which he professed complete ignorance, although he insisted on going with us to visit her with a ready apology to hand. When she answered the door, he kissed her on the cheek, and said, "Lovely to see you again, Liz!" No doubt prompted by the look on her face, he immediately apologised, took a couple of steps backwards and, suitably contrite, began again. All might have gone well from that point on, had we both been able to offer our congratulations to the cast of *The Shooting Range* following its opening night. Unfortunately, this was not to be the case since we both, and for a variety of reasons, found the experience irksome. All I can remember thinking, as we left the auditorium, is that the actors had been absolutely right in their original estimation of the play. Bernard's response, however, was loudly voiced as we approached the foyer, and so I deemed it inadvisable to join the company for their first night celebrations in the bar where our opinions, even if not offered, were bound to be sought; so we made what I thought was a discreet exit, fondly believing that our absence would not be noticed. Silly me! When Ursula approached Lesley the following day, she made it clear that while she was aware of Bernard's anti-social tendencies, she didn't think *I* would behave in such a churlish way myself. Lesley was left with no alternative but to tell her the truth, to which Ursula responded by saying that, whatever we thought of the play, we could at least have stayed on to say, "Well done!"; which was all very well as far as Bernard was concerned as he didn't have to live with the 'nippy-sweetie' legacy he bequeathed me when he left. As a footnote to what might otherwise be regarded as a fairly inconsequential story, I should add that, during a visit with Ursula to Perth Theatre only a few weeks earlier for the opening night of a musical show, she had said to Lesley, during their brief visit to the Ladies' Room after the curtain had come down, "Well, I suppose we'd better go backstage and lie through our teeth!" Need I say more?

Although it's difficult at this distance to make any sense of the rehearsal schedule in the early days and weeks of the season, given that the first three productions all opened in April, obviously we must have been required to work more or less simultaneously on all three. What I do remember, and very clearly, is that rehearsals and, subsequently, the performances of the Rattigan play provided a welcome relief from the Sisyphean task with which we were burdened in *A Cup of Kindness*. In fact, *While the Sun Shines* went on to become our favourite play of the season, a preference I believe we shared with our audiences. Set in 1943, it was first performed in that very same year when it played for well over a thousand performances at London's Globe Theatre. That a light-comedy about the pre-marital machinations of an Englishman, a Frenchman and an American scored such a success in the wake of the London Blitz, and with D-Day still a year away, is not really very surprising I suppose. That it should be revived 35 years later and meet with the same kind of response, and not simply as a curiosity but as a piece of living theatre, speaks volumes for the theatrical craftsmanship of its author, whose work had been more or less consigned to the wilderness during the revolutionary 'sixties'. In view of the increasing number of Rattigan revivals over the subsequent years, however, it would seem that 'Aunt Edna' lives on, along with her appetite for 'the well-made play.'

While the Sun Shines was sympathetically directed in Pitlochry by Brian Shelton, with Graham Pountney as the English soldier, who also happens to be the Earl of Harpenden, and Tim Swinton, who became one of our closer friends in the company, as the American, Lieutenant Mulvaney, whilst I was happily cast as Lieutenant Colbert, the archetypal Free Frenchman. Deborah Makepeace was the young lady around whom these bees buzzed, and Lesley, who had arguably been the only member of the cast in *A Cup of Kindness* whose laughs were obtained more or less legitimately as Kate, the eccentric maid, was now a blonde-bewigged and comely Mabel Crum, 'the trollop with a heart of gold'.

By the end of April, *The Tempest* had joined the list of plays already up and running, and although my concerns about recapturing lost innocence turned out to be largely unfounded, thanks to employing my imagination, our transfer from the rehearsal room to the stage gave rise to a dilemma with regard to the ethereal nature of the role. For some reason, Andrew McKinnon had introduced a horseshoe-shaped ramp as the centrepiece of his set, effectively trapping the actors in its semi-circular grasp at stage level, and leaving them with no alternative but to exit by the same extended uphill route they had taken to enter downhill. There was an alternative route, but that was reserved for the characters who inhabited the island, namely Prospero, Miranda and Caliban. Ariel, not being an inhabitant of anywhere but the elements, was obliged to make full use of the ramps. Still being relatively fleet of foot, I would have been quite happy to take this on board had it not been for the fact that the slatted timber of which they were constructed, creaked quite audibly at the lightest of footfalls. This was obviously quite acceptable as far as the mortals were concerned, but for an airy spirit who was meant to weigh nothing at all, it presented me with a problem which, short of sprouting wings, I could see no way of resolving. That a local newspaper critic chose to draw attention to Ariel's 'heavy footedness' was, of course, mean spirited, but it did at least bear witness to my fears. Not that I didn't relish playing the part again (especially when I was standing still!), and neither did I bear any serious grudge against Andrew, with whom I enjoyed a good working relationship, although I was not alone in reacting adversely when, quite late on in rehearsals, he came up with the idea of using *The Beach Boys* to provide background music. Fortunately, a chorus of gasps and more than a few raised eyebrows later, that notion bit the dust; but it was vaguely reminiscent of the never-to-be-mentioned-again 'Hogarthian' motif he attached to his production of *Twelfth Night* a few years earlier. The responsibility for the music in *The Tempest*, incidentally, and which mainly involves Ariel, was designated to Malcolm McKee, a member of the company who was also a fine pianist and an occasional composer. During the course of the season, both Lesley and I were to work ever more closely with him, but the bulk of that, and of our blossoming friendship was still to come when we embarked upon rehearsals for *Know Your Own Mind* by Arthur Murphy.

Arthur Murphy was an Irishman who made his stage début as an actor in the 1760s at Covent Garden in the role of Othello, and followed this with Hamlet, Richard III and Macbeth. He was then engaged by David Garrick at Drury Lane, where it was soon discovered that he lacked both stage presence and technique. Whether he lost these essential attributes on his way down the road, or whether he wrote his own reviews at Covent Garden is all unknown, but he subsequently gave up acting and devoted himself to writing plays. *Know Your Own Mind* was first produced in 1779, and would probably have enjoyed greater success than it did had Richard Brinsley Sheridan not had access to the finished script long before it was produced and had written a remarkably similar play entitled *The School for Scandal*, which opened three months later, and was hailed as a masterpiece. Whether this accident-prone play of Arthur Murphy's merited a revival some 200 years later is open to debate, but Brian Shelton obviously thought it did, since he had chosen to direct it.

Aside from the fact that I recall some of the sillier members of the Pitlochry company chose to refer to it as *Blow Your Own Nose*, I have no recollection at all of either the rehearsal period, or of the play in performance. This is not necessarily a criticism of the play or the process. It is somewhat strange, though, that when I managed to access a copy of the script before writing this, my memory remained unjogged, and not a single line of dialogue – and there were a good many of them assigned to the character of Dashwould – rang even the most distant of bells. Photographic evidence suggests that Dashwould was a dandyish character, something of a joker, but essentially a good egg, whereas Malvil, played by Michael Mackenzie, and looking like the victim of a Botox treatment gone wrong, was obviously the villain of the piece. Lesley is also in the photograph, taken outside the stage-door, as a sweetly bonneted Miss Melville, the poor relation in a play that was all about the machinations employed by the rich and privileged in the marriage stakes, as is *The School for Scandal*. Miss Melville was one more cameo role for Lesley, whose participation in *The Tempest* was limited to the part of Ceres, one of the three goddesses summoned by Prospero to bless the union between his daughter, Miranda, and Ferdinand. But her major challenge was yet to come.

The works of Bertolt Brecht were far from being a regular feature in the Pitlochry repertoire. In fact, only once before in its history had they staged a play by Brecht, and that was a relatively unknown piece called *Senora Carrar's Rifles* which, in any case, could hardly be described as typically Brechtian. But with Andrew McKinnon at the helm, and with a recently successful production of *Mother Courage* at Perth under his belt, it was hardly surprising that he chose to include *The Caucasian Chalk Circle* in the 1978 season. It was equally unsurprising, having witnessed the impact of Lesley's performance as Kattrin in *Mother Courage* that he would offer her the part of Grusha, the kitchen-maid around whom the story of *The Caucasian Chalk Circle* revolves. Brecht's epic demanded the employment of a large number of actors, and consequently it was the only play in the season which brought the entire company together. I, for my part, was cast as Arkadi Cheidze, the singer/narrator, which meant that I would be spending more time in Malcolm McKee's company, learning and rehearsing the songs he had composed – 28 in all – than I would with Andrew and the rest of the cast in the rehearsal room. Malcolm was an extremely gifted musician, but no Kurt Weill, so that when the play opened, and was received by a few of the critics with something less than enthusiasm for not being 'Brechtian' enough, it was the music that suffered most at their hands. 'Amateur operatic' was one of the phrases that galled, while 'more reminiscent of a stranded tour of an Ivor Novello musical' for some reason left me feeling flattered! It was Lesley Mackie, however, who triumphed, her performance greeted with enthusiasm by them all, and most notably by Cordelia Oliver in *The Guardian* who, while expressing reservations about the production, went on to write, 'Lesley Mackie might have been born to play Grusha ... whenever this gifted young actress is on stage, commonsensical sincerity personified, one's attention is held.'

With all five productions in which we were involved up and running by June 23rd, and with more than three months left before the season came to an end, it would be reasonable to assume that leisure activities would play some part in the spare time now at our disposal; early morning runs, for instance, instigated by my wife, and sunny afternoons on our lawn learning Italian for some long-forgotten reason at my instigation, as was the surprise party to celebrate her 27th birthday, although the surprise element was effectively removed when Jonathan Battersby apologised to her for not being able to come. We doubtless found other recreations; the occasional trip round the putting-green, and the even fewer visits to the tiny local cinema where I recall seeing Martin Scorcese's *New York, New York*, starring Robert deNiro and Liza Minnelli, and being sadly disappointed, having been entirely captivated by the same director's *Taxi Driver* only a year or so earlier. But all these diversions were essentially fleeting, and although I find it hard now to believe that playing five or six shows a week was not enough to justify my existence in Pitlochry, the 'roar of the greasepaint and the smell of crowd' obviously proved to be irresistible.

Having myself directed a short play called *Tidy*, one of a couple to be performed at lunch-time in the theatre foyer, and in both of which Lesley appeared, we got together with Malcolm McKee, and embarked upon a project of our own. Only recently, and for the first time in many years, I listened to a recording we made of the late-night entertainment we devised at that time, and performed on several occasions before the season came to an end; and besides being pleasantly surprised by much of it, I was struck by the sheer amount of reading, research and rehearsing that must have gone into preparing it, and at such short notice. It was essentially an anthology of poetry, music and prose, serious and comic, based on the subject of sleep, or the lack of it, dreams and nightmares, and it was called *Are We Keeping You Up?* How we managed to access the huge amount of material, used or discarded, whilst being cloistered in Pitlochry, and in those far-off days before the internet, is a mystery to me now, although I imagine the local library had a part to play in it. I remember that we had, quite coincidentally, brought with us a book we had been given as a present, called *Dreams About H.M. The Queen*, a compilation by Brian Masters from which we managed to lift a few examples, notably the one about the hitchhiker who managed to get a lift from a lorry driver who turned out to be the Queen in full regalia, and with whom he enjoyed a cup of tea when they stopped off at a transport café. Otherwise, we somehow managed to gather a variety of poems from the disparate pens of Robert Graves, Roger McGough, Dylan Thomas and Kathleen Raine, to name but a few, with the musical element of the show, largely in Malcolm's hands, covering an equally diverse selection, with songs like *If There Were Dreams To Sell* by John Ireland alongside Irving Berlin's *Count Your Blessings* (instead of sheep) and the Lennon/McCartney version of *Golden Slumbers*. I particularly remember duetting with Lesley on *Barcelona*, from Stephen Sondheim's musical, *Company,* in which the leading man, Bobby, tries to persuade the air-hostess with whom he has spent the night to come back to bed, although he knows she has a flight to catch, and when his persistence eventually pays off and she changes her mind, he is not best pleased! I have even more reason to remember my own waking nightmare when the moment came for me to launch myself into the *Nightmare Song* from Gilbert and Sullivan's *Iolanthe*. My God, how did I ever learn it! Perhaps I'd hoped that my performance would be likened to that of a stranded member of the D'Oyly Carte Opera Company, but unfortunately the show was never reviewed. It was, nevertheless, one of the highlights of our Pitlochry season, and our relationship with Malcolm McKee, who was a complete joy to work with, blossomed and endured.

One of the vagaries associated with the Pitlochry Festival Theatre, besides paying the female members of the company five pounds a week less than the male actors, was that there was to be a fortnight's gap between our first touring date in Inverness at the end of the season and the resumption of the tour, a gap that would be bridged by the payment, not of a holding salary, but by the holiday money the actors had earned throughout the rest of the season. For most of the company, unprepared, unable, or simply not interested in taking a holiday at that time, and more than likely counting on their holiday entitlement to tide them over between jobs, it was preposterous, but went unchallenged by Equity, our union. Lesley and I, having earned £145 a week between us, and living in shared accommodation, were not especially troubled by this. In fact, we had managed to save a little, and with our first wedding anniversary fast approaching, we decided to treat ourselves to a belated honeymoon, a week's package holiday on the Greek island of Kos. That I had already been offered the chance, after 14 years in the Wild Woods, to return to the River Bank as Ratty in David Conville's Christmas production of *Toad of Toad Hall* in the West End of London might also have prompted our decision. Meanwhile, following the curtain-call on the last night of the Pitlochry season, Kenneth Ireland came onto the stage and gave his annual address to the audience. "It has been a wonderful season," he said, and in fulsome vein, acknowledging us all as we stood there smiling, "and a wonderful company. Next year," he went on, "we hope to have an even better one!"

oOoOo

Twenty three

Why book a holiday on the moon when you can go to the Greek Island of Kos for a fraction of the price? Its lunar landscape was the first thing that struck us about the place as our coach bumped its way along the road from the airport to our hotel, only to find that the rooms were not ready, and after a whole night without sleep, lying around in the foyer was not the most promising start to our honeymoon. However, after managing to grab a few hours, and with our optimism restored, we headed out to make the most of our seven-day holiday.

Kos is the nearest island to the Turkish coast, and the recent conflict between Greece and Turkey meant that it was very much like a fortified garrison; the military presence was everywhere. Our first attempt at sunbathing was rudely interrupted by shouts of, "Mines! Mines!" We had obviously chosen the wrong beach and so we picked our way gingerly back towards the relative safety of the hotel pool. There was, however, a fate worse than death awaiting the unwary female tourist in the shape of seven thousand frustrated soldiers, many of whom were more or less out of control. On our first night out, we were joined very quickly by a group of soldiers who imbibed freely from our carafes and made Lesley the focus of their attentions. She was pestered in particular by a rather surly soldier who would not take 'No' for an answer. I did my best to deter him with comments like, "She is my wife" and, "Hands off", but all to no avail. In a final steely-eyed confrontation, the soldier exerted too much pressure on the wine glass he was holding. It was meant to be a macho gesture of defiance and he probably thought he was squeezing a beer can; either that or he was completely off his head. The glass shattered in his hand, blood spurted everywhere and he was taken off to a local hospital for stitches. His colleagues thought it was hilarious. With his departure Lesley became the quarry of their leader, the Captain, who had obviously attributed her lack of interest in his colleague to his lowly rank. He asked if she would meet him the following evening, and when she reminded him of her marital status, he said he would be quite happy to invite me along as well. Needless to say, we didn't take him up on that invitation. We seemed to have chosen an island that was bubbling over with sexual frustration, manifesting itself not only in night-clubs, but on the streets too where, alone or escorted, female tourists had no choice but to ignore the remarks and dodge the hands. This was, of course, easily attributable on Kos to its overwhelming military presence, but Greek Orthodoxy obviously had its part to play too, at least back in the 1970s, when native girls were still encouraged by their priests and their families to arrive at the altar *virgo intacta*, and who must have been severely pissed-off as their chances of arriving there at all dwindled in the face of easier prey. It was, in short, a somewhat bizarre honeymoon, however belated, but we returned to Scotland in good spirits, our attraction to Greek tavernas and our fondness for souvlaki, accompanied by a bottle of Demestika, having lost none of their allure. This might well have been due to the fact that what we returned to were the last few weeks of the Pitlochry tour, embracing Peterhead, Troon, Dumbarton, Livingstone and Musselburgh, made all the more miserable by the cold and rain-soaked climate that accompanied us. Courtesy of Rupert Brooke ... Εἴθε γενοίμην would I were on Kos again, on Kos again' – well, if not exactly on Kos again, at least somewhere the sun was shining.

An altogether different experience, just as bizarre in its way, was going back to London and moving into our first marital home at 137 Purves Road, the house in which I had spent virtually all of my childhood, and much of my adolescence. Not that I had ever ventured upstairs during those years when it was occupied by Mr and Mrs Smith, and it was a strange feeling, to say the least, bordering on trespass, when we climbed those stairs for the first time to make our home in what had been their domain. Clearly, my father's wishes had prevailed, and my mother welcomed us, if not exactly with open arms, certainly without any hint of her original reaction to the idea, which she appeared to have entirely forgotten. There was, of course, a great deal of work to be done in the way of painting and decorating, and I fondly recall Lesley, suitably masked and armed with a blow-torch, stripping the paint from the bannisters in an attempt to reveal the natural wood underneath, an exercise which, far from enhancing their appearance, left them crying out for a coat of paint. On many occasions she could also be found, wearing overalls and a woolly hat, at the top of a ladder wielding a paint-brush. In fact, I saw so little of my delightfully feminine wife during that time that I ended up calling her Douglas! Not that I didn't paper the odd wall and occasional ceiling myself although, unlike Lesley at that time, I did have other fish to fry as I returned to the River Bank in David Conville's Christmas production of *Toad of Toad Hall* at the Piccadilly Theatre. From a writer's point of view it would have been, of course, more amusing had I been cast as Mole, emerging from my hole in the ground, paint-brush in hand, having abandoned interior decoration in favour of life in the big wide world. However, and more happily, I was invited to return in my original role as Ratty, thus consigning to history my 'dismally charmless' portrayal of Mole in Birmingham three years earlier. Needless to say, since he was still alive, the part of Mole was to be played again by Richard Goolden. The other two leading players were David King as Badger, with whom I had last worked on the BBC Television Shakespeare series, *The Spread of the Eagle,* and Ian Talbot as Mr.Toad, who had been a member of Joan Knight's company at the Castle Theatre, Farnham back in 1965. *Toad of Toad Hall* being a matinées only production, we shared the theatre with Barry Humphries aka Dame Edna Everidge, that Australian doyen(ne) of comedy whose performance began by picking up from the stage an object which bore a striking resemblance to an oversized, and somewhat mottled, cucumber, which (s)he studied for a while before saying "It's probably a Toad's tool!"

While 1978 had been a relatively smooth ride, if only because most of it had happened in the same place, 1979 turned out to be somewhat bumpier. I'd scarcely had time enough to paper one wall after *Toad* had ended its run, before I was invited by Christopher Dunham, the Artistic Director at the Palace Theatre, Westcliff-on-Sea, to play the Narrator in the musical revue, *Side by Side by Sondheim.* It was Chris who had directed *Joseph and the Amazing Technicolor Dreamcoat* at Perth Theatre in 1974, a production that had not only received standing ovations at virtually every performance, but which had also been, for me, the seedbed of a life-changing relationship. Chris had, in fact, originally intended to play the Narrator himself, until he realised that it might just get in the way of his job as director and choreographer, and I can only endorse that decision and be grateful that he offered it to me. *Side by Side by Sondheim* had made its first appearance in 1976, the brainchild of David Kernan, who had played a leading role in the London production of Sondheim's *A Little Night Music,* and had recruited the talents of Ned Sherrin to write a linking script, and singers, Julia McKenzie and Millicent Martin to sing alongside him in an anthology of Stephen Sondheim's work. After a short, sell-out season at the Mermaid Theatre, it had transferred to the West End, where it ran for almost two years before travelling to Broadway with the original cast. Ned Sherrin, with whom I was destined to work more closely in the near future, demonstrated none of Christopher Dunham's reservations; not only directing the production but by reading his own script. But then again, *he* wasn't responsible for the choreography! It was a delightful experience and, having already become an admirer of Sondheim's contribution to musical theatre, I was well on the way to idolatry by the time it came to an end. My only regret was that I didn't get the chance to sing myself, although being paid to sit there and listen to Rosemary Williams singing *Another 100 People* from *Company* and *Losing My Mind* from *Follies* night after night was compensation enough. I was further rewarded when my front-of-house photograph was returned to me at the end of the run by Chris Dunham, who had written on the back if it, 'Who else could have been so much better than Ned Sherrin (or me for the matter!) - come back soon.'

It was a short trip from the sublime to Salisbury Playhouse, where I began rehearsals in April for another musical show called *Miss Leading Lady*, based on an 18th century play by Susanna Centlivre called *A Bold Stroke For A Wife*. On the face of it not a bad idea, and especially in the musical hands of Chris Littlewood whose background, knowledge and expertise as a composer as well as on the keyboard brought forth a number of songs and musical interludes echoing the style of several eminent composers of the late Baroque and early Classical period. However ingenious, I suppose it could have been suspected of having limited audience appeal, which might well have been one of the reasons that Chris and/or his director, Roger Clissold, decided to turn it into a musical within a musical in which a company of modern performers carry the so-called plot while rehearsing Mrs Centlivre's play. This notion was doubtless inspired by *A Chorus Line*, which had enjoyed a huge and recent success in London, and even possibly by more distant memories of *Kiss Me, Kate*. Whatever his undisputed musical gifts, however, Chris Littlewood was no Marvin Hamlisch, nor was he, indeed, a born again Cole Porter, and the end result was little short of catastrophic. The rehearsal period, presided over by the genial, but relatively ineffectual, Roger Clissold, resolved none of the problems arising from this dichotomy, and while tackling the characters from the original play (mine was 'Tradelove, an avaricious broker') was rewarding enough, playing their modern counterparts ('Bill' in my case) was nothing short of embarrassing, and excruciatingly so when we made our final choreographed entrance down through the auditorium wearing top hats and tails. If I needed any further excuse for my mortification, it was amply provided when we arrived on stage and, glancing down into the orchestra pit, I was greeted by the sight of Chris Littlewood, his head buried in his hands over the keyboard. On a more positive note, it was a pleasure to work with such an affable company of actors, the overwhelming majority of whom shared with me the same feelings about the show. Little did I know at the time that, within a few short weeks, I would be returning to the Playhouse, but against an entirely different backdrop, and one that would leave me with nothing but happy memories of my time there. However, on May 4th, even the shadow cast by having to go on playing *Miss Leading Lady* for another three weeks was eclipsed by an even darker one when, following a General Election, Margaret Thatcher took up residence in No.10 Downing Street as the first woman to become Prime Minister!

Meanwhile, Lesley's residence at 137 Purves Road had not, so far, opened many other doors for her in London, although Scotland still beckoned from time to time, and she returned on a couple of occasions to make television appearances, most notably as a Punk Rock singer in an episode of *Charles Endell Esquire,* a short-lived series starring Iain Cuthbertson, based on a character he had already played in an altogether more successful series called *Budgie,* which had co-starred the pop singer, Adam Faith. Lesley did audition, though, for Mary O'Malley's play, *Once a Catholic,* which was about to open in the West End. It was to be directed by Mike Ockrent, another of Joan Knight's protégés, whose star by that time was very much in the ascendant, and who went on to direct major productions on Broadway as well as in the West End. He and Lesley had worked together several years earlier when he was director of the Traverse Theatre in Edinburgh, and he had said to her, on parting, that he was determined to work with her again and sure enough, he arranged for Lesley to audition for the part of Mary Mooney, one of the three featured pupils in the Willesden Convent School where the play is set. That he had not yet achieved the stellar status as a director that lay in wait for him was clearly demonstrated when Mary O'Malley, providing a perfect blueprint for future casting directors, refused to consider Lesley for the role, simply because she didn't come from Willesden, and had never attended a convent school. She was, however, offered a summer season with the Perth Theatre Company, playing at the Adam Smith Theatre in Kirkcaldy, Fife, and whilst it would involve a degree of separation, not exactly what I was looking forward to, it was obviously the right thing for her to do, and especially since one of the three plays that made up the season was Coward's *Hay Fever,* giving her the opportunity to reprise the part of Jackie Coryton, one of her all-time favourites. Besides, I had nothing else lined up after *Miss Leading Lady* finished its run, and fondly imagined that I might be able to make the occasional trip up to Scotland myself.

It was on one such visit, while we were enjoying afternoon tea with Lesley's Auntie Nan and Uncle Archie in Dundee that I received a telephone call from Patrick Garland, inviting me to play opposite Timothy West in a biographical tribute to the orchestral conductor, Sir Thomas Beecham, at the Playhouse Theatre in Salisbury. *Make the Little Beggars Hop* had been conceived and written by Ned Sherrin and Caryl Brahms as a one-man show until they realised, possibly with Patrick's prompting, that there were far too many stories and anecdotes about Beecham's life that would have to come from somebody else's mouth. Hence they created another character, the Music Secretary, whose function was not only to tell those stories, but to interact with Beecham in this role and as any member of the orchestra who became the butt of his humour. And thus it was, having attended the opening night at the Adam Smith Theatre of the French farce *Boeing-Boeing,* in which Lesley played a most alluring air-hostess, I returned to London, and subsequently to Salisbury where rehearsals began at the beginning of July.

Timothy West and I got along famously from the start, and enjoyed a mutually supportive relationship which was, as far as I was concerned, the only reason my role existed, although I could well imagine that, with another actor playing Beecham, it could easily have turned out to be a one-sided relationship. After all, it was still, in essence at any rate, a one-man show, but rather than grudgingly accepting the need for another voice, Tim responded positively to the presence of another actor and, largely because of his enthusiasm, the character I was playing was allowed to become three-dimensional, and even to get the occasional laugh! It was just as well that we enjoyed working together as we were often left to our own devices while Patrick was engaged in a series of long-distance telephone calls to Rex Harrison, with whom he was about to embark on a Broadway revival of *My Fair Lady*. But, even when he was otherwise engaged, Patrick was entirely supportive, welcoming our independence, while providing us with the means to make it work. Along with designer Richard Marks, he had also provided us with the perfect setting. Within a false proscenium, a symphony orchestra with strings, brass and percussion all laid out with token instruments but lacking anyone to play them, was fronted by an enlarged conductor's podium from which Tim would address the audience before turning to conduct the invisible orchestra to the strains of Beecham's own recordings.

It was somewhat surprising given that Tim, having made something of a name for himself portraying such a diverse list of historical characters as Winston Churchill, Josef Stalin, Mikhail Gorbachev and King Edward VII, wasn't the first choice for the part of Thomas Beecham. For reasons best known to the authors, I suppose, it was offered to Arthur Lowe, he of *Coronation Street* and *Dad's Army* fame, who allegedly turned it down because they wouldn't allow his wife to join him on stage as a dancer.

Whether Arthur Lowe was aware that Beecham would have been disinclined to share the stage with a dancer in any case (hence the original title of the show), and to what music she could have danced in order to justify her presence there, remains a mystery, but his decision was nevertheless a wise one, and not only as far as I was concerned, but for the authors too, who came to see a final run-through before we opened, and who were given, thanks to Timothy West's superb performance, every reason to rejoice. As far as I can recall, they approved of my performance too, although I did receive one note from Caryl Brahms "You should not pronounce the final letter 's' when you talk about Beecham's romantic liaisons, Terry." I was about to hesitantly question this when Ned Sherrin said, "No, Caryl, you're wrong; the word has been anglicised." She made no comment, and I can only offer my belated thanks to Ned for rescuing me from a confrontation with that formidable little lady!

Make the Little Beggars Hop was not only well received by the Press and by the public in Salisbury, it also generated a good deal of interest elsewhere, so that by the time it closed we had every reason to hope that it might well have a life thereafter, a prospect to which we raised our glasses at a dinner-party Tim threw before we went our separate ways, and at which I had the pleasure of meeting his wife, the actress Prunella Scales, who will surely be remembered as John Cleese's wife in that wonderful yet-to-come TV comedy series, *Fawlty Towers*. It was also the occasion to raise my own private glass in gratitude to Patrick Garland, whose offer had successfully exorcised the spectre of *Miss Leading Lady* from my memories of the Salisbury Playhouse.

At some point towards the end of our tour with the Pitlochry Festival Company the previous year, Lesley had made a trip to London to meet Alan Dosser, the director assigned to a projected tour by the English 7:84 Company of a musical called *Bitter Apples*. For those who know little or nothing of its origins, the Scottish 7:84 Company came into being in 1971, the brainchild of John McGrath, whose passionate espousal of the political left gave rise to the company's name when, according to *The Economist*, 7% of the nation's population owned 84% of the country's wealth. The 7:84 Company no longer exists and neither does John McGrath, whose enduring legacy can best be demonstrated by his authorship of, amongst other works, *The Cheviot, The Stag and The Black, Black Oil*, a play about the historical exploitation of Scotland, its people and its resources. McGrath was a socialist crusader, and very much at the centre of his crusade was his determination to eschew the predominantly bourgeois commercial theatre in favour of taking popular, political theatre to venues shunned by the established national and regional companies. Scotland was his usual hunting-ground, but not in the case of *Bitter Apples*. Lesley enjoyed her meeting with Alan Dosser, the director, who told her that it had been John McGrath's express wish that she should play the part of Bessie. She was flattered, of course, although somewhat taken aback, given that she was not, at that time, a political animal of any persuasion, let alone the kind of 'lefty' with whom John McGrath was wont to work, and on the one and only occasion they had spoken to each other on the phone some years earlier, she had confessed, much to McGrath's surprise and disappointment, that she had never even heard of the revolutionary Socialist, John MacLean. On the train back to Scotland, following her meeting with Alan Dosser, she read the script with increasing unease. Bessie, it turned out, was one of the leaders of the Liverpool Liberation Army, around whom the story revolved, and quite clearly a pretty tough cookie. She came to the conclusion that McGrath's image of her had obviously been ingrained some years earlier when she had played Alison, the amply proportioned young leading lady in *Just Your Luck*, a BBC television *Play for Today* which was transmitted back in 1973; either that, or on stage as Billy Connolly's girl-friend, 'Hairy Mary from the Gorbals,' in *The Great Northern Welly-Boot Show* a few months earlier. In fact, to give him his due, had I not become acquainted with the comparatively lissom creature I had recently married, my memories of Lesley Mackie, even had I known who she was at the time, would have been confined to chubby Daisy Pringle in *The Wicker Man*. Anyway, by the time she arrived back in Scotland, having finished reading the script, she had decided she didn't want to do it for a variety of other reasons, one of which was that it was about two hours longer than it had any right to be. John McGrath, however, was not prepared to leave it at that, and what with Lesley's fondly recalled reluctance to say 'No', she finally succumbed to the pressure, albeit with serious misgivings. It was only a couple of weeks after our return to London that she heard the tour had been cancelled and that, having already committed to it, she was to be paid two weeks salary by way of compensation, so perhaps she'd made the right decision; if only that had been the end of the story. By the time *Bitter Apples* surfaced again, Lesley was already engaged in the season at Kirkcaldy which didn't come to an end until a fortnight after the 7:84 Company were due to start rehearsals. On this occasion, they had no option but to recast the part of Bessie, and Lesley had every reason to believe that she had finally heard the last of it. They were less than two weeks into rehearsal when the new Bessie was obliged to withdraw – for 'personal' reasons, John McGrath averred. He went on to assure Lesley that he was certain she'd be able to cope with what was left of the rehearsal period, if only she'd be free to start the following week. He already knew, of course, that her present engagement would have come to an end by then. Had I suspected an element of contrivance in all of this, my suspicions were not laid to rest when Lesley told me that she would have said 'No' if only she hadn't accepted the fortnight's hand-out; or would she, I wonder?

I high-tailed it up to Scotland as soon I could after leaving Salisbury, travelling by train on this occasion, our sturdy Rover 100 having arrived at what appeared to be its final resting place at the kerbside in Purves Road. The pittance we were paid for it was recompensed to some extent by the £110 we received from the private sale of its number-plate – 100 DBM! One of the several reasons for my hasty return was that Lesley had managed to locate a second-hand Fiat 128 at a very reasonable price by way of an overheard conversation in a sauna bath. That it failed to start due to faulty spark-plugs and that the door-lock broke the first time I used it, should have forewarned me about its quality. Indeed, it was never destined to be a favourite car of mine, although it was to be well and truly put through its paces over the next couple of months. My very first journey in it, undertaken on Tuesday, 21st August, was not back to London with Lesley, but on my own to Coventry, where I was due to start rehearsals the following day. It had been all but 20 years since I had left the Belgrade Theatre under something of a cloud, thanks to a strained relationship with a certain guest director, and consequently with the artistic director of the theatre with whom he shared the same proclivities. It was hardly surprising then that, even with a new team in charge, and a guest director I had worked with more congenially at the Crucible Theatre in Sheffield, I still felt a chill of apprehension when I first arrived at the stage door. Not that I had any reason to doubt the wisdom of my decision to return. The new joint directors, Ed Thomason and Keith Green, had invited Colin George to direct *Sleuth*, the opening production of their autumn season, and Colin had offered me the chance to play Milo Tindle again. It had been seven years since we had last worked together, and having no reason to believe he had seen me play it in Perth, I still have no idea why he offered it to me without so much as a meeting, let alone an audition. In any case, I was only too happy to be playing it again whatever had brought it about, and I was looking forward to working alongside a very different Andrew Wyke, in the shape of Ronald Lewis, a handsome Welshman I had seen a number of times on the cinema screen, and from whom I might be able to learn the truth about his rumoured affair with Vivien Leigh when they had played together on stage in Noël Coward's *South Sea Bubble* back in 1956!

Having ensconced myself in one of the theatre flats, a rare privilege enjoyed by only a very few actors when I was last there, I went to the rehearsal room where I was warmly greeted by Colin, and with whom I happily reminisced, not so much about our time together in Sheffield, but of our first meeting in Coventry when we had worked together as actors in *The Comedy of Errors* and *Treasure Island* with the Midland Theatre Company, a few years before the Belgrade Theatre was built. I have no idea how long it took before we realised that Ronald Lewis had not yet arrived, but obviously Colin had taken note of his protracted absence, and with a murmured apology, he finally took his leave, only to return a little while later with the news that Mr Lewis was experiencing some problems with his packing, and that it would be better for all concerned if we took the train to London, held the read-through in Ronald Lewis's flat, and then brought him back with us to Coventry. I must surely have thought it strange, to say the least, even if Colin had made it sound like a par for the course scenario. Memories of his credulous take on life when he was running the Crucible Theatre came flooding back, and although it didn't exactly ring alarm bells at the time, I certainly thought there was more to this than met the eye. I was reassured, up to a point, when we were admitted to Ronald Lewis's flat in Maida Vale I think, or was it Bayswater? Anyway, wherever it was, his suitcase was standing in the hallway, packed and ready to go, while he himself turned out to be a perfectly charming gentleman. In fact, the only question-mark that hung over me following a read-through of the play, in which he acquitted himself quite ably, was his seeming inability to put out a cigarette without immediately lighting another. As a smoker myself, and having been forewarned of his state of mind, I would have put it down to the stress of that particular situation, had I not caught sight of his heavily nicotine-stained fingers.

Rehearsals got off to a good start in Coventry the following day, and were rounded off with a convivial pint at the local pub before retiring to our respective flats, both on the same level of the block. Early rehearsals took place in a hall some little distance away from the theatre, and I recall being struck by the fact that I was having to walk more slowly so that he could keep up with me, although I wasn't exactly hurrying in the first place. I naturally wondered why someone in his early 50s, and who looked even younger, walked like an elderly man, although I wasn't unduly worried. It did occur to me, however, that although we were in the very early stages of rehearsal, and consequently just walking through the play, that Andrew Wyke would be required to spend the best part of Act Two climbing up and down stairs and generally rushing around like a blue-arsed fly. These considerations soon gave way to a growing suspicion that he was finding it difficult to learn the lines. Having played in *Sleuth* before, and only quite recently, the words obviously came back to me relatively easily, so I tried to keep these suspicions at bay for as long as I could. As the days went by, however, watching him lay his script aside, never more than an arm's length away, only to snatch it up again, clearly panic-stricken, I was finally convinced. And on one occasion, when I went to pick him up from his flat before heading off for rehearsals and found the door open and Ronnie fast asleep with a half-empty bottle of Scotch by his bedside, I knew we had a major problem on our hands. I didn't mention this to Colin, although I did confide in him my anxieties about the ever-present script, to which he characteristically responded with a laugh, and a scornful dismissal of my concerns, saying that Ronnie would learn the lines in his own good time and then proceed to act me off the stage. This was nonsense, of course, and when I told him that I was the only person who was in a position to see the sweat on his brow and witness the genuine panic in his eyes, he was equally dismissive.

The time had obviously come for me to call my agent who, after listening sympathetically to my concerns, suggested that my only option was to 'jump ship'. Pragmatic as always, Norman attached one caveat to this course of action, warning me that, in six months time, I would probably be remembered as an actor who is prone to walk out of shows, the reasons for my defection long forgotten. He added, as a kind of palliative, that he would have a word with Bill Kenwright, the theatre producer for whom Ronald Lewis had recently worked. This was obviously a way of discovering if Colin maybe had a point about Ronald Lewis's duplicity. Norman called me back a little later with

Kenwright's response, which was to tell me, in no uncertain terms, that Ronnie would never be able to learn the lines, and that I should make immediate contact with another actor, Ronald Leigh-Hunt, who had already played the part of Andrew Wyke on a couple of occasions and who, should he be available, would undoubtedly be more than happy to step into the breach. Since neither of these options, for obvious reasons, were open to me, I resolved to see it through, offering Ronnie as much support as I could.

It was only then, just a week away from our opening night, that Colin approached me and, without any reference to our previous conversation, or indeed any suggestion that it was a cause for concern, told me that arrangements had been made for someone to come and spend the weekend with Ronnie to help him with his lines, and that I should consequently take a couple of days off. On my way to the car park, weekend-bag in hand, I happened to bump into a lady I hadn't seen for many years, but whom I immediately recognised as Ann Spiers, former call-girl at the Old Vic, who had fought my corner and stolen my heart more than a quarter of a century earlier. It transpired that she was the 'someone' who had come to Ronnie's aid, and while I could only conjecture on the nature of their relationship, and without the familiar pang of jealousy I would have felt had I still been 15 years old, I was able to head for London happy in the certain knowledge that if anyone could leave Ronnie Lewis word-perfect and fleet-footed, it would be Annie Spiers! It could only have been with this in mind, given that in just two days time we would be embarking on technical rehearsals prior to opening on Thursday, that I was quite content to exchange my trials and tribulations for Lesley's as she came to the end of her first week on *Bitter Apples*.

It hadn't taken her long to realise that a great deal had happened to the script during the fortnight's rehearsal she had missed, and the part of Bessie had been cut to ribbons, leaving her with very little to 'get her teeth into'. The prospect of heading out on tour in such a dreary part did not fill her with a great deal of enthusiasm, and her only glimmer of hope, or so she said in the privacy of our home, was that with the play currently running at about five and half hours, Bessie might disappear altogether!

I drove her in to rehearsals the following day and stopped off to say 'hello' to Alan Dosser, an erstwhile client of Richard Hatton Ltd, where our paths had crossed back in the late '60s. He invited me to stay for what, indeed, turned out to be a marathon run-through. The plot, if you could call it a plot, spanned a period of ten years, from the heady left-wing idealism of 1968 to the growing disillusionment which had its apogee in 1978 with the ignominious fall of the Labour government, and the prospect of Thatcherism, and all that it stood for, on the not-too-distant horizon. Onto this already huge canvas far too many political events were sketched in, so that every member of the sizeable cast was required to play as many as four or five different parts as well as their own named characters as the story sprawled from Vietnam to Paris and from Chile to Wenceslas Square. Most memorably, at least as far as I was concerned, was when Lesley Mackie appeared as a fully-uniformed GI when she would surely have been more appropriately cast as a tiny Vietcong guerrilla! But as far as playing what was left of Bessie was concerned, I understood only too well her feelings about it. In one of our many telephone conversations over the next week or so, recalling the picture of 'Douglas' up a ladder when painting our ceiling, I suggested that she should don a woolly hat for the role, and I like to think that it went some way to making her feel more at home as a leader of the Liverpool Liberation Army. Musically, however, she was at her most relaxed, seeming to genuinely enjoy working with a group of talented musicians, and alongside her 'boy-friend', Matthew Kelly, all of 6ft 5ins tall, and consequently a partnership that promised a few welcome laughs.

When I returned to Coventry, and onto the stage for the first time, Ronnie appeared to be in good spirits, so clearly the visit from Ann Spiers had made a difference; but it wasn't to last. It was his grim determination to get the lines right that still dominated his thinking, so that he was all but incapable of anticipating, let alone addressing, the technical demands of the play. The absence of a script had been replaced by an ever-increasing reliance on the prompter, whose duties went beyond supplying him with his next line to reminding him from where it should be spoken, and with what props to hand. But my concerns remained, as usual, unaddressed, and I was left with no alternative but to adopt a stoical belief that Fate would surely step in and take a hand – which, in fact, is just what it did. Thursday arrived, and with the powers-that-be at home, heedlessly donning their dicky-bows in celebration of the season's opening night, I arrived at the theatre and went straight to Ronnie's dressing-room where I offered him what comfort I could by suggesting that we should think of it as a preview, staged for our benefit rather than for an audience, and that we should simply go out there and enjoy ourselves. I then retired to my own dressing-room where I was in the process of removing my jacket when I heard a crash from next-door. I rushed in, and found Ronnie stretched out on the floor, blood issuing from his forehead which had obviously come into contact with the sink as he fell; he was also foaming at the mouth. I knelt beside him, but having realised that he was all but unconscious, and not having a clue what to do about it, I went to the door and yelled out for Gladys, the lady who was in charge of the Green Room café. By the time she got down the stairs, Ronnie's complexion had attained a decidedly green hue, which she immediately diagnosed as something or other shared by her husband, suggesting that I should call an ambulance while she loosened his tie. Having regained consciousness by the time the ambulance men arrived, lifted him to his feet and led him gently to the door, he glanced at me and said, the same wan smile on his face: "This is your lucky day!" It was very soon after he had been taken away that I was approached by the front-of-house manager who asked what he should do about the audience, and since there was no-one else with any authority at present in the theatre, I said he should send them home. "On whose authority?" he asked. "Well, mine", I said, "I'm not about to do the play on my own." So off he went, and a little while later chaos erupted at the stage-door as Ed Thomason, Keith Green and Colin George burst in, all three dressed to kill and, having been informed that Ronnie was unlikely to be released from hospital tout de suite, Ed immediately suggested that Colin should go on in his place with a script. I, of course, demurred; it was, after all, a play with a good deal of action in it, requiring the use of both hands, not to mention a familiarity with the text. "Besides", I said, "the audience has been sent home!" There was a stunned silence, before Keith Green rushed off to have words with the front-of-house manager, while Ed and Colin were left to digest the news. A little while later, Keith returned, suitably chastened, and the four of us retired to Ed's office, where he poured four large brandies, and where we all sat, sadly deflated, and with no idea how the problem could be resolved, until I suddenly remembered Bill Kenwright's words. "Call Ronald Leigh-Hunt", I suggested, "He's played Andrew Wyke a couple of times before, and if he's free, he might be interested". Somewhat surprisingly, instead of finding his agent's contact details in *Spotlight*, the actors' directory, Ed came across his home telephone number there and called him immediately. Less than ten minutes later, Ronald Leigh-Hunt had agreed to take over the role of Andrew Wyke with two provisos: the first being that he wouldn't be available to take it on until the following Monday, and the second that he would only be able to play it for a week due to a previous contractual commitment in Sweden. Ed had no option but to accept and, to give him his due, he had handled the crisis with a calm authority which surely belied what he must have been feeling at the time. I don't recall anyone asking me, either then or later, how I had been inspired to suggest Ronald Leigh-Hunt, although I find it hard to believe that Colin George didn't at least have an inkling.

Following yet another unscheduled weekend with Lesley, prior to her somewhat reluctant departure for Liverpool where *Bitter Apples* was due to begin its tour, I returned to Coventry where, on Monday morning, Ronald Leigh-Hunt and I met for the very first time. Memories of his performance, or indeed of mine during that week, are understandably misty, if only because I began rehearsals the very next day with Colin George who had decided to take over the part of Andrew Wyke for the final week of the run. I do recall quite vividly, however, that the first problem Ronald and I encountered on that Monday morning, and which we resolved throughout the day with mutual deference, was that the set was very different from the one on which he had last played the part; it was, in fact, turned the other way around. On the plus side, the fact that Milo Tindle and Andrew Wyke themselves are strangers to each other at the beginning of the play provided a refreshing challenge to a relationship that is generally forged over a period of time in the rehearsal room. Both of us, as I recall, bent over backwards to accommodate the other, working our way through Act 1 in the morning and Act 2 in the afternoon with an easy assurance, born of a gentlemanly respect for each other, which allowed us to open on Monday evening to a full house, peopled almost entirely by ticket-holders from the cancelled first night, and whose reception could not have been warmer and more sympathetic. My third opening night (surely a record!), playing opposite Colin George on the following Monday, confirmed at the very least my memories of him, from as far back as 1955, as an extremely talented actor, deprived of the success he might well have enjoyed by the collapse of a lung, and thus obliging him to become a director instead.

I cannot, of course, move on without revealing what became of Ronald Lewis, whom I was sadly never to see again. It transpired that what he was suffering from was epilepsy, a fact he'd withheld for fear of invalidating his insurance for overseas engagements. But this was just the tip of the iceberg. His career, which had reached its peak in the 1950s and '60s with a string of film and television appearances in major roles, establishing him as something of a matinée idol, had gone into a decline. In fact, the very last time he had appeared on television before he came to the Belgrade Theatre had been in an episode of *Z*

Cars a year earlier, and then only in a very subsidiary role. The writing was already on the wall, of course, by the time we started working together, although I had no idea how serious his mental condition was, and it was not until some time later that I learned of his bankruptcy hearing and, in 1982, of his suicide in a Pimlico boarding-house. He was 53 when he died, and I can only say that, during our brief period together, and clearly the victim of numerous afflictions, in no way did he exploit his vulnerability, but remained always good-natured and courteous, virtues that must have been inherent for someone like Ann Spiers to take him under her wing.

How I found the time and the energy, meanwhile, to undertake several trips to Liverpool during the run of *Sleuth*, and especially in my Fiat 128, is a mystery to me now. I was obviously suffering the pangs of separation from my dear wife, but nevertheless playing Milo Tindle was a pretty tiring experience, and having to re-rehearse it with two entirely different partners as well as perform it every night beggars the imagination. On one occasion, I actually drove up to Liverpool after the curtain had come down at the Belgrade, in the hope of persuading Alan Dosser to release Lesley from her contract so that she could accept an offer from Clive Perry to appear in Alan Ayckbourn's *Bedroom Farce* at the Birmingham Rep. I knew, of course, that my powers of persuasion would probably meet with little success, so I wasn't at all surprised that, by the time I arrived at the Everyman Theatre, Alan Dosser was already well-oiled and way beyond negotiating anything except his way to the toilet. In any case, my journey had been undertaken principally as a labour of love, and since I did get to spend the night with Lesley, all was not in vain!

Sleuth ended its run on September 29th, as did *Bitter Apples* in Liverpool, and having rendezvoused at Corley Service Station, a short distance away from Coventry on the M6, Lesley and I headed for London, from where, after a weekend at home, Lesley re-joined the company in Nottingham. Having no imminent professional commitments, I was able to spend some time with her there, and on her subsequent tour dates, a pleasure restricted only by my weekly appointment at the Chadwick Street Labour Exchange! It was on one such occasion that I missed out on witnessing Matthew Kelly's inspired decision to expose himself on stage during the first night performance in Nottingham. He had done it before, Lesley told me, as a one-off example of 'Matthew Madness' in Liverpool, although he had no plans to repeat it until Alan Dosser, thinking that it added a little *je ne sais quoi* to the occasion, suggested he should keep it in, which he did, to the apparent delight of Liverpool audiences. But not so in Nottingham where there was a big reception on the opening night, the guests of honour being the Mayor and his entourage. Matt apparently skipped onto the stage, his dressing gown falling open as usual, and the entire block of Town Councillors got up and left. Headlines in the local paper the following morning read 'Actor's little slip shocks the sheriff!' It even got a mention on Ned Sherrin's late night radio show, so at least they got some publicity out of it. There was another 'free spirit' in the company, although not quite as much fun as Matthew. George Costigan's raison d'etre, it seemed, was to be as unpredictable as possible, the equally predictable consequences being that others could be affected by his cavalier approach. On one of the few occasions I saw the show, a couple of latecomers arrived during his opening speech, and with an eye to the main chance, he used their late arrival to his advantage, managing to get a few legitimate laughs. When I later commented on how well it had worked and suggested, not without a degree of humour, that in order to get the show off to a good start, it might be worth planting a couple of latecomers, George said, with a hint of disdain, "Oh, I couldn't possibly do the same thing twice." I was later brought up to date with a catalogue of his devices, all intended to 'ring the changes' and keep the other actors on their toes, and which included coming on stage backwards or from a totally different entrance, throwing himself onto the floor and playing an entire scene in that position, or not coming on at all. One night, he apparently entered clutching a toilet seat which he then placed over Lesley's head just as she was about to sing. When the tour of *Bitter Apples* finally came to an end several weeks later in Swindon without achieving the commercial success that John McGrath clearly had in mind when he conceived it, Lesley joined me in Chadwick Street.

It was not long, however, before I was invited to return to the River Bank as Ratty in *Toad of Toad Hall,* this time to be performed at the Old Vic, one of my all-time favourite theatres, and in which I hadn't appeared for many years. The leading members of the cast were the same as they had been the previous year, the only exception being that I would be replaced for the last week of the run so that I could join Timothy West for the West End premiere of *Make the Little Beggars Hop,* now called simply *Beecham.* Just before I left the Waterloo Road en route for Shaftesbury Avenue, I received a card from Richard Goolden, featuring E.H. Shepard's illustration of the four main characters from *The Wind in the Willows,* on the back of which he had written, after wishing me luck for *Beecham:* 'I would like to say what a very great delight it was to have done *Toad* once again with you. No one could have been nicer and more lovely to act with, and I hope we may do it again together if I live long enough!' Sadly, he didn't. He had first played the part of Mole in 1930, and had become so identified with the character that one could be forgiven for thinking the part had been originally created for him. In 1981, at the age of 86, Moley returned permanently to his hole in the ground, and was much missed on the River Bank.

oOoOo

Twenty four

If the 1970s had received mixed reviews, both professionally and personally, the '80s couldn't have got off to a more auspicious start when *Beecham* opened at the Apollo Theatre in Shaftesbury Avenue at the end of January. Not that the play itself escaped the occasional dig for failing to address the more serious aspects of Beecham's career in favour of his wit and his bombast. But it was well-received by most critics, and unquestionably enjoyed by large and appreciative audiences who would surely have been encouraged to dig deeper, had they a mind to. I can certainly claim, amongst other things, that it revealed to me, for the first time in my life, the unique genius of Wolfgang Amadeus Mozart, a revelation that was to stand me in good stead in the not-too-distant future. But there was no denying, of course, that *Beecham* was, first and foremost, meant to be an entertainment, and that the portrait painted by Ned and Caryl leaned heavily on his outrageously comic utterances, such as, 'Try everything once, except incest and folk-dancing,' and, 'The English do not care for music, but they absolutely love the noise it makes'; while on a more personal level, 'Sir Adrian Boult came round to see me this morning, positively reeking of Horlicks', and his description of Herbert von Karajan as 'a musical Malcolm Sargent', demonstrating a wicked disregard for the sensibilities of his peers. My undoubted favourite, though, was when he stopped the orchestra and, turning to the lady cellist, said, "Madam, you have between your legs an instrument capable of giving delight to thousands, and all you can do is scratch it!" Tim's reviews were all very positive, with headlines such as: 'Bravo! A West End triumph for Timothy' and 'This is Beecham in all his waggish majesty'; nor did I come out of it too badly. The scene in which I played an Australian radio interviewer, desperately trying to get some kind of response to my questions from an obdurately silent Beecham was much remarked upon and, according to one critic, 'The funniest in the play', while R.B.M. in The Stage wrote: 'In the sole supporting part, Terry Wale is faultless.' On the opening night, I was invited into Tim's dressing-room after the show to share with him the pleasure and the burden of a plethora of visitors, all of whom were enthusiastic, except for she who was the last to leave. Along with her small, though élite, coterie, prima ballerina Dame Alicia Markova (née Alice Marks) was graciously offered a chair from which she bestowed her somewhat patronising praise for his performance, received by Tim with characteristic charm and grace. She concluded by saying, with a condescending smile, that having worked with Sir Thomas on numerous occasions, she had never seen him lean on the podium the way Timothy did, an observation that Tim greeted with what appeared to be genuine interest, as if taking a serious note. It was only after the door had finally closed behind her that he turned, Beecham re-surfacing, and said, "And I've never seen a swan die like you do, either!"

We both enjoyed our time at the Apollo, not least, as far as I was concerned, for the unprecedented salary I was receiving of £300 a week! For Tim, who was clearly more accustomed to earning decent wages, it also provided a welcome refuge from the daily trials and tribulations of running the Prospect Theatre Company.

Beecham sadly closed after only three months, probably because of its somewhat limited commercial appeal. But it had been a happy time for both of us, and one that heralded – although we didn't know it at the time – a future for the show, extending over the next few years and including a number of one-night stands across the country, a major television production in which Tim actually got to conduct the Hallé Orchestra, and a trip to the other side of the world. Meanwhile, there were other things for me to look forward to.

I never suspected when I began to write this tome, and without taking into account how long it would take me to finish it, that my memory might well be somewhat impaired by this time, so I owe to Lesley a debt of gratitude for allowing me access to her diaries which have provided me with a largely accurate account of what has happened, where and when, since we became a couple. This probably explains why my most abiding memory of our holiday on the island of Rhodes is of an evening visit to a taverna where Lesley used her diary to prop up a wonky table-leg, and forgot to retrieve it, thereby depriving me of any documentary evidence for 1980. What I do recall however, and quite vividly, is that thanks to a relatively healthy bank balance following the run of *Beecham*, we booked a three-week holiday on that very island which we chose rather than any other of the numerous Greek islands that attracted us, for the simple reason that it provided us with a direct flight. When we arrived there, not having booked any accommodation, we allowed ourselves to be persuaded by another couple who had been on the same flight to share a taxi with them to a resort called Lindos, some thirty-odd miles away on the east coast. Having been dropped off in the village square, we bade farewell to our fellow-travellers and wandered away, carrying our suitcases down the narrow main street, lined with shops and galleries, to look for somewhere to stay. We couldn't have gone very far before a man, standing outside one of these shops, asked if we were looking for accommodation. He then locked the door behind him and led us to a nearby villa with an enclosed courtyard, featuring a lemon tree, beyond which were spacious living quarters which he offered to us for the equivalent of £5 a night.

Lindos has since then become one of the most frequently visited locations on the island of Rhodes, its side-streets, tavernas and night-clubs invariably thronged with day-trippers, whilst a never-ending stream of reluctant donkeys haul them up the steep gradient, lined with women selling lace, to the ancient acropolis that dominates the skyline. When we were there, the influx of day-trippers was pretty well restricted to one day a week from which we quickly learned to retreat to the comparative quiet and seclusion of St. Paul's Bay on the other side of the acropolis. For the most part, however, our days were spent wallowing in the sun-soaked environs of this delightful village, acquiring deep tans as we sunbathed on the sparsely populated main beach, and either swimming or venturing further out to sea aboard a pedalo, before returning to our villa where Lesley would pluck a lemon from the branches of our very own tree, the juice of which I would then employ in concocting her favourite aperitif, the *Bloody Mary*, before leisurely venturing out to select yet another taverna from the many alternatives in those maze-like lanes where we could enjoy our favourite Greek dishes along with a bottle of Demestika, and ending the evening in one of several clubs featuring bouzouki music. Sounds idyllic? Well, it certainly was, although it didn't stop us from justifying our otherwise hedonistic existence by visiting Rhodes town for a few days, and taking in something of its chequered history, its ancient origins, crusading knights, besieging Ottomans and colonial Italians.

Even without her diary it was not particularly difficult for Lesley to remember the rest of that year, involved as she was in a production of *Canterbury Tales* with the New Vic Theatre Company. The fact that I was free to accompany her on a significant number of her touring dates, and had seen the show a record-breaking 16 times before it reached the Roundhouse in London, at least speaks volumes for my lack of any other employment. I do recall this becoming something of an issue with Norman Boyack who, having long been separated from his business partner, Jeremy Conway, was experiencing periods of otherwise welcome isolation when he would plug the hole by seeking my opinion on a number of subjects, and even occasionally raising my expectations as an actor by calling me at home simply to ask me if I thought one or other of his clients was right for a certain part or, if he was feeling a bit low, did I have a joke to cheer him up? Norman had never been particularly adept at finding me work as an actor, although he was happy enough, given our shared history with Richard Hatton Ltd, to ask me to stand in for him when he felt in need of an occasional break. I'm fairly certain that it was he too who procured for me a brief association with Bernard Braden and Barbara Kelly, whose company, *Prime Performers*, represented a host of after-dinner speakers, amongst whom was my friend, Benny Green, an entertaining and expert speaker on a variety of subjects, but whose services were rarely called upon, while demands for the presence of Erica Roe, whose sole claim to fame was for running topless across the Twickenham rugby pitch were many and stentorian. I was later given to understand, however, that negotiations were all but terminated once it became clear that she would never bare her breasts in public again!

On the plus side, my occasional employment meant that I was able to spend more time with Lesley, and I particularly remember accompanying her on a day-trip to Boulogne, organised by Micky O'Donoghue, one of the founders of the New Vic Theatre, for the purpose of allowing the *Canterbury Tales* company to enjoy a day out together before getting down to work. Micky was a larger than life character whose cartoon-like personality would dominate the proceedings as The Miller in this updated version of Chaucer's tales, adapted by Phil Woods and Michael Bogdanov, who was also credited with directing it when it had premiered at the Young Vic Theatre, but whose contribution to the rehearsal process, at least as far as Lesley was concerned, was confined to the odd leer, or a slap on the bum. His name on the poster, however, was something of a coup as he had recently become an associate director at the National Theatre. Besides, he was 'one of the boys', and the New Vic Company was very much a boy's world. In fact, male chauvinism was rife amongst them, admirably suiting the tenor of the show which was, at its best, grotesquely funny. The main source of hilarity was Micky as the Miller, whose function was to disrupt the tranquillity of the Vicar's garden-party which was the setting for the play, with lewd remarks, bawdy jokes and general grossness. Four other members of the company, including Lesley as the Cook, had a tale to tell in which the others participated, and as the show was structured as a competition between these tales, they were each of them expected to accost members of the audience in the bar before the show to solicit their votes at the end of the evening. Micky, of course, was in his element and, although the Miller was excluded for obvious reasons from the official story-telling competition, he made many friends in the bar with his lewd and lascivious pre-show antics. Having then gone on to create havoc throughout the show, winning himself many more friends in the audience, he finally comes on stage, and, with their support, is reluctantly allowed to tell his tale. It is, of course, just as rude as everyone hopes, and the volume of the applause declares him the winner. With just a pretty folk song to sing, no jokes to tell, and no outrageous character to hide behind, Lesley's tale was on a hiding to nothing, or at least it was until they took the show to Edinburgh where, on home ground, and with a sizeable proportion of the audience made up of family and friends, she won hands down!

Canterbury Tales had actually launched its tour with a three-week run in Poole, on the Dorset coast, where I was happy (and available!) to take up all but permanent residence. It was July, our accommodation quite luxurious, and the weather was perfect. For Lesley, however, it was marred by the introduction of 'Street Theatre', in which all the company members were expected to participate. They called it *The Alternative Olympics*, but since Lesley had no particular skills in that area, she was at a loss to know what to do. Micky tore up telephone directories with his bare hands, Big John Labanowski lay on a bed of nails and stubbed out cigarettes on his tongue, Bev Willis did some roller-skating and Kate Versey swallowed chocolate wagon wheels whole! They finally came up with a stunt for Lesley which was to catch a flat iron in her teeth. She was introduced as 'The Mighty Microdot', at which point she flexed her muscles and bared her teeth to the assembled throng. The flat iron was attached to a long piece of elastic which she held between her teeth as one of the boys walked into the distance holding the iron until the elastic was taut. After a big build-up he shouted, "Are you ready?", at which point, as she opened her mouth to say, "Yes", the elastic popped out from between her teeth, and the boy fell backwards as the flat iron whacked him in the goolies! For some reason she found the experience embarrassing and, as the tour progressed, she gave it up in favour of handing out leaflets; and for much the same reason, I went out of my way never to watch *The Alternative Olympics* again!

Of all my memories of that tour, the one that stands out most indelibly is the week they spent in Bradford which, for some reason, I missed. After packing them in all over the country, they played the Alhambra Theatre to near empty houses, mainly because the Yorkshire Ripper was still at large and the city was living in fear. Few women dared to venture out alone in the evening, and I had already had a word with the lads in the company asking them to keep a look out for the girls during the Bradford week. "What do you take us for?", they chorused. Obviously I took them for a bunch of male chauvinist pigs, or I wouldn't have had to mention it in the first place. Wild horses could not have dragged them away from their pints, their dirty jokes and their late-night curries. However, Lesley was sharing digs with Jackie, the girl from the wardrobe department, so at least she had company, although they both still found the walk back at night quite unnerving. On the very last night, however, Jackie had arranged a lift back to London and Lesley was on her own, sinking under the weight of half a dozen plastic bags filled with all her bits and pieces from the dressing-room. It was apparently bitterly cold, and there wasn't a soul in sight as she made her way back to the digs, losing her way en route and, increasingly panic-stricken, seeing the shape of the Ripper in every lurking shadow. In fact, she very nearly stopped at a phone box to say goodbye to me. She kept on running, however, and finally made it, slamming the door behind her. Had she known that the most recent murder had taken place only a few hundred yards away, and that days later another would take place in the same area, I cannot begin to imagine what state she would have been in. Just for the record, Peter Sutcliffe (the Yorkshire Ripper) was finally caught on January 5th, 1981, and the citizens of Bradford breathed a sigh of relief.

By the time they reached the Roundhouse in London, I was happily ensconced on the River Bank as Ratty once more, returning to the Old Vic, and sharing the stage again with Ian Talbot as Toad and David King as Badger, while Mole's hole in the ground, having recently been vacated, was now occupied by Barrie Jamieson. *Toad of Toad Hall* being a matinées only show, I was able to visit the Roundhouse on a few more occasions, winning a well-deserved accolade from the company for my dedicated support during the tour. In truth, although Geoffrey Chaucer might well have been turning in his grave, I must have enjoyed the experience as it would have taken more than Lesley's presence on stage to persuade me to return as often as I did. A more Chaucerian reaction came, not surprisingly, from Patrick Garland who saw it at the Roundhouse and put me to shame by sending Lesley a card, saying that her performance was 'a good deed in a naughty world!' But then, *I* didn't go to Oxford University!

Before removing my rat's tail for the very last time, David Conville made me an offer I couldn't refuse, and I am not referring exclusively to the part of Don John in *Much Ado About Nothing,* tempting enough though it was, but to his suggestion that, if Lesley was interested in embarking on yet another tour so soon after returning to London, he would happily offer her the part of Margaret. Nothing could have been nicer as far as I was concerned, and Lesley needed no persuasion to pack her suitcase again.

Courtesy of Lesley's 1981 diary, I learned that the tour had come to an end in Aberystwyth on May 9th, and that it had been punctuated *en route* by welcome breaks. It was on one of these that I was called by Norman Boyack – not for advice on this occasion, nor yet for a cheerful jest, but to tell me that a client of his had decided to leave the cast of *Amadeus* prior to its transfer from the National Theatre to the West End, and to ask if I would be interested in taking over from him. I was naturally delighted that Norman had put on his agent's hat again on my behalf, while my only reservation about the prospect of working with Peter Hall again was quickly dispelled when he told me that restaging the production would be in the hands of his Assistant Director, Giles Block, with whom I had worked in Ludlow some 20 years earlier when he had been an actor. Following a meeting with Giles who had no need to think that far back, having seen me in *Beecham*, I was offered the part of one of the two Venticelli, the 'gentle breezes', with whom Antonio Salieri, the leading character, has a largely imaginary relationship as he plots the death of Wolfgang Amadeus Mozart. The Venticelli were, in fact, an extremely effective theatrical device, listening to Salieri's otherwise silent thoughts and, as streetwise purveyors of gossip, feeding him with the ways and means to translate them into deeds. They were otherwise involved as token guests at the court of the Austrian Emperor, Joseph II, and as the means, by virtue of frequent costume changes, of moving the action backwards and forwards from the late 18th century when Mozart was still alive to Salieri's deathbed confession in 1825.

By the time I started rehearsals, *Amadeus* had been running as part of the National Theatre repertoire since November 1979 with Paul Scofield as Salieri, Simon Callow as Mozart and Felicity Kendall as Constanze Mozart. The play, by Peter Shaffer, had received almost universally rhapsodic reviews, and had won five Tony Awards for the New York production which was still running on Broadway. For the West End run, the three leading characters were to be played by Frank Finlay as Salieri, Richard O'Callaghan as Mozart and Morag Hood as Constanze, and had I not already known who they were, Peter Hall's failure to acknowledge, let alone extend a greeting, to anyone other than those three on that first day would have informed me, at least of their 'star' status.

The rehearsal process, under the sympathetic stewardship of Giles Block, was a very enjoyable experience, made even more so for being aware that we would be reaping the benefits of an already well-established critical and popular success without any of the doubts and uncertainties that usually attend an opening night. I had signed a year-long contract from the date of our first performance at Her Majesty's Theatre, and I didn't entertain for a moment the possibility that I wouldn't still be there in a year's time; a dream come true, in fact. Moreover, I loved the play and its music; all the more so for having been schooled by Sir Thomas Beecham! In addition, the omni-present Venticelli provided exactly the right kind of parts; significant, yet relatively undemanding, that would allow me the time and space to live my life to the full and, who knows, even to find and afford the country cottage that Lesley and I had set our hearts on. In fact, the outlook was rosy, complemented as it was by my on-stage and dressing-room partnership with fellow Venticello, Dermot Crowley, who had played the part before I came along, and brought with him a good many stories about what it had been like to work alongside Scofield, whose energies, as Salieri, seemed to have been largely devoted to making the Venticelli laugh, which was certainly not destined to be one of Frank Finlay's ambitions!

Achieving what must have been something of a record, the new company played for all of two performances at the Olivier Theatre before travelling to Manchester for a week at the Palace Theatre, and finally opening at Her Majesty's on July 2nd to the anticipated acclaim of both press and public. Despite the fact that Peter Hall sent no first-night greetings to the company, nor made an appearance back-stage, the company duly celebrated the occasion. So, from a personal point of view, and short of a national catastrophe, I was able to look forward to a year's employment at £250 a week, rising to £275 after the first six months, not to mention driving to work every day with a more or less guaranteed free parking space in St. James's Square, just across the road from the theatre; a theatre, moreover, of many memories, fond and otherwise, where I had understudied Jeremy Spencer in *The Innocents* some 28 years earlier, and on the stage of which, between a matinée and evening performance, I had witnessed the production of my very first play. It was also, for the archives, the theatre in which I had seen the original London production of *West Side Story* in 1959, and in 1972, the opening night of Stephen Sondheim's seminal musical, *Company*. In other words, the prospect of enjoying a long run in a hugely successful play at such a theatre in the heart of London's West End augured well, and for the first few months I had no reason to question this precept, punctuated as it was in the early days by my frequent weekend visits to Coventry.

Following the tour of *Much Ado About Nothing*, Lesley had been having a pretty thin time of it workwise, so it was hardly surprising that she rose to the bait when she was offered several parts in *The Mystery Plays* which were to take place in the bomb-damaged ruins of the old cathedral in Coventry. Although she hadn't seen a script, she was persuaded to accept the director's tempting description of the parts on offer which, when she finally got to read it, a couple of days before rehearsals were due to start, fell far short of her expectations, not to mention the director's sales-pitch. The 'Meaty' Messenger in his gift had all of five lines to say, while Celedonius' Sister was a deaf mute, and the mother of a murdered baby had one song and that was a duet!

Nevertheless, ignoring my advice not to go, Lesley packed her bags and headed for Coventry, taking up residence in one of the Belgrade Theatre's little flats. Following the read-through, the director visited her in her flat and apologised for the late arrival of the script, frankly admitting that what he really wanted her there for was to supervise and lead the children's choir. He went on, applying balm, to say that he would do his very best to make the Messenger 'meatier' and that he would help her to make something more of the Deaf Mute, promises which came to nothing. As time went by, however, and the production took shape, she realised she was more than happy to remain on the sidelines. I myself never got to see the entire event, although I did manage to catch the pre-show pageants on one occasion, and gleaned enough from them to fully empathise with Lesley's preferred comfort zone. Being a timeless and universal story, the director had decided to ignore time and place. Fair enough, but when the Angel Gabriel appeared in a flying suit as a World War 1 pilot, and Herod played *Some Enchanted Evening* on the violin, credibility was strained to breaking point. In one of the pageants, Lesley played Daniel in the Lion's Den, wearing a three-piece suit, huge spectacles, and looking for all the world like an even smaller Ronnie Corbett. All four pageants happened simultaneously, giving audiences the chance to wander from one to the other. It was hardly surprising, however, that Adam and Eve, who wore nothing but body stockings, drew by far the biggest crowd, most of whom chose to stay where they were. It was, of course, a shame to see such a beautiful and poignant setting as the ruined Cathedral so sadly misused, and the fact that Coventry actually decided not to do *The Mystery Plays* the following year was, I think, a fitting postscript! Just for the record, the director's name was Michael Boyd, whose career path eventually led to the artistic directorship of the Royal Shakespeare Company – horses for courses.

On one of my fairly frequent trips up to Coventry during the following few weeks, I took the opportunity to view a cottage that was up for sale in the tiny Oxfordshire village of Milton, close to Banbury. For some reason, I had brought my old friend from Chichester days, Gordon Griffin, along with me and he was as enchanted as I was by the little doll's house that was up for sale. Lesley was equally charmed when I drove her down from Coventry to see it, and we decided to make an offer – subject, of course, to a surveyor's report. A clutch of cottages, situated on a slight mound, known as The Bank, hemmed our cottage in on either side and to the rear, depriving it of access, unless you were prepared to climb the mound or 'trespass' on next door's property. There was, moreover, no rear entrance at all, which was not in itself a problem, except that we were denied access to the back of the cottage, making any kind of maintenance impossible. Clearly, there were issues to be addressed, not to mention applying for a mortgage. The cottage was on the market for £19,500 and there was no question – long-term West End engagement notwithstanding – that we would be able to lay our hands on that kind of money. But we were determined to have it, no matter how long it took to resolve the problems. When Lesley was invited to appear at the Thorndike Theatre, Leatherhead, in a new play by Philip Guard called *A Criminal Suggestion* it was late September, and I was coming to the end of my third month in *Amadeus,* still relatively unperturbed, even by Frank Finlay's decision to treat the Venticelli, both on-stage and off, solely as figments of his imagination, making no eye contact with us at all, which was disorientating, to say the least. By the time *A Criminal Suggestion* came to an end, however, five months had gone by, and the cracks were beginning to show. I didn't know anything about it at the time, but what I was beginning to experience were the early signs of what is known – at least by me – as 'the long-run syndrome'. I think it would be true to say that, for the vast majority of stage actors, the chance of playing a decent part in a hugely successful play over a lengthy period of time, leaving the theatre every night with the thunderous approval of the audience ringing in your ears is such stuff as dreams are made on. That it should happen in a West End theatre from which you would return to your own home, free to carry on with your everyday life whilst enjoying financial security, is surely the crème de la crème. But it is the expectations born of that dream that conceal the whirlpool of disenchantment. The constant repetition of the same words over a long period of time is, of course, a common hurdle, and one which can manifest itself even in comparatively short runs, depending on the nature of the role and its contribution to the dramatic momentum of the play, not to mention the quality of the play itself.

The existence of the Venticelli was a theatrical device, subsumed, more or less, in the character of Salieri, later confirmed when they were done away with in the film version. That Frank Finlay's refusal to acknowledge our physical presence anticipated this, and was naturally disconcerting, but at least there were two of us, and both Dermot and I found ways and means of dealing with it in the months to come. Besides, we were occasionally let off the robotic leash to enjoy a degree of independence at various social gatherings in the Emperor Josef's

Vienna.

More surprisingly, and if only because it was the very last thing I expected, was the absence of camaraderie. Yes, I got to live at home, but then so did everybody else and, following the token celebrations on the opening night, that's where everybody went at the end of the show, returning in time for the half-hour call the next day to the virtual seclusion of their dressing-rooms. In a career spanning three decades, most of which I had spent away from home, and more often than not as a member of a company engaged in a season of plays, I took for granted the comradely nature of theatre where, throughout my life, friendships had been forged, many of them fleeting due to the nomadic nature of the business, but friendships nonetheless. It was an intrinsic part of life in the theatre as far as I was concerned, and the all but complete absence of togetherness at Her Majesty's Theatre over a period of months led to a sense of isolation which was off-set to a certain extent by sharing a dressing-room, and by the occasional encounters with other members of the company in the gap between matinée and evening performances. But it was certainly a combination of factors that led to my 'long-run syndrome'.

1981 Amadeus - Her Majesty's Theatre, with Dermot Crowley.

It was, and remains to this day, something of a mystery to me that Frank Finlay, all but alone in the company, appeared to survive intact. It was a subject that gave rise to some discussion, at least between Dermot and myself who spent most of our on-stage life in his company, that he never changed a gesture, an inflection or a movement throughout the entire run of the play. Was it because he believed he had achieved perfection on the opening night, and was never tempted to try something different? Or because he knew only too well that his survival depended upon creating a shell around himself, allowing nothing to penetrate it? Whether he had ever been a 'company' man was unknown to me, but he certainly made no effort to socialise during the run of *Amadeus*, leaving the theatre promptly every night without ever attending any of the few get-togethers that punctuated our lengthy stay. I can only surmise that, short of him being, by nature, anti-social, he had simply found and mastered a survival technique. Only on one occasion do I remember him personally addressing me when, late on in the run, he came up to me in the wings and congratulated me on my marriage. There was little point, I knew, in telling him that it was Dermot whose wedding had recently taken place, so I simply thanked him, and left it at that.

For obvious reasons, I never got to see Lesley in *A Criminal Suggestion*, although I was on the receiving end of blow-by-blow accounts when I picked her up nightly from the railway station after it had opened, and so could reasonably be forgiven for thinking that I *had* seen it. She and the author, Philip Guard, had worked together on a production of *The Fantasticks* in Scotland back in 1973, the year before she and I met, and he had specifically asked for her to play the part of Karen in *A Criminal Suggestion*, a yokel from Suffolk, and maid to the vivisectionist doctor who has, for personal reasons, decided to practise his skills on human beings rather than furry animals. His choice was happily endorsed by the play's director, John Doyle, with whom, coincidentally, I had worked when he was a member of the stage management team on the Perth Theatre tour of *The Government Inspector* in 1975. Had Philip's enthusiastic advocacy of Iain Cuthbertson for the role of the Doctor met with as happy an outcome, all might have gone well, but unfortunately Iain Cuthbertson turned it down, and Philip was left with no alternative but to play the part himself. Philip's reputation as an actor, as well as a playwright, was already well established, and there was little doubt that he would be able to acquit himself well in the role, but as the play was billed as 'a thriller', one of its essential ingredients was that the character of the Doctor should remain ambiguous for as long as possible. Well, Iain Cuthbertson was certainly built for the part, large and generously proportioned as he was, he could have been mistaken for Santa Claus on a good day, while Philip, slightly built and foxy-featured, was bound to be cast as the villain of the piece from his very first entrance. With less than enthusiastic newspaper reviews following the opening night, and by disappointingly small audiences, he became increasingly paranoid, accusing the management and the staff of going out of their way to wreck his play, not only by offering Iain Cuthbertson the derisory salary of £80 a week, but for withholding information about ticket sales and, according to Lesley, a not entirely unjustified complaint about the generally cavalier attitude exhibited towards the production, a paranoia that grew until he began to imagine that the whole world was against him, and reached its climax when, on leaving the theatre one night, he turned back and shouted up at the building, "I wish you cancer by Christmas!" Lesley, being Lesley, and having worked alongside him before, had a sneaking, if incomprehensible, fondness for Philip as he could be 'such wickedly entertaining company', and it was on their frequent train journeys back to London when he vented his wrath, the blow-by-blow accounts of which prompted this little detour.

I was perfectly happy, of course, when Lesley was asked to stay on at the Thorndike Theatre for the pantomime. Had I been aware, however, of the seeds that were being sown, I might well have tried to dissuade her, or at least have insisted that she find herself suitable accommodation in Leatherhead. But then again, maybe not, as I was given to understand quite early on in rehearsals, that the Musical Director of the pantomime had taken something of a shine to her, by no means an unfamiliar scenario, and in the normal course of events one that I would have handled with my usual insouciance. In all truth, I would not have liked to be married to a woman who no one else fancied! On this occasion, however, Lesley's tales of his attentions had an increasingly deleterious effect on my brain. This was not helped by her prolonged absences from home as she continued to play in *A Criminal Suggestion* at night while rehearsing the pantomime during the day. Some time later, when a visit to the doctor was deemed advisable, I was diagnosed with 'housewives' syndrome' which, when dovetailed with the 'long-run syndrome' (of which he had never heard!), was not too far from the truth. With Christmas fast approaching, shopping became a preoccupation, my days spent seething about other shoppers, mainly women, who never looked where they were going, and who never ever seemed to have their money ready to hand, causing endless delays at the checkout while they delved for their purses. With our mutual work commitments, I found it difficult to understand why we had decided to entertain so much over the Christmas period. The fact that we hadn't, and that Lesley had never suggested we would, should have culminated in an abject apology instead of which I ended up throwing the turkey I had just purchased at the wall; such was my state of mind, exacerbated by the arrival of winter. Picking up Lesley from the railway station late at night became more stressful with the arrival of snow, if only because the train was just as likely to arrive at Victoria as Waterloo, depending on the weather conditions, and in those otherwise halcyon days before the coming of mobile phones, the only way you could find out what station it would arrive at was to wait for it not to arrive and then head for the other one.

Jack and the Beanstalk opened at the Thorndike Theatre on Saturday, December 19th, followed by a party to which I was invited, and would have attended, had not my car lost a wheel outside Buckingham Palace, where I was obliged to wait in the freezing cold for the AA to arrive. A couple of weeks later, replete again with all four wheels, I drove down to Leatherhead after the show to join in their New Year celebrations, having instructed Lesley to tell the MD, in no uncertain terms, to keep his distance. That we had scarcely taken our seats before he came up and asked her to dance did not, in spite of the fact that she declined his invitation, augur well for the rest of the evening, a prophecy borne out when he later rose to announce the winner of 'The Naughty Knickers' award, the contestants gleaned from his privileged point of view in the orchestra pit. The winner, of course, was Lesley Mackie, and had I not entirely lost my sense of humour, I might have found it quite amusing when he presented her with a pair of tartan knickers. Contrarily, I would quite happily have stuffed them down his throat when, on the point of leaving, he suggested that he and I might meet for a drink one evening after *Amadeus*. I have no idea what I said, but it was obviously pretty rude, sparking a blazing row between Lesley and me on our way back to London.

For some unaccountable reason, I awoke the following morning feeling altogether stress-free. The sun had come out, albeit briefly, and I apologised profusely for my churlish behaviour the previous evening, and offered to drive her down to Leatherhead for her matinée performance. She demurred, but I insisted and finally she gave way. The sun had indeed come out, and while there was still a good deal of snow lying around, there was nothing to cause undue concern, until we reached the A3 where we were delayed on the southbound lane by much denser traffic than I had anticipated, the result of a heavier residue of snow than we had encountered on the London streets, much of it now thrown up onto my windscreen. Thanks to tradition, most Christmas shows played two performances daily, and I thanked providence for allowing me the luxury, whatever my other reservations, of a schedule that only demanded two matinées a week. I was pondering this, and weighing up the chances of arriving at the Thorndike Theatre in time for the half-hour call, when it suddenly occurred to me that this was a Saturday, and that I had a matinée myself. I was obviously in no position at the time to observe my reaction to this cataclysmic revelation, nor even now to describe it as objectively as Lesley, who was sitting next to me:

'We were heading slowly along the A3 when Terry suddenly went rigid and yelled, "I've got a matinée too!" Neither of us had remembered his matinée, which was due to begin 30 minutes later than mine. Suddenly all hell broke loose. "I'm driving the wrong way", he shouted. "Look for a taxi!" "A taxi?", I screamed back. "On the A3? You must be joking!" He was in a terrible state, skidding all over the road. I tried to calm him with time-honoured phrases like, "It's only a show", and "You've got an understudy!" But they were having no effect and I finally shrieked; "I don't want to die today! *Amadeus? Jack and the Beanstalk*? What does it all mean?" He dropped me at the stage-door 20 minutes before curtain-up and I left him, slumped over the steering-wheel.'

Lesley went into the theatre, telephoned Her Majesty's, and told them that I would not be there for the afternoon performance. Meanwhile, I managed to pull myself together, reconcile myself to the situation, and head back towards London. The traffic was a good deal less dense going back and, as I drove on, it occurred to me that there was a possibility, should it stay that way, that I might just make it in time for the show. I put my foot down and, as all reason evaporated, I determined that there was no other option. Screeching to a halt in St. James's Square, I belted across the road and into the stage door with two minutes to spare before the curtain was due to rise. I was, by this time, in no condition to go on stage, but there was no one there to stop me, so I rushed up the stairs, burst into my dressing-room, and all but tore the costume from my understudy's back. So if, perchance, Jim Bryce should happen to read this one day, I apologise again. I did buy him a bottle of whisky at the time, and I even suggested to the company manager that I could absent myself on another matinée day so that he could get to play the part, but short of a crisis situation, I was told it wouldn't be allowed.

Small comfort, however, is taken from discovering that you are not alone, and that there are others similarly afflicted. But it took a story from a neighbouring theatre to upstage my own, at least in dramatic terms, when Brenda Blethyn arrived in her dressing-room at the Comedy Theatre in Panton Street far too early one day when she was appearing in another long-running play called *Steaming*. She subsequently decided to fill in the time with a shopping expedition to Regent Street, during which she clearly suffered a mental aberration. She returned to Panton Street and, with time still to spare before the evening's performance, she decided to visit *The Stockpot*, a restaurant just across the road from the theatre, which she was just about to enter when the stage manager emerged from the theatre and called out to her, "Brenda, where are you going? We're in the middle of a matinée!" She allegedly collapsed and had to be carried in through the stage door.

The arrival of 1982 brought with it other diversions, including several Sunday night visits to theatres around the country with *Beecham*, and calls from Norman Boyack to sit in for him at his office – not to mention the best of 500 games of scrabble between Dermot and myself in our dressing-room, all of which provided a welcome distraction from the all-too-familiar lives of the Venticelli. And then, of course, there was the Falklands conflict which, for a variety of reasons, provided a powerful magnet. But by far the happiest of diversions was moving into our tiny cottage in Milton on which, after a bit of a struggle, we had finally managed to secure a mortgage. We had also managed to resolve the problems of access, but with parking space available in the nearby pub's spacious car-park, we were happy, more often than not, to climb the grassy mound to our own front gate.

Situated between the villages of Bloxham and Adderbury, Milton was little more than a hamlet, although it did possess a very pretty little church in which services were only rarely held. In fact, the only social gatherings that took place were in the pub which, as if to emphasise its isolation from the real world, was called *The Black Boy*, displayed for all to see by the presence on the road of an old inn-sign featuring, just in case you'd never seen one before, the portrait of a black boy! Our occasional visits to this pub were invariably greeted with a sudden silence from the local clientele, predominantly male, who obviously regarded us as aliens, or at least as people who must have stumbled across the place by accident. The cottage itself, up on 'The Bank', and soon to be christened *Wild Thyme*, became a haven as far as we were concerned, akin to a doll's house or, according to Lesley's father on a visit, more like a 'coo-shed'. But we treasured our times there, and even before the coming of the M40, it took us only an hour and a half in our newly acquired Renault 5 to reach it by way of High Wycombe, Woodstock and Oxford. Four miles further up the road was Banbury, where we were able to do most of our shopping, whilst driving westwards took us into the Cotswolds, that most beautiful of England's rural settings, and introducing us to delightful places like Bourton-on-the-Water, Moreton-in-Marsh, Broadway, Chipping Camden and, further north, through Evesham to our ultimate destination – Worcester.

For all the more or less general feelings of relief that our year-long contracts were coming to an end, there weren't too many people in the *Amadeus* company who understood my decision to accept an offer from the Swan Theatre in Worcester. I suppose they felt that, having established a presence in the West End, that's where I should have remained, instead of hiding myself away in the back-of-beyond at a theatre that few of them had even heard of. The fact that John Doyle had just become the artistic director there, and that his opening production was to be Kander & Ebb's musical *Cabaret*, in which he had offered me the role of Emcee, would have been tempting enough as far as I was concerned, but that he had invited Lesley, with the prospect of bigger parts to come, to enlist as one of the chorus of Kit Kat Girls, proved irresistible.

On Saturday, July 17th, I gave my last performance at Her Majesty's Theatre in a play I had been given every reason to believe was a contemporary masterpiece and, should I be accused of nursing a grudge, in a production that was undoubtedly excellent. However, I had not set eyes on the director for over a year until I stood in the wings prior to making my final entrance and saw, to my surprise, Peter Hall standing in the prompt corner. He happened to look around at that point, and our eyes met, blankly for a moment, until an all-too-familiar synthetic smile lit up his face as he said, "Hello, goodbye".

oOoOo

Twenty five

Any doubts I might have had about the wisdom of venturing into the back-of-beyond would have been quickly dispelled after only a few weeks in Worcester. Yes, the Swan Theatre was very much off the beaten track, even by provincial reckoning, but once there and finally ensconced, it became the centre of my universe, ultimately providing me with more pleasure and fulfilment than I have ever enjoyed in the theatre, before or since.

The Worcester Repertory Company shared the building with the local amateurs, many of whom dedicated much of their spare time to providing front-of-house staff for the theatre, demonstrating not only a united front, but also sound economic priorities. True as I'm sitting here writing this, there were occasions when even our Artistic Director could be found selling tickets. There was a welcome feeling of togetherness about the place even before the season got under way, only to be enhanced by the arrival of a company, the majority of whom would become long-term, and in many cases, lifelong friends. So much for the transience of theatrical relationships that such an upshot could only have been brought about, as with any successful team, by the personality and the input of its leader. In the months and, indeed, in the years to come, John Doyle would take his place alongside David William and Peter Dews (at his best!) as a good team captain.

I was aware, courtesy of Lesley's involvement in John's production of *A Criminal Suggestion* in Leatherhead, that he was already working at the Swan Theatre as Associate Director to the then Artistic Director, Patrick Masefield, although I'm not at all sure I knew that he was on the point of taking over from him. In fact, all I knew of John Doyle at that stage was of our professional relationship when he came to Perth as an Assistant Stage Manager in 1975. Of course, he may well have seen and heard Lesley and I singing in *Cowardy Custard* during that time or even – heaven help us – in *Cloud Nine*. But he must surely have heard me singing somewhere, sometime, or what in the world could have possessed him to offer me the role of the Master of Ceremonies, or Emcee as he is known in *Cabaret,* without so much as an audition? I can honestly say that it never occurred to me at the time to ask him and, modesty aside, given that he made the right decision, I have never questioned it until now. I'm simply very grateful that he did, and that I was free to take it on, as it turned out to be one of my all-time favourite acting experiences, enhanced as it was by playing alongside a superb company of actors in a production that might well have been seen as a flagship, had any of us known at the time that John's long-term future in the world of musical theatre would take him to the top of the tree. We were also blessed with Catherine Jayes, an especially warm-hearted and gifted lady, as Musical Director, with whom Lesley had already worked on the *Mystery Plays* in Coventry, as well as Sally Marshall, a choreographer who almost succeeded in making me look as if I could dance!

Kander & Ebb's *Cabaret* is, of course, an extremely powerful piece of theatre, based as it is on Christopher Isherwood's Berlin stories, and already seen as a play called *I Am a Camera* by John van Druten back in the early '50s in which I had been privileged to see Dorothy Tutin as Sally Bowles, a dizzy London ingenue, making a living in a Berlin night-club while, all around her, Nazism takes hold. Christine McKenna played it in Worcester, and acquitted herself well, especially with the musical element of the part, as in our duet, the *Money Song*, as well as *Don't Tell Mama* and, of course, the title song, *Cabaret*. Lesley may very well have hankered after the part at the outset, but as it turned out she really enjoyed being a member of the chorus line of Kit Kat Girls, which also involved her, along with the delightful Hilary Cromie, and myself as Emcee, in painting a picture of the ideal *ménage à trois* in the song, *Two Ladies*. She also got to bring the first act curtain down with her rendition, backed by the rest of the company, of that chilling hymn to the Fatherland, *Tomorrow Belongs to Me*. But it was in the second act that she really came into her own when, following that most poignant of scenes in which Fraulein Schneider is 'persuaded' to turn her back on the man she has decided to marry because he is a Jew, Emcee enters and embarks on a song in praise of his lover's attributes, entitled, *If You Could See Her Through My Eyes*, in which he is joined by a baby gorilla, banana in hand, who is clearly the object of his affections, and whose presence, as intended, manages to raise a good deal of welcome laughter until it is cut short by the last line of the song, 'If you could see her through my eyes – she wouldn't look Jewish at all.' Lesley couldn't have been happier with her lot, and in particular with the baby gorilla whose banana, as the run progressed, became a regular prize, awarded to the actor or actress responsible for perpetrating the most outstanding and amusing faux pas of the evening, nominations for which were submitted by those who had the time and the inclination, and for which the winner was awarded the gorilla's banana at the end of the night. I have no reason to believe that all this nonsense impaired the quality of the show, and neither (I hope) did our regular visits to *The Cellars*, a local niterie where we spent many a late night with members of the company, often staggering home in the wee small hours. Having suffered and endured the absence of camaraderie for so long at Her Majesty's Theatre, to rediscover it with a vengeance at the tiny Swan Theatre in Worcester was manna from heaven!

1982 Cabaret - The Swan Theatre as Emcee.

At the end of the short run, we had a little party at which John was going to present 'bananas' in various categories, and one that had been specially made, called the Golden Banana, for the person he felt had made the biggest contribution to the show. Almost everyone entertained hopes and had prepared acceptance speeches, but when it was awarded to Lesley, she was so overcome she could barely splutter out a "Thank you", never mind make a speech. It clearly meant a great deal to her, witnessed by the fact that the Golden Banana is still displayed on a shelf only a few feet away from where I am sitting now!

Cabaret was a wonderful show to work on, and an inspired choice with which to open the season, enjoying capacity audiences and, in the wake of Hollywood's lavish version, starring Liza Minnelli, very favourable reviews, although being staged in far-away Worcester did not tempt any of the more illustrious critics to dip their pens.

Looking even further back now, and recalling those distant days when I all but wept when the run of a play came to its end, I cannot recall another occasion since then when I felt as sad as I did when the curtain fell for the last time on *Cabaret*. Fortunately, I had been asked to stay on for John's next production, *Romeo and Juliet*, being made aware that, having reached the age of forty-four, I was no longer required to 'age-up' in order to play the part of Friar Laurence! It was, if my memory serves me right, an enjoyable experience, and something of a sinecure after the roller-coaster ride of *Cabaret* – at least it was for Friar Laurence!

Lesley had already taken her leave, albeit temporarily, and returned to the cottage where she was fully occupied putting the finishing touches to the décor, cycling into Bloxham on her fold-up bike to do the shopping, and contemplating, not only her return to Worcester and to the land of Oz where she would reprise her performance as Dorothy Gale at Christmas, but also to the prospect of playing Edith Piaf in Pam Gems' play about the French *chanteuse* which John Doyle had scheduled for the following Spring season. I had long known that Lesley had nurtured a desire to play Piaf ever since she and I first saw the play, an RSC production which transferred to the Piccadilly Theatre only four years earlier. Jane Lapotaire had played the part then, and had gone on to New York with it where she won a Tony Award for her performance, which was excellent, despite the fact that she bore little resemblance to Edith Piaf, either physically or vocally. Lesley was certainly built for the part, and having heard her on several occasions, and in several drinking establishments in and around Perth, singing *Milord*, albeit with the occasional misheard and guessed-at French word, I knew she would come nearer to re-creating the 'Little Sparrow' than ... well, anyone else I could think of. Anyway, thanks to John Doyle's perspicacity, Lesley now had the chance to play it, and it was with great zest and a gritty determination that she set herself the task of recapturing the spirit and the soul of Edith Piaf. She read everything that had ever been written about her, listening over and over to her recordings, and studying every photograph that featured the lady, in real life as well as on screen and on stage. She studied her interpretation of all the songs that would be featured in the play, sung in French, together with Piaf's occasionally idiosyncratic pronunciation to which she was determined to be faithful. For anyone unfamiliar with the play, it's worth pointing out that Pam Gems had chosen to write it in the English vernacular, so that one could easily be forgiven for thinking that Piaf was a cockney sparrow rather than a French one. But, given that the only viable alternative for an English-speaking audience was for them all to speak with French accents, it was a perfectly acceptable dramatic device, redressing the dichotomy through the songs which, when sung in French, accompanied by an accordion, and with Piaf's own unique style and delivery, would place the action firmly on French soil.

Meanwhile, *Romeo and Juliet* having run its course, and with Swan Theatre hosting a production of Ronald Harwood's play, *The Dresser,* in which neither of us appeared, Lesley and I flew off to Portugal where, in Albufeira, we celebrated our fifth wedding anniversary. After ten sun-soaked days, we returned to London and from there to Milton where we packed and drove to Worcester, moving into our first proper digs, a large and spacious house close to the theatre, presided over by a very sweet lady called Bette Lewis, one of the familiar figures on front-of-house duty at the 'Swan'. It was good to be back, even with the prospect, on the not-too-distant horizon, of giving two – and on a couple of occasions *three* – performances a day of *The Wizard of Oz* over the Christmas period.

Before embarking on that, however, and having just re-read my biography in the Swan Theatre programme which mentions a television appearance I had recently made, I think it's worth recording here, if only for historical reasons. It was an episode of a BBC2 series called *Animal Behaviour* in which I played the Dutch ornithologist, Niko Tinbergen. Those were the days, still long before computer technology, the internet and self-taping took over, when every casting director's and agent's desk was laden with four massive volumes of *The Spotlight Casting Directory*, containing photographs, biographies and contact details of every actor and actress who could afford to pay for it; and woe betide you if you couldn't, for without a doubt there were few, if any, agents who would consider representing you if you didn't appear in 'Spotlight'. Having said that, I can't imagine I was alone in believing that I was seldom, if ever, cast as a result of my half-page advertisement, until *Animal Behaviour* came along. They were obviously looking for someone who closely resembled Niko Tinbergen, and having just now accessed his photograph on 'Google' (how long before even that becomes an anachronism?), I can see where they were coming from, if only as a result of my prematurely grey hair! What I do remember, only too vividly, are the days when, perched on a cliff-edge somewhere on the Farne Islands, just off the Northumbrian coast, I was crouched over a host of nesting sea-birds, fearfully contemplating the waves that crashed onto the rocks just below my feet whilst being dived upon by flocks of angry and possessive mothers as I sought to fondle their offspring. On balance, I suppose, I should be thankful that it was not a programme about Brother Adam, the 19th century Benedictine bee-keeper, to whom I also bore a passing resemblance!

But back to Worcester, where I was to play the title role in *The Wizard of Oz*, as well as the Mayor of Munchkinland, alongside Ginni Barlow as the Good Fairy and Karen Mann as the Wicked Witch of the West, while Dorothy's friends, the Scarecrow, the Tin Man and the Cowardly Lion were played by Iain Lauchlan, Don Crerar and Charles Bell respectively. Charles, who had played Ernst Ludwig, the chillingly devoted Nazi adherent in *Cabaret*, was also John's associate director with whom, in that capacity, I was destined to work on several occasions over the next few months, and also, in the not-too-distant future, with our roles reversed, in my production of Bernard Pomerance's *The Elephant Man*. Charles was a great bonus to the company on both sides of the footlights.

I was, of course, already acquainted with Lesley Mackie's Dorothy Gale, having seen it at the Birmingham Rep six years earlier, a performance that had, in fact, prompted my marriage proposal; an eyebrow raising proposal, I can hear you say, given that Dorothy was meant to be at least ten years younger than even Lesley was at that time. Yet here she was, at the ripe old age of 31, being asked by an elderly back-stage helper if she'd left school yet. There was even a little girl in the audience who was so taken with her Dorothy that she wanted to meet her, and maybe even ask her to tea. When Lesley finally emerged, out of costume, the girl burst into tears, and cried, "But mummy, she's a lady!"

Unlike me, Lesley had not been nurtured on Judy Garland's performance, unimaginable as far as I was concerned, but a blessing in disguise, as she succeeded in making the part her very own. That's the way it was in Birmingham, and she went on to do it again at the Swan Theatre where it was, of course, a pleasure to be sharing the stage with her. My only truly abiding memory of *The Wizard of Oz*, apart from the number of performances we were obliged to give, severely restricting our late night visits to The Cellars, was on the last night, when Lesley and I climbed into the basket suspended from the invisible hot-air balloon that was to take us back to Kansas. After waving farewell to the citizens of Emerald City, we were rocketed towards the roof of the theatre as the guy-line securing the basket slipped through the fingers of the stage-hand in charge of it. I was only aware of the open-mouthed faces of the company as we shot skywards, briefly contemplating a genuine, and possibly fatal, journey to... well, somewhere over the rainbow!

I had obviously been aware of Lesley's quality as an actress from early on in our relationship, for no matter how attractive and alluring I had found her, which I obviously had, I know I would never have contemplated marriage had I not known her to be, at the very least, talented. This is by way of being an afterthought, as I don't believe I seriously considered it at the time, but the very notion of spending the rest of my life with a fellow professional whose work I did not hold in some esteem was unthinkable. No matter how subliminal this pre-condition had been, I was about to witness, at first hand, a performance that was at once instinctive, and yet at the same time so thoroughly researched, that there were occasions during rehearsals for *Piaf*, and certainly during performances, when I found it difficult to recognise the woman to whom I was married.

Many of Edith Piaf's characteristics were, as it happened, easily accessible to Lesley, and particularly the early ones when the young Edith Gassion took life as it came, with few expectations save for doing what she wanted to do, and dealing with the consequences. She was a high-spirited guttersnipe, sexually and socially uninhibited, who sang for her supper on the streets of Paris and shared her breakfast with whatever man she'd taken a fancy to the night before. But when night-club owner Louis Leplée came along and heard her singing, took her in hand, re-christened her 'La Môme Piaf' (the little sparrow), and featured her in his night-club, he paved her way to international stardom, a status and a life-style she was ill-equipped to deal with, recklessly leading to her untimely death, at the age of 47, the result of too much booze and too many drugs. It was in these later, and often ugly, stages of her life, that Lesley demonstrated an uncanny skill, transforming the character she had already created into a barely recognisable but totally credible pastiche of her former self. But it was her musical presentation of Piaf's songs that rubber-stamped for me the value of all those hours of study and research which won her the acclaim of audiences and critics alike, and from as far afield as *The Birmingham Post*: 'The central figure – brazen in her bawdiness, constant in her crudities, desperate in her loves, tragic in her loneliness – grabs our attention with her first expletive in the first minute. Not once does she let us off the hook. The result is riveting. Lesley Mackie makes Edith Piaf a Cockney sparrow with a Barbara Windsor laugh and a singing voice which holds and haunts and challenges, defying its audience to escape from its spell. At grips with life, her Piaf is a waif-like bundle of precocious unpredictability. At grips with the microphone, when Piaf is in concert, she is electrifying. It is a performance of stunning memorability, snatching every ounce of opportunity, and finally hitting us with *Non, Je Ne Regrette Rien*. There is implicit self-indulgence in a play which insists on giving us a dozen songs in French in one evening. The author is fortunate that they are in such excellent hands.'

My own contribution to the show, aside from playing a handful of cameo roles, including Louis 'Papa' Leplée, was in persuading John Doyle to have second thoughts about his decision, prompted no doubt by thrift, to dispense with the services of an accordionist, my own reason for questioning it being that, without that readily identifiable French sound, Lesley's desire to mirror, as authentically as possible, Piaf's vocal qualities and techniques, would be severely handicapped – especially when she was singing Michel Émer's *L'Accordéoniste*! The fact that both John, and Nick Hawkins, our congenial general manager, not only listened, but were persuaded to change their minds, says more about them, I think, than it does about me, since they were the ones who were left to balance the books! Not that it was an extravagant budget by any means; the scenery, designed by the resourceful Chris Crosswell was simplicity itself, which is how it should have been, focusing entirely on the personality of the central character and her journey, and dominated by a backcloth featuring a full-scale photograph of Edith Piaf herself, a daunting prospect for anyone less equipped than Lesley to emulate the original. It was a good, no-nonsense, production, well served by the indispensable Catherine Jayes, and by a company of actors who did their best to inhabit the sketchy characters provided by Ms. Gems. It was in such a role, as a boy-friend of Edith's by the name of Paul, that I witnessed a strange occurrence one evening. I was supposed to be sitting at a table in a night-club, listening to Edith sing a love song, *Mon Manège à Moi*, when an unfamiliar gesture caught my eye, and immediately reminded me of Judy Garland. I had, in years gone by, seen Garland in concert, both on stage and on television, and was as familiar with her physical techniques as any other dyed-in-the-wool fan. Given that Piaf's gestures were invariably dramatic, sharp and angular, the hands open and the fingers extended, it was hardly surprising that I was taken aback when she illustrated one particular moment in the song in a much more romantic, relaxed and sophisticated way. Whatever it was, it came and went in a moment; but it was enough. After giving it some little thought, I told John Doyle that I wanted to write a play for Lesley about Judy Garland, and being something of a fan himself – of both ladies – he offered me a thousand pounds to write it for the Swan Theatre.

By the time Lesley was invited to stay on at the Swan, at least for the next production, she had already accepted an offer to return to Leatherhead as Maggie Wylie in J.M.Barrie's Scottish classic, *What Every Woman Knows*, a part she 'was born to play', according to Roger Clissold, who was to be directing it. As it turned out, she would probably have been happier had she stayed on in Worcester for Noël Coward's *Tonight at 8.30*, re-titled *Tonight at 7.30* to avoid audiences arriving just in time for the second interval!

It was back in the mid 1930s that Coward had decided to reinstate the one-act play, not as a curtain-raiser for the main event, but as part of a programme made up of one-act plays. His reasons for this venture were many and varied, 'From the audience's point of view, a short play can be more appealing than a long one in that it can sustain a mood without technical creaking or over-padding while, from the other side of the footlights, the stimulus provided by playing several roles instead of only one will communicate itself to the audience, thereby ensuring that a good time be had by all'. There were originally three separate triple-bill programmes, giving companies the opportunity to pick and choose, and from which the Swan chose *Fumed Oak, The Astonished Heart* and *Hands Across the Sea,* and in which I got to play a variety of roles, from a down-trodden working-class husband who, having managed to save £500, finally walks out on the three women who have made his life a misery, to a sophisticated psychiatrist who falls desperately in love with his wife's friend, and finding he can't cope with the outcome, kills himself, and culminating with a Commander R.N. who co-hosts a gathering of strangers to which his well-travelled, but dotty wife had forgotten she'd invited them.

For the first time that season, John handed over the reins to Charles Bell, in whose safe and sympathetic hands we all happily took advantage of Coward's gift, fully endorsing his claim that, at least, a good time would be had by us and, if memory serves me right, by our audiences too. I was married in two of the plays to John Doyle's wife, Jacquie Crago, an excellent actress with whom I would go on to enjoy several more close relationships on stage as time went by. Ginni Barlow played my absent-minded wife, Piggie, in *Hands Across the Sea,* while Karen Mann was the fatal attraction in *The Astonished Heart.* The part of Elsie, my adenoidal daughter in *Fumed Oak,* originally earmarked for Lesley, was very well played by Hilary Cromie.

When John went on to offer me the title role in Chekhov's *Uncle Vanya,* his final production of the season, he presented me with my biggest challenge to date. How on earth could I possibly make this traditionally well-upholstered 47 year-old Russian landowner my own? My Jack Tanner in Shaw's *Man and Superman* at Perth had been dubbed 'Napoleonic' by one critic because I lacked the height usually associated with that particular character, but at least that was a viable alternative. As Vanya I could think of nothing, short of growing a beard, padding my torso and wearing a pair of muddy boots to meet people's expectations, or risk being dubbed 'miscast'. But obviously John did not share my misgivings, or he wouldn't have asked me to play it in the first place, so I simply went ahead on the premise that even the character of Vanya was open to interpretation; and so it was. I cannot, in all honesty, claim to have changed people's perceptions, but thanks to Chekhov's own reference to Vanya's predilection for wearing 'fine ties', and for saying, in his dispute with Stanislavsky, the play's original director, "Don't you understand that landowners dress better than we do?", I did manage to make the part my own, an opinion endorsed by John Slim of *The Birmingham Post,* when he wrote, 'In the title role, Terry Wale sets the going rate for fretting and fulminating, pushes it calculatedly close to the brink of believability, and somehow survives the essential impossibility of having to shout "Missed!" after twice shooting from close quarters at the man whose very existence is a goad.' So, thanks were due to Chekhov, and to John Doyle too for entrusting me with the part. In what turned out to be an extremely rewarding experience, I was well aware too, that I also owed a debt to those who shared it with me, and especially to Charles Bell, whose Astrov was the perfect foil, and to Jacquie Crago, whose quality as an actress was raised, even beyond my expectations, by her moving portrayal of Sonya. With this, I departed from Worcester, although not for long.

In a year that was to become one of the busiest I have ever spent in the theatre, it surprises me that we managed to find the time to go on two holidays abroad, the second obviously being somewhat longer than the first, bearing in mind how long it must have taken us to drive to Croatia and back by way of France, Switzerland and Italy, and with a couple of stopovers en route, one of which was particularly memorable when, what appeared to be a mass evacuation from the city of Milan forced me to take refuge on the centre island of a road from which there was no immediate escape. It finally transpired that the exodus had not been due to panic but from a football stadium, following a match involving AC Milan. By the time the traffic had dispersed, however, it was too late to seek accommodation, and so we were obliged to spend the rest of the night in our car, and without so much as a cup of tea!

I had long nurtured a desire to take Lesley to the place that had meant so much to me and which I hadn't visited myself for more than ten years. In the early summer of 1983, three years after the death of their much revered leader, President Tito, the seeds were already sown that would finally lead to the dismemberment of Yugoslavia, but for the moment it still existed and Croatia was still a part of it, as was Opatija, the delightful seaside town of such fond memories which was our destination. We could hardly have spent more than a week there before prior commitments obliged us to return home, stopping off briefly in Venice before driving back the way we came, while giving Milan a wide berth!

After crossing the channel we headed for London where I was to meet up with John Doyle who was holding auditions for the autumn season at the Swan. My only reason for being there was that it included a production of *The Elephant Man* which I had been invited to direct, and that finding a suitable actor to play the central role of John Merrick was not going to be a piece of cake. He had, in fact, been described by Frederick Treves, the doctor who exhibited him before the Pathological Society of London in 1884, as 'the most disgusting specimen of humanity' he had ever seen; and he had written somewhat later, that 'at no time had I met with such a degraded or perverted version of a human being'. In fact, as the day went by, the casting of Merrick presented what appeared to be insuperable problems, and was only resolved when John exercised his *droit de seigneur* by offering the part of Malcolm in his own production of *Macbeth* to an extremely personable, if rather low key young man called Malcolm Ward, who would also be cast in the complex and demanding role of Merrick. As Malcolm had demonstrated little that was particularly characterful at his audition it was clearly a tall order, and I was more than a little perturbed to be facing the prospect of working with an actor so miscast that the play would be bound to lose some of its impact, not to mention bereft of its credibility.

However, there were other things to distract me, at least for the time being. The season kicked off with an adaptation of Laurie Lee's autobiography, *Cider with Rosie,* in which I was to play the older Laurie Lee who acts largely as a narrator, followed by a studio production of *Stevie* by Hugh Whitemore, a play about the controversial woman writer, Stevie Smith, a three-hander with Jacquie Crago in the title role, while I was cast as 'The Man', who in fact turned out to be several of the men involved in Stevie's life. Only then came *The Elephant Man,* followed by *Macbeth*. Oh yes, and while I remember, I had also embarked upon a project which involved, amongst other things, reading and making notes on everything that had ever been written about Judy Garland, a marathon journey that was giving me second thoughts about the wisdom of writing a play about her.

Meanwhile, Lesley had gone back to Scotland for her brother's wedding from which she would return in due course having been diagnosed with a life-changing condition. I should perhaps explain how this came about. Well, it seems that at a family get-together on the day after the wedding she had become involved in a political debate about unemployment, and when her Auntie Bessie said that she had never come across the kind of people they were talking about, an incensed Lesley, aflame with her relatively recent left-wing leanings, said, before bursting into tears, "Well, you wouldn't, would you, not in Chislehurst!" The following morning, her mother came to her bedroom and suggested that she should see a doctor, making her concerns perfectly clear by adding that she had already made an appointment. The fact that Lesley had recently been suffering from excessive thirst which she had put down to the vocal demands of playing Edith Piaf, and that the condition had become steadily worse while she was in Leatherhead where she began to have persistent coughing fits, culminating on the last night of *What Every Woman Knows* when, as the final curtain came down on Maggie laughing with joy, she was actually choking fit to burst, she herself decided that a visit to the doctor might well be timely. She was on the point of returning to London when the results of a blood sample the doctor had sent to Ninewells Hospital in Dundee came through and she was advised to head straight to St.

Mary's Hospital in Paddington where a bed had been reserved for her in the Metabolic Unit and where, having been diagnosed with a severe potassium deficiency, plans were made for her immediate admission.

Neither Lesley nor I had any idea at that time what a potassium deficiency, however severe, entailed, but clearly it was being regarded as an emergency, and as far as I was concerned the immediate consequences were that whatever spare time I had would be spent alongside her in the Metabolic Unit, and occasionally taking her out, with strict instructions that she was not to go too far or to eat anything while she was away.

Needless to say, our little haven in Milton was out of bounds during this period, but there was little we could do about it. After all, I was about to embark, with some trepidation, on rehearsals for *The Elephant Man*. This was to be my first production under John Doyle's aegis, and he had cast an actor whose shortcomings had since grown arms and legs in my imagination. How on earth could this play survive without a credible John Merrick? It was at this point, with rehearsals a mere coffee-break away, that Malcolm Ward took me aside and asked if he could have a private word with me. Perhaps he too had become aware of the Herculean task ahead of him, and had come to hand in his notice. I took him into a side room where he told me he'd been doing a bit of work on Merrick's physical and vocal characteristics, and he'd like to know if he was on the right track; whereupon he turned and walked away from me, gradually changing shape, his hips and his shoulders moving in opposite directions, his arms and legs reflecting this imbalance. When he turned towards me I saw that his mouth was grotesquely twisted too, so that when he spoke, the words were slowly and painfully formed but with surprising clarity. Concealing my astonishment, I told him that he was very definitely on the right track, and that I was looking forward to seeing it develop. What I didn't tell him was that, against all the odds, and in a matter of a few minutes without any technical resources to hand, he had transformed himself into an entirely credible John Merrick. His performance, when the time arrived, not only fulfilled all of my new found expectations, but brought with it a compelling humanity that cried out to be released from the cruel fate Nature had imposed upon him.

I was blessed too with a strong supporting cast, led by Charles Bell as Frederick Treves, the prominent surgeon who became Merrick's guardian and friend, enriching his life with social contacts until his inevitable demise at the age of 27, the victim of multiple neurofibromatosis, for which, over a 100 years later, there is still no cure. Once again too, Chris Crosswell designed a setting that was both simple and effective, placing Merrick in his tiny room at the London Hospital centre stage, surrounded by a number of acting areas where related scenes could be played while maintaining that essential focus. So, all in all it was a rewarding experience; not only because it was my first full-scale professional production outside of Perth, but of which, although I say it myself, I believe I had good reason to be proud.

As if 1983 hadn't already given me plenty to dwell upon, it was now about to pile Pelion on Ossa when Lesley, against all medical advice, discharged herself from the Metabolic Unit at Paddington Hospital to go and reprise her *Piaf* at the Gateway Theatre in Chester at more or less the same time that I was invited to join Timothy West on a tour of New Zealand with *Beecham*.

Lesley and I were not alone in being mystified by the implications, let alone the reasons, for her potassium deficiency. All we knew was that it had reached a dangerously low level, and the only thing that the head of the Metabolic Unit knew was that her kidneys seemed to be disposing of it as quickly as she took it in. So unusual was her case, it seemed, that Professor Wynn was convinced that she must be practising some sort of self-abuse, such as taking diuretics in order to keep her weight down. The general consensus, however, was that unless she could get her potassium up to an acceptable level, her body's organs, and her heart in particular, could malfunction. Professor Wynn tried to persuade her that she was in no fit state to work, and that she should stay on and allow him to perform a kidney biopsy; but there was no way, short of a detention order, that Lesley was going to turn her back on the opportunity to play Edith Piaf again when she had clearly been living with this condition for some time, and no one knew what to make of it in any case. As she left St Mary's, carrying a ton of potassium and a drug called *Indomethacin*, the Professor said to her, "You must understand that you are a very sick woman, Mrs Wale". Had Mrs Wale known what she was about to be subjected to in Chester she would undoubtedly have opted for the kidney biopsy!

Despite being separated by 13,000 miles and several continents throughout most of her time in Chester, I was still around during the early stages of their association, and by the time I left, I already had an inkling of what lay in store for her. During a preliminary meeting with Sue Wilson at the Spotlight offices, and following a brief chat, she had made it clear to Lesley that she was being asked because she had so recently played it in a successful production and would therefore have a pretty good idea how it all worked, and some of the possible pitfalls.

She had also readily agreed that, with various versions of the script doing the rounds at that time, she would use the same one we had worked with at the Swan which differed in quite a few respects from the poorly crafted, and often gratuitously obscene, published version. Lesley even went so far as to suggest using her own script from which to make copies, but Ms Wilson declined the offer, and said she would be in touch if she couldn't get hold of it. We naturally assumed she would make contact with the Swan Theatre, from where she would be able to access a pristine copy, but when Lesley heard from her that she hadn't managed to get hold of one, having clearly not been in touch with anyone in Worcester, and had consequently ordered copies of the published version, she was dismayed. Not only was this to be the first broken promise but also the seedbed of a series of betrayals that were not only designed to undermine Lesley's self-confidence, but also to alienate her from some of the company who, having worked with Sue Wilson before, and ignorant of what had passed between her and Lesley, were hardly likely to bite the hand that fed them.

Following a hastily convened meeting in Chester where she spent an entire afternoon with the director juggling the two scripts, and achieving what amounted to little more than a compromise, she returned to our cottage, deeply depressed by the prospect of what lay ahead. My only comfort was that, in my absence, she would at least enjoy the support of our old friend from Pitlochry, Malcolm McKee, who had instigated the original meeting between Sue and Lesley and who, besides being the only member of the company she knew, was also to be her landlord for the duration. However, as a member of the coterie of actors regularly employed by Ms Wilson, he didn't see fit to offer Lesley any support when she was finally pushed near to breaking-point.

It could well have been a relatively trivial oversight when Ms Wilson failed to introduce Lesley to the rest of the company on the first day of rehearsal, but when, following the read-through, they were shown the costume and set designs, she began to realise that their first meeting, at which the director had appeared to take on board, and indeed sought, details of Lesley's previous experience, had been a sham. Why else would she have encouraged the costume designer to come up with an array of coats, hats, furs and feather boas for Piaf when she knew that the structure of the play allowed little or no time for multiple costume changes? The obvious sequel to this was provided when the elaborate set designs were displayed, consisting of a series of rostra which were to be trucked on and off between scenes, effectively interrupting the fragile structure of a play which demanded simplicity and a seamless transition from one short scene to the next. All of this had been discussed, and apparently agreed upon, at their first meeting, but to the rest of the company, who were clearly ignorant of what had gone before, Lesley may have come across as a bit of a prima donna who wouldn't let the director get on with her job. And you could hardly blame them while the said director went out of her way to allow, nay, even to encourage them to upstage Lesley, in theory as well as in practice. The opening of the play sees Piaf singing on a street corner, her audience consisting of nightclub owner, Louis Leplée, who finally moves up behind her and places a hand on her shoulder, whereupon she spins round and says, "Get your fuckin' hands off me, I ain't done nothin'." For some bizarre reason, the actor playing Leplée felt that it would work better if he didn't touch her, and when Lesley questioned the logic of this, Sue said that she should do as he suggested to see if it worked! That was on the first day of rehearsal, and things were destined to get worse; much worse, as time went by. Sadly, I was not to be around for much longer, although my telephone bills from New Zealand testify to the ongoing torment she suffered. It was left to one member of the company who was not entirely under the sway, to offer Lesley a sympathetic nod when she said, "You'll have to watch – the way things are going, the play should be called *Piaf's Mates!*"

A couple of days before I left to join Tim West at Heathrow Airport, I went to Chester where, besides sitting through a fairly uninspired production of *The Elephant Man*, I witnessed an excruciating example of the Gateway's policy to stage an open rehearsal of every production, allowing members of the public to pay 50p for the privilege of watching 'a normal rehearsal' at which, they were assured, no concessions would be made. Before it began, Lesley was not only instructed to avoid any argument with the director, but was also 'requested' to provide some entertainment by singing a few songs. Lesley complied with this if only to avoid any contention in the company, but I sat there, seething with anger, not only because of the conditions imposed upon her, but by the deliberate fabrication of the rehearsal process. The very last thing I wanted to do was to go away, leaving Lesley to deal with this nightmare scenario on her own. I dread to think, however, what might have happened had I remained!

oOoOo

Twenty six

It is doubtful, so many years later, that I would have been able to recall in any detailed way my visit to New Zealand, except I knew that at least I could refer to Timothy West's letters to his wife, compiled from his numerous travels away from home and published as a book entitled *I'm Here I Think, Where Are You?*, and in which I am quoted as saying on a bus journey following our arrival in Auckland, "What I can't understand is how we've flown thirteen thousand miles, and we're still in Thames Ditton". Given that my first impressions, and many subsequent ones, were of an unremittingly English suburban landscape in which I had never seen more gardens being mowed and hedgerows trimmed, this quote rings true, suggesting an immigrant community firmly entrenched in the past which was one of the long-lasting souvenirs I brought back home with me.

Imagine my surprise and delight when Lesley suddenly produced, over 30 years later, seemingly from out of nowhere, a pile of letters which I had written to her at the time, and which she had kept hidden away until now, furnishing me with the means to tell the story in my own contemporaneous words. For instance, I had completely forgotten that my journey to Heathrow Airport was via Purves Road from where I last spoke to Lesley before leaving. I was downstairs at the time with my mother and father so I felt a bit constrained, although I obviously said 'darling' a few times, and distinctly remember saying that our parting was as bad for me as it was for her, together with other intimacies and endearments. When I eventually hung up and my mother said, "Who was that?", my father's reaction, expressing disbelief, clearly demonstrated that he still hadn't come to terms with her steadily deteriorating mental condition and I, similarly lacking in foresight, was perfectly happy to see the funny side of it. I was reminded of this episode as I read the first of my letters, written on that very flight, which began appropriately from 'Somewhere over Kansas' and from which I have lifted the following quotes: ' …You'll have to forgive the handwriting if it gets a bit erratic; there's a fair bit of turbulence at the moment which affects even us first-class passengers! My dear, the stewardesses address you by name every time they bring you something – which is pretty nearly continuous. We had the customary champagne on arrival, since when we've consumed a bottle of red wine with our first meal - caviar and smoked salmon, then thick, rare roast beef with roast potatoes and Yorkshire pudding, followed by ice-cream with hot peaches! I guess we'll be due for a late-night snack soon, and when we change planes I imagine the process will repeat itself. About three hours ago, we flew over the North Pole – incredible sight – an endless wasteland of ice and ice-flows stretching as far as the eye could see; not even a polar bear to break the terrible bleakness of it'; followed by 'Aloha from Hawaii! It's about 3am and we've just taken off from Honolulu on the last leg of our trip. We're due to arrive in N.Z. at about 10 am. First-class or not, it's still a horrendous experience, and the only thing that makes it bearable is the food and drink. It's not entirely the time in the air, but the waiting time at airports that adds to the general misery. We had to hang around at Los Angeles for about 3 hours – a real pain, made worse by the fact that I didn't have a U.S. visa (Tim had an unexpired one from a previous visit), and I had to be escorted round the airport by an immigration official just in case I decided to become an illegal immigrant. So much for L.A. And then it took another 5 hours to reach Hawaii. There are times when you think you're going bananas, but it won't be nearly as bad coming back, 'cos at least I'll be coming home to you! I don't know whether to wish you luck or say I hope it went well, 'cos God knows when you'll receive this. Meanwhile I'm going to try to get a bit more sleep …' Then, from the Terrace Regency Hotel, Wellington … 'It's now 8am Sunday morning – 13 hours ahead of you. I collapsed into bed after a long hot bath at about 8 last night, and slept for nearly 11 hours, so the worst is over. But it's really a horrible experience, and one I wouldn't care to repeat! I don't know what happened to Friday – one minute it was Thursday night and the next it was Saturday morning! We arrived in Auckland at about 10.15am feeling fine, but it didn't last! Three Jumbos arrived at the same time, and it was chaotic. They let us through Passport & Immigration first but our baggage was the last to be unloaded, so there were hundreds of suitcases going round and round with nobody to pick them up while we stood around for nearly an hour waiting for ours to appear. Needless to say, we missed our connecting flight to Wellington. Don't let anyone tell you that the British are less efficient than anyone else, 'cos it just ain't true! It's just Tory propaganda to keep the workers feeling inferior! We were finally met by our producer, Stewart Macpherson, and driven to a hotel in Auckland for a bit of lunch and a press interview. I think we were both a bit gaga by then, and it took us a long time to answer even the simplest of questions. Then back to the airport, and a truly hair-raising flight to Wellington. The weather was atrocious – pissing down and gale-force winds. Another press interview at the hotel in Wellington before I returned to my room for a long hot bath. Poor Tim had to go and put all that make-up on and do a TV interview. God knows how he managed to get through it! I read a bit, shed a few tears to be so far away from my only love, then fell into a deep sleep ... Well, it's Sunday now, and things are looking a little better, although missing you has become a positive ache now, and I can't wait to start doing the show to distract me for a few hours. I went for a walk this morning and, it being Sunday, Wellington was pretty dead. We take so many things for granted at home – beautiful buildings, lovely shops, a sense of vitality. Here there's nothing to arrest the eye. Then I turned a corner, and there, sprayed on a wall in front of me in huge capital letters were the words CRUTCHLESS KNICKERS, and my first thought was that somebody else must have felt the same way I did about the place, only he'd come armed with a paint-spray! Tim assured me that it wasn't him, although he'd seen it too. The day cleared up a bit after that, and downtown Wellington looked quite jolly, probably livens up a bit during the week. Tuesday morning we fly to Christchurch, and I shall write again from there.'

It was from this point on that our telephone calls, at opposite ends of the day, began to play a more intimate part in our communications, and in which Lesley up-dated me on the Chester saga. But my concerns were not entirely confined to the treatment she was receiving there; she also had ongoing health issues in the aftermath of her stay in the Metabolic Unit. On leaving, she had been given a potassium-saving drug to take, which she later suspected was partly to blame for the nausea she was experiencing, together with an inability to eat. When she finally realised that her symptoms were not entirely caused by stress, she had written to St Mary's and was advised to stop taking Indomethacin immediately, because it might not be the right drug for her. But it didn't entirely set my mind at rest.

Meanwhile, Tim and I flew down to Christchurch on the South Island where we were scheduled to give only four performances. We opened on the Thursday evening to a small but appreciative house, and received a glowing review the following morning, but as Friday was a regional holiday, the box-office, situated in the Town Hall rather than at the theatre, was closed, and so we didn't benefit from it. As Tim said to me, "The only way you can tell the difference between Saturday and Sunday in Christchurch is on Sunday the churches are open". It became increasingly clear as the tour went on that the people of New Zealand, at that time anyway, were not remotely interested in going to the theatre. Tim had recently played the leading character in a TV series called *Brass* which had gone on to enjoy considerable success worldwide, and consequently he attracted a good deal of attention on the streets. Without reference to either Tim's letters or my own, I can recall quite vividly one such encounter when, having run out of superlatives for Tim's performance in *Brass*, the fan in question was graciously thanked by Tim, who went on to suggest that perhaps he might like to come and see our show. "Oh. I dunno about that", he said, "we don't go out much in the evenings". We didn't know it at the time, of course, but what we took for a very personal and idiosyncratic remark, turned out to be a statement on behalf of an entire population. As Tim said, with reference to the paucity of audiences throughout the tour, "What the country lacks in human beings, it more than makes up for in sheep!"

We hired a car for the first leg of our return journey to Wellington, finally arriving in Picton on the tip of the South Island where we embarked on the boat which would take us on a three-and-a-half hour voyage across Cook Strait to our destination. Thanks again to Tim's celebrity, we were royally entertained on board by a bunch of people, from the Purser, who provided us with a good deal of whisky in the wardroom, to the Captain, who then invited us up to the bridge to watch him perform the notoriously difficult piece of navigation out of Cook Sound and into the open sea. Tim's recorded account of this not only confirms my own memories of the occasion, but recalls it in considerably more entertaining detail than I could have done ... 'The Captain was amazing; lots of curly hair, no front teeth, extremely camp, falling about with high-pitched laughter ... "Starboard fifteen", he sang out. "I hope! What do I usually do here, John? Well, here goes. It might be all right. Midships! That always sounds good, doesn't it?" He did it beautifully, of course; then took us down to an enormous high tea with the officers, during which he slipped out briefly to bring her into Wellington harbour'; an episode worth recollecting if, for no other reason, it provided us with the rare opportunity to enjoy the company of kindred spirits.

So we returned to Wellington, and to the exorbitantly priced hotel in which we had stayed briefly on the trip down. Both Tim and I were somewhat concerned about this, and to the prospect of having to pay over the odds for accommodation elsewhere on the tour. I haven't a clue now how much I was being paid by the management, appropriately known as Stetson Productions, but I do remember that our producer, Stewart Macpherson, who was widely known as a man with very deep pockets and very short arms, told us that he had tried and failed to find us lodgings at an affordable price.

The theatre in Wellington was a good deal more appealing than the one in Christchurch, and our opening night was graced by an appreciative audience, if only because it was largely peopled by members of the New Zealand Symphony Orchestra. Tim came into my dressing-room before the show to tell me that we probably wouldn't be playing on Thursday or Friday, but we'd do one on Saturday, and if the bookings looked good, it would be extended to include the rest of the week. It was the weirdest system I had ever come across. How they planned to let the public know, short of dropping leaflets from a helicopter, was a mystery. However, as the newspaper review didn't appear the following morning, Stewart panicked, and decided to lose the two performances. Our week in Wellington was otherwise full of diversions; the weather was glorious, and social occasions were plentiful. My spirits were lifted, not least by a visit to another of the city's theatres to see a play called *Crimes of the Heart* by a new American playwright, Beth Henley, which was an absolute delight, and one I was ultimately destined to come to grips with myself as director on a couple of occasions.

We drove from Wellington to New Plymouth on the west coast, a distance of about 300 miles, having agreed a deal with Stetson Productions to exchange our mode of transport so that we might at least get to see something of the country rather than just fly over it, and maybe even enjoy a degree of independence, staying at the occasional motel, and generally suiting ourselves. Tim and I were seldom out of each other's company which, at least as far as I was concerned, was a boon.

My letter to Lesley from New Plymouth pretty well sums up my recollections of the place, if somewhat more accurately, and certainly more vehemently than if I were relying on memory alone: 'Well, we've just 'done' New Plymouth which means, as with most other places in New Zealand, a half-hour walk and a three hour coffee break! It's interesting to note the large proportion of Scots living here; street after street called things like Inverlochie Place, Braemar Avenue and Fintry Road. The larger towns, or cities as they have the cheek to call them, aren't really very much livelier, although we both have high hopes of Auckland next week. We're probably in for a terrible disappointment. Some distinguished British visitor remarked when he got home that he had been to New Zealand, but it was closed!' And so on to Tauranga, our final date before Auckland, and to the last letter I sent, 'which will probably reach you at about the same time I do.' Lesley was already commuting to Worcester, and while I had no reason to doubt that returning to the Swan Theatre would have a remedial effect on her, I was also sure that the psychological damage inflicted upon her in Chester would be a long time healing, which is why (if for no other reason) I was impatient to get back home. So even if Auckland didn't quite live up to expectations, it was at least blessed with the airport from which we would make that final journey. We were, however, given no reason to doubt its appeal when we stopped off for a coffee on our way to Tauranga, and met a Maori who was travelling in the opposite direction, desperate to put the hustle and bustle of Auckland behind him. Tim and I could hardly wait! Meanwhile, our performance in Tauranga went very well, or so my letter tells me, although it goes on to describe the audience as 'bizarre'. 'Not only did they all stand for 'The Queen', they sang it too!'

On our drive along the east coast, with the South Pacific Ocean on one side of us, we were overwhelmed, not only by the glorious weather, but by the breathtaking scenery that greeted us on the other side. In a country where the most familiar backdrop was of mind-numbing two-dimensional suburbia, the impact made by this unidentifiable and timeless scenery, was all the more surprising. Small wonder that it, and similar landscapes on the South Island, would in time become perfect film settings, one of them later chosen as the main location for the Middle Earth setting in Tolkien's *The Lord of the Rings*. We also visited Rotorua on our travels, and checked into a little motel before going out to dinner. Of course, Tim was recognised again and we were invited to join this group of people who, it transpired, were on some towel distribution company's outing. I return to my epistle now, the better to describe the event ... 'God, they were vulgar! There was this vast woman in sham velvet (a dog of a dress!) who sat there stuffing her face with ice cream, and went on and on about how wonderful New Zealand was; that it was the best country in the world, and so what if you couldn't get a meal after ten o'clock at night – everybody should be in bed by that time anyway, and getting up for a good, hearty breakfast at six in the morning, and so on, and so on. She was obviously trying to provoke us into some response. But since we were drinking their revolting sparkling wine, we just smiled politely, and tried to change the subject. We told them we were off to Auckland next week, and they all agreed that we'd enjoy that, and then one guy came out with the prize remark of the tour; "They're working very hard to make it historical!"'

The following morning we visited the thermal areas, for which

Rotorua is famed, described by Tim as 'a preposterous natural aberration', with steam hissing out of holes in the ground, and boiling mud with great spouts of stinking water shooting 20 or 30 feet into the air. And finally to Auckland.

By this time, only just over a week away from home, and nursing no desire ever to come back, I was able to rationalise my feelings about the place, at least to a certain extent. At first, it had just been a feeling of alienation which I could easily attribute to all sorts of things in myself; being away from Lesley at such a critical time being the foremost. But as the days passed, I began to see that there was, in fact, a New Zealand malaise. It was as though everyone who had come to live there from other parts of the world, and principally from the UK, had come in order to get away from various aspects of their native environment: the weather, strikes, immigration, or whatever. Their initial reasons for being there were essentially negative. Tim had said at one point that, whether you like it or not, Australians are undoubtedly positive, sometimes to a fault, whereas in New Zealand nothing impresses itself on you. Everyone talks about the political parties with complete equanimity. You may have voted for the National Party, but you don't get too worked up when, in power, they fail to live up to your expectations or, indeed, to their mandate. This kind of attitude is humorously summed up in one of Tim's published letters home, in which he writes: 'Yesterday's headline in *The Dominion:* 'Lange (Labour Party leader) Says Muldoon Tells Lies'. Today's headline: 'Muldoon Says Lange Tells Lies.' The sophisticated cut-and-thrust of New Zealand politics is a little dazzling till you get used to it.'

First impressions of Auckland were a distinct improvement on the rest of the country, or so my letter tells me – 'At least it's a proper city, with something approaching a night-life. They've even got nude massage parlours – two naked girls for $25!' Tim and I shared a large suite in a block of service apartments that week, which was provided with a balcony from where we made our separate spouse-bound telephone calls, at the end of one of which he came back into the sitting-room, looking distinctly down-in-the-mouth. "Why is it," he said, "that women never say they miss you?" I could only shrug sympathetically, not yet having suffered from that dereliction of duty, but not wishing to rub salt into his wound. The apartment block was also furnished with a swimming-pool on the roof, and for the best of reasons, I'll let Tim tell you about that: 'Today we took our towels and went up and lay in the warm sun. A number of bikini-clad nymphs wandered languidly around the edge of the pool, but without so much as a glance in our direction. I remarked on this, quietly but with perhaps a certain petulance. Terry indicated our room keys lying beside us, their large tags both displaying the same number, 19. "That and the pink towels", he said.'

Our week in Auckland was the best of our tour dates, where audiences were certainly larger and more appreciative than elsewhere. Nevertheless, I could barely wait for it to come to an end. Tim's overall summary of the tour, however, was certainly more benign than my memories of it are, highlighting the scenery and the hospitality we enjoyed, neither of which I could refute, any more than I could deny that my state of mind must have played a significant part in my perceptions.

Meanwhile, before bringing this episode to a close, I am tempted beyond resistance to round it off with Wynford Vaughan Thomas's verse, *Farewell to New Zealand,* which truly reflected my feelings at that time ...

> Super-suburbia of the Southern Seas,
> Nature's – and Reason's – true Antipodes,
> Hail, dauntless pioneers, intrepid souls,
> Who cleared the Bush – to make a lawn for bowls,
> And smashed the noble Maori to ensure
> The second-rate were socially secure!
> Saved by the Wowsers from the Devil's Tricks,
> Your shops, your pubs, your minds all close at six.
> Your battle-cry's a deep contented snore,
> You voted Labour, then you worked no more.
> The Wharfies' Heaven, the gourmet's Purgat'ry:
> Ice-cream on mutton, swilled around in tea!
> A Maori fisherman, the legends say,
> Dredged up New Zealand in a single day.
> I've seen the catch, and here's my parting crack -
> It's undersized; for God's sake throw it back!

I was obviously sorry to say goodbye to Tim, but it wasn't the last time *Beecham* would rear its head; far from it in fact.

It had been 11 years since I had last appeared in *Pinocchio* at the Crucible Theatre in Sheffield, where I had played the aged puppet-maker, Gepetto. At the Swan Theatre, Worcester, I had been cast as Jiminy Cricket, Pinocchio's agile and fleet-footed 'Conscience'. I suppose it ought to have been the other way around; however, as it happened, with Lesley playing the title role, we couldn't have been brought closer together.

1983 Pinnocchio - The Swan Theatre, with Lesley Mackie.

The details of my journey back to the UK and on to Worcester went unrecorded, and all I can recall with any clarity, besides spending a great deal of time in each other's arms, is that rehearsals had been underway for a week before I arrived, and that it was great to be back amongst so many friends. Lesley had been commuting during that week, and so she too scarcely had time to settle in; every day ending with a return trip to Chester, which she even now describes as the worst and unhappiest experience of her career. Both physically and vocally she could have done with a break, although the balm of returning to the Swan on a daily basis, plus the rigours of yet another demanding role did more to heal her psychologically than any vacation would have done.

In *Cabaret* and in *The Wizard of Oz* we had enjoyed the sympathetic input of Sally Marshall as choreographer, but on this occasion, John had engaged the services of Marcia Gresham and her partner, Alan Radcliffe. I had worked with Alan only a few months earlier when he played several parts in my production of *The Elephant Man* as well as the Porter in *Macbeth,* but his terpsichorean credentials were all but unknown to me. I remembered him as a perfectly likeable young man and they had clearly decided that dance was of paramount importance in the show. Lesley had already rehearsed her opening number before I arrived when she was given so many moves and steps to execute, that there wasn't much hope of her being able to sing at the same time, and it was only with the support of Catherine Jayes, not only our Musical Director on this occasion, but also the composer of a brand-new musical score, that the routine was simplified to give the song a chance.

Shortly after my arrival I too was introduced to a frenetic dance routine that was way beyond my abilities, and it was only again thanks to Cathy, stoical as always, that their demands on me were also toned down. Perhaps the explanation for their fervour was that they were making their début as choreographers, and they wanted to make a strong impression. Oh, I did miss Sally Marshall – which reminds me that some 17 years later, Sally's son, Gabriel, auditioned for the title role in the first screen adaptation of J. K. Rowling's Harry Potter films, and came pretty close to getting it, until he was beaten to the tape by Daniel Radcliffe, son of Alan and Marcia, so, whatever my personal feelings, they certainly created a very grounded and successful progeny, allowing them to take a back seat in the business from then on.

My abiding memory of *Pinocchio,* however, was of happy times, and of an incident involving Cathy, Lesley and myself, the only ones in the company to complain about the absence of a review in *The Stage* which eventually appeared a week later, and in which Cathy's music was described as 'derivative', while Lesley's performance was 'only superficially wooden', and my Jiminy Cricket was 'a tired old conscience whose jumping days are long gone'! I should perhaps mention that my brother, otherwise known as the Kenneth Tynan of North Harrow, brought his children to see the show, and was convinced that I must have had a trampoline in the wings, so agile was my performance!

The shadow cast by the Chester production was quickly dispelled when, in February 1984, we returned to Perth where, under Joan Knight's sympathetic direction, and alongside a company of actors who not only had minds of their own, but who knew perfectly well what the play was about, she rediscovered the joy of coming to grips with it again.

1984 Piaf - Perth Theatre, with Lesley Mackie.

Joan, accompanied by John Scrimger, Perth's Musical Director, had visited Chester where her misgivings about staging the play, largely due to the explicit nature of the dialogue, were overcome by Lesley's performance. She even acted upon Lesley's suggestion that they work from the Swan Theatre script, and also went thoughtfully out of her way to make sure that I would be there in a supportive role, once again playing Papa Leplée, as well as the other parts I'd played in Worcester. Lesley quickly settled into the production which, at least in Joan's hands, featured Edith Piaf as its central character.

Returning to Perth after a six-year absence was like a homecoming, which indeed it was as far as Lesley was concerned. A familiar warm and welcoming atmosphere pervaded, not that far removed, except in miles, from the more recently encountered ambience of the Swan Theatre, for which, in both cases, although from very different perspectives, the presence of Joan Knight and John

Doyle was largely responsible. John was shortly to move on from Worcester, and we never worked there again once he had gone, although I have good reason to remember that he took his brand of captaincy with him, while I have equally good reason to recall that Perth was never quite the same following Joan's departure some years later.

1984 Piaf - Perth Theatre, with Lesley Mackie.

Meanwhile, she had every reason to be happily relieved when her gamble paid off and *Piaf* became the hit of the season, with the 'House Full' sign becoming all but a fixture on the pavement outside the theatre. For Lesley, it was a wonderful and fulfilling episode, restoring her self-confidence, and finally allowing her to treat the never-to-be-forgotten events of Chester with at least a degree of sangfroid. The subsequent newspaper reviews obviously contributed to this with Mary Brennan of the Glasgow Herald writing, 'Miss Mackie fills the theatre with the intensity and immediacy of a legend', while Christopher Rainbow wrote in *The Times* that 'The tiny Lesley Mackie has so masterfully taken hold of the raw invigorating style and timbre of the legendary Edith Piaf that one is simply struck with amazement', while the local guru, Graham Fulton, surpassed himself by writing that it was a 'performance that was nothing short of remarkable'.

On the last night, some of the usherettes clubbed together and threw flowers down onto the stage from the Dress Circle, a memorable event, made all the more so when fellow-actor, Martyn James, muttered, "It's like working with Torvill and Dean!" On our way back to Dundee later that night, accompanied by Lesley's Uncle Archie, we were stopped at a police road check. The policewoman looked into the back of the car where Lesley sat, surrounded by flowers, and asked for her autograph, a fitting end to a triumphant evening, leading as it subsequently did, to five weeks incarceration in the Metabolic Unit at St. Mary's Hospital where they were still as keen to pursue their investigation into the cause, or causes, of her potassium deficiency as was Lesley. It turned out to be a gruelling few weeks, at the end of which they were no nearer to providing any answers.

The only plus side to her extended absence from home was that, for the very first time, I was left entirely alone and free to get on with writing my play about Judy Garland.

oOoOo

Twenty seven

It had been all but a year since John Doyle had commissioned me to write the play, a year in which I had read pretty well everything that had been written about Judy Garland, listened to every song she had ever recorded, and revisited many of the films in which she had appeared. What all of this research had told me, first and foremost, was that I had undertaken a mammoth task. When I wrote my ill-fated play about Jessica Mitford, epic though it was in many respects, it was entirely based on her own autobiographical account, whilst Judy Garland's life and career had been mulled over and written about by numerous biographers, most of whom had a very different story to tell about her, their views ranging from the reverential to the defamatory, often depending on whether or not the author had worked alongside her. I had determined to tell her story from beginning to end, but how was I to know what she was really like? I had, of course, seen *The Wizard of Oz* which was released the year after I was born, but it wasn't until I saw her in *A Star is Born* in 1954 that my teenage heart was stolen. I had subsequently seen her give two live performances, firstly at the Dominion Theatre in Tottenham Court Road, and then at the London Palladium where she previewed her legendary Carnegie Hall concert in 1961. I was obviously a dedicated fan, along with thousands of others, but did that qualify me to write a play about her? I had clearly been inspired by Lesley's portrayal of Edith Piaf, not to mention her two memorable appearances as Dorothy Gale in *The Wizard of Oz*, the first of which had led to a life-changing decision for both of us. But I had never so much as laid eyes upon the subject herself except from across the footlights or by way of the silver screen. But then again, a great many playwrights have chosen to write plays about historical characters, most of them long dead, and whose knowledge of them can only have been garnered by research. Judy Garland, however, had only died 14 years ago, and the world was still full of people who had known her and worked with her, not to mention close friends and members of her family, who were obviously better acquainted with her than I was. The same was, of course, true of Edith Piaf whose life story more or less covered the same years as Judy's. Pam Gems, in her play, however, chose to transplant 'La Môme Piaf' from Paris to London, bestowing on her a cockney accent, while the rest of the characters, despite their authentic origins, were more or less fictionalised, thus distancing her from any real biographical obligations.

In an otherwise extremely busy year, I had at least learned that, while Edith Piaf's character had remained essentially the same throughout her life, Judy Garland had been transformed, and finally destroyed, by expectations that were largely born of the fantasy world she had inhabited during her earlier years in Hollywood. It's worth mentioning, I think, if only as an example of this, that in 1951, the year in which she made her first major move from screen to stage, band leader Artie Shaw went to see her opening performance at New York's Palace Theatre, and told her later how moved he had been when, during her final song, *Over the Rainbow*, she had wept while singing the words 'If happy little bluebirds fly beyond the rainbow, why oh why can't I?' Given her history and her mind-set, it isn't hard to understand, not only why she cried at the end of that first night, but also to appreciate her reasons for fabricating the tears at every subsequent performance; not for nothing did she become known as 'Miss Show Business'.

Judy, born Frances Ethel Gumm, had been devastated by the premature death of her loving and caring father, leaving her at the mercy of an ambitious and overbearing mother who went on to place her child's destiny into the hands of Louis B. Mayer, the head of MGM studios, a man devoid of genuine sympathy who turned a blind eye to the drugs prescribed for her by studio medics to combat her inherent insomnia, thereby sowing the seeds of her future, and finally fatal, addiction. Small wonder, then, that she spent the rest of her life searching for, and failing to find, the man who could take her father's place, not only in her heart, but in her best interests, whatever those became. These people, far from being cyphers, or cartoons, were instrumental in shaping Judy Garland's life and career, and therefore had to be fleshed out in any play that purported to tell her story. What I also had to take on board before committing myself to a structure was the fact that, between 1936 when she was 14 years old, and 1963, she had appeared in 35 films, all of which had made some kind of impact on her life, some even contributing to her growing neuroses. There was no way, however, that I could cover that kind of a landscape, short of a documentary narration, which would stand a good chance of killing the drama stone dead. It was only then that I was inspired to introduce the two legendary Hollywood gossip-columnists, Hedda Hopper and Louella Parsons, into the action. They were, after all, well qualified to express their opinions about Judy's ups and downs, and also to vie with each other in capturing the headlines. In what was principally a biographical play, my brief sojourns with Hedda and Louella allowed me off the leash from time to time, for which relief I was truly thankful!

Meanwhile, Lesley's five-week incarceration in the Metabolic Unit came to an end without providing answers to her condition. Every time the doctors came up with a possible syndrome, another test would give the lie to it. It reached the stage, at one point, where they thought that if ever they found anyone with identical symptoms, they might have to recognise a new condition, and call it 'The Mackie Syndrome'. Lesley rather liked the sound of that, but it did nothing to alleviate her concerns. She was hearing so much about potassium and its functions within the human body that she began to believe she would be lucky to see the year out. The doctors finally accepted that, genetic or not, her case was unique, allowing her to survive at a lower level of potassium than what was considered the norm, although they stressed that if it was allowed to sink much lower it would inevitably put the heart under too much stress. Professor Wynn would undoubtedly have kept her there for even longer, so keen was he to get his hands on a piece of her kidney, but for obvious reasons Lesley wanted to get on with her life, and so she left.

With a deadline looming, we headed for Milton where, in the early spring of 1984, and in the comparative seclusion of *Wild Thyme*, I was able to concentrate on producing the first draft of my script. Our stay in the cottage was interrupted on several occasions by return visits to London, where we had been invited to attend a meeting of *The Judy Garland Fan Club*. This came about as the result of a fortuitous encounter at a book fair between Cathy Jayes and a man called Ken Sephton, who turned out to be a prominent member of the club, and who was happy to give Cathy his contact details. The club met twice a year, usually in a central London hotel where they spent a few hours watching films and TV 'Specials', gossiping, swapping memorabilia and generally wallowing in nostalgia. What was astonishing was that, although the lady had long gone, they still kept digging up new snippets of information and trivia to share with each other. I was, of course, well aware that amongst her audiences, both in the cinema and in the theatre, the overwhelming majority of her male admirers had been, and clearly still were, homosexual. I'm not sure I ever quite understood why that should have been the case, but it was certainly borne out by the members of *The Judy Garland Fan Club*, many of whom, and especially those sitting in the front row at that meeting whooped with joy and clapped their hands every time Judy opened her mouth. Most of them were gentle, charming, and keen to help. One of the gentlest and most helpful was Brian Glanville, whose official role was as projectionist and keeper of the films and archive material. He invited us to his little flat in Ealing to see some of his treasures, and we went there regularly throughout the summer, watching obscure footage of Judy with the *Meglin Kiddies* when she was still little Frances Ethel, and barely seven years old. We also saw her as the newly created Judy Garland at 14, fooling around with the other child stars in L.B. Mayer's swimming pool. Brian's flat was a shrine to Judy, with photos in every nook and cranny; he even had 'Judy Garland' roses on his veranda. His image of her was very precious to him, and we were aware from the outset that we would have to tread very carefully, although we did try to warn him that, while my play would be a celebration of her life, it would contain the 'lows' as well as the 'highs'. He responded by saying that he knew we would do nothing to harm Judy and, as far as I can recall, I smiled reassuringly, whilst privately hoping that, should my play ever reach the stage, Brian would be otherwise engaged during its run.

I was coming face to face with some of those 'lows' on a daily basis back at our cottage in which the tiny upstairs room next to our bedroom had been requisitioned as a study, while Lesley remained downstairs, glued to the television, watching endless re-runs of Judy's television appearances and interviews, a preoccupation punctuated by my occasional appearances with a page or two of the script, hot-off-the-press, for her perusal. There were occasions, it has to be said, when I abandoned my typewriter for other, more personal, reasons – when Judy's behaviour became so objectionable, for instance, that I couldn't bear to spend another minute in her company, or when I was so moved by the indignities imposed upon her that I couldn't see through my tears to type. Lesley's main dilemma lay, not surprisingly, in finding and relating to a character that was full of these inconsistencies. Edith Piaf had remained essentially the same person throughout her life, careless of her health, returning to sing again on the streets where she had been discovered even at the height of her fame. Her choice of songs, along with her untutored vocal qualities, were all predictably familiar. Besides which, being disadvantaged from birth, Piaf could be forgiven almost anything, whilst Judy, who appeared to have been given the keys to the kingdom and wilfully thrown them away, would be more likely to alienate an audience. I had learned on my own journey, however, that her essential frailty, born of childhood ailments, had been exacerbated by external factors, notably by her father's death, her mother's autocratic behaviour, and by being manipulated by studio bosses into becoming what they wanted her to be. Frances Ethel Gumm became Judy Garland, not even retaining her Christian name as Piaf did, but assuming a fictional identity which could be reinvented as time, place and circumstance demanded. Overwork and its consequent intake of prescribed drugs, allowing her to sleep on the one hand, and to wake up in time for an early start on the other, had its part to play too, not to mention, as time went by, the pressures of Hollywood celebrity culture. It was, as I was soon to discover, those very inconsistencies that made her who she was, and suggested to Lesley that if she tried too hard to rationalise her behavioural patterns by playing two consecutive scenes as if she were the same woman, then she had probably got it wrong. It was a fairly daunting prospect, I realised, but one that I knew she would take on board, whereas her ability to simulate Judy's vocal qualities was a different matter. For a start, Garland's voice was more difficult to capture, demanding a subtler approach and a greater variety of tone than Piaf's, and even more difficult to sustain on a nightly basis as the play would often demand a quietly restrained song following an hysterical outburst. Although I shared what I knew were Lesley's concerns too, I said nothing at the time, and she went on practising.

Somehow or other, in the midst of all this, I managed to reach the end of the story and sent my first draft to John, principally to meet the deadline rather than with any immediate expectations. It was, after all, about three and a half hours long, and contained more than 20 songs, which Lesley and I had managed to cut down from the original 33! But John responded enthusiastically, albeit with certain provisos, and scheduled it for production in the autumn season.

It's worth recalling that the repertory system, still flourishing back in 1984, did not allow for extensive rehearsal periods for the simple reason that, in most of the towns that boasted a repertory theatre, the potential audience would be drained after two to two and a half weeks, and eagerly awaiting the next production. The days of weekly rep had thankfully all but vanished by then, allowing for more ambitious productions, but even so, the time-scale for mounting a new play, and especially one with music at its centre, proved a daunting prospect for everyone involved. As well as meeting frequently to discuss rewrites and cuts to the script, a process which went on well after the play had opened, John and I were faced with the job of casting it. The production team was already on board, with Cathy Jayes as Musical Director, in whose hands lay the unenviable task of authenticating, with six instruments, Judy Garland's often big-band backings. There were occasions, once we had moved back to Worcester and were sharing digs with Cathy, when we came across her in the middle of the night, crouched on the floor where she had been scribbling out the parts, and where she had fallen fast asleep! We were also happy to learn to learn that Sally Marshall had returned as choreographer, and that Chris Crosswell was once again designing both sets and costumes. There were around 25 characters in the play, most of whom could be at least doubled, so we were looking for around 12 actors, all of whom would have to be able to sing passably well, and at least three of them, playing Judy's theatrical back-up group, 'The Boy Friends', would need to be able to dance too. We had no trouble at all casting Lewis Cowen, who had played the part of Herr Schultz in *Cabaret,* as Louis B. Mayer and, having subsequently seen him playing a decidedly non-Jewish role in Mike Leigh's play, *Abigail's Party,* as Judy's third, and most influential husband, Sid Luft. Hedda Hopper and Louella Parsons were to be played by Karen Mann, who had played the Wicked Witch of the West in *The Wizard of Oz,* and newcomer (at least to me), Caroline High. It was also a welcome opportunity to work again with Jacquie Crago as Judy's mother, and with Paul Milton, who had cut his teeth at the Swan Theatre as 'Little Louis' in *Piaf,* now cast in a number of roles, including the hotel bell-boy who shares the final scene of the play with Judy. Gordon Griffin, my friend from Chichester, whose skills as a pianist as well as an actor made him an obvious choice for the part of Roger Edens, Judy's musical mentor, also played the film director, Joe Mankiewicz.

Driving to Worcester at the end of one of our weekend visits to the cottage, we had barely put it behind us when Lesley started to sing *Do it Again,* a song featured on Garland's Carnegie Hall album, and which I had included in the show. I don't know how long it took me to realise that it was not Judy's voice I was listening to but Lesley's, and I all but stopped breathing. I had harboured my own doubts as time went by that she would be able to capture the elusive spirit of Judy Garland which found its outlet in the protean nature of her singing voice, yet there I was, hearing her sing in a very personal way something I had begun to believe might be beyond even her well-tried versatility. It was a moment to savour, and savour it I did, as I considered the very real possibility that she might now begin to inhabit the complexities of the character she was about to play.

Lesley's ongoing journey, however, encumbered as she was with such a gigantic role, was inevitably rougher and tougher than anyone else's as, with rehearsals well underway, she was the one most affected by the daily cutting and rewriting. Songs vanished and new ones appeared, while scenes we had both lavished so much care and attention on were discarded overnight. But everyone, it has to said, worked their socks off and somehow or other we honed it to an acceptable length in time to open. After six months of blood, sweat and tears, we finally had a play called *Judy* up and running, and scheduled to be given its World Premiere at the Swan Theatre, Worcester on September 13th, 1984. The following programme note, written in haste during rehearsals, still pretty well sums up, I think, my original conception of the play, and the driving force behind it:

'In a country whose constitution decrees 'The pursuit of happiness' to be the inalienable right of every citizen, the cost of failing to achieve it has ever been high. Nowhere in the U.S.A. does this hold more true than in the Hollywood of the 1930s and '40s, where success and failure were the only possible options, and where the casualty rate, in terms of drug-addiction, alcoholism and suicide were significantly higher than the national average. Judy Garland, at the tender age of 13, was admitted to this make-believe world, and almost immediately fell victim to its fairy-tale values. As cinema-goers our passport to fantasy was simply the price of a ticket, but for the people who provided us with our fantasies there was no escape. Never-Never Land was their home, and dreams were their reality. Such is the story of Judy Garland. At her funeral in 1969, more than 20,000 people lined the streets of New York to pay homage to her. Millions more mourned her across the world. They were weeping, not only for the loss of a unique artiste, but also for the little girl whose lifelong pursuit of happiness had turned her into a legend.'

Lesley received a well-deserved standing ovation on the opening night, followed by a plethora of rave reviews for a performance that was 'mostly like the real thing, and occasionally so much like the real thing, the resemblance is uncanny' – and for the play, 'a perfect vehicle for Miss Mackie's remarkable talents'. While Gareth Lloyd Evans wrote in *The Guardian*: 'It was not an impersonation but a stunning acting performance. It fully deserved the standing ovation which, at the end, followed the yearning, dying fall of *Over the Rainbow*', and in the *The Evesham Advertiser*, 'I fully expect *Judy* and Lesley Mackie to be major West End stars within a year'.

Buoyed up as we were by *The Evesham Advertiser's* expectations, together with all the other positive reactions, there was no sign of any West End interest, nor any visitors, as far as we knew, from beyond the purlieus of Worcestershire throughout its two and a half week run, except for friends and family, of course. Naturally, we had dreams about its future, most of them concerning what it might do for Lesley's career south of the border, but we were not so unworldly as to think that it would be second nature for producers and casting directors to mount expeditions into the provincial wilderness without any incentive beyond a few good reviews, and it seemed we were right. Neither had it been surprising to learn that Brian Glanville's reaction to the play had been unenthusiastic, to say the least.

WORCESTER REPERTORY COMPANY
13-29 SEPTEMBER
☆ WORLD PREMIER ☆

Judy

BY TERRY WALE
A musical play on the life story of Judy Garland

After watching it, and having gone out for a while into the Malvern Hills to be alone with his thoughts, he returned home, after leaving us a note expressing his dismay and disbelief that I could have written such things about her. There was nothing we could do at that stage to make things better, although I did write to him shortly afterwards, feigning humour by suggesting that he should maybe write his own version, and call it *Saint Judy*! The other side of the coin revealed that two gentlemen, one from Leicester and the other from Manchester, had come to see the final matinée. They had, it transpired, spent years waiting for something to come along that might fill the gap left by Judy's death and, as it turned out, our play was the answer to their prayers. They were Reg Needle and David Mars, both of them members of *The Judy Garland Fan Club*, although we only knew of this when, some little while later, a copy of the club magazine, containing the following review landed on our door-mat: 'It would take a very detached person not to be moved with compassion by what is shown of Judy in this very fine play. There is no attempt to whitewash Judy, to keep her in the 'Dorothy' mould, and yet even at the end, running right through the self-destructive instincts and abuses, there still was the shining light of childlike innocence... and it is to Lesley Mackie's credit that we are able to perceive it'. Needless to say, Reg and David were soon to become our very dear friends!

Although I returned to Worcester for the very last day of the play's all too brief run at the Swan Theatre, I left for Scotland at the end of its first full week in order to begin rehearsals for *Amadeus* in Perth. I knew, of course, that Roger Kemp had already been invited to direct it, but as it happened, his increasing deafness had lead him to realise he would be severely handicapped as director of a play in which music played such an integral part. Coming as it did at the last minute, it might have been too daunting a prospect for me too had I not already known the play inside out!

By the time I arrived, of course, the actors had already been cast, and I had every reason to be happy about that too. *Amadeus* followed Clive Perry's production of O*liver,* from the cast of which I inherited a few heavyweights of a certain age who, while they may not have enjoyed the professional standing of Willoughby Goddard and Mark Dignam from the original production, were not without the experience or the authority to have earned a place in the court of the Austrian Emperor Joseph, who was to be played by James McClure, a contemporary of Lesley's at the Royal Scottish Academy of Music and Drama (RSAMD), and an erstwhile neighbour of ours in Kensal Rise. I knew little of his previous work, but he couldn't have been better cast. In fact, it became difficult to believe, with his easy assumption of majesty and his delivery of Peter Shaffer's dialogue, autocratic and loftily humorous, that the part hadn't been written with him in mind. As if this wasn't enough to be going on with, I was also gifted with a Mozart, in the hands of Iain Stuart-Robertson, who was at least as impressive as Richard O'Callaghan was at Her Majesty's Theatre.

At the centre of the play, however, is Antonio Salieri, the well-established court composer who finds himself sidelined by the arrival of Wolfgang Amadeus Mozart, whose silly adolescent giggles, smutty humour and generally inappropriate behaviour mask a genius whose musical gifts render Salieri's compositions pedestrian by contrast, and provoke in him the desire to humiliate, cuckold and finally to murder his tormentor. In casting Martyn James as Salieri, Joan had made good her choice of a local actor, and one moreover who enjoyed audience popularity in Perth. Martyn's reputation, however, was founded mainly on laughter, and no matter how agonising it was for his Salieri to listen to a piece of Mozart's music, he would be sure to make his audience laugh, or at least smile. In what otherwise was a most favourable review, Joyce McMillan of *The Scotsman* wrote: 'Where it departs from standard practice is in the unambitious casting of that genial pantomime villain, Martyn James, as the possessed Salieri; he handles the courtly puppet show of the dramatised sequences – the   black comedy of social relations with the foul-mouthed and giggling Mozart – well enough, but he is inclined to treat Salieri's lush linking monologues – which must be taken to contain the philosophical meat of the play – with a combination of twinkly coyness and semi-comic theatrical rant which hardly inclines one to take them seriously'.

I was blessed with a wonderful set designer, Nigel Hook, and with the stolid support of Simon Sewell who lit the stage beautifully as always, together with a cast and crew that did me proud, both on-stage and off. Joyce McMillan went on to say, 'What I feel about this Perth Theatre production, skilfully and gracefully directed by Terry Wale, is that I never wish to see a better one.'

Meanwhile, I had returned to Worcester to see the final performance of *Judy*, and to bid a fond farewell to all those who had played a part in its success, and in particular to John Doyle whose contribution from day one had been incalculable. It was sad, of course, to see it close after a mere two and a half weeks without knowing if it had any kind of a future, and especially from Lesley's point of view. Well, we could but hope!

As far as the immediate future was concerned, Lesley had been offered the part of Principal Boy in *Jack and the Beanstalk* at the Eden Court Theatre in Inverness by Jimmy Logan, the well-known Scottish comedian, actor and impresario, who was to be starring as Dame Trott, Jack's mother. As Jack was one of only two Principal Boys who could feasibly be played by someone as petite as Lesley and Jimmy knew her work well, it was no surprise that he offered her the role. What inspired him, however, to offer me the part of the Wicked Uncle, aside from being Lesley's husband, I had no way of knowing but, without mentioning my 'pantophobic' propensities, I crossed my fingers behind my back and told him I was otherwise engaged. It was only when I learned that the 'Wicked Uncle' went hand-in-hand with playing the 'Busy Bee', and dressed like one, that my guilty conscience evaporated, and I felt entirely justified in saying that I was going to be too busy rewriting my script for *Judy*. Jimmy Logan, as it happened, was a great admirer of Judy Garland. In fact, his younger sister, the jazz-singer Annie Ross, had appeared alongside Judy in the 1943 film, *Presenting Lily Mars*, a family link he treasured.

My time in Inverness proved to be something of a mixed blessing, the town itself uneasily reminding me of the featureless cities of New Zealand. In Scotland, however, history is never far away. Culloden Moor, for instance, where Bonnie Prince Charlie's army was decimated in 1746, was but a stone's throw, while only a short drive away was Loch Ness where you could spend a pleasurable hour or two taking pictures of the iconic Urquhart Castle, and of the Loch itself, in the vain hope of capturing at least a fleeting image of the monster! I have few other memories of my time there, and hardly any at all of my infrequent visits to the Eden Court Theatre except for Lesley flaunting her legs at both ends of the beanstalk, and a very touching moment when Jimmy Logan sang *Unforgettable* to his departing cow. But by far my most abiding memory is of the friendship we forged with George Duffus, who was playing Simple Simon. George was a stand-up comedian, while holding down a 'proper' job as an Insurance Salesman in Dundee. Lesley and he, Dundonians both, knew of each other, although their paths had never crossed, but their immediate rapport in the rehearsal room threatened to backfire when he turned up at a restaurant where Lesley and I were being treated to dinner by Jimmy and his lady-friend, and proceeded to vilify the staff and the management in an extremely cantankerous way for providing drinks that were over-priced, and especially the Rémy Martin brandies he had ordered. Clearly he had been drinking before he arrived, and although I already knew that he owned a hostelry of his own and was bound to have opinions, I had heard enough, and refused the drink he offered to buy me, while even Lesley was sadly disillusioned by his overbearing manner. It was somewhat later the next day that I learned from Lesley that he had been waiting at the stage door the following morning to offer his apologies to all and sundry for his reported sins, which he himself could barely recall. For some reason he was particularly contrite with Lesley, offering to take us both out for a meal, and promising not to argue about anything, whatever the quality or price. Had he but known it, a mega task awaited him in the shape of a newly-opened restaurant in the centre of town where the choice of wine was restricted, not by grape nor by country of origin, but by the fact that they only had two bottles left following a large party earlier in the day. George merely raised his eyebrows, and ordered them both. Things went from bad to worse as the meal progressed. The food, served on cold plates, was unappetising to say the least, while Lesley was offered tartare sauce to go with her steak. At the end of the meal, the waiter was quite nonplussed when we ordered a liqueur, saying that he would have to go over to the bar which was due to close in two minutes. But George still kept his cool, simply asking him if he might make the effort. As the liqueur glasses were still on order, we were eventually given our drinks in half-pint mugs. Just before we left, a man appeared from out of nowhere, looked at George, and said, "You're George Duffus and you're not fuckin' funny!" George smiled benignly. It was the perfect end to the evening and, together with a parcel containing a bottle of Rémy and two crystal glasses awaiting Lesley in her dressing-room the following day, the perfect launching-pad for a friendship that was to last, not just for the next few weeks when we became pretty well inseparable, but for the rest of his sadly curtailed life.

My fleeting visit to London, and a welcome return to *Beecham*, anticipated our final departure from Inverness by little more than a week, as pantomimes that far north didn't enjoy the longevity enjoyed by other theatres in towns less likely to be rendered inaccessible by snowfall. Suddenly, we were back in London, facing zero prospects, not to mention a flat that was in dire need of care and attention. My father, already overburdened by my mother's declining mental and physical condition, had nonetheless embarked upon a major conversion of our upstairs accommodation into a self-contained flat with its own front door, so that our stairway, previously banistered, was now separated from the downstairs flat by a wall, turning the downstairs passageway into a dark tunnel. He had also arranged for our tiny kitchenette, or scullery, to be knocked through to the rear bedroom, thus creating a very welcome and spacious kitchen/dining area. Most of this had been achieved in our absence – when we were at the cottage, in Worcester or in Scotland. But the sorry truth of it, as we were to discover, was that the work had been entrusted to a couple of ne'er-do-wells who had left the flat in what can only be described as a rough and ready condition. My father had received a substantial Council grant to accomplish the renovation, so it hadn't cost him a great deal, but, not for the first time, and probably not for the last, I question my own blinkered outlook whilst all this was going on. Short of getting the workmen back to finish what they had left undone, we were faced with a large number of soul-destroying and time-consuming domestic jobs, coming at a time when there were no work prospects on the horizon for either of us, and with the all-too-short life of *Judy* seemingly having come to an end, no real professional reason for Lesley to go on living down south. But did it even cross my mind that my father had provided us with rent-free accommodation in London, of all places, for the past six years, and intended to go on doing so at no little cost to himself, while suffering the privations, not to mention the frequent abuse brought about by my mother's dementia? Somehow I don't think so, or even if it did, I'm pretty sure that I never offered him the support that was due to him.

It has to be said that the first three months of 1985 were, for a variety of reasons, the most dystopian we had lived through since we were married. Then there were Lesley's frequent visits to the hospital for blood tests and potassium checks, and her frustration at not being able to make contact with her new agent. All of this, however, was put on a back-burner while we embarked upon a more immediate task, only a little less painful, which was selling our cottage, a luxury we felt we could no longer afford.

It was in April, while Lesley was visiting family and friends in Scotland, and I was doing my best to spruce up the cottage for potential buyers, that I received a phone call from John David, the Bristol Old Vic's Artistic Director. It soon came to light that, unrecognised and unannounced, he had seen *Judy* in Worcester, and was thinking of staging it himself in Bristol. The only condition attached to this was that Lesley Mackie would be free, and willing to play the part again. I was, of course, in a position as her husband to assure him that she had no other commitments during September and October, and that I had every reason to believe she would be perfectly happy to play it again, which was, of course, the understatement of the year.

It was shortly after this, with contracts signed and sealed, that John David came to us again with the news that he had been approached by Alan Strachan, artistic director of London's Greenwich Theatre, suggesting a co-production deal that would enable *Judy* to be played at Greenwich immediately following its run in Bristol. Notwithstanding the paltry salary she was offered, Lesley agreed, if only because the Greenwich Theatre was one step nearer to the West End, a prophetic observation that was borne out when the Greenwich Theatre programme announced it as 'A Bristol Old Vic/Greenwich

Theatre Co-Production in Association with Bill Kenwright'.

We were in fairly dire financial straits by the time an offer was made for the cottage on June 23rd, but even knowing that it would be some weeks before completion, and having already borrowed some money from Lesley's parents, ostensibly to pay our tax bill, we decided to push out the boat and book a holiday on Crete instead. After all, with a six week engagement in Bristol on the cards, followed by an eight week season in Greenwich, Lesley surely deserved the buttress that only a fortnight's holiday on a Greek island could provide.

Even so, and with only a few weeks to go before rehearsals were due to start, we returned from our lazy, sun-soaked holiday to face more irritating and nerve-racking delays before completion took place on August 23rd. We then hired a van and made two separate trips, transferring our goods and chattels from Milton to London, creating something of a logjam in our flat that would have to be dealt with in due course. We were obviously sorry to say goodbye to *Wild Thyme*. We had only been there for three years, and for much of that time we had lived and worked elsewhere. Nevertheless, the happy memories of our more or less secluded times together in that tiny doll's house would have a long lasting effect and, in the years to come, prompt us to revisit Milton and enjoy a drink at *The Black Boy* whenever we were in that neck of the woods. For the time being, however, we had other fish to fry and, having recklessly used some of the profits from the sale to exchange my well-worn blue Renault 5 for a brand new magenta coloured one, we headed for Bristol, where Lesley embarked on an altogether longer journey down 'The Yellow Brick Road'.

oOoOo

Twenty eight

I was, of course, sorry that John Doyle wouldn't be directing *Judy* at Bristol; but then again, if John David hadn't made his own journey to Worcester, its première at the Swan Theatre might well have been the beginning and the end of the story. Personal reasons aside, and given that it was fairly obvious from day one that he and I would not enjoy a similar rapport, I had no reason to doubt that my play was in safe hands. At least John David had the nous and the resources to expand on the Swan Theatre's budgetary limitations without turning his back on John Doyle's legacy. He was obviously well aware, for instance, of the huge contribution made by Cathy Jayes to the original production, not to mention the time it would take to replicate it, so he did not hesitate to engage her services as Musical Director; and for similar reasons, having briefly flirted with the notion of a 'star name', he invited Lewis Cowen to play again the roles of Louis B. Mayer and Sid Luft. Nor did he hesitate to take advantage of local talent, swelling the company with several recent graduates from the Bristol Old Vic Theatre School, mainly to be seen in the casting of the 'Boyfriends', Judy Garland's supporting chorus throughout her concert years, introducing her to her audience with a mixture of song and dance. Five in number now, instead of just three, they were also entrusted with a number of supporting roles in the play, and were chosen first and foremost for their quality as actors, whilst also being tried and tested for their singing and dancing abilities by Cathy and Gail Gordon, Bristol's own choreographer.

On one of several trips to Bristol prior to rehearsals, Lesley had met up with Dawn, who had decided to make her home there, it being eight years since Charles had died, and she had obviously never entertained any serious thoughts about moving away. When Lesley met her for lunch, she was accompanied by her friend, a lady called Mary Wilkins, who offered Lesley a room in her house not too far away from the theatre, an offer she was only too happy to accept, and which I was only too happy to share with her on my occasional, and fleeting, visits to Bristol from Guildford where I had been engaged to direct a production of *Cinderella* (the original fairy-story, I hasten to add, and not the pantomime!), for the Musical Theatre course at the Guildford School of Acting. Although initiated by the choreographer, Angela Hardcastle, with whom I had previously worked at Salisbury, the actual offer was made by Michael Gaunt, the Principal of GSA, who subsequently invited me to direct Alan Ayckbourn's *Way Upstream* for the Third Year Acting course. I was obviously unaware at the time of what this venture into pastures new would mean to me, but I remain grateful to Angela for opening that particular door for me.

In the gap between these two productions, and before heading back to Perth to direct Willy Russell's *One for the Road*, I was able to spend a reasonable amount of time in Bristol, dealing with last minute rewrites when I wasn't ferrying Lesley to and from a succession of interviews for various newspapers and magazines, radio and television programmes. On one occasion we drove up to Greenwich Park where she cavorted around with photographers snapping away, an inconvenient distraction that was rewarded the following day when one of the tabloids referred to her as 'lovely, leggy Lesley Mackie'! But by far the most stressful was our joint appearance on BBC Breakfast Television, which meant driving to London the night before so that we could be collected from home at 5am the following morning, appearing in front of the cameras at a time of day when neither of us were at our best, either to look at or to listen to! The schedule was gruelling, and all the more so for Lesley, but we were naturally delighted to be getting so much publicity.

By far the most inspirational contribution John David made to the staging of the play was the opening scene in which Judy, in top hat and tails, sings *Born in a Trunk* from *A Star is Born*, telling the story of a woman, not a million light-years removed from herself, who makes the journey from childhood to seasoned performer. This provides a launching-pad for the actress playing Judy when, following an onstage change of costume witnessed by the audience at the end of the song, she becomes the teenage newcomer to MGM. But instead of simply having her come on stage and sing directly to the audience, John opened with a film studio set-up, including cameras and sound-booms, all manned by members of the company as film-crew, into which Judy wanders, her back to the audience, taking her place in front of a camera and backed by the familiar 'Stand by!' routine, culminating in 'Action!' at which point the music starts and she begins to speak the intro ... "Thank you, thank you very much, I can't express it any other way; but with this awful trembling in my heart, I just can't find another thing to say. I'm happy that you liked the show; I'm grateful you liked me, and I'm sure to you the tribute seemed quite right ..." As she then begins to sing, she turns away from the camera to face the audience for the first time. John David was certain that Lesley's striking resemblance to Judy Garland would make a significant impact on the audience when she turned to face them, and he was right; the show couldn't have got off to a better start.

1985 Judy - Bristol Old Vic. Lewis Cowen, Lesley Mackie & Michael Gardiner

I was there on the opening night, of course, although I was far too busy pacing up and down at the back of the auditorium watching the audience to take much notice of what was happening on stage. When we did *Judy* in Worcester, audiences were already kindly disposed towards us and were likely to look on anything we did with grace and favour, but here in Bristol we were strangers; not to mention the fact that the Bristol production succeeded in attracting a wider audience, some of them from as far afield as London, and whose sophisticated response to it was anybody's guess. As it happened, I needn't have worried as Lesley's performance was again rewarded with a standing ovation, reaffirmed by local newspaper critic, Jeremy Brien: 'This moving and magical musical biography bids to provide the Bristol Old Vic with their biggest hit for quite some time ... Judy is played, indeed lived, by actress-singer Lesley Mackie, known mainly on the repertory circuit, but honoured on her first night in Bristol by a rare standing ovation. Terry Wale ... was obviously inspired by his wife's remarkable physical resemblance to Judy Garland in her adult and declining years, plus her ability to convey the innocence and dormant waywardness of her *Wizard of Oz* days. Yet there is more than this in Mackie's totally stunning performance' and from David Foot in the *Guardian*: 'Indeed a star is born. Her name is Lesley Mackie ... Miss Mackie has more than a technically good voice and plaintive presence. She gives us, in this tour de force performance, a vivid characterisation, all the way from 'chubby little hunchback' to abrasive lush'; while from Eric Shorter in The Daily Telegraph: 'The author, Terry Wale, and the actress, Lesley Mackie aim so daringly at a spitting stage image that the singer seems to live again ... the famous triumphs and the dressing-room torments are thus new-minted ... Miss Mackie is (for me) a revelation, a reincarnation, a blazing theatrical personality'; and not to forget the review broadcast on the local radio station, *Severn Sound*: 'If you don't get down to the Bristol Theatre Royal before October 19th', the critic said, 'you will be missing the best British musical for years!'

Although I would have welcomed the prospect of remaining in Bristol to share with Lesley and the rest of the company the success *Judy* was enjoying, I had no option but to leave for Perth where rehearsals were due to begin on *One for the Road*. There were other more pressing reasons why I would rather have stayed on in Bristol where Lesley would again be left to play an enormously demanding role without my support. My only concrete memory of that rehearsal period in Perth was breaking rehearsals at 4pm on one particular Friday, and standing in the wings at the Bristol Theatre Royal, 420 miles down the road, watching the closing scenes of *Judy* with both Lesley and I clearly running on adrenalin.

By the time I finally returned to Bristol, following the opening night of *One for the Road*, Bill Kenwright had already visited Lesley in her dressing-room, and told her there was a good chance *Judy* might transfer to the West End following its run in Greenwich, should a suitable theatre become available at that time. Lesley had meanwhile undergone theatrical surgery, replacing her agent with a man of good repute and a favourable track-record, Larry Dalzell, who offered to take her on after seeing the show, a transplant she could hardly refuse.

Our final night in Bristol was as exciting as our first, made all the more so when Lesley's family came all the way from Dundee to see it, greeting her achievement with no faint praise. With several weeks to spare before we were due to re-rehearse it for Greenwich, we took the opportunity to follow them back to Scotland for a short break, during which we both went to see the final performance of *One for the Road*.

Larry Dalzell could not improve upon the £125 a week Lesley was offered at Greenwich but, following a heart-felt plea from Lesley to Alan Strachan, at least a space in the wardrobe department was found and cleared which not only provided her with room to change, but also allowed her a little privacy as well. This lack of space, both offstage and on was our biggest problem at Greenwich. At both the Swan Theatre and the Theatre Royal, having played in the wings during the first act, the band was trucked onto the stage just before the interval, and remained there for the rest of the play. In Greenwich there was simply not enough wing space to accommodate them. In fact, the only available space was underneath the stage, from where Cathy had no contact with the performance during the first act except by way of earphones and a TV monitor. This was also, of course, a setback as far as the production was concerned, if only because the band couldn't be trucked on during the action, and had to wait for the interval to be relocated. But even without the band, there was little enough room onstage to accommodate the set which meant that it ended up almost flush with one of the side walls so that all entrances and exits had to be made from the other side where there was all of four feet to spare, largely taken up with furniture from the show, piled up and downloaded as required. Lesley's quick-changes, of which there were several, consequently had to be undertaken on top of beds, under tables and in cupboards. At one point, she had to clamber over a double bed, crawl under a curtain and enter, looking serene, to sing *Better Luck Next Time*!

As if this wasn't enough to be going on with, after returning to our flat one evening following a technical rehearsal, Lesley decided to visit a local chip shop on her return from which she was mugged, thrown to the ground when she protested, and her handbag stolen. Her initial concern had been for her voice when the man approached her from behind and threw an arm around her throat, but she was obviously distressed by the whole incident when she arrived home, not least by having seen her fish and chips scattered across the pavement! I called the police, and went off to search for any items that might have fallen from her handbag, and came across her spectacles which were lying in the gutter. I was about to retrieve them when a car pulled in and I heard a crunch. After thanking God for His divine intervention, I went off down the road to see if I could find any witnesses. The police meanwhile arrived, and Lesley was able to tell them that her attacker was a young man of West Indian origin wearing a woolly hat. But since most of the population of Kensal Rise was made up of young West Indians wearing woolly hats, they didn't hold out too much hope in the event of an identity parade. As a postscript to this unresolved episode, my father suggested that Lesley should put in a claim for damages to the Criminal Injuries Board, and over a year later when we had all but forgotten about it, she received a cheque for over £400, which more than covered all the items she had lost, including her fish and chips!

In spite of all this, the play opened on December 18th to enthusiastic applause and a standing ovation for Lesley. The subsequent reviews were the best we'd received so far, and coming from London critics, the most influential as far as the future was concerned. Eric Shorter, who was fast becoming an aficionado, wrote in the *Daily Telegraph*: '*Judy* is a surprising pleasure at Greenwich Theatre. It was a surprising pleasure at Bristol in the autumn ... more surprising now because it stands up so well to a second viewing ... should Lesley Mackie take all the credit? Her resemblance to the singer is eerily exact, not only physically but also vocally. The phrasing of the songs, the sense of breathless spontaneity, the self-pity behind the brave, button-holing chatter as she addresses us from the footlights with the orchestra behind her – all this is uncannily memorable ... she doesn't so much impersonate Judy Garland as achieve a kind of theatrical reincarnation', while a few days later Clive Hirschorn of the *Sunday Express* wrote: 'For an actress to attempt to play Garland at any stage of her turbulent career requires a certain foolhardy courage. But to portray her from the age of 12 to her death at the age of 47, well, that's surely courting disaster. And yet, in *Judy*, a diminutive newcomer called Lesley Mackie attempts and magnificently achieves the impossible ... it is an astonishing tour de force, powerfully fuelled by author Terry Wale's hard-hitting canter through the high and low spots of his subject's variegated career'. And as for Martin Hoyle in the *Financial Times*: 'Biography, not hagiography. This fairy-tale cum horror story of Judy Garland gains immensely from the script's avoidance of tear-jerking; but emotion there is, first in the songs and then in the familiar Hollywood fable of *Beauty and the Beast* – in reverse. Villains include Louis B. Mayer, raging at his studio's loss of Deanna Durbin, and reluctant to use the 14 year-old Garland, 'the chubby little hunchback who sings like an old lady.' Lewis Cowen convinces as both this monstrous exploiter, and the best intentioned of the star's husbands, Sid Luft, who selflessly battled against Garland's drug-addiction. We see the roots of the problem as the teenager takes 'little magic pills' for vivacity (and to quell that figure-filling appetite), watch her insecurely fishing for compliments, and witness the total collapse of confidence that resulted in her final suspension from MGM ... which provides an effective Act 1 curtain as a harder, brighter Judy leads a troupe of Chorus Boys in *Get Happy*. The apparent clichés of showbiz fiction – pushful mother, bitchy journalists (notably an incisive Hedda Hopper from Alison Skilbeck), and a raddled and crumpled star clutching at hotel bell-boys for company in the small hours – emerge with freshness and conviction. The excellent script is unwaveringly American, down to the careful omission of the perfect tense ... Lesley Mackie's performance is magnificent'. And from Michael Ratcliffe of the *New Statesman* ... 'Something remarkable is happening at Greenwich Theatre where Terry Wale's *Judy* has arrived for the Christmas season, and an actress holds us in the pathetic history of a great singer ... switching with volatile ease between panic, humour, hectic brilliance, charm, cunning and despair ... *Judy* is Mr. Wale's first stage play, but his grasp of theatrical shape is instinctive ... Witty, too. Hedda Hopper (Alison Skilbeck) and Louella Parsons (Caroline Holdaway) provide a malicious and queenly chorus throughout, often very funny, their prophecies sometimes gloriously wrong: 'A family don't want to leave St. Louis and they wind up not having to; what kind of a movie can you make of *that*?' And finally from Malcolm Hay in *Time Out* ... 'a performance fit to send critics rummaging through their stock of superlatives'.

I happened to be in the foyer of Greenwich Theatre one evening shortly after we had opened, when Benny Green arrived. Benny and I had been friends for a long time, going all the way back to the Open Air Theatre, Regent's Park, where I had played alongside his actress wife, Toni Kanal, who was with him too on this occasion, and I joined them for a drink. I was well aware, of course, that Benny wrote reviews for the theatrical magazine, *What's On*, and knowing that he had never been a great admirer of Judy Garland, I could only hope that he was taking time off from his duties simply to come and see my play which he had tacitly given me to understand that he thought I was mad to have taken on in the first place!

For those who are perhaps too young, or were else too distracted by lesser mortals, I should perhaps point out that Benny Green, as well as presiding over a regular Sunday afternoon programme on Radio 2 over a period of 20 years in which he aired his uncompromising views on popular music in his equally uncompromising North London accent, also wrote numerous books on subjects as diverse as jazz and cricket, and from W.S. Gilbert to Fred Astaire by way of P.G. Wodehouse and Max Miller. Not only that, but he wrote lyrics and devised theatrical entertainments, while his gift for anecdote enlivened many a radio and TV panel show. Benny was a jazz saxophonist in his early days, and went on to be voted 'most promising new jazz musician' in a *Melody Maker* poll of 1953 before going on to join the *Ronnie Scott Orchestra*. His days as a working saxophonist, however, were numbered. The coming of Rock 'n Roll brought to an end the Golden Age of Popular Music and made it even more difficult for jazz musicians to make a living. So Benny retired and, as he once said, he never went back to work, he just pursued his hobbies! I had no idea when I first met him, of course, precisely what his friendship would come to mean to me. I was awed by his encyclopædic knowledge on a wide variety of subjects, dumbstruck by his passionate enthusiasm for all the things he cared about, and sometimes taken aback by his red-blooded condemnation of everything he perceived to be third-rate and tawdry. Over the years, in an increasingly dumbed-down world, Benny's standards became a beacon, his tireless enthusiasm an inspiration, and his impeccable taste in popular music a point of reference for those amongst us who might otherwise have thought our preference for Gershwin and Sinatra merely old-fashioned.

As you might well be able to imagine by now, I spent the rest of that evening in a state of inner turmoil for, if indeed he did mean to submit a review to *What's On*, I knew he would not be influenced either way by our friendship. Benny Green, as I had every reason to know, took no prisoners! At the end of the show, I saw him emerge from the auditorium, and – wonder of wonders – he was wiping the tears from his eyes. He said very little at the time, but this is an extract from the review he submitted to *What's On*: 'I thought the Greenwich audience slightly circumspect. They only cheered. I expected them to stand, jump, climb up the walls, light torches and form a processional down Greenwich High Street, carrying Miss Mackie on a golden throne. That may yet come ... In the meantime, *Judy* contains the most startlingly accomplished musical-dramatic performance I can recall by any actress not world-famous'.

Bill Kenwright's increasingly frequent appearances suggested that a West End transfer was now well and truly on the cards, and while no theatre had as yet been mentioned, his proprietorial input, reserved for John David's, Lesley's and my ears only, made it transparently clear that he was now in the driving seat. The first bombshell he dropped was to insist that Cathy Jayes be replaced as Musical Director, a bitter pill as far as Lesley and I were concerned until he justified it by saying that in her concert years Judy Garland had never appeared on stage with a female MD. He was quite right, of course, but although we took his point it was difficult to go on working alongside Cathy with both of us keeping our mouths shut while fervently hoping that another job would crop up for her before the big day arrived.

In the course of my ongoing relationship with Bill Kenwright, I was to learn quite a lot about the man who had graduated from actor to producer, not least about his unpredictable behaviour which became only too predictable. He could be disarmingly frank and open at times, even about himself; but in the same vein he could pull the wool over your eyes with a convincing display of charismatic charm. Knowing little or nothing about him at the time, except for being the man who had, via Norman Boyack, provided me with the solution to the problems we encountered during those stormy days of *Sleuth* at the Belgrade Theatre more than six years earlier, he was also the only producer to show an interest in taking *Judy* into the West End.

It was only a few days before we ended our run at Greenwich on February 8th, that we received the news we had been waiting for; the Strand Theatre (now the Novello) was going to be our next home and, with a bit of luck, for some months to come. Ironically, as it turned out, our only real concern at the time was that after seven weeks of full houses at Greenwich, just down the road so to speak, our audience potential might have been somewhat impaired. But we didn't let it get in the way of our dream come true. Driving down to Greenwich one day via the Strand where we parked the car and looked up at the theatre, right in the heart of London's West End, we pictured Lesley's name up in lights.

Our first surprise, however, came about when a few of the younger actors in the company, playing Judy's 'Boyfriends' and a number of other roles, decided to call it a day after Greenwich, obviously not wanting to tie themselves to a year-long contract. It was a shame as far as we were concerned, as most of them, besides being good lads, had brought a great deal to the production, not only as singer/dancers but also as actors, only now to be replaced by some who may well have been light on their feet, but who didn't match up in the acting stakes. On a more positive note, however, their departures allowed us to bring back into the cast our friend from Worcester, Paul Milton, playing the same roles as he had at the Swan Theatre, as well as David Bauckham, also from the original production, and a definite bonus as Arthur Freed, Judy's friend and mentor at MGM. Bill certainly came up trumps there, along with his casting of Buster Skeggs as Louella Parsons, who had all the appropriate credentials. Fate was also kind to Cathy Jayes, and to us, by providing her with an irresistible offer from elsewhere before the transfer became more than a pipe dream.

To give him his due, Bill provided us with an excellent Musical Director, Callum McLeod, who not only made good Bill's point about Judy Garland's onstage propensity for male MDs, but also endowed the show with a very accomplished, and extremely personable young musician. It was Callum who took us to meet the man who was to undertake some new orchestral arrangements and when we visited Alexander (Sandy) Faris at his home in North London, where he accompanied Lesley as she sang *You're Nearer*, the Rodgers and Hart song that brings Judy Garland's first concert appearance to a close, I was completely won over. It's a very simple and gentle love song, which is why I chose it in the first place, but Sandy Faris's arrangement had enhanced it with such skill and sensitivity, that I'm sure Judy herself would have been as moved to tears by it as I was. It was only in the aftermath of this meeting that I learned of Sandy Faris's musical background; not only classically trained as a pianist and conductor, but the composer of a host of musicals, not to mention the theme music for the hugely successful TV series, *Upstairs, Downstairs*. In fact, I only had one major musical issue with the inclusion in the line-up of a keyboard synthesiser. I hasten to add that electronic keyboards have improved beyond measure since 1986 when its vague resemblance to a piano, let alone all the other instruments it imitated, in my opinion, would have undermined the authenticity of every piece of music in the show. Lesley tells me that I threw a tantrum, of which I have no memory, while I do remember very clearly the musician packing up his keyboard and leaving without any protest from Callum, John David, or even from Bill Kenwright, so I must at least have made my point!

It was during rehearsals that we were invited by Bill to attend the opening night of another of his musical productions at Sadler's Wells Theatre. It was called *Jeanne*, the story of Joan of Arc, upon which we had been given to believe he had invested £400,000, while the budget for *Judy* was only £150,000, a ludicrous amount by all accounts for a musical. I had to be restrained by my wife from leaving at the interval, although I was finally glad that I stayed, as I would have missed out on the prison scene in which the heroine, in male attire, and sporting a wig that was a cross between a badger and a Davy Crockett hat, was advised by her fellow prisoners to 'wear a skirt', a musical number that bore a striking resemblance to Cole Porter's *Be a Clown*; not to mention missing the final tableau in which, tied to a stake with the flames lapping around her, she sang 'Where Will I Be Tomorrow?' The reviews for the show well and truly endorsed my own opinion of it, and it closed just five weeks later; an unfortunate end, not only for the actors, but for the producer who lost his entire investment, which didn't bode too well for the future of *Judy*.

Our main concern at that time, however, and with our own first night fast approaching, was that having already covered the show in Greenwich, it was unlikely that many of the London critics would return. This concern was exacerbated by the management deciding to open *Judy* on March 26th, only a few days before Easter weekend, so that even if we did manage to get a few reviews, how many people would be around in London to read them, and how many of those would have already seen it during its seven-week season at Greenwich? As it happened, there were more reviews than we had bargained for, although our other premonition was not too wide of the mark. In normal circumstances, greeted at breakfast by these kind of reviews, it would be hard to believe that we wouldn't go on to enjoy full houses for a considerable length of time: 'A further burst of applause for *Judy*, Terry Wale's song-punctuated dramatisation of the Judy Garland story ... Lesley Mackie is brilliant'... 'Miss Mackie is simply terrific .... In her West End début, tiny Lesley Mackie is so successful in recreating the looks, style and voice of Judy Garland that I swear at times I believed she was the real thing' ... 'This musical biography of the girl who soared over the rainbow before crash-diving to the grave is a show-us-then challenge to its star, and star Miss Mackie is this morning, after a sentiment-spurred yet well-deserved standing ovation'.

And from Eric Shorter, having now become a zealot: 'If ever a show was born in a trunk it is *Judy*. A legend on the road long before it reached the Strand, Lesley Mackie's interpretation of Judy Garland bears such an eerie likeness to the star's own style that the evening might be the upshot of a séance. It isn't however just for Miss Mackie's performance that I find the show worth a third visit. It is Terry Wale's skills as the author ... knowing when to bring in a song (and which one), knowing how to vary the tone from self-pity to witty commentary, and how to make the outsiders interesting. Hedda

Hopper and Louella Parsons can be particularly apt ... but it is finally Miss Mackie we applaud for sustaining our sympathy so easily. *Over the Rainbow*, sung with heartrending truth to character from the footlights, draws our tears; and the supporting company, led by Lewis Cowen as Louis B Mayer and Sid Luft, dances attendance on the pathetic case-history with understandable loyalty'.

Even more memorable was the story of Lesley's parents who had arrived at Kings Cross from Dundee and taken a taxi to the Strand Theatre. It turned out that the cabbie had been to see a preview performance and had loved the show so much that, when he discovered that Lesley Mackie was their daughter, he refused to accept their fare – a rare gift from a London taxi-driver!

Sadly, as it happened, and for a variety of reasons, full houses and a long run were not to be our lot. Even so, we might well have survived for longer had our Prime Minister not allowed the U.S. to use Britain as a base from which to bomb Libya, emptying the streets of London, and particularly of Americans fearing vengeance around every street corner. Only those shows that had already been running for a long time were able to survive yet another of Margaret Thatcher's heedless policies, and *Judy* was not one of them. But there were other reasons, closer to home, that made a long run even less feasible. It was perfectly understandable, given the stresses and strains of a West End opening, that Lesley felt a little queasy at the first-night party, and even when she awoke the following morning feeling, if anything, worse than the night before, it was still too easy to shrug it off as a passing trauma. In the light of what came to pass, it's difficult to understand why we allowed ten days to go by without seeking medical advice, and more especially when her condition began to affect her onstage as well as off. Our GP visited us the following morning and thought, subject to further investigation, that it might be gastroenteritis. It being a Wednesday, Lesley subsequently played two shows without being able to eat anything.

London was awash with rain at the time which not only did little to encourage lengthy queues at the box-office, but also succeeded in washing away anything advertising the show at the West End ticket booth. We were made aware of this by Annette Cook, who was surely Lesley's most stalwart fan, and subsequently a close friend, clocking up 53 trips to see the show during its all-too-brief run. Other shows were suffering too, of course, but at least many of them were being advertised on the front of London's buses. When I happened to bump into Bill Kenwright on the street one day, and suggested that it might well be worth investing in this mobile publicity, he appeared to be genuinely sympathetic, "Yes, absolutely; what a pity they've stopped doing it now." By the time I discovered that they hadn't stopped doing it, and that Bill had obviously been misinformed, it was too late to do anything about it.

1986 Lesley Mackie as Judy.

Meanwhile, Lesley's ongoing nausea had finally been diagnosed as food poisoning, and she was told to stick to fluids until the bug had left her system. Somewhere along the way, in the run-up to our opening night, she had left the theatre and grabbed a chicken sandwich from a nearby café, which was the only thing she could think of to blame; but with all of three weeks having passed since she had felt the first stirrings, her memories of exactly where she had purchased it were a little hazy. To make matters worse, she then contracted a throat infection and was given a massive dose of antibiotics which had the effect of killing off what little resistance she had left. Being a consummate professional, her overriding concern was to go on playing Judy Garland at every performance come what may, a compulsion made even more inescapable by the fact that, for some reason best known to the management, she had no understudy.

Despite her throat infection she got off to a good start on Monday evening, a performance which ended with a standing ovation which boosted her morale. This was to be the beginning of a week which culminated in what became known – by us at any rate – as 'Black Friday'. There was a thwarted attempt to lay down a few tracks for the proposed album of the show with Lesley marking her way through some of the numbers simply to help set the tempi. The following morning, as she could barely rise from her bed, I went on ahead to the Redan studios and filled in until she arrived, remaining with her until all the instrumental parts were 'in the can'. The only thing left to do was to get the 'vocals' and the piano part down, but it would obviously be a few days before she would be able to cope vocally with anything more than the demands of the show.

On the Thursday and in Lesley's own words: 'I was playing the most demanding role of a lifetime, and feeling fit to drop. Twice I had to stop during the show, once during a song, and again in the middle of a long speech to the audience recounting Judy's early days at MGM studios, when I found myself telling them about my own plight and how bad I was feeling. I somehow managed to stagger through to the end, comforted by the fact that at least the audience now understood what I was going through. As it happened, someone told me afterwards that he had thought it was all part of the show. I was beginning to think that maybe Judy's life and mine were growing too close for comfort!'

'Black Friday' finally arrived, beginning with a trip to the television studio in Shepherd's Bush where Lesley had been invited to appear as a guest on the *Wogan* show before heading straight for the theatre for Friday night's performance. She was clearly in a bad way, totally dehydrated and barely able to function when we arrived at the studio, and the very notion that she would be able to get up and sing at all, let alone for ten million television viewers, was fanciful to say the least. Sue Lawley, who was standing in for Terry Wogan on that occasion, came into the dressing-room to ask if she was going to be able to make it, but Lesley couldn't even reply. If memory serves me right, I had gone in search of some kind of medicine from a local pharmacy and may well have telephoned Bill Kenwright's office while I was out; hence the miraculous appearance of a Doctor Diamond who gave her an injection, as a result of which she was able to stagger through to the make-up department. I had, by this time, retired to an upstairs viewing room where I stood, poised for a quick descent to the studio floor, my eyes glued to the television monitor on which, at any moment, Lesley would (or would not) appear.

Geoffrey Boycott's long-winded interview, aptly reminiscent of many of his innings in front of the stumps as England's opening batsman, finally came to an end, and Sue Lawley introduced Lesley. The lights came up, the band started to play, and there she was, singing, "Forget your troubles, come on get happy" while I stood there, rooted to the spot, marvelling at her fortitude, knowing that it was only I who really knew how much it was costing her. That old theatrical adage, 'The Show Must Go On', had surely never been more stringently applied. With whatever it was that Doctor Diamond had injected her having served its purpose, combined with 'Doctor Theatre', she managed to get through that evening's performance. But by the time I drove her home she was beginning to hallucinate. Her body went into spasm, and I finally phoned the Metabolic Unit at St Mary's Hospital. So overcome was I by her condition that I omitted to say she was still suffering from the effects of a severe bout of food poisoning which was, after all, entirely responsible for the state she was now in, and about which they had no knowledge. They thought it sounded like a severe case of flu, and suggested that I bring her in the following morning if she showed no signs of improvement. Early the next morning, I drove her to the hospital where, having lost all the minerals from her body, and all but comatose by the time we arrived, she was quickly put on a drip, later telling me that she felt an immediate surge of relief as the fluids and vitamins started to flow through her.

It was now Saturday, and consequently a matinée day at the Strand, so I realised that I had to phone Bill Kenwright to let him know what was going on. In the absence of an official understudy, a girl in the company who was playing a tiny part, had been delegated to learn Judy's lines – just in case Lesley broke a leg! Having sent instructions to her to prepare to go on for the matinée, Bill came down from Liverpool, probably sacrificing an afternoon at Goodison Park watching his beloved Everton play football. Leaving Lesley in very capable hands, I went down to the theatre to give the girl a bit of moral support, only too aware that she was faced with a daunting prospect to say the least, bearing no resemblance whatsoever to Judy Garland either physically or, as it turned out, vocally, and without anything more than a cursory rehearsal. I was therefore somewhat taken aback to find a perfectly calm young lady, welcoming her date with destiny, and betraying no nervousness whatsoever. I was about to discover that her sublime confidence was totally misplaced. I stayed for as long as I could before making a panic-stricken exit when she ran on to sing *Zing! Went the Strings of My Heart* crammed into Lesley's little sailor-suit, and sounding like someone who'd never even heard of Judy Garland. The only thing I can remember now (and will surely never be able to forget) is rushing into the hospital and leaning over Lesley's prostrate form, still all wired up, imploring her to come back, "Lesley, she can't do it! You cannot let her go on on a Saturday night!" Who knows but I might well have dragged her from her bed had I not been dragged away myself by a doctor who told me, in no uncertain terms, that if I wanted to see my wife collapse on stage I was going the right way about it – hence Dr. Levy's surprise when he saw her later in the day and said, "Oh, so you're still with us are you, Mrs Wale?" That she went on to discharge herself from the hospital the very next day, and against all advice, so that she could prepare herself to return to the theatre again by Monday, speaks volumes, not only for her professional commitment, but also for her refusal, and mine too for that matter, to take her condition seriously enough. There is no denying that we had both become blinkered; we simply couldn't bring ourselves to believe that some kind of ailment would put an end to our dream. Back at the theatre I was greeted by an extremely disgruntled company, one of whom was on the point of refusing to go on, as he had found the experience of working alongside a virtually unrehearsed 'understudy' totally embarrassing. But he was persuaded to carry on, and the young lady went on to perform before the biggest audience of the entire run, many of whom greeted the announcement that Lesley Mackie would not be appearing with loud groans.

It had been on the cards for some time that I was going to have to leave London for a few weeks to direct a production of T.S.Eliot's *The Family Reunion* at the Everyman Theatre in Cheltenham where John Doyle, having left Worcester, was now Artistic Director. Of course, this came about before the recent dramatic turn of events made it all but impossible to turn my back on Lesley, and if it hadn't been for her mother, who embarked on yet another journey from Dundee to take my place, I don't know how we would have dealt with it. As it happened, and with what I now look back upon with something approaching disbelief, I nevertheless commuted from Cheltenham to London, a round-trip of more than 200 miles, even if not on a daily basis, certainly with a frequency that I would have dismissed as a fantasy had it not been for Lesley's diary entries. Why I felt I had to do this when her Mum was dancing attendance on her, morning, noon and night, remains a mystery, obviously motivated by concern, but one that took its toll on my energy levels. *The Family Reunion* would have been a difficult enough play to direct in any case, so it's hardly surprising that, with these other distractions, my memories of the experience are somewhat sketchy – or at least they were until only the other day when I happened to come across a programme which not only provided me with a cast list, but with a programme note, credited to me, about the nature of the play: its origins, its latter-day success in the wake of its initial failure, and Eliot's own autobiographical slant on it. It is undoubtedly well-written and equally well-researched (all three paragraphs of it), so unless John Doyle took pity on me and wrote it himself, generously giving me the credit, I must surely claim it as my own!

I do know for a fact that it was on that very first Monday when Lesley returned to the theatre, dragging herself from bed and still suffering bouts of nausea, that she was told Bill Kenwright had chosen to ditch the album, consigning the musical arrangements already laid down, and the time spent on them, to the proverbial dustbin from which Lesley's subsequent attempts to rescue them were to no avail. Understandably, he didn't want to spend any more on a show that was on the brink of closure.

Lesley, of course, had her mother to thank for sustaining her through those few traumatic weeks, accompanying her to the theatre, remaining with her throughout the show, more often than not in her dressing-room but occasionally offering her support from the front row of the stalls, and for providing her with the sustenance that she obviously needed, even when it invariably ended up down the toilet. I was, of course, made aware of all this, although more often than not from a distance as rehearsals in Cheltenham became more demanding with the approach of an opening night, and in any case only Lesley can provide the subjective account that this story demands:

'Each night brought new terrors. My reactions followed a pattern. I felt very nervous at the beginning, but as the act gathered momentum, my adrenalin started flowing, and I usually came off at the end of Act One on a 'high'. By the time the interval was over, I was scared to go back on again, and it was left to Mum to cajole and encourage me, and I don't know what I would have done without her. I was managing, but only just, to keep body and soul together. As I began to feel a little stronger, I decided to face the underground, but when Mum and I alighted at Covent Garden, we discovered that the lift had broken down, so we had to face an endless climb up hundreds of stairs. I had to stop before we were even halfway up, and wondered how I could possibly find the strength to get through the show. On another occasion when Lewis was onstage with me, I suddenly found that my breathing was very shallow and fast, and it went out of control, almost to the point of being unable to speak or sing, but I comforted myself in the knowledge that the audience might not notice, as Judy was often breathy in her delivery. Never having suffered this before, I did not realise that what I was experiencing was a sudden and overwhelming feeling of anxiety, known as a panic attack. I had returned to work too soon, and my body was just saying – Enough!'

As if all of this was not enough to contend with, and with London being all but bereft of American visitors, the last people we would have welcomed to the city were Liza Minnelli and Lorna Luft, Judy Garland's daughters. Looking back after all these years it is hardly surprising that they felt discomfited by the larger than life cut-out of their mother in her *Get Happy* costume staring down at them from the front of the Strand Theatre, just a stone's throw from the Savoy Hotel where Liza was staying. I find it hard to believe, however, that she knew nothing of my play before she crossed the Atlantic and, had it not been for press intrusion, which we did our best to discourage, who knows but she might well have gone back home following her appearance at the London Palladium without joining the campaign that was to cast a lengthy shadow over the final days of *Judy*. Goodness knows, neither Lesley nor I would have expected them to come and see the show, but journalists being journalists, they could not leave well enough alone, and whilst Liza waited until she got back home before she 'let slip the dogs of war', Lorna was quoted in a tabloid headline saying 'It Will Be A Cold Day In Hell Before I Go To See That Play!' She turned down an invitation to meet up with Lesley on a breakfast television programme, a decision welcomed by Lesley who was doing all she could to remain on her feet without the added stress of a confrontation with Lorna Luft, who was a tough cookie and very much her father's daughter. We were to get a taste of Sid Luft's job-description as being in the 'suit' business a little later on, but meanwhile both ladies returned to New York where, as representative of the Garland Estate, Liza instructed her lawyers to take action, expressing her concerns about a play she had neither seen nor read. Thankfully, Norman Boyack came to the rescue and provided a lawyer to represent us so we struck lucky, and it all came to nothing with both sets of lawyers ending up good friends. Not that it was the end of the story as far as we were concerned. In fact, the flak we had been getting from the girls paled into insignificance when Sid appeared on the scene.

I was in the middle of a dress rehearsal in Cheltenham when I heard from Lesley that she had been summoned to a meeting with Kenwright, who had received a call from Sid Luft, Lorna's father and Judy's third husband, who was about to issue us with a writ, citing various matters that had come to his attention. On one particular evening as Lesley left the stage-door, she had been accosted by a couple of large men who, in mildly threatening tones, told her that Sid was not going to be happy when they reported back to him about the way Judy was portrayed in the second half of the play. She said she was sorry about that, but that she hadn't written the play, and bade them goodnight. Had they not introduced themselves as representatives of Group Five, an organisation that had something to do with Judy and Sid's financial affairs, they might easily have passed for a couple of Mafiosi, making it clear that Sid had no reason to come and see the show, having briefed his henchmen to inform him of anything he could possibly sue us for. In their subsequent telephone conversations, Sid told Bill that he wanted cuts and changes made, and in particular, he objected to certain words and phrases used to describe him in the play. Bill had tried to explain that it was Hedda Hopper, the gossip columnist, who described him as 'a gangster, a mobster, and a no-good drunken bum!', but as she and Louella Parsons had already been discredited in the play as strangers to truth, no one took what they said seriously. I had, in any case, gone out of my way to paint a sympathetic portrait of Sid, a loving and caring husband, doing everything in his power to pull Judy back from the abyss. But Sid, whose only legitimate grounds for suing me would have been for flattery, was clearly not listening. He also demanded that we pull down all our publicity posters, as he owned the rights to the photograph Bill had used, taken from the cover on Judy Garland's *Miss Showbusiness* album.

Our journey along the 'Yellow Brick Road', by way of Worcester, Bristol and Greenwich without encountering any major obstacles, only to arrive in Oz where, following great previews, a fabulous opening night and excellent reviews, we were to weather a political storm causing audiences to disappear, followed by the onset of a debilitating sickness, and only five weeks later to wind up with the entire Garland family on our backs, made the looming prospect of an early closure less heartbreaking than it might otherwise have been. A couple of weeks later, Bill also received a call from Warner Brothers, a call which opened with the immortal line, "Have you ever had a lobotomy Mr Kenwright? Well, we're about to give you one." It was gangster talk, and they should have been told to mind their manners, or words to that effect, but the redoubtable Bill Kenwright was curiously unnerved by it. They went on to demand that we omit the song *Born in a Trunk* which, in partnership with Sid Luft, they claimed to own. This was the bitterest pill of all from my point of view, and not only because it was the perfect song with which to open the play, but it was merely an excerpt. In any case, the notice, having already gone up, Bill should surely have told them that the show was coming off and allowed Lesley to go on singing it for the last two weeks, instead of insisting that it had to be removed at once. I was still in faraway Cheltenham when I was asked to suggest an alternative, Lesley having already shown little enthusiasm for the idea of transplanting Irving Berlin's *Better Luck Next Time*, and even less with *Over the Rainbow*, which would have ruined the end of the play as well as the beginning. I was devastated, of course, as it would mean losing the opening scene in front of the movie cameras and her on-stage costume change. In fact, the only option that was left open to me was to scrap the musical element entirely, and to open the play with Judy's parents discussing their daughter's future; not exactly the most engaging scene on which to take the curtain up, but that's what we were stuck with for the rest of the run.

We had been on edge for some time, waiting and wondering, even before the notice had gone up, with Lesley hearing one thing from Bill and another from Nigel, the Front of House Manager, who came into her dressing-room and told her that while Bill felt he had no option but to bring *Judy* off, the Strand management was more than willing to sustain the loss for a little while longer. At the same time she was hearing from Bill that he was doing everything to keep *Judy* afloat, but that the Strand was desperate to bring in another show. Nigel had, in fact, already told her that they had a production of *Cabaret* lined up and waiting in the wings, but that the management were more than willing to give us a few more weeks. Bill went on to say that if and when our show went down he would be the last man to leave the ship, and he'd still be singing *Mammy*! Whatever the truth, the notice went up on May 9th which meant that *Judy* would close in two weeks.

All this had happened while I was in the process of bringing my production of *The Family Reunion* to fruition. It opened on May 15th, was well received and went on to enjoy a successful run, thanks largely, or so I thought, given my ongoing distractions, to the quality of the performances, although John Doyle's invitation to return and direct several more productions at the Everyman Theatre in the not-too-distant future led me to believe that maybe my contribution to its success had not been quite as marginal as I had feared.

Back in London, Lesley was managing to give a performance every evening, but sadly missing out when it came to the many publicity opportunities that were on offer but which would inevitably dwindle once the show had closed. She was invited to take part in *Night of a Hundred Stars*, and also to contribute to a Leonard Bernstein tribute evening, singing *I Feel Pretty* alongside other West End 'stars', but she didn't want to put at risk the quality of her performance at the Strand.

She did, however, manage a trip to Birmingham accompanied by her mother, where she appeared on *The Pebble Mill Show*, and for the very first time began to feel that she was on the mend, although too late for the publicity to do us any good, or for her recovery to be enjoyed on stage for longer than a few more performances.

It was while Bill was on the receiving end of threats and intimidating calls from Warner Bros, that Lesley's agent, Larry Dalzell, also had a call from them asking for photographs and reviews of the show, as they were considering her for the movie they were soon to be making of Judy's life. A little later, having sent a batch of photos, Larry received another call which ended with the voice at the other end saying, "But perhaps your client won't be interested in playing the part when she hears we're gonna sue her husband!" Needless to say, no film was made, and neither was I ever sued.

If only Bill Kenwright, or we for that matter, had known that over the next twenty-odd years my play would be performed in a number of countries across the world without raising so much as an eyebrow, he might well have consigned Sid Luft's following telegram to the waste-paper basket where, without ever having seen the show, or read my script, it truly belonged:

'This will confirm to serve notice of your unauthorized use of literary property, photographs and materials, including, but not limited to, that certain copyrighted composition owned by the undersigned, *Born in a Trunk*, that certain photograph of Judy Garland and her signature contained thereon as copyrighted by Capitol Records under the title of *Miss Show Business* of which the undersigned is the lawful owner, that certain photograph of Judy Garland and James Mason from the undersigned's production of *A Star is Born* as copyrighted by Warner Bros. Pictures, and certain literary material from the biography *Judy* copyrighted by Gerald Frank of which the undersigned is co-owner, in connection with your production of *Judy* by Terry Wale. In addition, you have, without permission or authorization, portrayed my person in your production and have caused slander and defamed my person. Therefore, based upon the foregoing, demand is hereby made to cease and desist in your unauthorized use of the aforesaid property and your failure to do so will necessitate taking further appropriate legal action. You will also be held accountable for your slanderous action to my person. You will be contacted by my solicitors in England. Govern yourself accordingly. Sid Luft'.

There were two standing ovations on our last day, and at the end of the final show, a couple of men ran down the centre aisle and handed Lesley bouquets of flowers. She reached down and shook their hands and for a few moments, felt that surge of love for her audience that Judy herself must have felt so often. Given two full houses and such an enthusiastic response, Bill must have been as bewildered by our closure as we were. I had written the play for Lesley, and she had rewarded me with a performance that was way beyond even *my* expectations, during the course of which she had suffered immeasurably, even visiting death's door on one occasion, and to what end? We had both hoped that it would have a positive effect on her future career, but had enough people seen it? It was with mixed feelings that we drove away from the Strand Theatre that night, seeing the lights that illuminated Lesley's name plunged into darkness.

Among our souvenirs is a framed photograph of the Strand Theatre frontage with Lesley's name, forever in lights, and in the corner a written message, somewhat faded now, and inscribed here before it disappears altogether 'To the best actress of <u>any</u> year, in <u>any</u> musical, with love and admiration. Bill'.

oOoOo

Twenty nine

Larry Dalzell was an agent of the old school, a true gentleman of impeccable taste. It naturally followed that, while he was keen to exploit her recent success, he advised Lesley not to accept an offer to take over the role of Grizabella in *Cats* for the simple reason that she would be just one in a succession of actresses to have played the part in that long-running musical, and that she would simply come and go without arousing much interest. I naturally went along with him, persuading Lesley to accept his advice. The fact that she had been offered a six-month contract playing a major, yet relatively undemanding, role in the West End would, in the circumstances, have been the ideal job, although Larry and I would have needed a crystal ball to foresee those circumstances. It was hardly surprising then, given his elitist predilections, that he responded with enthusiasm to an offer from none other than Frank Dunlop for Lesley to play Fatima, the soubrette in Weber's opera, *Oberon,* scheduled to play for a mere three performances at the Edinburgh Festival, followed by a week in Frankfurt, and winding up with a few days at Tanglewood in the USA. For better or worse it was discovered, shortly afterwards, that the lead baritone, Benjamin Luxon, and another cast member had recording commitments, cutting the rehearsal period to ten days which, Frank felt, was too short for a non-opera singer to cope with. In the end, Larry was undoubtedly more disappointed than Lesley that it didn't work out.

In the wake of a fairly traumatic few months, what we needed – and what Lesley's physical and mental condition demanded, or so I thought – was a stress-free break from it all. So I proposed a leisurely drive down to the south of France which, with me at the wheel, and with Lesley having nothing to do but enjoy the scenery, would surely provide the balm she needed. Just before we were due to leave, Lesley went into town to meet Larry for lunch but had felt nauseous, and was unable to eat. Arriving at Piccadilly Circus tube station on her way back home she all but collapsed, and with her heart pounding and gasping for breath, she thought she might be having a heart attack. It being Piccadilly, where all kinds of people fall over for all kinds of reasons, no one offered to assist her, so she fought her demons and finally managed to board a train bound for Paddington, where she ran all the way to St. Mary's Hospital and, after climbing four flights of stairs to avoid using the lift, she staggered into the now familiar Metabolic Unit, and gave them a breathless explanation. One of the doctors there suggested that what she had suffered was a full-blown panic attack, lesser versions of which she had already experienced. She had, as she later told me, felt like she was dying, and needless to say was not enthusiastic about the prospect of a holiday abroad. I remained obdurately convinced, however, that it would provide the perfect panacea, and so it was that on Sunday June 8th we left for Dover.

It would be too easy for me to look back on our holiday in France as halcyon, were it not for Lesley's diary which catalogues the daily traumas, together with the persistent rain that accompanied us on our drive down towards the Mediterranean coast. Not only that, but the relief she felt every time we entered even the smallest of towns, and the dread she experienced every time we left it behind, distancing her from the next chemist's shop. She was obviously becoming quite an expert on the French pharmaceutical system, quickly realising that the chemist with the cross outside was of no use to her, there being no trained pharmacist within, and that it was only the one with the 'snake' insignia that held out any comfort. This problem got worse as we approached the mountain ranges of southern France, which are not famous for chemist shops of any kind!

I have vivid memories of my own, however, when it came to her problems with food: glancing across to the passenger seat on a number of occasions as she rummaged in her bag for a chunk of bread to gnaw, and thinking, 'Here we go again!', seeking out a restaurant in the early evening when her hunger pangs began to take hold, and suspecting that if it took too long to find one, she wouldn't be able to eat anything. This syndrome persisted, with occasional let-ups, for much of our holiday, climaxing on our return journey in Aix-en-Provence which, for some reason, was teeming with visitors, making it all but impossible to book a room for the night. Anyway, we ended up driving out of town where we soon came across a roadside inn which not only served decent enough food, but provided a television room where we were able to watch France beat Italy 2-0 in the 1986 World Cup!

I have, nonetheless, some very fond memories, often supported by photographic evidence, of happier and sunnier days on our tour of the French Riviera, from Cannes to Nice, and on to Fréjus, crossing the border very briefly into Italy, before heading home by way of Paris, by which time, if memory serves me right, Lesley had all but put her malaise behind her – well, for the time being anyway. She even began to enjoy her food again, albeit for the most part, of the Chinese variety.

Aside from the other myriad distractions of Paris, we took the opportunity to embark on the Piaf trail, not only for nostalgic reasons, but also to provide Lesley with some back-up in the event of a London revival of Pam Gems' play. Hence the photographs I took of her sitting on the steps of 72 Rue de Belleville, upon which, according to a plaque above the door, Edith Piaf had been born, and subsequently on a visit to the Père Lachaise cemetery where, along with a number of other famous people, she was buried. Having taken with us a small bouquet, we waited for some time as a man we took to be a cemetery employee, tended her grave with a great deal more loving care than you might have expected. That he turned out to be no such thing, but a fervent fan who had taken it upon himself to cherish her final resting place, provided an uplifting end to our stay in Paris, and to our potpourri of a holiday in France.

Apart from Lesley's prestigious appearance alongside Peter Ustinov and Juliet Stevenson in Battersea Park where she made a short speech and released some doves as part of UNICEF's campaign on behalf of refugees, plus an invitation from Christopher Dunham for me to return to Westcliff as director of Agatha Christie's *The Hollow,* there was little or nothing else on the horizon for either of us – apart, that is, from an offer made by John Ginman for us both to take part in a cabaret celebrating the 21st anniversary of the Swan Theatre where, following in the footsteps of John Doyle, he had become Artistic Director.

On our return to London, Lesley presented herself at the Metabolic Unit, desperately in need of some reassurance that her body was returning to something approaching normal. She was there for several days while they undertook various tests, revealing little or nothing, until she came back home, looking a good deal better and somewhat rounder and more buxom than when she went in. It was relatively easy for her to dismiss the lateness of her period as just one of the symptoms of her recent condition, the only possible alternative being nothing but a pipe dream. Until *Judy* came along and took over our lives, we had devoted a good deal of our time to investigating the possibility of having a baby, and had all but given up hope, short of *in vitro* fertilisation, donor sperm or adoption. It wasn't, in fact, until we went up to Worcester to rehearse for the anniversary cabaret that I became aware of Lesley's sudden craving for pickled onions. This clue went hand-in-hand with her realisation that the little black dress she had chosen to wear onstage was tighter than she remembered it. We succeeded, however, in putting our hopes on hold until, having enjoyed our brief sojourn at the Swan Theatre, we returned to London where we finally discovered that she was, indeed, pregnant.

People like to tell you, when you have been waiting and trying for a baby, that it usually happens when you are completely relaxed and stop thinking about it. But nothing could have been less relaxing than the holiday we had just taken. Lesley was recovering from food poisoning and suffering from acute anxiety symptoms, while I was living on a knife-edge from day to day, yet here she was, just after her 35th birthday, and pregnant with our first baby. Maybe it had something to do with the magic of Paris, but given the approximate date of conception, it was more likely to have been in that hotel near Aix-en-Provence when, after watching the World Cup match, we had celebrated the French victory just as Edith Piaf would have done. Now we were filled with wonder and trepidation as the reality of it sunk in.

Of course, taking over the role of Grizabella in *Cats* for six months would have been the perfect job. Even Larry Dalzell, had he known what was about to happen, would probably have acquiesced. But it didn't stop him from advising Lesley not to accept an offer from Tom Fleming to play Maggie in a touring production of *What Every Woman Knows* for the Scottish Theatre Company, for the simple reason that she would be 26 weeks pregnant when the tour came to an end, and he was concerned about the risks involved at that stage. So protective was he, in fact, that Tom Fleming asked her if Larry was a member of her family!

On the home front, my father was naturally delighted by the news, given that he had every reason to believe that his first-born had no intention of ever becoming a father. Lesley and I had been married for nine years by this time, a good deal of which we had spent under his roof, and yet we had never shared with him our desire to become parents. In any case, my brother and his wife, Annette, already had three children, so he wasn't entirely bereft of grandchildren. Nonetheless, he was overjoyed by the prospect of having a baby around the house, if only because it would restore a sense of purpose and pleasure to his life, all but frustrated by my mother's inexorable decline into dementia.

It was around about this time that I embarked upon a new writing project. Having devoted a large part of my life over the previous three years to what was essentially a play with music I still hankered after writing a musical. I was certainly keen to try my hand at writing the book and the lyrics, alongside a composer yet to be named, for an original musical, the subject of which had presented itself to me when I read a book called *The Small Woman*, a biography, written by Alan Burgess, of Gladys Aylward. I naturally recognised the story, having seen the technicolor biopic back in the late '50s when it was called *The Inn of the Sixth Happiness*, starring Ingrid Bergman in the leading role. Gladys Aylward, as it turned out, had been a diminutive creature, a parlourmaid from North London, who had turned her back on family and friends to take a hair-raising journey by train across Russia and Siberia to China, where she was to embark on her God-given task as a missionary, culminating in her fabled trek through the mountains at the head of a large number of Chinese children, as she led them to safety from the advancing Japanese forces, singing *Knick Knack Paddy Whack* as they went. It wasn't, of course, until I read Alan Burgess's book that I realised how gloriously miscast Ingrid Bergman had been; how much more poignant would the story have been had the character been cast with someone bearing a closer resemblance to the original, at least in terms of background, education and height. In other words, a perfect part for Lesley – once our baby had been born, of course! Having written to Alan Burgess via his agent, we were subsequently invited to meet him at his home, where we were warmly welcomed, and given carte blanche to go ahead with the adaptation, and from which we eventually departed with a signed copy of his book, and his best wishes for what lay ahead.

Some time later, having written the first 15 pages, along with some drafted lyrics where I felt a song was appropriate, I became aware that *Gladys, the Musical*, for all its crowd-pulling appeal, not to mention a stage full of little Chinese children, was going to require an expansive and expensive production. With this in mind, I sent a copy of what I had written to Cameron Mackintosh, already the most successful theatrical producer of musicals in London, simply to test the water, and to receive at least a glimmer of interest. My timing could not have been worse, however, for the simple reason that his production of *Miss Saigon* was already in the pipeline, and clearly the West End could not play host to two oriental musicals at the same time – or at least that's what he said. Our disappointment, however, was tempered, at least in my case, by the dawning realisation that I was finding it increasingly difficult to relate to the leading character. Not that I didn't admire her for her courage and her tenacity, but because she was possessed of a religious fervour with which I found it increasingly difficult to empathise. I am reminded now, even if I wasn't at the time, of a similar impasse I had experienced back in the '60s when I had begun to write a play about James Nayler, the charismatic Quaker who, in Cromwellian times, was seduced by his followers into believing that he was the Son of God; a compelling subject, best written (and I still wonder why it hasn't been) by someone with religious convictions. In any event, I suppose I should have been thankful that I had only written 15 pages about Gladys which, short of a divine revelation, are now permanently consigned to a trunk in our loft devoted to memorabilia.

It came as a complete surprise to me when I was invited by Bill Kenwright to direct a production of *The Wind in the Willows* at the Mermaid Theatre. Obviously, my long association with *Toad of Toad Hall* had played a part in this, but it transpired, however, that the idea had not come from Bill, but from David Conville who had been responsible for the adaptation, and had decided, for some reason or other, not to direct it himself. This is conjecture, of course, borne out by the fact that the set had already been designed, and the music already composed, before the reins were handed over to me.

Meanwhile, our relationship with Bill, having survived the trials and tribulations of *Judy's* untimely closure, Lesley in particular was keen for the whole saga to end on a sweet note, so we took both Bill and Norman Boyack out for a meal, during which Lesley and Bill had even discussed the possibility of getting together for a West End revival of *Piaf;* and only a couple of nights later we were among his guests at the Savoy Hotel. He said that he had invited his ten closest mates which made us feel that we were still included in his inner circle, as did his invitations to attend the first nights of his many productions. Little by little, of course, as the months passed, we found ourselves relegated from the stalls to the upper circle, and finally out onto the street.

My few weeks in Westcliff, having provided me with a temporary emollient, were quickly dispelled when Bill provided me with an office and a desk of my own upon which, awaiting my arrival, was a pile of Spotlight casting directories. I was then instructed to cast the four leading characters in the play with actors who had achieved star status, or were at least well-known to television audiences. Four days later, having submitted numerous suggestions all of which had proved to be in vain for one reason or another, but largely – as I was later to learn – because of the meagre salaries they were being offered for playing two shows a day, I was instructed to cast it myself.

Staggering out of the office after yet another exhausting, yet somewhat more successful day, I was greeted by Bill who took my hand, into the palm of which he placed what turned out to be £50, and said, "Take the wife out to dinner!" Needless to say, I did.

To give him his due, Bill had at least made sure that *Judy* had been seen by the entire panel of the Olivier Awards judges, as Lesley heard on November 5th that she had been nominated for *Best Performance by an Actress in a Musical*. This was great news, of course, although all but six months had passed since *Judy* had closed, and so it was extremely unlikely she would win it. It was gratifying nonetheless for *Judy* to be remembered, and for Lesley's performance to go down in theatrical history, even if only as a footnote. It was, in fact, the best thing that could have happened in the circumstances, given that her pregnancy had left her with nothing much to do except to attend regular ante-natal classes, read baby books, and do the shopping.

Following a get-together at Drury Lane where she had her photograph taken along with all the other Olivier Award nominees, she started to draft an acceptance speech which at least gave her something else to do, even if she never got to deliver it; and with Elaine Paige in *Chess*, which was still running, Maureen Lipman in *Wonderful Town*, still running, and Angela Richards in *Side by Side by Sondheim*, which closed only two months earlier, I could not but share those misgivings with her. Nevertheless, I was more than happy to see her enjoy being in the limelight again, however fleetingly. I was happy too, of course, to note that my 'play with music' had now been officially categorised as a 'musical', not only in the Theatre Critics nominations, but by none other than Laurence Olivier!

It was on the evening of December 7th, a week before the first night of *The Wind in the Willows*, that Lesley and I made our way to what was then the Royalty Theatre for the televised Olivier Awards ceremony; for obvious reasons a shared occasion which I will now, for equally obvious reasons, let Lesley share with you ...

'I was heavily pregnant by this time, and Mum had warned me not to jump up too suddenly if I won in case I hastened the arrival of the baby. I told her not to hold her breath, as the odds were stacked against me. I was under no illusions; I was a rank outsider, and I knew it. I was just thrilled to have been nominated, and to be part of such a prestigious event. We slipped into the theatre, totally ignored by the press who were flocking around the more famous nominees, and Terry and I headed into the auditorium and took our seats in the front stalls. Our innate knowledge that we were not in the running was compounded by the fact that I was the only nominee who had not been invited to sing. I was told that they would try to include me, but priority would be given to those shows still running. As I sat there with butterflies and a baby in my tummy, I was a little relieved that I did not have to participate in the evening's entertainment. Maureen Lipman said afterwards that she would never put herself through such an experience again. She had to sing before the announcement, which is probably the lesser of the two evils, as it must be pretty tough to get up there and sing if you've just heard that you haven't won. Whichever way you look at it, it must be preferable just to sit there and watch the show until it reaches your category. Having said that, Terry and I were so nervous that we were unable to concentrate, and afterwards we could remember very little of the events on stage. It was indeed a star-studded night. Lord Olivier himself was there, although he was old and frail by that time and had to be helped to his feet by his wife, Joan Plowright, to acknowledge the plaudits of his fellow-actors. As he waved graciously down at us from his box, there was no doubt that, as far as the theatrical world was concerned, we were in the presence of 'royalty'! Numerous awards were handed out, and we were treated to excerpts from various shows. Finally, Alan Bates came on to read out the nominations for *Best Performance By An Actress In A Musical,* and then read out the names of the four nominees: Elaine Paige, Maureen Lipman, Angela Richards, and me. Miss Paige and Miss Lipman had already sung songs from their respective shows as part of the evening's entertainment, and Miss Richards was due to sing something a little later on. As the four names were announced, the camera flashed onto each one of us, and despite the fact that I knew I wasn't going to win, I felt tense as Alan Bates opened the dreaded envelope, and read, "And the winner is . . Lesley Mackie!" Ignoring my mother's advice, I shot up as though I had been scalded, finally putting an end to the myth that winners know in advance! I also remembered to kiss my husband before waddling up to the podium where I collected my award, made my speech while choking back floods of emotion and waddled off in the wrong direction. We had been given strict instructions to exit stage right if we won, but by this point I was overwhelmed, and Alan Bates had to chase after me into the auditorium to get me back on stage. Michael Crawford also won an Olivier Award for his performance in *Phantom of the Opera,* and it seemed as if every newspaper in the world wanted a picture of us together. I think he was as emotional as I was! I spent the rest of the evening in a complete and utter daze.'

Looking back on it now, and with Lesley's more indelible memories to prompt me, not to mention a very heavy trophy that would sit on our bookcase for all to see, and for the rest of our lives, I knew that she had climbed a mountain, reached the summit and, in spite of all the setbacks, had finally been rewarded. Whatever happened, nothing could take away our joint achievement on that wonderful and memorable night.

1986 Olivier Award winners. Lesley Mackie and Michael Crawford.

Certainly, her gift to me had been a performance that by some mysterious process had grown and evolved into an uncanny reincarnation of Judy Garland at every stage of her life. There were those, of course, who believed that she must have had some kind of relationship with Judy from beyond the grave. There was even a medium who wanted her to book a session so that she could talk to

Judy herself. But, disregarding that kind of psychic nonsense, I knew that it was the outcome of what can only be described as great acting. I have witnessed many fine stage performances in my time, from a seat in the auditorium or alongside me on stage, but only a handful of great ones; and by great, I mean performances that transported me, took my breath away, and made the hairs on the back of my neck to stand on end, not understanding where such qualities came from. In chronological order, or as near to it as my memory allows, the truly great performances that I have witnessed, other than Laurence Olivier's *Titus Andronicus* and, more surprisingly, his Archie Rice in John Osborne's *The Entertainer*, was Leonard Rossiter in Brecht's *The Resistible Rise of Arturo Ui*. There have undoubtedly been many other great performances that I was not privileged to see, and for those amongst you who may well take issue with what is essentially a subjective shortlist, I have no hesitation in adding Lesley Mackie as Judy Garland. And I should make it quite clear that prejudice plays no part in this accolade. No one but I was in a position to witness the extraordinary journey she made, the troughs as well as the crests; times when I thought that I had gone too far by presenting her with a character too life-spanning for any one actress to accomplish, when I suspected that the idiosyncrasies of Garland's voice, and her unpredictable nature, were beyond Lesley's reach. Even when Lesley was ill and shouldn't have been up there on-stage at all, soldiering on against all medical advice, she managed to convince the audience that it was Judy Garland's infirmities she was suffering from, when I knew only too well the hell she was going through. Lesley's portrayal of Judy Garland was, in fact, nothing short of a metamorphosis, and the fact that her achievement had been rewarded six months later with a major award was a truly wonderful and unexpected dénouement. There was no doubt we had both reached a pinnacle in our professional lives, and with an even more unexpected baby on the way, in our private lives too.

Only one small glitch marred the occasion; Bill Kenwright had already confided to Lesley that he thought the Olivier Award should go to her, although he rather hoped it wouldn't, for the simple reason that *Wonderful Town*, another of his productions, was still up and running, and would receive a welcome box-office boost if Maureen Lipman won it. Fair enough, I guess, but his wish hadn't been granted, and the seating arrangements for dinner at a nearby hotel had clearly been changed at the last minute so that Maureen and Lesley were no longer at the same table. When we saw the seating plan on our arrival Lesley and I had been moved from Bill's celebrity table to join his relatives and friends at another. While I could appreciate his reasons for doing this, I couldn't help wondering why he had seated us at the same table to begin with, unless he was sure Maureen was going to win, and he knew Lesley was more likely to take it on the chin.

I was aware of how fit and well Lesley appeared to be – stress-free and blooming, as nature intended, but the very last thing I expected, given all that had led up to it. The Olivier Award had, of course, been partly responsible for this, and while she may not have been working, she was made to feel back in the swim with a couple of television interviews requiring trips to Scotland: for Grampian Television in Aberdeen, and somewhat later to Glasgow where she actually sang *Over the Rainbow* and *La Vie en Rose* on the Jimmy Mack Show. According to Lesley, it was the Olivier Award that sustained her throughout the rest of her pregnancy, keeping her name alive for a little longer. Sod's Law, of course, that it should have happened just when her career seemed to have taken off, but that's show business for you!

As February gave way to March, and having just celebrated my 49th birthday at our favourite Chinese restaurant in Acton, we decided it was time to make a decision about the baby's name, in the unlikely event that it should it turn out to be a girl. We knew, of course, with the absolute certainty of instinct, that it was going to be a boy, and that his name would be Oliver Barnaby. Having chosen Dickens as our inspiration for the boy's names, we turned to Shakespeare, and finally came up with Katherine or Kate from *The Taming of the Shrew*. Unfortunately, however, Katherine Wale sounded too much like a firework, whilst Kate had only one syllable, as did her surname, so we opted for Katy, an old and tried name with which we were perfectly happy, and in any case it was purely academic, as Lesley knew full well that it was Oliver Barnaby she was carrying.

Gone were the days when a prospective father would pace about at the foot of the stairs, waiting for a voice from above telling him that the baby had arrived. I had, in fact, been present at Lesley's final ante-natal class where I had learned what my role would likely be, and so here I was, averse from childhood to the sight of blood, about to assist at the birth of my first child, and just hoping I would be able to remain upright long enough to see it through!

The whole labour lasted for 24 hours. As the hours dragged on, Lesley realised that there would be no more squatting for her. She clamped her nose to the gas and air, lay down, and there she stayed.

I did my best, supplying ice cubes to suck, wet sponges to cool her down, and gentle encouragement. I didn't have time to feel squeamish, and only managed the odd brief respite to grab a sandwich, make a phone call or have a fag! After so many hours of labour, she eventually felt that she could no longer cope with gas and air alone, so she caved in and begged for an epidural, which the midwife topped up every couple of hours. Once they accepted she was almost at the end of her rope, she was told there were two options – a bit more pushing and forceps delivery, or a Caesarean Section. Having come so far, she would have been disappointed not to have a 'normal' birth and, in any case, she did not relish a major operation, so she opted for what she thought would be the more bearable option.

The best thing you can say is that, at least, it's a productive pain, and with the aid of the epidural and forceps, Katy Violet Wale finally made her entrance at 5am on March 18th 1987.

My father with Katy.

oOoOo

Thirty

Having now embarked upon my octogenarian years, I am faced with the daunting prospect of encapsulating over 30 years of memories into as few pages as possible!

As far as Lesley was concerned, the road to stardom had become a cul-de-sac. Another of our dreams had come true, of course, but at what cost? It was Lesley, of course, who had to put up with the never-ending demands of little Katy Violet more incessantly than I did. Well, someone had to make a living!

Somewhat ironically, the next couple of years were destined to be among the busiest of our professional lives together, juggling Katy between us where feasible, depending on my father to baby-sit on occasions, and Lesley's itinerant and stalwart mother to stand in when neither of us was available.

That I became a doting father for the first time at the ripe old age of 49 is somewhat grudgingly remembered as the occasion when, having taken Katy on her first holiday abroad the following year, she got a bit fractious on the flight; I picked her up and carried her up and down the aisle a few times until a lady who'd been watching us and smiling warmly, said, "I can see Grandad's very proud."

I managed to procure an interview with Raphael Jago, Principal of the Webber-Douglas Academy of Dramatic Art, hoping that he might be persuaded to offer me a production or two in South Kensington, a mere bus ride away from home and cradle. I had an ongoing association with the Webber-Douglas for the next six years, during which time I directed a variety of plays, mainly in the Chanticleer Theatre. My fondest memory, however, is reserved for Stephen Sondheim's *Company*, even though I suspected it might be too ambitious a project for a bunch of students untrained in musical theatre. It was going to be virtually impossible, of course, to find a young actress to follow in the footsteps of Elaine Stritch, a mature lady whose performance as Joanne in the original West End production had been all but show-stopping. There was, however, a young lady whose comparative maturity amongst such a young cast, qualified her for the role, and in which she defied augury with a performance that did not make me once lament the absence of Miss Stritch. Her name was Samantha Spiro, whose subsequent career in Musical Theatre has so far won her two Olivier Awards!

Katy was barely six weeks old when John Doyle approached Lesley with an offer to play the leading role in a revival of *Bells Are*

Ringing at the Everyman Theatre in Cheltenham followed by a run at Greenwich Theatre. Given that John had probably been as disappointed as we were that it wasn't he who had taken Judy into the West End, it was hardly surprising that he wanted to provide Lesley with another vehicle with which they might make a similar journey together. It featured a number of evergreen songs, including *Just in Time*, and *The Party's Over*. However, it was, in short, a musical that didn't really merit a West End revival, let alone provide an inspired vehicle for Lesley who nevertheless brought to it, according to *The Mail on Sunday* review: 'an irresistibly winsome talent ... if the show doesn't ring my bell, Ms. Mackie certainly lights my candle.'

We had been looking for an opportunity to exploit the Olivier Award before it became ancient history; we were only too well aware that memories are notoriously short in our business. Lesley had, of course, long nursed a desire to play Edith Piaf again, an ambition enthusiastically endorsed by Alan Strachan who went on to set up a meeting with the author, Pam Gems, a meeting which she cancelled at the last minute with an excuse so implausible we were left thinking there was more to it than met the eye; and there certainly was – as we were to find out later!

In the meantime Ronald S. Lee, in collaboration with Stoll Moss was in the process of casting a revival of Lerner and Loewe's *Brigadoon*, and asked if Lesley would be interested in the role of Meg Brockie. If *Bells are Ringing* had proved to be somewhat old-fashioned, *Brigadoon* was, by the same token, antique. It was however, and almost everyone agreed, a lavish and entertaining production, with a 40-strong cast fronted by a 25 piece orchestra, and it made for happy listening as well as providing some extremely energetic and watchable Scottish dances. Jeff, played by Robin Nedwell, and without a single song to sing, is left to fend off the advances of man-mad Meg Brockie who, according to various critics, 'almost stops the show with her interpretation of *The Love of My Life*' ... 'delightfully effervescent' ... 'frantically funny'... 'vibrant and maturely mischievous'; and just in case you missed the point 'a superb performance from the impish Lesley Mackie'.

The show went on to open at the Victoria Palace in London on October 25th 1988, where it would run for the next nine months, by which time, however, a more significant change had taken place in our lives when, in June 1989, we moved to Brighton – well, to Hove actually! By the time we moved into 20, Molesworth Street, *Brigadoon* was fast approaching the end of its run, and so it was only for a limited amount of time that Lesley was able to enjoy the comparative comfort of travelling up to London by train, alighting at Victoria Station, crossing the road and walking through the stage door, a journey moreover that took less time than it had when we lived in London.

1989 brought an unexpected treat with Yorkshire Television's decision to film *Beecham*, bringing Timothy West and me together again for the first time since our tour of New Zealand, and in what turned out to be a fairly lavish production. We rehearsed in London and recorded it at the YTV studios in Leeds where it was enhanced by the presence of the entire Hallé Orchestra. It provided a lasting and faithful record of Ned and Caryl's dramatisation, and of Tim's performance, which would otherwise have become but a distant memory for those who only saw it on stage.

On January 13th 1990, less than two months away from her 80th birthday, my mother died. It was not entirely surprising given her long downhill journey, but a sad occasion nonetheless, leaving nothing of her real self behind but a few black and white photographs to remind me of the beauty and the vitality she had once possessed.

Lily Wale and TW

There then came an offer from Joan Knight to return to Perth for a production of Garson Kanin's *Born Yesterday* which I would direct with Lesley in the leading role of dumb-blonde Billie Dawn, played in the original Broadway production and in the 1950 film version by Judy

Holliday. So we embarked on what turned out to be a delightful journey, with a blonde-wigged Lesley adding Billie Dawn to her list of all-time favourite roles.

It was around this time that Joan broached the subject of a *Piaf* revival and her struggle to obtain the rights. We discovered that the problems we had encountered were because Elaine Paige held the rights to the play pending her decision to go ahead with it in London. However, after a bit of persuasion, we somehow got permission for a production, limited to Perth, in the Spring of 1991, and we both became involved (I was directing on this occasion!) in preparation for an imminent revival, where it had last been seen seven years earlier. On this occasion, we were blessed with a terrific set, designed by Nigel Hook, a splendid evocation of back-street Paris with its street-lamps and tenements. Moreover, Lesley's performance was, if anything, more powerful than it had been before, leaving me in no doubt (had I ever entertained one) that it was she who should play it in the West End.

She was then invited by Benny Green to take up the mantle of Judy Garland again in a concert he had devised called *Two Smart Girls*, featuring the songs of Judy Garland and Deanna Durbin who had enjoyed a brief professional relationship during their early days at MGM in 1936. Lesley was to sing the Garland songs and Maria Kesselman to take on the role of Deanna Durbin, while the narrative was to be delivered by Benny Green in his familiar witty and off the cuff style. After a couple of out of town bookings, their achievement was crowned on Sunday, June 2nd, when they performed it at the Queen Elizabeth Hall on the South Bank.

The icing on the cake that year was when we were invited to tour *Judy* in the Summer, starting in Perth and directed by Clive Perry. Rehearsals began on August 5th, and for the first time we had two genuinely middle-aged gossip columnists. An old friend of Lesley's from drama school days, Anne Downie, was to play Hedda Hopper while that Perth stalwart, Janet Michael, was cast as Louella Parsons, an ideal role for her. Not only that, but we actually had six 'Boyfriends', none of whom were trained dancers, but who proved to be the best troupe we ever had, thanks largely to choreographer Tony Ellis.

As we embarked on the second week of rehearsals, the results of a pregnancy test came through, and proved positive. The exacting demands of playing Judy Garland again were daunting enough, never mind in the early stages of pregnancy – and not only that, but she had also agreed to return to Perth in November to play Jane in Alan Ayckbourn's *Absurd Person Singular*, followed by Jack in *Jack and the*

Beanstalk! From Joan's point of view, a five-month pregnant 'Jane' would be perfectly acceptable, while a seven-month pregnant 'Jack' trying to climb up a beanstalk would not only be too risky, but too large a pill for the audience to swallow! The timing of all this aside, of course, Lesley and I were delighted; a second child was, after all, no longer a dream but a fait accompli.

Judy opened on August 30th, with a performance that not only led to a standing ovation from the audience but to a joyful response from the entire company, demonstrating a genuine *joie de vivre* that was to accompany us throughout the tour. Looking back it was interesting that Clive had managed to gather together such a multi-talented company from the limited resources of Perth Theatre. And it wasn't just the actors; we had a wonderful set and costumes, courtesy of Nigel Hook and Alex Reid, while the musical arrangements from the West End production, most of which we had managed to get hold of, were placed in the nimble-fingered hands of John Scrimger as Musical Director. This was, without doubt, the production we had hoped for.

1991 Judy - Perth Theatre. Lesley Mackie with 'Boyfriends'.

Our week in Glasgow left us all in a state of euphoria, and wishing we could have extended it. Lesley's new agent, Jean Diamond, having flown up from London, was there on the first night which could not have been more warmly received by the audience, nor greeted with such a number of enthusiastic reviews, one of which we have treasured over the years, written by Mary Lockhart in *The Glasgow Herald*: 'Lesley Mackie's Judy Garland, sometimes sexy, sometimes seedy, always vulnerable, excites, infuriates, delights and breaks the heart'.

Our tour came to an end at the Whitehall Theatre in Dundee. The last night was unforgettable, according to Lesley, who said that she was so choked that she could barely sing *Over the Rainbow* at the end, a finale that was greeted with one last standing ovation. Dundee was, after all, Lesley's home town, an appropriate place to bring an end to the journey. An unparalleled company of actors had been assembled, together with a production team that would have graced any West End stage, not to mention a plethora of new ideas, one of the most inspirational being Lesley's brief appearance early on in the play as the 12 year-old Dorothy in *The Wizard of Oz* being welcomed to Munchkinland, when Lesley had just celebrated her 40th birthday, and was pregnant with her second child.

On a journey back to Hove from Dundee, where I had been directing Terence Rattigan's *In Praise of Love*, I stopped off in Whitley Bay, a seaside village close to Newcastle, where I had arranged a meeting with Derek Jones, who ran an audio book company there called Soundings. It was entirely due to my friend from Chichester days, Gordon Griffin, a Tynesider himself, and one of the first readers to be employed by Soundings, that I was taken into Derek's office and asked to read out loud an extract from a London based novel by Harry Bowling entitled *Conner Street's War*, which I was then invited to come back and record. While not exactly 'life-changing', my return visits to Whitley Bay over the next 27 years provided me with an alternative outlet as an actor, recording around 250 books; the most memorable of which will always be a series of novels written by Cynthia Harrod Eagles, tracing the life and career of Bill Slider, a policeman based in Shepherd's Bush, during the course of which she dedicated one of her omnibus editions to me as 'The voice of Bill Slider'.

Following a labour that was reminiscent, if not decidedly worse than the one she'd suffered five years earlier, Oliver Duncan Wale made his first appearance at 1am on Friday, April 10th 1992 in the East Sussex County Hospital where the staff were run off their feet with only four midwives attending to eight births, one of which was an emergency Caesarean. Moreover, it was General Election day and some of the hospital staff, already stretched beyond their limits, became increasingly dispirited as seat after seat fell to the Tories.

With Katy now at school and a new addition to the family, it was time for a major re-think. We enjoyed living in Hove, but our work invariably took us elsewhere and, significantly, most of it was to Scotland. Besides, Lesley's Mum and Dad had been travelling the length and breadth of the country to be of assistance ever since Katy was born, and would surely not be able to keep it up for much longer. So a plan to move to Scotland began to take shape, although it would be almost a year before we finally said goodbye to the Sussex coast.

Still harbouring hopes of a West End *Piaf*, and having fondly imagined Ms Paige might have second thoughts, we then saw a photograph of her in the *Daily Express* standing, as Lesley had, at Edith's grave in the Père Lachaise cemetery, confirming her intention and leaving Lesley in tears. As a postscript to this episode, I went to see *Piaf* when it later played in Glasgow, and in my opinion it was nothing more nor less than an evening with Elaine Paige in disguise, and culminating in a rendition of *Non, Je Ne Regrette Rien* that was very obviously designed to bring the curtain down on a celebration of Elaine's talent as a chanteuse rather than as a requiem for a long-lost legend.

It was late in 1992 that Joan offered Lesley the title role in Willy Russell's *Shirley Valentine*, and invited me to direct it. Her reason for bringing up the subject some six months earlier than it was due to be staged was to give Lesley ample time to learn the part, the play itself being a monologue and therefore a mammoth undertaking.

Having decided to accomplish our move before rehearsals were due to begin, the new year was given over to selling our house, and finding another to live in north of the border. We found one in Perth, where we must have been very happy, as I'm writing this today more than 25 years later in a downstairs room of that same house, used as a study, and toying with the idea of turning it into a downstairs bedroom, if and when I am no longer able to climb the stairs!

With six year-old Katy installed at Kinnoull Primary School, a ten minute walk away, and a baby-sitter found to look after Ollie, we began rehearsals for *Shirley Valentine*. Having started rehearsals in our living room in Hove, we now had a rehearsal room, a Stage Manager, and the outlines of two perfect sets (designed by Geoffrey Scott), the first act set in Shirley's kitchen, and the second, following the interval, on the beach of a Greek island.

'From the scene-setting James Taylor song at the beginning with Lesley Mackie herself on tape accompanied on guitar by theatre manager Marcus Ford, there was an awareness of a special event ... A little actress with a big heart and an even larger talent is entirely wowing the town at Perth Theatre. Let it be heard loud and clear – you miss this performance and play at your peril ... it is to the actress's credit and husband Terry Wale as her director, that she times and paces the solo performance with a perfection that thoroughly deserved the ovation at the end.'

I was playing Spettigue in John Doyle's production of *Charley's Aunt* at the Theatre Royal in York when I had a call from Andrew McKinnon, offering me the part of 'Professor' Otto Marvuglia in a play called *Grand Magic* by the Italian playwright, Eduardo de Filippo. The story of *Grand Magic* begins with the arrival of a wandering magician/conjurer and his acolytes onto the terrace of the Grand Hotel Metropole where he is about to entertain the guests. While preparing his equipment he is visited by a member of the hotel staff who tells him that he and the wife of a hotel guest, mutually attracted, would like to spend some little time alone with each other, and suggests that the conjurer makes her disappear, for which service he will be amply rewarded. Not averse to making a bit on the side, Marvuglia agrees to do it on the understanding that, once they have satisfied their mutual desires, she will come back. That she and the young man run away, never to return, provides the substance of the second act in which Marvuglia is left to convince the husband that she was never there in the first place. With monologues of Shavian length, crammed to bursting with gobbledegook, Marvuglia reduces him to a pale and hollow-eyed wreck, and finally presents him with a magic casket which, he says, contains his wife who, should he ever dare to open it, will cease to exist.

This synopsis will have made clear, I hope, the nightmare scenario I had to live through during every performance when I was faced with the prospect of having to remember the meaningless mumbo-jumbo which Marvuglia summons up to impair the husband's sanity; it certainly impaired mine. Looking back, however, I'm glad that I played it. *Grand Magic* was a very impressive piece of theatre, and the Perth production was well received; well, at least by the critics it was!

Two years after playing in Charley's Aunt at the Theatre Royal in York I returned to appear in Giles Havergal's adaptation of Graham Green's novel, *Travels With My Aunt*. It goes without saying, of course, that *Travels With My Aunt* is meant to be outrageous and funny, but bearing in mind that only three actors were engaged to play 20 characters, the task that faced Bernard Lloyd, James Woolley and myself was gruelling to say the least. 'Bernard Lloyd, Terry Wale and James Woolley are a masterclass in how to fascinate and amuse an audience for two hours without breaking sweat ... a superb challenge for actors – and a delight for theatregoers who want to stretch their imagination.' (*The Stage*)

I soon discovered that our move to Perth had been beneficial in more ways than one when it turned out that my frequent trips to Whitley Bay took half the time it had taken me to get there from Brighton. I was also anxious to replace the large slice of my life that had been taken up with student productions at the Webber-Douglas Academy. It was to be at Queen Margaret University College Drama Department in Edinburgh where I embarked on a series of productions that included, most memorably, Stephen Sondheim and James Lapine's musical, *Into The Woods*, and not only because it was a favourite of mine, but that it would also provide me with the chance to work alongside resident choreographer, Tony Ellis, again, and also allowed me to engage the services of our new friend Michael Ellacott as pianist under the baton of Musical Director, Marion McNeill.

It was on one of my trips down to Whitley Bay that I gave one of the students, Michael Harrison, a lift to his home in Newcastle, during which he told me in no uncertain terms, that his real ambition was not to be as an actor but a producer. *Into The Woods* was, in fact, his last appearance before graduating, following which he embarked upon his chosen profession, kicking it off in 2001 with a production of *Born to Sing*, a musical anthology devised and directed by myself, and starring Lesley Mackie as Edith Piaf and Judy Garland. But unlike our earlier version of the show, called *Legends*, accompanied on piano by George Donald, this one was provided, thanks to our fledgling producer, with a theatrical setting and a six-piece band which went on to enjoy a successful tour following its premiere at the Whitley Bay Playhouse, an even more appropriate venue now that Lesley had joined me there as a reader of audio books.

Michael Harrison went on to realise his ambition, initially as a prolific producer of pantomimes under the banner of *Qdos Entertainment*. It was, however, under the banner of Michael Harrison Productions that in 2006 Lesley went on to play one of the three ladies who occupy the stage in a Scottish tour of *The Vagina Monologues* by Eve Ensler, which turned out to be a compelling experience, playing to full houses throughout the tour. Just for the record, Michael's entrepreneurial career led to him reaching Number 8 in the recent Stage 100 (the 100 most influential people working in the theatre and performing arts).

Despite continuing to work in rep and on tour, it was clear that our professional lives had not been changed by the Olivier Award, as I always hoped and felt it would. However, in 1985, just prior to our transfer from the Bristol Old Vic to Greenwich with *Judy*, I had been approached by a German literary agency called *Litag* based in Bremen. They were seeking permission to translate my play into German, and to represent me in any prospective European sales which eventually led to productions, not only in Germany, but in Austria, Sweden, Denmark, New Zealand, and even in Japan. The royalties were a great bonus during the years when our children were young and the work was not too abundant. In 2011 we actually went to Vienna to see one of the foreign language productions at the Kammerspiele Theatre. The language barrier left me without much of a clue as to where we were in the play, but it was different, it was fun, and they were very welcoming – I even had to rise at the end as the playwright and wave to the Grand Circle!

By 1996, Andrew McKinnon had left, and Michael Winter had decided to swap the Mercury Theatre in Colchester for Perth. We did a few productions during his tenure; the highlight of Lesley's season being when she played Proserpine Garnett in Shaw's *Candida*, as a result of which she was nominated for a TMA/Barclays Award for Best Supporting Actress.

It was some little while later, in December 1996, that Joan Knight died, and while I cannot help but nurse reservations about her multifaceted persona, I will never forget the opportunities, the challenges and the rewards I received at her hands over the years, and most of all for inviting me to Perth in the first place, allowing Lesley and I to meet, a serendipitous event for both of us that would otherwise probably never have happened.

Sadly too, and less than a year later in 1997, my father died. I drove down in order to register his death, and to make arrangements for his funeral – which was somewhat bleak due to the absence of flowers which were all but extinct as Dad's funeral happened to coincide with Princess Diana's. Well, at least he had made it to his 90th birthday which was ten years more than my mother had achieved.

Out of the blue, I was offered the part of Spinetti, an Italian Mafia boss whose arrival and departure from the lochside village of Glendarroch spanned two episodes in the long-running Scottish television soap-opera, *High Road*. Spinetti's reason for being there was to meet up with his illegitimate son, and advise him to set his sights somewhat higher than as a barman at the local inn. At the end of my brief visit, I suggested (only half-jokingly) to the producer that maybe the character should return, take over the sleepy village of Glendarroch, and turn it into the Las Vegas of Scotland. Only a few months later I was invited back for one more episode – the final one – and it was only then that I realised he had taken me at my word; I was back with a surveyor in tow! Rumours were rife at that time that *High Road* was about to be axed, but it didn't even occur to me that I would be chosen as the axe.

When Lesley was invited by Michael Winter to play Miss Hannigan in his production of *Annie* in 2001, Katy decided she would audition for one of the orphans. We were both cautiously enthusiastic when she was offered the title role, but she met the challenge with confidence, and she sang all the songs most attractively. More to the point, and ominously, she got better and better as the run went on, and there seemed to be little hope of deflecting her from an acting career. Oh yes, and Lesley was pretty good as Miss Hannigan too! Our attempts to deflect Oliver from going down the same path as his sister led to his mother's decision to introduce him to something more physical by way of joining a junior training course at McDiarmid Park, home of St. Johnstone Football Club, at the age of 6, introducing Ollie - and myself – to what would become a passion. Due to the sad lack of sporting activities at school, I volunteered to play referee at the local recreation ground after school on Tuesdays for him and his classmates, and was astounded, not to say deeply moved, when I was presented with the Parent of the Year Award for my services to football! Oliver not only went on to become a fervent supporter of St. Johnstone, but devoted himself as time went by, to donating his services to the club by writing match previews and interviewing their players one by one for publication in their programmes.

Having auditioned for a part in the musical *Oliver* at Perth Theatre, he wound up being offered the title role in his first professional production. Like Katy, who played the title role in *Annie*, Ollie shared the stage with his mother who, it may be remembered, used to play title roles herself! On this occasion she took on a variety of parts, including Mrs. Sowerberry, and even disported herself as a chorus-girl, but will be best remembered as Old Sal, the beggar-woman who dies, and is dragged off-stage by her feet! Katy and I went together to the first night, and when Ollie stood alone on stage and sang *Where is Love?*, all I could do was listen and watch him through a veil of tears!

I was obviously not entirely happy about the prospect of yet one more member of the family taking on a part-time job and calling it a career. With this in mind, and inclined towards one of the alternatives, I remember leaning over his sleeping form on one occasion and whispering in his ear, "Oliver Wale QC, Oliver Wale QC" but to little effect.

Lesley's appearance as an over-the-hill Cinderella at the Oran Mor in Glasgow as part of its *A Play A Pie and a Pint* season, was an unqualified success, and especially so with me, a lifelong pantophobe. It was extremely funny, well cast and full of witty songs. Its greatest strength, however, was that it only lasted 50 minutes. In the wake of Lesley's personal triumph, she was asked by the producer if I had written anything for her since 1985, and if so, would I be willing to cut it to the required length for a lunchtime production.

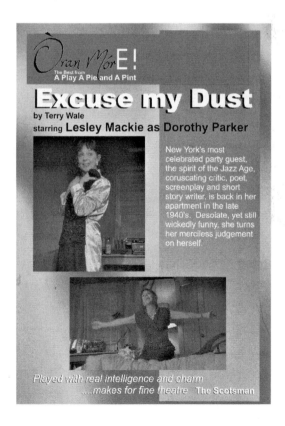

Oran MorE!
The Best from
A Play A Pie and A Pint

Excuse my Dust

by Terry Wale
starring **Lesley Mackie as Dorothy Parker**

New York's most celebrated party guest, the spirit of the Jazz Age, coruscating critic, poet, screenplay and short story writer, is back in her apartment in the late 1940's. Desolate, yet still wickedly funny, she turns her merciless judgement on herself.

Played with real intelligence and charm ...makes for fine theatre The Scotsman

And so it came to pass that my one-woman play about Dorothy Parker was seen for the very first time. In truth, I had all but given up on it ever seeing the light of day up here where, despite her Scottish ancestry, Mrs Parker was all but *terra incognita*. Well, its reception at the Oran Mor was enthusiastic to say the least. I had directed it myself with a helping hand from our old friend and fellow director Charles Bell. I was doubly rewarded by seeing Dorothy Parker uncannily brought to life by one of those rare talents that make your work seem even better than you thought it was. The play went on to enjoy a short tour before ending up at the Edinburgh Festival Fringe, accompanied by positive reviews, pretty well summed up by Joyce McMillan's in *The Scotsman:* 'Wale's Parker – played with real intelligence and charm by that fine Scottish stage-star, Lesley Mackie ... it makes for fine theatre; ·by far the sharpest, most entertaining and most moving of all the female mid-life dramas Oran Mor has presented this season.'

The success that *Excuse My Dust* enjoyed, albeit on a limited excursion, culminated in my promise to write another play for Lesley. She asked, in return, that I make the character 75 years old as, based on my previous record, it would probably take me that long to write it!

Katy graduated from her HNC course in Acting & Performance with an A pass. Her determination to become an actress finally came to fruition when she started applying to drama colleges up and down the country, and was finally offered a place on the BA (Hons) Acting course at the Arts Educational School in Chiswick. For several months, most of my days – and Lesley's too – were taken up with fund-raising, haunted by the prospect of yet another day writing yet more letters addressed to trust funds, charitable trusts, professional organisations and local council funding bodies, and all the while fearing that we wouldn't be able to raise enough to send her there, an outcome which, for some reason, Katy refused to take seriously. There was no telling her that it was an impossible dream. Amazingly enough, and with the help of a couple of local trust funds, we almost did it – or at least it was becoming a possibility. Having put it all in place, she made plans to head for London at the start of September.

Within a few weeks, however, her hard work and dedication having been spotted by the staff, she was awarded the last of the much sought after DaDAs (Dance and Drama Awards). To be able to study on a three year course at one of the best drama schools in London and to achieve this without a student loan and to finish without oodles of debt, was incredible.

Oliver, meanwhile, achieved better results in his GCSEs than we had any reason to expect. 'A' Levels were to come, of course, and we could only hope that he might begin to take life a bit more seriously. He left school to a standing ovation following his rendition of *My Way* and settled into Dundee University, where he quickly acquired his own radio show every Wednesday at 1pm, and was taken on as male vocalist with the University big band. Oh yes, and he was reading English Literature, Film Studies and Psychology!

In the original production of Tennessee Williams' *A Streetcar Named Desire*, the actor who played the Doctor, whose only appearance is in the final scene, was asked in a newspaper interview what the play was about. "Well", he said, "it's about this doctor ..." I still fondly remember sitting in my dressing-room waiting for my entrance as that very same doctor, accompanied by my wife in the equally small role of the Nurse, both of us acutely aware, following an article in the local paper welcoming us both back to Perth Theatre after a lengthy absence, that there must have been several people out there who had been looking forward to seeing us for the last two and a quarter hours. I should add, for those who may be taken aback by this seeming downturn in Lesley's fortunes as an actress, that she was solely there to show me where the stage was and to nudge me when it was my turn to speak! She had, in fact, already been asked to appear in Perth's Christmas production of *The Snow Queen* in which she was to play the considerably larger and more demanding parts of a Crow and a Polar Bear! Heigh-ho, the glamorous life!

The following year, Katy returned home, sporting her newly acquired BA to make her début as a professional actress as Princess Peekaboo in *Aladdin* at Perth Theatre; coincidentally, the Empress, her mother, was played by her own mother!

Inescapably, the shadow of *The Wicker Man* loomed large again when *Cowboys for Christ*, now retitled *The Wicker Tree*, went before the cameras, with a very frail <u>Sir</u> Christopher Lee, who had almost grown too old for the part while waiting for it to happen. For various economic reasons it had become what is known as a low-budget picture although, as far as I could make out, this was only reflected in the fees that were offered to the cast. To my relatively inexperienced eye, it was a fairly lavish production. Since Lesley was the sole remaining member of the cast from *The Wicker Man*, it is hardly surprising that she had already been cast as Daisy again, although whether Daisy the Cook was intended to be a more mature version of the chubby schoolgirl she had played back in 1973, we never discovered.

My own involvement had come about when Robin Hardy offered me the part of a trade union convener whose background, I was assured, was not necessarily Scottish, which was something of a relief, although short-lived. When I received the script, I saw that the character's name was Murdoch Renfrew, a good old Cockney name if ever I heard one! Just for the record – the film was only released on DVD.

Our children's independence was well established by this time, although with Oliver living just a few miles down the road in Dundee we saw a great deal more of him than we did of Katy, who was now experiencing an actor's most dreaded malady, and had consequently become the most sought after nanny in West London. It didn't take her too long to decide that an actor's life was not for her; so she decided to become a theatrical agent.

But before she made a final decision, she had one last engagement. Full of anticipation, we headed down south to see dear old Brighton, visit a few friends and, of course, to catch her show before it ended. It was lovely to have the chance to see Katy playing Cinderella in *Into the Woods*, especially as we knew we might never see her on stage again. Although she gave a very good performance, with it being a profit-share, at the end of the run she only received £100 for eight weeks' work, and I don't think for one moment that she thought she had made the wrong decision in becoming an agent! Neither did we – as we had paid for her upkeep throughout the run!

Oliver's progress in Dundee, besides embarking on a Creative Writing course in his third year, also saw him, in partnership with guitarist, Jamie Harris, singing songs of his own making at various gigs around the town, and when asked what they were known as, they simply looked at each other and shrugged, thus becoming known from that moment on as *The Shrugs*. They went on to record several discs, inevitably rising to the occasion when St. Johnstone were in the running for the Scottish Cup, and Ollie wrote a song called *Fair Maid*, which was played for all to hear at Celtic Park stadium in 2014 following St Johnstone's victory over Dundee United, winning the Scottish Cup for the very first time in its 130 year history. With football and music being his abiding passions to this very day, it's worth noting that Oliver graduated from Dundee University with an MA!

2011 brought the Edith Piaf cabaret to Perth Theatre, despite the fact that we had done it on a number occasions before, and as recently as the year before (and the year before that) to capacity audiences in the 100 seat theatre bar. I was somewhat surprised then when Lesley, with bare-faced effrontery, decided to book the 400 seat theatre on that occasion. That it sold out and earned her an enthusiastic ovation spoke volumes, not only for the popularity of Edith Piaf up here, whose songs they must have known backwards by then, and in French, but also for the fact that Lesley had announced that it was possibly her farewell performance – ha ha!

As I approach my 70th anniversary as an actor, I am prompted to bring this chapter to a close by recalling a visit to the Care Home in which Lesley's father spent his last days. On my way out, there being no member of the staff in the reception area to open the barrier for me, I waited for the somewhat corporeal lady who had just arrived to open it from the outside, which she did. I thanked her, and was about to make my way to the main exit when she grabbed hold of me, and said, "Oh, no you don't!" Whereupon she wrapped her arms around me, and obviously mistaking me for an inmate trying to escape, she started calling for help as I struggled to free myself. It took several members of the staff to arrive and laugh it off before she let me go, and without so much as an apology.

2011 Death of a Salesman - Perth Theatre, Richard Addison, TW and Ron Emslie.

Thus it was, and with no wish to outstay my welcome, or to end up playing dead bodies, that I announced my farewell to the stage when I accepted an offer from Ian Grieve to play Ben in Arthur Miller's *Death of a Salesman* at Perth Theatre in 2012. In fact I could not have chosen a more fitting way to bring the curtain down, and not only because Ben is a ghost, but because it's a great play; arguably one of Miller's best.

It turned out to be a fine production with a company of actors, led inspirationally from the first read-through by Ron Emslie as Willy Loman, who turned out to be so well cast, and such a pleasure to work with, that it was indeed a truly memorable swansong.

oOoOo

Epilogue

Had I not chosen to embark on this lengthy saga when I did, I would now have very few memories, not only of the distant past, but having reached that time of life when memory is prone to be more fallible, of more recent events too. Hence this epilogue which I am writing, not only as a postscript, but to acknowledge my debt to those who made my journey more rewarding, both personally and professionally, than it otherwise might have been.

Looking back across the last 70 or so years I have enjoyed a life and a career that would probably never have come about had it not been for a certain school teacher who not only introduced me to William Shakespeare, but who opened the door for me to embark on a lifelong journey that, even in my wildest dreams, I would probably never have contemplated.

Thus it is that I have chosen to go back to the very beginning, describing a circle that began when Peter Wright cast me as Ariel in The Tempest at Kilburn Grammar School, and has come to an end, as did that airy spirit's with Prospero's words:

My Ariel, chick,
That is thy charge: then to the elements
Be free, and fare thou well!

Printed in Poland
by Amazon Fulfillment
Poland Sp. z o.o., Wrocław

63322252R00304